CHAPTER SIX
Evaluation
Evaluate a subject by applying standards held in common with your readers and by justifying your judgments.

- Choose an appropriate su[bject ...]
- Present a subject to reade[rs ...]
- Assert a clear, authoritative judgment, qualifying it as necessary.
- Give reasons for a judgment, based on recognized standards.
- Support reasons with evidence from a subject and by comparing or contrasting a subject to similar subjects.
- Organize an essay through logically related reasons.
- Signal explicitly the stages of an evaluative argument.

CHAPTER SEVEN
Speculating about Causes or Effects
Attempt to convince readers that certain causes or effects offer a plausible explanation for an event, trend, or phenomenon.

- Choose an event, trend, or phenomenon that remains open to speculation about its possible causes or effects.
- Present a subject to be speculated about.
- Propose likely causes or effects.
- Support proposed causes or effects with facts, examples, statistics, cases, quotes from authorities, or anecdotes.
- Anticipate readers' questions and preferred causes or effects, counterarguing as needed.
- Organize an essay through a logical sequence of causes or effects.
- Signal explicitly the stages of cause or effect reasoning.

CHAPTER EIGHT
Proposal to Solve a Problem
Attempt to convince readers to support a proposed course of action.

- Choose a problem that needs solving and come up with a feasible solution.
- Describe a problem and solution.
- Give reasons why readers should support a solution.
- Support each reason with examples, facts, analogies, cases, scenarios, statistics, quotes from authorities, or anecdotes.
- Anticipate readers' questions and preferred solutions, counterarguing as needed.
- Organize an essay through logically ordered reasons.
- Signal explicitly the stages in an argument to support a solution.

CHAPTER NINE
Position Paper
Attempt to convince readers to take seriously a position on a current issue.

- Choose an arguable issue and define it carefully.
- Assert a position on an issue.
- Give reasons why readers should take a position seriously.
- Support each reason with examples, facts, analogies, statistics, anecdotes, or quotes from authorities.
- Anticipate readers' questions and their positions on an issue, counterarguing as needed.
- Organize an essay through logically ordered reasons.
- Signal explicitly the stages in an argument taking a position.

SIXTH EDITION

READING CRITICALLY WRITING WELL

A READER AND GUIDE

Rise B. Axelrod
University of California, Riverside

Charles R. Cooper
University of California, San Diego

BEDFORD/ST. MARTIN'S
Boston ♦ New York

For Bedford/St. Martin's

Senior Developmental Editor: John Elliott
Senior Production Editor: Shuli Traub
Production Supervisor: Jennifer Wetzel
Marketing Manager: Brian Wheel
Art Director/Cover Designer: Lucy Krikorian
Text Design: Wanda Kossak
Copy Editor: Wendy Polhemus-Annibell
Composition: Pine Tree Composition, Inc.
Printing and Binding: RR Donnelley & Sons Company

President: Charles H. Christensen
Editorial Director: Joan E. Feinberg
Editor in Chief: Nancy Perry
Director of Marketing: Karen R. Melton
Director of Editing, Design, and Production: Marcia Cohen
Managing Editor: Erica T. Appel

Library of Congress Control Number: 2001090572

Manufactured in the United States of America.

7 6 5 4
f e

For information, write: Bedford/St. Martin's, 75 Arlington Street, Boston, MA 02116
(617-399-4000)

ISBN: 0–312–39047–5

Acknowledgments

Laurie Abraham. "Divorced Father." From *Reinventing Home* by Laurie Abraham et al. Copyright © 1991 by Laurie Abraham. Used by permission of Dutton Signet, a division of Penguin Putnam, Inc.

Tony Adler. "The Grin Game." From *Chicago* magazine, 1998. Reprinted by permission of the author.

Natalie Angier. "Intolerance of Boyish Behavior." Taken from *The New York Times,* July 24, 1994. Originally published as "The Debilitating Malady Called Boyhood." Copyright © 1994 by The New York Times Company. Reprinted by permission.

Acknowledgments and copyrights are continued at the back of the book on pages 615–16, which constitute an extension of the copyright page.

Preface

Read, read, read. . . .Just like a carpenter who works as an apprentice and studies the master. Read!

— WILLIAM FAULKNER

I went back to the good nature books that I had read. And I analyzed them. I wrote outlines of whole books — outlines of chapters — so that I could see their structure. And I copied down their transitional sentences or their main sentences or their closing sentences or their lead sentences. I especially paid attention to how these writers made transitions between paragraphs and scenes.

— ANNIE DILLARD

In these quotations, the Nobel Prize–winning novelist William Faulkner and the Pulitzer Prize–winning novelist and essayist Annie Dillard tell us what many authors know intuitively—that reading critically helps writers learn to write well.

Our goal throughout the sixth edition of *Reading Critically, Writing Well* continues to be to teach students how to read critically: to pay close attention to how texts work. We believe that as college students become better readers, they will also become more effective writers. To help students read and write better, we provide extensive instruction in reading as well as comprehensive guidance in writing.

FEATURES

The special features of *Reading Critically, Writing Well* include:

Eight Different Types of Real-World Writing

Each assignment chapter (Chapters 2 through 9) focuses on a specific genre or type of writing that students will encounter during college and on the job. There are four personal and explanatory genres (autobiography, observation, reflection, and explanation of concepts) and four argumentative genres (evaluation, speculation about causes or effects, proposal to solve a problem, and position on an issue). Some of the reading and writing assignments give students opportunities to think deeply about their own experiences and perceptions, while other assignments require them to think about points of view other than their own.

Engaging Readings That Provoke Response and Reward Analysis

The readings have been carefully selected to show students how other writers—published authors as well as students—have approached each type of writing presented in *Reading Critically, Writing Well.* Varying in length and difficulty, the fifty-six readings encompass interesting topics that are likely to stimulate lively class discussion and student writing, such as whether teenagers should work while attending school, why some people like horror films, what inspires loyalty to a religion, why it is so difficult for some young people to break out of dead-end jobs, whether racial profiling is justified, what unexpected economic and social consequences result from state lotteries, and how gender expectations impact individuals. To show students strong writing by their peers, every chapter includes at least two essays written by students in composition courses. (One chapter includes three.)

Many of the readings are trusted favorites by distinguished writers like Audre Lorde, Annie Dillard, David Quammen, Amitai Etzioni, John McPhee, Deborah Tannen, Jonathan Kozol, Michael Kinsley, Rick Bragg, and Brent Staples.

Guided Activities That Teach Critical Reading

This text brings critical reading and writing together by engaging students in two fundamental ways of reading: *Reading for Meaning* and *Reading Like a Writer.* While *Reading for Meaning* gives students insight into how readers will construct meanings from their writing, *Reading Like a Writer* teaches them how to construct their own texts rhetorically to influence their readers' understanding and response. The two strategies are introduced in Chapter 1, developed further in the Guide to Reading at the beginning of each chapter, and applied to every reading selection throughout the text. Persisting with these two critical reading strategies, students gain confidence in their ability to write essays of their own in the same genres this book explores.

Reading for Meaning Activities

As writing instructors, we recognize that many students need help reading for meaning. Some students read superficially, barely skimming the surface, while others do not go beyond the meanings that resonate with their own experience. We developed the *Reading for Meaning* activities to help students get the gist of a reading, but also to suggest how they can reread for further meanings. We want students to gain confidence that they can construct meanings from any text, and we want them to persist at constructing meanings beyond initial impressions and personal connections.

Although the *Reading for Meaning* activities that follow each reading are organized identically, each one is designed specifically to help students explore and respond to the particular meanings of the reading it accompanies. As students complete these activities, they learn to perform an active role in constructing meaning. This kind of exploratory writing stimulates thinking, especially when it is sustained for at least a page.

We prompt exploratory writing in two ways:

Start Making Meaning. Students are first asked to write about a particular aspect of a reading, such as the significance of an autobiographical event or the main reasons for taking a position on an issue. We designed this part of the activity to ensure that students get the gist of the reading. Students are then asked to continue writing about anything else, either in the reading itself or in their own experience, that contributes to their understanding of the reading. This part of the activity gives students a point of departure to explore additional meanings.

If You Are Stuck. If students are unable to extend their meaning-making for a page, they may skim a variety of suggestions offered in *If You Are Stuck.* We designed this part of the activity to draw attention to different aspects of a reading, such as problematic assertions, intriguing examples, graphic design elements and visuals, and astute word choices. This activity also encourages students to explore ways in which their own points of view differ from or correspond to the points of view in the reading. Furthermore, it invites students to relate the reading to their own experience in a way that deepens their understanding of the reading.

In addition to teaching students to read closely and critically, the *Reading for Meaning* activities also give students useful insights about writing. Students nearly always recognize, for example, that writers seek to influence readers' thinking and feeling in particular ways and that writers choose their words and writing strategies carefully to achieve these purposes. Students also usually notice that writers attempt to direct readers' attention to key ideas and that the more precisely these ideas are named, defined, and supported, the more likely readers are to understand them. These and other insights, absorbed through much reading for meaning, complement the more recognizably rhetorical principles students learn from our *Reading Like a Writer* activities.

Reading Like a Writer Activities

These activities shift student focus from exploring and developing meanings of a reading selection to analyzing and evaluating how the writer presents meaning. By completing these activities, students learn how to read rhetorically, examining and assessing the effectiveness of the writer's choices in light of the purpose and audience.

The Guide to Reading at the beginning of each chapter presents several *Reading Like a Writer* activities that introduce the rhetorical strategies typical of the genre. Each subsequent essay in a chapter is followed by one *Reading Like a Writer* activity, inviting students to learn more about a particular strategy introduced in the Guide to Reading. Altogether, each chapter invites students to complete nine or ten focused rhetorical analyses of readings in the same genre.

Every *Reading Like a Writer* activity directs students to a specific part of a reading—a few sentences or paragraphs—so that students lose no time wondering where to begin their analysis. Many activities show students the first step to take. At least one activity in every chapter invites students to compare two or more readings in the chapter. Because they are focused and accessible, these activities make it possible for even the most inexperienced readers to complete them and engage in a serious program of rhetorical learning. Each *Reading Like a Writer* activity has two parts:

Analyze. Students note and annotate a rhetorical feature of the reading. For example, they may be asked to underline the active verbs in several paragraphs to see how a writer dramatizes an autobiographical event or to outline a causal argument to see how the writer sequences causes in order of importance or plausibility. Students may also be asked to consider the strategy's possible effect on the intended readers—for example, judging the persuasiveness of a counterargument in a position paper or deciding whether a comparison/contrast helps explain a concept. This part of the activity teaches students how to identify and think about writers' use of rhetorical strategies.

Write. Students write to present what they have learned by analyzing one particular feature of a reading. They explain or describe what they have noticed and evaluate its effectiveness by citing examples from the reading. Thus they learn to illustrate and support their generalizations with specific details from the text.

Guides to Writing That Support Students' Composing

As writing instructors, we know that students need help writing essays. To provide support for students, each *Reading Critically, Writing Well* chapter concludes with a comprehensive Guide to Writing that escorts students through every stage of writing from choosing a topic and gathering information and ideas, to offering constructive criticism of a classmate's draft, to revising and then editing and proofreading an essay. In our experience, all students—from the most anxious, inexperienced writers to the most confident, expert writers—benefit in some way from the Guides to Writing.

Grounded in research on composing and in learning theory, each Guide to Writing is effective because it:

- scaffolds students' learning about a genre, providing temporary support so that students can focus on one stage of writing at a time.
- provides prompts so that students can learn the kinds of questions they need to ask themselves.

- applies the rhetorical knowledge gleaned from reading to writing an essay in a genre.
- helps students engage in constructive critical readings of their classmates' writing.
- shows students how to organize their work and follow through to the end.

Activities That Ask Students to Reflect on Their Learning

Research has shown that when students reflect on their learning, they clarify their understanding and remember what they have learned longer. Reflecting also enables students to think critically about what they have learned and how they have learned it. *Reading Critically, Writing Well* provides two opportunities for students to reflect on their learning and also to discuss what they have learned with others. These activities are placed at important transitions in each chapter:

- *Reviewing What Makes [this kind of essay] Effective* appears after the readings and before the Guide to Writing. It invites students to look back at one essay they admire and to think about how it achieves its purpose.
- *Reflecting on What You Have Learned* appears at the end of the chapter and invites students to think about the essay they wrote and what influenced their writing.

Complete Catalog of Proven Critical Reading Strategies

In addition to the two critical reading strategies—*Reading for Meaning* and *Reading Like a Writer*—highlighted in every chapter, *Reading Critically, Writing Well* offers students an array of additional reading strategies. These strategies include annotating, outlining, summarizing, paraphrasing, contextualizing, and evaluating the logic of an argument. They are presented in Appendix 1, A Catalog of Critical Reading Strategies, where they are briefly illustrated. Following one reading in each assignment chapter, one of these various strategies is introduced, encouraging students to use this additional strategy to extend meaning or to deepen a rhetorical analysis.

Guidelines for Research and Documentation

Appendix 2 includes guidelines for finding and evaluating library and Internet sources and integrating them into an essay, as well as the most current MLA and APA guidelines for documenting them. It also includes coverage of field research.

Index to Methods of Development

The readings in *Reading Critically, Writing Well* are categorized by genre—by social function or writer's purpose. Writers usually employ a combination of rhetorical strategies to achieve their purposes but may emphasize a specific method of development in a particular genre, such as narration in autobiographical essays (Chapter 2) and argument in position papers (Chapter 9). The Index to Methods of Development categorizes entire readings as well as specific passages within readings that employ particular methods of development that instructors may want to emphasize.

Comprehensive Instructor's Manual

The Instructor's Manual offers a variety of course plans for teaching with *Reading Critically, Writing Well,* along with a panoply of practical suggestions for using the *Reading Like a Writer* activities together with the Guide to Writing. There is also a discussion of general teaching strategies, such as using reading journals, small groups, portfolios, and computers, as well as an annotated bibliography of research, theory, and practice that has influenced *Reading Critically, Writing Well.*

NEW TO THIS EDITION

In this edition, we have tried, as always, to make the book more engaging and useful for you and your students. In book reviews, bookstores, and university libraries, we broadened our usual wide search for new readings. In our own files and published collections of student essays and in dozens of essays submitted by instructors, we sought additional models of student writing. We looked for current subjects and stimulating content, and we looked for good models of the genres students will be learning about. This search for new readings was also influenced by our desire that some of the readings include illustrations, so that students could see how they need to apply critical-thinking skills to visual as well as verbal texts—and how, when appropriate, they can use visuals to enhance the rhetorical effect of their own essays. We also wanted to ease students' struggles to integrate text sources successfully into their essays. Finally, we sought a design that would make the book easier to live with for a semester by making it easier for students—and instructors—to navigate our somewhat complex chapters.

Following is a summary of the major new features of *Reading Critically, Writing Well*:

New Readings

There are twenty-nine new readings, over half of the total number, more than we have ever replaced in a new edition. New authors, including John Edge, Ian Frazier, Mari Matsuda, Randall Kennedy, and Suzanne Winckler, take on new subjects that range from reflections on butchering the meat we eat to definitions of nanotechnology and rave culture; speculations about why most quiz-show contestants are men and what makes a serial killer; a proposal for how to conserve resources and reduce pollution while saving money; and arguments for banning hate speech on college campuses, ending the anti-tobacco crusade, and lifting speed limits on interstate highways.

Reviewers asked for more student essays, and we happily complied. As mentioned earlier, each chapter's set of readings now includes two or three student essays, a total of seventeen in the book, twelve of them new. Following the last student essay in every chapter, students are invited to respond by reading for meaning and reading like a writer without the guidelines following the other readings. These assignments challenge students to think in a more independent way as they apply the critical-reading skills they have developed through the directed activities earlier in the chapter.

New Support for Using Sources

In previous editions of *Reading Critically, Writing Well,* Appendix 2, Strategies for Research and Documentation, has provided guidelines for finding and evaluating sources and citing them in an essay. Many students, however, also need help with the crucial intermediate stages of using source material, between initial scanning of possibilities and final formatting of citations. To this end, in this edition we have added a major new section, "Integrating Sources with Your Own Writing," which provides students with comprehensive support for deciding whether to quote, paraphrase, or summarize and how to quote, integrate quotations syntactically and punctuate them, and paraphrase and summarize. As noted earlier, we have also updated the section on MLA and APA citation styles to include the latest guidelines for electronic as well as other kinds of sources.

Attention to Visuals

With technology making it increasingly easy to add visual images to verbal texts, students need guidance on how to think critically about visuals as they encounter, choose, and use them. Consequently, we have added readings to most chapters that demonstrate various ways to enhance writing by incorporating visual elements. Following these readings, we invite students to think about what the visuals contribute to their understanding of the reading. In addition, in every chapter's Guide to Writing, we have added an invention activity, "Considering Visuals"; and to Reading a Draft Critically, we have added a step, "Evaluate the effectiveness of visuals."

New Design

In keeping with our increased attention to visual elements of writing, we have again updated the design of the book to make it more attractive and easier for both you and your students to use. Adding a second color and typeface makes it possible to distinguish the Guide to Reading and Guide to Writing more clearly from the readings in each chapter and to locate key sections that students need to review or refer to frequently, such as the Writing Assignment, the Special Reading Strategy, and the guidelines for Reading a Draft Critically.

ACKNOWLEDGMENTS

We first want to thank our students at the University of California, San Diego; University of Nevada, Reno; California State University, San Bernardino; and University of California, Riverside, who have been generous and frank with their advice. Some of them contributed essays to this text. We also owe a debt of gratitude to the many reviewers and questionnaire respondents who made suggestions for the revision. They include Tarisa A.M. Matsumoto, Iowa State University; Kip Strasma, Illinois Central College; Jacqueline A. Blackwell, Hampton University; Carmen M. Fye, California State University; Carol Leigh Rydell, Montana State University; Larry Severeid, College of Eastern Utah; Edis Kittrell, Montana State University; Sheryl D. McGough, Iowa State University; Maria A. Clayton, Middle Tennessee State University; Randall Vaughn Fishel, Hawaii Pacific University; Maribeth Winslow, Ivy Technical State College; Daniel Ding, Ferris State University; David Chapman, Samford University; Margaret G. Lee, Hampton University; Suzanne V. Shephard, Broome Community College; Clement Lau, Hawaii Pacific University; L. Leigh Westerfield, Indiana University; Sandra H. Howerton, Edgecombe Community College; Douglas L. Okey, Spoon River College; Bill Doyle, Florida Gulf Coast University; and Mary Dell Heathington, North Central Texas College.

To the editorial, production, and marketing crew at Bedford/St. Martin's, we wish to convey our deepest appreciation. We want to thank our developmental editor, John Elliott, for his many contributions and good humor, as well as Nancy Perry for over twenty years of friendship, encouragement, and sound advice. Sincere thanks go especially to Wendy Polhemus-Annibell, for her insightful editing; Wanda Kossak, for her helpful, creative new design; and to Shuli Traub, for her smooth coordination of the production process. We are indebted to Erica Appel for patient, inventive reschedulings of our publication date. Thanks also to Sandy Schechter for her work on permissions and to Brian Wheel for his enthusiasm in marketing the book.

Finally, Charles dedicates this book to his daughter Susanna, a member of the editorial board at the Sacramento *Bee* and the 2002 Journalism Fellow, Public Policy Institute of California. Susanna is an exemplary writer-in-the-world — well informed, curious, collaborative, personally courageous, and master of her genres. Rise wishes to dedicate this book with love to her mother, Edna Borenstein, who always told her to do the best she could — and had faith that she would.

Rise B. Axelrod
Charles R. Cooper

Contents

CHAPTER 6 Evaluation 250

CHAPTER 

Introduction

Reading Critically, Writing Well is designed to help prepare you for the special demands of learning in college, where all your reading should be critical reading—not only understanding what you read but also analyzing and evaluating it.

When you read a text critically, you alternate between two points of view: seeking to understand the text on its own terms and questioning the text's ideas and authority. Putting your questions aside even temporarily allows you to be open to new ideas. But reading critically requires that eventually you examine every idea—your own as well as those of others—skeptically.

Learning to read critically also helps you to write well. It leads you to a fuller understanding of the subject you plan to write about, enabling you to go beyond the obvious, to avoid superficiality and oversimplification. In addition, reading critically helps you anticipate what readers will expect and what questions they may have in mind as they read your writing.

Knowing your readers' expectations for the kind of essay you are writing helps you plan your essay with readers in mind. For example, if you are explaining an unfamiliar concept, you can assume your readers will expect concrete examples and comparisons to help them grasp the new and abstract idea. If you are arguing a position on a current issue, you know that readers will expect you not merely to assert your position but also to support it with facts, statistics, expert testimony, or other relevant evidence. In turn, knowing your readers' expectations will help you anticipate their questions. If you expect readers to accept certain of your ideas but to be skeptical about others, you can support with specific details, examples, or quotations those parts of your essay that present your most unfamiliar or controversial ideas.

Being able to anticipate how readers will respond does not mean that as a writer you always seek to please readers. In fact, good writing often challenges readers. But to challenge readers' assumptions, you need to know what they expect.

You will learn from the activities in this book that reading critically and writing well are intellectually demanding tasks that require your time and effort. Speed-reading may be the best strategy when you need to get the gist of an article or sort through a pile of possible sources. But when you need to understand new ideas or to evaluate complex arguments, when you are reading to prepare for class discussion or to write an essay, then you need to read more slowly and thoughtfully. Rereading is also essential.

The same principles apply to writing. Some kinds of writing can be dashed off in a single draft. The more practiced you are in a given kind of writing, the more efficient your writing process will be. If you write a lab report every week for a term, you should be able to write one rather quickly. If you know how to study for essay exams and have written them often, you should become quite adept at them. But when you need to do a kind of writing you have not mastered or to write about new and difficult material, then you will need more time to develop and organize your ideas.

Slowing down your reading and writing probably sounds like a bad idea to you right now, especially as you begin a new term and have just been told how much course work you will have to do. This book offers practical and efficient ways to meet this challenge by introducing basic strategies for reading critically and writing well.

Reading Critically

After you read each selection in *Reading Critically, Writing Well,* you will practice two basic strategies for reading critically: *reading for meaning* and *reading like a writer.* These strategies offer different but complementary ways of looking at a text.

When you read for meaning, you look at a text in terms of its ideas and information in order to understand and respond critically to what is being said. When you read like a writer, your focus shifts from meaning to rhetoric, from *what* is being communicated to *why* and *how* it is communicated. Although experienced readers may combine these two ways of reading—simultaneously reading for meaning and reading like a writer—we separate them here to give you an opportunity to refine your critical reading skills.

In Chapters 2 through 9, you will be asked to read a variety of essays in these two ways. Strategies such as summarizing, outlining, and evaluating the logic of an argument will be introduced to extend and deepen your repertoire of critical reading skills. Appendix 1 presents a complete catalog of these strategies.

READING FOR MEANING

When you read, your primary effort is to make the characters on the page or computer screen meaningful. But as you know from your experience as a reader, a text may be more meaningful or less so depending on your familiarity with the words that are used, as well as your knowledge of the subject and the kind of text or genre you are reading. If you have some knowledge about an issue currently being debated, for example, then an essay arguing for a position on that issue is likely to be relatively easy to read and full of meaning for you. If, however, you know nothing about the issue or the positions people have been taking on it, then the essay will probably be more difficult to read and less obviously meaningful.

Reading for meaning requires you to use your knowledge and experience to create meaning. You must bring to the text your knowledge about the subject and genre, your beliefs and values, your personal experience, as well as the historical and cultural contexts you share with others. Reading with this rich context helps you to see many possibilities for meaning in a text. Therefore, you will not be surprised that what you find meaningful in a given reading may overlap to some extent with what others find meaningful in the same reading, but also retain your own unique stamp.

As a reader, you are not a passive receptacle into which meaning is poured. Instead, as your eyes move across a text, you actively construct meaning from it, contributing your own relevant knowledge and point of view while also seeking to assimilate the text's new ideas and information. This highly significant and culturally important activity is what we mean by reading for meaning.

Annotating as you read is a powerful method for making sure you have something relevant to say about a given text. It helps concentrate your attention on the text's language and leaves you with a record of the insights, reactions, and questions that occurred to you in the process of reading for meaning. Annotating simply involves marking the page as you read. You note what you think is important in a reading, what you think it means, and what ideas and questions it raises for you. Annotating is easy to do. All it takes is a text you can write on and something to write with. Here are just a few ways to annotate a text:

- Highlight or underline key words and sentences.
- Bracket important passages.
- Connect related ideas with lines.
- Circle words to be defined.
- Outline the main ideas in the margin.
- Write brief comments and questions in the margin.

Some readers mark up the text extensively, while others mark only the parts they consider significant or problematic. What is important is not how you annotate or even how much you annotate, but *that* you annotate. The simple act of marking the page as you read makes it more likely that you will read closely and attentively. There is no right or wrong way to annotate. (For an example of annotating, see Appendix 1, pp. 519–24.)

After annotating, *exploratory writing* is a powerful way of developing your ideas about an essay. You will find that the very act of composing sentences leads you to clarify and extend your ideas, discovering new insights and raising new questions. The key to productive exploratory writing is to refrain from censoring yourself. Simply write at least a page. The goal at this stage is to allow ideas to flow freely.

We recommend, then, a two-step procedure: annotating as you read, followed by exploratory writing that develops meanings for a text. You can extend your understanding by adding a third step—conversing with others who have also read the essay. Your instructor will likely give you opportunities, whether in class or online, to discuss the reading with other students.

Previewing the Reading for Meaning Activities

A Reading for Meaning activity follows each reading in the book. Turn to one of these activities now. As you can see, each Reading for Meaning activity consists of two sections: (1) *Start Making Meaning* and (2) *If You Are Stuck.*

Start Making Meaning

This section asks you to begin constructing meaning by writing about an important aspect of the type of essay you are studying, such as the event's significance in an autobiographical essay or the reasons in a position paper. Then, you are encouraged to write about any meanings you see in the essay. Think of this writing as exploratory—following your thoughts to see where they lead, without being overly concerned about word choice, grammar, or spelling. Your aim is simple: Write until you have written at least a page. If you cannot think of anything else to write, try to expand on your annotations, reread and respond to an intriguing passage, or write about one of the suggestions offered in If You Are Stuck.

If You Are Stuck

To help you write at least a page about the essay's possible meanings, the If You Are Stuck section offers several suggestions focusing on different aspects of the essay. You could respond to one or more of these suggestions or use them as a springboard for your own insights about the essay. You might have no need for these suggestions; they are offered only to help you think about the reading in different ways.

READING LIKE A WRITER

Reading like a writer shifts your focus from constructing meanings for a reading to analyzing and evaluating how its meanings are presented. Reading like a writer, you look closely at rhetoric—the ways writers make their ideas understandable and seek to influence readers.

To read rhetorically, you need to think about writing in terms of its purpose and audience. Writers make many choices when they write, choices that frequently depend on the writer's reason(s) for writing and the particular readers being addressed. When you read like a writer, you examine the writer's choices and assess their effectiveness in light of the writer's purpose and audience. This kind of reading helps you make rhetorically effective choices in your own writing.

When you read like a writer, you follow the same simple procedure as you do for reading for meaning: annotating, followed by writing.

Previewing the Reading like a Writer Activities

A Reading like a Writer activity follows each selection in the book. Turn to one of these activities now. As you can see, each Reading like a Writer activity consists of one or two introductory paragraphs followed by two sections: *Analyze* and *Write*.

Analyze

The instructions in this section typically ask you to reread specific paragraphs in the reading and to underline or bracket certain words or sentences. These annotations, which you make as you read like a writer, focus on the characteristic textual features and rhetorical strategies of the genre—or type of writing—you are studying. Your aim is to use annotating as a way to begin analyzing the features and strategies typical of the genre and to begin evaluating how well they work in a particular reading.

Write

Here you are asked to write several sentences about what you discovered in analyzing and evaluating a reading's features and strategies in terms of how well they achieve the writer's purpose. Writing even a few sentences can help you develop your analysis and evaluation of a reading.

Writing Well

The following section introduces you to the essay-length writing you will do when you undertake the major assignments in Chapters 2 through 9 of *Reading Critically, Writing Well.* As you might guess, the briefer writing activities following every reading (Reading for Meaning and Reading like a Writer) prepare you to write your own full-length essay.

Before previewing the essay assignments, pause to think about your own writing experience in high school, college, or on the job.

THINKING ABOUT YOUR PAST WRITING EXPERIENCE

1. *Recall* the last time you wrote something fairly difficult, long, or complicated. It may have been an assignment at school or at work, or it may have been something you initiated yourself. Do not choose something written under strict time limits, such as an in-class essay exam.
2. *Write* several sentences describing how you went about planning and writing. Begin by briefly explaining your purpose for writing and identifying your intended readers. *Note* any assumptions you made about your readers' knowledge of the subject or their expectations of your writing.

You can use one or more of the following questions if you need help remembering how you went about completing the writing. But do not restrict yourself to these questions. Write down whatever comes to mind as you think about your past writing experience.

- How long did it take before you started putting your ideas on paper?
- What kind of plan did you have? How did your plan evolve as you worked?
- What did you change as you were writing? What changes, if any, did you make after completing your first draft?
- What role did other people play in helping you develop your ideas and plans?

THE WRITING ASSIGNMENTS

As you work through the assignments in Chapters 2 through 9 of *Reading Critically, Writing Well,* you will learn how to write the following genres or types of essays:

Autobiography (Chapter 2): telling readers about important events and people in your life

Observation (Chapter 3): presenting to readers your firsthand reports about intriguing new places, people, and activities

Reflection (Chapter 4): exploring for readers the larger social implications of your experience or observation

Explaining concepts (Chapter 5): defining for readers the meaning and importance of key ideas

Evaluation (Chapter 6): arguing to convince readers that your judgment of a movie, book, performance, essay, noteworthy person, or other subject is justifiable

Speculation about causes or effects (Chapter 7): arguing to convince readers that certain causes or effects plausibly explain some event, trend, or phenomenon

Proposal to solve a problem (Chapter 8): arguing to convince readers to accept or seriously consider your proposed solution to a problem

Position paper (Chapter 9): arguing to convince readers to accept or seriously consider your position on a controversial issue

Each of these writing assignments identifies a genre of writing done every day by countless writers. More than mere school writing exercises, they are real-world writing situations like those you will encounter in college and at work. Pause now to learn a bit more about these assignments.

Previewing the Writing Assignments

Look at the different writing genres that are represented in this book. On the second or third page of each assignment chapter (Chapters 2 through 9) is a brief set of Writing Situations. Read this section in all of the chapters to get a quick sense of the different kinds of writing. Then write several sentences responding to the following questions:

1. Which of these genres have you already written?
2. With which of these genres have you had the most experience? Where and when did you write this kind of essay? What was most challenging about writing it?
3. What other genres would you like to learn to write? Why do they interest you?

THE GUIDES TO WRITING

Following the Readings section of Chapters 2 through 9 in *Reading Critically, Writing Well,* a Guide to Writing helps you complete the writing assignment. These guides reflect the fact that writing is a process of discovery. As writers, we rarely if ever begin with a complete understanding of the subject. We put together some information and ideas, start writing, and let the writing lead us to understanding. While writing helps us achieve greater understanding, it also raises questions and unexpected complexities, which, in turn, can inspire more writing and, nearly always, generate further ideas and insights.

Experienced writers have learned to trust this fascinating discovery process because they know that writing is an unsurpassed way of thinking. Writing helps you discover, explore, develop, and refine your ideas in a way that cannot compare with sitting around and thinking about a subject. Because writing leaves a record of your thinking, it reduces the burden of remembering and allows you to direct all your energy toward solving the immediate problem. By rereading what you have written, you can figure out where you became derailed or recall points that you forgot were important or see new possibilities you did not notice before.

The Guide to Writing for each assignment leads you through the complex, creative process of discovery: Invention, Drafting, Reading a Draft Critically, Revising, and Editing and Proofreading. Because it helps to approach the first draft of an essay with some notes and other brief writings in hand, the first writing activity in each guide is called *invention,* a term used since classical Greek times to describe speakers' and writers' attempts to discover what they know and might say about a subject. Because *drafting* is most efficient and productive when you clarify your purpose and plan in advance, the Guide to Writing helps you set goals and organize your draft. Also, because nearly any draft can benefit from the advice of thoughtful readers, guidelines are included to help you and your classmates *read each other's drafts critically.* And because *revising* gives you the opportunity to develop your ideas and to make your writing communicate more clearly and effectively, each Guide to Writing includes suggestions for improving your draft. Finally, because you want your finished essay to conform to the conventions of grammar, mechanics, punctuation, spelling, and style, each guide concludes with advice on *editing and proofreading* your essay.

Before reading about the resources offered to support your invention, drafting, critical reading, revising, and editing and proofreading, take time to preview a Guide to Writing.

Previewing a Guide to Writing

Turn to one of the Guides to Writing toward the end of any writing assignment chapter. Skim the guide, reading the headings and the first paragraph in each major section to get an idea of what the guide offers.

Invention

Invention begins with finding a subject to write about. The Considering Ideas for Your Own Writing section following each reading, together with the suggestions in the Guide to Writing, will help you list several possible subjects. This act of listing possibilities is itself inventive because one item often suggests the next, and as the list grows you come to understand your options better and can therefore more confidently choose a subject. In each chapter, you will find suggestions that will help you make a good choice and understand the implications of developing the subject you choose.

Because each writing situation makes unique demands on writers, the invention activities in each chapter differ. To see how the invention activities differ from one kind of writing to the next, compare the activities under Invention in two or three chapters—for example, in Chapter 2 on autobiography, Chapter 5 on explaining concepts, and Chapter 9 on arguing positions.

The immediate advantage of this genre-specific invention is that it stimulates your thinking, getting you writing days before you begin drafting your essay. Although you will usually need no more than two hours to complete these invention activities, it is best to spread them over several days. As soon as you start writing the first few sentences about a subject, your mind goes to work on it, perhaps even offering ideas and insights when you are going about your daily activities, not consciously thinking about the subject. More invention writing will inspire more ideas. Your understanding of the subject will deepen and the possibilities will become more wide-ranging and subtle. An assignment that may have seemed daunting will become intellectually invigorating, and you will have pages of invention notes with which to launch your draft.

Drafting

After working on invention, you may be eager to begin drafting your essay. If, however, you are having difficulty making the transition from jotting down invention notes to writing a first draft, the Guide to Writing in each chapter will show you how to set achievable goals and devise a tentative plan that will ease the process of drafting. The guide's Drafting section offers several activities, including Setting Goals and Organizing Your Draft. To set goals, you need to ask yourself questions about your purpose and audience, such as how to interest readers in your subject, describe a person vividly, or counterargue effectively. As you establish your goals, you will also be reminded of the strategies that you saw other writers in the chapter use to accomplish similar goals in their essays. Organizing Your Draft points out how the other writers in the chapter organize their essays and suggests that you make a scratch outline to develop a tentative plan for your own essay.

Reading a Draft Critically

Reading a draft with a critical eye enables you to give a classmate's draft an informed reading. Your critical reading can be supportive and helpful because as a writer yourself you can give the kind of advice writers most need when they have written a draft but are unsure what is working and what needs improvement. In the case of revising a position paper, for example, writers may need advice on how to clarify the position, strengthen the argument, anticipate readers' objections, tighten the logic, and so on. These are the essentials for arguing convincingly for a position on a controversial issue.

The Reading a Draft Critically section invites you to make practical use of all you have learned about reading a genre. It also invites you to try out your newly acquired expertise and even to show off a bit—all while doing a classmate a big favor. Part of the favor you provide is the written record of your critical reading that you hand over to your classmate, a record the classmate can refer to the next day or next week when revising his or her essay. You do yourself a favor as well. Like your classmate, you too will revise an essay in the same genre. As you read your classmate's essay critically, you will be reflecting intensely on your own just-completed draft. The more thoughtful and comprehensive your critical reading, the more likely you will be to discover ways to strengthen your own draft.

Revising

Revising offers the great opportunity of rethinking what you have written, given your purpose and your readers' needs and expectations. Assume you will want to make changes and add new material at this stage. Be prepared to cut sentences, move sentences, and reorder paragraphs. You provide the brainpower, and the computer provides the technology to make dramatic changes easy. The Revising section offers a range of suggestions for you to consider, along with the advice you received from your classmates and instructor.

Editing and Proofreading

Editing and proofreading are like taking a last look at yourself in the mirror before going out. You have given some thought to what you would wear and how you would look; now you check to make sure everything is the way you want it. When you write an essay, you spend a lot of time and energy planning, drafting, and revising; now you want to check to make sure that there are no glaring mistakes in grammar, punctuation, word choice, spelling, or matters of style. If you are unsure whether you have made a mistake or how to fix it, consult a writer's guidebook or handbook, another student, or your writing instructor.

Thinking about Your Learning

We know from research that if learning is not reviewed, reflected on, and consolidated, it soon fades and might not be available when new occasions arise for using or applying it. Therefore, in each assignment chapter, we provide two occasions for you to pause and reflect on what you have learned.

Reviewing What Makes Essays Effective

The first occasion for thinking about your learning comes after the Readings section in each assignment chapter. For example, in Chapter 9, Position Paper, this section is titled Reviewing What Makes Position Papers Effective. You are asked to choose one reading from the chapter that seemed to you a particularly good example of its genre, to reread it critically in light of all you have learned about the genre, and then to write a page or more justifying your choice. This activity enables you to review the characteristic features and rhetorical strategies of the genre you are about to write. Coming where it does, *before* the Guide to Writing, this activity helps you complete the transition from thinking like a reader to thinking like a writer.

Reflecting on What You Have Learned

This final occasion for thinking about your learning comes at the end of each assignment chapter, where you are invited to describe what you are most pleased with in your final essay and to explain what contributed to this achievement. It reminds you that there is much you have learned and much to learn about writing—from reading others' work, from writing your own essays, and from collaborating with other writers.

CHAPTER 2

Autobiography

Autobiography involves telling stories about key events in your life and describing people who played important roles in it. Whether writing about an exhilarating childhood game or a difficult relationship, you should evoke for readers a vivid impression to help them see what you saw, hear what you heard, and feel what you felt. To write autobiography, therefore, you need to revisit the past, immersing yourself in the sights, sounds, and other sensations of memory. You also need to think deeply about the meaning of your experience—why it was and still is significant to you. Thinking deeply about the significance of important events and people in your life can help you discover something about the forces within yourself and within society that have helped to shape who you are and what is important to you.

While writing about your own life can be both enjoyable and instructive, so too can reading about other people's lives. As readers, we often take pleasure in seeing reflections of our own experience in other people's autobiographical writing. We enjoy recognizing similarities between the people and the events we have known and those that we read about. But sometimes the differences can be far more thought-provoking. For example, we may see how certain conditions—such as whether we grew up in the suburbs or the city; whether we are male or female; whether we are of African American, European, Asian, or of mixed descent—can profoundly affect our lives and perspectives. Autobiography sometimes affirms our preconceptions, but it is most effective when it leads us to question our certainties, challenging us to see ourselves and others in a new light.

Whether you are reading or writing autobiography, it is important to remember that autobiography is public, not private. While it involves self-presentation and contributes to self-knowledge, it does not require writers to make unwanted self-disclosures. Autobiographers compose themselves for readers; they fashion a self in words, much as a novelist creates a character. As readers, we come to "know" the people we read about by the way they are portrayed. Consequently, when you write autobiography, you have to decide how to portray yourself. This decision depends on whom you expect to read your essay (your audience) and what you want to communicate to readers (your purpose).

As you work through this chapter, you will learn more about autobiography by reading several different examples of it. You will see that some autobiographical essays center on a single event that occurred over a brief period of hours or days, while other essays focus on a person who played a significant role in the writer's life. Whether you decide to tell a story about a remembered event or to write about another person, you will practice two of the most basic writing strategies—narration and description. As you will see in later chapters of this book, narration and description can play a role not only in autobiography but also in providing explanations and advancing arguments.

Whether you choose to write about an event or a person, your study of the readings in this chapter will give you ideas for writing effective autobiography. As you read and write about the selections, keep in mind the following assignment, which sets out the goals for writing an autobiographical essay. To support your writing of this assignment, the chapter concludes with a Guide to Writing Autobiography.

THE WRITING ASSIGNMENT

Autobiography

Write an autobiographical essay about a significant event or person in your life. Choose the event or person with your readers in mind: The subject should be one that you feel comfortable presenting to others and that will lead readers to reflect on their own lives or on the differences between their personal experiences and your own. Present your experience dramatically and vividly so that readers can imagine what it was like for you. Through a careful choice of words and details, convey the meaning and importance in your life—the autobiographical significance—of this event or person.

WRITING SITUATIONS FOR AUTOBIOGRAPHY

You may think only scientists, novelists, politicians, movie stars, and other famous people write their autobiographies. But autobiographical writing is much more widespread, as the following examples indicate:

- As part of her college application, a high-school senior includes a brief autobiographical essay that conveys her reasons for wanting to study science and become a researcher. In the essay, she recalls what happened when she did her first scientific experiment on the nutritional effects of different breakfast cereals on mice.

- Asked to recall a significant early childhood memory for an assignment in a psychology class, a college student writes about a fishing trip he took as a nine-year-old. He reflects on the significance of the trip—it was the first trip he took alone with his father and it began a new stage in their relationship.
- As part of a workshop on management skills, a business executive writes about a person who influenced his ideas about leadership. As he explores his memory and feelings, he realizes that he mistook fear for admiration. He recognizes that he has been emulating the wrong model, an autocratic leader who got people to perform by intimidating them.

A Guide to Reading Autobiography

This guide introduces you to autobiographical writing. By completing all the activities in it, you will prepare yourself to learn a great deal from the other readings in this chapter about how to read and write an autobiographical essay. The guide to reading focuses on a brief but powerful piece of autobiography by Annie Dillard. You will read Dillard's autobiographical essay twice. First, you will read it for meaning, seeking to grasp the significance of the event for Dillard—what it meant to her both at the time she experienced it and years later when she wrote about it—as well as the meaning it holds for you. Then, you will reread the essay like a writer of autobiography, analyzing the parts to see how Dillard crafts her essay and to learn the strategies she uses to make her autobiographical writing effective. These two activities—reading for meaning and reading like a writer—follow every reading in this chapter.

ANNIE DILLARD

A Chase

Annie Dillard (b. 1945) is a prolific writer whose first book, Pilgrim at Tinker Creek *(1974), won the Pulitzer Prize for nonfiction writing. Since then, she has written meditations on nature and religion, including* For the Time Being *(1999); several collections of poetry, most recently* Mornings like This *(1996); a novel,* The Living *(1992); an account of her work as a writer,* The Writing Life *(1989); and an autobiography,* An American Childhood *(1987), from which the following reading is excerpted.*

"A Chase" relates an event that occurred one snowy morning when the seven-year-old Dillard and a friend were chased relentlessly by an adult stranger at whom they had been throwing snowballs. Dillard admits that she was terrified at the time, and yet she asserts that she has "seldom been happier since." As you read, think about how this paradox helps you grasp the autobiographical significance of this experience for Dillard. Annotate anything that helps you appreciate the drama and significance of the event. Annotating involves writing on the text as you read—noting parts you think are important, identifying words or references you do not know, and writing comments and questions in the margin. (To learn more about annotating, see Appendix 1, pp. 518–24.)

Some boys taught me to play football. This was fine sport. You thought up a new strategy for every play and whispered it to the others. You went out for a pass, fooling everyone. Best, you got to throw yourself mightily at someone's running legs. Either you brought him down or you hit the ground flat out on your chin, with your arms empty before you. It was all or nothing. If you hesitated in fear, you would miss and get hurt: you would take a hard fall while the kid got away, or you would get kicked in the face while the kid got away. But if you flung yourself wholeheartedly at the back of his knees—if you gathered and joined body and soul and pointed them diving fearlessly—then you likely wouldn't get hurt, and you'd stop the ball. Your fate, and your team's score, depended on your concentration and courage. Nothing girls did could compare with it. 1

Boys welcomed me at baseball, too, for I had, through enthusiastic practice, what was weirdly known as a boy's arm. In winter, in the snow, there was neither baseball nor football, so the boys and I threw snowballs at passing cars. I got in trouble throwing snowballs, and have seldom been happier since. 2

On one weekday morning after Christmas, six inches of new snow had just fallen. We were standing up to our boot tops in snow on a front yard on trafficked Reynolds Street, waiting for cars. The cars traveled Reynolds Street slowly and evenly; they were targets all but wrapped in red ribbons, cream puffs. We couldn't miss. 3

I was seven; the boys were eight, nine, and ten. The oldest two Fahey boys were there—Mikey and Peter—polite blond boys who lived near me on Lloyd Street, and who already had four brothers and sisters. My parents approved Mikey and Peter Fahey. Chickie McBride was there, a tough kid, and Billy Paul and 4

Mackie Kean too, from across Reynolds, where the boys grew up dark and furious, grew up skinny, knowing, and skilled. We had all drifted from our houses that morning looking for action, and had found it here on Reynolds Street.

5 It was cloudy but cold. The cars' tires laid behind them on the snowy street a complex trail of beige chunks like crenellated castle walls. I had stepped on some earlier; they squeaked. We could not have wished for more traffic. When a car came, we all popped it one. In the intervals between cars we reverted to the natural solitude of children.

6 I started making an iceball—a perfect iceball, from perfectly white snow, perfectly spherical, and squeezed perfectly translucent so no snow remained all the way through. (The Fahey boys and I considered it unfair actually to throw an iceball at somebody, but it had been known to happen.)

7 I had just embarked on the iceball project when we heard tire chains come clanking from afar. A black Buick was moving toward us down the street. We all spread out, banged together some regular snowballs, took aim, and, when the Buick drew nigh, fired.

8 A soft snowball hit the driver's windshield right before the driver's face. It made a smashed star with a hump in the middle.

9 Often, of course, we hit our target, but this time, the only time in all of life, the car pulled over and stopped. Its wide black door opened; a man got out of it, running. He didn't even close the car door.

10 He ran after us, and we ran away from him, up the snowy Reynolds sidewalk. At the corner, I looked back; incredibly, he was still after us. He was in city clothes: a suit and tie, street shoes. Any normal adult would have quit, having sprung us into flight and made his point. This man was gaining on us. He was a thin man, all action. All of a sudden, we were running for our lives.

11 Wordless, we split up. We were on our turf; we could lose ourselves in the neighborhood backyards, everyone for himself. I paused and considered. Everyone had vanished except Mikey Fahey, who was just rounding the corner of a yellow brick house. Poor Mikey, I trailed him. The driver of the Buick sensibly picked the two of us to follow. The man apparently had all day.

12 He chased Mikey and me around the yellow house and up a backyard path we knew by heart: under a low tree, up a bank, through a hedge, down some snowy steps, and across the grocery store's delivery driveway. We smashed through a gap in another hedge, entered a scruffy backyard and ran around its back porch and tight between houses to Edgerton Avenue; we ran across

Edgerton to an alley and up our own sliding woodpile to the Halls' front yard; he kept coming. We ran up Lloyd Street and wound through mazy backyards toward the steep hilltop at Willard and Lang.

13 He chased us silently, block after block. He chased us silently over picket fences, through thorny hedges, between houses, around garbage cans, and across streets. Every time I glanced back, choking for breath, I expected he would have quit. He must have been as breathless as we were. His jacket strained over his body. It was an immense discovery, pounding into my hot head with every sliding, joyous step, that this ordinary adult evidently knew what I thought only children who trained at football knew: that you have to fling yourself at what you're doing, you have to point yourself, forget yourself, aim, dive.

14 Mikey and I had nowhere to go, in our own neighborhood or out of it, but away from this man who was chasing us. He impelled us forward; we compelled him to follow our route. The air was cold; every breath tore my throat. We kept running, block after block; we kept improvising, backyard after backyard, running a frantic course and choosing it simultaneously, failing always to find small places or hard places to slow him down, and discovering always, exhilarated, dismayed, that only bare speed could save us—for he would never give up, this man—and we were losing speed.

15 He chased us through the backyard labyrinths of ten blocks before he caught us by our jackets. He caught us and we all stopped.

16 We three stood staggering, half blinded, coughing, in an obscure hilltop backyard: a man in his twenties, a boy, a girl. He had released our jackets, our pursuer, our captor, our hero: he knew we weren't going anywhere. We all played by the rules. Mikey and I unzipped our jackets. I pulled off my sopping mittens. Our tracks multiplied in the backyard's new snow. We had been breaking new snow all morning. We didn't look at each other. I was cherishing my excitement. The man's lower pants legs were wet; his cuffs were full of snow, and there was a prow of snow beneath them on his shoes and socks. Some trees bordered the little flat backyard, some messy winter trees. There was no one around: a clearing in a grove, and we the only players.

17 It was a long time before he could speak. I had some difficulty at first recalling why we were there. My lips felt swollen; I couldn't see out of the sides of my eyes; I kept coughing.

18 "You stupid kids," he began perfunctorily.

19 We listened perfunctorily indeed, if we listened at all, for the chewing out was redundant, a mere formality, and beside the

point. The point was that he had chased us passionately without giving up, and so he had caught us. Now he came down to earth. I wanted the glory to last forever.

20 But how could the glory have lasted forever? We could have run through every backyard in North America until we got to Panama. But when he trapped us at the lip of the Panama Canal, what precisely could he have done to prolong the drama of the chase and cap its glory? I brooded about this for the next few years. He could only have fried Mikey Fahey and me in boiling oil, say, or dismembered us piecemeal, or staked us to anthills. None of which I really wanted, and none of which any adult was likely to do, even in the spirit of fun. He could only chew us out there in the Panamanian jungle, after months or years of exalting pursuit. He could only begin, "You stupid kids," and continue in his ordinary Pittsburgh accent with his normal righteous anger and the usual common sense.

21 If in that snowy backyard the driver of the black Buick had cut off our heads, Mikey's and mine, I would have died happy, for nothing has required so much of me since as being chased all over Pittsburgh in the middle of winter—running terrified, exhausted—by this sainted, skinny, furious redheaded man who wished to have a word with us. I don't know how he found his way back to his car.

READING FOR MEANING

Write to create meanings for Dillard's autobiographical essay.

Start Making Meaning

Begin by explaining what you think the significance of this event is for Dillard and what her purpose or purposes are in choosing to write about it in the way that she does. Continue by writing about anything else in the selection or in your experience that contributes to your understanding of Dillard's story.

If You Are Stuck

If you cannot write at least a page, consider writing about

- why Dillard states proudly, "We all played by the rules" (paragraph 16), speculating about how we come to know what "rules" to play by.
- why Dillard uses such words as "hero" (paragraph 16) and "sainted" (paragraph 21) to describe the man who chased her, even though she dismisses

what he said when he finally caught her as "redundant, a mere formality, and beside the point" (paragraph 19).

- how a particular scene—such as the iceballing scene (paragraphs 5–8) or the confrontation scene (paragraphs 15–21)—contributes to your understanding of the event's significance for Dillard.
- your impression of childhood and gender roles in the United States at the time of Dillard's story (the 1950s), perhaps in comparison with the childhood and gender roles of your own generation.

READING LIKE A WRITER

This section leads you through an analysis of Dillard's autobiographical writing strategies: *narrating the story, presenting people, describing places,* and *conveying the autobiographical significance.* For each strategy you will be asked to reread and annotate part of Dillard's essay to see how she uses the strategy to accomplish her particular purpose.

When you study the selections later in this chapter, you will see how different autobiographers use these same strategies for different purposes. The Guide to Writing Autobiography near the end of the chapter suggests ways you can use these strategies in your own writing.

Narrating the Story

Whether focusing on a single event or a person, writers nearly always tell a story or several brief stories called *anecdotes.* Stories are so pervasive in our culture, indeed in most cultures, that we are all familiar with what makes a story effective. A well-told story draws readers in by arousing their curiosity and often keeps them reading by building suspense or drama, making them want to know what will happen next.

Storytellers use a variety of techniques to dramatize events. One way is to speed up the action and heighten the tension. This activity will help you see how Dillard uses active verbs and other verb forms to make her story dramatic.

Analyze

1. *Reread* paragraphs 12 and 13, underlining as many verbs and verbals as you can. Do not worry if you miss some. Verbals are verb forms that usually end in *ing* as in "staggering" and "coughing" (paragraph 16), or *ed,* as in "blinded" (16) and "smashed" (8), or that begin with *to,* as in "to fling" and "to point" (13).
2. *Put a second line* under the verbs or verbals that name an action. For example, the verb "chased" in the following sentence names an action (double

underline), whereas the verb "knew" does not name an action (single underline): "He chased Mikey and me around the yellow house and up a backyard path we knew by heart . . ." (paragraph 12).

3. *Find* two or three sentences in which the action verbs and verbals help you imagine the drama of the chase.

Write

Write several sentences explaining what you have learned about Dillard's use of verbs and verbals to represent action and to make her narrative dramatic. *Use examples* from paragraphs 12 and 13 to support your explanation.

Presenting People

Autobiographers describe people by depicting what they look like, by letting readers hear how they speak, and by characterizing their behavior and personality. Often, one or two specific details about the way a person looks, dresses, talks, or acts will be sufficient to give readers a vivid impression of the person. As you will see when you read the essays later in this chapter by Laurie Abraham, Amy Wu, and Brad Benioff, even autobiographical essays that focus on a person rather than a single event tend to use only a few well-chosen details to present the person.

To see how Dillard presents people, let us look at the descriptions of the neighborhood boys in paragraph 4. Notice that she gives each boy a brief descriptive tag: "Mikey and Peter—polite blond boys who lived near me on Lloyd Street" and "Chickie McBride . . . a tough kid, and Billy Paul and Mackie Kean too, from across Reynolds, where the boys grew up dark and furious, grew up skinny, knowing, and skilled." The details "blond" and "skinny" create a visual image, whereas "polite," "tough," and "knowing" convey Dillard's characterizations or evaluations of the boys. These characterizations or evaluations contribute not only to the impression we get of each boy but also to our understanding of his significance in the writer's life. (As you will see later in the chapter, such characterizations are one way writers convey autobiographical significance.)

Analyze

1. In paragraphs 10, 16, and 21, *find* and *underline* words and phrases that visually describe the man. Also *put brackets around* words and phrases that characterize or evaluate the man.

2. *Look* at paragraph 18 and the last sentence of paragraph 20, where Dillard presents the man through dialogue. *Underline* the details used to describe

how the man looks and sounds. Also *put brackets around* words and phrases used to characterize or evaluate what the man says and how he says it.

3. *Think about* how Dillard's presentation of the man in these five paragraphs helps you see him in your mind's eye and understand his role in the chase.

Write

Based on your analysis, *write* several sentences examining Dillard's use of descriptive details and characterizations to present the man. *Use examples* from the words and phrases you underlined and bracketed to support your ideas.

Describing Places

Whether autobiography centers on an event or a person, it nearly always includes some description of places. Writers make a remembered place vivid by naming memorable objects they want readers to see there and by detailing these objects. For examples of *naming* and *detailing*, look at paragraph 3, where Dillard describes what it looked like on that particular morning after Christmas. Notice that Dillard uses naming to point out the snow, Reynolds Street, and the cars. She also adds details that give information about these objects: "*six inches* of *new* snow," "*trafficked* Reynolds Street," "cars traveled . . . *slowly* and *evenly*."

To make her description evocative as well as vivid, Dillard adds a third describing strategy: *comparing*. In paragraph 5, for example, she describes the trail made by car tires in the snow as being "like crenellated castle walls." The word *like* makes the comparison explicit and identifies it as a simile. Dillard also uses implicit comparisons, called metaphors, such as when she calls the cars "targets all but wrapped in red ribbons, cream puffs" (paragraph 3).

Analyze

1. *Examine* how Dillard uses naming and detailing to describe the "perfect iceball" in paragraph 6. What does she name it and what details does she add to specify the qualities that make an iceball "perfect"?

2. Then *look closely* at the two comparisons in paragraphs 3 and 5. *Notice* also the following comparisons in other paragraphs: "smashed star" (8), "sprung us into flight" (10), "mazy backyards" (12), "every breath tore my throat" (14), and "backyard labyrinths" (15). Choose any single comparison—simile or metaphor—in the reading and *think about* how it helps you imagine what the place was like for Dillard on that day.

Write

Write a few sentences explaining how Dillard uses the describing strategies of *naming, detailing,* and *comparing* to help you imagine what the places she presents seemed like during the chase. *Give at least one example* from the reading of each describing strategy.

Conveying the Autobiographical Significance

Autobiographers convey the significance of an event or a person in two ways: by *showing* and by *telling.* Through your analyses of how Dillard narrates the story, presents people, and describes places, you have looked at some of the ways she *shows* the event's significance. This activity focuses on what Dillard *tells* readers.

When Dillard writes in the opening paragraphs about boys teaching her to play football and baseball, she is telling why these experiences were memorable and important. Autobiographers usually tell both what they remember thinking and feeling *at the time* and what they think and feel now *as they write about the past.* Readers must infer from the ideas and the writer's choice of words whether a phrase or sentence conveys the writer's past or present perspective, remembered feelings and thoughts or current ones. For example, look at the following sentences from paragraph 1: "You thought up a new strategy for every play and whispered it to the others. You went out for a pass, fooling everyone." The words "whispered" and "fooling" suggest that here Dillard is trying to reconstruct a seven-year-old child's way of speaking and thinking. In contrast, when she tells us that football was a "fine sport" and what was fine about it—"Your fate, and your team's score, depended on your concentration and courage"—we can infer from words such as "fate," "concentration," and "courage" that Dillard is speaking from her present adult perspective, telling us what she may have sensed as a child but now can more fully understand and articulate.

To determine the autobiographical significance of the remembered event or person, then, readers need to pay attention to what Dillard tells about the significance—both her remembered feelings and thoughts and her present perspective.

Analyze

1. *Reread* paragraphs 19–21, where Dillard comments on the chase and the man's "chewing out." *Put brackets around* words and phrases that tell what the adult Dillard is thinking as she writes about this event from her past. For example, in the first sentence of paragraph 19, "perfunctorily," "redundant," and "a mere formality" may seem to you to be examples of adult language, rather than words a seven-year-old would use.

2. Then *underline* words and phrases in the same paragraphs that seem to convey thoughts and feelings that Dillard remembers from when she was a child.

Write

Write several sentences explaining what you have learned about the event's significance for Dillard. What does she tell readers about the thoughts and feelings she had as a child as well as the thoughts and feelings she has now as an adult looking back on the experience? *Quote* selected words and phrases from your underlining and bracketing, indicating what identifies them as either remembered or present-perspective thoughts and feelings.

Readings

AUDRE LORDE

That Summer I Left Childhood Was White

Audre Lorde (1934–1992) wrote ten volumes of poetry, including The Black Unicorn *(1978) and the posthumous* The Marvelous Arithmetics of Distance *(1994), which was nominated for a National Book Critics Circle Award. Among her five works of prose are* Sister Outsider: Essays and Speeches *(1984) and a best-selling autobiography,* Zami: A New Spelling of My Name *(1982), from which this reading is excerpted.*

In "That Summer I Left Childhood Was White," Lorde recalls an incident that occurred in 1947, when she was thirteen. Remembering what happened and how her family reacted to the event, Lorde reflects on the silence, even within her own family, about the injustice of racism in America.

Before you read, consider what you know about the history of racism in the United States during and after World War II. Did you know, for example, that a million African American men and women served in the military during the war, but that the military was not integrated until 1948? Did you know that it did not become illegal to refuse service in a restaurant on the basis of race until the Civil Rights Act of 1964?

The first time I went to Washington, D.C., was on the edge of the summer when I was supposed to stop being a child. At least that's what they said to us all at graduation from the eighth grade. My sister Phyllis graduated at the same time from high school. I don't know what she was supposed to stop being. But as graduation presents for us both, the whole family took a Fourth of July trip to Washington, D.C., the fabled and famous capital of our country. 1

It was the first time I'd ever been on a railroad train during the day. When I was little, and we used to go to the Connecticut shore, we always went at night on the milk train, because it was cheaper. 2

Preparations were in the air around our house before school was even over. We packed for a week. There were two very large suitcases that my father carried, and a box filled with food. In fact, my first trip to Washington was a mobile feast; I started eating as 3 soon as we were comfortably ensconced in our seats, and did not stop until somewhere after Philadelphia. I remember it was Philadelphia because I was disappointed not to have passed by the Liberty Bell.

4 My mother had roasted two chickens and cut them up into dainty bite-size pieces. She packed slices of brown bread and butter and green pepper and carrot sticks. There were little violently yellow iced cakes with scalloped edges called "marigolds," that came from Cushman's Bakery. There was a spice bun and rock-cakes from Newton's, the West Indian bakery across Lenox Avenue from St. Mark's School, and iced tea in a wrapped mayonnaise jar. There were sweet pickles for us and dill pickles for my father, and peaches with the fuzz still on them, individually wrapped to keep them from bruising. And, for neatness, there were piles of napkins and a little tin box with a washcloth dampened with rosewater and glycerine for wiping sticky mouths.

5 I wanted to eat in the dining car because I had read all about them, but my mother reminded me for the umpteenth time that dining car food always cost too much money and besides, you never could tell whose hands had been playing all over that food, nor where those same hands had been just before. My mother never mentioned that Black people were not allowed into railroad dining cars headed south in 1947. As usual, whatever my mother did not like and could not change, she ignored. Perhaps it would go away, deprived of her attention.

6 I learned later that Phyllis's high school senior class trip had been to Washington, but the nuns had given her back her deposit in private, explaining to her that the class, all of whom were white, except Phyllis, would be staying in a hotel where Phyllis "would not be happy," meaning, Daddy explained to her, also in private, that they did not rent rooms to Negroes. "We will take you to Washington, ourselves," my father had avowed, "and not just for an overnight in some measly fleabag hotel."

7 American racism was a new and crushing reality that my parents had to deal with every day of their lives once they came to this country. They handled it as a private woe. My mother and father believed that they could best protect their children from the realities of race in america and the fact of american racism by never giving them name, much less discussing their nature. We were told we must never trust white people, but why was never explained, nor the nature of their ill will. Like so many other vital pieces of information in my childhood, I was supposed to know without being told. It always seemed like a very strange injunction coming from my mother, who looked so much like one of those

people we were never supposed to trust. But something always warned me not to ask my mother why she wasn't white, and why Auntie Lillah and Auntie Etta weren't, even though they were all that same problematic color so different from my father and me, even from my sisters, who were somewhere in-between.

8 In Washington, D.C., we had one large room with two double beds and an extra cot for me. It was a back-street hotel that belonged to a friend of my father's who was in real estate, and I spent the whole next day after Mass squinting up at the Lincoln Memorial where Marian Anderson had sung after the D.A.R.[1] refused to allow her to sing in their auditorium because she was Black. Or because she was "Colored," my father said as he told us the story. Except that what he probably said was "Negro," because for his times, my father was quite progressive.

9 I was squinting because I was in that silent agony that characterized all of my childhood summers, from the time school let out in June to the end of July, brought about by my dilated and vulnerable eyes exposed to the summer brightness.

10 I viewed Julys through an agonizing corolla of dazzling whiteness and I always hated the Fourth of July, even before I came to realize the travesty such a celebration was for Black people in this country.

11 My parents did not approve of sunglasses, nor of their expense.

12 I spent the afternoon squinting up at monuments to freedom and past presidencies and democracy, and wondering why the light and heat were both so much stronger in Washington, D.C., than back home in New York City. Even the pavement on the streets was a shade lighter in color than back home.

13 Late that Washington afternoon my family and I walked back down Pennsylvania Avenue. We were a proper caravan, mother bright and father brown, the three of us girls step-standards in-between. Moved by our historical surroundings and the heat of the early evening, my father decreed yet another treat. He had a great sense of history, a flair for the quietly dramatic and the sense of specialness of an occasion and a trip.

14 "Shall we stop and have a little something to cool off, Lin?"

15 Two blocks away from our hotel, the family stopped for a dish of vanilla ice cream at a Breyer's ice cream and soda fountain. Indoors, the soda fountain was dim and fan-cooled, deliciously relieving to my scorched eyes.

[1]*D.A.R.:* Daughters of the American Revolution, an organization of women descended from Americans who aided in the achievement of American Independence. *(Ed.)*

Corded and crisp and pinafored, the five of us seated ourselves one by one at the counter. There was I between my mother and father, and my two sisters on the other side of my mother. We settled ourselves along the white mottled marble counter, and when the waitress spoke at first no one understood what she was saying, and so the five of us just sat there. 16

The waitress moved along the line of us closer to my father and spoke again. "I said I kin give you to take out, but you can't eat here. Sorry." Then she dropped her eyes looking very embarrassed, and suddenly we heard what it was she was saying all at the same time, loud and clear. 17

Straight-backed and indignant, one by one, my family and I got down from the counter stools and turned around and marched out of the store, quiet and outraged, as if we had never been Black before. No one would answer my emphatic questions with anything other than a guilty silence. "But we hadn't done anything!" This wasn't right or fair! Hadn't I written poems about Bataan and freedom and democracy for all? 18

My parents wouldn't speak of this injustice, not because they had contributed to it, but because they felt they should have anticipated it and avoided it. This made me even angrier. My fury was not going to be acknowledged by a like fury. Even my two sisters copied my parents' pretense that nothing unusual and anti-american had occurred. I was left to write my angry letter to the president of the united states all by myself, although my father did promise I could type it out on the office typewriter next week, after I showed it to him in my copybook diary. 19

The waitress was white, and the counter was white, and the ice cream I never ate in Washington, D.C., that summer I left childhood was white, and the white heat and the white pavement and the white stone monuments of my first Washington summer made me sick to my stomach for the whole rest of that trip and it wasn't much of a graduation present after all. 20

READING FOR MEANING

Write to create meanings for Lorde's autobiographical essay.

Start Making Meaning

Begin by explaining what you think the significance of this event is for Lorde and what her purpose or purposes are in choosing to write about it in the way that she does. Continue by writing about anything else in the selection or in your experience that contributes to your understanding of Lorde's story.

If You Are Stuck

If you cannot write at least a page, consider writing about

- what surprised you as you read the story and what you could have predicted—and why.
- the young Lorde's reaction to being denied service at the ice-cream counter compared to her parents' reactions.
- this essay as a coming-of-age story, enabling the young Lorde to see herself and others differently or to act differently.
- the young Lorde's "fury" at injustice in relation to your own personal experience of injustice.

READING LIKE A WRITER

CONVEYING THE AUTOBIOGRAPHICAL SIGNIFICANCE THROUGH SHOWING AND TELLING

Lorde uses the two strategies of *showing* and *telling* to convey significance. She *shows* how she and her family felt about being denied service at the ice-cream parlor in the way she describes their reactions to the event: "Straight-backed and indignant, one by one, my family and I got down from the counter stools and turned around and marched out of the store, quiet and outraged, as if we had never been Black before" (paragraph 18). Notice that Lorde combines showing through descriptive details like "straight-backed," "marched," and "quiet" with telling through words like "indignant" and "outraged." The showing and telling combine in this paragraph to present a dramatic moment that is full of significance.

In addition, the phrase "as if we had never been Black before" tells readers indirectly and sarcastically about the young Lorde's frustration. In subsequent sentences where she complains about her family's refusal to "speak of this injustice" (paragraph 19), Lorde tells readers directly what she felt at the time as well as what she feels now looking back on the event. For example, Lorde tells that her parents responded to her questions with what she felt at the time was "a guilty silence" (paragraph 18). From her adult perspective, however, Lorde understands and can tell readers why her parents remained silent about the injustice they experienced: "not because they had contributed to it, but because they felt they should have anticipated it and avoided it" (paragraph 19).

Analyze

1. *Reread* paragraphs 8–12, where Lorde describes sightseeing in Washington, D.C. *Underline* any words and phrases that you think tell the significance of the event.
2. Then *underline* any words and phrases that show the significance through descriptive details.
3. *Review* your underlinings and *single out* the two or three that best convey the autobiographical significance of Lorde's story.

Write

Write several sentences explaining the autobiographical significance that Lorde shows and tells in these five paragraphs. *Give two or three examples* from your underlining to support your explanation.

A SPECIAL READING STRATEGY

Contextualizing

Contextualizing is a special strategy used to read for meaning. You use it to look for differences between the values and attitudes you bring to your reading of a text and those represented in a text such as Lorde's, which was written in an earlier era (the early 1980s) about an event that occurred even earlier (in the late 1940s). To contextualize about Lorde's essay, you would need to think about questions such as these:

- What images, ideas, and information come to mind when you think about racism against African Americans in America (particularly in the South) during the post–World War II period of the late 1940s and throughout the 1950s? How does Lorde's autobiographical writing reinforce or contradict those images, ideas, and information?
- Lorde wrote her autobiography in the early 1980s, and you are reading it twenty years later in the early 2000s. What was happening in America at the time Lorde was writing? What connections do you imagine Lorde wanted her contemporary readers to make? What connections can you make to your own time?

See Appendix 1 (p. 536) for detailed guidelines on using contextualizing as a critical reading strategy.

CONSIDERING IDEAS FOR YOUR OWN WRITING

Like Lorde, consider writing about an event that you were looking forward to but that turned out differently than you had expected—perhaps a dreadful disappointment or a delightful surprise. There are many possibilities: a vacation, a swim meet, a band performance, summer camp, or an interview for an after-school job. The event may have taken you to a new place (moving to a new city, changing schools, visiting family) or put you in a new social situation (joining a school team or club, taking part in a play, working in a political campaign). You might also consider writing about an event when your reactions, like Lorde's, differed significantly from those of your friends or family. If you have encountered racism, sexism, ageism, or some other injustice, you might take this opportunity to write about the experience. For example, you may have been stopped and questioned by the police simply because of your race (an example of racial profiling).

RICK BRAGG

100 Miles per Hour, Upside Down and Sideways

Rick Bragg (b. 1959) has worked as Miami bureau chief and national correspondent for the New York Times *and has also reported for the* Los Angeles Times, *the* St. Petersburg Times, *the* Birmingham News, *and the* Anniston *(Alabama)* Star. *He received a Pulitzer Prize for his feature writing as well as the American Society of Newspaper Editors' Distinguished Writing Award. Bragg has also been a Nieman Fellow at Harvard University and has taught writing there as well at Boston University and the University of South Florida. In addition to a collection of his newspaper stories,* Somebody Told Me *(2000), Bragg has published two autobiographical works:* Redbirds: Memoirs from the South *(1998) and a best-selling account of his small-town Alabama upbringing in a poor family,* All Over but the Shoutin' *(1997), from which this reading is excerpted.*

"100 Miles per Hour, Upside Down and Sideways" recounts what happened one Saturday night when the teenage Bragg raced his souped-up "muscle car" into a ditch. Note that he begins by recalling his youthful desire to "slingshot" himself "faster and faster." As you read, think about what this metaphor suggests about the event's autobiographical significance.

Since I was a boy I have searched for ways to slingshot myself into the distance, faster and faster. When you turn the key on a car built for speed, when you hear that car rumble like an approaching storm and feel the steering wheel tremble in your hands from all that power barely under control, you feel like you can run away from anything, like you can turn your whole life into an insignificant speck in the rearview mirror. 1

In the summer of 1976, the summer before my senior year at Jacksonville High School, I had the mother of all slingshots. She was a 1969 General Motors convertible muscle car with a 350 V-8 and a Holley four-barreled carburetor as long as my arm. She got about six miles to the gallon, downhill, and when you started her up she sounded like Judgment Day. She was long and low and vicious, a mad dog cyclone with orange houndstooth interior and an eight-track tape player, and looked fast just sitting in the yard under a pine tree. I owned just one tape, that I remember, *The Eagles' Greatest Hits.* 2

I worked two summers in the hell and heat at minimum wage to earn enough money to buy her and still had to borrow money 3 from my uncle Ed, who got her for just nineteen hundred dollars mainly because he paid in hundred-dollar bills. "You better be careful, boy," he told me. "That'un will kill you." I assured him that, Yes, Sir, I would creep around in it like an old woman.

4 I tell myself I loved that car because she was so pretty and so fast and because I loved to rumble between the rows of pines with the blond hair of some girl who had yet to discover she was better than me whipping in the breeze. But the truth is I loved her because she was my equalizer. She raised me up, at least in my own eyes, closer to where I wanted and needed to be. In high school, I was neither extremely popular nor one of the great number of want-to-bes. I was invited to parties with the popular kids, I had dates with pretty girls. But there was always a distance there, of my own making, usually.

5 That car, in a purely superficial way, closed it. People crowded around her at the Hardee's. I let only one person drive her, Patrice Curry, the prettiest girl in school, for exactly one mile.

6 That first weekend, I raced her across the long, wide parking lot of the TG&Y, an insane thing to do, seeing as how a police car could have cruised by at any minute. It was a test of nerves as well as speed, because you actually had to be slowing down, not speeding up, as you neared the finish line, because you just ran out of parking lot. I beat Lyn Johnson's Plymouth and had to slam on my brakes and swing her hard around, to keep from jumping the curb, the road and plowing into the parking lot of the Sonic Drive-In.

7 It would have lasted longer, this upraised standing, if I had pampered her. I guess I should have spent more time looking at her than racing her, but I had too much of the Bragg side of the family in me for that. I would roll her out on some lonely country road late at night, the top down, and blister down the blacktop until I knew the tires were about to lift off the ground. But they never did. She held the road, somehow, until I ran out of road or just lost my nerve. It was as if there was no limit to her, at how fast we could go, together.

8 It lasted two weeks from the day I bought her.

9 On Saturday night, late, I pulled up to the last red light in town on my way home. Kyle Smith pulled up beside me in a loud-running Chevrolet, and raced his engine. I did not squall out when the light changed—she was not that kind of car—but let her rpm's build, build and build, like winding up a top.

10 I was passing a hundred miles per hour as I neared a long sweeping turn on Highway 21 when I saw, coming toward me, the blue lights of the town's police. I cannot really remember what happened next. I just remember mashing the gas pedal down hard,

halfway through that sweeping turn, and the sickening feeling as the car just seemed to lift and twist in the air, until I was doing a hundred miles per hour still, but upside down and sideways.

11 She landed across a ditch, on her top. If she had not hit the ditch in just the right way, the police later said, it would have cut my head off. I did not have on my seat belt. We never did, then. Instead of flinging me out, though, the centrifugal force—I had taken science in ninth grade—somehow held me in.

12 Instead of lying broken and bleeding on the ground beside my car, or headless, I just sat there, upside down. I always pulled the adjustable steering wheel down low, an inch or less above my thighs, and that held me in place, my head covered with mud and broken glass. The radio was still blaring—it was the Eagles' "The Long Run," I believe—and I tried to find the knob in the dark to turn it off. Funny. There I was in an upside-down car, smelling the gas as it ran out of the tank, listening to the tick, tick, tick of the hot engine, thinking: "I sure do hope that gas don't get nowhere near that hot manifold," but all I did about it was try to turn down the radio.

13 I knew the police had arrived because I could hear them talking. Finally, I felt a hand on my collar. A state trooper dragged me out and dragged me up the side of the ditch and into the collective glare of the most headlights I had ever seen. There were police cars and ambulances and traffic backed up, it seemed, all the way to Piedmont.

14 "The Lord was riding with you, son," the trooper said. "You should be dead."

15 My momma stood off to one side, stunned. Finally the police let her through to look me over, up and down. But except for the glass in my hair and a sore neck, I was fine. Thankfully, I was too old for her to go cut a hickory and stripe my legs with it, but I am sure it crossed her mind.

16 The trooper and the Jacksonville police had a private talk off to one side, trying to decide whether or not to put me in prison for the rest of my life. Finally, they informed my momma that I had suffered enough, to take me home. As we drove away, I looked back over my shoulder as the wrecker dragged my car out of the ditch and, with the help of several strong men, flipped it back over, right-side up. It looked like a white sheet of paper someone had crumpled up and tossed in the ditch from a passing car.

17 "The Lord was riding with that boy," Carliss Slaughts, the wrecker operator, told my uncle Ed. With so many people saying that, I thought the front page of the *Anniston Star* the next day would read: LORD RIDES WITH BOY, WRECKS ANYWAY.

I was famous for a while. No one, no one flips a convertible at a hundred miles per hour, without a seat belt on, and walks away, undamaged. People said I had a charmed life. My momma, like the trooper and Mr. Slaughts, just figured God was my copilot. 18

The craftsmen at Slaughts' Body Shop put her back together, over four months. My uncle Ed loaned me the money to fix her, and took it out of my check. The body and fender man made her pretty again, but she was never the same. She was fast but not real fast, as if some little part of her was still broken deep inside. Finally, someone backed into her in the parking lot of the Piggly Wiggly, and I was so disgusted I sold her for fourteen hundred dollars to a preacher's son, who drove the speed limit. 19

READING FOR MEANING

Write to create meanings for Bragg's autobiographical essay.

Start Making Meaning

Begin by explaining what you think the significance of this event is for Bragg and what his purpose or purposes are in choosing to write about it in the way that he does. Continue by writing about anything else in the selection or in your experience that contributes to your understanding of Bragg's story.

If You Are Stuck

If you cannot write at least a page, consider writing about

- the car's importance as an "equalizer" for Bragg, perhaps relating to your own experience or observation of the concern with status in high school.
- Bragg's initial reaction to the accident, as described in paragraph 12.
- why Bragg sold the car after having it repaired.
- how your personal experience with a car accident or other brush with death helps you understand Bragg's experience.

READING LIKE A WRITER

NARRATING THE STORY

When autobiographers narrate a story about a particular event in their lives, they often introduce the event by establishing a context for it and conclude by reflecting on it. Bragg introduces the event in paragraphs 1–8 and reflects on what happened in paragraphs 17–19. In paragraphs 9–16, he narrates the story of his car accident. Between the opening context and the concluding reflections, the story unfolds roughly in chronological order.

This activity will help you see how Bragg uses a variety of writing strategies to mark the passage of time in his narrative and keep readers oriented. One strategy is to refer to clock or calendar time, as when Bragg signals the beginning of his narrative and situates the event in time with the phrase "On Saturday night." Another strategy he uses is to indicate the relation in time between one action and another with a transition, such as "when" in paragraph 10. The most pervasive strategy Bragg uses for marking time is verb tense, which indicates when an action occurred in relation to other actions. You may not know the technical names of the different verb tenses, but your experience speaking English should help you recognize the relationships the tenses signify. For example, the simple past tense of the phrase "I *pulled* up" (paragraph 9) identifies an action that began and ended sometime in the past. The past perfect tense in "they informed my momma that I *had suffered* enough" (paragraph 16) indicates that Bragg's suffering occurred or began before the police informed his mother. The conditional tense in "If she had not hit the ditch in just the right way, the police later said, it *would have cut* my head off" (paragraph 11) shows that this action is "contrary to fact"—it did not actually occur. The past progressive tense in "I *was passing* a hundred miles per hour . . . when I saw . . . the blue lights of the town's police" (paragraph 10) indicates that Bragg's acceleration to that speed and his seeing the lights occurred simultaneously.

Analyze

1. *Reread* paragraphs 9–16, underlining the time markers—clock or calendar time, transitional words and phrases, and different verb tenses—that Bragg uses to mark the passage of time in his story.

Write

Write a few sentences explaining what you have learned about the way Bragg uses time markers to narrate the story. *Give examples* from your underlining to support your explanation. What kinds of time markers does he rely on most? How well do the time markers work to mark the passage of time in the story and to help readers, like yourself, follow the chronology?

Compare

Compare the way Bragg organizes his essay to the way Annie Dillard or Audre Lorde organizes hers. Does Dillard or Lorde, like Bragg, divide her reading into three sections: establishing a context, narrating the event, and reflecting on it? What kinds of markers does she use to indicate the passage of time and to keep readers oriented? How well do the time markers work?

CONSIDERING IDEAS FOR YOUR OWN WRITING

Like Bragg, you might consider writing about a traumatic event, something that endangered your life (a car accident or a mugging, for example). Another possibility is to choose an event that changed your perspective, making you look at yourself or others in a new light. You might consider an event that made you feel the need to identify yourself with a particular community, such as an ethnic group, a political or religious group, or a group of students or co-workers. Or you might choose an event that had the opposite effect—making you want to disconnect yourself from or to give up trying to be accepted by a particular group at school, at work, or in the community.

LAURIE ABRAHAM

Divorced Father

Laurie Abraham (b. 1965), a journalist who specializes in public health issues, wrote this portrait of her father for a collection of autobiographical essays titled Reinventing Home: Six Working Women Look at Their Home Lives *(1991). She also edited a second essay collection,* Reinventing Love: Six Women Talk about Love, Lust, Sex, and Romance *(1998), and wrote an exposé of health care for seniors,* Mama Might Be Better off Dead: The Failure of Health Care in Urban America *(1993).*

As the title "Divorced Father" suggests, Abraham focuses on her father shortly after her parents were divorced. As you read and annotate the essay, note Abraham's feelings about how the divorce changed her father and affected her relationship with him.

I have seen tears in my father's eyes twice: during the premiere of the Waltons' Christmas special and on the drive to his new apartment. If I had asked about the tears in his eyes the morning he left home, he probably would have blamed them on the sun. It was a too-bright day in June when my father left home, exactly eighteen years after my parents were married. He took his clothes, the old black-and-white TV, the popcorn popper, a pot and skillet, and a few other things. It took only two trips in the brown Pinto station wagon to move half of my father's life. Not that he couldn't have claimed his share of the tables, chairs, and pictures—but he chose to leave the fallout of two decades of acquiring with my mother. 1

From a house full of things, he went to an apartment of four empty rooms carpeted in gold-and-white shag. Soon, though, a queen-sized bed jutted from the middle of his bedroom wall, a butcher-block table with four matching chairs sat in the dining room, and an L-shaped brown velvet sofa dwarfed the 19-inch TV. He never bought a picture, a coffee-table, a knickknack or anything that said, "Harold Abraham lives here." A few things that my dad had claimed from the divorce, however, definitely bore his mark: cocktail glasses printed with the Dow Jones Industrial Average; four plastic beer mugs (one with the Bud Man, another with "Michelob" tastefully printed in gold); a stoneware coffee mug with sailboats. But these weren't the possessions of a father of two with a master's degree and a CPA degree. These were pieces of "Abe," that hard-drinking wild boy who wore garlic around his neck for a week to gain admission to a fraternity 2 that stole a cow for a pet, a fraternity that was banned from the campus the year after my father left.

3 Money certainly didn't prevent my father from decorating his apartment. He usually had enough of it, and when he didn't, he spent it anyway. Surprisingly, the explanation for the starkness of his home came to me from people who have less in common with my father than my mother did: low-income teenagers who picked up trash and trimmed grass in a government jobs program.

4 "Where do you stay?" several of them asked me during the summer that I worked as their supervisor. At first I wondered about their word choice: I always asked new acquaintances where they lived, not where they stayed. But after listening to them all summer I understood why "stay" was the most appropriate word to describe their experiences. They were always moving, from their mother's apartment, to their grandmother's, to an aunt's. None of these places was necessarily bad, just temporary. These kids didn't live at East Seventy-fifth and Superior, they stayed there for a time. My father was doing that, too—staying. He had no intention of living in his apartment, or calling it home. It was a way station between his first wife and the one to come—except on Sundays. When his girls came to visit, my dad rushed to throw together a home.

5 I know little about my father's childhood, but I won't forget the few memories that he's let slip over the years. He slept in a dresser drawer because his family could not afford a crib. His dad never said to him, "Harold, how was school today?" He went without many of the furnishings that make up a home, never mind the nurturing. Making a home for his children was important so that he could give us what he never got. He did his best—for us and for the boy whose parents never quite made it to his high school football games.

6 But since he had been deprived of the emotional sustenance that makes a home a home, my father was never quite sure what to do with my sister and me once he had us. He relied on food—the most straightforward kind of nurturing—to turn his bachelor's apartment into a home. Breakfast was pancakes. In the beginning, when all three of us were trying to fight off sadness and before my sister and I grew to resent the Sunday morning call, "Your father's here," he flipped them. By high school, the pancakes didn't fly and I slumped in my chair, suffering from the six-pack I had downed the night before. By dinner I'd usually recovered enough to enjoy either spaghetti with Ragú sauce or Kentucky Fried Chicken—always carryout; the restaurant wasn't

home. These dishes were hearty but deliciously junky, the kind of food men with few cooking skills and one chance a week to win their children's approval are apt to serve. Between meals, we'd eat some more: popcorn or pizza rolls while watching football on TV, or ice cream after an awkward, time-filling walk in the woods.

7 My father's homemaking hit full stride at Christmas, when shortcomings we never could ignore became that much more obvious and sad. First, we'd pick the right tree with my mother. Then, another tree with Dad, if we could arrange a time that was "mutually convenient." To the scratchy strains of "Christmas in Killarney," a Ray Conniff album my parents bought when they were first married, we pushed the lights onto the prickly branches of a spruce or Scotch pine. (We never used garden gloves with my father, although my mother used them; he probably didn't own a pair anyway.) My father's half of the ornaments included a few of the "good" ones—the papier-mâché Santa, the Ohio State football helmet trimmed with holly—but he also had his share of the back-of-the-tree duds such as clear plastic teardrops, one for each of the twelve days of Christmas. Most years, decorating the tree with Dad was fun, but to my sister and me, it wasn't our real tree in our real home. It was what we put up with Dad so he wouldn't be lonely at Christmas.

8 Long after I began to consider the two times I saw my father almost cry, I realized that there might be a connection between the tears of moving day and those provoked by the Waltons' Christmas show. Its plot was this: Pa Walton was lost during a snowstorm on Christmas Eve. A man was cut off from his family. I doubt back then, watching that show, that Dad imagined one day he would be driving away from his wife and girls, but somehow he identified. And what my father missed the most when he left home was something the Waltons had plenty of—people. That's what my father was forced to give up: lots of people around, people he might not necessarily be close to (like my mom), but who were present. He didn't want to struggle to build a new family from scratch; he needed to be plopped down in the middle of one. And so he was, finally. His second wife comes from a large and raucous family, and my dad has three new stepchildren. Large Christmas Eve parties at his new wife's home have become something of a tradition for us.

9 For me, the parties are events. I wear red, or something that stands out in a crowd of relatives I see once a year. Yet although I always have a good time, I still feel that my real Christmas is the next day at treeside, in those more intense, heartfelt moments

with my mother. Spending the day with my mother is what I want, but I do not think I could enjoy myself if my father were alone on Christmas. He would never ask my sister or me to spend part of the day with him; he is too proud. Instead, he would call us around eleven in the morning to wish us "Merry Christmas" in a loud voice. His conversation would be punctuated by laughs that seemed to end before they started. I knew from experience that when he wasn't talking, he was gritting his teeth slightly, tightening the line of his jaw. "Love you big bunches," he would say rapidly, before hanging up. Then the phone would ring again right away. He had forgotten to tell me that I left my sweatshirt at his apartment. "Oh, thanks, Dad; I'll get it next time we come over," I would say.

"Okay, then. Merry Christmas." 10

"Merry Christmas, Dad." 11

I am grateful to my new stepfamily for sheltering my father and me from this coldest cold. Without them, my father would get lost in the snow. 12

READING FOR MEANING

Write to create meanings for Abraham's portrait of her father.

Start Making Meaning

Begin by explaining what you think the significance of Abraham's relationship with her father is during the period about which she is writing, and what her purpose or purposes are in choosing to write about her father in the way that she does. Continue by writing about anything else in the selection or in your experience that contributes to your understanding of Abraham's essay.

If You Are Stuck

If you cannot write at least a page, consider writing about

- the picture you get of Abraham's father from the list of things he took to his new apartment (paragraphs 1 and 2).
- the contrast between the two different Christmas memories (paragraphs 7 and 8).
- the distinction between where you stay and where you live (paragraph 4).

- your impression of what Abraham's childhood was like after her parents divorced or after her father possibly remarried, perhaps comparing her experience with your own or a friend's.

READING LIKE A WRITER

NARRATING ANECDOTES AND RECURRING ACTIVITIES

Writers usually can recall many experiences that might be used to describe a person who played a significant role in their lives. Some of these experiences are onetime occurrences that, like a snapshot, catch the person at a particular place and time. The stories writers tell about onetime occurrences, such as someone tripping and dropping the cake at a birthday party, are called *anecdotes*. Other experiences occur more than once, often on a regular basis with only a little variation over a period of time. Stories writers tell about what usually happened rather than what once happened, such as several stories of a particular person tripping or dropping things, suggesting clumsiness, are called *recurring activities*. As you analyze Abraham's use of anecdotes and recurring activities, you will see how they differ and what each contributes to the portrait of her father.

Analyze

1. *Reread* paragraph 1, where Abraham tells a brief anecdote about her father, and paragraph 6, where she presents a recurring activity central to life with him after the divorce.
2. *Try to figure out* what makes paragraph 1 an anecdote and paragraph 6 a recurring activity. *Underline* the language that lets you know.

Write

Write several sentences describing how the anecdote and recurring activity differ, pointing to specific details in each paragraph to illustrate the differences. Then *speculate about* what each strategy contributes to Abraham's portrait of her father.

Compare

Like Abraham, the author of the next selection, Amy Wu, uses anecdotes and recurring activities to present a person. Quickly read Wu's essay, looking closely at the anecdote in paragraph 3, beginning with the word "Once," and the recurring activities she presents in paragraphs 6–9. Then *compare* how Abraham and Wu use these two narrative strategies.

CONSIDERING IDEAS FOR YOUR OWN WRITING

Consider writing about a close relative, friend, or co-worker whose life or whose relationship with you was somehow transformed. Perhaps you know someone who had to deal with an illness or a disability, someone who acknowledged an addiction and worked to overcome it, somone who lost a job or had to learn a new profession, someone who moved to a new country and had to adapt to the cultural differences. You might try to think of "before and after" anecdotes, through which you could dramatize the change in order to help readers appreciate what it was like for the person and how it affected you. If the change made you feel alienated from the person, you might focus on how you reacted, perhaps how you tried to rebuild the relationship or simply accepted the change. Think about how a change in another person changed you as well. What did you have to learn or relearn?

AMY WU

A Different Kind of Mother

Amy Wu (b. 1976) wrote this essay when she was seventeen years old, just before entering New York University, where she majored in political science and journalism. Since then, she has worked for news organizations, for Internet companies, and as a freelance writer, publishing articles in the New York Times, *the* New York Daily News, Asian Week, *and other publications. This essay was originally published in 1993 in* Chinese American Forum, *a quarterly magazine.*

As the title "A Different Kind of Mother" indicates, Wu wants readers to understand her special relationship with her mother. Notice, as you read, the cultural differences Wu points out between her "Chinese" mother and "American" friends' mothers. What significance do you think she wants readers to draw from these differences?

1 My best friend once asked me what it was like being brought up by a Chinese mother. Surprisingly, I could find no answer. I found myself describing my mother's beauty—the way my mother's hair was so silky and black, how her eyes were not small and squinty, but shaped like perfect almonds. How her lips and cheeks were bright red even if she put on no makeup.

Amy Wu and Her Mother

2 But unlike my friends, who see my mother as a Chinese mother, I see my mother as simply "my" mother. The language between any mother and daughter is universal. Beyond the layers of arguments and rhetoric, and beyond the incidents of humiliation and misunderstandings, there is a love that unites every mother and daughter.

3 I am not blind, however, to the disciplinary differences between a culture from the west and a culture from the east. Unlike American mothers, who encourage their young children to speak whatever is on their mind, my mother told me to hold my tongue. Once, when I was 5 or 6, I interrupted my mother during a dinner with her friends and told her that I disliked the meal. My

mother's eyes transformed from serene pools of blackness into stormy balls of fire. "Quiet!" she hissed, "do you not know that silent waters run deep?" She ordered me to turn my chair to the wall and think about what I had done. I remember throwing a red-faced tantrum before my mother's friends, pounding my fists into the rug, and throwing my utensils at the steaming dishes. Not only did I receive a harsh scolding, but a painful spanking. By the end of that evening, I had learned the first of many lessons. I learned to choose my words carefully before I opened my undisciplined mouth.

4 Whenever my friends and I strike up conversations about our mothers in the cafeteria or at slumber parties, I find myself telling them this story. Nevertheless, they respond to my story with straight and pale faces. "How," one of my friends asked, "can a mother be so cruel?" "You mean she beat you in front of other people?" another asked. My best friend told me that her mother disciplined her children wisely instead of abusing them. She sat them on her lap, patiently explaining what they had done wrong. She didn't believe in beating children into submission.

5 What my American friends cannot understand, however, is how my mother's lessons have become so embedded within me, while my friends have easily forgotten their mother's words. My mother's eyes are so powerful, her fists so strong, that somehow I cannot erase her words of advice. To this day, I choose my words carefully before I speak, unlike so many of my friends whose words spill out aimlessly when they open their mouths. My mother says that American girls are taught to squabble like chickens, but a Chinese girl is taught how to speak intelligently.

6 Only lately have I also discovered that Chinese mothers show their love in different ways. Ever since I was a little girl, my mother has spent hours cooking intricate dishes. I remember Friday evenings she would lay out the precious china her mother had given her as a wedding present—how she laid down the utensils and glasses so meticulously, how she made sure there was not a crease in the tablecloth.

7 She would spend the entire day steaming fish, baking ribs, cutting beef into thin strips, and rolling dough to make dumplings. In the evening, her work of labor and art would be unveiled. My father and I and a few Chinese neighbors and friends would be invited to feast on my mother's work of art.

8 I remember how silent my mother was as she watched her loved ones devour her labor of love. She would sit back, with a small smile on her face. She would nibble at the food in her dish while urging others to eat more, to take seconds, and thirds and

fourths. "Eat, eat!" she would order me. I dared not tell her I was too full.

9 She would fill my bowl with mounds of rice and my dish with endless vegetables, fish, and fried delicacies. A Chinese mother's love flows from the time and energy she puts into forming a banquet. A Chinese mother's love comes through her order to eat more.

10 My American friends laugh so hard that tears come out of their eyes, when I tell them how my Chinese mother displays her love. "So she wants you to get fat!" one screamed. They said that their mothers showed love by hugging them tightly, buying them clothes, and kissing them on the cheeks.

11 Deep inside, I know that my mother does show her love, except she does it when she thinks I am asleep. Every so often, she will tiptoe into my dark room, sit on the edge of my bed, and stroke my hair. When I am awake, however, she is like a professor constantly hounding her prize student and expecting only the best. All throughout my childhood, she drilled me on lessons of cleanliness and respect.

12 A few years ago at my Grandpa Du's 67th birthday party, I ran up to my grandfather and planted a wet, juicy kiss on his right cheek. To this day, I can easily remember the horrified looks on my relatives' faces. My grandfather turned pale for a second and then smiled meekly. He nodded his head and quickly sat down.

13 Later that evening, my mother cornered me against the wall. "Do you not know that respect to elderly is to bow!" she screamed. Her face turned bright purple. My excuses of "I didn't know . . ." were lost in her powerful words.

14 From that day on, I bowed to anyone Chinese and older than I. I have learned that respect for the elderly earns a young person a different kind of respect. These days, my grandfather points to me and tells my little cousins to follow my example. "She has been taught well," he tells them.

15 It saddens me that my Chinese mother is so often misunderstood. After she threw my friends out during my twelfth birthday party, because they refused to take off their shoes, they saw her as a callous, cruel animal. One of my friends went home and told her father that I had an abusive mother. Her father even volunteered to call the child welfare department. They never dared to step foot in my house again.

16 My mother has given me so many fine values and morals because of her way of teaching me. I choose words carefully before I speak. I am careful to speak and act toward the elderly a certain way. Without my mother's strong words and teachings, I believe that I would be a rather undisciplined person who didn't value

life greatly. I would most likely have been spoiled and callous and ignorant. I have also learned that there is more than one definition of love between a mother and a daughter.

READING FOR MEANING

Write to create meanings for Wu's autobiographical essay.

Start Making Meaning

Begin by explaining what you think the significance of her mother is for Wu and what her purpose or purposes are in choosing to write about her mother in the way that she does. Continue by writing about anything else in the selection or in your experience that contributes to your understanding of Wu's essay.

If You Are Stuck

If you cannot write at least a page, consider writing about

- the tug of war Wu felt between her mother's values and expectations, on the one hand, and those of her friends, on the other hand.
- what the photograph adds to your understanding of Wu's relationship with her mother.
- cultural or ethnic differences in the ways children are expected to behave toward adults, in the ways people are expected to show affection toward others, or in any other ways you have noticed.
- the importance of ritual occasions, such as holiday meals in Wu's family—perhaps relating her family's rituals to your own family's.

READING LIKE A WRITER

PRESENTING A PERSON THROUGH DIALOGUE

Autobiographers often use dialogue to present people and to shed light on relationships. Dialogue reconstructs conversation, either through *direct quotation* to emphasize the speaker's choice of words or through *indirect quotation*—*paraphrasing* and *summarizing* to focus on the substance of what was said instead of the precise words that were used. Effective dialogue gives readers an impression of the speaker's character or personality as well as how he or she relates to others. In this reading, Wu alternates between reporting two kinds of conversations, those she had about her mother with friends and those she had with her mother. This activity focuses on the conversations with her mother.

When writers compose dialogue, they usually include descriptive details depicting the speaker's tone of voice, facial expression, and hand gestures. For example, in paragraph 3, Wu describes her mother's physical reaction to her interruption with these details: "My mother's eyes transformed from serene pools of blackness into stormy balls of fire." And she characterizes her mother's response, "Quiet!," by describing her tone: "she hissed." These descriptive details convey the mood and emotion as well as the content of the conversation.

Analyze

1. *Reread* paragraphs 3, 8, and 13, where Wu uses dialogue to present her conversations with her mother. *Put brackets around* the dialogue—noting both the parts that are quoted and those that are paraphrased or summarized. Then *underline* any details that describe the speakers.
2. *Review* the bits of dialogue you bracketed and the details you underlined. *Single out* one or two examples that seem particularly effective in presenting Wu's mother and Wu's relationship with her.

Write

Write several sentences explaining what you have discovered about Wu's use of dialogue. From your annotations, *give two or three examples* to show how the quoted language and the details contribute to the dialogue's effectiveness.

CONSIDERING IDEAS FOR YOUR OWN WRITING

Autobiographers often write about people with whom they have close and somewhat complicated relationships. Like Wu, you might choose to present a person about whom you felt (and maybe still feel) strong and conflicting emotions, such as love, anger, disapproval, admiration, envy, disappointment, or hurt. Try to recall particular events or conversations with the person that you could use to help readers understand why the person aroused strong feelings or conflicting emotions in you. Another possibility is to write about a parent, a guardian, a counselor, a minister, or some other older person who influenced you deeply, for good or ill. Consider also someone who passed on to you a sense of your family history or culture.

BRAD BENIOFF

Rick

Brad Benioff was a first-year college student when he wrote the following essay for an assignment in his composition class. Like Laurie Abraham and Amy Wu in the two preceding selections, Benioff focuses his essay on a memorable person: his high-school water polo coach, Rick Rezinas.

As you read, notice how Benioff uses dialogue to dramatize his relationship with Rick.

I walked through the dawn chill, shivering as much from nervousness as from the cold. Steam curled up from the water in the pool and disappeared in the ocher morning light. Athletes spread themselves about on the deck, lazily stretching and whispering to each other as if the stillness were sacred. It was to be my first practice with the high school water polo team. I knew nothing about the game, but a friend had pushed me to play, arguing, "It's the most fun of any sport. Trust me." He had awakened me that morning long before daylight, forced me into a bathing suit, and driven me to the pool. 1

"Relax," he said. "Rick is the greatest of coaches. You'll like him. You'll have fun." 2

The mythical Rick. I had heard of him many times before. All the older players knew him by his first name and always spoke of him as a friend rather than a coach. He was a math teacher at our school, and his classes were very popular. Whenever class schedules came out, everyone hoped to be placed in Mr. Rezinas's class. He had been known to throw parties for the team or take them on weekend excursions skiing or backpacking. To be Rick's friend was to be part of an exclusive club, and I was being invited to join. And so I looked forward with nervous anticipation to meeting this man. 3

My friend walked me out to the pool deck and steered me toward a man standing beside the pool. 4

"Rick," announced my friend, "I'd like you to meet your newest player." 5

Rick was not a friendly looking man. He wore only swim trunks, and his short, powerful legs rose up to meet a bulging torso. His big belly was solid. His shoulders, as if to offset his front-heaviness, were thrown back, creating a deep crease of excess muscle from his sides around the small of his back, a crease like a huge frown. His arms were crossed, two medieval maces 6 placed carefully on their racks, ready to be swung at any moment. His round cheeks and chin were darkened by traces of black whiskers. His hair was sparse. Huge, black, mirrored sunglasses replaced his eyes. Below his prominent nose was a thin, sinister mustache. I couldn't believe this menacing-looking man was the legendary jovial Rick.

He said nothing at first. In those moments of silence, I felt more inadequate than ever before in my life. My reflection in his glasses stared back at me, accusing me of being too skinny, too young, too stupid, too weak to be on his team. Where did I get the nerve to approach him with such a ridiculous body and ask to play water polo, a man's game? Finally, he broke the silence, having finished appraising my meager body. "We'll fatten him up," he growled. 7

Thus began a week of torture. For four hours a day, the coach stood beside the pool scowling down at me. I could do nothing right. 8

"No! No! No!" He shook his head in disgust. "Throw the damn ball with your whole arm! Get your goddamn elbow out of the water!" 9

Any failure on my part brought down his full wrath. He bellowed at my incompetence and punished me with pushups and wind sprints. Even when I was close to utter exhaustion, I found no sympathy. "What the hell are you doing on the wall?" he would bellow. "Coach . . . my side, it's cramped." 10

"Swim on it! If you can't take a little pain, then you don't play!" With this, he would push me off the wall. 11

He seemed to enjoy playing me against the older, stronger players. "Goddamn it, Brad! If someone elbows or hits you, don't look out at me and cry, 'It's not fair.' Push back! Don't be so weak!" I got elbowed around until it seemed that none of my internal organs was unscathed. He worked me until my muscles wouldn't respond, and then he demanded more. 12

"You're not trying! Push it!" 13

"Would you move? You're too slow! Swim!" 14

"Damn it! Get out and give me twenty!" 15

It took little time for me to hate both the game and the man who ruled it. 16

I reacted by working as hard as I could. I decided to deprive him of the pleasure of finding fault with me. I learned quickly and started playing as flawlessly as possible. I dispensed with looking tired, showing pain, or complaining of cramps. I pushed, hit, and elbowed back at the biggest of players. No matter how flawless or aggressive my performance, though, he would find fault and let 17 me know it. He was never critical of other players. He would laugh and joke with the other players; but whenever he saw me, he frowned.

18 I decided to quit.

19 After a particularly demanding practice, I walked up to this tyrant. I tried to hold his gaze, but the black glasses forced me to look down.

20 "Coach Rezinas," I blurted, "I've decided that I don't want to play water polo." His scowl deepened. Then after a moment he said, "You can't quit. Not until after the first game." And he walked away. The dictator had issued his command.

21 There was no rule to keep me from quitting. Anger flushed through me. Somehow I would get revenge on this awful man. After the first game? Okay. I would play. I would show him what a valuable player I was. He would miss my talents when I quit. I worked myself up before the first game by imagining the hated face: the black glasses, the thin mustache, the open, snarling mouth. I was not surprised that he placed me in the starting lineup because I was certain he would take me out soon. I played furiously. The ball, the goal, the opposition, even the water seemed to be extensions of Rick, his face glaring from every angle, his words echoing loudly in my ears. Time and time again I would get the ball and, thinking of his tortures, fire it toward the goal with a strength to kill. I forgot that he might take me out. No defender could stand up to me. I would swim by them or over them. Anger and the need for vengeance gave me energy. I didn't notice the time slipping by, the quarters ending.

22 Then, the game ended. My teammates rushed out to me, congratulating and cheering me. I had scored five goals, a school record for one game, and shut out the other team with several key defensive plays. Now I could get revenge. Now I could quit. I stepped out of the pool prepared with the words I would spit into his face: "I QUIT!"

23 As I approached him, I stopped dead. He was smiling at me, his glasses off. He reached out with his right hand and shook mine with exuberance.

24 "I knew you had it in you! I knew it!" he laughed.

25 Through his laughter, I gained a new understanding of the man. He had pushed me to my fullest potential, tapping into the talent I may never have found in myself. He was responsible for the way I played that day. My glory was his. He never hated me. On the contrary, I was his apprentice, his favored pupil. He had brought out my best. Could I really hate someone who had done that much for me? He had done what he had promised: he had

fattened me up mentally as well as physically. All this hit me in a second and left me completely confused. I tried to speak, but only managed to croak, "Coach . . . uh . . . I, uh . . ." He cut me off with another burst of laughter. He still shook my hand.

"Call me Rick," he said. 26

READING FOR MEANING

Write to create meanings for Benioff's autobiographical essay.

Start Making Meaning

Begin by explaining what you think the significance of his coach is for Benioff and what his purpose or purposes are in choosing to write about Rick in the way that he does. Continue by writing about anything else in the selection or in your experience that contributes to your understanding of Benioff's essay.

If You Are Stuck

If you cannot write at least a page, consider writing about

- Rick's coaching style, perhaps comparing it with other styles of coaching or teaching.
- the notion that how you see yourself reflected in another person's eyes affects what you value or devalue in yourself.
- how being male or female may affect your reading of and response to this essay.
- this reading as a coming-of-age story, one that enables Benioff to see the role Rick played in his life.

READING LIKE A WRITER

DESCRIBING A PERSON THROUGH VISUAL DETAILS

Visual description enables readers to see the person and to get a sense of how that person appears to others. For example, providing vivid details of someone's facial features could show whether a person looks others directly in the eye or looks down on others. This activity will help you see how Benioff uses visual description to give readers a picture of Rick as well as an understanding of his significance to the writer.

Analyze

1. *Reread* paragraph 6, where Benioff describes Rick. *Notice* that the writer makes only two general statements characterizing Rick, in the first and last sentences of the paragraph. The remaining sentences in this paragraph offer visual details and images describing Rick's appearance. Because Rick is wearing only swim trunks and sunglasses, Benioff concentrates on the appearance of Rick's body.
2. *Underline* the parts of Rick's body Benioff singles out, beginning with "legs" and "torso" in the second sentence. Then *put a wavy line* under each visual detail Benioff uses to describe the parts of Rick's body, beginning with "short, powerful" and "bulging" in sentence 2.
3. *Put a star* by the two comparisons: a simile in sentence 2 (a simile makes an explicit comparison by using the word *like* or *as*), and a metaphor in sentence 3 (a metaphor implicitly compares two items by describing one in terms of the other).

Write

Write several sentences explaining the impression you get of Rick as seen through Benioff's eyes. *Quote* the visual details and comparisons that contribute most to this impression.

CONSIDERING IDEAS FOR YOUR OWN WRITING

Think about the coaches, teachers, employers, and other mentors who have influenced your life. Choose one of these people, and consider how you can describe what that person taught you and how he or she went about it. As a writer aiming to describe this individual's significance in your life, how would you reveal what you learned about the person and about yourself? Or as an alternative, you might consider someone with whom you have had continuing disagreements or conflicts, and then speculate on how you can describe your relationship with that person.

NICOLE BALL

Sticks and Stones

Nicole Ball was a first-year college student when she wrote this essay for her composition course. You may recognize that her title alludes to the childhood retort to verbal insults hurled by other children: "Sticks and stones can break my bones, but words can never harm me." As the title suggests, Ball recounts an event in which she and her brother finally reacted to a bully on the school bus. As you read, consider what you would have done in their position.

The other readings in this chapter are followed by reading and writing activities. Following this reading, however, you are on your own to decide how to read for meaning and read like a writer.

1 James Nichols was short and scrawny, the smallest kid in the entire eighth grade class. But he had a foul mouth and a belligerent attitude to make up for it. And he was a bully.

2 James sat in the front seat of the school bus, relegated there by the bus driver after some infraction or other. The driver, a balding, heavy-set man who paid little or no attention to the charges he shuttled back and forth, rarely spoke and, except for that act of discipline, seemed disinclined to do anything else. The punishment, however, didn't seem to faze James; in fact, he reveled in it. Sitting in the front put him at the head of all the action and surrounded him with easy victims: those too timid or meek to trespass into the "tough" zone at the back of the bus.

3 I was a year older than James and, though not very tall myself, was at least a foot taller than he was. But by my last year in junior high school, I had a terrible complexion, a mouthful of braces, and a crippling shyness. I sat in the second seat on the school bus, only because I couldn't get any closer to the front.

4 My brother, Greg, who was a year younger, generally sat with me because while he was a bit shorter, and much more confident, he had no more desire to mix with the cigarette-toting crowd in the back of the bus than I did. And although we didn't always get along well at home, we both felt that it was nice to have someone to sit with on the bus, even if we didn't talk much.

5 In our junior high, as in all junior highs, skill at socializing outranked skill in classes. And since Greg and I were both social outcasts, we endured our share of teasing and taunts. But James Nichols set out to top them all.

At first, of course, his words were easy to ignore, mostly because they were nothing new. But as his taunts grew louder and nastier, he developed the habit of kneeling on his seat and leaning over the back to shout his unrelenting epithets down upon us. The kids in the back of the bus relished every moment of our humiliation, often cheering him on. James puffed up with pride over his cruelty. The bus driver never said a word, though he could not have helped but hear the barrage of insults. Inside, I seethed. 6

"Ignore him," my parents insisted. "He'll eventually stop when he realizes that you're not going to react." Their words were well meant, but didn't help. The taunts continued and even intensified when we got to school. Upon arrival, the buses lined up in front of the school building, waiting until exactly 8:10 to release their passengers. Those long moments sitting in the parking lot, staring at the red plastic seat in front of me, praying for the bell to ring so I could escape James were pure torture. 7

Each morning, Greg and I would flee from the bus. "I can't take this much more," I would rage under my breath. Oh how I longed to tear James to pieces. And although I knew I would never physically attack James, I felt better imagining myself doing so. Greg, though, would never respond to my frustrated exclamations, which only added to my wrath. After all, didn't he hate James too? But more often than not, I was just too furious to care what Greg might have been thinking. 8

The showdown, I suppose, was inevitable. 9

One morning as we sat in the school parking lot, James took his taunting too far. I don't remember what he said, but I remember what he did. He pulled a long, slender wooden drumstick from his pocket. He started to tap Greg on the top of the head, each hit emphasizing every syllable of his hateful words. My brother stared straight ahead. James laughed. The kids in the back of the bus laughed. The bus driver ignored everything. 10

My anger boiled over. "Don't you touch him!" I shrieked, striking out and knocking the drumstick from James's hand. At that moment, I didn't care that my parents had advised us to ignore James. I didn't care that everyone turned to gape at me. I didn't care that even the bus driver glanced up from his stony reverie. I only wanted James to leave my brother alone. As the stick clattered to the floor, audible in the sudden silence, I bit my lip, uncertain of what I had done and afraid of what might result. 11

My mistake, of course, was thinking my screams would end the taunts. The crowd at the back of the bus waited to see James's reaction. With his authority threatened, James turned on me like a viper. 12

"Shut up, bitch!" he hissed. Coming from a home where "shut up" was considered strong language, James's swear word seemed the worst of all evils. 13

My eyes wide, I shuddered but didn't respond. Words were words, and if I had done nothing else, at least I had caused the bully to revert to words instead of actions. I turned my face to the window, determined to ignore his insults for the few remaining minutes before school. But a movement from Greg caught my eye, and I looked back. 14

In one swift movement, Greg reached into the front seat, grabbed James by the coat, yanked him out into the aisle, pulled him down, and delivered two quick, fierce jabs to James's face. Then he released him without a word and settled back into his seat. James, for once in his life, was speechless. His cheek flaming red from where the blows had struck, he stared at my brother without moving until the bus driver clicked open the doors a moment later, indicating we could go into school. 15

My parents heard about the incident, of course, and called the assistant principal about the entire matter. When the vice principal questioned my brother, Greg's explanation was simple: "He called Nicole a swear word, and no one calls my sister that." Greg had never said anything more touching. 16

I have heard it said that violence never solves anything, and it didn't. The bus driver was advised to keep an eye on James, but no admonition would have spurred the driver to interfere in anything. The teasing went on, cruel as ever, until James threatened to slit our throats with a knife he swore he had hidden in his locker at school. After that, even though a locker search turned up nothing, my parents drove us to school every morning, and my mother talked to us about what to do if James ever pulled a knife on us at school. 17

But for me an imagined weapon paled when compared with the vivid memory of the complete silence on the bus, the blazing red mark on James's face, the calm little smile that tugged at the edges of my brother's mouth, and the click of the bus doors as they opened to free us. 18

READING FOR MEANING

Write to create meanings for Ball's autobiographical story about her and her brother's encounter with a bully.

READING LIKE A WRITER

Autobiographers focusing on a remembered event or person

- narrate the event or anecdotes.
- present people.
- present places.
- convey autobiographical significance.

You have seen how important these autobiographical writing strategies are in the readings you have read, written about, and discussed in this chapter. Focus on one of these strategies in Ball's story and analyze it carefully through close rereading and annotating. Then write several sentences explaining what you have learned, giving specific examples from the reading to support your explanation. Add a few sentences evaluating how successfully Ball uses the strategy to dramatize the experience for her readers.

REVIEWING WHAT MAKES AUTOBIOGRAPHY EFFECTIVE

In this chapter, you have been learning how to read autobiographical essays for meaning and how to read them like a writer. Before going on to write a piece of autobiography, pause here to review and contemplate what you have learned about the elements of effective autobiography.

Analyze

Choose one reading from this chapter that seems to you especially effective. Before rereading the selection, *jot down* one or two reasons you remember it as an example of good autobiographical writing.

Reread your chosen selection, adding further annotations about what makes it a particularly successful example of autobiography. *Consider* the selection's purpose and how well it achieves that purpose for its intended readers. (You can make an informed guess about the intended readers and their expectations by noting the publication source of the essay.) Then *focus* on how well the essay

- narrates the story.
- presents people.
- describes places.
- conveys the autobiographical significance.

You can review all of these basic features in the Guide to Reading Autobiography (p. 14).

Your instructor may ask you to complete this activity on your own or to work with a small group of other students who have chosen the same reading. If you work with others, allow enough time initially for all group members to reread the selection thoughtfully and to add their annotations. Then *discuss* as a group what makes the selection effective. *Take notes* on your discussion. One student in your group should then report to the class what the group has learned about the effectiveness of autobiographical writing. If you are working individually, write up what you have learned from your analysis.

Write

Write at least a page, supporting your choice of this reading as an example of effective autobiographical writing. *Assume* that your readers—your instructor and classmates—have read the selection but will not remember many details about it. They also might not remember it as especially successful. Therefore, you will need to *refer* to details and specific parts of the essay as you explain how it works as autobiography and as you justify your evaluation of its effectiveness. You need not argue that it is the best reading in the chapter or that it is flawless, only that it is, in your view, a strong example of the genre.

A Guide to Writing Autobiography

The readings in this chapter have helped you learn a great deal about autobiographical writing. You have seen that some autobiographies tell dramatic stories, while others present vivid portraits of people who played a significant role in the writer's life. Whether the focus is on events or people, you have discovered that the overall purpose for writers of autobiography is to convey the significance—both the meaning and the importance—of their past experience. In so doing, autobiographers often present themselves as individuals affected by social and cultural influences.

As a reader of autobiography, you have examined how autobiographers convey through their writing drama and vividness as well as significance. But you may have also found that different readers interpret the significance of an autobiographical selection differently. In other words, you have seen how the meanings readers make are affected by their personal experience as well as their social and cultural contexts.

Having learned how autobiographers invest their writing with drama, vividness, and significance and how readers interpret and respond to autobiographical writing, you can now approach autobiography more confidently as a writer. You can more readily imagine the problems you must solve as a writer of autobiography, the materials and possibilities you have to work with, the choices and decisions you must make. This Guide to Writing offers detailed suggestions for writing autobiographical essays and resources to help you solve the special challenges this kind of writing presents.

INVENTION

The following invention activities will help you choose a memorable *event* or an important *person* to write about, recall details about your subject, and explore its significance in your life. Completing these activities will produce a record of remembered details and thoughts that will be invaluable as you draft your essay.

Choosing a Subject

Rather than limiting yourself to the first subject that comes to mind, take a few minutes to consider your options. By listing as many subjects as you can, you will have a variety of possible topics to choose from for your autobiographical essay. List the most promising subjects you can think of, beginning with any you listed for the Considering Ideas for Your Own Writing activities following the readings in this chapter. Here are some additional ideas to consider:

Events

- A difficult situation, such as when you had to make a tough choice, when someone you admired let you down (or you let someone else down), or when you struggled to learn or understand something
- An event that shaped you in a particular way or that revealed an aspect of your personality you had not seen before, such as your independence, insecurity, ambition, or jealousy
- An occasion when something did not turn out as you thought it would, such as when you expected to be criticized but were praised or ignored instead, or when you were convinced you would succeed but failed
- An event in which a single encounter with another person changed the way you view yourself, changed your ideas about how you fit into a particular group or community, or led you to consider seriously someone else's point of view

People

- Someone who helped you develop a previously unknown or undeveloped side of yourself
- Someone who led you to question assumptions or stereotypes you had about other people
- Someone who surprised or disappointed you
- Someone in a position of power over you, or someone over whom you had power
- Someone who made you feel you were part of a larger community or had something worthwhile to contribute, or, conversely, someone who made you feel alienated or like an outsider

Choose a subject that you feel comfortable sharing with your instructor and classmates. The subject also should be one that you want to try to remember in detail and to think about in terms of what it means to you. You may find the choice easy to make, or you may have several equally promising possibilities. In making a final choice, it may help to think about your readers and what you would want them to learn about you from reading about the event or person.

Developing Your Subject

The following activities will help you develop your subject by recalling actions that happened during the event or by telling anecdotes that reveal something about the person. These activities will also help you recall details of the place and people. Each activity takes only a few minutes but will help you produce a fuller, more focused draft.

Recalling the Event or Person. *If you have chosen to write about an **event**, begin by writing for five minutes, simply telling what happened.* Do not worry about telling the story dramatically or even coherently.

*If you have chosen to write about a **person**, begin by listing anecdotes you could tell about the person.* Then choose one anecdote that reveals something important about the person or your relationship, and write for five minutes telling what happened.

Presenting Important People. *If you have chosen to write about a **person**, list aspects of the person's appearance and dress, ways of walking and gesturing, tone of voice and mannerisms—anything that would help readers see the person as you remember her or him.*

*If you have chosen to write about an **event**, recall other people who were involved, and write a brief description of each person.*

Reconstructing Dialogue. *Write a few lines of dialogue that you could use to convey something important about the event or to give readers an impression of the person you have chosen to write about.* You may use direct quotation, enclosing the words you remember being spoken in quotation marks, or you may use indirect quotation, paraphrasing and summarizing what was said. Try to re-create the give-and-take quality of normal conversation in the dialogue.

Describing Important Places. *Identify the place where the event happened or a place you associate with the person, and detail what you see in the scene as you visualize it.* Try to recall specific sensory details: size, shape, color, condition, and texture of the scene or memorable objects in it. Imagine the place from head-on and from the side, from a distance and from close-up.

Considering Visuals. *Consider whether visuals—photographs, postcards, ticket stubs—would strengthen your presentation of the event or person.* If you submit your essay electronically to other students and your instructor, or if you post it on a Web site, consider including photographs as well as snippets of film or sound or other memorabilia that might give readers a more vivid sense of the time, place, and people about which you are writing. Visual and audio materials are not at all a requirement of an effective autobiographical essay, as you can tell from the readings in this chapter, but they could add a new dimension to your writing. If you want to use photographs or recordings of people, though, be sure to request their permission.

Reflecting on Your Subject

The following activities will help you think about the significance of your subject by recalling your remembered feelings and thoughts as well as exploring your present perspective. The activities will also help you consider your purpose in writing about this subject and formulate a tentative thesis statement.

Recalling Your Feelings and Thoughts. *Write for a few minutes, trying to recall your thoughts and feelings when the event was occurring or when you knew the person.* What did you feel—in control or powerless, proud or embarrassed, vulnerable, detached, judgmental? How did you show or express your feelings? What did you want others to think of you at the time? What did you think of yourself? What were the immediate consequences for you personally?

Exploring Your Present Perspective. *Write for a few minutes, trying to express your present thoughts and feelings as you look back on the event or person.* How have your feelings changed? What insights do you now have? What does your present perspective reveal about what you were like at the time? Try looking at the event or person in broader, cultural or social terms. For example, consider whether you or anyone else upset gender expectations or felt out of place in some way.

Considering Your Purpose. *Write for several minutes exploring what you want your readers to understand about the significance of the event or person.* Use the following questions to help clarify your thoughts:

- What will writing about this event or person enable you to suggest about yourself as an individual? What will it let you suggest about the social and cultural forces that helped shape you—for example, how people exercise power over one another, how family and community values and attitudes have an impact on individuals, or how economic and social conditions influence our sense of self?
- What do you not understand fully about the event or relationship? What about it still puzzles you or seems contradictory? What do you feel ambivalent about?
- What about your subject do you expect will seem familiar to your readers? What do you think will surprise them, perhaps getting them to think in new ways or to question some of their assumptions and stereotypes?

Formulating a Tentative Thesis Statement. *Review what you wrote for Considering Your Purpose and add another two or three sentences that will help you convey to readers the significance of the event or person in your life.* Try to write sentences that do not just summarize what you have written, but that also extend your insights and reflections. These sentences may be contradictory because they express ambivalent feelings. They also must necessarily be partial and speculative because you may never understand fully the event's or person's significance.

Keep in mind that readers do not expect you to begin your essay with the kind of explicit introductory thesis statement typical of argumentative essays. None of the readings in this chapter offers to readers an explicit thesis statement explaining the event or person's significance. Instead, the readings convey the significance by combining showing with telling in their narration of events and descriptions of people and places. And yet it is possible for readers to infer from each reading an implied thesis or impression of the significance. For example, some readers might decide that Dillard wants readers to think that what was most significant and memorable about the event was the way the man threw himself into the chase, showing that childlike enthusiasm sometimes can survive into adulthood. Other readers might focus on the idea that what was significant was that the man as well as the children "all played by the rules," and that when people play by the rules they act with honor and nobility (paragraph 16). If, like you, Dillard had tried to write a few sentences about the significance she hoped to convey in writing about this small but memorable event in her life, she might have written sentences like these.

Nearly all first attempts at stating a thesis are eventually revised once drafting gets under way. Writing the first draft helps autobiographers discover what they think and feel about their subject and find ways to convey its significance without ever spelling it out directly. Just because there is no explicit thesis statement in an autobiography does not mean that the essay lacks focus or fails to convey significance.

DRAFTING

The following guidelines will help you set goals for your draft, plan its organization, choose relevant details, and decide how to begin.

Setting Goals

Establishing goals for your draft before you begin writing will enable you to make decisions and work more confidently. Consider the following questions now, and keep them in mind as you draft. They will help you set goals for drafting as well as recall how the writers you have read in this chapter tried to achieve similar goals.

- *How can I present my subject vividly and memorably to readers?* Should I rely on dialogue to present people and relationships, as Wu and Benioff do? Or should I concentrate on presenting action rather than dialogue, like Dillard and Bragg? Can I use visual or other sensory details, as Lorde and Abraham do, to give readers a vivid impression of the person and place while also establishing the significance of my subject?
- *How can I help readers understand the meaning and importance of the event or person?* Can I use the symbolism of the place, as Lorde does with Washington, D.C., to underscore the significance of the event? Can I build the suspense, as Dillard does, in a way that lets readers vicariously share the excitement I felt at the time?
- *How can I avoid superficial or one-dimensional presentations of my experience and my relations with others?* Knowing that my readers will not expect easy answers about what makes the event or person significant, how can I satisfy their expectations for writing that has some depth and complexity? How might I employ one or more of the strategies illustrated by the writers I have read in this chapter—the paradox in Dillard's feeling both terror and pleasure as she is chased by the man in the black Buick; the contradictions Lorde sets up in relating her parents' behavior and their beliefs; Benioff's love-hate relationship with the coach? What contradictions, paradoxes, or ironies exist in my own story?

Organizing Your Draft

With goals in mind, plan your draft by making a tentative outline. Although your plan may change as you write and revise your draft, outlining before you begin drafting can help you get organized. If you are uncertain about how to organize your material, review how some of the writers in this chapter organize their autobiographical essays.

For an *event*, outline the sequence of main actions, from the beginning to the end of the event.

For a *person*, outline the order of the recurring activities, or anecdotes you will use to present the person, interspersing relevant character traits, physical details, and dialogue.

Choosing Relevant Details

The invention activities helped you generate many details, probably more than you can use. To decide which details to include in your draft and which to leave out, consider how well each detail contributes to the overall impression you want to create. But before you discard any details that seem irrelevant, think again about what they might suggest about the significance of your subject. Sometimes, seemingly irrelevant details or ones that do not fit neatly can lead you to new insights.

Writing the Beginning

In order to engage your readers' interest from the start, consider beginning with an arresting bit of dialogue or a compelling graphic description (as Benioff does when he describes the swimming pool in the early morning light), with a startling action or a vivid memory (as Abraham does when she recalls the two times she saw her father cry), or with some background information (as Lorde does when she explains why her family decided to go to Washington, D.C.). You might have to try two or three different beginnings before finding a promising way to start, but do not agonize for too long over the first sentence. Try out any possible beginning and see where it takes you.

READING A DRAFT CRITICALLY

Getting a critical reading of your draft will help you see how to improve it. Your instructor may schedule class time for reading drafts, or you may want to ask a classmate or a tutor in the writing center to read your draft. Ask your reader to use the following guidelines and to write out a response for you to consult during your revision.

Read for a First Impression

1. Read the draft without stopping to annotate or comment, and then write two or three sentences giving your general impression.
2. Identify one aspect of the draft that seems especially effective.

Read Again to Suggest Improvements

1. Recommend ways to make the narrative more dramatic and telling. For a draft presenting an *event*:
   - Point to any scenes where the action seems to drag or become confusing.
   - Suggest places where the drama might be intensified—by adding a close-up, using more active verbs, or shifting the placement of background information or descriptive detail, for example.
   - Indicate where dialogue could add drama to a confrontation scene.

   For a draft using anecdotes or recurring activities to present a *person*:
   - Note which anecdotes and recurring activities seem especially effective in illustrating something important about the person or the relationship.

- Point to one weak anecdote or recurring activity and suggest how it could be made more effective, such as by adding graphic details and dialogue or by telling how it relates to the person's significance.
- Indicate any passages where direct quotations could be more effectively presented indirectly, through paraphrase or summary, or by combining a striking quote with summary.

2. Indicate any areas where improving dull or weak description could more vividly or effectively convey the dominant impression of the essay.
   - Describe the impression you get from the writer's description of the event or person.
   - Identify one or two passages where you think the description is especially vivid; for example, where the visual details and images help you picture the event or person.
   - Point to any passages where the description could be made more vivid or where it seems to contradict the impression you get from other parts of the essay.
3. Suggest how the autobiographical significance could be developed.
   - Briefly explain your understanding of the significance, indicating anything that puzzles or surprises you about the event or person.
   - Note any word choice, contradiction, or irony—in the way people and places are described or in the way the story is told—that alerts you to a deeper meaning that the writer could develop.
   - Point to any passages where the writer needs to clarify the historical, social, or cultural dimensions of the experience or relationship.
4. Suggest how the organizational plan could be improved. Consider the overall plan of the essay, perhaps by making a scratch outline (see Appendix 1, p. 529, for an example).
   - For an *event*, indicate any passages where narrative transitions or verb tense markers are needed to make the story unfold more logically and clearly.
   - For a *person*, suggest where topic sentences or transitions could be added or where the writer could more clearly indicate what impression of the person the anecdotes or recurring activities are intended to convey.

5. Evaluate the effectiveness of visuals.
   - Look at any visuals in the essay, and tell the writer what they contribute to your understanding of the event or person.
   - If any visuals do not seem relevant, or if there seem to be too many visuals, identify the ones that the writer could consider dropping, explaining your thinking.
   - If a visual does not seem to be appropriately placed, suggest a better place for it.

REVISING

This section offers suggestions for revising your draft, suggestions that will remind you of the possibilities for developing an engaging, coherent autobiography. Revising means reenvisioning your draft, trying to see it in a new way, given your purpose and readers, in order to develop your autobiography.

The biggest mistake you can make while revising is to focus initially on words or sentences. Instead, first try to see your draft as a whole in order to assess its likely impact on your readers. Think imaginatively and boldly about cutting unconvincing material, adding new material, and moving material around. Your computer makes even drastic revisions physically easy, but you still need to make the mental effort and decisions that will improve your draft.

You may have received help with this challenge from a classmate or tutor who gave your draft a critical reading. If so, keep this feedback in mind as you decide which parts of your draft need revising and what specific changes you could make. The following suggestions will help you solve problems and strengthen your essay.

To Make the Narrative More Dramatic and Telling

- If the story seems to meander and have no point, focus the action so that it builds up more directly toward the climax.
- Where the narrative drags or the tension slackens, try using more active verbs, more dialogue, or shorter sentences.
- Where background information or descriptive detail interrupts the drama or slows the pace, consider cutting or moving it.
- If the purpose of an anecdote or a recurring activity is not clear, make explicit what it illustrates.

- If the exact words in a conversation are not striking or important, use indirect instead of direct dialogue or combine the two, paraphrasing or summarizing most of what was said but including a memorable phrase or notable word.

To Present People Vividly

- Where more graphic description is needed, give visual details showing what the person looks like or how the person gestures.
- If any detail seems inconsistent or contradictory, cut it or use it to develop the significance.
- If the description does not convey the impression you want it to convey, consider cutting some descriptive details and adding others, or rethinking the impression you want your writing to convey and the significance it suggests.

To Describe Places Vividly

- If any details about an important place do not fit together well and do not contribute to the dominant impression or reinforce the significance, omit them from the essay.
- Where readers cannot visualize the place, add more sensory detail.
- Where the description distracts from the action, cut or move the description.
- Where the point of view is confusing, consider simplifying it.

To Convey the Autobiographical Significance

- If readers may not understand the significance of the person or event, look for passages where you could convey it more directly.
- If the significance seems too pat or simplistic, consider whether you could develop contradictions or allow for ambivalence.
- If readers may not understand the importance of the social, cultural, or historical context, consider giving background information to reveal its influence.

To Make the Organizational Plan More Effective

- If readers may be confused about what happened when, add transitions or verb tense markers.

- If readers may not see clearly how the anecdotes or recurring activities contribute to the portrait of the person, add forecasting statements or topic sentences to clarify what those elements demonstrate.

EDITING AND PROOFREADING

After you have revised your essay, be sure to spend some time checking for errors in usage, punctuation, and mechanics and considering matters of style. If you keep a list of errors you typically make, begin by checking your draft against this list. Ask someone else to proofread your essay before you print out a copy for your instructor or send it electronically.

From our research on student writing, we know that essays dealing with autobiographical subjects have a high percentage of errors in verb tense and punctuation. You should proofread your narration for verb tense errors and your description for punctuation errors—such as comma splices and missing commas after introductory elements. Check a writer's handbook for help with these potential problems.

REFLECTING ON WHAT YOU HAVE LEARNED

Autobiography

In this chapter, you have read critically several pieces of autobiography and have written one of your own. To better remember what you have learned, pause now to reflect on the reading and writing activities you completed in this chapter.

1. *Write* a page or so reflecting on what you have learned. *Begin* by describing what you are most pleased with in your essay. Then *explain* what you think contributed to your achievement. *Be specific* about this contribution.
   - If it was something you learned from the readings, *indicate* which readings and specifically what you learned from them.
   - If it came from your invention writing, *point out* the section or sections that helped you most.
   - If you got good advice from a critical reader, *explain* exactly how the person helped you—perhaps by helping you understand a particular problem in your draft or by adding a new dimension to your writing.
2. Now *reflect* more generally on how you tend to interpret autobiographical writing, your own as well as other writers'. *Consider*

some of the following questions: In reading for meaning, do you tend to find yourself interpreting the significance of the event or person in terms of the writer's personal feelings, sense of self-esteem, or psychological well-being? Or do you more often think of significance in terms of larger social or economic influences—for example, whether the writer is male or female, rich or poor, suburban or urban, African American or Anglo? Where do you think you learned to interpret the significance of people's stories about themselves and their relationships—from your family, friends, television, school?

CHAPTER 

Observation

Certain kinds of writing are based on fresh observation or direct investigation. Travel writers, for example, may profile a place they have visited; naturalists may describe phenomena they have observed undisturbed in nature. Investigative reporters or clinical psychologists may write up interviews with individuals, while cultural anthropologists may write ethnographies of groups they have studied in depth. Much of what we know about people and the world we learn from this kind of writing.

Writing about your own observations offers special challenges and rewards. It requires you to pay more attention than you normally do to everyday activities. You need to look with all your senses and give your curiosity free rein. Taking a questioning or inquiring stance will enable you to make discoveries in even the most mundane settings. In addition, it helps to take voluminous notes because you might not know what is significant until you begin to sort through the observations and quotations you have collected. That way, after the work of observing and interviewing is done, another kind of equally challenging and rewarding work can begin — making meaning of the bits and pieces you have gathered. Analyzing and synthesizing your notes, you interpret your subject, deciding what you want to tell your readers about it. These activities of close observation and careful notetaking, combined with thoughtful analysis and imaginative synthesis, form the basic strategies of researching and learning in many areas of college study.

When writing about your observations, you will have an immediate advantage if you choose a place, an activity, or a person that is new to readers. But even if the subject is familiar, you can still intrigue and inform readers by presenting it in a new light or by focusing on a specific aspect of the subject. By focusing on certain details, you not only help readers imagine what the place looks, sounds, and smells like or picture how the people dress, gesture, and talk, but you also create an impression that conveys your idea or interpretation of the subject.

The readings in this chapter will help you learn a lot about observational writing. From the readings and from the ideas for writing that follow each reading, you will get ideas for your own observational essay. As you read and write about the selections, keep in mind the following assignment, which sets out the goals for writing an observational essay. To support your writing of this assignment, the chapter concludes with a Guide to Writing Observational Essays.

THE WRITING ASSIGNMENT

Observation

Write an observational essay about an intriguing place, person, or activity in your community. Your essay may be a brief profile of an individual based on one or two interviews; a description of a place or activity observed once or twice; or a longer, more fully developed profile of a person, place, or activity based on observational visits and interviews conducted over several days. Observe your subject closely, and then present what you have learned in a way that both informs and engages readers.

WRITING SITUATIONS FOR OBSERVATIONAL ESSAYS

As we indicated earlier, many people — including travel writers, investigative reporters, clinical psychologists, and cultural anthropologists — write essays based on observations and interviews. In your other college courses, you may have an opportunity to write an observational essay like one of the following:

- For an art history course, a student writes about a local artist recently commissioned to paint outdoor murals for the city. The student visits the artist's studio and talks with him about the process of painting murals, large pictures painted on walls or the sides of buildings. The artist invites the student to spend the following day as a part of a team of local art students and neighborhood volunteers working on the mural under the artist's direction. This firsthand experience helps the student profile the artist, present some of the students, and give readers a clear impression of the process of collaboration involved in mural painting.
- For a journalism course, a student profiles a typical day in the life of an award-winning scientist. He spends a day observing the scientist at home and at work, and he then interviews colleagues, students, and family, as well as the scientist herself. Her daily life, he learns, is very much like that of other working mothers — a constant effort to balance the demands of her career against the needs of her family. He conveys this idea in his essay by

alternating between details about the scientist's work and those about her family life.

- For a sociology class, a student writes about a controversial urban renewal project to replace decaying but repairable houses with a library and park. To learn about the history of the project, she reads newspaper reports and interviews people who helped plan the project as well as some neighborhood residents and activists who oppose it. She also tours the site with the project manager to see what is actually being done. In addition to presenting different points of view about the project, her essay describes the library and park in detail, including pictures of the neighborhood before the project and drawings of what it will look like afterward. She seeks to give the impression that the project manager has succeeded in winning neighborhood support and that most residents will be pleased with the completed project.

A Guide to Reading Observational Essays

This guide introduces you to observational writing. By completing all of the activities in it, you will prepare yourself to learn a great deal from the other readings in this chapter about how to read and write an observational essay. The guide focuses on "Soup," an intriguing profile of Mr. Yeganeh and his unique New York City restaurant, Soup Kitchen International. You will read this observational essay twice. First, you will read it for meaning, looking closely at the essay's content and ideas. Then, you will read the essay like a writer, analyzing its parts to see how the writer crafts the essay and to learn the strategies that make it vivid and informative. These two activities — reading for meaning and reading like a writer — follow every reading in this chapter.

THE NEW YORKER

Soup

"Soup" was published anonymously in a 1989 issue of the New Yorker, *a magazine read by many people across the country who enjoy cartoons, short stories, music and art reviews, political and social commentary, and profiles of people and places. The subject of this essay is Albert Yeganeh, the creative and demanding owner/chef of a small take-out restaurant that serves only soup. In 1995, Yeganeh's restaurant inspired an episode of the then-popular television program* Seinfeld.

The writer of "Soup" relies extensively on dialogue quoted from the interview to keep the focus on Yeganeh's personality and ideas.

Readers can readily imagine the reporter interviewing Yeganeh, writing down soup names and ingredients, observing people in line, and even standing in line as well for a bowl of soup.

As you read, annotate anything that helps you imagine Yeganeh and his Soup Kitchen International.

When Albert Yeganeh says "Soup is my lifeblood," he means it. And when he says "I am extremely hard to please," he means that, too. Working like a demon alchemist in a tiny storefront kitchen at 259-A West Fifty-fifth Street, Mr. Yeganeh creates anywhere from eight to seventeen soups every weekday. His concoctions are so popular that a wait of half an hour at the lunchtime peak is not uncommon, although there are strict rules for conduct in line. But more on that later. 1

"I am psychologically kind of a health freak," Mr. Yeganeh said the other day, in a lisping staccato of Armenian origin. "And I know that soup is the greatest meal in the world. It's very good for your digestive system. And I use only the best, the freshest ingredients. I am a perfectionist. When I make a clam soup, I use three different kinds of clams. Every other place uses canned clams. I'm called crazy. I am not crazy. People don't realize why I get so upset. It's because if the soup is not perfect and I'm still selling it, it's a torture. It's *my* soup, and that's why I'm so upset. First you clean and then you cook. I don't believe that ninety-nine per cent of the restaurants in New York know how to clean a tomato. I tell my crew to wash the parsley *eight* times. If they wash it five or six times, I scare them. I tell them they'll go to jail if there is sand in the parsley. One time, I found a mushroom on the floor, and I fired that guy who left it there." He spread his arms, and added, "This place is the only one like it in . . . in . . . the whole earth! One day, I hope to learn something from the other places, but so far I haven't. For example, the other day I went to a very fancy restaurant and had borscht. I had to send it back. It was *junk.* I could see all the chemicals in it. I never use chemicals. Last weekend, I had lobster bisque in Brooklyn, a very well-known place. It was *junk.* When I make a lobster bisque, I use a whole lobster. You know, I never advertise. I don't have to. All the big-shot chefs and the kings of the hotels come here to see what *I'm* doing." 2

As you approach Mr. Yeganeh's Soup Kitchen International from a distance, the first thing you notice about it is the awning, which proclaims "Homemade Hot, Cold, Diet Soups." The second thing you notice is an aroma so delicious that it makes you want to take a bite out of the air. The third thing you notice, in front of the kitchen, is an electric signboard that flashes, saying, 3

"Today's Soups . . . Chicken Vegetable . . . Mexican Beef Chili . . . Cream of Watercress . . . Italian Sausage . . . Clam Bisque . . . Beef Barley . . . Due to Cold Weather . . . For Most Efficient and Fastest Service the Line Must . . . Be Kept Moving . . . Please . . . Have Your Money . . . Ready . . . Pick the Soup of Your Choice . . . Move to Your Extreme . . . Left After Ordering."

4 "I am not prejudiced against color or religion," Mr. Yeganeh told us, and he jabbed an index finger at the flashing sign. "Whoever follows that I treat very well. My regular customers don't say anything. They are very intelligent and well educated. They know I'm just trying to move the line. The New York cop is very smart — he sees everything but says nothing. But the young girl who wants to stop and tell you how nice you look and hold everyone up — *yah!*" He made a guillotining motion with his hand. "I tell you, I hate to work with the public. They treat me like a slave. My philosophy is: The customer is always wrong and I'm always right. I raised my prices to try to get rid of some of these people, but it didn't work."

5 The other day, Mr. Yeganeh was dressed in chef's whites with orange smears across his chest, which may have been some of the carrot soup cooking in a huge pot on a little stove in one corner. A three-foot-long handheld mixer from France sat on the sink, looking like an overgrown gardening tool. Mr. Yeganeh spoke to two young helpers in a twisted Armenian-Spanish barrage, then said to us, "I have no overhead, no trained waitresses, and I have the cashier here." He pointed to himself theatrically. Beside the doorway, a glass case with fresh green celery, red and yellow peppers, and purple eggplant was topped by five big gray soup urns. According to a piece of cardboard taped to the door, you can buy Mr. Yeganeh's soups in three sizes, costing from four to fifteen dollars. The order of any well-behaved customer is accompanied by little waxpaper packets of bread, fresh vegetables (such as scallions and radishes), fresh fruit (such as cherries or an orange), a chocolate mint, and a plastic spoon. No coffee, tea, or other drinks are served.

6 "I get my recipes from books and theories and my own taste," Mr. Yeganeh said. "At home, I have several hundreds of books. When I do research, I find that I don't know anything. Like cabbage is a cancer fighter, and some fish is good for your heart but some is bad. Every day, I should have one sweet, one spicy, one cream, one vegetable soup — and they *must* change, they should always taste a little different." He added that he wasn't sure how extensive his repertoire was, but that it probably includes at least eighty soups, among them African peanut butter,

Greek moussaka, hamburger, Reuben, B.L.T., asparagus and caviar, Japanese shrimp miso, chicken chili, Irish corned beef and cabbage, Swiss chocolate, French calf's brain, Korean beef ball, Italian shrimp and eggplant Parmesan, buffalo, ham and egg, short rib, Russian beef Stroganoff, turkey cacciatore, and Indian mulligatawny. "The chicken and the seafood are an addiction, and when I have French garlic soup I let people have only one small container each," he said. "The doctors and nurses love that one."

7 A lunch line of thirty people stretched down the block from Mr. Yeganeh's doorway. Behind a construction worker was a man in expensive leather, who was in front of a woman in a fur hat. Few people spoke. Most had their money out and their orders ready.

8 At the front of the line, a woman in a brown coat couldn't decide which soup to get and started to complain about the prices.

9 "You talk too much, dear," Mr. Yeganeh said, and motioned her to move to the left. "Next!"

10 "Just don't talk. Do what he says," a man huddled in a blue parka warned.

11 "He's downright rude," said a blond woman in a blue coat. "Even abusive. But you can't deny it, his soup is the best."

READING FOR MEANING

Write to create meanings for this observational essay on Albert Yeganeh and his Soup Kitchen International.

Start Making Meaning

Begin by listing Yeganeh's most memorable or surprising qualities. Continue by writing about anything else in the selection or in your experience that contributes to your understanding of Yeganeh and his restaurant.

If You Are Stuck

If you cannot write at least a page, consider writing about

- what Yeganeh thinks of the work he does and its importance, giving examples of his views.
- Yeganeh's often-stated business principle, "The customer is always wrong" (paragraph 4). You may also want to reflect on your own experience as a fast-food customer or worker in light of Yeganeh's principle. If you do so, connect your personal experience explicitly to Yeganeh's principle.

- Yeganeh's apparent obsession with quality, possibly connecting it with your own or someone else's perfectionism.
- the personal work ethic and small-business values that Yeganeh stands for as compared with your own work experience.

READING LIKE A WRITER

This section guides you through an analysis of the observational writing strategies illustrated in "Soup": *describing places and people, organizing the observations, engaging and informing readers,* and *conveying an impression of the subject.* For each strategy you will be asked to reread and annotate part of the essay to see how that particular strategy works in "Soup."

When you study the selections later in this chapter, you will see how different writers use these same strategies. The Guide to Writing Observational Essays near the end of the chapter suggests ways you can use these strategies in your own writing.

Describing Places and People

Observational writing, like autobiography (Chapter 2), succeeds by presenting the subject vividly and concretely. Writers of observation usually describe both places and people, although they may emphasize one over the other. Visual details usually predominate in an observational essay, but some writers complement these by describing sounds, smells, tastes, and even textures and temperatures.

Observational writers present people through visual details and action — how they look, how they dress, how they move, what they do. They also show how people talk and interact with one another, often including both direct quotations from their notes and paraphrases of what people have said. To gain a sense of an individual's personality, readers usually need only a few details indicating the person's tone of voice, facial expression, style of dress, or movements.

Analyze

1. *Reread* the description of Yeganeh and his establishment in paragraph 5, and *underline* all of the words and phrases used to describe them. To get started, *underline* the phrases "dressed in chef's whites" and "orange smears," which describe Yeganeh. Then *underline* "carrot" and "huge," which describe one of the soups and one of the utensils. Now *underline* the remaining words and phrases in paragraph 5 that describe Yeganeh and his soup kitchen. You will notice that the writer relies on visual details in this paragraph.

2. *Review* the visual details you underlined. *Single out* two or three that seem most vivid to you or that best help you imagine Soup Kitchen International as different from other fast-food places you have visited.

Write

Write several sentences explaining what you have discovered about the essay's use of visual details to present Yeganeh and his restaurant. From your annotations in paragraph 5, *give examples* of the details you find to be especially vivid or memorable. Then *explain* why they work so well for you.

Organizing the Observations

Observational writers typically present their subjects either narratively, as a more or less chronological story of their observations, or topically, as groups of related information the writer wants readers to know about the subject. "Soup" is a good example of topical organization. Some observational essays in this chapter are arranged narratively, as you will discover when you analyze John McPhee's observations of an outdoor farmers' market. While a narrative plan offers certain advantages — engaging readers and providing the drama of a good novel or movie — a topical plan keeps the focus firmly on the information.

Analyze

1. *Make a scratch outline* of "Soup," identifying the topics in the order in which they appear. *Notice* that some paragraphs have more than one topic; paragraph 2, for instance, raises several topics: the health benefits of soup, Yeganeh's perfectionism, his emphasis on cleanliness, and how his restaurant compares to others. (For an example of scratch outlining, see Appendix 1, p. 529.)

2. *Note* in your outline whether the source of the topic is the writer's interviews, the writer's firsthand observations, or both.

Write

Write several sentences commenting on what types of topics are presented, which sources they come from, and how effectively they are sequenced. Then *write a few more sentences* answering these questions: How does the sequence of topics contribute to or inhibit your growing understanding of Soup Kitchen International as you read through the essay? Which topics does the writer introduce and then drop? Which topics does he return to later?

Engaging and Informing Readers

Along with presenting their subjects vividly and organizing material effectively, observational writers strive both to engage or interest their readers and to inform them about the subject. Readers expect to learn something new from observational writing, and they anticipate savoring this learning experience. To accomplish these intertwined goals of engaging and informing readers, writers must pace the flow of information while engaging readers' interests. Strategies for engaging readers include beginning with an arresting image or statement, using active verbs, reporting unusual activities and events, and reporting revealing interview material.

Much of the information in observational writing tends to come from interviews and to be presented as quoted statements or conversations, as in "Soup." Information can also come from the writer's observations and background reading and may be quoted or summarized. Strategies for presenting information include identifying and defining new terms, listing, dividing into parts, classifying or grouping, and comparing or contrasting. A writer of observation needs to consider carefully what readers are likely to know about the subject as well as what will interest or even amuse them.

Analyze

1. *Skim the reading,* thinking about the pace of information. *Note* the overall quantity of the information, the different types of information, and whether the information comes at readers so fast they might be confused or so slow they might lose interest. *Put an "X"* in the margin by any information that seems to you to come too fast or too slow for readers who have never been to Soup Kitchen International.

2. *Skim the reading again,* this time looking for anything you think *New Yorker* readers, including yourself, might find engaging or amusing. *Put a checkmark* next to these spots.

Write

Write several sentences describing how the author of "Soup" informs and engages readers. *Cite examples* from your annotations. *Point out* what seems most and least successful about the pace of information and the attempts to engage readers.

Conveying an Impression of the Subject

Readers expect observational essays to convey a particular impression or interpretation of the subject. They want to know the writer's insight into the subject after having spent time observing the place and interviewing people.

To convey an impression, writers carefully select details of the place and people and put these details together in a particular way. They may also explicitly express an attitude toward the subject as well as an interpretation or evaluation of it, announcing these at the beginning, weaving them into the ongoing observations, or presenting them in the conclusion. More often, however, writers convey an impression by implication. The author of "Soup," for example, does not state an interpretation or evaluation directly but implies it through the quotes, the descriptive details, and the little drama presented at the end.

Analyze

1. *Underline* any words or phrases that suggest the author's attitudes toward or feelings about Yeganeh as a human being, cook, and businessman.
2. *Note in the margin* any interpretation or evaluation of Yeganeh and his way of doing business implied by what he says and does.

Write

Write several sentences identifying the overall impression you have of Yeganeh and his Soup Kitchen International. *Quote* two or three phrases or sentences from the essay that convey this impression most strongly, and *identify* briefly the attitude, interpretation, or evaluation you see in each phrase or sentence.

Readings

JOHN LELAND

Monster Factory

John Leland (b. 1959), a reporter at the New York Times, *writes for the style department in the newspaper's weekly House and Home section. He has also been a senior editor at* Newsweek, *editor in chief at* Details *magazine, and music critic for* Newsday, *a suburban New York newspaper.*

In the following reading, which appeared in Newsweek *in 2000, Leland writes about a school for aspiring professional wrestlers. Unlike some writers of observational essays, such as the author of "Soup," who spend time observing the place and talking with different people but who do not participate in the activity, Leland fully participates in his subject. Along with the instructor and students, he practices the holds, deceptions, and other strategies required for success in the World Wrestling Federation (WWF). Instead of organizing by topic the information he wants to pass on, as does the author of "Soup," Leland organizes narratively; that is, he tells the story of the four days he spent taking lessons at the wrestling school. Leland's subject gives him the advantage of reporting on a place likely to be unfamiliar to nearly all of his readers.*

As you read, notice how the writer focuses on the specific wrestling moves students must learn and on insider knowledge about professional wrestling. Also reflect on times when you were introduced to a completely new sport or other activity.

Cliff Compton, as he is known professionally, stands 6 feet 1½ inches, weighs 215 pounds and owns his own gym — on the whole, not the sort of guy I'd choose to tussle with. But on a cold morning in January, the two of us square off in an unheated cinder-block hangar in south Jersey. "Come on, *Newsweek*," taunts an onlooker helpfully. "It's time to get slammed." 1

Cliff and I circle each other warily, then tie up in the center of the ring — our arms locked at each other's necks and elbows, bodies torqued in opposition. With a nod for me to jump up, Cliff lifts me off the mat, raising me horizontally at chin level. Then, like the man says, it is time to get slammed. For an instant I am in free fall, until *wham!* the concussive thump of a 40-year-old back slamming flat against the dirty canvas. I take inventory of the damage: nothing I can't walk away from. Let's do it again, from the top. Tie up; lift; *wham!* So goes another lesson at the 2

Monster Factory, a place that gives full meaning to the phrase, School of Hard Knocks.

3 In the world of professional wrestling, some men are born to cartoon greatness. But most learn it in institutions like the Monster Factory, one of a couple of dozen schools across the country where guys like Cliff learn the fine art of making it look real. For $3,500, "Pretty Boy" Larry Sharpe, a former top pro himself, molds able bodies into what they hope will be the next generation of WWF superstars. The lessons usually take about six to eight months, but Larry and his deputy, Ed Atlas, have agreed to run me through a four-day crash course, or as long as I can hang. I'm down for pain, I say, but not lasting injury. Ed smiles at the first part.

4 Larry has trained some of the top names in wrestling, including the Big Show and King Kong Bundy, but on this day, a

SCHOOL OF HARD KNOCKS: Like the man says, it is time to get slammed. Wham! I'm on the canvas.

half-dozen lesser mortals pace the ring: beer distributors, security guards, bodybuilders, schoolteachers. We start with the basic "bump": fold your arms across your chest, tuck in your chin and fall flat on your back. And again. Most rings have a coiled spring under the center to absorb some of the impact, but this one relies on the natural give of the plywood, which is covered by an inch and a half of foam padding. The goal is to land flat, distributing the shock over as broad an area as possible. It is the wrestling student's first act of faith. Like fledgling actors or musicians, my classmates believe unshakably that from this humble tumble lies the road to stone-cold greatness. "I'm positive that I'm going to do it," says Ryan Miller, 19, a butcher who has emptied his savings to pursue this dream. "I met Ravishing Rick Rude when I was 7 years old. I said right then, 'I want to be a wrestler'."

5 Larry offers a frank assessment of my prospects. At 49, he has bleached hair, a giant cigar and a shiny Cadillac. Because of a run-in with the gout, he drinks only champagne. "You're not going to walk out of here and get a job with the WWF, that's for sure," he says in his flat south Jersey accent. After decades as a "heel" — the guy fans love to hate — he communicates in the broad, expressive gestures of his profession. "If you concentrate, work hard, I can teach you how to wrestle. You would wrestle part-time and make your money back." After this counsel, it is my turn to inflict some damage. I fling Jack McFadden, 31, an interior designer, against the ropes (he helps), then guide him through an aerial flip over my hip: my first hip toss. As he crashes to the canvas, "selling" the pain with a so-so paroxysm, I can see how guys get hooked. Jack whips me wrenchingly against a turnbuckle, to Ed's withering appraisal. "That's better, *Newsweek,*" he yells. "It still sucked, but it wasn't ridiculous." This is the nicest thing he ever says to me, and I take it as a compliment.

6 Larry and Ed work on the basics: always twist your opponent's left arm; two squeezes on your hand signal that it's time for you to take over; keep your posture theatrically upright to play to the cheap seats, even in a side headlock. If you hurt your opponent for real, he might "get a receipt," or return the favor. "It's like a waltz," yells Ed, counting off a one-two-three rhythm. "Your opponent is really your partner."

7 Though it is premature, Larry agrees to steer me toward my gimmick, or ring persona. A good gimmick exaggerates one facet of a wrestler's real personality. Larry sizes me up as a heel. This is good news. Heels generate the emotional energy, or "heat," in any match, and are usually the "ring generals," directing the moves

(most wrestlers plan their opening and closing sequences, improvising in between). "With you," says Larry, warming to the subject, "your personality is slightly introverted; your posture is not outstanding. You could be a sneak or a tricky guy that would hide gimmicks. You could take a beating, then every once in a while pull something dirty and sneaky and underhanded. Maybe a thumb to the Adam's apple, or hiding brass knuckles or a roll of dimes in your tights." Who wouldn't love this game?

8 By the fourth morning, however, I reassess the damage. My ankles are on fire, my calves cramped. My right temple throbs from an inadvertent kick. My ribs hurt when I inhale, and I have to lift my head with my hands to get out of bed. Critics of professional wrestling scoff that the daring feats are all bogus, but wrestling fans buy into a trickier illusion: that a man can tumble headlong onto a table from 10 feet above and not be hurt — *because everyone knows wrestling is fake.* In fact, that man is in pain. For my last day, I decide, I will just watch.

9 As they run through the moves, Ryan takes a nasty header onto his face. A student named Anthony aggravates a separated shoulder. A rope comes loose, nearly spilling everyone onto the concrete. Larry offers bags of ice (everybody has already signed a release waiving his right to sue) and sympathy. "You gotta love the pain," says Ronnie Koreck, a beefy insurance adjuster from Pennsylvania. Though he is 37, Ronnie assures me that he has lined up sponsors to help him reach the next level, wrestling in gyms and VFW halls for small paychecks en route to the top.

10 It is this faith that offsets the day's pains, and the next day's as well. No one teases me for wimping out. I say my farewell, but I will long remember my days in the squared circle. Every time I get out of bed.

READING FOR MEANING

Write to create meanings for Leland's observations of the wrestling school.

Start Making Meaning

Begin by listing and describing the specific wrestling moves the writer is required to practice. Continue by writing about anything else in the selection or in your experience that contributes to your understanding of Leland's observations.

If You Are Stuck

If you cannot write at least a page, consider writing about

- the different backgrounds of Leland's fellow students and their motivations for coming to the Monster Factory.
- what the photograph adds to your understanding of Leland's experiences at the wrestling school.
- the concept of having a "gimmick" in wrestling (paragraph 7), describing the gimmick Larry assigns the writer, and, if possible, noting one or two kinds of work you know about for which it is important to have a gimmick in addition to skills and knowledge.
- your own experience of being introduced to a challenging activity, physical or mental, connecting your personal experience explicitly to Leland's and to the principles that seem important to Leland's instructors, such as "'concentrate, work hard'" (paragraph 5) and "'You gotta love the pain'" (9).

READING LIKE A WRITER

DESCRIBING PEOPLE THROUGH SPECIFIC NARRATIVE ACTION

Leland describes the Monster Factory and the people there by detailing how they look. For example, he describes the school as a "cinder-block hangar" (paragraph 1) and the ring as "plywood . . . covered by an inch and a half of foam padding" (4). In paragraph 5, he describes Larry, his coach, as someone with "bleached hair" who always seems to be smoking a "giant cigar." He also describes Larry by the kind of car he drives ("a shiny Cadillac") and his drinking preferences ("only champagne"). Writers of observational essays nearly always rely on strategies like these to help readers imagine places and people. But they have available still another important strategy: specific narrative action, describing people through the ways they move, gesture, and talk. Because Leland is profiling a very physical kind of sports training, we expect him to make repeated use of specific narrative action.

Analyze

1. *Reread* paragraphs 2 and 9, and *underline* words or phrases that show people's movements or gestures. *Also underline* any quoted talk. To get started, *underline* "circle each other," "tie up," and "arms locked" at the beginning of paragraph 2.
2. *Review* the words and phrases you underlined, and *think about* how they present the students' interactions, some of the basic activities of

wrestling, and Larry Sharpe. *Note in the margin* any ideas you come up with as well as which actions and talk best help you understand the wrestling instruction given at the Monster Factory.

Write

Write several sentences explaining how Leland makes use of specific narrative action to describe his subject, giving examples from your annotations of the most vivid and revealing actions.

CONSIDERING IDEAS FOR YOUR OWN WRITING

Leisure or educational activities that bring people together briefly for special training offer good material for observational essays. Given your time constraints for researching and writing the essay, consider choosing an activity or course that meets only a few times (one to five times is typical) on evenings or weekends. The offerings reflect people's diverse interests and differ somewhat from community to community: dog training, motorcycle riding, indoor climbing, skating, dancing, cooking, holiday decorating, stress reduction, conflict resolution, computer software training, public speaking, speed reading. You can find these and other classes advertised in newspapers and listed in your college's extension-course catalog. Ask the instructor for permission to observe the class, and arrange to interview the instructor for a few minutes before or after class. Be bold in approaching two or three students to discover why they enrolled in the class and what they have to say about it. Take careful notes on your observations of at least one class meeting. Like Leland, consider enrolling in the class yourself.

JOHN T. EDGE

I'm Not Leaving Until I Eat This Thing

John T. Edge (b. 1962) is director of the Southern Foodways Alliance at the University of Mississippi, where he coordinates an annual conference on southern food. Food writer for the national magazine Oxford American, *he has also written for* Cooking Light, Food & Wine, *and* Gourmet. *He has published two books,* A Gracious Plenty: Recipes and Recollections from the American South *(1999) and* Southern Belly *(2000), a portrait of southern food told through profiles of people and places.*

This reading first appeared in a 1999 issue of Oxford American *(where the illustration on p. 87 appeared) and was reprinted in 2000 in* Utne Reader. *Edge focuses his considerable observational writing skills on an unusual manufacturing business in a small Mississippi town — Farm Fresh Food Supplier. He introduces readers to the company's workers and its pig products, a best-seller being pickled pig lips, which are sometimes bottled in vivid patriotic and special-events colors. Like Leland, Edge participates in his subject — not by joining in the activities at Farm Fresh, but by attempting to eat a pig lip at Jesse's Place, a nearby "juke" bar. You will see that the reading begins and ends with this personal experience.*

As you read, enjoy Edge's struggle to eat a pig lip, and pay attention to the information Edge offers about the history and manufacture of pickled pig lips at Farm Fresh.

It's just past 4:00 on a Thursday afternoon in June at Jesse's Place, a country juke 17 miles south of the Mississippi line and three miles west of Amite, Louisiana. The air conditioner hacks and spits forth torrents of Arctic air, but the heat of summer can't be kept at bay. It seeps around the splintered doorjambs and settles in, transforming the squat particleboard-plastered roadhouse into a sauna. Slowly, the dank barroom fills with grease-smeared mechanics from the truck stop up the road and farmers straight from the fields, the soles of their brogans thick with dirt clods. A few weary souls make their way over from the nearby sawmill. I sit alone at the bar, one empty bottle of Bud in front of me, a second in my hand. I drain the beer, order a third, and stare down at the pink juice spreading outward from a crumpled foil pouch and onto the bar. 1

I'm not leaving until I eat this thing, I tell myself. 2

Half a mile down the road, behind a fence coiled with razor wire, Lionel Dufour, proprietor of Farm Fresh Food Supplier, is loading up the last truck of the day, wheeling case after case of pickled pork offal out of his cinder-block processing plant and into a semitrailer bound for Hattiesburg, Mississippi. 3

His crew packed lips today. Yesterday, it was pickled sausage; the day before that, pig feet. Tomorrow, it's pickled pig lips again. Lionel has been on the job since 2:45 in the morning, when he came in to light the boilers. Damon Landry, chief cook and maintenance man, came in at 4:30. By 7:30, the production line was at full tilt: six women in white smocks and blue bouffant caps, slicing ragged white fat from the lips, tossing the good parts in glass jars, the bad parts in barrels bound for the rendering plant. Across the aisle, filled jars clatter by on a conveyor belt as a worker tops them off with a Kool-Aid-red slurry of hot sauce, vinegar, salt, and food coloring. Around the corner, the jars are capped, affixed with a label, and stored in pasteboard boxes to await shipping. 4

Unlike most offal — euphemistically called "variety meats" — lips belie their provenance. Brains, milky white and globular, look like brains. Feet, the ghosts of their cloven hoofs protruding, look like feet. Testicles look like, well, testicles. But lips are different. Loosed from the snout, trimmed of their fat, and dyed a preternatural pink, they look more like candy than like carrion. 5

At Farm Fresh, no swine root in an adjacent feedlot. No viscera-strewn killing floor lurks just out of sight, down a darkened 6 hallway. These pigs died long ago at some Midwestern abattoir. By the time the lips arrive in Amite, they are, in essence, pig Popsicles, 50-pound blocks of offal and ice.

7 "Lips are all meat," Lionel told me earlier in the day. "No gristle, no bone, no nothing. They're bar food, hot and vinegary, great with a beer. Used to be the lips ended up in sausages, headcheese, those sorts of things. A lot of them still do."

8 Lionel, a 50-year-old father of three with quick, intelligent eyes set deep in a face the color of cordovan, is a veteran of nearly 40 years in the pickled pig lips business. "I started out with my daddy when I wasn't much more than 10," Lionel told me, his shy smile framed by a coarse black mustache flecked with whispers of gray. "The meatpacking business he owned had gone broke back when I was 6, and he was peddling out of the back of his car, selling dried shrimp, napkins, straws, tubes of plastic cups, pig feet, pig lips, whatever the bar owners needed. He sold to black bars, white bars, sweet shops, snowball stands, you name it. We made the rounds together after I got out of school, sometimes staying out till two or three in the morning. I remember bringing my toy cars to this one joint and racing them around the floor with the bar owner's son while my daddy and his father did business."

9 For years after the demise of that first meatpacking company, the Dufour family sold someone else's product. "We used to buy lips from Dennis Di Salvo's company down in Belle Chasse," recalled Lionel. "As far as I can tell, his mother was the one who came up with the idea to pickle and pack lips back in the '50s, back when she was working for a company called Three Little Pigs over in Houma. But pretty soon, we were selling so many lips that we had to almost beg Di Salvo's for product. That's when we started cooking up our own," he told me, gesturing toward the cast-iron kettle that hangs from the rafters by the front door of the plant. "My daddy started cooking lips in that very pot."

10 Lionel now cooks lips in 11 retrofitted milk tanks, dull stainless-steel cauldrons shaped like oversized cradles. But little else has changed. Though Lionel's father has passed away, Farm Fresh remains a family-focused company. His wife, Kathy, keeps the books. His daughter, Dana, a button-cute college student who has won numerous beauty titles, takes to the road in the summer, selling lips to convenience stores and wholesalers. Soon, after he graduates from business school, Lionel's younger son, Matt, will take over operations at the plant. And his older son, a veterinarian, lent his name to one of Farm Fresh's top sellers, Jason's Pickled Pig Lips.

"We do our best to corner the market on lips," Lionel told me, his voice tinged with bravado. "Sometimes they're hard to get from the packing houses. You gotta kill a lot of pigs to get enough lips to keep us going. I've got new customers calling every day; it's all I can do to keep up with demand, but I bust my ass to keep up. I do what I can for my family — and for my customers. 11

"When my customers tell me something," he continued," just like when my daddy told me something, I listen. If my customers wanted me to dye the lips green, I'd ask, 'What shade?' As it is, every few years we'll do some red and some blue for the Fourth of July. This year we did jars full of Mardi Gras lips — half purple, half gold," Lionel recalled with a chuckle. "I guess we'd had a few beers when we came up with that one." 12

Meanwhile, back at Jesse's Place, I finish my third Bud, order my fourth. *Now,* I tell myself, my courage bolstered by booze, *I'm ready to eat a lip.* 13

They may have looked like candy in the plant, but in the barroom they're carrion once again. I poke and prod the six-inch arc of pink flesh, peering up from my reverie just in time to catch the barkeep's wife, Audrey, staring straight at me. She fixes me with a look just this side of pity and asks, "You gonna eat that thing or make love to it?" 14

Her nephew, Jerry, sidles up to a bar stool on my left. "A lot of people like 'em with chips," he says with a nod toward the pink juice pooling on the bar in front of me. I offer to buy him a lip, and Audrey fishes one from a jar behind the counter, wraps it in tinfoil, and places the whole affair on a paper towel in front of him. 15

I take stock of my own cowardice, and, following Jerry's lead, reach for a bag of potato chips, tear open the top with my teeth, and toss the quivering hunk of hog flesh into the shiny interior of the bag, slick with grease and dusted with salt. Vinegar vapors tickle my nostrils. I stifle a gag that rolls from the back of my throat, swallow hard, and pray that the urge to vomit passes. 16

With a smash of my hand, the potato chips are reduced to a pulp, and I feel the cold lump of the lip beneath my fist. I clasp the bag shut and shake it hard in an effort to ensure chip coverage in all the nooks and crannies of the lip. The technique that Jerry uses — and I mimic — is not unlike that employed by home cooks mixing up a mess of Shake 'n Bake chicken. 17

I pull from the bag a coral crescent of meat now crusted with blond bits of potato chips. When I chomp down, the soft flesh 18 dissolves between my teeth. It tastes like a flaccid cracklin', unmistakably porcine, and not altogether bad. The chips help, providing texture where there was none. Slowly, my brow unfurrows, my stomach ceases its fluttering.

19 Sensing my relief, Jerry leans over and peers into my bag. "Kind of look like Frosted Flakes, don't they?" he says, by way of describing the chips rapidly turning to mush in the pickling juice. I offer the bag to Jerry, order yet another beer, and turn to eye the pig feet floating in a murky jar by the cash register, their blunt tips bobbing up through a pasty white film.

READING FOR MEANING

Write to create meanings for Edge's observations of packing pig lips at Farm Fresh Food Supplier and eating them at Jesse's Place.

Start Making Meaning

Begin by describing a pig lip and explaining how Farm Fresh obtains and packs pig lips. Continue by writing about anything else in the selection or in your experience that contributes to your understanding of Edge's observations.

If You Are Stuck

If you cannot write at least a page, consider writing about

- retelling the story of Edge's struggle to eat a pig lip and never getting beyond the first bite.
- the impression Edge conveys of Lionel Dufour (in paragraphs 3, 4, and 7–12).
- an unusual food you tried but never came to like, connecting your experience of first trying it to Edge's experience with pig lips.
- what the photograph adds to your understanding of Edge's observations about pig-lip manufacturing and consumption.

READING LIKE A WRITER

ENGAGING AND INFORMING READERS BY REPORTING PARTICIPATION

Readers of observational essays expect to be engaged or entertained as well as informed. Writers have many strategies available to them to engage readers, one effective strategy being to report a personal experience with the subject, either prior to writing about it or as a participant during the research on the subject. Consider that the unsigned writer of "Soup" never tells readers about his or her interest in soup or experience eating soup. The writer might have stayed in the line, placed an order, and then enjoyed one of Yeganeh's soups, later including among the observations just how the soup smelled and tasted. Perhaps the writer chose not to do so because he or she wanted to keep the focus on Yeganeh's encyclopedic knowledge of soup, high standards, and brusque treatment of customers. Not a participant, the writer remains an observer of Soup Kitchen International and never gets personally involved in preparing or consuming the soups. By contrast, both John Leland and John Edge set out to learn about their subjects by participating in them, Leland taking wrestling lessons, and Edge attempting to eat a pig lip at the kind of bar in the South where pig lips are served. Leland appropriately organizes his observations around his own wrestling lessons. Edge, however, frames — begins and ends — his observations of pig-lip packing and marketing with the relatively full story of his humorous attempt to eat one pig lip.

Analyze

1. *Reread* paragraphs 1, 2, and 13–19, where Edge tells the story of his attempt to eat a pig lip. *Notice* how he sets up the time and place, describes the bar, and locates himself in the bar. Then, in paragraphs 13–19, *notice* the roles of other characters in the story and the importance of reported conversation. *Underline* details that inform you about the appearance, texture, smell, and taste of the pig lip. (These strategies you may have learned about and used in your own essay in Chapter 2.)

2. *Reflect* on the relation of the bar story to the profile of Farm Fresh Food Supplier in paragraphs 3–12. *Make notes in the margin* about what you learn from the story about pig lips that you cannot find out from paragraphs 3–12. Also *note in the margin* any places in the story that influenced your engagement with or interest in the subject of pig lips.

Write

Write several sentences explaining what you have learned about the use of personal experience in reporting observations.

CONSIDERING IDEAS FOR YOUR OWN WRITING

Consider writing about a place that serves, produces, or sells something unusual, perhaps something that, like Edge, you could try yourself to discover more about for the purpose of informing and engaging your readers. If no such place comes to mind, you could browse the Yellow Pages of your local phone directory for ideas. One example is a company that produces or packages some special ethnic or regional food and/or a local cafe that serves it. There are many other possibilities: acupuncture clinic, caterer, novelty toy and balloon store, microbrewery, chain-saw dealer, boatbuilder, talent agency, ornamental iron manufacturer, bead store, manicure or nail salon, aquarium and pet fish supplier, auto-detailing shop, tattoo parlor, scrap-metal recycler, fly-fishing shop, handwriting analyst, dog- or cat-sitting service, photo restorer, burglar alarm installer, Christmas tree farm, wedding specialist, reweaving specialist, wig salon. You need not evaluate the quality of work at the place as part of your observational essay. Instead, keep the focus on informing readers about the service or product the place offers. Relating a personal experience with the service or product is a good idea but not a requirement of an observational essay.

JOHN McPHEE

The New York Pickpocket Academy

John McPhee (b. 1931) lives in Princeton, New Jersey, where he occasionally teaches a writing workshop in the "literature of fact" at Princeton University. He is highly regarded as a writer of profiles — in-depth reporting about people, places, and activities — and is a shrewd observer and masterful interviewer. In his profiles, McPhee ingeniously integrates information from observations, interviews, and research into engaging, readable prose. Readers marvel at the way he explains such complex subjects as experimental aircraft or modern physics and discovers the complexities of such ordinary subjects as bears or oranges. Among his books are Oranges *(1967),* The Control of Nature *(1989),* Assembling California *(1993),* Irons in the Fire *(1997), and* Annals of the Former World *(1998).*

The following selection, from the collection of essays Giving Good Weight *(1979), is part of a longer profile of New Jersey farmers who sell produce at open-air farmers' markets in New York City. The narrator of the story is McPhee himself, weighing and sacking produce, all the while looking beyond the zucchini and tomatoes for material that might interest readers.*

As you read, notice the many details McPhee provides about the people and the place: the vegetables and trucks and hats and colors and sounds of the market. Notice, too, the great variety of examples he presents of crime and honesty, some happening before his eyes and some told to him by people at the market.

1 Brooklyn, and the pickpocket in the burgundy jacket appears just before noon. Melissa Mousseau recognizes him much as if he were an old customer and points him out to Bob Lewis, who follows him from truck to truck. Aware of Lewis, he leaves the market. By two, he will have made another run. A woman with deep-auburn hair and pale, nervous hands clumsily attracts the attention of a customer whose large white purse she is rifling. Until a moment ago, the customer was occupied with the choosing of apples and peppers, but now she shouts out, "Hey, what are you doing? Your hand is in my purse. What are you doing?" The auburn-haired woman not only has her hand in the purse but most of her arm as well. She withdraws it, and with intense absorption begins to finger the peppers. "How much are the peppers? Mister, give me some of these!" she says, looking up at me with a gypsy's dark, starburst eyes. "Three pounds for a dollar," I tell her, with a swift glance around for Lewis or a cop. When I look back, the pickpocket is gone. Other faces have filled

in — people unconcernedly examining the fruit. The woman with the white purse has returned her attention to the apples. She merely seems annoyed. Lewis once sent word around from truck to truck that we should regularly announce in loud voices that pickpockets were present in the market, but none of the farmers complied. Hodgson shrugged and said, "Why distract the customers?" Possibly Fifty-ninth Street is the New York Pickpocket Academy. Half a dozen scores have been made there in a day. I once looked up and saw a well-dressed gentleman under a gray fedora being kicked and kicked again by a man in a green polo shirt. He kicked him in the calves. He kicked him in the thighs. He kicked him in the gluteal bulge. He kicked him from the middle of the market out to the edge, and he kicked him into the street. "Get your ass out of here!" shouted the booter, redundantly. Turning back toward the market, he addressed the curious. "Pickpocket," he explained. The dip did not press charges.

2 People switch shopping carts from time to time. They make off with a loaded one and leave an empty cart behind. Crime on such levels is a part of the background here, something in the urban air, so many parts per million. The condition is accepted with a resignation that approaches nonchalance.

3 Most thievery is petty and is on the other side of the tables. As Rich describes it, "Brooklyn, Fifty-ninth Street, people rip off stuff everywhere. You just expect it. An old man comes along and puts a dozen eggs in a bag. Women choosing peaches steal one for every one they buy — a peach for me, a peach for you. What can you do? You stand there and watch. When they take too many, you complain. I watched a guy one day taking nectarines. He would put one in a plastic bag, then one in a pocket, then one in a pile on the ground. After he did that half a dozen times, he had me weigh the bag."

4 "This isn't England," Barry Benepe informed us once, "and a lot of people are pretty dishonest."

5 Now, in Brooklyn, a heavyset woman well past the middle of life is sobbing pitifully, flailing her arms in despair. She is sitting on a bench in the middle of the market. She is wearing a print dress, a wide-brimmed straw hat. Between sobs, she presents in a heavy Russian accent the reason for her distress. She was buying green beans from Don Keller, and when she was about to pay him she discovered that someone had opened her handbag — even while it was on her arm, she said — and had removed several books of food stamps, a telephone bill, and eighty dollars in cash. Lewis, in his daypack, stands over her and tells her he is sorry. He said, "This sort of thing will happen wherever there's a crowd."

Another customer breaks in to scold Lewis, saying, "This is the biggest rip-off place in Brooklyn. Two of my friends were pick-pocketed here last week and I had to give them carfare home." 6

Lewis puts a hand on his forehead and, after a pensive moment, says, "That was very kind of you." 7

The Russian woman is shrieking now. Lewis attends her like a working dentist. "It's all right. It will be O.K. It may not be as bad as you think." He remarks that he would call the police if he thought there was something they could do. 8

Jeffrey Mack, eight years old, has been listening to all this, and he now says, "I see a cop." 9

Jeffrey has an eye for cops that no one else seems to share. (A squad car came here for him one morning and took him off to face a truant officer. Seeing his fright, a Pacific Street prostitute got into the car and rode with him.) 10

"Where, Jeffrey?" 11

"There," Jeffrey lifts an arm and points. 12

"Where?" 13

"There." He points again — at trucks, farmers, a falafel man. 14

"I don't see a policeman," Lewis says to him. "If you see one, Jeffrey, go and get him." 15

Jeffrey goes, and comes back with an off-duty 78th Precinct cop who is wearing a white apron and has been selling fruits and vegetables in the market. The officer speaks sternly to the crying woman. "Your name?" 16

"Catherine Barta." 17

"Address?" 18

"Eighty-five Eastern Parkway." 19

Every Wednesday, she walks a mile or so to the Greenmarket. She has lived in Brooklyn close to half her life, the rest of it in the Ukraine. Heading back to his vegetables, the officer observes that there is nothing he can do. 20

Out from behind her tables comes Joan Benack, the baker, of Rocky Acres Farm, Milan, New York — a small woman with a high, thin voice. Leaving her tropical carrot bread, her zucchini bread, her anadama bread, her beer bread, she goes around with a borrowed hat collecting money from the farmers for Catherine Barta. Bills stuff that hat, size 7 — the money of Alvina Frey and John Labanowski and Cleather Slade and Rich Hodgson and Bob Engle, who has seen it come and go. He was a broker for Merrill Lynch before the stock market imploded, and now he is a blond-bearded farmer in a basketball shirt selling apples that he grows in Clintondale, New York. Don Keller offers a dozen eggs, and one by one the farmers come out from their trucks to fill Mrs. Barta's shopping cart with beans and zucchini, apples, eggplants, 21 tomatoes, peppers, and corn. As a result, her wails and sobs grow louder.

22 A man who gave Rich Hodgson a ten-dollar bill for a ninety-five-cent box of brown eggs asks Rich to give the ten back after Rich has handed him nine dollars and five cents, explaining that he has smaller bills that he wants to exchange for a twenty. Rich hands him the ten. Into Rich's palm he counts out five ones, a five, and the ten for a twenty and goes away satisfied, as he has every reason to be, having conned Rich out of nine dollars, five cents, and a box of brown eggs. Rich smiles at his foolishness, shrugs, and sells some cheese. If cash were equanimity, he would never lose a cent. One day, a gang of kids began taking Don Keller's vegetables and throwing them at the Hodgson truck. Anders Thueson threw an apple at the kids, who then picked up rocks. Thueson reached into the back of the truck and came up with a machete. While Hodgson told him to put it away, pant legs went up, switchblades came into view. Part of the gang bombarded the truck with debris from a nearby roof. Any indication of panic might have been disastrous. Hodgson packed deliberately, and drove away.

23 Todd Jameson, who comes in with his brother Dan from Farmingdale, New Jersey, weighed some squash one day, and put it in a brown bag. He set the package down while he weighed something else. Then, reaching for the squash, he picked up an identical bag that happened to contain fifty dollars in rolled coins. He handed it to the customer who had asked for the squash. Too late, Todd discovered the mistake. A couple of hours later, though, the customer — "I'll never forget him as long as I live, the white hair, the glasses, the ruddy face" — came back. He said, "Hey, this isn't squash. I didn't ask for money, I asked for squash." Whenever that man comes to market, the Jamesons give him a bag full of food. "You see, where I come from, that would never, never happen," Todd explains. "If I made a mistake like that in Farmingdale, no one — no one — would come back with fifty dollars' worth of change."

24 Dusk comes down without further crime in Brooklyn, and the farmers are packing to go. John Labanowski — short, compact, with a beer in his hand — is expounding on his day. "The white people are educating the colored on the use of beet greens," he reports. "A colored woman was telling me today, 'Cut the tops off,' and a white woman spoke up and said, 'Hold it,' and told the colored woman, 'You're throwing the best part away.' They go on talking, and pretty soon the colored woman is saying, 'I'm seventy-three on Monday,' and the white says, 'I don't believe a

word you say.' You want to know why I come in here? I come in here for fun. For profit, of course, but for relaxation, too. I like being here with these people. They say the city is a rat race, but they've got it backwards. The farm is what gets to be a rat race. You should come out and see what I — " He is interrupted by the reappearance in the market of Catherine Barta, who went home long ago and has now returned, her eyes hidden by her wide-brimmed hat, her shopping cart full beside her. On the kitchen table, at 85 Eastern Parkway, she found her telephone bill, her stamps, and her cash. She has come back to the farmers with their food and money.

READING FOR MEANING

Write to create meanings for McPhee's observations of the vegetable market.

Start Making Meaning

Begin by listing the types of crime McPhee observes at the farmers' market (described in paragraphs 1–5 and 22). Continue by writing about anything else in the selection or in your experience that contributes to your understanding of McPhee's observations.

If You Are Stuck

If you cannot write at least a page, consider writing about

- what happens to Catherine Barta and how people at the market treat her.
- the Todd Jameson anecdote in paragraph 23.
- the attitudes of the farmers who work at the market toward the crimes committed there. You may want to reflect on your own attitude toward "petty thievery" in light of the attitudes of the farmers. If you do so, connect your attitude to some of the farmers' attitudes.
- the notion that theft is part of the everyday experience of urban living but is not part of life in suburbia or small-town America.

READING LIKE A WRITER

ORGANIZING THE OBSERVATIONS

McPhee uses a narrative organization to present his observations chronologically, as they occur along a time line. His story begins "just before noon" (first sentence of paragraph 1) and ends as "dusk comes down" (first sentence of paragraph 24). To keep readers from getting confused about what is happening as the narrative moves along, McPhee uses narrative time markers. These markers include words and phrases that note the time of day (such as "noon" and "by two" in sentences 1 and 4 of paragraph 1) or indicate when something happened relative to when something else happened (such as "until a moment ago" and "but now" in sentence 6). This easy-to-follow chronological structure pushes readers along, keeping them on track as they are catapulted into the noisy, crowded world of the farmers' market.

For most of the essay, the narrative moves forward in time. But McPhee's narrative is not simple. He interweaves into his narrative of what happened that afternoon references to events that occurred at various points in the past. In the middle of paragraph 1, for example, the phrases "Lewis once sent word" and "I once looked up and saw" refer to events that occurred sometime before this particular afternoon. These references to earlier events give McPhee's narrative a thick fabric, enabling readers to imagine not only the swirl of activities occurring that afternoon but also what the market has been like on other occasions when McPhee was there observing the activity.

Analyze

1. *Skim* the selection and *underline* the time markers, beginning with "just before noon" in the opening sentence of the essay.
2. *Note in the margin* which time markers refer to events that occurred that afternoon and which occurred in the past.

Write

Write several sentences describing how McPhee uses time markers to help readers understand which events occurred that afternoon and which occurred at other times. How effectively do the time markers keep you oriented? *Indicate* any passages in the essay where you are confused about when something happened.

Compare

To understand the difference between narrative and topical organization in observational writing, *compare* McPhee's narrative plan with the topical organization used in "Soup" (pp. 72–75). Given the subject and the writer's purpose in each essay, what advantages and disadvantages do you see in the type of organization chosen?

Write several sentences speculating about why each writer chose the particular organizational plan. Instead of working chronologically, could McPhee have organized the essay topically by the various types of crime he observes at the market, using anecdotes as examples of each type? Could the *New Yorker* writer have told the story of a typical day at the soup kitchen, weaving the various topics he discusses into the narrative of a day? *Consider* these alternatives and *speculate about* why the writers might have chosen the plans they did.

CONSIDERING IDEAS FOR YOUR OWN WRITING

Public scenes crowded with people and action offer good material for observational essays. Crowds also present problems, mainly because of their huge size and scope: So many people are present and so much is happening at once, the observer may not be able to decide where to focus. Notice how McPhee solves this problem by remaining in one location, the stall where he is selling vegetables. The action takes place in one small area of a huge market, focusing on only a few people and events.

You could likewise find such a focus for an observational essay in some large public scene. Here are a few examples to start you thinking: the souvenir sellers or groundskeepers at a baseball game; a lifeguard station at a beach; an unusual store or restaurant at a shopping mall; one stall at a flea market; a small group of riders from the same club at a Harley-Davidson motorcycle reunion; one section of your college library; an ice-skating rink at a city park; a musician, vendor, or guard in a subway station. You need not seek to find some unexpected activity, like the pickpocketing at the Brooklyn farmers' market, but you could probably interest readers in the people and activities in one limited area of a public place — as a way of giving them a distinct impression of the large, complex public space.

AMANDA COYNE

The Long Good-Bye: Mother's Day in Federal Prison

Amanda Coyne (b. 1966), a native of Colorado, is a graduate of the University of Iowa and is studying for a master's degree in Iowa's nonfiction writing program. Coyne has worked as a waitress, an assistant in a nursing home, a teacher, a public relations associate, and a public policy analyst. She wrote "The Long Good-Bye," her first piece of published writing, for the May 1997 issue of Harper's, *a monthly magazine that publishes profiles of interesting people and places, autobiographical and reflective essays, and informative reports on current social and political issues.*

As Coyne explains in the essay, her observations are based on a one-day visit to a minimum security women's prison where her sister is incarcerated. She writes about her sister and other women in a similar situation to inform readers and to awaken their concern about the injustice of prison terms for people, especially girlfriends and wives, who aided drug dealers.

As you read, pay particular attention to Coyne's focus on two inmates, Jennifer (her sister) and Stephanie, and their relationships with their sons.

You can spot the convict-moms here in the visiting room by the way they hold and touch their children and by the single flower that is perched in front of them — a rose, a tulip, a daffodil. Many of these mothers have untied the bow that attaches the flower to its silver-and-red cellophane wrapper and are using one of the many empty soda cans at hand as a vase. They sit proudly before their flower-in-a-Coke-can, amid Hershey bar wrappers, half-eaten Ding Dongs, and empty paper coffee cups. Occasionally, a mother will pick up her present and bring it to her nose when one of the bearers of the single flower — her child — asks if she likes it. And the mother will respond the way that mothers always have and always will respond when presented with a gift on this day. "Oh, I just love it. It's perfect. I'll put it in the middle of my Bible." Or, "I'll put it on my desk, right next to your school picture." And always: "It's the best one here." 1

But most of what is being smelled today is the children themselves. While the other adults are plunking coins into the vending machines, the mothers take deep whiffs from the backs of their children's necks, or kiss and smell the backs of their knees, or take 2 off their shoes and tickle their feet and then pull them close to their noses. They hold them tight and take in their own second scent — the scent assuring them that these are still their children and that they still belong to them.

3 The visitors are allowed to bring in pockets full of coins, and today that Mother's Day flower, and I know from previous visits to my older sister here at the Federal Prison Camp for women in Pekin, Illinois, that there is always an aberrant urge to gather immediately around the vending machines. The sandwiches are stale, the coffee weak, the candy bars the ones we always pass up in a convenience store. But after we hand the children over to their mothers, we gravitate toward those machines. Like milling in the kitchen at a party. We all do it, and nobody knows why. Polite conversation ensues around the microwave while the popcorn is popping and the processed-chicken sandwiches are being heated. We ask one another where we are from, how long a drive we had. An occasional whistle through the teeth, a shake of the head. "My, my, long way from home, huh?" "Staying at the Super 8 right up the road. Not a bad place." "Stayed at the Econo Lodge last time. Wasn't a good place at all." Never asking the questions we really want to ask: "What's she in for?" "How much time's she got left?" You never ask in the waiting room of a doctor's office either. Eventually, all of us — fathers, mothers, sisters, brothers, a few boyfriends, and very few husbands — return to the queen of the day, sitting at a fold-out table loaded with snacks, prepared for five or so hours of attempted normal conversation.

4 Most of the inmates are elaborately dressed, many in prison-crafted dresses and sweaters in bright blues and pinks. They wear meticulously applied makeup in corresponding hues, and their hair is replete with loops and curls — hair that only women with the time have the time for. Some of the better seamstresses have crocheted vests and purses to match their outfits. Although the world outside would never accuse these women of making haute-couture fashion statements, the fathers and the sons and the boyfriends and the very few husbands think they look beautiful, and they tell them so repeatedly. And I can imagine the hours spent preparing for this visit — hours of needles and hooks clicking over brightly colored yards of yarn. The hours of discussing, dissecting, and bragging about these visitors — especially the men. Hours spent in the other world behind the door where we're not allowed, sharing lipsticks and mascaras, and unraveling the occasional hair-tangled hot roller, and the brushing out and

lifting and teasing . . . and the giggles that abruptly change into tears without warning — things that define any female-only world. Even, or especially, if that world is a female federal prison camp.

While my sister Jennifer is with her son in the playroom, an inmate's mother comes over to introduce herself to my younger sister, Charity, my brother, John, and me. She tells us about visiting her daughter in a higher-security prison before she was transferred here. The woman looks old and tired, and her shoulders sag under the weight of her recently acquired bitterness. 5

"Pit of fire," she says, shaking her head. "Like a pit of fire straight from hell. Never seen anything like it. Like something out of an old movie about prisons." Her voice is getting louder and she looks at each of us with pleading eyes. "My *daughter* was there. Don't even get me started on that place. Women die there." 6

John and Charity and I silently exchange glances. 7

"My daughter would come to the visiting room with a black eye and I'd think, 'All she did was sit in the car while her boyfriend ran into the house.' She didn't even touch the stuff. Never even handled it." 8

She continues to stare at us, each in turn. "Ten years. That boyfriend talked and he got three years. She didn't know anything. Had nothing to tell them. They gave her ten years. They called it conspiracy. Conspiracy? Aren't there real criminals out there?" She asks this with hands outstretched, waiting for an answer that none of us can give her. 9

The woman's daughter, the conspirator, is chasing her son through the maze of chairs and tables and through the other children. She's a twenty-four-year-old blonde, whom I'll call Stephanie, with Dorothy Hamill hair and matching dimples. She looks like any girl you might see in any shopping mall in middle America. She catches her chocolate-brown son and tickles him, and they laugh and trip and fall together onto the floor and laugh harder. 10

Had it not been for that wait in the car, this scene would be taking place at home, in a duplex Stephanie would rent while trying to finish her two-year degree in dental hygiene or respiratory therapy at the local community college. The duplex would be spotless, with a blown-up picture of her and her son over the couch and ceramic unicorns and horses occupying the shelves of the entertainment center. She would make sure that her son went to school every day with stylishly floppy pants, scrubbed teeth, and a good breakfast in his belly. Because of their difference in 11 skin color, there would be occasional tension — caused by the strange looks from strangers, teachers, other mothers, and the bullies on the playground, who would chant after they knocked him down, "Your Momma's white, your Momma's white." But if she were home, their weekends and evenings would be spent together transcending those looks and healing those bruises. Now, however, their time is spent eating visiting-room junk food and his school days are spent fighting the boys in the playground who chant, "Your Momma's in prison, your Momma's in prison."

12 He will be ten when his mother is released, the same age my nephew will be when his mother is let out. But Jennifer, my sister, was able to spend the first five years of Toby's life with him. Stephanie had Ellie after she was incarcerated. They let her hold him for eighteen hours, then sent her back to prison. She has done the "tour," and her son is a well-traveled six-year-old. He has spent weekends visiting his mother in prisons in Kentucky, Texas, Connecticut (the Pit of Fire), and now at last here, the camp — minimum security, Pekin, Illinois.

13 Ellie looks older than his age. But his shoulders do not droop like his grandmother's. On the contrary, his bitterness lifts them and his chin higher than a child's should be, and the childlike, wide-eyed curiosity has been replaced by defiance. You can see his emerging hostility as he and his mother play together. She tells him to pick up the toy that he threw, say, or to put the deck of cards away. His face turns sullen, but she persists. She takes him by the shoulders and looks him in the eye, and he uses one of his hands to swat at her. She grabs the hand and he swats with the other. Eventually, she pulls him toward her and smells the top of his head, and she picks up the cards or the toy herself. After all, it is Mother's Day and she sees him so rarely. But her acquiescence makes him angrier, and he stalks out of the playroom with his shoulders thrown back.

14 Toby, my brother and sister and I assure one another, will not have these resentments. He is better taken care of than most. He is living with relatives in Wisconsin. Good, solid, middle-class, churchgoing relatives. And when he visits us, his aunts and his uncle, we take him out for adventures where we walk down the alley of a city and pretend that we are being chased by the "bad guys." We buy him fast food, and his uncle, John, keeps him up well past his bedtime enthralling him with stories of the monkeys he met in India. A perfect mix, we try to convince one another. Until we take him to see his mother and on the drive back he asks the question that most confuses him, and no doubt all the other children who spend much of their lives in prison visiting

rooms: "Is my Mommy a bad guy?" It is the question that most seriously disorders his five-year-old need to clearly separate right from wrong. And because our own need is perhaps just as great, it is the question that haunts us as well.

15 Now, however, the answer is relatively simple. In a few years, it won't be. In a few years we will have to explain mandatory minimums, and the war on drugs, and the murky conspiracy laws, and the enormous amount of money and time that federal agents pump into imprisoning low-level drug dealers and those who happen to be their friends and their lovers. In a few years he might have the reasoning skills to ask why so many armed robbers and rapists and child-molesters and, indeed, murderers are punished less severely than his mother. When he is older, we will somehow have to explain to him the difference between federal crimes, which don't allow for parole, and state crimes, which do. We will have to explain that his mother was taken from him for five years not because she was a drug dealer but because she made four phone calls for someone she loved.

16 But we also know it is vitally important that we explain all this without betraying our bitterness. We understand the danger of abstract anger, of being disillusioned with your country, and, most of all, we do not want him to inherit that legacy. We would still like him to be raised as we were, with the idea that we live in the best country in the world with the best legal system in the world — a legal system carefully designed to be immune to political mood swings and public hysteria; a system that promises to fit the punishment to the crime. We want him to be a good citizen. We want him to have absolute faith that he lives in a fair country, a country that watches over and protects its most vulnerable citizens: its women and children.

17 So for now we simply say, "Toby, your mother isn't bad, she just did a bad thing. Like when you put rocks in the lawn mower's gas tank. You weren't bad then, you just did a bad thing."

18 Once, after being given this weak explanation, he said, "I wish I could have done something really bad, like my Mommy. So I could go to prison too and be with her."

19 It's now 3:00. Visiting ends at 3:30. The kids are getting cranky, and the adults are both exhausted and wired from too many hours of conversation, too much coffee and candy. The fathers, mothers, sisters, brothers, and the few boyfriends, and the very few husbands are beginning to show signs of gathering the trash. The mothers of the infants are giving their heads one last whiff before tucking them and their paraphernalia into their respective

carrying cases. The visitors meander toward the door, leaving the older children with their mothers for one last word. But the mothers never say what they want to say to their children. They say things like, "Do well in school," "Be nice to your sister," "Be good for Aunt Berry, or Grandma." They don't say, "I'm sorry I'm sorry I'm sorry. I love you more than anything else in the world and I think about you every minute and I worry about you with a pain that shoots straight to my heart, a pain so great I think I will just burst when I think of you alone, without me. I'm sorry."

We are standing in front of the double glass doors that lead to the outside world. My older sister holds her son, rocking him gently. They are both crying. We give her a look and she puts him down. Charity and I grasp each of his small hands, and the four of us walk through the doors. As we're walking out, my brother sings one of his banana songs to Toby. 20

"Take me out to the — " and Toby yells out, "Banana store!" 21

"Buy me some — " 22

"Bananas!!" 23

"I don't care if I ever come back. For it's root, root, root for the — " 24

"Monkey team!" 25

I turn back and see a line of women standing behind the glass wall. Some of them are crying, but many simply stare with dazed eyes. Stephanie is holding both of her son's hands in hers and speaking urgently to him. He is struggling, and his head is twisting violently back and forth. He frees one of his hands from her grasp, balls up his fist, and punches her in the face. Then he walks with purpose through the glass doors and out the exit. I look back at her. She is still in a crouched position. She stares, unblinking, through those doors. Her hands have left her face and are hanging on either side of her. I look away, but before I do, I see drops of blood drip from her nose, down her chin, and onto the shiny marble floor. 26

READING FOR MEANING

Write to create meanings for Coyne's observations of children visiting their mothers in federal prison.

Start Making Meaning

Begin by describing your impression of the two inmates, Jennifer and Stephanie, and their relationships with their sons. Include details from the reading to support your impression. Continue by writing about anything else in the selection or in your experience that contributes to your understanding of Coyne's observations.

If You Are Stuck

If you cannot write at least a page, consider writing about

- the homey details used to describe the visiting room and the impression they convey to you (paragraphs 1–4).
- the interactions among the people who have brought children to visit the inmate mothers.
- the idea that a person may be good, even though his or her behavior may be bad (paragraph 17), as Coyne believes to be the case with her sister. You may want to test this idea against your personal experience. If you do so, connect it explicitly to Coyne's example.
- Coyne's criticism of the criminal justice system (paragraphs 15 and 16), stating whether you agree or disagree with it and giving reasons and support from your knowledge or personal experience. Be sure to relate your ideas to Coyne's.

READING LIKE A WRITER

DESCRIBING PEOPLE

Writers of observational essays often focus their observations on people, alone or interacting with others. To present people, writers can choose from a repertoire of strategies. They may tell us how people look and dress, characterize their behavior or emotions, let us hear them talk, show them gesturing and moving, or compare them to other people. One of the most vividly described people in this reading is Ellie, Stephanie's six-year-old son. Coyne describes him mainly through his actions — his movements and gestures.

Analyze

1. *Reread* paragraphs 13 and 26, and *underline* the details that enable you to imagine Stephanie's son, Ellie. *Underline* details about his age, comparisons to other people, characterizations of his emotions, and details about his movements and gestures.
2. In the margin beside these paragraphs, *make notes* about the impression you get of Ellie and his relationship with his mother from the details you underlined.

Write

Write several sentences explaining how Coyne describes Ellie, giving examples from your annotations. *Add a few more sentences* identifying what you think is the most effective part of the description and explaining why you think it works so well.

CONSIDERING IDEAS FOR YOUR OWN WRITING

You might write about a public place where you can observe parents and children interacting, such as a neighborhood playground, a beach, a restaurant, or a toy store. Another possibility is to visit a place where people live in a communal setting, such as a hospital, a home for the elderly, or a halfway house. Alternatively, you might consider places where people see each other routinely but do not know each other very well; for example, a gym, a night course at the local community college, or a Little League baseball game.

A SPECIAL READING STRATEGY

Scratch Outlining

Outlining, especially scratch outlining, is an easy and surprisingly helpful strategy for reading critically. To outline a long and complicated essay like "The Long Good-Bye: Mother's Day in Federal Prison," you must distinguish between the essay's main ideas and its many supporting details and examples. Turn to the reading strategy Outlining in Appendix 1 (p. 527) and follow the guidelines there for scratch outlining.

BRIAN CABLE

The Last Stop

Brian Cable wrote the following observational essay when he was a first-year college student. His observations are based on a one-time visit to a mortuary, or funeral home, a subject he views with both seriousness and humor. Hoping as he enters the mortuary not to end up as a participant that day, he records what he sees and interviews two key people, the funeral director and the embalmer. In reporting his observations, he seems equally concerned with the burial process — from the purchase of a casket to the display of the body — and the people who manage this process.

As you read, notice how the writer presents the place and people and how he attempts to heighten readers' interest in the mortuary by considering it in the larger, social context of peoples' beliefs about death and burial.

Let us endeavor so to live that when we come to die even the undertaker will be sorry.

— MARK TWAIN

Death is a subject largely ignored by the living. We don't discuss it much, not as children (when Grandpa dies, he is said to be "going away"), not as adults, not even as senior citizens. Throughout our lives, death remains intensely private. The death of a loved one can be very painful, partly because of the sense of loss, but also because someone else's mortality reminds us all too vividly of our own. 1

Thus did I notice more than a few people avert their eyes as they walked past the dusty-pink building that houses the Goodbody Mortuaries. It looked a bit like a church — tall, with gothic arches and stained glass — and somewhat like an apartment complex — low, with many windows stamped out of red brick. 2

It wasn't at all what I had expected. I thought it would be more like Forest Lawn, serene with lush green lawns and meticulously groomed gardens, a place set apart from the hustle of day-to-day life. Here instead was an odd pink structure set in the middle of a business district. On top of the Goodbody Mortuaries sign was a large electric clock. What the hell, I thought, mortuaries are concerned with time, too. 3

I was apprehensive as I climbed the stone steps to the entrance. I feared rejection or, worse, an invitation to come and stay. The door was massive, yet it swung open easily on well-oiled hinges. "Come in," said the sign. "We're always open." Inside was a cool 4 and quiet reception room. Curtains were drawn against the outside glare, cutting the light down to a soft glow.

5 I found the funeral director in the main lobby, adjacent to the reception room. Like most people, I had preconceptions about what an undertaker looked like. Mr. Deaver fulfilled my expectations entirely. Tall and thin, he even had beady eyes and a bony face. A low, slanted forehead gave way to a beaked nose. His skin, scrubbed of all color, contrasted sharply with his jet black hair. He was wearing a starched white shirt, gray pants, and black shoes. Indeed, he looked like death on two legs.

6 He proved an amiable sort, however, and was easy to talk to. As funeral director, Mr. Deaver ("call me Howard") was responsible for a wide range of services. Goodbody Mortuaries, upon notification of someone's death, will remove the remains from the hospital or home. They then prepare the body for viewing, whereupon features distorted by illness or accident are restored to their natural condition. The body is embalmed and then placed in a casket selected by the family of the deceased. Services are held in one of three chapels at the mortuary, and afterward the casket is placed in a "visitation room," where family and friends can pay their last respects. Goodbody also makes arrangements for the purchase of a burial site and transports the body there for burial.

7 All this information Howard related in a well-practiced, professional manner. It was obvious he was used to explaining the specifics of his profession. We sat alone in the lobby. His desk was bone clean, no pencils or paper, nothing — just a telephone. He did all his paperwork at home; as it turned out, he and his wife lived right upstairs. The phone rang. As he listened, he bit his lips and squeezed his Adam's apple somewhat nervously.

8 "I think we'll be able to get him in by Friday. No, no, the family wants him cremated."

9 His tone was that of a broker conferring on the Dow Jones. Directly behind him was a sign announcing "Visa and Master Charge Welcome Here." It was tacked to the wall, right next to a crucifix.

10 "Some people have the idea that we are bereavement specialists, that we can handle the emotional problems which follow a death: Only a trained therapist can do that. We provide services for the dead, not counseling for the living."

11 Physical comfort was the one thing they did provide for the living. The lobby was modestly but comfortably furnished. There were several couches, in colors ranging from earth brown to pastel blue, and a coffee table in front of each one. On one table lay some magazines and a vase of flowers. Another supported an

aquarium. Paintings of pastoral scenes hung on every wall. The lobby looked more or less like that of an old hotel. Nothing seemed to match, but it had a homey, lived-in look.

"The last time the Goodbodies decorated was in '59, I believe. It still makes people feel welcome." 12

And so "Goodbody" was not a name made up to attract customers but the owners' family name. The Goodbody family started the business way back in 1915. Today, they do over five hundred services a year. 13

"We're in *Ripley's Believe It or Not,* along with another funeral home whose owners' names are Baggit and Sackit," Howard told me, without cracking a smile. 14

I followed him through an arched doorway into a chapel that smelled musty and old. The only illumination came from sunlight filtered through a stained glass ceiling. Ahead of us lay a casket. I could see that it contained a man dressed in a black suit. Wooden benches ran on either side of an aisle that led to the body. I got no closer. From the red roses across the dead man's chest, it was apparent that services had already been held. 15

"It was a large service," remarked Howard. "Look at that casket — a beautiful work of craftsmanship." 16

I guess it was. Death may be the great leveler, but one's coffin quickly reestablishes one's status. 17

We passed into a bright, fluorescent-lit "display room." Inside were thirty coffins, lids open, patiently awaiting inspection. Like new cars on the showroom floor, they gleamed with high-gloss finishes. 18

"We have models for every price range." 19

Indeed, there was a wide variety. They came in all colors and various materials. Some were little more than cloth-covered cardboard boxes, others were made of wood, and a few were made of steel, copper, or bronze. Prices started at $400 and averaged about $1,800. Howard motioned toward the center of the room: "The top of the line." 20

This was a solid bronze casket, its seams electronically welded to resist corrosion. Moisture-proof and air-tight, it could be hermetically sealed off from all outside elements. Its handles were plated with 14-karat gold. The price: a cool $5,000. 21

A proper funeral remains a measure of respect for the deceased. But it is expensive. In the United States the amount spent annually on funerals is about $2 billion. Among ceremonial expenditures, funerals are second only to weddings. As a result, practices are changing. Howard has been in this business for forty 22 years. He remembers a time when everyone was buried. Nowadays, with burials costing $2,000 a shot, people often opt instead for cremation — as Howard put it, "a cheap, quick, and easy means of disposal." In some areas of the country, the cremation rate is now over 60 percent. Observing this trend, one might wonder whether burials are becoming obsolete. Do burials serve an important role in society?

23 For Tim, Goodbody's licensed mortician, the answer is very definitely yes. Burials will remain in common practice, according to the slender embalmer with the disarming smile, because they allow family and friends to view the deceased. Painful as it may be, such an experience brings home the finality of death. "Something deep within us demands a confrontation with death," Tim explained. "A last look assures us that the person we loved is, indeed, gone forever."

24 Apparently, we also need to be assured that the body will be laid to rest in comfort and peace. The average casket, with its inner-spring mattress and pleated satin lining, is surprisingly roomy and luxurious. Perhaps such an air of comfort makes it easier for the family to give up their loved one. In addition, the burial site fixes the deceased in the survivors' memory, like a new address. Cremation provides none of these comforts.

25 Tim started out as a clerk in a funeral home but then studied to become a mortician. "It was a profession I could live with," he told me with a sly grin. Mortuary science might be described as a cross between pre-med and cosmetology, with courses in anatomy and embalming as well as in restorative art.

26 Tim let me see the preparation, or embalming, room, a white-walled chamber about the size of an operating room. Against the wall was a large sink with elbow taps and a draining board. In the center of the room stood a table with equipment for preparing the arterial embalming fluid, which consists primarily of formaldehyde, a preservative, and phenol, a disinfectant. This mixture sanitizes and also gives better color to the skin. Facial features can then be "set" to achieve a restful expression. Missing eyes, ears, and even noses can be replaced.

27 I asked Tim if his job ever depressed him. He bridled at the question: "No, it doesn't depress me at all. I do what I can for people and take satisfaction in enabling relatives to see their loved ones as they were in life." He said that he felt people were becoming more aware of the public service his profession provides. Grade-school classes now visit funeral homes as often as they do police stations and museums. The mortician is no longer regarded as a minister of death.

Before leaving, I wanted to see a body up close. I thought I could be indifferent after all I had seen and heard, but I wasn't sure. Cautiously, I reached out and touched the skin. It felt cold and firm, not unlike clay. As I walked out, I felt glad to have satisfied my curiosity about dead bodies, but all too happy to let someone else handle them. 28

READING FOR MEANING

Write to create meanings for Cable's observational essay.

Start Making Meaning

Begin by explaining briefly what you learned from the reading about the activities that take place at the funeral home. Continue by writing about anything else in the selection or in your experience that contributes to your understanding of Cable's observations.

If You Are Stuck

If you cannot write at least a page, consider writing about

- the gap between your expectations about funeral and burial procedures and what actually happens at Goodbody Mortuaries.
- Cable's attitude toward Mr. Deaver and Tim.
- a funeral, burial, or cremation service that you attended recently, comparing your experience to the procedures at Goodbody Mortuaries.
- your beliefs about death and burial (or cremation) as compared with those expressed by Mr. Deaver and Tim.

READING LIKE A WRITER

CONVEYING AN IMPRESSION OF THE SUBJECT

Writers of observational essays are more than reporters. They do seek to inform readers about a subject, but they go further to convey to readers their impression of a subject. The impression is like an interpretation of the subject or an insight into it. Writers may create an impression in several ways: by revealing their attitude toward the place and people there, by stating their impression directly, or by implying an impression through the way they describe the subject. Readers may not find a sentence beginning "My impression is . . . ," but they will nevertheless get a distinct impression of the subject.

Analyze

1. *Underline* words and phrases in the essay that suggest Cable's attitudes toward or feelings about Goodbody Mortuaries. *Be selective;* in a successful essay, every detail reveals the author's attitude, but certain details will be especially revealing.
2. *Note in the margin* what your underlinings seem to reveal about Cable's attitude toward his subject.

Write

Write several sentences explaining the impression you get about Goodbody Mortuaries, supporting your explanation with examples from the reading. Then *add a few sentences* evaluating how successful you think Cable is in conveying an impression of the funeral home.

CONSIDERING IDEAS FOR YOUR OWN WRITING

Think of places or activities about which you have strong preconceptions or with which you have had little or no experience, and yet have been curious about, or perhaps even put off by. Maybe in your neighborhood there is an upscale gym where you assume participants are interested primarily in posing for and competing with each other, a day-care center where you assume the teachers are idealistic and devoted to the children, a tattoo parlor where you assume all the clients are young, an acupuncture clinic where you doubt there is any scientific basis for the treatments, or a fast-food place where you expect that nearly all employees find their jobs onerous and unrewarding. Or perhaps on your campus there is a tutoring center where you assume tutors do students' work for them, a student counseling center where you have been led to believe that students are not treated with sympathy and understanding, or an office that seems to schedule campus events at times that make it difficult for commuter students to participate. Because many readers would likely share your preconceptions and curiosity, you would have a relatively easy time engaging their interest in the subject. How would you test your preconceptions through your observations and interviews? How might you use your preconceptions to capture readers' attention, as Cable does?

MELANIE PAPENFUSS

Behind the Sugar Curtain

Melanie Papenfuss wrote this essay when she was a first-year college student. Her title suggests that even people in her part of the country, the high plains of North Dakota where sugar-beet farming is widespread, know little about how beets are harvested and delivered for processing. Therefore, she confidently draws the curtain aside to show readers how much there is to learn about a common activity that is very important to the economy of the region.

The other readings in this chapter are followed by reading and writing activities. Following this reading, however, you are on your own to decide how to read for meaning and read like a writer.

1 Ten-thirty on a Friday night I pull into my cousin Blaine's farmyard. The old white two-story house is dark. I grab my overnight bag from the backseat and quickly make my way into the house. Silence. I know Blaine is home: his pick-up is in the driveway. I flick on the kitchen light and look around. What a mess!

2 During beet season, which runs from the first week in October until all the beets are out of the ground, I expect the house to be messy, but nothing like this. A red and white cooler is sitting on the table, half open. Through the crack I can see empty sandwich bags, two cans of Coke, and an empty bag of Ruffles potato chips. On the counter sits a box of Wheaties and a carton of milk, still waiting to be put away. Dishes are piled high in the sink. My eyes wander to the living room. The hide-a-bed is laying out, obviously being used regularly. Dirty laundry is scattered about.

3 "Melanie, is that you?"

4 From the bedroom, Blaine walks out, wearing a pair of old basketball shorts. Dark brown hair, matted on one side of his head and sticking out on the other, sleepy eyes, and a groggy voice materialize before my eyes.

5 "You're just getting up?" I stare in disbelief.

6 "Ya," he replies while rubbing the sleep from his eyes. As an afterthought he looks at what he is wearing, or not wearing. "Let me get dressed."

7 He returns with a red turtleneck, red and black flannel shirt, and faded Wrangler jeans. The left side of his upper lip curls into a cocky smirk. "Do you think you can handle an all-nighter?"

8 Before I can answer he continues. "What do you want to bring to eat — sandwiches, chips, cookies, Rice Krispies bars, Coke, Pepsi, Dr. Pepper?"

"I thought this was for twelve hours, not twelve days!" I respond. 9

Quickly he throws together four salami and cheese sandwiches, a bag of chips, some Rice Krispies bars, and a six-pack of Coke. After the food supply is safely tucked away, we go into the living room to catch a weather report. 10

The announcer blasts, "For all you farmers, you can expect clear skies. Those stars will shine tonight!" 11

Blaine jumps out of his chair and flicks the TV off. "That's all I needed to hear. Let's go." 12

He grabs the cooler and his red St. Thomas Standard jacket and walks out the door. I shut off the lights and quickly follow. 13

We reach the field at 11:15 p.m. All I can see from the road is a large light emanating from the middle of the field. I look closer, and alongside the bright light I can see orange parking lights suspended in mid-air. Blaine turns into the field and heads toward the light. 14

A gruff voice comes from the CB. "Blaine, is that you?" 15

"Ya, John, and I have a passenger tonight. You remember Melanie, don't ya?" Blaine looks at me and winks. 16

"I sure do," John replies with a chuckle. A large older man with silver hair and wire-rimmed glasses, John is the owner of all the beets. "Kevin should be back with the truck in about fifteen minutes. You can take over then." 17

We pass the machine producing the light. It is a 4440 John Deere tractor with four headlights. Behind it a weird-looking contraption is being pulled. It looks like a plow or cultivator but with a long armlike structure that rises up and disappears into the box. 18

"What is that thing behind the tractor?" 19

Blaine laughs, "That 'thing' is the beet lifter. It pulls the beets up and into the truck box." 20

"Oh." 21

We reach the other side of the field, and Blaine stops the pickup. I turn and watch the beet lifter inch its way across the field. It reminds me of a snail creeping up and down the glass of a fish tank. 22

It's not long before I see headlights coming from the north. It is Kevin's truck. He turns into the field, comes halfway in, and stops. I am confused. Patiently I wait for him to continue toward us, but he doesn't. Instead I see his box begin to lift slowly into the air. 23

"What is he doing?" 24

"Do you mean Kevin?" I nod yes. "He's dumping the leftover dirt." Blaine shifts his body toward me and focuses his attention 25 on my question. "You see, after you unload your beets at the plant, the dirt and beets are separated by the grab rollers and you get your dirt back. So then you put it back in the field it came from."

26 As Kevin drives toward us, Blaine grabs the cooler and tilts his head in the direction of the truck. "That's where we're spending the night, so take everything you need."

27 The beet truck is a yellow-and-brown Mack truck. To get into the cab, I have to step onto a runner that is a foot and a half off the ground. There is even a handle on the left side that is perpendicular to the ground. The inside of the cab is small. There are two seats that squeak as you sit down. Between the seats is a cubbyhole for storage. On the steering wheel is a stainless steel knob to help the driver turn.

28 Blaine turns the radio on to KFGO, a country station. "Jason's truck is full; that means we take over."

29 Jason, I think, must be the other driver. Blaine pushes in the clutch and grinds the gears into first. The truck jerks to a slow start. Carefully Blaine pulls the truck box underneath the lifter and CBs to John to tell him we're ready.

30 Before long I hear the thudding of the beets in the empty box. "How do you know when to pull forward or move back to allow the beets to fill the truck evenly?"

31 "Do you see those arrows?" Blaine says, pointing out his window to a panel of orange arrows attached to the tractor. "When I need to speed up or slow down, John flicks a switch and the appropriate arrow lights up."

32 "Oh."

33 After a few rounds (a round is one row of beets that runs the entire length of the field), the truck is loaded. Now we head north on the small country road for a mile until we reach a paved road. There we turn east. It's twelve miles to the Crystal Sugar Beet Plant in Drayton, North Dakota.

34 "How fast do you go?"

35 "With a full load I don't like to go over fifty. Empty I will go sixty to sixty-five."

36 On the road to the plant we meet many empty trucks. Blaine can tell me who is driving and where they are heading by seeing only the headlights and the color of the truck.

37 After twenty minutes, we reach the road that will take us to the plant. We get in line with a few other trucks. Their boxes are heaping with beets.

38 "Is our truck heaping too?"

39 Amused, Blaine replies, "Yes."

"Why don't the beets fly off when you are going down the highway?" 40

"Because each beet weighs five to ten pounds. They're too heavy to fly off." 41

It takes only a few minutes to reach the scale house. When we get up to the scale house window, Blaine rummages through some index cardlike metal plates and hands one to the woman in the window. I hear a stamp, and she gives Blaine a slip of paper. 42

"What did you just do? What's that metal thing?" 43

"This metal thing is a number plate," Blaine explains patiently. "It is recorded by the scale house. The number tells them who owns the beets in the truck and how heavy the truck is when it's loaded." 44

I turn and look to see where we are going. We are driving on a single-lane paved road, but at the end it branches out into eight separate roads, spread out like the bristles of a broom. At the end of each is an orange machine (the piler); trucks are driving up onto them. 45

Again we wait behind other trucks. When it's our turn, a man in a hardhat signals for us to pull ahead. Slowly Blaine releases the clutch and drives the big truck onto the piler. There are railings on each side of us and I don't think we'll fit, but I am wrong. Behind the truck the ramp is being raised so it is perpendicular to the ground. Then Blaine gets a signal that tells him to back up so the truck box gate is against the inclined ramp. When this is done, Blaine can then begin to raise the truck bed and dump the beets. Once the beets are dumped, the piler separates the excess dirt from the beets. From there the beets go up a long conveyor belt and are piled on many other beets. The dirt is brought to a type of holding bin and is then dumped back into the truck after it comes off the piler. 46

We make our way back up the broom bristle and head for the scale house. Blaine hands the woman in the window the paper with his loaded weight, and she stamps it with his empty weight. We have been carrying 44,000 pounds of beets — twenty-two tons! 47

"So, now you've seen what goes on during beet season. What do you think?" 48

"I never knew all the things that go on," I said in amazement. "How many more loads will we get to do before your shift is over?" 49

"Probably five or six more if we have no breakdowns. Do you want to go home or keep going?" 50

"Are you kidding?" I reply eagerly. "Pass me a Coke, would ya?" 51

READING FOR MEANING

Write to create meanings for Papenfuss's observations of sugar-beet harvesting.

READING LIKE A WRITER

Writers of observational essays

- describe places and people.
- organize or sequence the observations in a particular way.
- engage and inform readers.
- convey an impression of the subject.

You have seen how important these observational writing strategies are in the readings you have read, written about, and discussed in this chapter. Focus on one of these strategies in Papenfuss's essay and analyze it carefully through close rereading and annotating. Then write several sentences explaining what you have learned, giving specific examples from the reading to support your explanation. Add a few sentences evaluating how successfully Papenfuss uses the strategy to help readers unfamiliar with sugar-beet harvesting learn about it.

REVIEWING WHAT MAKES OBSERVATIONAL ESSAYS EFFECTIVE

In this chapter, you have been learning how to read observational essays for meaning and how to read them like a writer. Before going on to write an observational essay, pause here to review and contemplate what you have learned about the elements of effective observational writing.

Analyze

Choose one reading from this chapter that seems to you especially effective. Before rereading the selection, *jot down* one or two reasons you remember it as an example of good observational writing.

Reread your chosen selection, adding further annotations about what makes it a particularly successful example of observation. *Consider* the selection's purpose and how well it achieves that purpose for its intended readers. (You can make an informed guess about the intended readers and their expectations by noting the publication source of the essay.) Then *focus* on how well the essay

- details places and people.
- organizes the observations.

- engages and informs readers.
- conveys an impression of its subject.

You can review all of these basic features in the Guide to Reading Observational Essays (p. 72).

Your instructor may ask you to complete this activity on your own or to work with a small group of other students who have chosen the same reading. If you work with others, allow enough time initially for all group members to reread the selection thoughtfully and to add their annotations. Then *discuss* as a group what makes the selection effective. *Take notes* on your discussion. One student in your group should then report to the class what the group has learned about the effectiveness of observational writing. If you are working individually, write up what you have learned from your analysis.

Write

Write at least a page, supporting your choice of this reading as an example of effective observational writing. *Assume* that your readers — your instructor and classmates — have read the selection but will not remember many details about it. They also might not remember it as especially successful. Therefore, you will need to *refer* to details and specific parts of the essay as you explain how it works and as you justify your evaluation of its effectiveness. You need not argue that it is the best reading in the chapter or that it is flawless, only that it is, in your view, a strong example of the genre.

A Guide to Writing Observational Essays

The readings in this chapter have helped you learn a great deal about observational writing. You have seen that writers of observational essays present unfamiliar places and people. You have also seen that they collect large amounts of information and ideas from visits and interviews, which must be sorted, organized, and integrated into a readable draft. This Guide to Writing is designed to help you through the stages of invention, drafting, revising, and editing, as you gather the material you will need and solve problems you encounter as you write.

INVENTION

The following invention activities will help you choose a subject, research and reflect on your subject, plan and make observations, and decide on the impression you want your essay to convey to readers. Each activity is easy to do and takes only a few minutes. If you can spread out the activities over several days, you will have adequate time to understand what you must do to present your subject in an engaging and informative way. Keep a written record of your invention work to use later when you draft and revise the essay.

Choosing a Subject

List the subjects you are interested in observing. To make the best possible choice and have alternatives in case the subject you choose requires too much time or is inaccessible, you should have a list of several possible subjects. You might already have a subject in mind, possibly one you listed for the Considering Ideas for Your Own Writing activities following the readings in this chapter. Here are some other suggestions that will help you think of possible topics:

People

- Anyone doing work that you might want to do — city council member, police officer, lab technician, computer programmer, attorney, salesperson
- Anyone with an unusual job or hobby — dog trainer, private detective, ham radio operator, race car driver, novelist
- A campus personality — coach, distinguished teacher, newspaper editor, oldest or youngest student
- Someone recently recognized for community service or achievement

Places

- Small-claims court, consumer fraud office, city planner's office
- Bodybuilding gym, weight-reduction clinic, martial arts school
- Hospital emergency room, campus health center, hospice, psychiatric unit
- Recycling center, airport control tower, theater, museum, sports arena

Activities

- Tutoring, registering voters, rehearsing for a play, repairing a car
- An unconventional sports event — dog's frisbee tournament, chess match, amateur wrestling or boxing meet, dogsledding, log sawing and splitting, ice-fishing contest, Olympics for people with disabilities
- A team practicing a sport or other activity (one you can observe as a curious outsider, not as an experienced participant)
- A community improvement project — graffiti cleaning, tree planting, house repairing, church painting, road or highway litter collecting
- Special courses — rock climbing, folk dancing, dog training, truck driving

Select a topic about which you are genuinely curious. Be sure to check on accessibility, requesting permission to visit one or more times to make detailed observations and to interview key people. Above all, choose a subject that interests you — and one that you think will appeal to your readers. Keep in mind that the more unfamiliar the subject is for readers, the easier it will be for you to interest them in it. If you choose a subject familiar to readers, try to focus on some aspect of it likely to be truly informative, even surprising, to them.

Researching Your Subject

The writing and research activities that follow will enable you to gather information and ideas about your subject.

Making a Schedule. *Set up a tentative schedule for your observational and interview visits.* Figure out first the amount of time you have to complete your essay. Then determine the scope of your project — a onetime observation, an interview with follow-up, or multiple observations and interviews. Decide what visits you will need to make, whom you will need to interview, and what library or Internet work you might want to do to get background information about your subject. Estimate the time necessary for each, knowing you might need to schedule more time than anticipated.

Make phone calls to schedule visits. When you write down your appointments, be sure to include names, addresses, phone numbers, dates and times, and any special arrangements you have made for each visit. (Consult the section Field Research, pp. 558–63, in Appendix 2 for helpful guidelines on observing, interviewing, and taking notes.)

Exploring Readers' and Your Own Preconceptions. *Write for several minutes about your readers' as well as your own assumptions and expectations.* For example, ask questions like these about your readers: Who are they? What are they likely to think about the subject? What would they want to know about it? Also reflect on yourself: Why do you want to research this subject? What do you expect to find out about it? What aspects of it do you expect to be interesting or entertaining?

Visiting a Place. *During your visit, take notes on what you observe.* Do not try to impose order on your notes at this stage; simply record whatever you notice. Pay special attention to visual details and other kinds of details (sounds, smells) that you can draw on later to describe the place and people.

Interviewing a Person. *Prepare for the interview by writing out some preliminary questions.* But do not be afraid of abandoning your script during the interview. Listen carefully to what is said and ask follow-up questions. Take notes; if you like and your subject agrees, you may also tape-record the interview.

Gathering Information. *If you do background reading, take careful notes and keep accurate bibliographic records of your sources.* Try to pick up relevant fliers, brochures, or reports at the place you observe. In addition, you might want to do some research on the Internet or in your college library. (See the sections Library Research, pp. 563–70, and Internet Research, pp. 570–75, in Appendix 2 for help.)

Reflecting on Your Subject

After you research your subject, consider your purpose for writing about it and formulate a tentative thesis statement.

Considering Your Purpose. *Write for several minutes about the impression of the subject you want to convey to your readers.* As you write, try to answer this question: What makes this subject worth observing? Your answer to this question might change as you write, but a preliminary answer will give your writing a direction to follow, or what journalists commonly call an "angle" on the subject. This angle will help you choose what to include as well as what to emphasize in your draft. Use the following questions to help clarify the impression you want your essay to convey:

- What visual images or other sensory details of the subject stand out in your memory? Think about the feelings these images evoke in you. If they evoke contradictory feelings, consider how you could use them to convey to readers the complexity of your feelings about the place, people, or activities you observed.
- What is most surprising about your observations? Compare the preconceptions you listed earlier with what you actually saw or heard.
- What interests you most about the people you interviewed? Compare the direct observations you made about them with the indirect or secondhand information you gathered about them.

Formulating a Tentative Thesis Statement. *Review what you wrote for Considering Your Purpose and add another two or three sentences that will bring into focus the impression you want to give readers about the person, place, or activity on which you are focusing.* This impression is based on an insight into, interpretation of, or idea about the person, place, or activity you have gained while observing it. Try to write sentences that do not summarize what you have already written but that express a deeper understanding of what impression you want to make on your readers.

Keep in mind that readers do not expect you to begin your observational essay with the kind of explicit thesis statement typical of argumentative essays. None of the readings in this chapter offers to readers an explicit statement of the impression the writer hopes to convey about the subject. Instead, the writers convey an impression through the ways they describe their subjects, select information to share with readers, or narrate the story of their experiences with the subject. And yet it is possible for readers to infer from each reading an impression of the subject. For example, some readers might decide that John Leland wants to convey the impression that professional wrestling requires the most careful planning and cooperation between wrestlers, that "Your opponent is really your partner," as one of the instructors says. Other readers might decide that Leland wants to convey the impression that wrestling students seem willing to undergo a lot of pain for an uncertain return on their investments in an expensive, prolonged training program. If, like you, Leland had tried to write a few sentences about the impression he hoped to convey following his four days at the Monster Factory, he might have written sentences like these.

Nearly all first attempts to state an impression to be conveyed, to focus a jumble of notes and remembered observations, or to state a thesis are eventually revised once drafting gets under way. Writing the first draft helps writers of observational essays discover their main impression and find ways to convey that impression without ever stating it directly. Just because there is no explicit thesis statement in an observational essay does not mean that it lacks focus or fails to convey an impression of its subject.

Considering Visuals. *Consider whether visuals — photographs you take, drawings you make, copies of revealing illustrative materials you picked up at the place observed — would strengthen your observational essay.* If you submit your essay electronically to other students and your instructor, or if you post it to a Web site, consider including snippets of your interviews or sounds from the place (if you make use of a tape recorder in your project) or your own digital photographs or video. Remember to ask permission to make visual or audio records: Some persons may be willing to be interviewed or share printed material but reluctant to allow photographs or recordings. Visual and audio materials are not at all a requirement of an effective observational essay, as you can tell from the readings in this chapter, but they could add a new dimension to your writing.

DRAFTING

The following guidelines will help you set goals for your draft and plan its organization.

Setting Goals

Establishing goals for your draft before you begin writing will enable you to make decisions and work more confidently. Consider the following questions now, and keep them in mind as you draft. They will help you set goals for drafting as well as recall how the writers you have read in this chapter tried to achieve similar goals.

- *How can I help my readers imagine the subject?* In addition to describing visual details, as all of the authors in this chapter do, should I evoke other senses, in the way that Edge describes how a pig lip smells and tastes and what its unusual texture is? Should I characterize people by their clothes, facial expressions, and talk, as McPhee, Coyne, and Cable do? Should I use surprising metaphors or similes, as the author of "Soup" does in describing Yeganeh's "working like a demon alchemist" or as Leland does when he compares the wrestling students to musicians and actors, "Like fledgling actors or musicians, my classmates believe unshakably that from this humble tumble lies the road to stone-cold greatness"?
- *How can I engage my readers?* Should I focus on dramatic interactions among people, as McPhee does? Should I begin with a dramatic moment, as Leland does? A poignant image, as Coyne does? A surprising statement, as

in "Soup"? Personal experience with the subject, as Edge does? Humor, as Leland, Edge, and Cable all do?

- *How can I present and distribute the information so that readers do not become either bored or overwhelmed?* Should I present some information through reported conversation, as in "Soup"? Some as part of a personal experience story of participating in the subject, as Leland, McPhee, and Edge do? Some from interviews, as Edge and Cable do? Some as observed visual and other details, as all the authors in this chapter do?
- *How should I organize my observations?* Should I organize the observations topically in groups of related information, as the author of "Soup" and Edge and Cable do? Or should I arrange them in a chronological narrative order, as McPhee, Leland, and Coyne do?
- *How can I convey the impression I want to leave with my readers?* Should I convey it explicitly, or should I try to convey an impression indirectly — by my choice of words, descriptive details, and the story, as all of the authors in this chapter do?

Organizing Your Draft

With your goals in mind, reread the notes you took about the place and people, and decide how to organize them — grouped into topics or put in chronological order. If you think a topical organization would work best, try grouping your observations and naming the topic of each group. If you think narrating what happened would help you organize your observations, make a time line and note where the information would go. You might want to try different kinds of outlines before settling on a plan and drafting your essay.

Writers who use a narrative structure usually follow a simple, straightforward chronology. Coyne, Leland, and Cable, for example, present activities observed over a limited period — a few hours or a few days — in the order in which they occurred. Writers may also punctuate their main narrative with additional events that occurred on other occasions: McPhee, for example, recounts what happened over a few hours at the Brooklyn farmers' market while also weaving in other stories about the market that took place at different times in the past. Coyne provides a lot of background information about the two families she juxtaposes.

Writers who organize their observations topically must limit the number of topics they cover. The author of "Soup," for example, focuses on Yeganeh's ideas about soup and his attitudes toward customers. Leland limits his attention to aspects of the training regimen at the Monster Factory and to wrestling moves, while Edge concentrates on the history and process of bottling and selling pig lips.

READING A DRAFT CRITICALLY

Getting a critical reading of your draft will help you see how to improve it. Your instructor may schedule class time for reading drafts, or you may want to ask a classmate or a tutor in the writing center to read your draft. Ask your reader to use the following guidelines and to write out a response for you to consult during your revision.

Read for a First Impression

1. Read the draft without stopping to annotate or comment, and then write two or three sentences giving your general impression.
2. Identify one aspect of the draft that seems particularly effective.

Read Again to Suggest Improvements

1. Suggest ways of making descriptions of places and people more vivid.
   - Find a description of a place, and suggest what details could be added to objects in the scene (location, size, color, and shape) or what sensory information (look, sound, smell, taste, and touch) could be included to help you picture the place.
   - Find a description of a person, and indicate what else you would like to know about the person's dress, facial expression, tone of voice, and gestures.
   - Find reported conversation, and note whether any of the quotes could be paraphrased or summarized without losing impact.
   - Find passages where additional reported conversation could enhance the drama or help bring a person to life.
2. Recommend ways of making the organization clearer or more effective.
   - If the essay is organized chronologically, look for passages where the narrative seems to wander pointlessly or leaves out important information. Also suggest cues that could be added to indicate time sequence (*initially, then, afterward*).
   - If the essay is organized topically, mark topics that get too much or too little attention, transitions between topics that need to be added or clarified, and topics that should be placed elsewhere.
   - If the essay alternates narration with topical information, suggest where transitions could be made smoother or sequencing could be improved.
3. Suggest how the essay could be made more engaging and informative.

- If the essay seems boring or you feel overwhelmed by too much information, suggest how the information could alternate with vivid description or lively narration. Also consider whether any of the information could be cut or simplified.
- List any questions you still have about the subject.

4. Suggest ways to make the impression conveyed to you more focused and coherent.
   - Tell the writer what impression you have of the subject.
   - Point to key information that supports your impression, so that the writer knows how you arrived at it.
   - Point to any information that makes you doubt or question your impression.
5. Evaluate the effectiveness of visuals.
   - Look at any visuals in the essay, and tell the writer what they contribute to your impression of the subject and your understanding of the observations.
   - If any visuals do not seem relevant, or if there seem to be too many visuals, identify the ones that the writer could consider dropping, explaining your thinking.
   - If a visual does not seem to be appropriately placed, suggest a better place for it.

REVISING

This section offers suggestions for revising your draft, suggestions that will remind you of the possibilities for developing a vivid, informative observational essay. Revising means reenvisioning your draft, trying to see it in a new way, given your purpose and readers, in order to develop your observations.

The biggest mistake you can make while revising is to focus initially on words or sentences. Instead, first try to see your draft as a whole in order to assess its likely impact on your readers. Think imaginatively and boldly about cutting unconvincing material, adding new material, and moving material around. Your computer makes even drastic revisions physically easy, but you still need to make the mental effort and decisions that will improve your draft.

You may have received help with this challenge from a classmate or tutor who gave your draft a critical reading. If so, keep this feedback in mind as you decide which parts of your draft need revising and what specific changes you could make. The following suggestions will help you solve problems and strengthen your essay.

To Make Your Description of Places and People More Vivid

- Cull your notes for additional details you could supply about people and objects in the scene.
- If your notes are sparse, consider revisiting the place to add to your visual observations, or try imagining yourself back at the place and write about what you see.
- Consider where you could add details about sounds, smells, or textures of objects.
- Identify where a simile or metaphor would enrich your description.
- Review reported conversations to make sure you directly quote only the language that conveys personality or essential information; paraphrase or summarize other conversations.
- Show people interacting with each other by talking, moving, or gesturing.

To Make the Organization Clearer and More Effective

- If the essay is organized chronologically, keep the narrative focused and well-paced, adding time markers to clarify the sequence of events.
- If the essay is organized topically, make sure it moves smoothly from topic to topic, adding transitions where necessary.
- If the essay alternates narration with topical information, make sure the sequence is clear and easy to follow.

To Make the Essay More Engaging and Informative

- If the essay bores or overwhelms readers, cut information that is obvious or extraneous, and consider alternating blocks of information with descriptive or narrative materials.
- If readers have questions about the subject, try to answer them.
- If the essay seems abstract, provide specific definitions, examples, and details.

To Strengthen the Impression Your Essay Conveys

- If readers get an impression of the subject you did not expect, consider what may have given them that impression. You may need to add or cut material.
- If readers are unable to identify an impression, look for ways to make clearer the impression you want to convey.

EDITING AND PROOFREADING

After you have revised your essay, be sure to spend some time checking for errors in usage, punctuation, and mechanics and considering matters of style. If you keep a list of errors you typically make, begin by checking your draft against this list. Ask someone else to proofread your essay before you print out a copy for your instructor or send it electronically.

From our research on student writing, we know that observational essays tend to have errors in the use of quotation marks, when writers quote the exact words of people they have interviewed. Check a writer's handbook for help with this problem.

REFLECTING ON WHAT YOU HAVE LEARNED

Observation

In this chapter, you have read critically several observational essays and have written one of your own. To better remember what you have learned, pause now to reflect on the reading and writing activities you completed in this chapter.

1. *Write* a page or so assessing what you have learned. *Begin* by describing what you are most pleased with in your essay. Then *explain* what you think contributed to your achievement. *Be specific* about this contribution.
   - If it was something you learned from the readings, *indicate* which readings and specifically what you learned from them.
   - If it came from your invention writing, interview, or observations, *point out* the parts that helped you most.
   - If you got good advice from a critical reader, *explain* exactly how the person helped you — perhaps by helping you understand a particular problem in your draft or by adding a new dimension to your writing.
2. Now *reflect* more generally on the genre of observational writing. Observational essays may seem impartial and objective, but they inevitably reflect the writer's interests, values, and other characteristics, such as gender and ethnicity or cultural heritage. For example, readers would expect a vegetarian to write a very different profile of a cattle ranch from one a beef lover would write. *Identify* a reading in the chapter where the writer's attitudes or characteristics seemed to influence the choice of subject, the observations,

and the essay. *Explain* briefly how this influence is apparent to you. Then *consider* the following questions about your own project: How did your interests, values, or other characteristics influence your choice of subject, your observations, and your interactions with the people you interviewed? In your essay itself, how do these influences show through? If you tried to keep them hidden, *explain* briefly why. How could these influences be made more visible in your essay, and do you wish you had made them more visible? *Explain* why briefly.

CHAPTER 

Reflection

Like autobiographical and observational writing, reflective writing is based on the writer's personal experience. Reflective writers present something they did, saw, overheard, or read. They try to make their writing vivid so that the reader can imagine what they experienced. But unlike writers of autobiography and observation, their goal is not primarily to present their experience so that the reader can imagine it. Reflective writers, instead, present their experience in order to explore its possible meanings. They use events in their lives and people and places they have observed as the occasions or springboards for thinking about society — how people live and what people believe.

In this chapter, for example, one writer tells what happened one evening when he was taking a walk and he noticed a woman react to him with evident fear. This experience, and others like it, leads him to think about popular stereotypes concerning gender and race. Another writer recalls how upset his son was after a visit to the orthodontist. This event makes him wonder where the idea that everyone should have an "ideal set of teeth" comes from and why he and his wife put their son through torture to achieve this questionable ideal. Still another writer, who observed a spate of news reports on dysfunctional families, muses over the idea that families are not always the safe haven we like to think they are.

As you can see from these few examples, the subjects reflective essays explore are wide ranging. Reflective writers may think about social change with its many opportunities and challenges (changes in the family, in ways to perfect the body, and in the notion of community in the Internet age). They may examine cultural customs in our culturally diverse society (such as those related to eating, dating, and child rearing). They may explore traditional virtues and vices (pride, jealousy, and compassion) or common hopes and fears (the desire for intimacy and the fear of it).

These subjects may seem far reaching, but writers of reflection have relatively modest goals. They do not attempt to exhaust their subjects, nor do they set themselves up as experts. They simply try out their ideas. One early meaning of the word *essay*, in fact, was "to try out." Reflective essays are exercises, experiments, simply opportunities to explore ideas informally and tentatively.

Reflective writing is enjoyable to write and read precisely because it is exploratory and creative. Reflective writing can be as stimulating as a lively conversation. It often surprises us with its insights and unlikely connections and encourages us to look in new ways at even the most familiar things, examining with a critical eye what we usually take for granted.

The readings in this chapter will help you learn a good deal about reflective writing. From the readings and from the suggestions for writing that follow each reading, you will get ideas for your own reflective essay. As you read and write about the selections, keep in mind the following assignment, which sets out the goals for writing a reflective essay. To support your writing of this assignment, the chapter concludes with a Guide to Writing Reflective Essays.

THE WRITING ASSIGNMENT

Reflection

Write a reflective essay based on something you experienced or observed. Describe this occasion vividly so that readers can understand what happened and will care about what you have to say about it. In reflecting on the particular occasion, make some general statements exploring its possible meanings or cultural significance. Consider what the occasion might imply about how people in our society behave toward one another, what they value, and what assumptions or stereotypes they may hold consciously or unconsciously. Think of reflective writing as a stimulating conversation in which you seek to expose — and perhaps question — your readers' attitudes and beliefs as well as your own.

WRITING SITUATIONS FOR REFLECTIVE ESSAYS

Writers use a wide range of particular occasions to launch their reflections. These occasions nearly always lead them to reflect on some aspect of contemporary culture, as the following examples indicate:

- A former football player writes a reflective essay for his college alumni magazine about his experience playing professional sports. He recounts a specific occasion when he sustained a serious injury but continued to play because he knew that playing with pain was regarded as a sign of manliness.

As he reflects on what happened, he recalls that he first learned the custom of playing with pain from his father but that the lesson was reinforced later by coaches and other players. He wonders why boys playing sports are taught not to show pain but encouraged to show other feelings like aggression and competitiveness. Taking an anthropological view, he sees contemporary sports as equivalent to the kind of training Native American boys traditionally went through to become warriors. This comparison leads him to question whether sports training today prepares boys (and perhaps girls, too) for the kinds of roles they need to play in contemporary society.

- Writing for a political science course, a student reflects on her first experience voting in a presidential election. She begins by describing a recent conversation with friends about how people decide to vote for one presidential candidate over another. They agreed that most people they know seem to base their decisions on trivial, even bizarre, reasons, rather than on a candidate's experience, voting record in previous offices, character, or even campaign promises. For example, one friend knew someone who voted for a presidential candidate who reminded her of her grandfather, while another friend knew someone who voted against a candidate because he did not like the way the candidate dressed. The writer then reflects on the humorous as well as the serious implications of such voting decisions.
- A first-year college student, in an essay for his composition course, reflects on a performance of his high-school chorus that far surpassed the members' expectations. He describes their trip to the statewide competition and their anxious rehearsals before the performance and, during the competition, their unexpected feelings of confidence, their precision and control, and the exuberance of the performance. He considers factors that led to their success, such as fear of embarrassment, affection for their teacher, the excitement of a trip to the state capital, and the fact that they had rehearsed especially attentively for weeks because the music was so challenging and the competition so fierce. After considering possible reasons for their success, the writer concludes with some ideas about the special pleasures of success where cooperation and individual creativity are essential.

A Guide to Reading Reflective Essays

This guide introduces you to reflective writing. By completing all the activities in it, you will prepare yourself to learn a great deal from the other readings in this chapter about how to read and write a reflective essay. The guide focuses on a brief but powerful piece of reflection by Brent Staples. You will read Staples's reflective essay twice. First, you will read it for meaning, seeking to understand Staples's experience, to follow his reflections, and to discover your own ideas about stereotyping and fear of others. Then, you will read the essay like a writer, analyzing the parts to see how Staples crafts his essay and to learn the strategies he uses to make his reflective writing effective. These two activities — reading for meaning and reading like a writer — follow every reading in this chapter.

BRENT STAPLES

Black Men and Public Space

Brent Staples (b. 1951) earned his Ph.D. in psychology from the University of Chicago and went on to become a journalist, writing for several magazines and newspapers, including the Chicago Sun-Times. *In 1985, he became assistant metropolitan editor of the* New York Times, *where he is now a member of the editorial board. His autobiography,* Parallel Times: Growing Up in Black and White, *was published in 1994.*

The following essay originally appeared in Ms. *magazine in 1986, under the title "Just Walk on By." Staples revised it slightly for publication in* Harper's *a year later under the present title. The particular occasion for Staples's reflections is an incident that occurred for the first time in the mid-1970s, when he discovered that his mere presence on the street late at night was enough to frighten a young white woman. Recalling this incident leads him to reflect on issues of race, gender, and class in the United States. (If you are interested in learning more about the issue of racial profiling that Staples brings up in this essay, be sure to read the selection by Randall Kennedy in* *Chapter 9, pp. 471–78.)*

As you read, think about why Staples chose the new title, "Black Men and Public Space."

My first victim was a woman — white, well dressed, probably in her late twenties. I came upon her late one evening on a deserted street in Hyde Park, a relatively affluent neighborhood in an otherwise mean, impoverished section of Chicago. As I swung onto the avenue behind her, there seemed to be a discreet, uninflammatory distance between us. Not so. She cast back a worried glance. To her, the youngish black man — a broad six feet two inches with a beard and billowing hair, both hands shoved into the pockets of a bulky military jacket — seemed menacingly close. After a few more quick glimpses, she picked up her pace and was soon running in earnest. Within seconds she disappeared into a cross street. 1

That was more than a decade ago. I was twenty-two years old, a graduate student newly arrived at the University of Chicago. It 2 was in the echo of that terrified woman's footfalls that I first began to know the unwieldy inheritance I'd come into — the ability to alter public space in ugly ways. It was clear that she thought herself the quarry of a mugger, a rapist, or worse. Suffering a bout of insomnia, however, I was stalking sleep, not defenseless wayfarers. As a softy who is scarcely able to take a knife to a raw chicken — let alone hold one to a person's throat — I was surprised, embarrassed, and dismayed all at once. Her flight made me feel like an accomplice in tyranny. It also made it clear that I was indistinguishable from the muggers who occasionally seeped into the area from the surrounding ghetto. That first encounter, and those that followed, signified that a vast, unnerving gulf lay between nighttime pedestrians — particularly women — and me. And I soon gathered that being perceived as dangerous is a hazard in itself. I only needed to turn a corner into a dicey situation, or crowd some frightened, armed person in a foyer somewhere, or make an errant move after being pulled over by a policeman. Where fear and weapons meet — and they often do in urban America — there is always the possibility of death.

In that first year, my first away from my hometown, I was to become thoroughly familiar with the language of fear. At dark, shadowy intersections, I could cross in front of a car stopped at a traffic light and elicit the *thunk, thunk, thunk, thunk* of the driver — black, white, male, or female — hammering down the door locks. On less traveled streets after dark, I grew accustomed to but never comfortable with people crossing to the other side of the street rather than pass me. Then there were the standard unpleasantries with policemen, doormen, bouncers, cabdrivers, and others whose business it is to screen out troublesome individuals *before* there is any nastiness. 3

I moved to New York nearly two years ago and I have remained an avid night walker. In central Manhattan, the near-constant crowd cover minimizes tense one-on-one street encounters. Elsewhere — in SoHo, for example, where sidewalks are narrow and tightly spaced buildings shut out the sky — things can get very taut indeed. 4

After dark, on the warrenlike streets of Brooklyn where I live, I often see women who fear the worst from me. They seem to have set their faces on neutral, and with their purse straps strung across their chests bandolier-style, they forge ahead as though bracing themselves against being tackled. I understand, of course, that the danger they perceive is not a hallucination. Women are particularly vulnerable to street violence, and young black males are drastically overrepresented among the perpetrators of that 5 violence. Yet these truths are no solace against the kind of alienation that comes of being ever the suspect, a fearsome entity with whom pedestrians avoid making eye contact.

6 Over the years, I learned to smother the rage I felt at so often being taken for a criminal. Not to do so would surely have led to madness. I now take precautions to make myself less threatening. I move about with care, particularly late in the evening. I give a wide berth to nervous people on subway platforms during the wee hours, particularly when I have exchanged business clothes for jeans. If I happen to be entering a building behind some people who appear skittish, I may walk by, letting them clear the lobby before I return, so as not to seem to be following them. I have been calm and extremely congenial on those rare occasions when I've been pulled over by the police.

7 And on late-evening constitutionals I employ what has proved to be an excellent tension-reducing measure: I whistle melodies from Beethoven and Vivaldi and the more popular classical composers. Even steely New Yorkers hunching toward nighttime destinations seem to relax, and occasionally they even join in the tune. Virtually everybody seems to sense that a mugger wouldn't be warbling bright, sunny selections from Vivaldi's *Four Seasons.* It is my equivalent of the cowbell that hikers wear when they know they are in bear country.

READING FOR MEANING

Write to create meanings for Staples's reflections about how people react to him in public spaces.

Start Making Meaning

Begin by listing some of the ways Staples tries to alleviate people's fear of him and commenting on his feelings about these encounters. Continue by writing about anything else in the selection or in your experience that contributes to your understanding of Staples's reflections.

If You Are Stuck

If you cannot write at least a page, consider writing about

- whether Staples accurately assesses the woman's feelings in the first encounter he describes, perhaps speculating about how you would feel in this woman's position.

- the extent to which in your view Staples's problem results from social tensions related to race, class (income level), or gender.
- an experience you have had in which racial, gender, age, or other differences caused tension, comparing your experience with that of Staples or one of the people he encountered.
- whether in your experience the fear of strangers operates the same way in suburban or small-town public spaces as it does for Staples in an urban setting.

READING LIKE A WRITER

This section guides you through an analysis of Staples's reflective writing strategies: *presenting the particular occasion, developing the reflections, maintaining topical coherence,* and *engaging readers.* For each strategy you will be asked to reread and annotate part of Staples's essay to see how he uses the strategy in "Black Men and Public Space."

When you study the selections later in this chapter, you will see how different writers use these same strategies for different purposes. The Guide to Writing Reflective Essays near the end of the chapter suggests ways you can use these strategies in your own writing.

Presenting the Particular Occasion

Reflective writers present a particular occasion — something they experienced or observed — to introduce their general reflections. They may describe the occasion in detail, or they may sketch it out quickly. The key in either case is to present the occasion in a vivid and suggestive way that encourages readers to want to know more about the writer's thoughts. To succeed at presenting the occasion vividly, writers rely on the same narrating and describing strategies you practiced in Chapter 2 (Autobiography) and Chapter 3 (Observation).

Staples lets readers know from the word *first* in the introductory phrase ("My first victim") that what happened on this occasion happened again later. But he focuses in the opening paragraph on this first occasion, the one that started his reflections. Staples presents this first event in vivid detail, trying to give readers a sense of the surprise and anxiety he felt at the time. In addition to helping readers imagine what happened, Staples tries to present the event in a way that suggests the larger meanings he will develop in subsequent paragraphs. Looking closely at how he saw the woman and how she saw him helps readers understand his ideas about what happened.

Analyze

1. *Reread* the opening sentence of paragraph 1, where Staples describes the person he encountered. *Notice* that even before he identifies her by gender,

he uses the word "victim" to name her. Then *underline* the details he gives to describe this person and the actions she takes.

2. Now *turn to* the places in paragraph 1 where Staples describes himself as the woman saw him. *Put brackets around* the names used to identify him, and *underline* the details used to describe him physically as well as the actions he takes.

3. *Review* the details you have underlined; then *choose* three or four details that you think help make this particular occasion especially vivid and dramatic.

Write

Write several sentences explaining what you have learned about how Staples uses this event to create a dramatic occasion that helps to introduce his reflections. *Support* your explanation with some of the details you singled out.

Developing the Reflections

While the particular occasion introduces the subject, the reflections explore the subject by developing the writer's ideas. For example, what occasions Staples's reflections is an event that occurred when his mere presence on the street frightened a woman into running away from him. He uses this particular event to introduce the general subject: fear resulting from racial stereotyping. As he explains, "It was in the echo of that terrified woman's footfalls that I first began to know the unwieldy inheritance I'd come into" (paragraph 2). Throughout the rest of the essay, Staples examines this "inheritance" from various angles, using a range of reflective writing strategies: He expresses his different feelings at being misperceived as a threat; he explains the effects of racial stereotyping, including the danger to himself; he gives examples of other occasions when people react to him with fear or hostility; and, finally, he lists the "precautions" he takes to make himself appear "less threatening" (paragraph 6). These are just some of the strategies writers use to develop their reflections. This activity will help you see how Staples uses examples to illustrate and explain his ideas.

Analyze

1. *Look at* the opening sentence of paragraph 3, where Staples introduces the idea that there is a "language of fear." *Reread* the rest of the paragraph to see how the writer uses examples to help readers understand what he means.

2. Now *look at* paragraphs 6 and 7, where Staples writes about the "precautions" he takes to make himself seem "less threatening." *Mark* the examples, and *choose* one or two that you think work especially well to help readers understand what he means.

Write

Write several sentences explaining what you have learned about Staples's use of examples, pointing to the examples you think are especially effective.

Maintaining Topical Coherence

Reflective essays explore ideas on a subject by turning them this way and that, examining them first from one perspective and then from another, and sometimes piling up examples to illustrate the ideas. Such essays may seem rambling, with one idea or example added to another in a casual way. It is not always clear where the writer is going, and the essay may not seem to end conclusively. This apparently casual organization is deceptive, however, because in fact the reflective writer has arranged the parts carefully to give the appearance of a mind at work.

While each new idea or example may seem to turn the essay in an unexpected new direction, reflective writers use what we call *topical coherence* to make the parts of a reflective essay connect to the central subject. An important way of achieving topical coherence is to refer to the subject at various points in the essay by repeating certain key words or phrases associated with the subject. In the opening anecdote that presents the particular occasion, Staples dramatizes the woman's fear of him. He does not use the word "fear," however, until the end of paragraph 2. He then repeats that word twice: at the beginning of paragraph 3, in the phrase "language of fear," and at the beginning of paragraph 5. He also concludes the latter paragraph with a phrase that indicates how others, particularly women, see him: as "a fearsome entity." In addition, Staples uses several related words, such as "terrified" and "frightened" (paragraph 2) as well as "nervous" and "skittish" (6). By repeating the word "fear" and words related to it, Staples highlights the subject of his reflections.

Another way reflective writers achieve topical coherence is through carefully placed transitions. Staples, as you will see in this activity, uses time and place markers to introduce a series of examples illustrating the fear he engenders in others simply because of his race and gender.

Analyze

1. *Skim* paragraphs 2, 3, 4, and 6, and *put brackets around* the time and place markers. *Begin* by bracketing the time marker "more than a decade ago" and the place marker "at the University of Chicago" in the opening sentence of paragraph 2.

2. *Notice* how many different times and places Staples refers to with these markers.

Write

Write several sentences explaining how Staples uses time and place markers to help maintain topical coherence. *Support* your explanation with examples from the reading.

Engaging Readers

Readers of reflective essays, like readers of autobiographical and observational writing, expect writers to engage their interest. In fact, most readers have no pressing reason to read reflective writing. They choose to read an essay because something about it catches their eye — a familiar author's name, an intriguing title, an interesting graphic or drop quote. Journalists typically begin feature articles, ones that do not deal with "hard" news, with what they call a *hook,* designed to catch readers' attention. The particular occasion that opens many reflective essays often serves this purpose. Staples's opening phrase, "My first victim," certainly grabs attention.

But once "caught," readers have to be kept reading. One of the ways reflective writers keep readers engaged is by projecting an image of themselves — sometimes called the *writer's persona* or *voice* — that readers can identify with or at least find interesting. Staples, for example, uses the first-person pronouns *my* and *I* to present himself in his writing and to speak directly to readers. In paragraph 2, for example, he describes himself as "a softy" and explains how he felt when he realized that the woman was so frightened by him that she ran for her life. Like most reflective writers, Staples tries to make himself sympathetic to readers so that they will listen to what he has to say.

Analyze

1. *Reread* the essay looking for places where you get a sense of Staples as a person, and in the margin briefly *describe* the impression you get.
2. *Think about* what engages you or draws you into the essay.

Write

Write several sentences about the impressions you get of Staples from reading this essay, exploring how these impressions affect your interest in his ideas.

Readings

SUZANNE WINCKLER

A Savage Life

Suzanne Winckler (b. 1946) is a freelance writer. She has written several volumes in the Smithsonian Guides to Natural America *series (including* The Plains States *[1998],* The Great Lakes States *[1998], and* The Heartland *[1997]) and has co-authored three books in the Our Endangered Planet series (on* Antarctica *[1992],* Population Growth *[1991], and* Soil *[1993]). In addition, her essays have been published in many newspapers and magazines, such as* Audubon, *the* Atlantic Monthly, *the* Kansas City Star, *and the* New York Times Magazine, *in which "A Savage Life" appeared originally in 1999.*

Before you read Winckler's reflections on killing chickens, think about how distant most of us are from the processes of raising and butchering the food we eat and how that distance might affect our attitudes toward these activities.

1 Every few years I butcher chickens with a friend named Chuck who lives near the farm my husband and I own in northern Minnesota. Chuck buys chicks and takes care of them for the 10 weeks it takes them to mature. I share in the feed costs, but my main contribution — for which I get an equal share of birds — is to help slaughter them.

2 One day last fall, Chuck, two other friends and I butchered 28 chickens. We worked without stopping from 10 A.M. to 6 P.M. By the time it was over we had decapitated, gutted, plucked, cleaned and swaddled each bird in plastic wrap for the freezer. We were exhausted and speckled with blood. For dinner that night we ate vegetables.

3 Butchering chickens is no fun, which is one reason I do it. It is the price I pay for being an omnivore and for eating other meat, like beef and pork, for which I have not yet determined a workable way to kill.

4 The first time I caught a chicken to chop its head off, I noticed, as I cradled it in my arms, that it had the heft and pliability of a newborn baby. This was alarming enough, but when I beheaded it, I was not prepared to be misted in blood or to watch it bounce on the ground. Headless chickens don't run around. They thrash with such force and seeming coordination that they sometimes turn back flips. When I first saw this, three things became clear to me.

I realized why cultures, ancient and contemporary, develop elaborate rituals for coping with the grisly experience of killing any sentient creature. I understood why so many people in my largely bloodless nation are alarmed at the thought of killing anything (except insects) even though they eat with relish meat other people process for them. I saw why a small subset of my contemporaries are so horrified by the thought of inflicting pain and causing death that they maintain people should never kill anything. 5

One risk I run in this self-imposed food-gathering exercise is leaving the impression, or perhaps even furtively feeling, that I am superior to the omnivores who leave the killing of their meat to someone else. I don't think I am. Slaughtering my own chickens is one of two opportunities (gardening is the other) where I can dispense with the layers of anonymous people between me and my food. I have no quarrel with them. I just don't know who they are. They are not part of my story. 6

Killing chickens provides narratives for gathering, cooking and sharing food in a way that buying a Styrofoam package of chicken breasts does not. I remember the weather on the days we have butchered our chickens, and the friends over the years who've come to help, who have included a surgical nurse, a cell biologist, a painter of faux interiors, a Minnesota state representative who is also a logger, a zoologist, a nurse with Head Start and a former Army medic who now runs the physical plant at a large hospital. I can measure the coming of age of my partner's two kids, who were tykes the first time we butchered chickens 10 years ago, and who this go-round were well into puberty with an array of pierced body parts. 7

My mother, who was born in 1907, belonged to the last generation for whom killing one's food was both a necessity and an ordinary event. Her family raised chickens for the purpose of eating them, and her father taught all his children to hunt. My survival does not depend on killing chickens, but in doing so I have found that it fortifies my connection to her. It also allows me to cast a tenuous filament back to my feral past. In 1914, Melvin Gilmore, an ethnobotanist wrote, "In savage and barbarous life the occupation of first importance is the quest of food." Having butchered my own chickens, I now feel acquainted with the savage life. 8

As exhilarating as this may be, I do not thrill at the prospect of beheading chickens. Several days before the transaction, I circle around the idea of what my friends and I will be doing. On the assigned morning, we are slow to get going. There are knives and cleavers to sharpen, vats of water to be boiled in the sauna house, tables and chairs to set up, aprons and buckets to gather, an order of assembly to establish. In their own ritual progression, these 9 preparations are a way to gear ourselves up. I feel my shoulders hunch and my focus is narrow. It is like putting on an invisible veil of resolve to do penance for a misdeed. I am too far gone in my rational Western head to appropriate the ritual of cultures for whom the bloody business of hunting was a matter of survival. But butchering chickens has permitted me to stand in the black night just outside the edge of their campfire, and from that prospect I have inherited the most important lesson of all in the task of killing meat: I have learned to say thank you and I'm sorry.

READING FOR MEANING

Write to create meanings for Winckler's reflections on killing chickens for food.

Start Making Meaning

Begin by listing the three things that Winckler says became clear to her after the first time she beheaded a chicken (paragraph 5). Continue by writing about anything else in the selection or in your experience that contributes to your understanding of Winckler's reflections.

If You Are Stuck

If you cannot write at least a page, consider writing about

- the idea that killing her food connects Winckler to her mother's generation as well as to the more distant past (paragraph 8).
- the ritual Winckler and her friends follow (paragraph 9), perhaps relating Winckler's ritual to other group rituals in which you participate.
- why you think Winckler chooses to butcher the chickens she eats, perhaps speculating on why she does not just become a vegetarian.
- how your own feelings about eating meat help you understand Winckler's choice to participate in this ritual.

READING LIKE A WRITER

PRESENTING THE PARTICULAR OCCASION

Reflections are often triggered by a onetime event or observation. In the previous reading, for example, you saw how Brent Staples started thinking about his subject as a result of a particular event, and how he uses the time marker "late one evening" (paragraph 1) to let readers know this was a onetime event. Later in his essay, however, Staples refers to other occasions to make the point that what he became aware of on that particular night unhappily became a frequent occurrence. Similarly, Winckler begins her essay by referring to a recurring event, something she does "every few years." Then, in paragraph 2, she recounts a particular occasion signaled by the time marker "One day last fall." In paragraph 4, she recalls a second particular occasion, one that happened before the occasion narrated in the second paragraph. This activity will help you analyze the strategies Winckler uses to present these two particular occasions.

Analyze

1. *Look closely* at the occasion presented in paragraph 2. *Underline* the descriptive details and narrative actions Winckler uses to present what happened on this occasion.
2. Now *turn to* the event presented in paragraph 4. *Underline* the descriptive details and narrative actions Winckler uses here to present what happened.
3. *Review* the two events in paragraphs 2 and 4, and *choose* the one that you think makes the greatest impact on you as a reader.

Write

Write several sentences explaining how Winckler's descriptive details and narrative actions give the event you chose its impact. *Support* your explanation with examples from your annotations.

CONSIDERING IDEAS FOR YOUR OWN WRITING

Winckler's reflections may lead you to reflect on your own personal, familial, cultural, or religious traditions regarding food preparation and consumption. Consider any particular occasions you associate with certain kinds of foods. You also might consider reflecting on rituals more generally, such as the "rituals for coping" with painful or distasteful experiences that Winckler mentions in paragraph 5. You could reflect on the ways rituals are used to celebrate important occasions (such as drinking champagne on New Year's Eve), to signify a change in social status (a wedding or graduation), or to mark a significant stage in life (a bar mitzvah, confirmation, or other coming-of-age ceremony). Other subjects you could consider involve history and culture: Following Winckler's lead in calling her mother's "the last generation for whom killing one's food was both a necessity and an ordinary event" (paragraph 8), you could explore differences between your own and preceding generations. Alternatively, you could reflect on how people in the United States or in other countries maintain the kinds of traditions Winckler's mother grew up following.

TONY ADLER

The Grin Game

Tony Adler (b. 1954) teaches drama criticism at DePaul University and has been a theater critic for more than fifteen years for various publications, including the Chicago Tribune *and* Chicago *magazine. A graduate of Carnegie-Mellon University, he is also a published poet and has been an artist in residence at the Chicago Council on Fine Arts.*

In "The Grin Game," written for Chicago *magazine in 1998, Adler reflects on his son's orthodontia. If you wore braces, you might want to take a few minutes before reading the essay to recall your own experience.*

The older of my two sons has been wearing braces for about a year and a half. He's wearing them now, though they may be off by the time you read this. 1

Let's hope so. Let's all get in a circle and pray on it. 2

They were supposed to have come off this past summer. He was assured that he'd be metal-free by the start of seventh grade. But then came that crucial appointment in early August when everything got screwed up. Seems a young orthodontist checked my boy's teeth and told him his treatment was proceeding right on target, only to be overruled by his supervisor. The head man's analysis meant that my boy would spend most of September behind bars. 3

I wasn't present for this disastrous consultation. I was in the waiting room reading magazines. I knew something had gone wrong only when my boy charged past me on his way out the door. 4

Now, my son isn't the maudlin type. You have to cut through a thick layer of bravado and then another of wrath before you can really pierce him. But he was utterly disconsolate when I finally found him in the front seat of our car. Eighteen months of sharp metal! Aching jaws! Torquemadan[1] headgear! Rubber bands! All faithfully, faithfully borne! And now this . . . *betrayal* — made even more bitter by the wryly offered assurance that his braces would have come off on schedule if only he had followed instructions. 5

That was when I began to wonder about this whole orthodontics thing. 6

I could no longer remember what had been so wrong with my son's mouth in the first place. Or why it had seemed so absolutely necessary that he undergo a process that countless 7

[1]*Torquemada:* the Spanish inquisitor general and an expert torturer. *(Ed.)*

human generations had managed to live without. All I knew for sure was that the procedure had been recommended by our son's dentist — a man with a toupee and penchant for voguish therapies who always seemed to have just got back from a ski vacation. He sent us to a colleague who literally videotaped my boy's mouth to take us on a journey through it, stopping here and there to point out formations that would have to be rethought.

8 This orthodontic auteur[2] had big plans, requiring a commitment of many years and lots of money. Basically, he wanted our first-born child. My wife and I found it funny in an appalling sort of way.

9 But we didn't laugh it off completely, did we? It didn't occur to us to think that, like our ancestors, we might manage to live without it, too.

10 Orthodontia corrects malocclusions: irregularities of bite caused by the position of the teeth or the formation of the jaw. Overbites, underbites, off-center bites, rotations, gaps, crowding.

11 Its medical value is mainly preventive. Crowded teeth are harder to clean and therefore more susceptible to decay; teeth that

[2]*auteur:* the author or creative genius behind a work of art. *(Ed.)*

point the wrong way can hinder proper chewing and, consequently, digestion; a misaligned jaw can cause joint pain. I've even read that wayward growth patterns can lead to blocked air passages, causing sleep apnea.

12 But that's the worst of the worst-case scenarios. Though malocclusions don't go away on their own, they don't necessarily trigger serious complications, either — and our boy didn't look to us like somebody whose palate was going to suffocate him. To us simple folk his smile looked interesting. Handsome, even.

13 And yet, no, we didn't laugh it off completely. It's amazing, when you think about it: how hot we were to correct a problem we couldn't see, on the say-so of people we found slightly comical.

14 What's even more amazing is that getting our dentist's say-so was really just a formality. We settled on a well-reputed suburban orthodontist who sat us down and (using low-tech drawings) explained that our son had a mild case of buckteeth complicated by a two-millimeter "midline discrepancy" — a minor misalignment of the upper and lower teeth.

15 He also suggested that intervention now might spare our boy dreadful problems later, but he was just riffing at that point. He needn't have bothered. Braces were a foregone conclusion, a perceived necessity, and the thing we were shopping for wasn't a more precise diagnosis — or a better orthodontist — or even a cheaper price — but an environment in which we could feel comfortable carrying out this rite of passage. We were no more going to let our boy miss braces than his bar mitzvah.

16 My wife and I are hardly the only parents ever to have succumbed to the siren call of orthodontics. According to the Web site promoting Masel Industries, a company that makes "fun" orthodontic products, "Over 70 percent of U.S. teenagers wear braces sometime, including many teenage movie stars." Even without the sleazy Hollywood reference, that's an incredible statistic — suggesting that what was once an elective procedure connoting affluence is now a cultural given.

17 The anecdotal evidence is even stronger: Just try thinking of a kid who isn't under an orthodontist's care. The field isn't limited to teens, either. Despite a lack of conclusive research, a growing orthodontic faction maintains, like the Jesuits, that a mouth is easier to train when you catch it early. Hence grade schoolers are now a growth market for orthodontists.

18 And so are adults. Back when getting braces meant having a clunky band of metal wrapped around each tooth, grownups were less apt to endure the procedure. Now the bands are gone: Compact brackets are affixed directly to the tooth instead. This less obtrusive hardware, and a decline in costs relative to inflation (current prices start at $3,000), has created a boom in braces for

dentally challenged adults — whose poster girl, of course, is Paula Corbin Jones.

19 But improved technology and lower prices alone can't explain orthodontics' new status. Braces still hurt. They still make eating a chore. They still look goofy. And they still take years and years to do the job. You can start seeing an orthodontist before your eighth birthday and never finish till your 24th.

20 And yet we do it, unquestioningly. Why?

21 "The norm in which children are growing up today is different from the norm in which their parents and certainly their grandparents grew up," says Dr. Chester Handelman, a Loop orthodontist and a clinical associate professor of orthodontics at the University of Illinois at Chicago.

22 "When children look at their teeth, they're heavily influenced by what they see in adults, they're influenced by what they see in the advertising media, they're influenced by what they see in their older brothers and sisters, and [orthodontics] becomes . . . psychosocial: having to do with how they feel about themselves in relationship to a social situation."

23 In short, pretty teeth are more than a luxury now. They're an identity.

24 Handelman observes that with more access to orthodontics and other aesthetics-enhancing procedures, the dental bar gets raised higher all the time.

25 Able to discern — and attain — finer and finer degrees of perfection, we find it more difficult to tolerate finer and finer degrees of variation. This worries Handelman and other orthodontists who insist that they have no control over the cosmetic fanaticism exhibited by some of their customers.

26 "It's the patients' goals that are driving the profession and not the profession driving the patients," says Handelman. "It's the patients that are demanding perfection."

27 This claim of helplessness is undoubtedly sincere, coming from a thoughtful man like Handelman. But it also rings hollow in the face of sales pitches like Masel Industries' Web site.

28 The essential fact is that orthodontia invites cosmetic fanaticism by suggesting the possibility of a kind of platonic mouth, flawless in line and proportion. "The ideal set of teeth," declares one medical dictionary, "are straight, regularly spaced with neither overlap nor gaps, and exactly the right size for the jaws. The occlusion . . . is such that the upper teeth slightly overlap the lower teeth and the points (cusps) of the molars mesh with the spaces between opposing teeth." The tone of this passage puts me in mind of the Renaissance courtier Baldassare Castiglione, defining perfect love.

29 What parent would deny his child a shot at such perfection? What parent would condemn his baby to a life of second-tier jobs and dumpy lovers, when the antidote is available?

30 "In the era of the absolute image," declared Joan Juliet Buck in a recent *New Yorker* story about Princess Diana,[3] "imperfections of the body are sins." It follows that naughty children without braces go to absolute-image hell.

31 And that being so, it's no wonder my wife and I never thought twice about redesigning our boy's mouth. Even now, we can't bring ourselves to resist: Our second son has buckteeth as bad as his brother's. There's no doubt in my mind that he'll get braces when the time comes.

32 Still, every once in a while I think of certain beloved sinners like my mother, who never had orthodontia and went through life with a pronounced gap between her two front teeth. Mom never looked all that tormented to me. Just the opposite: Her unreconstructed smile expressed the vivacity and mischief that were part of her character. And she flashed it often. Evidently, imperfection suited her.

33 Perfection, on the other hand, can be an awful burden. There's a beautiful young woman I know with a gorgeous smile. She told me she had been happy to get braces — overjoyed — because of the marvelous transformation she knew they would work on her. After a couple of years, the braces came off and she hurried to the mirror. What she saw was a disappointment. Sure, her smile was big and full and bright. It's just that she had imagined something better.

READING FOR MEANING

Write to create meanings for Adler's reflections on orthodontia and the quest for perfection.

Start Making Meaning

Begin by summarizing the medical reasons for having orthodontia. Continue by writing about anything else in the selection or in your experience that contributes to your understanding of Adler's reflections.

If You Are Stuck

If you cannot write at least a page, consider writing about

- the idea that having braces is a "rite of passage" (paragraph 15).
- the idea that "pretty teeth are more than a luxury now. They're an identity" (paragraph 23).

[3]Diana suffered from an eating disorder. *(Ed.)*

- what the cartoon drawing adds to your understanding of Adler's reflections.
- your own experience with orthodontia or other ways to perfect your body, exploring how your experience helps you think about Adler's reflections in this essay.

READING LIKE A WRITER

ENGAGING READERS

Knowing that they have to attract readers' interest, reflective writers try to present the particular occasion for their reflections in a dramatic or otherwise engaging way. Sometimes they use the title of their essay to attract readers (like Barbara Ehrenreich's surprising question "Are Families Dangerous?" in the following selection). Or they may compose an arresting opening sentence (such as Wendy Lee's "When my friend told me that her father had once compared her to a banana, I stared at her blankly" later in this chapter). Adler's primary strategy to engage readers in his reflection is to use humor — directed at others as well as at himself.

Analyze

1. *Reread* the essay, noting in the margin places where you think Adler uses humor. *Identify* where he turns the humor on others and where he turns it on himself.
2. *Reflect* on how Adler's uses of humor affects your willingness to read his essay and your openness to his ideas.

Write

Write several sentences explaining what you have learned from Adler's essay about using humor to engage readers. *Support* your explanation with examples from the reading.

CONSIDERING IDEAS FOR YOUR OWN WRITING

Adler's essay suggests many different subjects for reflection. An obvious subject is perfections, the idea that we are in an "era of the absolute image" (paragraph 30). Jumping off of Adler's comments about his "orthodontic auteur" (paragraph 8), you could write about experts (in any field) or you could focus on attitudes about expertise, especially in medical or other emergencies. Another subject suggested by this essay is fads, what Adler calls "voguish therapies" in health or diet (paragraph 7). Finally, you might reflect on what parents do to or require from their children — such as taking sports like Little League baseball too seriously or insisting that their teenagers attend college or work an after-school or summer job.

BARBARA EHRENREICH

Are Families Dangerous?

Barbara Ehrenreich (b. 1941) is the author of many books, including Fear of Falling: The Inner Life of the Middle Class *(1989),* The Worst Years of Our Lives: Irreverent Notes from a Decade of Greed *(1990), and* Blood Rites: Origins and History of the Passions of War *(1997). Her essays have appeared in such journals and magazines as* American Scholar, Atlantic Monthly, *and* New Republic, *and. she writes a weekly column for* Time *magazine and the* Guardian, *a British newspaper.*

The following essay was published in Time *in 1994. The occasion for Ehrenreich's reflections is three well-publicized cases of family violence: Brothers Erik and Lyle Menendez, convicted of murdering their parents, claimed their parents abused them; Lorena Bobbitt cut off her husband's penis because he abused her; and O. J. Simpson abused his wife, Nicole, but was found not guilty of murdering her.*

As you read, notice how Ehrenreich weaves these cases in and out of her reflections about how dangerous, even deadly, some families can be. You will find yourself drawn into intense reflection about your own family and into evaluation of Ehrenreich's ideas.

1 A disturbing subtext runs through our recent media fixations. Parents abuse sons — allegedly at least, in the Menendez case — who in turn rise up and kill them. A husband torments a wife, who retaliates with a kitchen knife. Love turns into obsession, between the Simpsons anyway, and then perhaps into murderous rage: the family, in other words, becomes personal hell.

2 This accounts for at least part of our fascination with the Bobbitts and the Simpsons and the rest of them. We live in a culture that fetishes the family as the ideal unit of human community, the perfect container for our lusts and loves. Politicians of both parties are aggressively "pro-family," even abortion-rights bumper stickers proudly link "pro-family" and "pro-choice." Only with the occasional celebrity crime do we allow ourselves to think the nearly unthinkable: that the family may not be the ideal and perfect living arrangement after all — that it can be a nest of pathology and a cradle of gruesome violence.

3 It's a scary thought, because the family is at the same time our "haven in a heartless world." Theoretically, and sometimes actually, the family nurtures warm, loving feelings, uncontaminated by greed or power hunger. Within the family, and often only within the family, individuals are loved "for themselves," whether or not they are infirm, incontinent, infantile or eccentric. The

strong (adults and especially males) lie down peaceably with the small and weak.

4 But consider the matter of wife battery. We managed to dodge it in the Bobbitt case and downplay it as a force in Tonya Harding's life. Thanks to O. J., though, we're caught up now in a mass consciousness-raising session, grimly absorbing the fact that in some areas domestic violence sends as many women to emergency rooms as any other form of illness, injury or assault.

5 Still, we shrink from the obvious inference: for a woman, home is, statistically speaking, the most dangerous place to be. Her worst enemies and potential killers are not strangers but lovers, husbands and those who claimed to love her once. Similarly, for every child like Polly Klaas who is killed by a deranged criminal on parole, dozens are abused and murdered by their own relatives. Home is all too often where the small and weak fear to lie down and shut their eyes.

6 At some deep, queasy, Freudian level, we all know this. Even in the ostensibly "functional," nonviolent family, where no one is killed or maimed, feelings are routinely bruised and often twisted out of shape. There is the slap or put-down that violates a child's shaky sense of self, the cold, distracted stare that drives a spouse to tears, the little digs and rivalries. At best, the family teaches the finest things human beings can learn from one another — generosity and love. But it is also, all too often, where we learn nasty things like hate and rage and shame.

7 Americans act out their ambivalence about the family without ever owning up to it. Millions adhere to creeds that are militantly "pro-family." But at the same time millions flock to therapy groups that offer to heal the "inner child" from damage inflicted by family life. Legions of women band together to revive the self-esteem they lost in supposedly loving relationships and to learn to love a little less. We are all, it is often said, "in recovery." And from what? Our families, in most cases.

8 There is a long and honorable tradition of "anti-family" thought. The French philosopher Charles Fourier taught that the family was a barrier to human progress; early feminists saw a degrading parallel between marriage and prostitution. More recently, the renowned British anthropologist Edmund Leach stated that "far from being the basis of the good society, the family, with its narrow privacy and tawdry secrets, is the source of all discontents."

9 Communes proved harder to sustain than plain old couples, and the conservatism of the '80s crushed the last vestiges of lifestyle experimentation. Today even gays and lesbians are eager to get married and take up family life. Feminists have learned to

couch their concerns as "family issues," and public figures would sooner advocate free cocaine on demand than criticize the family. Hence our unseemly interest in O. J. and Erik, Lyle and Lorena: they allow us, however gingerly, to break the silence on the hellish side of family life.

10 But the discussion needs to become a lot more open and forthright. We may be stuck with the family — at least until someone invents a sustainable alternative — but the family, with its deep, impacted tensions and longings, can hardly be expected to be the moral foundation of everything else. In fact, many families could use a lot more outside interference in the form of counseling and policing, and some are so dangerously dysfunctional that they ought to be encouraged to disband right away. Even healthy families need outside sources of moral guidance to keep the internal tensions from imploding — and this means, at the very least, a public philosophy of gender equality and concern for child welfare. When, instead, the larger culture aggrandizes wife beaters, degrades women or nods approvingly at child slappers, the family gets a little more dangerous for everyone, and so, inevitably, does the larger world.

READING FOR MEANING

Write to create meanings for Ehrenreich's reflections on the dangers in families.

Start Making Meaning

Begin by listing the dangers in families that Ehrenreich implies or states in paragraphs 1–6. Continue by writing about anything else in the selection or in your experience that contributes to your understanding of Ehrenreich's reflections.

If You Are Stuck

If you cannot write at least a page, consider writing about

- the advice Ehrenreich gives in her conclusion (paragraph 10), where she restates her main points about the dangers in families and comments on how to minimize them.
- the ideas of the "anti-family" thinkers (paragraph 8), restating their arguments, giving your reaction, and supporting your views with comments and examples.

- the reaction you think Ehrenreich expects to get from her readers, supporting your hunches with details or quotations from the reading.
- the extent to which your experience with a family (your own or one you know) supports or does not support Ehrenreich's ideas.

READING LIKE A WRITER

MAINTAINING TOPICAL COHERENCE

Because writers of reflective essays aim to try out ideas, their essays may appear organized by a "first I had this idea and then I had another idea" principle. The reflective essay therefore may seem rambling and loosely organized, and yet readers seldom become confused. They are able to track the writer's meandering thoughts without getting derailed because of the ways writers maintain topical coherence. As we saw earlier in the essay by Brent Staples, one of the main ways writers establish topical coherence is by repeating a key word or phrase related to the general subject. Recall that Staples writes about the fear his mere presence engenders in others merely because of his race and gender. This activity will help you analyze the way Ehrenreich uses word repetition to help her readers keep in mind and never lose track of her central subject: the family.

Analyze

1. *Skim* Ehrenreich's essay, underlining each instance of the word *family* or *families.*
2. In paragraphs 4 and 5, where the word *family* does not appear, *underline* any words that you associate with family.

Write

Write several sentences reporting what you have learned about Ehrenreich's use of word repetition to maintain topical coherence. *Cite examples* from the reading.

A SPECIAL READING STRATEGY

Outlining

Outlining can be an especially useful strategy for reading reflective essays because they tend to pile up ideas and examples, often in a seemingly random order. Making a scratch outline of Ehrenreich's essay, identifying the main idea in each paragraph, will help you discover what she is saying about families. For help with outlining, see Appendix 1, pages 527–29.

CONSIDERING IDEAS FOR YOUR OWN WRITING

Ehrenreich's essay suggests several different kinds of subjects you might consider. For example, she points out that families in reality seldom live up to our idea of the perfect family. You could reflect on something else that falls short of expectations. Think of an experience you have had that was disappointing, such as a conflict with a friend, co-worker, or sibling; a job, class, or school that turned out to be less satisfying than you had hoped; a type of new technology that had great promise but was full of bugs. Ehrenreich mentions other subjects you could explore in your own reflective essay, such as "a child's shaky sense of self" (paragraph 6). Your own experience as a child might suggest a particular occasion you could use to reflect on how children develop a sense of individuality and self-worth. You could also explore your ideas of what an ideal society would be like and perhaps reflect on where your ideas about the ideal society come from.

IAN FRAZIER

Dearly Disconnected

Ian Frazier (b. 1951) wrote for the satirical Harvard Lampoon *when he was a student at Harvard and then went on to become a staff writer for the* New Yorker. *He has written many books, including* Family *(1994),* Coyote vs. Acme *(1996), and* Lamentation of the Father *(2000), and has edited two important collections,* The Best American Essays: 1997 *(1997) and* They Went: The Art and Craft of Travel Writing *(1991). His most recent book,* On the Rez *(2000), reflects on contemporary life on an Indian reservation.*

In "Dearly Disconnected," originally published in Mother Jones *in 2000, Frazier reflects on the loss of public pay phones. Before you read, think about your own experiences and associations with this "almost-vanished" form of technology.*

Before I got married I was living by myself in an A-frame cabin in northwestern Montana. The cabin's interior was a single high-ceilinged room, and at the center of the room, mounted on the rough-hewn log that held up the ceiling beam, was a telephone. I knew no one in the area or indeed the whole state, so my entire social life came to me through that phone. The woman I would marry was living in Sarasota, Florida, and the distance between us suggests how well we were getting along at the time. We had not been in touch for several months; she had no phone. One day she decided to call me from a pay phone. We talked for a while, and after her coins ran out I jotted the number on the wood beside my phone and called her back. A day or two later, thinking about the call, I wanted to talk to her again. The only number I had for her was the pay phone number I'd written down. 1

The pay phone was on the street some blocks from the apartment where she stayed. As it happened, though, she had just stepped out to do some errands a few minutes before I called, and she was passing by on the sidewalk when the phone rang. She had no reason to think that a public phone ringing on a busy street would be for her. She stopped, listened to it ring again, and picked up the receiver. Love is pure luck; somehow I had known she would answer, and she had known it would be me. 2

Long afterwards, on a trip to Disney World in Orlando with our two kids, then aged six and two, we made a special detour to Sarasota to show them the pay phone. It didn't impress them much. It's just a nondescript Bell Atlantic pay phone on the cement wall of a building, by the vestibule. But its ordinariness and 3 even boringness only make me like it more; ordinary places where extraordinary events have occurred are my favorite kind. On my mental map of Florida that pay phone is a landmark looming above the city it occupies, and a notable, if private, historic site.

4 I'm interested in pay phones in general these days, especially when I get the feeling that they are about to go away. Technology, in the form of sleek little phones in our pockets, has swept on by them and made them begin to seem antique. My lifelong entanglement with pay phones dates me. When I was young they were just there, a given, often as stubborn and uncongenial as the curbstone underfoot. They were instruments of torture sometimes. You had to feed them fistfuls of change in those pre-phone-card days, and the operator was a real person who stood maddeningly between you and whomever you were trying to call. And when the call went wrong, as communication often does, the pay phone gave you a focus for your rage. Pay phones were always getting smashed up, the receivers shattered to bits against the booth, the coin slots jammed with chewing gum, the cords yanked out and unraveled to the floor.

5 You used to hear people standing at pay phones and cursing them. I remember the sound of my own frustrated shouting confined by the glass walls of a phone booth — the kind you don't see much anymore, with a little ventilating fan in the ceiling that turned on when you shut the double-hinged glass door. The noise that fan made in the silence of a phone booth was for a while the essence of romantic, lonely-guy melancholy for me. Certain specific pay phones I still resent for the unhappiness they caused me, and others I will never forgive, though not for any fault of their own. In the C concourse of the Salt Lake City airport there's a row of pay phones set on the wall by the men's room just past the concourse entry. While on a business trip a few years ago, I called home from a phone in that row and learned that a friend had collapsed in her apartment and was in the hospital with brain cancer. I had liked those pay phones before, and had used them often; now I can't even look at them when I go by.

6 There was always a touch of seediness and sadness to pay phones, and a sense of transience. Drug dealers made calls from them, and shady types who did not want their whereabouts known, and otherwise respectable people planning assignations, and people too poor to have phones of their own. In the movies, any character who used a pay phone was either in trouble or contemplating a crime. Pay phones came with their own special atmospherics and even accessories sometimes — the predictable bad smells and graffiti, of course, as well as cigarette butts, soda

cans, scattered pamphlets from the Jehovah's Witnesses, and single bottles of beer (empty) still in their individual, street-legal paper bags. Mostly, pay phones evoked the mundane: "Honey, I'm just leaving. I'll be there soon." But you could tell that a lot of undifferentiated humanity had flowed through these places, and that in the muteness of each pay phone's little space, wild emotion had howled.

Once, when I was living in Brooklyn, I read in the newspaper that a South American man suspected of dozens of drug-related contract murders had been arrested at a pay phone in Queens. Police said that the man had been on the phone setting up a murder at the time of his arrest. The newspaper story gave the address of the pay phone, and out of curiosity one afternoon I took a long walk to Queens to take a look at it. It was on an undistinguished street in a middle-class neighborhood, by a florist's shop. By the time I saw it, however, the pay phone had been blown up and/or firebombed. I had never before seen a pay phone so damaged; explosives had blasted pieces of the phone itself wide open in metal shreds like frozen banana peels, and flames had blackened everything and melted the plastic parts and burned the insulation off the wires. Soon after, I read that police could not find enough evidence against the suspected murderer and so had let him go. 7

The cold phone outside a shopping center in Bigfork, Montana, from which I called a friend in the West Indies one winter when her brother was sick; the phone on the wall of the concession stand at Redwood Pool, where I used to stand dripping and call my mom to come and pick me up; the sweaty phones used almost only by men in the hallway outside the maternity ward at Lenox Hill Hospital in New York; the phone by the driveway of the Red Cloud Indian School in South Dakota where I used to talk with my wife while priests in black slacks and white socks chatted on a bench nearby; the phone in the old wood-paneled phone booth with leaded glass windows in the drugstore in my Ohio hometown — each one is as specific as a birthmark, a point on earth unlike any other. Recently I went back to New York City after a long absence and tried to find a working pay phone. I picked up one receiver after the next without success. Meanwhile, as I scanned down the long block, I counted half a dozen or more pedestrians talking on their cell phones. 8

It's the cell phone, of course, that's putting the pay phone out of business. The pay phone is to the cell phone as the troubled and difficult older sibling is to the cherished newborn. People even treat their cell phones like babies, cradling them in their palms and beaming down upon them lovingly as they dial. You 9 sometimes hear people yelling on their cell phones, but almost never yelling at them. Cell phones are toylike, nearly magic, and we get a huge kick out of them, as often happens with technological advances until the new wears off. Somehow I don't believe people had a similar honeymoon period with pay phones back in their early days, and they certainly have no such enthusiasm for them now. When I see a cell-phone user gently push the little antenna and fit the phone back into its brushed-vinyl carrying case and tuck the case inside his jacket beside his heart, I feel sorry for the beat-up pay phone standing in the rain.

10 People almost always talk on cell phones while in motion — driving, walking down the street, riding on a commuter train. The cell phone took the transience the pay phone implied and turned it into VIP-style mobility and speed. Even sitting in a restaurant, the person on a cell phone seems importantly busy and on the move. Cell-phone conversations seem to be unlimited by ordinary constraints of place and time, as if they represent an almost-perfect form of communication whose perfect state would be telepathy.

11 And yet no matter how we factor the world away, it remains. I think this is what drives me so nuts when a person sitting next to me on a bus makes a call from her cell phone. Yes, this busy and important caller is at no fixed point in space, but nevertheless I happen to be beside her. The job of providing physical context falls on me; I become her call's surroundings, as if I'm the phone booth wall. For me to lean over and comment on her cell-phone conversation would be as unseemly and unexpected as if I were in fact a wall; and yet I have no choice, as a sentient person, but to hear what my chatty fellow traveler has to say.

12 Some middle-aged guys like me go around complaining about this kind of thing. The more sensible approach is just to accept it and forget about it, because there's not much we can do. I don't think that pay phones will completely disappear. Probably they will survive for a long while as clumsy old technology still of some use to those lagging behind, and as a backup if ever the superior systems should temporarily fail. Before pay phones became endangered I never thought of them as public spaces, which of course they are. They suggested a human average; they belonged to anybody who had a couple of coins. Now I see that, like public schools and public transportation, pay phones belong to a former commonality our culture is no longer quite so sure it needs.

13 I have a weakness for places — for old battlefields, car-crash sites, houses where famous authors lived. Bygone passions should always have an address, it seems to me. Ideally, the world would

be covered with plaques and markers listing the notable events that occurred at each particular spot. A sign on every pay phone would describe how a woman broke up with her fiance here, how a young ballplayer learned that he had made the team. Unfortunately, the world itself is fluid, and changes out from under us; the rocky islands that the pilot Mark Twain was careful to avoid in the Mississippi are now stone outcroppings in a soybean field. Meanwhile, our passions proliferate into illegibility, and the places they occur can't hold them. Eventually pay phones will become relics of an almost-vanished landscape, and of a time when there were fewer of us and our stories were on an earlier page. Romantics like me will have to reimagine our passions as they are — unmoored to earth, like an infinitude of cell-phone messages flying through the atmosphere.

READING FOR MEANING

Write to create meanings for Frazier's reflections on public pay phones.

Start Making Meaning

Begin by explaining why you think Frazier is saddened by the loss of public pay phones. Continue by writing about anything else in the selection or in your experience that contributes to your understanding of Frazier's reflections.

If You Are Stuck

If you cannot write at least a page, consider writing about

- your understanding of and reactions to Frazier's nostalgic "weakness for places" (paragraph 13).
- how characters in movies contribute to Frazier's association of pay phones with "seediness and sadness" (paragraph 6).
- Frazier's idea that pay phones are "public spaces" and what he means when he writes that "like public schools and public transportation, pay phones belong to a former commonality our culture is no longer quite so sure it needs" (paragraph 12). (If you have read the essay by Brent Staples, you might compare Frazier's and Staples's ideas about "public space.")
- your own experience of "ordinary places where extraordinary events have occurred" (paragraph 3), indicating how your experience helps you understand Frazier's reflections.

READING LIKE A WRITER

DEVELOPING THE REFLECTIONS THROUGH EXAMPLES

Writers rely on a number of essential strategies to develop their reflections, perhaps the most common one being illustration or example. Like Brent Staples, Frazier relies on both brief examples and extended example to illustrate and explain his ideas. In the last sentence of paragraph 4; for instance, Frazier gives a series of brief examples to explain what he means in the opening clause: "Pay phones were always getting smashed up, the receivers shattered to bits against the booth, the coin slots jammed with chewing gum, the cords yanked out and unraveled to the floor." On the other hand, Frazier uses an extended example in paragraphs 1–3 to introduce his reflections on pay phones in general.

Analyze

1. *Reread* paragraphs 5–8, noting in the margin the examples Frazier gives. In your marginal notes, *distinguish* the brief examples from the extended examples.
2. *Underline* the general statement that each example is meant to illustrate.

Write

Write several sentences explaining what you have learned about how Frazier uses brief and extended examples to develop his reflections.

CONSIDERING IDEAS FOR YOUR OWN WRITING

Like Frazier's reflections on pay phones, you might consider a particular occasion or general subject involving an everyday object that people usually take for granted, using your experiences or observations to reflect on the cars people drive, the appliances they buy, or the homes they live in. Or following Frazier's suggestion that movies influenced his ideas about pay phones, you might reflect on a particular movie or a group of movies that influenced the way people think of a particular part of the country, like New York City or the Midwest, or a certain kind of work, such as the practice of law or medicine. Another possibility suggested by Frazier's essay is to reflect on how things have changed over time. Consider changes you have witnessed, such as those in technology, music, recreation, and styles of dress.

WENDY LEE

Peeling Bananas

Wendy Lee wrote the following essay when she was a high-school student, and in 1993 it was published in Chinese American Forum, *a quarterly journal of news and opinion. In the essay, Lee reflects on growing up in America as the child of parents born in China. While she focuses mainly on going to school, her interest is larger: to discover how she can be American without losing the knowledge and experience of her Chinese heritage.*

As you read, reflect on how you might hold on to the special qualities of your family or ethnic group while at the same time becoming part of a larger regional or national community.

When my friend told me that her father had once compared her to a banana, I stared at her blankly. Then I realized that her father must have meant that outside she had the yellow skin of a Chinese, but inside she was white like an American. In other words, her appearance was Chinese, but her thoughts and values were American. Looking at my friend in her American clothes with her perfectly straight black hair and facial features so much like my own, I laughed. Her skin was no more yellow than mine. 1

In kindergarten, we colored paper dolls: red was for Indians, black for Afro-Americans, yellow was for Chinese. The dolls that we didn't color at all — the white ones — were left to be Americans. But the class wanted to know where were the green, blue or purple people? With the paper dolls, our well-meaning teacher intended to emphasize that everyone is basically the same, despite skin color. Secretly I wondered why the color of my skin wasn't the shade of my yellow Crayola. After we colored the dolls, we stamped each one with the same vacant, smiley face. The world, according to our teacher, is populated by happy, epidermically diverse people. 2

What does it mean to be a Chinese in an American school? One thing is to share a last name with a dozen other students, so that you invariably squirm when roll-call is taken. It means never believing that the fairy-tales the teacher read during story time could ever happen to you, because you don't have skin as white as snow or long golden hair. "You're Chinese?" I remember one classmate saying. "Oh, I *really* like Chinese food." In the depths of her over-friendly eyes I saw fried egg-rolls and chow mein. Once, for show-and-tell, a girl proudly told the class that one of her ancestors was in the picture of George Washington crossing the 3

Delaware. I promptly countered that by thinking to myself, "Well, my grandfather was Sun Yat-Sen's[1] physician, so THERE."

4 In my home, there is always a rather haphazard combination of the past and present. Next to the scrolls of black ink calligraphy on the dining room wall is a calendar depicting scenes from the midwest; underneath the stacked Chinese newspapers, the *L.A. Times*. In the refrigerator, next to the milk and butter, are tofu and bok choy from the weekly trips to the local Chinese supermarket. Spoons are used for soup, forks for salad, but chopsticks are reserved for the main course. I never noticed the disparity between my lifestyle and that of white Americans — until I began school. There, I became acquainted with children of strictly Caucasian heritage and was invited to their homes. Mentally I always compared the interiors of their homes to my own and to those of my mother's Chinese friends. What struck me was that their homes seemed to have no trace of their heritages at all. But nearly all Chinese-American homes retain aspects of the Chinese culture; aspects that reflect the yearning for returning home Chinese immigrants always have.

5 Chinese immigrants like my parents have an unwavering faith in China's potential to truly become the "middle kingdom," the literal translation of the Chinese words for China. They don't want their first-generation children to forget the way their ancestors lived. They don't want their children to forget that China has a heritage spanning thousands of years, while America has only a paltry two hundred. My mother used to tape Chinese characters over the words in our picture books. Ungratefully my sister and I tore them off because we were more interested in seeing how the story turned out. When she showed us her satin Chinese dresses, we were more interested in playing dress-up than in the stories behind the dresses; when she taught us how to use chopsticks, we were more concentrated on eating the Chinese delicacies she had prepared. (Incidentally, I still have to remind myself how to hold my chopsticks properly, though this may merely be a personal fault; I can't hold a pencil properly either.)

6 After those endless sessions with taped-over books and flashcards, my mother packed us off to Chinese School. There, we were to benefit from interaction with other Chinese-American children in the same predicament — unable to speak, read, or write Chinese nicely. There, we were supposed to make the same progress we made in our American schools. But in its own way,

[1]*Sun Yat-Sen* (1866–1925): revolutionary leader of China and first president of the Chinese Republic (1911–1912). (*Ed.*)

Chinese School is as much of a banana as are Chinese-Americans. A Chinese School day starts and ends with a bow to the teacher to show proper reverence. In the intervening three hours, the students keep one eye on the mysterious symbols of Chinese characters on the blackboard and the other on the clock. Their voices may be obediently reciting a lesson, but silently they are urging the minute hand to go faster. Chinese is taught through the American way, with workbooks and homework and tests. Without distinctive methods to make the experience memorable and worthwhile for its students, Chinese School, too, is in danger of becoming completely Americanized. Chinese-American kids, especially those in their teens, have become bewitched by the American ideal of obtaining a career that makes lots and lots of money. Their Chinese heritage probably doesn't play a big part in their futures. Many Chinese-Americans are even willing to shed their skins in favor of becoming completely American. Certainly it is easier to go forward and become completely American than to regress and become completely Chinese in America.

7 Sometimes I imagine what it would be like to go back to Taiwan or mainland China. Through eyes misty with romantic sentiment, I can look down a crooked, stone-paved street where a sea of black-haired and slanted-eyed people are bicycling in tandem. I see factories where people are hunch-backed over tables to manufacture plastic toys and American flags. I see fog-enshrouded mountains of Guilin, the yellow mud of Yangtze River, and the Great Wall of China snaking across the landscape as it does in the pages of a *National Geographic* magazine. When I look up at the moon, I don't see the pale, impersonal sphere that I see here in America. Instead, I see the plaintive face of Chang-Oh, the moon goddess. When I look up at the moon, I may miss my homeland like the famous poet Li Bai did in the poem that every Chinese School student can recite. But will that homeland be America or China?

8 When the crooked street is empty with no bicycles, I see a girl standing across from me on the other side of the street. I see mirrored in her the same perfectly straight black hair and facial features that my Chinese-American friend has, or the same that I have. We cannot communicate, for I only know pidgin Mandarin whereas she speaks fluent Cantonese, a dialect of southern China. Not only is the difference of language a barrier, but the differences in the way we were brought up and the way we live. Though we look the same, we actually are of different cultures, and I may cross the street into her world but only as a visitor. However, I also realize that as a hybrid of two cultures, I am unique, and perhaps that uniqueness should be preserved.

READING FOR MEANING

Write to create meanings for Lee's reflections on the difficulties of embracing two different cultures.

Start Making Meaning

Begin by restating briefly the occasion for Lee's reflections and by listing two or three experiences by which Lee remains aware of her Chinese ethnicity. Continue by writing about anything else in the selection or in your experience that contributes to your understanding of Lee's reflections.

If You Are Stuck

If you cannot write at least a page, consider writing about

- the traces of Lee's Chinese heritage that she encounters at home, perhaps comparing them to the signs of your ethnic heritage (African, Mexican, Italian, Cambodian, German, or some other) in your home.
- the insights that occur to Lee as she imagines a trip to Taiwan or China (paragraphs 7 and 8).
- Lee's assumption that there is a white American ethnicity or culture that stands in contrast to Chinese ethnicity.
- your personal experience of feeling different ethnically or in some other way, comparing it to Lee's experience.

READING LIKE A WRITER

DEVELOPING REFLECTIONS THROUGH COMPARISON AND CONTRAST

In reflective writing, insights and ideas are central; yet writers cannot merely list ideas, regardless of how fresh and daring their ideas might be. Instead, writers must work imaginatively to develop their ideas, to explain and elaborate them, to view them from one angle and then another. One well-established way to develop ideas is through comparison and contrast.

Analyze

1. *Review* the comparisons and contrasts in paragraphs 4, 6, and 8 of Lee's essay.
2. *Choose one* of these paragraphs to analyze more closely. What exactly is being compared or contrasted? *Underline* details that highlight the comparisons and contrasts.

Write

Write several sentences describing how Lee uses comparisons and contrasts to develop her ideas. From the one paragraph you chose to analyze, *identify* the terms (the items being compared) of the comparison or contrast and the ideas they enable Lee to develop.

Compare

Reread paragraphs 9–10 of Ian Frazier's essay about public pay phones (pp. 158–59). *Underline* the details that highlight the comparisons and contrasts Frazier makes. Then *write* several sentences comparing Frazier's and Lee's uses of comparison and contrast to develop their reflections.

CONSIDERING IDEAS FOR YOUR OWN WRITING

Consider reflecting on your own ethnicity, beginning the essay, like Lee does, with a concrete occasion. If you are among the "white Caucasians" Lee mentions, you may doubt that you have an ethnicity in the sense that Lee has one. Consider, however, that Asians do not comprise a single ethnicity. Among Asian Americans, there are many distinctly different ethnicities, as defined by their countries or regions of origin: Chinese, Japanese, Korean, Cambodian, Vietnamese, and Philippine, among others. "White Caucasians" also represent many national origins: German (still the single largest American immigrant group), Swedish, Russian, Polish, Irish, Italian, British, Greek, and French, to mention only a few. In all of these immigrant groups, as well as others, intermarriage and acculturation to whatever is uniquely American have blurred many of the original ethnic distinctions. Nevertheless, Lee's reflections remind us of the likelihood that in nearly every American family there remain remnants of one or more national or regional ethnicities. This idea for writing invites you to reflect on whatever meanings remain for you personally in your ethnic identities.

KATHERINE HAINES

Whose Body Is This?

Katherine Haines wrote this essay for an assignment in her first-year college composition course. As the title suggests, the writer reflects on her dismay and anger about American society's obsession with the perfect body — especially the perfect female body. As you read, note the many kinds of details Haines uses to develop her reflections.

The other readings in this chapter are followed by reading and writing activities. Following this reading, however, you are on your own to decide how to read for meaning and read like a writer.

1 *"Hey Rox, what's up? Do you wanna go down to the pool with me? It's a gorgeous day."*

2 *"No thanks, you go ahead without me."*

3 *"What? Why don't you want to go? You've got the day off work, and what else are you going to do?"*

4 *"Well, I've got a bunch of stuff to do around the house . . . pay the bills, clean the bathroom, you know. Besides, I don't want to have to see myself in a bathing suit — I'm so fat."*

5 Why do so many women seem obsessed with their weight and body shape? Are they really that unhappy and dissatisfied with themselves? Or are these women continually hearing from other people that their bodies are not acceptable?

6 In today's society, the expectations for women and their bodies are all too evident. Fashion, magazines, talk shows, "lite" and fat-free food in stores and restaurants, and diet centers are all daily reminders of these expectations. For instance, the latest fashions for women reveal more and more skin: shorts have become shorter, to the point of being scarcely larger than a pair of underpants, and the bustier, which covers only a little more skin than a bra, is making a comeback. These styles are only flattering on the slimmest of bodies, and many women who were previously happy with their bodies may emerge from the dressing room after a run-in with these styles and decide that it must be diet time again. Instead of coming to the realization that these clothes are unflattering for most women, how many women will simply look for different and more flattering styles, and how many women will end up heading for the gym to burn off some more calories or to the bookstore to buy the latest diet book?

7 When I was in junior high, about two-thirds of the girls I knew were on diets. Everyone was obsessed with fitting into the smallest

size miniskirt possible. One of my friends would eat a carrot stick, a celery stick, and two rice cakes for lunch. Junior high (and the onset of adolescence) seemed to be the beginning of the pressure for most women. It is at this age that appearance suddenly becomes important. Especially for those girls who want to be "popular" and those who are cheerleaders or on the drill team. The pressure is intense; some girls believe no one will like them or accept them if they are "overweight," even by a pound or two. The measures these girls will take to attain the body that they think will make them acceptable are often debilitating and life threatening.

8 My sister was on the drill team in junior high. My sister wanted to fit in with the right crowd — and my sister drove herself to the edge of becoming anorexic. I watched as she came home from school, having eaten nothing for breakfast and at lunch only a bag of pretzels and an apple (and she didn't always finish that), and began pacing the oriental carpet that was in our living room. Around and around and around, without a break, from four o'clock until dinnertime, which was usually at six or seven o'clock. And then at dinner, she would take minute portions and only pick at her food. After several months of this, she became much paler and thinner, but not in any sort of attractive sense. Finally, after catching a cold and having to stay in bed for three days because she was so weak, she was forced to go to the doctor. The doctor said she was suffering from malnourishment and was to stay in bed until she regained some of her strength. He advised her to eat lots of fruits and vegetables until the bruises all over her body had healed (these were a result of vitamin deficiency). Although my sister did not develop anorexia, it was frightening to see what she had done to herself. She had little strength, and the bruises she had made her look like an abused child.

9 This mania to lose weight and have the "ideal" body is not easily avoided in our society. It is created by television and magazines as they flaunt their models and latest diet crazes in front of our faces. And then there are the Nutri-System and Jenny Craig commercials, which show hideous "before" pictures and glamorous "after" pictures and have smiling, happy people dancing around and talking about how their lives have been transformed simply because they have lost weight. This propaganda that happiness is in large part based on having the "perfect" body shape is a message that the media constantly sends to the public. No one seems to be able to escape it.

10 My mother and father were even sucked in by this idea. One evening, when I was in the fifth grade, I heard Mom and Dad

calling me into the kitchen. Oh no, what had I done now? It was never good news when you got summoned into the kitchen alone. As I walked into the kitchen, Mom looked up at me with an anxious expression; Dad was sitting at the head of the table with a pen in hand and a yellow legal pad in front of him. They informed me that I was going on a diet. A diet!? I wanted to scream at them, "I'm only ten years old, why do I have to be on a diet?" I was so embarrassed, and I felt so guilty. Was I really fat? I guess so, I thought, otherwise why would my parents do this to me?

11 It seems that this obsession with the perfect body and a woman's appearance has grown to monumental heights. It is ironic, however, that now many people feel that this problem is disappearing. People have begun to assume that women want to be thin because they just want to be "healthy." But what has happened is that the sickness slips in under the guise of wanting a "healthy" body. The demand for thin bodies is anything but "healthy." How many anorexics or bulimics have you seen that are healthy?

12 It is strange that women do not come out and object to society's pressure to become thin. Or maybe women feel that they really do want to be thin, and so go on dieting endlessly (they call it "eating sensibly"), thinking this is what they really want. I think if these women carefully examined their reasons for wanting to lose weight — and were not allowed to include reasons that relate to society's demands, such as a weight chart, a questionnaire in a magazine, a certain size in a pair of shorts, or even a scale — they would find that they are being ruled by what society wants, not what they want. So why do women not break free from these standards? Why do they not demand an end to being judged in such a demeaning and senseless way?

13 Self-esteem plays a large part in determining whether women succumb to the will of society or whether they are independent and self-assured enough to make their own decisions. Lack of self-esteem is one of the things the women's movement has had to fight the hardest against. If women didn't think they were worthy, then how could they even begin to fight for their own rights? The same is true with the issue of body size. If women do not feel their body is worthy, then how can they believe that it is okay to just let it stay that way? Without self-esteem, women will be swayed by society and will continue to make themselves unhappy by trying to maintain whatever weight or body shape society is dictating for them. It is ironic that many of the popular women's magazines — *Cosmopolitan, Mademoiselle, Glamour* — often feature articles on self-esteem and how essential it is and how to

improve it, and then in the same issue give the latest diet tips. This mixed message will never give women the power they deserve over their bodies and will never enable them to make their own decisions about what type of body they want.

"Rox, why do you think you're fat? You work out all the time, and you just bought that new suit. Why don't you just come down to the pool for a little while?" 14

"No, I really don't want to. I feel so self-conscious with all those people around. It makes me want to run and put on a big, baggy dress so no one can tell what size I am!" 15

"Ah, Rox, that's really sad. You have to learn to believe in yourself and your own judgment, not other people's." 16

READING FOR MEANING

Write to create meanings for Haines's reflections on the American obsession with having "the 'ideal' body" (paragraph 9).

READING LIKE A WRITER

Writers of reflective essays

- present the particular occasion.
- develop the reflections.
- maintain topical coherence.
- engage readers.

You have seen how important these reflective writing strategies are in the readings you have read, written about, and discussed in this chapter. Focus on one of these strategies in Haines's essay and analyze it carefully through close rereading and annotating. Then write several sentences explaining what you have learned, giving specific examples from the reading to support your explanation. Add a few sentences evaluating how successfully Haines uses the strategy to reflect on society's obsession with the perfect body.

REVIEWING WHAT MAKES REFLECTIVE ESSAYS EFFECTIVE

In this chapter, you have been learning how to read reflective essays for meaning and how to read them like a writer. Before going on to write a reflective essay, pause here to review and contemplate what you have learned about the elements of effective reflective essays.

Analyze

Choose one reading from this chapter that seems to you especially effective. Before rereading the selection, *jot down* one or two reasons you remember it as an example of good reflective writing.

Reread your chosen selection, adding further annotations about what makes it a particularly successful example of reflection. *Consider* the selection's purpose and how well it achieves that purpose for its intended readers. (You can make an informed guess about the intended readers and their expectations by noting the publication source of the essay.) Then *focus* on how well the essay

- presents the particular occasion.
- develops the reflections.
- maintains topical coherence.
- engages readers.

You can review all of these basic features in the Guide to Reading Reflective Essays (p. 133).

Your instructor may ask you to complete this activity on your own or to work with a small group of other students who have chosen the same reading. If you work with others, allow enough time initially for all group members to reread the selection thoughtfully and to add their annotations. Then *discuss* as a group what makes the selection effective. *Take notes* on your discussion. One student in your group should then report to the class what the group has learned about the effectiveness of reflective writing. If you are working individually, write up what you have learned from your analysis.

Write

Write at least a page, supporting your choice of this reading as an example of effective reflective writing. *Assume* that your readers — your instructor and classmates — have read the selection but will not remember many details about it. They also might not remember it as especially successful. Therefore, you will need to *refer* to details and specific parts of the essay as you explain how it works and as you justify your evaluation of its effectiveness. You need not argue that it is the best reading in the chapter or that it is flawless, only that it is, in your view, a strong example of the genre.

A Guide to Writing Reflective Essays

The readings in this chapter have helped you learn a great deal about reflective writing. At its best, the reflective essay is interesting, lively, insightful, and engaging — much like good conversation — and it avoids sounding pretentious or preachy in its focus on basic human and social issues that concern us all. Writers of reflection are not reluctant to say what they think or to express their most personal observations.

As you develop your reflective essay, you can review the readings to see how other writers use various strategies to solve problems you might also encounter. This Guide to Writing is designed to help you through the various decisions you will need to make as you plan, draft, and revise your reflective essay.

INVENTION

The following invention activities will help you find a particular occasion and a general subject, test your choices, present the particular occasion, and develop your reflections. Taking some time now to consider a wide range of possibilities will pay off later when you draft your essay, giving you confidence in your choice of subject and in your ability to develop it effectively.

Finding a Particular Occasion and a General Subject

As the selections in this chapter illustrate, writers of reflection usually center their essays on one (or more than one) event or occasion. They connect this occasion to a subject they want to reflect on. In the process of invention, however, the choice of a particular occasion does not always come before the choice of a general subject. Sometimes writers set out to reflect on a general subject (such as envy or friendship) and must search for the right occasion (an image or anecdote) with which to particularize it.

Start by listing several possible occasions and the general subjects they suggest in a two-column chart, as shown in the following example:

Particular Occasions	*General Subjects*
I met someone covered by tattoos.	Body art or self-mutilation
I saw the film *Fight Club.*	Masculinity and male bonding
I am amazed by people's personal revelations on talk shows.	Desire for celebrity status

While shopping for clothes, I couldn't decide what to buy and let the salesperson pressure me.	Indecisiveness and low self-esteem

For particular occasions, consider conversations you have had or overheard; memorable scenes you observed, read about, or saw in a movie or on television; and other incidents in your own or someone else's life that might lead you to reflect more generally. Then consider the general subjects suggested by the particular occasions — human qualities such as compassion, vanity, jealousy, and faithfulness; social customs for dating, eating, and working; abstract notions such as fate, free will, and imagination.

In making your chart, you will find that a single occasion might suggest several subjects and that a subject might be particularized by a variety of occasions. Each entry will surely suggest other possibilities for you to consider. Do not be concerned if your chart starts to look messy. A full and rich exploration of possible topics will give you confidence in the subject you finally choose and in your ability to write about it. If you have trouble getting started, review the Considering Ideas for Your Own Writing activities following the readings in this chapter. As further occasions and subjects occur to you over the next two or three days, add them to your chart.

Testing Your Choices

Review your chart, and choose a particular occasion and a general subject you now think look promising. To test whether your choices will work, write for fifteen minutes or so, exploring your thoughts. Do not make any special demands on yourself to be profound or even to be coherent. Just write your ideas as they come to mind, letting one idea suggest another. Your aims are to determine whether you have enough to say about the occasion and subject and whether they hold your interest. If you discover that you do not have very much to say about the occasion or that you quickly lose interest in the subject, choose another set of possibilities and try again. It might take a few preliminary explorations to find the right occasion and subject.

Presenting the Particular Occasion

The following activities will help you recall details about the particular occasion for your reflection. Depending on the occasion you have decided to write about, choose Narrating an Event or Describing What You Observed.

Narrating an Event. *Write for five to ten minutes narrating what happened during the event.* Try to make your story vivid so that readers can imagine what it was like. Describe the people involved in the event — what they looked like, how they acted, what they said — and the place where it occurred.

Describing What You Observed. *Write for five or ten minutes describing what you observed.* Include as many details as you can recall so that your readers can imagine what you experienced.

Developing Your Reflections

To explore your ideas about the subject, try an invention activity called *cubing.* Based on the six sides of a cube, this activity leads you to turn over your subject as you would a cube, looking at it in six different ways. Complete the following activities in any order, writing for five minutes on each one. Your goal is to invent new ways of considering your subject.

Generalizing. *Consider what you have learned from the event or experience that will be the occasion for your reflections.* What ideas does it suggest to you? What does it suggest about people in general or about the society in which you live?

Giving Examples. *Illustrate your ideas with specific examples.* What examples would best help your readers understand your ideas?

Comparing and Contrasting. *Think of a subject that could be compared with yours, and explore the similarities and the differences.*

Extending. *Take your subject to its logical limits, and speculate about its implications.* Where does it lead?

Analyzing. *Take apart your subject.* What is it made of? How are the parts related to one another? Are they all of equal importance?

Applying. *Think about your subject in practical terms.* How can you use it or act on it? What difference would it make to you and to others?

Considering Your Purpose. *Write for several minutes about your purpose for writing this essay.* As you write, try to answer the question: What do I want my readers to think about the subject after reading my essay? Your answer to this question may change as you write, but thinking about your purpose now may help you decide which of your ideas to include in the essay. Use the following questions to help clarify your purpose:

- Which of your ideas are most important to you? Why?
- How do your ideas relate to one another? If your ideas seem contradictory, consider how you could use the contradictions to convey to readers the complexity of your ideas and feelings on the subject.
- Which of your ideas do you think will most surprise your readers? Which are most likely to be familiar?
- Is the particular occasion for your reflections likely to resonate with your readers' experience and observation? If not, consider how you can make the particular occasion vivid or dramatic for readers.

Formulating a Tentative Thesis Statement. *Review what you wrote for Considering Your Purpose and add another two or three sentences that will bring into focus your reflections.* What do they seem to be about? Try to write sentences that indicate what you think is most important or most interesting about the subject, what you want readers to understand from reading your essay.

Keep in mind that readers do not expect you to begin your reflective essay with the kind of thesis statement typical of an argumentative essay, which asserts an opinion the writer then goes on to support. None of the readings in this chapter begins with an explicit statement of the writer's main idea. They all begin with a particular occasion followed by ideas suggested by the occasion. Brent Staples, for example, follows the particular occasion with a general statement of his main idea: "It was in the echo of that terrified woman's footfalls that I first began to know the unwieldy inheritance I'd come into — the ability to alter public space in ugly ways" (paragraph 2). He then explores this rather abstract idea, indicating that his "unwieldy inheritance" is racial stereotyping and the fear it engenders in others. Similarly, Suzanne Winckler follows the particular occasion with the reflection that "Butchering chickens . . . is the price I pay for being an omnivore" (paragraph 3). Barbara Ehrenreich also introduces her main idea after presenting the particular occasion: "We live in a culture that fetishes the family as the ideal unit of human community. . . . Only with the occasional celebrity crime do we allow ourselves to think the nearly unthinkable: that the family may not be the ideal and perfect living arrangement after all — that it can be a nest of pathology and a cradle of gruesome violence" (2).

As you explore your ideas and think about the particular occasion for your reflections, you can expect your ideas to change. The fun of writing a reflective essay is that you can share with readers your thinking process, taking them along for the ride.

Considering Visuals. *Consider whether visuals — cartoons, photographs, drawings — would help readers understand and appreciate your reflections.* If you submit your essay electronically to other students and your instructor, or if you post it on a Web site, you might also consider including snippets of film or sound. You could construct your own visuals, scan materials from books and magazines, or download them from the Internet. Visual and audio materials are not at all a requirement of an effective reflective essay, as you can tell from the readings in this chapter, but they could add a new dimension to your writing. If you want to use photographs or recordings of people, though, be sure to request their permission.

DRAFTING

The following guidelines will help you set goals for your draft and plan its organization.

Setting Goals

Establishing goals for your draft before you begin writing will enable you to make decisions and work more confidently. Consider the following questions now, and keep them in mind as you draft. They will help you set goals for drafting as well as recall how the writers you have read in this chapter tried to achieve similar goals.

- *How can I present the particular occasion vividly and in a way that anticipates my reflections?* Should I narrate the event, like Staples does? Refer to shocking events in the news, like Ehrenreich? Create an imaginary dialogue, like Haines?
- *How can I best develop my reflections?* Should I include brief and extended examples, like all of the writers in this chapter do? Should I use comparisons and contrasts, like Frazier and Lee? Refer to authorities and history, like Ehrenreich? Create an imaginary or conversational scene, like Lee and Haines?
- *How can I maintain topical coherence?* Like all the writers in this chapter, how can I make clear the connections between my ideas or insights and the examples that develop them? How can I keep my readers on track as they follow the course of my reflections?
- *How can I engage and hold my readers' interest?* Should I reveal the human interest and social significance of my subject by opening my essay with a dramatic event, like Staples and Winckler do? Should I start with a personal reminiscence, like Frazier does? A reminder of bizarre and troubling events in the news, like Ehrenreich? A familiar dialogue, like Haines? An ethnic stereotype, like Staples and Lee? Like all the writers in this chapter, should I reveal my personal commitment to the subject, and should I attempt to inspire my readers to think deeply about their own lives?

Organizing Your Draft

You might find it paradoxical to plan a type of essay that does not aim to reach conclusions or that seeks to give readers the impression that it is finding its way as it goes. And yet you have seen in the readings in this chapter that reflective essays, at least after they have been carefully revised with readers in mind, are usually easy to follow. Part of what makes a reflective essay easy to read is its topical coherence, such as the repetition of key words and phrases that keep the reader's focus on the subject that is being explored in the essay. Writers often develop coherence as they draft and revise their essays, but there are some ways in which planning can also help. For example, one approach to planning is to begin with the particular occasion, outlining the sequence of events in a way that emphasizes the main point you want the occasion to make. After figuring out how you will present the particular occasion, you could choose one idea you want to develop in detail or list several ideas you think your essay will touch on, possibly indicating how each idea relates to the one that follows. Sometimes when writers go this far in planning, they are actually drafting segments of the essay, discovering a tentative plan as they write.

Another approach to planning begins with the ideas you want to discuss. You could consider various ways of sequencing your ideas. For example, you could start with an obvious idea, one you expect most readers would think of. Then, you could develop the idea in unexpected ways or build a train of ideas that leads in a surprising direction. Yet another approach is to pair ideas with examples, and develop a sequence of pairs that explores different aspects of your subject or tries out different points of view on it. Remember that the goal of planning is to discover what you want to say and a possible way of organizing your ideas. Planning a reflective essay can be especially challenging because the process of reflecting is itself a process of discovery: You won't really know what you want your essay to say until you've drafted and revised it. But if you think of planning simply as a way of getting started and remember that you will have a lot of opportunity to reorganize your ideas and develop them further, planning can become an extremely pleasurable and creative activity.

READING A DRAFT CRITICALLY

Getting a critical reading of your draft will help you see how to improve it. Your instructor may schedule class time for reading drafts, or you may want to ask a classmate or a tutor in the writing center to read your draft. Ask your reader to use the following guidelines and to write out a response for you to consult during your revision.

Read for a First Impression

1. Read the draft without stopping to annotate or comment, and then write two or three sentences giving your general impression.
2. Identify one aspect of the draft that seems especially effective.

Read Again to Suggest Improvements

1. Suggest ways of presenting the occasion more effectively.
   - Read the paragraphs that present the occasion for the reflections, and tell the writer if the occasion dominates the essay, taking up an unjustified amount of space, or if it needs more development.
   - Note whether this occasion suggests the significance or importance of the subject, and consider how well it prepares readers for the reflections by providing a context for them.
   - Tell the writer what in the occasion works well and what needs improvement.
2. Help the writer develop the reflections.
   - Look for two or three ideas that strike you as especially interesting, insightful, or surprising and tell the writer what interests you about them. Then, most important, suggest ways these ideas might be developed further through examples, comparisons or contrasts, social implications, connections to other ideas, and so on.
   - Identify any ideas you find uninteresting, explaining briefly why you find them so.
3. Recommend ways to strengthen topical coherence.
   - Skim the essay, looking for gaps between sentences and paragraphs, those places where the meaning does not carry forward smoothly. Mark each gap with a double slash (//), and try to recommend a way to make the meaning clear.
   - Skim the essay again, looking for irrelevant or unnecessary material that disrupts coherence and diverts the reader's attention. Put brackets around this material, and explain to the writer why it seems to you irrelevant or unnecessary.
   - Consider the essay as a sequence of sections. Ask yourself whether some of the sections could be moved to make the essay easier to follow. Circle any section that seems out of place and draw an arrow to where it might be better located.
4. Suggest ways to further engage readers.
   - Point out parts of the essay that draw you in, hold your interest, inspire you to think, challenge your attitudes or values, or keep you wanting to read to the end.
   - Try to suggest ways the writer might engage readers more fully. Consider the essay in light of what is most engaging for you in the essays you have read in this chapter.

5. Evaluate the effectiveness of visuals.
   - Look at any visuals in the essay, and tell the writer what they contribute to your understanding of the writer's reflections.
   - If any visuals do not seem relevant, or if there seem to be too many visuals, identify the ones that the writer could consider dropping, explaining your thinking.
   - If a visual does not seem to be appropriately placed, suggest a better place for it.

REVISING

This section offers suggestions for revising your draft, suggestions that will remind you of the possibilities for developing an engaging, coherent, reflective essay. Revising means reenvisioning your draft, trying to see it in a new way, given your purpose and readers, in order to develop your reflections.

The biggest mistake you can make while revising is to focus initially on words or sentences. Instead, first try to see your draft as a whole in order to assess its likely impact on your readers. Think imaginatively and boldly about cutting uninteresting material, adding new material, and moving material around. Your computer makes even drastic revisions physically easy, but you still need to make the mental effort and decisions that will improve your draft.

You may have received help with this challenge from a classmate or tutor who gave your draft a critical reading. If so, keep this feedback in mind as you decide which parts of your draft need revising and what specific changes you could make. The following suggestions will help you solve problems and strengthen your essay.

To Present the Particular Occasion More Effectively

- If the occasion for your reflections seems flat or too general and abstract, expand it with interesting details.
- If the occasion fails to illustrate the significance of your subject, revise it to do so.
- If the occasion seems not to anticipate the reflections that follow, revise it or come up with a new, more relevant occasion.

To Develop the Reflections More Fully

- If promising ideas are not yet fully developed, provide further examples, anecdotes, contrasts, and so on.

- If certain ideas now seem too predictable, drop them and try to come up with more insightful ideas.
- If your reflections do not move beyond personal associations, extend them into the social realm by commenting on their larger implications — what they mean for people in general.

To Strengthen Topical Coherence

- If there are distracting gaps between sentences or paragraphs, try to close them by revising sentences.
- If one section seems not to follow from the previous one, consider reordering the sequence of sections.

To Better Engage Readers

- If your beginning — typically the presentation of the occasion — seems unlikely to draw readers in, make its event more dramatic, its comments less predictable, or its significance more pointed. If you cannot see how to make it more interesting, consider another beginning.
- If your reflections seem unlikely to lead readers to reflect on their own lives and their interactions with other people, try to carry your ideas further and to develop them in more varied ways.

EDITING AND PROOFREADING

After you have revised your essay, be sure to spend some time checking for errors in usage, punctuation, and mechanics and considering matters of style. If you keep a list of errors you typically make, begin by checking your draft against this list. Ask someone else to proofread your essay before you print out a copy for your instructor or send it electronically.

From our research on student writing, we know that essays reflecting on a particular occasion have a relatively high frequency of unnecessary shifts in verb tense and mood. Consult a writer's handbook for information on unnecessary verb shifts, and then edit your essay to correct any shifts that you find.

REFLECTING ON WHAT YOU HAVE LEARNED

Reflection

In this chapter, you have read critically several reflective essays and have written one of your own. To better remember what you have learned, pause now to reflect on the reading and writing activities you completed in this chapter.

1. *Write* a page or so reflecting on what you have learned. *Begin* by describing what you are most pleased with in your essay. Then *explain* what you think contributed to your achievement. *Be specific* about this contribution.

   - If it was something you learned from the readings, *indicate* which readings and specifically what you learned from them.
   - If it came from your invention writing, *point out* the section or sections that helped you most.
   - If you got good advice from a critical reader, *explain* exactly how the person helped you — perhaps by helping you understand a particular problem in your draft or by adding a new dimension to your writing.

2. Now *reflect* more generally on reflective essays, a genre of writing that has been important for centuries and is still practiced in our society today. *Consider* some of the following questions: How comfortable do you feel relying on your own experience or observations as a basis for developing ideas about general subjects or for developing ideas about the way people are and the ways they interact? How comfortable are you with merely trying out your own personal ideas on a subject rather than researching it or interviewing people to collect their ideas? How comfortable is it to adopt a conversational rather than a formal tone? How would you explain your level of comfort? How might your gender or social class or ethnic group have influenced the ideas you came up with for your essay? What contribution might reflective essays make to our society that other genres cannot make?

CHAPTER 5

Explaining Concepts

Essays explaining concepts feature a kind of explanatory writing that is especially important for college students to understand. Each of the essays you will analyze in this chapter explains a single concept, such as *parthenogenesis* in biology, *rave* in popular culture, and *dating* in sociology. For your own explanatory essay, you will choose a concept from your current studies or special interests.

For you as a college student, a better understanding of how to read and write explanations of concepts is useful in several ways. It gives you strategies for critically reading the textbooks and other concept-centered material in your college courses. It helps give you confidence to write a common type of essay examination and paper assignment. And it acquaints you with the basic strategies or modes of development common to all types of explanatory writing: definition, classification or division, comparison and contrast, process narration, illustration, and causal explanation.

A *concept* is a major idea or principle. Every field of study has its concepts: physics has quantum theory, subatomic particles, the Heisenberg principle; psychiatry has neurosis, schizophrenia, narcissism; composition has invention, heuristics, recursiveness; business management has corporate culture, micromanagement, and direct marketing; and music has harmony and counterpoint. Concepts include abstract ideas, phenomena, and processes. Concepts are central to the understanding of virtually every subject — we create concepts, name them, communicate them, and think with them.

As you work through this chapter, keep in mind that we learn a new concept by connecting it to what we have previously learned. Good explanatory writing, therefore, must be incremental, adding bit by bit to the reader's knowledge. Explanatory writing goes wrong when the flow of new information is either too fast or too slow for the intended readers, when the information is too difficult or too simple, or when the writing is digressive or just plain dull.

The readings in this chapter will help you see what makes explanatory writing interesting and informative. From the readings and from the ideas for writing that follow each reading, you will get ideas for writing your own essay about a concept. As you read and write about the selections, keep in mind the following assignment, which sets out the goals for writing an essay explaining a concept. To support your writing of this assignment, the chapter concludes with a Guide to Writing Essays Explaining Concepts.

THE WRITING ASSIGNMENT

Explaining Concepts

Choose a concept that interests you enough to study further. Write an essay explaining the concept. Consider carefully what your readers already know about the concept and how your essay can add to their knowledge.

WRITING SITUATIONS FOR ESSAYS EXPLAINING CONCEPTS

Writing that explains concepts is familiar in college and professional life, as the following examples show:

- For a presentation at the annual convention of the American Medical Association, an anesthesiologist writes a report on the concept of *awareness during surgery.* He presents evidence that patients under anesthesia, as in hypnosis, can hear; and he reviews research demonstrating that they can perceive and carry out instructions that speed their recovery. He describes briefly how he applies the concept in his own work: how he prepares patients before surgery, what he tells them while they are under anesthesia, and what happens as they recover.
- A business reporter for a newspaper writes an article about *virtual reality.* She describes the lifelike, three-dimensional experience created by wearing gloves and video goggles wired to a computer. To help readers understand this new concept, she contrasts it with television. For investors, she describes which corporations have shown an interest in the commercial possibilities of virtual reality.
- As part of a group assignment, a college student at a summer biology camp in the Sierra Nevada mountains reads about the condition of mammals at birth. She discovers the distinction between infant mammals that are *altricial* (born nude and helpless within a protective nest) and those that are *precocial* (born well-formed with eyes open and ears erect). In her part of a group report, she develops this contrast point by point, giving many

examples of specific mammals but focusing in detail on altricial mice and precocial porcupines. Domestic cats, she points out, are an intermediate example — born with some fur but with eyes and ears closed.

A Guide to Reading Essays Explaining Concepts

This guide introduces you to concept explanation. By completing all of the activities in it, you will prepare yourself to learn a great deal from the other readings in this chapter about how to read and write an essay explaining a concept. The guide focuses on an engaging essay by the science writer David Quammen, "Is Sex Necessary? Virgin Birth and Opportunism in the Garden." You will read Quammen's essay twice. First, you will read it for meaning, looking closely at its content and ideas. Then, you will reread the essay like a writer, analyzing the parts to see how Quammen crafts his essay and to learn the range of strategies he employs to make his concept explanation effective. These two activities — reading for meaning and reading like a writer — follow every reading in this chapter.

DAVID QUAMMEN

Is Sex Necessary? Virgin Birth and Opportunism in the Garden

David Quammen (b. 1948) is a novelist and nature writer who writes a column for the magazine Outside, *and has published articles in* Smithsonian Magazine, Audubon, Esquire, Rolling Stone, *and* Harper's. *His books include the novel* The Soul of Viktor Tronko *(1987) and an edited collection (with Burkhard Bilger) of outstanding writing in his specialties,* The Best American Science and Nature Writing 2000 *(2000). Several collections of his own writing have also been published, including* Natural Acts: A Sidelong View of Science and Nature *(1985),* Wild Thoughts from Wild Places *(1998), and* Boilerplate Rhino: Nature in the Eye of the Beholder *(2001).*

The readers of Outside *have special interests in nature, outdoor recreation, and the environment, but few have advanced training in ecology or biology. In this essay, originally published as a column in* Outside *and reprinted in* Natural Acts, *Quammen gives us a nonscientist's introduction to parthenogenesis — not only to the facts of it but also to its significance in nature.*

As you read, annotate anything that helps you understand the concept of parthenogenesis. Notice also Quammen's attempts to amuse as well as inform, and think about how his playfulness might help or get in the way of readers' understanding of the concept.

1 *Birds do it, bees do it,* goes the tune. But the songsters, as usual, would mislead us with drastic oversimplifications. The full truth happens to be more eccentrically nonlibidinous: Sometimes they *don't* do it, those very creatures, and get the same results anyway. Bees of all species, for instance, are notable to geneticists precisely for their ability to produce offspring while doing *without.* Likewise at least one variety of bird — the Beltsville Small White turkey, a domestic dinnertable model out of Beltsville, Maryland — has achieved scientific renown for a similar feat. What we are talking about here is celibate motherhood, procreation without copulation, a phenomenon that goes by the technical name *parthenogenesis.* Translated from the Greek roots: virgin birth.

2 And you don't have to be Catholic to believe in this one.

3 Miraculous as it may seem, parthenogenesis is actually rather common throughout nature, practiced regularly or intermittently by at least some species within almost every group of animals except (for reasons still unknown) dragonflies and mammals. Reproduction by virgin females has been discovered among reptiles, birds, fishes, amphibians, crustaceans, mollusks, ticks, the jellyfish clan, flatworms, roundworms, segmented worms; and among insects (notwithstanding those unrelentingly sexy dragonflies) it is especially favored. The order *Hymenoptera,* including all bees and wasps, is uniformly parthenogenetic in the manner by which males are produced: Every male honeybee is born without any genetic contribution from a father. Among the beetles, there are thirty-five different forms of parthenogenetic weevil. The African weaver ant employs parthenogenesis, as do twenty-three species of fruit fly and at least one kind of roach. The gall midge *Miastor* is notorious for the exceptionally bizarre and grisly scenario that allows its fatherless young to see daylight: *Miastor* daughters cannibalize the mother from inside, with ruthless impatience, until her hollowed-out skin splits open like the door of an overcrowded nursery. But the foremost practitioners of virgin birth — their elaborate and versatile proficiency unmatched in the animal kingdom — are undoubtedly the aphids.

4 Now no sensible reader of even this can be expected, I realize, to care faintly about aphid biology *qua* aphid biology. That's just asking too much. But there's a larger rationale for dragging you aphidward. The life cycle of these little nebbishy sap-sucking insects, the very same that infest rose bushes and house plants, not only exemplifies *how* parthenogenetic reproduction is done; it also very clearly shows *why.*

5 First the biographical facts. A typical aphid, which feeds entirely on plant juices tapped off from the vascular system of young

leaves, spends winter dormant and protected, as an egg. The egg is attached near a bud site on the new growth of a poplar tree. In March, when the tree sap has begun to rise and the buds have begun to burgeon, an aphid hatchling appears, plugging its sharp snout (like a mosquito's) into the tree's tenderest plumbing. This solitary individual aphid will be, necessarily, a wingless female. If she is lucky, she will become sole founder of a vast aphid population. Having sucked enough poplar sap to reach maturity, she produces — by *live birth* now, and without benefit of a mate — daughters identical to herself. These wingless daughters also plug into the tree's flow of sap, and they also produce further wingless daughters, until sometime in late May, when that particular branch of that particular tree can support no more thirsty aphids. Suddenly there is a change: The next generation of daughters are born with wings. They fly off in search of a better situation.

6 One such aviatrix lands on an herbaceous plant — say a young climbing bean in some human's garden — and the pattern repeats. She plugs into the sap ducts on the underside of a new leaf, commences feasting destructively, and delivers by parthenogenesis a great brood of wingless daughters. The daughters beget more daughters, those daughters beget still more, and so on, until the poor bean plant is encrusted with a solid mob of these fat little elbowing greedy sisters. Then again, neatly triggered by the crowded conditions, a generation of daughters are born with wings. Away they fly, looking for prospects, and one of them lights on, say, a sugar beet. (The switch from bean to beet is fine, because our species of typical aphid is not inordinately choosy.) The sugar beet before long is covered, sucked upon mercilessly, victimized by a horde of mothers and nieces and granddaughters. Still not a single male aphid has appeared anywhere in the chain.

7 The lurching from one plant to another continues; the alternation between wingless and winged daughters continues. But in September, with fresh tender plant growth increasingly hard to find, there is another change.

8 Flying daughters are born who have a different destiny: They wing back to the poplar tree, where they give birth to a crop of wingless females that are unlike any so far. These latest girls know the meaning of sex! Meanwhile, at long last, the starving survivors back on that final bedraggled sugar beet have brought forth a generation of males. The males have wings. They take to the air in quest of poplar trees and first love. *Et voilà.* The mated females lay eggs that will wait out the winter near bud sites on that poplar tree, and the circle is thus completed. One single aphid hatching — call her the *fundatrix* — in this way can give rise in the course of a year, from her own ovaries exclusively, to roughly a zillion aphids.

Well and good, you say. A zillion aphids. But what is the point of it? 9

The point, for aphids as for most other parthenogenetic animals, is (1) exceptionally fast reproduction that allows (2) maximal exploitation of temporary resource abundance and unstable environmental conditions, while (3) facilitating the successful colonization of unfamiliar habitats. In other words the aphid, like the gall midge and the weaver ant and the rest of their fellow parthenogens, is by its evolved character a galloping opportunist. 10

This is a term of science, not of abuse. Population ecologists make an illuminating distinction between what they label *equilibrium* and *opportunistic* species. According to William Birky and John Gilbert, from a paper in the journal *American Zoologist:* "Equilibrium species, exemplified by many vertebrates, maintain relatively constant population sizes, in part by being adapted to reproduce, at least slowly, in most of the environmental conditions which they meet. Opportunistic species, on the other hand, show extreme population fluctuations; they are adapted to reproduce only in a relatively narrow range of conditions, but make up for this by reproducing extremely rapidly in favorable circumstances. At least in some cases, opportunistic organisms can also be categorized as colonizing organisms." Birky and Gilbert also emphasize that "The potential for rapid reproduction is the essential evolutionary ticket for entry into the opportunistic lifestyle." 11

And parthenogenesis, in turn, is the greatest time-saving gimmick in the history of animal reproduction. No hours or days are wasted while a female looks for a mate; no minutes lost to the act of mating itself. The female aphid attains sexual maturity and, bang, she becomes automatically pregnant. No waiting, no courtship, no fooling around. She delivers her brood of daughters, they grow to puberty and, zap, another generation immediately. If humans worked as fast, Jane Fonda today would be a great-grandmother. The time saved to parthenogenetic species may seem trivial, but it is not. It adds up dizzyingly: In the same time taken by a sexually reproducing insect to complete three generations for a total of 1,200 offspring, an aphid (assuming the *same* time required for each female to mature, and the *same* number of progeny in each litter), squandering no time on courtship or sex, will progress through six generations for an extended family of 318,000,000. 12

Even this isn't speedy enough for some restless opportunists. That matricidal gall midge *Miastor,* whose larvae feed on fleeting eruptions of fungus under the bark of trees, has developed a startling way to cut further time from the cycle of procreation. Far from waiting for a mate, *Miastor* does not even wait for maturity. When food is abundant, it is the *larva,* not the adult female fly, 13 who is eaten alive from inside by her own daughters. And as those voracious daughters burst free of the husk that was their mother, each of them already contains further larval daughters taking shape ominously within its own ovaries. While the food lasts, while opportunity endures, no *Miastor* female can live to adulthood without dying of motherhood.

14 The implicit principle behind all this nonsexual reproduction, all this hurry, is simple: Don't argue with success. Don't tamper with a genetic blueprint that works. Unmated female aphids, and gall midges, pass on their own gene patterns virtually unaltered (except for the occasional mutation) to their daughters. Sexual reproduction on the other hand, constitutes, by its essence, genetic tampering. The whole purpose of joining sperm with egg is to shuffle the genes of both parents and come up with a new combination that might perhaps be more advantageous. Give the kid something neither Mom nor Pop ever had. Parthenogenetic species, during their hurried phases at least, dispense with this genetic shuffle. They stick stubbornly to the gene pattern that seems to be working. They produce (with certain complicated exceptions) natural clones of themselves.

15 But what they gain thereby in reproductive rate, in great explosions of population, they give up in flexibility. They minimize their genetic options. They lessen their chances of adapting to unforeseen changes of circumstance.

16 Which is why more than one biologist has drawn the same conclusion as M. J. D. White: "Parthenogenetic forms seem to be frequently successful in the particular ecological niche which they occupy, but sooner or later the inherent disadvantages of their genetic system must be expected to lead to a lack of adaptability, followed by eventual extinction, or perhaps in some cases by a return to sexuality."

17 So it *is* necessary, at least intermittently (once a year, for the aphids, whether they need it or not), this thing called sex. As of course you and I knew it must be. Otherwise surely, by now, we mammals and dragonflies would have come up with something more dignified.

READING FOR MEANING

Write to create meanings for Quammen's explanation of parthenogenesis.

Start Making Meaning

Begin by writing a few sentences briefly explaining parthenogenesis. Continue by writing about anything else in the selection or from your own knowledge or experience that contributes to your understanding of parthenogenesis.

If You Are Stuck

If you cannot write at least a page, consider writing about

- the process of parthenogenesis in aphids (paragraphs 5–8).
- the advantages of nonsexual as compared with sexual reproduction (paragraphs 10–14).
- the distinction between equilibrium and opportunistic species (paragraph 11).
- how the theory of evolution helps explain parthenogenesis.

READING LIKE A WRITER

This section guides you through an analysis of Quammen's explanatory writing strategies: *devising a readable plan, using appropriate explanatory strategies, integrating sources smoothly,* and *engaging readers' interest.* For each strategy you will be asked to reread and annotate part of Quammen's essay to see how he uses the strategy in "Is Sex Necessary?"

When you study the selections later in this chapter, you will see how different writers use these same strategies. The Guide to Writing Essays Explaining Concepts near the end of the chapter suggests ways you can use these strategies in your own writing.

Devising a Readable Plan

Experienced writers of explanation know that readers often have a hard time making their way through new and difficult material and sometimes give up in frustration. Writers who want to avoid this scenario construct a reader-friendly plan by dividing the information into clearly distinguishable topics. They also give readers road signs — forecasting statements, topic sentences, transitions, and summaries — to guide them through the explanation.

Writers often provide a forecasting statement early in the essay to let readers know where they are heading. Forecasting statements can also appear at the beginnings of major sections of the essay. Topic sentences announce each segment of information as it comes up, transitions (such as *in contrast* and *another*) relate what is coming to what came before, and summaries to remind readers what has been explained already. Quammen effectively deploys all of these strategies.

Analyze

1. *Underline* the last sentence in paragraph 4, the first sentence in paragraph 5, all of the sentences in paragraph 9, and the first sentence in paragraph 10.

2. *Consider* these the key sentences in Quammen's effort to devise a readable plan and make that plan unmistakably clear to readers. *Make notes* in the margin by these sentences about how they forecast, announce topics, make transitions, and offer brief summaries. (These strategies are defined in the preceding paragraph.)

Write

Write several sentences, explaining how Quammen makes use of forecasting statements, transitions, brief summaries, and topic sentences to reveal his overall plan to readers. *Give examples* from the reading to support your explanation. Then, considering yourself among Quammen's intended readers, *write a few more sentences* evaluating how successful the writer's efforts are for you.

Using Appropriate Explanatory Strategies

When writers organize and present information, they rely on strategies we call the building blocks of explanatory essays: defining, classifying or dividing, comparing and contrasting, narrating a process, illustrating, and reporting causes or effects. The strategies a writer chooses are determined by the topics covered, the kinds of information available, and the writer's assessment of readers' knowledge about the concept. Following are brief descriptions of the writing strategies that are particularly useful in explaining concepts:

Defining: briefly stating the meaning of the concept or any other word likely to be unfamiliar to readers

Classifying or dividing: grouping related information about a concept into two or more discrete groups and labeling each group, or dividing a concept into its constituent parts to consider each part separately

Comparing and contrasting: pointing out how the concept is similar to and different from a related concept

Narrating a process: presenting procedures or a sequence of steps as they unfold over time to show the concept in practice

Illustrating: giving examples, relating anecdotes, listing facts and details, and quoting sources to help readers understand a concept

Reporting causes or effects: identifying the known causes or effects related to a concept

Quammen makes good use of all these fundamentally important explanatory strategies: defining in paragraphs 1, 8, and 11; classifying in paragraphs 10 and 11; comparing and contrasting in paragraphs 11–14 (as well as establishing the analogy between insects and humans that runs through the essay); narrating a process in paragraphs 5–8; illustrating in paragraph 3; and reporting known effects in paragraphs 12–14.

Analyze

1. *Review* Quammen's use of each explanatory strategy described in the preceding paragraph, and *select one* to analyze more closely.
2. *Make notes* in the margin about how Quammen uses that one strategy and what special contribution it makes to your understanding of parthenogenesis within the context of the whole reading.

Write

Write several sentences explaining how the strategy you have analyzed works in this essay to help readers understand parthenogenesis.

Integrating Sources Smoothly

In addition to drawing on personal knowledge and fresh observations, writers often do additional research about the concepts they are trying to explain. Doing research in the library and on the Internet, writers immediately confront the ethical responsibility to their readers of locating relevant sources, evaluating them critically, and representing them without distortion. You will find advice on meeting this responsibility in Appendix 2, pages 579–614.

Developing an explanation sentence by sentence on the page or the screen, writers confront a different challenge in using sources: how to integrate source material smoothly into their own sentences and to cite the sources of those materials accurately, sometimes using formal citation styles that point readers to a full description of each source in a list of works cited at the end of the essay.

How writers cite or refer to research sources depends on the writing situation they find themselves in. Certain formal situations, such as college assignments or scholarly publications, have prescribed rules for citing sources. As a student, you may be expected to cite your sources formally because your writing will be judged in part by what you have read and how you have used your reading. For more informal writing occasions — newspaper and magazine articles, for example — readers do not expect writers to include page references or publication information, only to identify their sources. In this chapter's readings, Deborah Tannen, Beth Bailey, Linh Kieu Ngo, and Lyn Gutierrez cite their sources formally; David Quammen, Christopher Farley, and Michael Lemonick cite their sources informally.

Writers may quote, summarize, or paraphrase their sources: quoting when they want to capture the exact wording of the original source; summarizing to convey only the gist or main points; and paraphrasing when they they want to include most of the details in some part of the original. Whether they quote, summarize, or paraphrase, writers try to integrate source material smoothly into their writing. For example, they deliberately vary the way they introduce borrowed material, avoiding repetition of the same signal phrases (*X said, as Y put it*) or sentence pattern (a *that* clause, use of the colon).

Analyze

1. *Look closely* at paragraphs 11 and 16, where Quammen quotes sources directly.
2. *Put brackets* ([ ]) *around* the signal phrase or key part of a sentence pattern that he uses to introduce each quotation, noticing how he integrates the quotation into his sentence.

Write

Write a few sentences describing how Quammen introduces and integrates quotations into his writing. *Give examples* from your annotations in paragraphs 11 and 16.

Engaging Readers' Interest

Most people read explanations of concepts because they are helpful for work or school. They do not generally expect the writing to entertain, but simply to inform. Nevertheless, explanations that keep readers engaged with lively writing are usually appreciated. Writers explaining concepts may engage readers' interest in a variety of ways. For example, they may remind readers of what they already know about the concept. They may show readers a new way of using a familiar concept or dramatize that the concept has greater importance than readers had realized. They can connect the concept, sometimes through metaphor or analogy, to common human experiences. They may present the concept in a humorous way to convince readers that learning about a concept can be painless, or even pleasurable.

Quammen relies on many of these strategies to engage his readers' interest. Keep in mind that his original readers could either read or skip his column. Those who enjoyed and learned from previous Quammen columns would be more likely to try out the first few paragraphs of this one, but Quammen could not count on their having any special interest in parthenogenesis. He has to try to generate that interest — and rather quickly, in the first few sentences or paragraphs.

Analyze

Reread paragraphs 1–4, and *note in the margin* the various ways Quammen reaches out to interest readers in his subject.

Write

Write several sentences explaining how Quammen attempts to engage his readers' interest in parthenogenesis. To support your explanation, give examples from your annotations in paragraphs 1–4. What parts seem most effective to you? Least effective?

Readings

CHRISTOPHER JOHN FARLEY

Rave New World

Christopher John Farley (b. 1967) is a senior writer covering arts and entertainment and chief music critic at Time, *the weekly newsmagazine. Occasionally reporting on national affairs as well, Farley has written feature articles on the militia movement, civil rights, and antismoking legislation. A novel,* My Favorite War, *appeared in 1996. He has won awards for his writing from the National Association of Black Journalists and the Deadline Club of New York, and his work is featured in* Step into a World: A Global Anthology of the New Black Literature *(2000).*

In this reading, published in Time *in 2000, Farley introduces readers to the concept of rave culture, which has developed around music and dance events known as raves. To help those of his readers who are in their forties or older understand the concept, he compares and contrasts rave culture with the Beat culture of the 1950s. He seems concerned to show that the media exaggerate certain features of rave and Beat in order to turn the somewhat distorted portrayal to its own ends. Consequently, as he explains rave to readers, he tries to correct what he assumes to be limited or even incorrect ideas they may have picked up, especially about the part ecstasy and other drugs play in rave culture.*

Before you read, reflect on what you know about rave culture or other new forms of music or dance. How did you first hear about them? If you have participated in them yourself, was your experience what you expected it to be?

It's hard to talk to women at raves, says Ben Wilke. The big beats drown out small talk. If you really need to, you can go to a "chill-out" room for get-to-know-you conversation. And if you really need them, there's "a moderate amount of drugs," says the 17-year-old from Houston. But for him, raves are "all about the music." Says Wilke: "Real party kids don't do drugs. We go to dance and have a good time." He goes on: "A lot of people don't understand it, but the guitar thing's been done. Electronic music is all I listen to. It beats my heart." 1

First we had the Beat Generation; now we have the Beats-per-Minute Generation. And it's not just about ecstasy. 2

Simply defined, a rave is a party — often an all-night-long party — at which some form of electronic, or "techno," music is 3 played, usually by a deejay. A rave can be as small as 25 people or larger than 25,000. And while raves have been around for a decade, the rituals, visuals and sounds associated with raves have finally started to exert a potent influence on pop music, advertising and even computer games. Several new films about raves are either in theaters or coming soon, including the British comedy *Human Traffic* and the documentaries *Better Living Through Circuitry* and *Rise,* a study of the rave scene in New Orleans. Says Jason Jordan, co-author of *Searching for the Perfect Beat,* a new book about raves and visual art: "Rave culture is youth culture right now."

4 "Rave culture is affecting pop culture in ways similar to the Beat Generation — and it's being misinterpreted in the same way," says Greg Harrison, director of the new movie *Groove,* a fictional take on the rave scene. "In the case of the Beats, a complex and subtle ethos was distilled by pop culture to marijuana, goatees and poetry. I would argue that just as there was much more to the Beats, there's something more subtle and interesting about the rave scene."

5 To find a rave, you can pick up one of the artfully rendered flyers at cafés or cool record stores like Other Music in New York city or Atomic Music in Houston. Or you might surf the Net and check out sites like *ravedata.com* or *raves.com.* Or you might just ask a friend in the know. Raves have traditionally been held in venues without permits or permission, giving them an outlaw allure. Today, however, an increasing number of raves are legal ones, and places like Twilo in New York City specialize in recreating the rave feel in legitimate clubs. "The New York club scene was not about music until Twilo opened," says Paul van Dyk, a popular deejay who specializes in trance — a soft, transporting form of techno and one of the genre's many, many offshoots.

6 Ravers often wear loose, wide-legged jeans that flare out at the bottom. Knick-knacks from childhood, like suckers, pacifiers and dolls, are common accessories. Dancers, sweating to the music all night, often carry bottles of water to battle dehydration, which can be aggravated by ecstasy. Attendees sometimes dress in layers so clothes can be stripped off if the going gets hot, and blue and green flexible glow sticks are popular. One sound you'll hear if the party's going right: a communal whoop of approval when the deejay starts riding a good groove. "The first rock-'n'-roll shows were dance events," says 6th Element promoter Matt E. Silver, who has worked with best-selling electronica acts such as Chemical Brothers and Prodigy. "Now it's about deejay culture." In the movie *Groove,* the filmmakers refer to that connection between

THE LOOK Plastic beads and pacifiers are part of the fashion as well as wide-legged pants for extra movement

deejay and dancer, between promoter and satisfied raver, as "the nod." Many rave promoters and deejays don't do it for the money. They do it for the nod.

7 One electronic musician who is definitely getting the nod these days is the American deejay-composer Moby. Most deejays a decade ago were faceless shadows lurking behind turntables. Now deejays associated with the rave scene — like Van Dyk, Armand Van Helden, Keoki and BT — are artists, celebrities, superstars. "If Stravinsky were alive today, this is the kind of music he'd make," says BT, who composed music for the rave movie *Go* (1999) as well as the PlayStation game *Die Hard Trilogy.* "It just affords you a broader sonic palette to work from."

8 Moby has used his palette skillfully. He got his start as a deejay, but he also sings and plays with a backing band when he's on tour. His 1995 album *Everything Is Wrong* sold about 125,000 copies. His critically acclaimed new album *Play,* which samples old blues songs and sets them to futuristic beats, has already gone platinum. The rave scene is catching on with a new generation of fans, Moby believes, because it offers an alternative to today's version of bubblegum. "The consolidation of all the different record companies under big multinational parent companies," he says, has spawned the current crush of mass-produced teen pop acts. "Your BMGs, your Sonys, your Time Warners . . . nothing against these companies, but they buy music companies and they expect music to perform the way that, say, snack cakes or liquid paper performs. There's so much commercial emphasis on

disposable pop music that I think it leaves a lot of people desperately looking for other types of musical expression."

9 One of the most creative ways in which rave culture expresses itself is its party flyers. These handouts are to raves what graffiti art is to hip-hop and psychedelic posters were to the acid rock of the '70s. They give vision to rave's sounds. Sometimes — much like rappers' sampling old songs — they appropriate corporate logos with ironic visual twists. The MasterCard logo becomes "MasterRave," or Rice Krispies becomes "Rave Krisp E's." Other flyers employ 3-D images and wild metallic hues that draw inspiration from sci-fi films, anime, even the rounded, flower-power imagery of the Summer of Love. "In a lot of ways it's one of the most modern visual art forms you can see," says Eric Paxton Stauder, a member of Dots per Minute, a network of designers that focuses on rave flyers. "Stylistically, you see things in flyers that you don't see other places — uses of line work and fontography. It's open and unrestricted, and it's a testing ground for combining visual elements together."

10 Rave iconography is already being co-opted by Madison Avenue, which has learned all about digging up the underground and selling the dirt. TV ads for Toyota's Echo have the trippy look and feel of rave flyers (Toyota is sponsoring a U.S. tour of British electronica acts Groove Armada and Faze Action). Every song on Moby's 18-track album *Play* has been licensed, popping up in ads for the last episode of *Party of Five,* movies like *The Beach* and commercials for Nissan's Altima sedan and Quest minivan. Donna Karan's DKNY label plans to use deejay John Digweed's song *Heaven Scent* to promote a fragrance with the same name.

11 Wayne Friedman, entertainment-marketing reporter for *Advertising Age,* says today's admakers look to tap into underground movements quickly so that they can make use of sounds and images that aren't necessarily familiar but that pique interest. Acts like Moby fit the bill. Says Friedman: "It's almost like you can't be overly commercial when you're trying to make commercials."

12 Many ravers are wary and weary of the media's embrace. In particular, many believe that the press is more interested in writing about drugs than about the music — and that the press coverage is partly to blame for the supposed ecstasy boom. Says Jon Reiss, director of *Better Living Through Circuitry:* "The media hype says if you want to do drugs, come to these parties. So all these kids come to the parties looking for drugs. It becomes a self-fulfilling prophecy."

13 Indeed, some of the biggest acts associated with the rave scene say they are drug free. Van Dyk says he was introduced to electronic music in East Germany, when he secretly tuned in to West German radio as a kid. He didn't need drugs to enjoy the

music then, so he figures he doesn't need them now. Moby says he tried smoking pot when he was 11 or 12 so he could hang out with the "cool kids," but that was pretty much the end of his experimentation. Says Moby: "I've never tried ecstasy, I've never tried cocaine, I've never tried heroin. I don't think there's anything ethically wrong with drug use, but the reason I stay away from it is that I value my brain too much. I don't want to trust my synapses to some stranger that I met in a nightclub. I hope to use my brain for the rest of my life."

14 We hope he does too. Every few years somebody says electronic music is going to break out, that electronic acts are going to storm the charts. A couple of years ago, Prodigy and the Chemical Brothers were supposed to lead the charge. They sold well, but few like-minded acts shared their success. This year it's Moby, and perhaps acts like Alice Deejay and others will follow. Maybe this time rave culture is here to stay . . . or maybe it'll slip safely back into the underground with alternative rock. With horrifyingly generic teen-pop acts blaring out from MTV's *Total Request Live* day in and day out, it's a wonder more kids haven't turned to drugs to escape the awful racket. Sure, a fair amount of electronica is wordless wallpaper, but slip on Moby's soulful, cerebral *Play,* and you won't need any substances to get high. The music will take you there all by itself.

READING FOR MEANING

Write to create meanings for Farley's explanation of raves.

Start Making Meaning

Begin by listing the major features of a rave. Continue by writing about anything else in the selection or in your experience that contributes to your understanding of Farley's explanation.

If You Are Stuck

If you cannot write at least a page, consider writing about

- the party-flyer art that is part of rave culture.
- the special role of deejays in rave culture.
- what the photograph adds to your understanding of rave culture.
- a recent rave you attended or movie you saw in which a rave is represented, comparing and contrasting it to Farley's description of raves.

READING LIKE A WRITER

ENGAGING READERS' INTEREST

Explanatory writing aimed at nonspecialist readers usually makes an effort to engage those readers' interest in the information offered. David Quammen, for example, writing for a popular magazine, exerts himself to be engaging, even entertaining. Also writing for a popular magazine, Farley attempts to engage and hold readers' interest, to draw them in at the beginning and keep them turning the pages until the end. Like Quammen, he weaves these attempts into the flow of information. While they are not separate from the information — for information itself, even dryly presented, can be engaging for readers — direct attempts to engage are nevertheless a recognizable feature of Farley's explanation. For example, he anticipates some readers' concerns about drugs at rave parties, emphasizes what is new and novel about rave culture, focuses on rave personalities like Moby, and connects rave culture to advertisements for products with which readers are familiar.

Analyze

1. *Reread* paragraphs 7, 8, and 13, where Farley focuses on the well-known rave deejay Moby.
2. *Make notes* in the margin about how Farley presents Moby so as to make him seem interesting to readers and to engage readers further with the information about rave culture revealed in these paragraphs.

Write

Write several sentences explaining how Farley presents a celebrity in order to inform readers about rave culture and to make the information seem more engaging. *Give examples* from the reading to illustrate your explanation.

CONSIDERING IDEAS FOR YOUR OWN WRITING

Many aspects of popular culture need explaining. Consider movie genres. Readers who have seen two or three movies that seem to them alike in important ways may have seen movies in the same genre; for example, horror, science fiction, martial arts, film noir, animal, high school, musical, or war. Television also has its genres: police shows, situation comedies, talk shows, TV churches, courtroom dramas, docudramas, game shows, cartoon programs, children's educational programs, sports talk shows, and many others. Any one of these genres is a concept that some readers would like to know more about. Each genre has a history, many current examples, and articles and books analyzing what makes it a genre, a special type of movie or television program. You could choose a genre you especially like and are very familiar with. When you begin researching it, you will probaby be surprised at how much is known about it as a genre. In your essay, do not evaluate examples of the genre. Instead, keep your focus on explaining the characteristics of the genre. Alternatively, you could choose an emerging style of dance or popular music.

MICHAEL D. LEMONICK

Will Tiny Robots Build Diamonds One Atom at a Time?

Michael D. Lemonick (b. 1954) is a senior writer at Time *magazine, where he specializes in science, medicine, and health. Topics of his twenty-seven cover stories since 1986 have included the Exxon* Valdez *oil spill, emerging viruses, and the McCaughey septuplets. He has written two books on astronomy,* The Light at the Edge of the Universe *(1995) and* Other Worlds: The Search for Life in the Universe *(1998), and has twice won a writing award from the American Association for the Advancement of Science.*

In this reading, published in Time *in 2000, Lemonick introduces readers to a futuristic-scientific concept — nanotechnology. It is so revolutionary and novel that nearly all of his readers will have difficulty grasping it because it leaps so far ahead of their current knowledge. Lemonick compares it only to biotechnology but briefly, and he then goes on to say how little similarity there really is between the two concepts. Consequently, his explanation necessarily remains somewhat abstract and for that reason quite challenging. You need not attempt to understand everything on first reading. Instead, aim for a good general idea of nanotechnology and its benefits and dangers.*

Before you read, reflect on what you know about the function of human cells and about DNA, molecules, and atoms.

On its face, the notion seems utterly preposterous: A single technology so incredibly versatile that it can fight disease, stave off aging, clean up toxic waste, boost the world's food supply and build roads, automobiles and skyscrapers — and that's only to start with. Yet that's just what the proponents of nanotechnology claim is going to be possible, maybe even before the century is half over. 1

Crazy though it sounds, the idea of nanotechnology is very much in the scientific mainstream, with research labs all over the world trying to make it work. Last January President Clinton even declared a national Nanotechnology Initiative, promising $500 million for the effort. 2

In fact, nanotechnology has an impeccable and longstanding scientific pedigree. It was back in 1959 that Richard Feynman, arguably the most brilliant theoretical physicist since Einstein, gave a talk titled "There's Plenty of Room at the Bottom," in which he suggested that it would one day be possible to build machines so tiny they would consist of just a few thousand atoms. (The term 3 nanotechnology comes from nanometer, or a billionth of a meter; a typical virus is about 100 nanometers across.)

4 What would such a machine be good for? Construction projects, on the tiniest scale, using molecules and even individual atoms as building blocks. And that in turn means you can make literally anything at all, from scratch — for the altering and rearrangement of molecules is ultimately what chemistry and biology come down to, and manufacturing is simply the process of taking huge collections of molecules and forming them into useful objects.

5 Indeed, every cell is a living example of nanotechnology: not only does it convert fuel into energy, but it also fabricates and pumps out proteins and enzymes according to the software encoded in its dna. By recombining dna from different species, genetic engineers have already learned to build new nanodevices — bacterial cells, for example, that pump out medically useful human hormones.

6 But biotechnology is limited by the tasks cells already know how to carry out. Nanotech visionaries have much more ambitious notions. Imagine a nanomachine that could take raw carbon and arrange it, atom by atom, into a perfect diamond. Imagine a machine that dismembers dioxin molecules, one by one, into their component parts. Or a device that cruises the human bloodstream, seeks out cholesterol deposits on vessel walls and disassembles them. Or one that takes grass clippings and remanufactures them into bread. Literally every physical object in the world, from computers to cheese, is made of molecules, and in principle a nanomachine could construct all of them.

7 Going from the principle to the practical will be a tall order, of course, but nanomechanics have already shown that it's possible, using tools like the scanning tunneling electron microscope, to move individual atoms into arrangements they'd never assume in nature: the IBM logo, for example, or a map of the world at one ten-billionth scale, or even a functioning submicroscopic guitar whose strings are a mere 50 nanometers across. They've also designed, though not yet built, minuscule gears and motors made of a few score molecules. (These should not be confused with the "tiny" gears and motors, built with millions of molecules, that have already been constructed with conventional chip-etching technique. Those devices are gargantuan compared with what will be built in the future.)

8 Within 25 years, nanotechnologists expect to move beyond these scientific parlor tricks and create real, working nanomachines, complete with tiny "fingers" that can manipulate mole-

cules and with minuscule electronic brains that tell them how to do it, as well as how to search out the necessary raw materials. The fingers may well be made from carbon nanotubes — hairlike carbon molecules, discovered in 1991, that are 100 times as strong as steel and 50,000 times as thin as a human hair.

9 Their electronic brains could themselves be made from nanotubes, which can serve both as transistors and as the wires that connect them. Or they may be made out of DNA, which can be altered to carry instructions that nature never intended. Armed with the proper software and sufficient dexterity, a nanorobot, or nanobot, could construct anything at all.

10 Including copies of itself. To accomplish any sort of useful work, you'd have to unleash huge numbers of nanomachines to do every task — billions in every bloodstream, trillions at every toxic-waste site, quadrillions to put a car together. No assembly line could crank out nanobots in such numbers.

11 But nanomachines could do it. Nanotechnologists want to design nanobots that can do two things: carry out their primary tasks, and build perfect replicas of themselves. If the first nanobot makes two copies of itself, and those two make two copies each, you've got a trillion nanobots in no time, each one operating independently to carry out a trillionth of the job.

12 But as any child who's seen Mickey Mouse wrestle with those multiplying broomsticks in *The Sorcerer's Apprentice* can tell you, there's a dystopian shadow that hangs over this rosy picture: What if the nanobots forget to stop replicating? Without some sort of built-in stop signal, the potential for disaster would be incalculable. A fast-replicating nanobot circulating inside the human body could spread faster than a cancer, crowding out normal tissues; an out-of-control paper-recycling nanobot could convert the world's libraries to corrugated cardboard; a rogue food-fabricating nanobot could turn the planet's entire biosphere into one huge slab of Gorgonzola cheese.

13 Nanotechnologists don't dismiss the danger, but they believe they can handle it. One idea is to program a nanobot's software to self-destruct after a set number of generations. Another is to design nanobots that can operate only under certain conditions — in the presence of a high concentration of toxic chemicals, for example, or within a very narrow range of temperature and humidity. You might even program nanobots to stop reproducing when too many of their fellows are nearby. It's a strategy nature uses to keep bacteria in check.

14 None of that will help if someone decides to unleash a nanotech weapon of some sort — a prospect that would make

WHAT IS NANOTECHNOLOGY?

Nanotechnology is the science of creating molecular-size machines that manipulate matter one atom at a time. The name comes from nanometer – one one-billionth of a meter – which is roughly the size of these tiny devices.

The idea dates back to a 1959 speech by physicist Richard Feynman in which he proposed manipulating matter atom by atom and was championed most famously in K. Eric Drexler's 1986 book *Engines of Creation.*

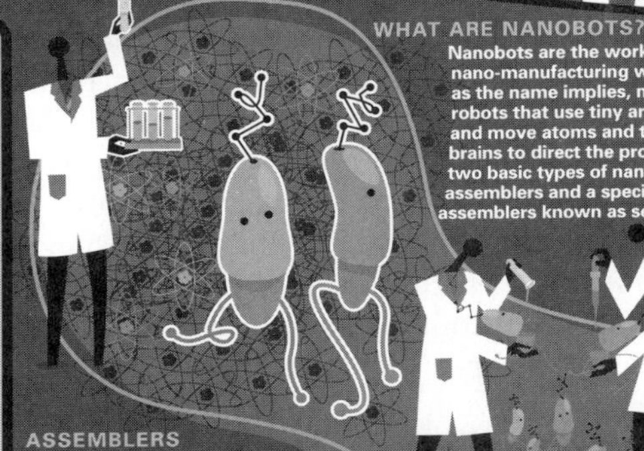

WHAT ARE NANOBOTS?

Nanobots are the workhorses of the nano-manufacturing world. They are, as the name implies, nanometer-scale robots that use tiny arms to pick up and move atoms and tiny electronic brains to direct the process. There are two basic types of nanobots: general assemblers and a special class of assemblers known as self-replicators.

ASSEMBLERS

These cell-sized robots may be equipped with fingers for manipulating matter, probes for distinguishing one atom or molecule from another and programs to tell the robots what to do.

SELF-REPLICATORS

To build anything of any size, you need a lot of assemblers, and constructing them one by one is expensive and laborious. So most assemblers will need the additional ability to make copies of themselves. To make a skyscraper, for example, a handful of assemblers would first clone themselves into an army of trillions of tiny robots, then start building (see NIGHTMARE SCENARIO).

TOP-DOWN

BOTTOM-UP

THE TWO SIDES OF MANUFACTURING

The conventional approach is top-down: starting with large clumps of steel, wood, plastic, masonry and shaping them into the forms you want. Nanotechnology is, by contrast, bottom-up: stacking individual atoms into useful shapes. We know that the bottom-up approach is possible because that's what biology does, assembling proteins from individual atoms and molecules, putting them together to form cells and layering cells upon cells to form large, complex objects such as sperm whales and giant Sequoia trees.

THE APPLICATIONS

Everything in the physical world is made of atoms. Nanobots manipulate atoms. Thus nanobots could in principle make anything from apples to airplanes. Nanobots will probably be made from carbon nanotubes, a new form of carbon that is astonishingly versatile.

NANOTUBES

Carbon molecules form a hexagonal mesh that curls into a cylinder like a tube of chicken wire. About 100 times as strong as steel and 50,000 times as thin as a human hair, they can serve as the structure of a nanobot. Acting as semiconductors, nanotubes are also ideal for building a nanobot's tiny microprocessor brain.

MOLECULAR MEDICINE

Streaming through the body by the billions, nanobots could chip plaque from arteries, gang up on bacteria and viruses, scour toxins from the bloodstream, repair broken blood vessels – and dozens of jobs doctors haven't dreamed of yet.

ENVIRONMENTAL CLEANUP

Specialized nanobots dumped into an oil spill, a toxic-waste site or even a polluted stream could seek out and find dangerous molecules, remove them or change their chemical structure one by one to render them harmless – or even beneficial.

ELECTRONICS

The advantages of smaller computers – more speed, more memory – are well known. But building matchbox-size supercomputers is too delicate a job for conventional mass manufacturing. Nanobots could do it easily, laying down circuits (made of nanotubes) molecule by molecule without a single mistake.

FUTURISTIC MATERIALS

A diamond's extraordinary clarity and strength make it an ideal building material, but also terribly hard to work with. Nanobots, however, could make diamonds in any shape at all – a sheet a few millimeters thick, say, to make a scratchproof window. And because the basic feedstock is ordinary carbon, these diamonds are as cheap as glass.

NIGHTMARE SCENARIO

Self-replication is the best way to build a few trillion nanobots in a hurry: each one makes two more, and each of those makes two and so on. But if they don't stop, the entire planet could rapidly be reduced to a teeming mass of robots. Nanotechnologists plan to program their tiny creations to stop reproducing after a certain point. but it takes only one rogue self-replicator to cause a disaster. If you thought computer viruses were a problem. . .

computer viruses seem utterly benign by comparison. Indeed, some critics contend that the potential dangers of nanotechnology outweigh any potential benefits. Yet those benefits are so potentially enormous that nanotech, even more than computers or genetic medicine, could be the defining technology of the coming century. It may be that the world will end up needing a nanotech immune system, with police nanobots constantly at microscopic war with destructive bots.

One way or another, nanotechnology is coming. 15

READING FOR MEANING

Write to create meanings for Lemonick's explanation of nanotechnology.

Start Making Meaning

Begin by devising your own two- or three-sentence definition of nanotechnology. Continue by writing about anything else in the selection or in your experience that contributes to your understanding of nanotechnology.

If You Are Stuck

If you cannot write at least a page, consider writing about

- what a nanomachine or nanobot is and what it may be able to do.
- how nanotechnology differs from biotechnology (paragraphs 5 and 6).
- how a nanobot may be able to copy itself and why it will be important for it to do so (paragraphs 10, 11, and 13).
- what the visual on pages 204–205 contributes to your understanding of nanotechnology.

READING LIKE A WRITER

DEVISING A READABLE PLAN

Think of a readable plan as fundamentally a logical, interrelated sequence of topics. One topic or main idea or point follows the preceding topics in a way that makes sense to readers. In addition, as you may have seen in analyzing the David Quammen reading about the concept of parthenogenesis, it helps readers greatly if the sequence is visibly cued by forecasting statements, topic sentences, transitions, and brief summaries. These important strategies can do nothing to rescue an illogical sequence of topics, however. You can learn more about how writers devise readable plans by outlining their essays.

Analyze

1. *Make a scratch outline* of the Lemonick reading. To create the scratch outline, *write* a phrase identifying the topic of each of the fifteen paragraphs. (For an example of scratch outlining, turn to Appendix 1, p. 529.)

2. *Divide* your outline into the following four parts: Part 1, paragraphs 1–3; Part 2, paragraphs 4–6; Part 3, paragraphs 7–11; Part 4, paragraphs 12–15. Finally, *write* a phrase or two that describes the common or related topics in each part.

Write

Write several sentences explaining how Lemonick creates a readable plan by grouping his topics into related parts. *Evaluate* briefly whether Lemonick seems to have found an ideal sequence for these fifteen topics, whether you see logical gaps among them, or whether you think one or more topics would fit better somewhere else in the sequence.

CONSIDERING IDEAS FOR YOUR OWN WRITING

Like Lemonick, consider writing about a technological concept. He mentions several possibilities: molecules, genetic engineering, biotechnology, atoms, recombinant DNA, and chip-etching techniques. There are many possibilities in computer science: cyberspace, local area networks, and virtual reality, for example. Within the field of automotive design, you might consider ergonomics, torque, aerodynamics, or fuel injection. In aeronautics there are such concepts as static pressure, lift, drag, airfoils, stalls, and dynamic stability. In mechanical engineering there are cumulative fatigue, load capacity, hardness testing, and corrosion control. If you have an interest in some other technology, a beginner's handbook or textbook would offer you several concepts to consider writing about.

Consider also the many concepts in academic disciplines you may be studying. For example, specialists in anthropology rely on the concepts of arranged marriages, serial monogamy, patrilineal/matrilineal descent, grouping, animism, rite of passage, genocide, acculturation, ethnocentrism, marriage, kinship, and ethnic identity. Researchers and students in sociology rely on the concepts of social control, construction of the self, socialization, social groups, stratification, mobility, and inequality.

DEBORAH TANNEN

Marked Women

Deborah Tannen (b. 1945), who holds the title of University Professor in Linguistics at Georgetown University, has written more than a dozen books and scores of articles. Although she does write technical works in linguistics, she also writes for a more general audience on the ways that language reflects the society in which it develops, particularly the society's attitudes about gender. Both her 1986 book, That's Not What I Meant!: How Conversational Style Makes or Breaks Your Relations with Others, *and her 1990 book,* You Just Don't Understand: Women and Men in Conversation, *were bestsellers.* The Argument Culture: Moving from Debate to Dialogue *was published in 1998. The following selection comes from an article that was originally published in the* New York Times Magazine *in 1993.*

In this essay, Tannen explains the concept of markedness, a "staple of linguistic theory." Linguistics — the study of language as a system for making meaning — has given birth to a new discipline called semiology, *the study of any system for making meaning. Tannen's essay embodies this shift, as it starts with a verbal principle (the marking of words) and applies it to the visual world (the marking of hairstyle and clothing).*

As you read the opening paragraphs, notice how Tannen unpacks the meaning of what various conference participants are wearing.

Some years ago I was at a small working conference of four women and eight men. Instead of concentrating on the discussion I found myself looking at the three other women at the table, thinking how each had a different style and how each style was coherent. 1

One woman had dark brown hair in a classic style, a cross between Cleopatra and Plain Jane. The severity of her straight hair was softened by wavy bangs and ends that turned under. Because she was beautiful, the effect was more Cleopatra than plain. 2

The second woman was older, full of dignity and composure. Her hair was cut in a fashionable style that left her with only one eye, thanks to a side part that let a curtain of hair fall across half her face. As she looked down to read her prepared paper, the hair robbed her of bifocal vision and created a barrier between her and the listeners. 3

The third woman's hair was wild, a frosted blond avalanche falling over and beyond her shoulders. When she spoke she 4 frequently tossed her head, calling attention to her hair and away from her lecture.

5 Then there was makeup. The first woman wore facial cover that made her skin smooth and pale, a black line under each eye and mascara that darkened already dark lashes. The second wore only a light gloss on her lips and a hint of shadow on her eyes. The third had blue bands under her eyes, dark blue shadow, mascara, bright red lipstick and rouge; her fingernails flashed red.

6 I considered the clothes each woman had worn during the three days of the conference: In the first case, man-tailored suits in primary colors with solid-color blouses. In the second, casual but stylish black T-shirts, a floppy collarless jacket and baggy slacks or a skirt in neutral colors. The third wore a sexy jump suit; tight sleeveless jersey and tight yellow slacks; a dress with gaping armholes and an indulged tendency to fall off one shoulder.

7 Shoes? No. 1 wore string sandals with medium heels; No. 2, sensible, comfortable walking shoes; No. 3, pumps with spike heels. You can fill in the jewelry, scarves, shawls, sweaters — or lack of them.

8 As I amused myself finding coherence in these styles, I suddenly wondered why I was scrutinizing only the women. I scanned the eight men at the table. And then I knew why I wasn't studying them. The men's styles were unmarked.

9 The term "marked" is a staple of linguistic theory. It refers to the way language alters the base meaning of a word by adding a linguistic particle that has no meaning on its own. The unmarked form of a word carries the meaning that goes without saying — what you think of when you're not thinking anything special.

10 The unmarked tense of verbs in English is the present — for example, *visit.* To indicate past, you mark the verb by adding *ed* to yield *visited.* For future, you add a word: *will visit.* Nouns are presumed to be singular until marked for plural, typically by adding *s* or *es,* so *visit* becomes *visits* and *dish* becomes *dishes.*

11 The unmarked forms of most English words also convey "male." Being male is the unmarked case. Endings like *ess* and *ette* mark words as "female." Unfortunately, they also tend to mark them for frivolousness. Would you feel safe entrusting your life to a doctorette? Alfre Woodard, who was an Oscar nominee for best supporting actress, says she identifies herself as an actor because "actresses worry about eyelashes and cellulite, and women who are actors worry about the characters we are playing." Gender markers pick up extra meanings that reflect common association with the female gender: not quite serious, often sexual.

Each of the women at the conference had to make decisions about hair, clothing, makeup and accessories, and each decision carried meaning. Every style available to us was marked. The men in our group had made decisions, too, but the range from which they chose was incomparably narrower. Men can choose styles that are marked, but they don't have to, and in this group none did. Unlike the women, they had the option of being unmarked. 12

Take the men's hair styles. There was no marine crew cut or oily longish hair falling into eyes, no asymmetrical, two-tiered construction to swirl over a bald top. One man was unabashedly bald; the others had hair of standard length, parted on one side, in natural shades of brown or gray or graying. Their hair obstructed no views, left little to toss or push back or run fingers through and, consequently, needed and attracted no attention. A few men had beards. In a business setting, beards might be marked. In this academic gathering, they weren't. 13

There could have been a cowboy shirt with string tie or a three-piece suit or a necklaced hippie in jeans. But there wasn't. All eight men wore brown or blue slacks and nondescript shirts of light colors. No man wore sandals or boots; their shoes were dark, closed, comfortable, and flat. In short, unmarked. 14

Although no man wore makeup, you couldn't say the men didn't wear makeup in the sense that you could say a woman didn't wear makeup. For men, no makeup is unmarked. 15

I asked myself what style we women could have adopted that would have been unmarked, like the men's. The answer was none. There is no unmarked woman. 16

There is no woman's hair style that can be called standard, that says nothing about her. The range of women's hair styles is staggering, but a woman whose hair has no particular style is perceived as not caring about how she looks, which can disqualify her from many positions, and will subtly diminish her as a person in the eyes of some. 17

Women must choose between attractive shoes and comfortable shoes. When our group made an unexpected trek, the woman who wore flat, laced shoes arrived first. Last to arrive was the woman in spike heels, shoes in hand and a handful of men around her. 18

If a woman's clothing is tight or revealing (in other words, sexy), it sends a message — an intended one of wanting to be attractive, but also a possibly unintended one of availability. If her clothes are not sexy, that too sends a message, lent meaning by the knowledge that they could have been. There are thousands of cosmetic products from which women can choose and myriad ways 19 of applying them. Yet no makeup at all is anything but unmarked. Some men see it as a hostile refusal to please them.

20 Women can't even fill out a form without telling stories about themselves. Most forms give four titles to choose from. "Mr." carries no meaning other than that the respondent is male. But a woman who checks "Mrs." or "Miss" communicates not only whether she has been married but also whether she has conservative tastes in forms of address — and probably other conservative values as well. Checking "Ms." declines to let on about marriage (checking "Mr." declines nothing since nothing was asked), but it also marks her as either liberated or rebellious, depending on the observer's attitudes and assumptions.

21 I sometimes try to duck these variously marked choices by giving my title as "Dr." — and in so doing risk marking myself as either uppity (hence sarcastic responses like "Excuse *me!*") or an overachiever (hence reactions of congratulatory surprise like "Good for you!").

22 All married women's surnames are marked. If a woman takes her husband's name, she announces to the world that she is married and has traditional values. To some it will indicate that she is less herself, more identified by her husband's identity. If she does not take her husband's name, this too is marked, seen as worthy of comment: She has *done* something; she has "kept her own name." A man is never said to have "kept his own name" because it never occurs to anyone that he might have given it up. For him using his own name is unmarked.

23 A married woman who wants to have her cake and eat it too may use her surname plus his, with or without a hyphen. But this too announces her marital status and often results in a tongue-tying string. In a list (Harvey O'Donovan, Jonathan Feldman, Stephanie Woodbury McGillicutty), the woman's multiple name stands out. It is marked.

24 I have never been inclined toward biological explanations of gender differences in language, but I was intrigued to see Ralph Fasold bring biological phenomena to bear on the question of linguistic marking in his book *The Sociolinguistics of Language.* Fasold stresses that language and culture are particularly unfair in treating women as the marked case because biologically it is the male that is marked. While two X chromosomes make a female, two Y chromosomes make nothing. Like the linguistic markers *s, es,* or *ess,* the Y chromosome doesn't "mean" anything unless it is attached to a root form — an X chromosome.

Developing this idea elsewhere Fasold points out that girls are born with full female bodies, while boys are born with modified female bodies. He invites men who doubt this to lift up their shirts and contemplate why they have nipples. 25

In his book, Fasold notes "a wide range of facts which demonstrates that female is the unmarked sex." For example, he observes that there are a few species that produce only females, like the whiptail lizard. Thanks to parthenogenesis, they have no trouble having as many daughters as they like. There are no species, however, that produce only males. This is no surprise, since any such species would become extinct in its first generation. 26

Fasold is also intrigued by species that produce individuals not involved in reproduction, like honeybees and leaf-cutter ants. Reproduction is handled by the queen and a relatively few males; the workers are sterile females. "Since they do not reproduce," Fasold said, "there is no reason for them to be one sex or the other, so they default, so to speak, to female." 27

Fasold ends his discussion of these matters by pointing out that if language reflected biology, grammar books would direct us to use "she" to include males and females and "he" only for specifically male referents. But they don't. They tell us that "he" means "he or she," and that "she" is used only if the referent is specifically female. This use of "he" as the sex-indefinite pronoun is an innovation introduced into English by grammarians in the eighteenth and nineteenth centuries, according to Peter Mühlhäusler and Rom Harré in *Pronouns and People.* From at least about 1500, the correct sex-indefinite pronoun was "they," as it still is in casual spoken English. In other words, the female was declared by grammarians to be the marked case. 28

Writing this article may mark me not as a writer, not as a linguist, not as an analyst of human behavior, but as a feminist — which will have positive or negative, but in any case powerful, connotations for readers. Yet I doubt that anyone reading Ralph Fasold's book would put that label on him. 29

I discovered the markedness inherent in the very topic of gender after writing a book on differences in conversational style based on geographical region, ethnicity, class, age, and gender. When I was interviewed, the vast majority of journalists wanted to talk about the differences between women and men. While I thought I was simply describing what I observed — something I had learned to do as a researcher — merely mentioning women and men marked me as a feminist for some. 30

When I wrote a book devoted to gender differences in ways of speaking, I sent the manuscript to five male colleagues, asking 31 them to alert me to any interpretation, phrasing, or wording that might seem unfairly negative toward men. Even so, when the book came out, I encountered responses like that of the television talk show host who, after interviewing me, turned to the audience and asked if they thought I was male-bashing.

32 Leaping upon a poor fellow who affably nodded in agreement, she made him stand and asked, "Did what she said accurately describe you?" "Oh, yes," he answered. "That's me exactly." "And what she said about women — does that sound like your wife?" "Oh, yes," he responded. "That's her exactly." "Then why do you think she's male-bashing?" He answered, with disarming honesty, "Because she's a woman and she's saying things about men."

33 To say anything about women and men without marking oneself as either feminist or anti-feminist, male-basher or apologist for men seems as impossible for a woman as trying to get dressed in the morning without inviting interpretations of her character.

34 Sitting at the conference table musing on these matters, I felt sad to think that we women didn't have the freedom to be unmarked that the men sitting next to us had. Some days you just want to get dressed and go about your business. But if you're a woman, you can't, because there is no unmarked woman.

READING FOR MEANING

Write to create meanings for Tannen's essay on the concept of markedness.

Start Making Meaning

Begin by listing two or three examples of markedness from paragraphs 1–8 in Tannen's essay, explaining briefly how these examples help you understand the concept. Continue by writing about anything else in the selection or in your experience that contributes to your understanding of markedness.

If You Are Stuck

If you cannot write at least a page, consider writing about

- the near-impossibility for a woman to escape marking (paragraphs 16–23).
- what one marked style in hair and clothes might look like for men.
- other examples of markedness, associated not with gender but with age, ethnicity, social class, income level, or anything else you can think of.

- Tannen's assumption that this essay may mark her "as a feminist — which will have positive or negative, but in any case powerful, connotations for readers" (paragraphs 29–33).

READING LIKE A WRITER

EXPLAINING THROUGH ILLUSTRATION

Because concepts are abstractions, mental not physical realities, they tend to be hard to grasp. One way to explain a concept is through illustration. Examples, anecdotes, descriptive detail, and specific facts and figures provide concrete images that help readers grasp or visualize concepts. Writers explaining concepts usually give several brief examples and sometimes also present an extended example. In his essay explaining parthenogenesis (pp. 184–88), David Quammen cites several examples of parthenogenetic species (paragraphs 2 and 3) and develops the example of the aphid over several paragraphs (4–8) so that readers can understand fully what is involved in the process of parthenogenesis. The following activity invites you to examine Tannen's use of a variety of brief examples to explain the concept of markedness.

Analyze

1. *Reread* paragraphs 1–8, and *make notes* in the margin about how Tannen creates through examples the three types of marked women. *Consider* what types of examples she uses for each type of marking.
2. *Examine* the first two sentences in paragraph 19 to see how she connects the examples in paragraphs 1–8 to the concept of markedness.

Write

Write several sentences explaining how Tannen uses examples to explain the abstract concept of markedness. *Cite examples* from paragraphs 1–8 to illustrate your explanation. Then *write a few more sentences* evaluating how effective the examples in these paragraphs are in introducing you to the concept of markedness.

CONSIDERING IDEAS FOR YOUR OWN WRITING

If you are taking a course concerned with language and society, you might want to learn about and then explain another linguistic concept such as semantics, language acquisition, connotation, or discourse community; or a semiotic concept such as signification, code, iconography, ideology, or popular culture. Related fields with interesting concepts to learn and write about are gender studies and sociology. Gender studies is concerned with such concepts as gender, femininity, masculinity, identity formation, objectification, intersubjectivity, nonsexist language, androgyny, domesticity, patriarchy, and the construction of desire. Sociology studies group dynamics and social patterns using concepts such as socialization, the family, role model, community, cohort, social stratification, positivism, dysfunctional families, and status.

BETH L. BAILEY

Dating

Beth L. Bailey (b. 1957) is associate professor in American studies at the University of New Mexico, where she holds the prestigious title of Regents Lecturer. She has also taught at Barnard College and at the University of Indonesia. A historian, she has written several scholarly books on nineteenth- and twentieth-century American culture, including The First Strange Place: The Alchemy of Race and Sex in World War II Hawaii *(1992);* Sex in the Heartland *(1999), the story of the sexual revolution of the 1960s in the small university town of Lawrence, Kansas; and* The Columbia Guide to America in the 1960s *(2001), with David Farber. "Dating" comes from Bailey's first book,* From Front Porch to Back Seat: Courtship in Twentieth-Century America *(1988).*

Bailey tells us that she first became interested in studying courtship attitudes and behavior when, as a college senior, she appeared on a television talk show to defend co-ed dorms, which were then relatively new and controversial. She was surprised when many people in the audience objected to co-ed dorms not on moral grounds, but out of fear that too much intimacy between young men and women would hasten "the dissolution of the dating system and the death of romance."

Before you read Bailey's historical explanation of dating, think about the attitudes and behavior of people your own age in regard to courtship and romance.

One day, the 1920s story goes, a young man asked a city girl if he might call on her (Black, 1924, p. 340). We know nothing else about the man or the girl — only that, when he arrived, she had her hat on. Not much of a story to us, but any American born before 1910 would have gotten the punch line. "She had her hat on": those five words were rich in meaning to early twentieth century Americans. The hat signaled that she expected to leave the house. He came on a "call," expecting to be received in her family's parlor, to talk, to meet her mother, perhaps to have some refreshments or to listen to her play the piano. She expected a "date," to be taken "out" somewhere and entertained. He ended up spending four weeks' savings fulfilling her expectations. 1

In the early twentieth century this new style of courtship, dating, had begun to supplant the old. Born primarily of the limits and opportunities of urban life, dating had almost completely replaced the old system of calling by the mid-1920s — and, in so doing, had transformed American courtship. Dating moved courtship into the public world, relocating it from family parlors 2 and community events to restaurants, theaters, and dance halls. At the same time, it removed couples from the implied supervision of the private sphere — from the watchful eyes of family and local community — to the anonymity of the public sphere. Courtship among strangers offered couples new freedom. But access to the public world of the city required money. One had to buy entertainment, or even access to a place to sit and talk. Money — men's money — became the basis of the dating system and, thus, of courtship. This new dating system, as it shifted courtship from the private to the public sphere and increasingly centered around money, fundamentally altered the balance of power between men and women in courtship.

3 The transition from calling to dating was as complete as it was fundamental. By the 1950s and 1960s, social scientists who studied American courtship found it necessary to remind the American public that dating was a "recent American innovation and not a traditional or universal custom." (Cavin, as cited in "Some," 1961, p. 125). Some of the many commentators who wrote about courtship believed dating was the best thing that had ever happened to relations between the sexes; others blamed the dating system for all the problems of American youth and American marriage. But virtually everyone portrayed the system dating replaced as infinitely simpler, sweeter, more innocent, and more graceful. Hardheaded social scientists waxed sentimental about the "horse-and-buggy days," when a young man's offer of a ride home from church was tantamount to a proposal and when young men came calling in the evenings and courtship took place safely within the warm bosom of the family. "The courtship which grew out of the sturdy social roots [of the nineteenth century]" one author wrote, "comes through to us for what it was — a gracious ritual, with clearly defined roles for man and woman, in which everyone knew the measured music and the steps" (Moss, 1963, p. 151).

4 Certainly a less idealized version of this model of courtship had existed in America, but it was not this model that dating was supplanting. Although only about 45 percent of Americans lived in urban areas by 1910, few of them were so untouched by the sweeping changes of the late nineteenth century that they could live that dream of rural simplicity. Conventions of courtship at that time were not set by simple yeoman farmers and their families but by the rising middle class, often in imitation of the ways of "society." . . .

5 The call itself was a complicated event. A myriad of rules governed everything: the proper amount of time between

invitation and visit (a fortnight or less); whether or not refreshments should be served (not if one belonged to a fashionable or semi-fashionable circle, but outside of "smart" groups in cities like New York and Boston, girls *might* serve iced drinks with little cakes or tiny cups of coffee or hot chocolate and sandwiches); chaperonage (the first call must be made on daughter and mother, but excessive chaperonage would indicate to the man that his attentions were unwelcome); appropriate topics of conversation (the man's interests, but never too personal); how leave should be taken (on no account should the woman "accompany [her caller] to the door nor stand talking while he struggles into his coat") ("Lady," 1904, p. 255).

6 Each of these "measured steps," as the mid-twentieth century author nostalgically called them, was a test of suitability, breeding, and background. Advice columns and etiquette books emphasized that these were the manners of any "well-bred" person — and conversely implied that deviations revealed a lack of breeding. However, around the turn of the century, many people who did lack this narrow "breeding" aspired to politeness. Advice columns in women's magazines regularly printed questions from "Country Girl" and "Ignoramus" on the fine points of calling etiquette. Young men must have felt the pressure of girls' expectations, for they wrote to the same advisers with questions about calling. In 1907, *Harper's Bazaar* ran a major article titled "Etiquette for Men," explaining the ins and outs of the calling system (Hall, 1907, pp. 1095–97). In the first decade of the twentieth century, this rigid system of calling was the convention not only of the "respectable" but also of those who aspired to respectability.

7 At the same time, however, the new system of dating was emerging. By the mid-1910s, the word *date* had entered the vocabulary of the middle-class public. In 1914, the *Ladies' Home Journal,* a bastion of middle-class respectability, used the term (safely enclosed in quotation marks but with no explanation of its meaning) several times. The word was always spoken by that exotica, the college sorority girl — a character marginal in her exoticness but nevertheless a solid product of the middle class. "One beautiful evening of the spring term," one such article begins, "when I was a college girl of eighteen, the boy whom, because of his popularity in every phase of college life, I had been proud gradually to allow the monopoly of my 'dates,' took me unexpectedly into his arms. As he kissed me impetuously I was glad, from the bottom of my heart, for the training of that mother who had taught me to hold myself aloof from all personal familiarities of boys and men" ("How," 1914, p. 9).

8 Sugarcoated with a tribute to motherhood and virtue, the dates — and the kiss — were unmistakably presented for a middle-class audience. By 1924, ten years later, when the story of the unfortunate young man who went to call on the city girl was current, dating had essentially replaced calling in middle-class culture. The knowing smiles of the story's listeners had probably started with the word *call* — and not every hearer would have been sympathetic to the man's plight. By 1924, he really should have known better. . . .

9 Dating, which to the privileged and protected would seem a system of increased freedom and possibility, stemmed originally from the lack of opportunities. Calling, or even just visiting, was not a practicable system for young people whose families lived crowded into one or two rooms. For even the more established or independent working-class girls, the parlor and the piano often simply didn't exist. Some "factory girls" struggled to find a way to receive callers. The *Ladies' Home Journal* approvingly reported the case of six girls, workers in a box factory, who had formed a club and pooled part of their wages to pay the "janitress of a tenement house" to let them use her front room two evenings a week. It had a piano. One of the girls explained their system: "We ask the boys to come when they like and spend the evening. We haven't any place at home to see them, and I hate seeing them on the street" (Preston, 1907, p. 31).

10 Many other working girls, however, couldn't have done this even had they wanted to. They had no extra wages to pool, or they had no notions of middle-class respectability. Some, especially girls of ethnic families, were kept secluded — chaperoned according to the customs of the old country. But many others fled the squalor, drabness, and crowdedness of their homes to seek amusement and intimacy elsewhere. And a "good time" increasingly became identified with public places and commercial amusements, making young women whose wages would not even cover the necessities of life dependent on men's "treats" (Peiss, 1986, pp. 75, 51–52). Still, many poor and working-class couples did not so much escape from the home as they were pushed from it.

11 These couples courted on the streets, sometimes at cheap dance halls or eventually at the movies. These were not respectable places, and women could enter them only so far as they, themselves, were not considered respectable. Respectable young women did, of course, enter the public world, but their excursions into the public were cushioned. Public courtship of middle-class and upper-class youth was at least *supposed* to be

chaperoned; those with money and social position went to private dances with carefully controlled guest lists, to theater parties where they were a private group within the public. As rebels would soon complain, the supervision of society made the private parlor seem almost free by contrast. Women who were not respectable did have relative freedom of action — but the trade-off was not necessarily a happy one for them.

12 The negative factors were important, but dating rose equally from the possibilities offered by urban life. Privileged youth, as Lewis Erenberg shows in his study of New York nightlife, came to see the possibility of privacy in the anonymous public, in the excitement and freedom the city offered (1981, pp. 60–87, 139–42). They looked to lower-class models of freedom — to those beyond the constraints of respectability. As a society girl informed the readers of the *Ladies' Home Journal* in 1914: "Nowadays it is considered 'smart' to go to the low order of dance halls, and not only be a looker-on, but also to dance among all sorts and conditions of men and women. . . . Nowadays when we enter a restaurant and dance place it is hard to know who is who" ("A Girl," 1914, p. 7). In 1907, the same magazine had warned unmarried women never to go alone to a "public restaurant" with any man, even a relative. There was no impropriety in the act, the adviser had conceded, but it still "lays [women] open to misunderstanding and to being classed with women of undesirable reputation by the strangers present" (Kingsland, May 1907, p. 48). Rebellious and adventurous young people sought that confusion, and the gradual loosening of proprieties they engendered helped to change courtship. Young men and women went out into the world *together,* enjoying a new kind of companionship and the intimacy of a new kind of freedom from adult supervision.

13 The new freedom that led to dating came from other sources as well. Many more serious (and certainly respectable) young women were taking advantage of opportunities to enter the public world — going to college, taking jobs, entering and creating new urban professions. Women who belonged to the public world by day began to demand fuller access to the public world in general. . . .

14 Between 1890 and 1925, dating — in practice and in name — had gradually, almost imperceptibly, become a universal custom in America. By the 1930s it had transcended its origins: Middle America associated dating with neither upper-class rebellion nor the urban lower classes. The rise of dating was usually explained, quite simply, by the invention of the automobile. Cars had given youth mobility and privacy, and so had brought about the system.

This explanation — perhaps not consciously but definitely not coincidentally — revised history. The automobile certainly contributed to the rise of dating as a *national* practice, especially in rural and suburban areas, but it was simply accelerating and extending a process already well under way. Once its origins were located firmly in Middle America, however, and not in the extremes of urban upper- and lower-class life, dating had become an American institution.

15 Dating not only transformed the outward modes and conventions of American courtship, it also changed the distribution of control and power in courtship. One change was generational: the dating system lessened parental control and gave young men and women more freedom. The dating system also shifted power from women to men. Calling, either as a simple visit or as the elaborate late nineteenth-century ritual, gave women a large portion of control. First of all, courtship took place within the girl's home — in women's "sphere," as it was called in the nineteenth century — or at entertainments largely devised and presided over by women. Dating moved courtship out of the home and into man's sphere — the world outside the home. Female controls and conventions lost much of their power outside women's sphere. And while many of the conventions of female propriety were restrictive and repressive, they had allowed women (young women and their mothers) a great deal of immediate control over courtship. The transfer of spheres thoroughly undercut that control.

16 Second, in the calling system, the woman took the initiative. Etiquette books and columns were adamant on that point: it was the "girl's privilege" to ask a young man to call. Furthermore, it was highly improper for the man to take the initiative. In 1909 a young man wrote to the *Ladies' Home Journal* adviser asking, "May I call upon a young woman whom I greatly admire, although she had not given me the permission? Would she be flattered at my eagerness, even to the setting aside of conventions, or would she think me impertinent?" Mrs. Kingsland replied: "I think that you would risk her just displeasure and frustrate your object of finding favor with her." Softening the prohibition, she then suggested an invitation might be secured through a mutual friend (Kingsland, 1909, p. 58). . . .

17 Contrast these strictures with advice on dating etiquette from the 1940s and 1950s: An advice book for men and women warns that "girls who [try] to usurp the right of boys to choose their own dates" will "ruin a good dating career. . . . Fair or not, it is the way of life. From the Stone Age, when men chased and captured their women, comes the yen of a boy to do the pursuing.

You will control your impatience, therefore, and respect the time-honored custom of boys to take the first step" (Richmond, 1958, p. 11). . . .

18 This absolute reversal of roles almost necessarily accompanied courtship's move from woman's sphere to man's sphere. Although the convention-setters commended the custom of woman's initiative because it allowed greater exclusivity (it might be "difficult for a girl to refuse the permission to call, no matter how unwelcome or unsuitable an acquaintance of the man might be"), the custom was based on a broader principle of etiquette (Hart and Brown, 1944, p. 89). The host or hostess issued any invitation; the guest did not invite himself or herself. An invitation to call was an invitation to visit in a woman's home.

19 An invitation to go out on a date, on the other hand, was an invitation into man's world — not simply because dating took place in the public sphere (commonly defined as belonging to men), though that was part of it, but because dating moved courtship into the world of the economy. Money — men's money — was at the center of the dating system. Thus, on two counts, men became the hosts and assumed the control that came with that position.

20 There was some confusion caused by this reversal of initiative, especially during the twenty years or so when going out and calling coexisted as systems. (The unfortunate young man in the apocryphal story, for example, had asked the city girl if he might call on her, so perhaps she was conventionally correct to assume he meant to play the host.) Confusions generally were sorted out around the issue of money. One young woman, "Henrietta L.," wrote to the *Ladies' Home Journal* to inquire whether a girl might "suggest to a friend going to any entertainment or place of amusement where there will be any expense to the young man." The reply: "Never, under any circumstances." The adviser explained that the invitation to go out must "always" come from the man, for he was the one "responsible for the expense" (Kingsland, Oct. 1907, p. 60). This same adviser insisted that the woman must "always" invite the man to call; clearly she realized that money was the central issue.

21 The centrality of money in dating had serious implications for courtship. Not only did money shift control and initiative to men by making them the "hosts," it led contemporaries to see dating as a system of exchange best understood through economic analogies or as an economic system pure and simple. Of course, people did recognize in marriage a similar economic dimension — the man undertakes to support his wife in exchange for her filling various roles important to him — but marriage was a permanent relation-

ship. Dating was situational, with no long-term commitments implied, and when a man, in a highly visible ritual, spent money on a woman in public, it seemed much more clearly an economic act.

22 In fact, the term *date* was associated with the direct economic exchange of prostitution at an early time. A prostitute called "Maimie," in letters written to a middle-class benefactor/friend in the late nineteenth century, described how men made "dates" with her (Peiss, 1986, p. 54). And a former waitress turned prostitute described the process to the Illinois Senate Committee on Vice this way: "You wait on a man and he smiles at you. You see a chance to get a tip and you smile back. Next day he returns and you try harder than ever to please him. Then right away he wants to make a date, and offer you money and presents if you'll be a good fellow and go out with him" (Rosen, 1982, p. 151). These men, quite clearly, were buying sexual favors — but the occasion of the exchange was called a "date."

23 Courtship in America had always turned somewhat on money (or background). A poor clerk or stockyards worker would not have called upon the daughter of a well-off family, and men were expected to be economically secure before they married. But in the dating system money entered directly into the relationship between a man and a woman as the symbolic currency of exchange in even casual dating.

24 Dating, like prostitution, made access to women directly dependent on money. . . . In dating, though, the exchange was less direct and less clear than in prostitution. One author, in 1924, made sense of it this way. In dating, he reasoned, a man is responsible for all expenses. The woman is responsible for nothing — she contributes only her company. Of course, the man contributes his company, too, but since he must "add money to balance the bargain" his company must be worth less than hers. Thus, according to this economic understanding, she is selling her company to him. In his eyes, dating didn't even involve an exchange; it was a direct purchase. The moral "subtleties" of a woman's position in dating, the author concluded, were complicated even further by the fact that young men, "discovering that she must be bought, [like] to buy her when [they happen] to have the money" (Black, 1924, p. 342).

25 Yet another young man, the same year, publicly called a halt to such "promiscuous buying." Writing anonymously (for good reason) in *American Magazine*, the author declared a "one-man buyer's strike." This man estimated that, as a "buyer of feminine companionship" for the previous five years, he had "invested" about $20 a week — a grand total of over $5,000. Finally, he

wrote, he had realized that "there is a point at which any commodity — even such a delightful commodity as feminine companionship — costs more than it is worth" ("Too-high," 1924, pp. 27, 145–50). The commodity he had bought with his $5,000 had been priced beyond its "real value" and he had had enough. This man said "enough" not out of principle, not because he rejected the implications of the economic model of courtship, but because he felt he wasn't receiving value for money.

In . . . these economic analyses, the men are complaining about the new dating system, lamenting the passing of the mythic good old days when "a man without a quarter in his pocket could call on a girl and not be embarrassed," the days before a woman had to be "bought" ("Too-high," 1924, pp. 145–50). In recognizing so clearly the economic model on which dating operated, they also clearly saw that the model was a bad one — in purely economic terms. The exchange was not equitable; the commodity was overpriced. Men were operating at a loss. 26

Here, however, they didn't understand their model completely. True, the equation (male companionship plus money equals female companionship) was imbalanced. But what men were buying in the dating system was not just female companionship, not just entertainment — but power. Money purchased obligation; money purchased inequality; money purchased control. 27

The conventions that grew up to govern dating codified women's inequality and ratified men's power. Men asked women out; women were condemned as "aggressive" if they expressed interest in a man too directly. Men paid for everything, but often with the implication that women "owed" sexual favors in return. The dating system required men always to assume control, and women to act as men's dependents. 28

Yet women were not without power in the system, and they were willing to contest men with their "feminine" power. Much of the public discourse on courtship in twentieth-century America was concerned with this contestation. Thousands of sources chronicled the struggles of, and between, men and women — struggles mediated by the "experts" and arbiters of convention — to create a balance of power, to gain or retain control of the dating system. These struggles, played out most clearly in the fields of sex, science, and etiquette, made ever more explicit the complicated relations between men and women in a changing society. 29

References

A Girl. (1914, July). Believe me. *Ladies' Home Journal,* 7.

Black, A. (1924, August). Is the young person coming back? *Harper's,* 340, 342.

Erenberg, L. (1981). *Steppin' out.* Westport, Conn.: Greenwood Press.
Hall, F. H. (1907, November). Etiquette for men. *Harper's Bazaar,* 1095–97.
Hart, S., & Brown, L. (1944). *How to get your man and hold him.* New York: New Power Publications.
How may a girl know? (1914, January). *Ladies' Home Journal,* 9.
Kingsland. (1907, May). *Ladies' Home Journal,* 48.
———. (1907, October). *Ladies' Home Journal,* 60.
———. (1909, May). *Ladies' Home Journal,* 58.
Lady from Philadelphia. (1904, February). *Ladies' Home Journal,* 255.
Moss, A. (1963, April). Whatever happened to courtship? *Mademoiselle,* 151.
Peiss, K. (1986). *Cheap amusements: Working women and leisure in turn-of-the-century New York.* Philadelphia: Temple University Press.
Preston, A. (1907, February). After business hours — what? *Ladies' Home Journal,* 31.
Richmond, C. (1958). *Handbook of dating.* Philadelphia: Westminster Press.
Rosen, R. (1982). *The Lost Sisterhood: Prostitution in America, 1900–1918.* Baltimore: Johns Hopkins University Press, 1982.
Some expert opinions on dating. (1961, August). *McCall's,* 125.
Too-high cost of courting. (1924, September). *American Magazine,* 27, 145–50.

READING FOR MEANING

Write to create meanings for Bailey's explanation of dating.

Start Making Meaning

Begin by listing the differences between calling and dating. Continue by writing about anything else in the selection or in your experience that contributes to your understanding of the concept of dating as Bailey explains it.

If You Are Stuck

If you cannot write at least a page, consider writing about

- how "lower-class" and "middle-class" values have shaped the current conception and practice of dating (paragraphs 7–14).
- the identification of a "good time" with "public places and commercial amusements" (paragraphs 10 and 11).
- the connection between money and power in dating (paragraphs 25–27).
- the contrasts between the dating system in the early decades of the twentieth century as described by Bailey and the courtship system you know today, connecting your contrasts to specific features of the early system.

READING LIKE A WRITER

EXPLAINING THROUGH COMPARISON/CONTRAST

One of the best ways of explaining something new is to relate it, through comparison or contrast, to something that is familiar or well known. A *comparison* points out similarities between items; a *contrast* points out differences. Sometimes writers use both comparison and contrast; sometimes they use only one or the other. Bailey uses comparison and contrast a little differently. She is not explaining something new to readers by relating it to something already known to them. Instead, she is explaining something already known — dating — by relating it to something that is unknown to most readers — calling, an earlier type of courtship. Since she is studying dating as a sociologist, this historical perspective enables her to consider the changing relationship between men and women and what it tells us about changing social and cultural expectations and practices.

Analyze

1. *Reread* paragraphs 15–19, and *put a line* under the sentences that assert the points of the contrast Bailey develops in these paragraphs. To get started, *underline* the first and last sentences in paragraph 15. Except for paragraph 17, you will find one or two sentences in the other paragraphs that assert the points.

2. *Examine closely* the other sentences to discover how Bailey develops or illustrates each of the points of the contrast between calling and dating.

Write

Write several sentences reporting what you have learned about how Bailey develops the contrast between calling and dating. *Give examples* from paragraphs 15–19 to support your explanation. *Write a few more sentences* evaluating how informative you find Bailey's contrast given your own knowledge of dating. What parts are least and most informative? What makes the most informative part so successful?

Compare

Compare Bailey's use of comparison/contrast to help explain the concept of dating with Quammen's use of it to explain parthenogenesis (paragraphs 12–15, pp. 187–88). *Write several sentences* explaining how the comparison or contrast helps you understand parthenogenesis. *Write a few more sentences* reporting what you have learned about how different writers use comparison/contrast in explanatory essays.

CONSIDERING IDEAS FOR YOUR OWN WRITING

Like Bailey, you might choose a concept that tells something about current or historical social values, behaviors, or attitudes. To look at changing attitudes toward immigration and assimilation, for example, you could write about the concept of the melting pot and the alternatives that have been suggested. Some related concepts you might consider are multiculturalism, race, ethnicity, masculinity or femininity, heterosexuality or homosexuality, and affirmative action.

LINH KIEU NGO

Cannibalism: It Still Exists

Linh Kieu Ngo wrote this essay when he was a first-year college student. In it, he explains a concept of importance in anthropology and of wide general interest — cannibalism, the eating of human flesh by other humans. Most Americans may know about survival cannibalism, but few may know about the importance historically of dietary and ritual cannibalism. Ngo explains all of these types in his essay.

Before you read, think about any examples of survival cannibalism you may have read about.

Fifty-five Vietnamese refugees fled to Malaysia on a small fishing boat to escape communist rule in their country following the Vietnam War. During their escape attempt, the captain was shot by the coast guard. The boat and its passengers managed to outrun the coast guard to the open sea, but they had lost the only person who knew the way to Malaysia, the captain. 1

The men onboard tried to navigate the boat, but after a week fuel ran out and they drifted farther out to sea. Their supply of food and water was gone; people were starving, and some of the elderly were near death. The men managed to produce a small amount of drinking water by boiling salt water, using dispensable wood from the boat to create a small fire near the stern. They also tried to fish, but had little success. 2

A month went by, and the old and weak died. At first, the crew threw the dead overboard, but later, out of desperation, the crew turned to human flesh as a source of food. Some people vomited as they attempted to eat it, while others refused to resort to cannibalism and see the bodies of their loved ones sacrificed for food. Those who did not eat died of starvation, and their bodies in turn became food for others. Human flesh was cut out, washed in salt water, and hung to dry for preservation. The liquids inside the cranium were eaten to quench thirst. The livers, kidneys, heart, stomach, and intestines were boiled and eaten. 3

Five months passed before a whaling vessel discovered the drifting boat, looking like a graveyard of bones. There was only one survivor. 4

Cannibalism, the act of human beings eating human flesh (Sagan 2), has a long history and continues to hold interest and create controversy. Many books and research reports offer examples of cannibalism, but a few scholars have questioned whether cannibalism was ever practiced anywhere, except in cases of ensuring 5 survival in times of famine or isolation (Askenasy 43–54). Recently, some scholars have tried to understand why people in the West have been so eager to attribute cannibalism to non-westerners (Barker, Hulme, and Iversen). Cannibalism has long been a part of American popular culture. For example, Mark Twain's "Cannibalism in the Cars" tells a humorous story about cannibalism by well-to-do travelers on a train stranded in a snowstorm, and cannibalism is still a popular subject for jokes ("Cannibal Jokes").

6 If we assume there is some reality to the reports about cannibalism, how can we best understand this concept? Cannibalism can be broken down into two main categories: exocannibalism, the eating of outsiders or foreigners, and endocannibalism, the eating of members of one's own social group (Shipman 70). Within these categories are several functional types of cannibalism, three of the most common being survival cannibalism, dietary cannibalism, and religious and ritual cannibalism.

7 Survival cannibalism occurs when people trapped without food have to decide "whether to starve or eat fellow humans" (Shipman 70). In the case of the Vietnamese refugees, the crew and passengers on the boat ate human flesh to stay alive. They did not kill people to get human flesh for nourishment, but instead waited until the people had died. Even after human carcasses were sacrificed as food, the boat people ate only enough to survive. Another case of survival cannibalism occurred in 1945, when General Douglas MacArthur's forces cut supply lines to Japanese troops stationed in the Pacific Islands. In one incident, Japanese troops were reported to have sacrificed the Arapesh people of northeastern New Guinea for food in order to avoid death by starvation (Tuzin 63). The most famous example of survival cannibalism in American history comes from the diaries, letters, and interviews of survivors of the California-bound Donner Party, who in the winter of 1846 were snowbound in the Sierra Nevada Mountains for five months. Thirty-five of eighty-seven adults and children died, and some of them were eaten (Hart 116–17; Johnson).

8 Unlike survival cannibalism, in which human flesh is eaten as a last resort after a person has died, in dietary cannibalism, humans are purchased or trapped for food and then eaten as a part of a culture's traditions. In addition, survival cannibalism often involves people eating other people of the same origins, whereas dietary cannibalism usually involves people eating foreigners.

9 In the Miyanmin society of the west Sepik interior of Papua, New Guinea, villagers do not value human flesh over that of pigs or marsupials because human flesh is part of their diet (Poole 17). The Miyanmin people observe no differences in "gender, kinship, ritual status, and bodily substance"; they eat anyone, even their

own dead. In this respect, then, they practice both endocannibalism and exocannibalism; and to ensure a constant supply of human flesh for food, they raid neighboring tribes and drag their victims back to their village to be eaten (Poole 11). Perhaps, in the history of this society, there was at one time a shortage of wild game to be hunted for food, and because people were more plentiful than fish, deer, rabbits, pigs, or cows, survival cannibalism was adopted as a last resort. Then, as their culture developed, the Miyanmin may have retained the practice of dietary cannibalism, which has endured as a part of their culture.

Similar to the Miyanmin, the people of the Leopard and Alligator societies in South America eat human flesh as part of their cultural tradition. Practicing dietary exocannibalism, the Leopard people hunt in groups, with one member wearing the skin of a leopard to conceal the face. They ambush their victims in the forest and carry their victims back to their village to be eaten. The Alligator people also hunt in groups, but they hide themselves under a canoelike submarine that resembles an alligator, then swim close to a fisherman's or trader's canoe to overturn it and catch their victims (MacCormack 54). 10

Religious or ritual cannibalism is different from survival and dietary cannibalism in that it has a ceremonial purpose rather than one of nourishment. Sometimes only a single victim is sacrificed in a ritual, while at other times many are sacrificed. For example, the Bangala tribe of the Congo River in central Africa honors a deceased chief or leader by purchasing, sacrificing, and feasting on slaves (Sagan 53). The number of slaves sacrificed is determined by how highly the tribe members revered the deceased leader. 11

Ritual cannibalism among South American Indians often serves as revenge for the dead. Like the Bangalas, some South American tribes kill their victims to be served as part of funeral rituals, with human sacrifices denoting that the deceased was held in high honor. Also like the Bangalas, these tribes use outsiders as victims. Unlike the Bangalas, however, the Indians sacrifice only one victim instead of many in a single ritual. For example, when a warrior of a tribe is killed in battle, the family of the warrior forces a victim to take the identity of the warrior. The family adorns the victim with the deceased warrior's belongings and may even force him to marry the deceased warrior's wives. But once the family believes the victim has assumed the spiritual identity of the deceased warrior, the family kills him. The children in the tribe soak their hands in the victim's blood to symbolize their revenge of the warrior's death. Elderly women from the tribe drink the victim's blood and then cut up his body for roasting and eating (Sagan 53–54). By sacrificing a victim, the people of the tribe 12 believe that the death of the warrior has been avenged and the soul of the deceased can rest in peace.

13 In the villages of certain African tribes, only a small part of a dead body is used in ritual cannibalism. In these tribes, where the childbearing capacity of women is highly valued, women are obligated to eat small, raw fragments of genital parts during fertility rites. Elders of the tribe supervise this ritual to ensure that the women will be fertile. In the Bimin-Kuskusmin tribe, for instance, a widow eats a small, raw fragment of flesh from the penis of her deceased husband in order to enhance her future fertility and reproductive capacity. Similarly, a widower may eat a raw fragment of flesh from his deceased wife's vagina along with a piece of her bone marrow; by eating her flesh, he hopes to strengthen the fertility capacity of his daughters borne by his dead wife, and by eating her bone marrow, he honors her reproductive capacity. Also, when an elder woman of the village who has shown great reproductive capacity dies, her uterus and the interior parts of her vagina are eaten by other women who hope to further benefit from her reproductive power (Poole 16–17).

14 Members of developed societies in general practice none of these forms of cannibalism, with the occasional exception of survival cannibalism when the only alternative is starvation. It is possible, however, that our distant-past ancestors were cannibals who through the eons turned away from the practice. We are, after all, descended from the same ancestors as the Miyanmin, the Alligator, and the Leopard people, and survival cannibalism shows that people are capable of eating human flesh when they have no other choice.

Works Cited

Askenasy, Hans. *Cannibalism: From Sacrifice to Survival.* Amherst: Prometheus, 1994.

Barker, Francis, Peter Hulme, and Margaret Iversen, eds. *Cannibalism and the New World.* Cambridge: Cambridge UP, 1998.

"Cannibal Jokes." *The Loonie Bin of Jokes.* 22 Sept. 1999 <http://www.looniebin.mb.ca/cannibal.html>.

Hart, James D. *A Companion to California.* Berkeley: U of California P, 1987.

Johnson, Kristin., "New Light on the Donner Party." 28 Sept. 1999 <http://www.metrogourmet.com/crossroads.KJhome.html>.

MacCormack, Carol. "Human Leopard and Crocodile." Ed. Paula Brown and Donald Tuzin. *The Ethnography of Cannibalism.* Washington: Society of Psychological Anthropology, 1983. 54–55.

Poole, Fitz John Porter. "Cannibals, Tricksters, and Witches." Ed. Paula Brown and Donald Tuzin. *The Ethnography of Cannibalism.* Washington: Society of Psychological Anthropology, 1983. 11, 16–17.

Sagan, Eli. *Cannibalism.* New York: Harper, 1976.

Shipman, Pat. "The Myths and Perturbing Realities of Cannibalism." *Discover* Mar. 1987: 70 +.

Tuzin, Donald. "Cannibalism and Arapesh Cosmology." Ed. Paula Brown and Donald Tuzin. *The Ethnography of Cannibalism.* Washington: Society of Psychological Anthropology, 1983. 61–63.

Twain, Mark. "Cannibalism in the Cars." *The Complete Short Stories of Mark Twain.* Ed. Charles Neider. New York: Doubleday, 1957. 9–16.

READING FOR MEANING

Write to create meanings for Ngo's explanation of cannibalism.

Start Making Meaning

Begin by listing two or three key facts about the three types of cannibalism Ngo reports on: survival, dietary, and religious. Continue by writing about anything else in the selection or in your experience that contributes to your understanding of cannibalism.

If You Are Stuck

If you cannot write at least a page, consider writing about

- the information offered about survival cannibalism in the opening anecdote (paragraphs 1–4).
- the most surprising example you encountered in the reading, describing it briefly and giving your reaction to it.
- what you already knew about cannibalism before reading and what new information you are most likely to remember from the reading.
- whether you might resort to cannibalism in order to survive.

READING LIKE A WRITER

INTEGRATING SOURCES SMOOTHLY

When writers explain concepts to their readers, they nearly always rely in part on information gleaned from sources in a library or on the Internet. When they do so, they must acknowledge these sources. Within their essays, writers must find ways to integrate smoothly into their own sentences the information borrowed from each source and to acknowledge or cite each source. When you analyzed David Quammen's essay, you learned that writers rely on certain signal phrases and sentence structures to integrate quoted materials smoothly into their essays. Sometimes, however, writers do not quote a source but instead summarize or paraphase it. (See Appendix 1, pp. 530–33, for examples of summarizing and paraphrasing.) When they do so, they may acknowledge the source of the summarized or paraphrased material through signal phrases or special sentence structures, or they may use a formal style of parenthetical citation. Ngo relies on both these strategies. (Ngo's parenthetical citations refer to sources in the works-cited list at the end of his essay.)

Analyze

1. In paragraphs 7 and 9, *notice* how Ngo sets up a sentence to integrate the quoted phrases.
2. *Put a checkmark* in the margin by each instance of parenthetical citation in paragraphs 5, 6, and 9–13. *Notice* where these citations are located in Ngo's sentences and the different forms they take.
3. *Make notes* in the margin about similarities and differences you observe in Ngo's use of parenthetical citations.

Write

Write a few sentences explaining how Ngo integrates quoted phrases into his sentences and makes use of parenthetical citations. *Illustrate* your explanation with examples from the reading.

CONSIDERING IDEAS FOR YOUR OWN WRITING

Consider writing about some other well-established human taboo or practice, such as ostracism, incest, pedophilia, murder, circumcision, celibacy or virginity, caste systems, a particular religion's dietary restrictions, adultery, stealing, gourmandism, or divorce.

A SPECIAL READING STRATEGY

Summarizing

Summarizing, a potent reading-for-meaning strategy, is also a kind of writing you will encounter in your college classes and on the job. By rereading Ngo's essay on cannibalism with an eye toward finding its main ideas, you can do the groundwork for writing a summary of it. Taking the time to write a summary will help you remember what you have read and could help you explain to others the important ideas in Ngo's essay. For detailed guidelines on writing an extended summary, see Appendix 1 (pp. 530–31).

LYN GUTIERREZ

Music Therapy

Lyn Gutierrez wrote this essay when she was a first-year college student. In it she presents an alternative form of healing — music therapy — from a variety of perspectives: by tracing its historical development, by providing institutional and individual definitions, by explaining a music therapist's training, by detailing when and how music therapy is used, and by outlining a music therapy session. Gutierrez builds logically on each piece of information until she has provided readers a comprehensive view of her subject.

The other readings in this chapter are followed by reading and writing activities. Following this reading, however, you are on your own to decide how to read for meaning and read like a writer.

Why do department stores play music for their customers? Why does the dentist let patients pick music to listen to while in the chair? Why do companies have music playing for the callers waiting on hold? Why do most people listen to music while driving? The answer is simple: music is therapeutic — it can relax, rejuvenate, calm, and energize. 1

During and after World War I and World War II, musicians visited veterans hospitals around the country in an effort to lift the spirits of patients suffering from physical and emotional trauma. The performers would sing, dance, play instruments, and perform skits. Doctors noticed positive physical and emotional patient responses to the music; it wasn't long before these facilities were hiring musicians to perform on a regular basis. In 1944, Michigan State University offered the first formal degree in music therapy. The desire to expand the use of music therapy resulted in the formation of the National Association for Music Therapy (NAMT) in 1950. Twenty-one years later, in 1971, the American Association for Music Therapy (AAMT) was established. In 1998, NAMT joined forces with AAMT to form the American Music Therapy Association (AMTA). Today, AMTA boasts 5,000 members. 2

AMTA defines music therapy as "the prescribed use of music by a qualified person to effect positive changes in the psychological, physical, cognitive, or social functioning of individuals with health or educational problems" ("FAQs"). Bruce Martin, a registered and board-certified music therapist working in Vancouver, Washington, defines music therapy as "an arts therapy which has been used to help people withstand pain and provide relaxation 3 and recreation. It is used in every stage of human development, from birth through death. Music therapy is used to maintain, restore, or increase a person's social, physical, or mental well-being" ("Sound Therapy Works"). Whether derived from an institutional definition or a personal one, the primary goal of music therapy is clearly to promote well-being.

4 But a music therapist does not simply decide one day to pick up a guitar and visit a hospital. A music therapist must complete an approved college curriculum,[1] including courses in anatomy, psychology, sociology, biology, special education, and music history and theory. Once the student has earned a degree in music therapy and has completed an internship, he or she may become either a registered music therapist (RMT) or a certified music therapist (CMT). The music therapist may then elect to participate in a national board examination to become certified by the Certification Board for Music Therapists. Once board certified, the music therapist may choose to practice in nursing homes, schools, institutions, hospitals, hospices, correctional facilities, drug and alcohol rehabilitation centers, community mental health centers, or agencies assisting developmentally disabled persons, or he or she may decide to go into private practice.

5 Within the institutions listed in the previous paragraph, music therapy has been used in various ways; for example, music therapy has been used in general hospitals to relieve pain in conjunction with anesthesia or pain medication, promote physical rehabilitation, and counteract apprehension or fear. Nursing homes use music therapy with elderly persons "to increase or maintain their level of physical, mental, and social/emotional functioning" ("FAQs"). Schools will also hire music therapists to provide music therapy services that are listed on the Individualized Education Plan for mainstreamed special learners. And in psychiatric facilities, music therapy is used to allow individuals "to explore personal feelings, make positive changes in mood and emotional states, have a sense of control over life through successful experiences, practice problem solving, and resolve conflicts leading to stronger family and peer relationships" ("FAQs").

6 Regardless of the settings in which they work, music therapists follow certain standards of practice, have a number of nonmusical goals, and may use a variety of musical tools in an effort to restore a patient's or group's physical, psychological, and/or emotional health. In any field that strives to be ethical and professional, standards of practice help define professionalism. This is no less true of music therapists. Among those practices a music therapist should engage in are (1) individualized assessments for

each client; (2) recommendations for or against treatment based on the assessment; (3) written, time-specific goals and objectives for each client; (4) a written treatment plan specifying music-therapy strategies and techniques that will be used to address the goals and objectives; (5) regular music-therapy sessions, with strategies and techniques chosen on the basis of the assessment and goals; (6) regular reevaluation of the effectiveness of the interventions being used; (7) written documentation; and (8) dismissal of the client from music therapy when the services are no longer necessary or appropriate (Brunk and Coleman).

Beyond embracing the profession's standards of practice, a music therapist will identify specific non-musical goals applicable to the patient with whom the therapist is working. Such non-musical goals may include "improving communication skills, decreasing inappropriate behavior, improving academic and motor skills, increasing attention span, strengthening social and leisure skills, pain management and stress reduction. Music therapy can also help individuals on their journey of self-growth and understanding" (Lindberg). 7

Music therapists may also use their instruments — their musical tools — in a number of therapeutic ways. For example, they may encourage a person to express feelings and emotions through music. Therapists believe that teaching a person to write music or play an instrument can be an emotional release and improve basic motor skills. Therapists also believe that listening to a song can relieve stress, counteract depression, and increase pain tolerance; singing can improve verbal skills, express emotions, and increase social skills; and banging on a drum can relieve tension and improve hand-eye coordination. Therapists advocate music for counteracting anxiety and fear, relieving tension and pain during the birthing process, and relaxing patients before and after surgery. 8

Once at work, there is no typical session for a music therapist. The therapist must evaluate each client and the result sof each session with the clients' needs in mind. Improving a person's musical abilities is not the primary goal of music therapy. There are no specific steps to follow, as every person and each circumstance is different. A therapist must draw on his or her own education in and experience with music therapy to encourage the development of the person. For example, in conducting a group session on relaxation through awareness and communication, two additional music therapists may be involved — one to guide the initial exploration and participate in the primary musical movement, and one to improvise for the second musical movement and the relax- 9 ation. The first musical movement, using energetic, rhythmic music, acts as a warm-up in which everyone participates. The therapists encourage everyone, especially new members to the session, to stand, since once the music starts, individuals may not have the courage to rise and move about. The second musical movement is improvised atonally — to avoid any musical associations — in response to the patients' associations to a specific stimulus. The music therapist will usually allow the individual who is least able to express him- or herself physically or verbally to choose the stimulus (which may vary among tactile stimuli, visual stimuli, symbols, or even quotations) so that the person feels he or she has invested in the session. When each member of the session has shared some association to the stimulus, the playing therapist improvises music — arrhythmically and atonally — to consciously reflect the ideas and feelings expressed by the group, or to echo unexpressed, unverbalized feelings within the group. During the remainder of the session, the lead therapist works with patients, ultimately guiding them through a series of relaxation exercises (Priestley 78–81).

10 In 1966, 22 years after Michigan State University offered the first formal degree in music therapy, Juliette Alvin wrote, "Music therapy has become a more or less recognized ancillary therapy and a remedial means [of addressing patient ailments]. [. . .][A] number of physicians, psychologists, educationalists and musicians are taking an interest in the subject" (104). And even today, while music therapists claim that their work improves the overall health of a patient and "[w]hile there is a broad literature covering the application of music therapy as reported in the medical press, there is an absence of valid clinical research material from which substantive conclusions may be drawn" (Aldridge 83). But this does not mean we should dismiss music therapy as a valid medical alternative. For while there are few cross-cultural studies supporting the claims of music therapists, within the field of nursing — where much of the research has been developed — music is recognized as an additional and useful therapeutic procedure (Aldridge 84).

11 Society is constantly looking for new and innovative ways to assist people in improving their way of life and bettering their physical and emotional circumstances. Music therapists believe that they offer an effective alternative to conventional medicine.

Note

1. A list of institutions that offer degrees in music therapy may be found at <http://www.musictherapy.org/Career/Schools.html>.

Works Cited

Aldridge, David. *Music Therapy Research and the Practice of Medicine.* Bristol, PA: Jessica Kingsley Publishers, 1996.

Alvin, Juliette. *Music Therapy.* New York: Humanities Press, 1966.

Brunk, Betsey, and Kathleen Coleman. "Medical Music Therapy." 1997. 2 Mar. 1998 <http://home.att.net/~bkbrunk/medic.html>.

———. "What to Expect from a Music Therapist." 1997. 2 Mar. 1998 <http://home.att.net/~bkbrunk/mtbc.html>.

"FAQs about Music Therapy." 1 Jan. 1998 <http://www.musictherapy.org/FAQs.html#DESCRIBE_A_SESSION>.

Lindberg, Kathering MT-BC. "Music Therapy Info Link." 8 Apr. 1997. 2 Mar. 1998 <http://members.aol.com/kathysl/questions.html>.

Priestley, Mary. *Music Therapy in Action.* New York: St. Martin's Press. 1975.

"Sound Therapy Works." 1997. 2 Mar. 1998 <http://www.pacifier.com/~stwmt/stw.html>.

READING FOR MEANING

Write to create meanings for Gutierrez's explanation of music therapy.

READING LIKE A WRITER

Writers of essays explaining concepts

- devise a readable plan.
- use appropriate explanatory strategies.
- integrate sources smoothly into the writing.
- engage readers' interest.

You have seen how important these explanatory writing strategies are in the readings you have read, written about, and discussed in this chapter. Focus on one of these strategies in Gutierrez's essay and analyze it carefully through close rereading and annotating. Then write several sentences explaining what you have learned, giving specific examples from the reading to illustrate your explanation. Add a few sentences evaluating how successfully Gutierrez uses the strategy to explain music therapy.

REVIEWING WHAT MAKES ESSAYS EXPLAINING CONCEPTS EFFECTIVE

In this chapter, you have been learning how to read essays explaining concepts for meaning and how to read them like a writer. Before going on to write an essay explaining a concept, pause here to review and contemplate what you have learned about the elements of effective concept explanations.

Analyze

Choose one reading from this chapter that seems to you especially effective. Before rereading the selection, *jot down* one or two reasons you remember it as an example of good concept explanation.

Reread your chosen selection, adding further annotations about what makes it a particularly successful example of concept explanation. *Consider* the selection's purpose and how well it achieves that purpose for its intended readers. (You can make an informed guess about the intended readers and their expectations by noting the publication source of the essay.) Then *focus* on how well the essay

- devises a readable plan.
- uses appropriate explanatory strategies.
- integrates sources smoothly into the writing.
- engages readers' interest.

You can review all of these basic features in the Guide to Reading Essays Explaining Concepts (p. 184).

Your instructor may ask you to complete this activity on your own or to work with a small group of other students who have chosen the same essay. If you work with others, allow enough time initially for all group members to reread the selection thoughtfully and to add their annotations. Then *discuss* as a group what makes the selection effective. *Take notes* on your discussion. One student in your group should then report to the class what the group has learned about the effectiveness of essays explaining concepts. If you are working individually, write up what you have learned from your analysis.

Write

Write at least a page, justifying your choice of this reading as an example of effective concept explanation. *Assume* that your readers — your instructor and classmates — have read the selection but will not remember many details about it. They also might not remember it as especially successful. Therefore, you will need to *refer* to details and specific parts of the essay as you explain how it works and as you justify your evaluation of its effectiveness. You need not argue that it is the best reading in the chapter or that it is flawless, only that it is, in your view, a strong example of the genre.

A Guide to Writing Essays Explaining Concepts

The readings in this chapter have helped you learn a great deal about essays explaining concepts. The readings also have helped you understand new concepts and learn more about concepts with which you are already familiar. Now that you have seen how writers use explanatory strategies that are appropriate for their readers, anticipating what their readers are likely to know, you can approach this type of writing confidently. This Guide to Writing will help you at every stage in the process of composing an essay explaining a concept — from choosing a concept and organizing your explanatory strategies to evaluating and revising your draft.

INVENTION

The following invention activities will help you choose a concept, consider what your readers need to know, explore what you already know, and gather and sort through your information.

Choosing a Concept

List different concepts you could explain and then choose the one that interests you and would be likely to interest your readers. To make the best choice and have alternatives in case the first choice does not work out, you should have a full list of possibilities. You might already have a concept in mind, possibly one suggested to you by the Considering Ideas for Your Own Writing activities following the readings in this chapter. Pause now to review the dozens of suggested concepts in those activities. Here are some other concepts from various fields of study for you to consider:

- *Literature:* representation, figurative language, canon, postcolonialism, modernism, irony, epic
- *Philosophy:* Platonic forms, causality, syllogism, existentialism, nihilism, logical positivism, determinism, phenomenology
- *Business management:* autonomous work group, quality circle, management by objectives, zero-based budgeting, benchmarking, focus group
- *Psychology:* phobia, narcissism, fetish, emotional intelligence, divergent/convergent thinking, behaviorism, Jungian archetype
- *Government:* one person/one vote, minority rights, federalism, communism, theocracy, popular consent, exclusionary rule, political machine, political action committee

- *Biology:* photosynthesis, ecosystem, plasmolysis, phagocytosis, DNA, species, punctuated evolution, homozygosity, diffusion
- *Art:* composition, cubism, iconography, Pop Art, conceptual art, public sculpture, graffiti, forgery, auction, Dadaism, surrealism, expressionism
- *Math:* Mobius transformation, boundedness, null space, eigenvalue, complex numbers, integral, exponent, polynomial, factoring, Pythagorean theorem, continuity, derivative, infinity
- *Physical sciences:* gravity, mass, weight, energy, quantum theory, law of definite proportions, osmotic pressure, first law of thermodynamics, entrophy, free energy, fusion
- *Public health:* alcoholism, epidemic, vaccination, drug abuse, contraception, prenatal care, AIDS education
- *Environmental studies:* acid rain, recycling, ozone depletion, sewage treatment, toxic waste, endangered species
- *Sports psychology:* Ringelman effect, leadership, cohesiveness, competitiveness, anxiety management, aggression, visualization, runner's high
- *Law:* arbitration, strike, minimum wage, liability, reasonable doubt, sexual harassment, nondisclosure agreement, assumption of evidence
- *Meteorology:* jet stream, hydrologic cycle, El Niño, Coriolis effect, Chinook or Santa Ana wind, standard time system, tsunami
- *Nutrition and health:* vegetarianism, bulimia, diabetes, food allergy, aerobic exercise, obesity, Maillard reaction

Choose a promising concept to explore, one that interests you and that you think would interest your readers. You might not know very much about the concept now, but the guidelines that follow will help you learn more about it so that you can explain it to others.

Analyzing Your Readers

Write for a few minutes, analyzing your potential readers. Begin by identifying your readers and what you want them to know. Even if you are writing only for your instructor, you should consider what he or she knows about your concept. Ask yourself the following questions to stimulate your thinking: What might my potential readers already know about the concept or about the field of study to which it applies? What new, useful, or interesting information about the concept could I provide for them? What questions might they ask?

Researching the Concept

Even if you know quite a bit about the concept, you may want to do additional library or Internet research or consult an expert. Before you begin, check with your instructor for special requirements, such as submitting photocopies of your written sources or using a particular documentation style.

Exploring What You Already Know about the Concept. *Write for a few minutes about the concept to discover what you know about it.* Pose any questions you now have about the concept and try to answer questions you expect your readers would have.

Finding Information at the Library or on the Internet. *Learn more about your concept by finding sources, taking notes or making copies of relevant material, and keeping a working bibliography.* Before embarking on research, review any materials you already have at hand that explain your concept. If you are considering a concept from one of your courses, find explanatory material in your textbook and lecture notes. (See Appendix 2, Strategies for Research and Documentation, for detailed guidance on finding information at a library and on the Internet.)

Consulting Experts. *Identify one or more people knowledgeable about the concept or the field of study in which it is used, and request information from them.* If you are writing about a concept from a course, consult the professor, teaching assistant, or other students. If the concept relates to your job, consider asking your supervisor. If it relates to a subject you have encountered on television, in the newspaper, or on the Internet, you might email the author or post a query at a relevant Web site. Consulting experts can answer your questions as well as lead you to other sources — Web sites, chatrooms, articles, and books.

Focusing Your Explanation. *With your own knowledge of the concept and that of your readers in mind, consider how you might focus your explanation.* Determine how the information you have gathered so far could be divided. For example, if you were writing about the concept of schizophrenia, you might focus on the history of its diagnosis and treatment, its symptoms, its effects on families, the current debate about its causes, or the current preferred methods of treatment. If you were writing a book, you might want to cover all these aspects of the concept, but in a relatively brief essay you can focus on only one or two of them.

Confirming Your Focus. *Choose a focus for your explanation and write several sentences justifying the focus you have chosen.* Why do you think this focus will appeal to your readers? What interests you about it? Do you have enough information to plan and draft your explanation? Do you know where you can find any additional information you need?

Formulating a Working Thesis. *Draft a thesis statement.* A working thesis — as opposed to a final, revised thesis — will help you begin drafting your essay purposefully. The thesis in an essay explaining concepts simply announces the concept and focus of the explanation. Here are three examples from the readings.

- "What we are talking about here is celibate motherhood, procreation without copulation, a phenomenon that goes by the technical name *parthenogenesis.* Translated from the Greek roots: virgin birth" (Quammen, paragraph 1).
- "Each of the women at the conference had to make decisions about hair, clothing, makeup and accessories, and each decision carried meaning. Every style available to us was marked. The men in our group had made decisions, too, but the range from which they chose was incomparably narrower. Men can choose styles that are marked, but they don't have to, and in this group none did. Unlike the women, they had the option of being unmarked" (Tannen, paragraph 12).
- "Cannibalism can be broken down into two main categories: exocannibalism, the eating of outsiders or foreigners, and endocannibalism, the eating of members of one's own social group (Shipman 70). Within these categories are several functional types of cannibalism, three of the most common being survival cannibalism, dietary cannibalism, and religious and ritual cannibalism" (Ngo, paragraph 6).

Notice that Ngo's thesis statement not only announces the concept, but also forecasts the main topics he will take up in the essay. Forecasts, though not required, can be helpful to readers, especially when the concept is unfamiliar or the explanation is complicated.

Considering Visuals. *Consider whether visuals — tables, graphs, drawings, photographs — would make your explanation clearer.* You could construct your own visuals; download materials from the Internet; copy images from print sources like books, magazines, and newspapers; or scan into your essay visuals from books and magazines. Visuals are not at all a requirement of an essay explaining a concept, as you can tell from the readings in this chapter, but they could add a new dimension to your writing.

DRAFTING

The following guidelines will help you set goals for your draft and plan its organization.

Setting Goals

Establishing goals for your draft before you begin writing will enable you to make decisions and work more confidently. Consider the following questions now, and keep them in mind as you draft. They will help you set goals for drafting as well as recall how the writers you have read in this chapter tried to achieve similar goals.

- *How can I begin engagingly so as to capture my readers' attention?* Should I try to be amusing, like Quammen? Should I begin with an anecdote, as Tannen, Bailey, and Ngo do? Should I begin by quoting a knowledgable person, like Farley does? Should I present a surprising fact, as Lemonick does? Should I, like Gutierrez, begin by asking rhetorical questions?
- *How can I orient readers so they do not get confused?* Should I provide an explicit forecasting statement, as Ngo does? Should I add transitions to help readers see how the parts of my essay relate to one another, as Ngo and Bailey do? Should I use rhetorical questions and summary statements, as Quammen does?
- *How should I conclude my explanation?* Should I frame the essay by echoing the opening at the end, as Quammen and Tannen do? Should I speculate about the future of the concept, as Farley and Lemonick do?

Organizing Your Draft

With goals in mind, make a tentative outline of the topics you now think you want to cover as you give readers information about the concept. You might want to make two or three different outlines before choosing the one that looks most promising. Try to introduce new material in stages, so that readers' understanding of the concept builds slowly but steadily. Keep in mind that an essay explaining a concept is made up of four basic parts:

1. An attempt to engage readers' interest in the explanation
2. The thesis statement, announcing the concept and the way it will be focused and perhaps also forecasting the sequence of topics
3. An orientation to the concept, which may include a description or definition of the concept
4. The information about the concept, organized around a series of topics that reflect how the information has been divided up

An attempt to gain readers' interest could take as little space as two or three sentences or as much as four or five paragraphs. The thesis statement and definition are usually quite brief, sometimes only a few sentences. One topic may require one or several paragraphs, and there can be few or many topics, depending on how the information has been divided up.

Consider tentative any outline you do before you begin drafting. Never be a slave to an outline. As you draft, you will usually see ways to improve on your original plan. Be ready to revise your outline, shift parts around, or drop or add parts as you draft.

READING A DRAFT CRITICALLY

Getting a critical reading of your draft will help you see how to improve it. Your instructor may schedule class time for reading drafts, or you may want to ask a classmate or a tutor in the writing center to read your draft. Ask your reader to use the following guidelines and to write out a response for you to consult during your revision.

Read for a First Impression

1. Read the draft without stopping to annotate or comment, and then write two or three sentences giving your general impression.
2. Identify one aspect of the draft that seems particularly effective.

Read Again to Suggest Improvements

1. Consider whether the concept is clearly explained and focused.
   - Restate briefly what you understand the concept to mean, indicating if you have any uncertainty or confusion about its meaning.
   - Identify the focus of the explanation and assess whether the focus seems appropriate, too broad, or too narrow for the intended readers.
   - If you can, suggest another, possibly more interesting, way to focus the explanation.
2. Recommend ways of making the organization clearer or more effective.
   - Indicate whether a forecasting statement, topic sentences, or transitions could be added or improved.
   - Point to any place where you become confused or do not know how something relates to what went before.
   - Comment on whether the conclusion gives you a sense of closure or leaves you hanging.
3. Consider whether the content is appropriate for the intended readers.
   - Point to any place where the information might seem too obvious to readers or too elementary for them.

- Circle any words that the writer should define or that you do not think need to be defined.
- Think of unanswered questions readers might have about the concept. Try to suggest additional information that should be included.
- Recommend new strategies the writer could usefully adopt: comparing the concept to a concept more familiar to readers, dividing some of the information into smaller or larger topics, reporting known causes or effects of the concept, giving further facts or examples, or narrating how a part of the concept actually works. Explain how the writer could make use of the strategy.

4. Assess whether quotations are integrated smoothly and acknowledged properly.
   - Point to any place where a quotation is not smoothly integrated into the writer's sentence and offer a revision.
   - Indicate any quotations that would have been just as effective if put in the writer's own words.
   - If sources are not acknowledged correctly, remind the writer to consult Appendix 2.
   - If you can, suggest other sources the writer might consult.
5. Evaluate the effectiveness of visuals.
   - Look at any visuals in the essay, and tell the writer what they contribute to your understanding of the concept explanation.
   - If any visuals do not seem relevant, or if there seem to be too many visuals, identify the ones that the writer could consider dropping, explaining your thinking.
   - If a visual does not seem to be appropriately placed, suggest a better place for it.

REVISING

This section offers suggestions for revising your draft, suggestions that will remind you of the possibilities for developing a lively, engaging, and informative essay explaining a concept. Revising means reenvisioning your draft, trying to see it in a new way, given your purpose and readers, in order to develop your concept explanation.

The biggest mistake you can make while revising is to focus initially on words or sentences. Instead, first try to see your draft as a whole in order to assess its likely impact on your readers. Think imaginatively and boldly about cutting unconvincing material, adding new material, and moving material around. Your computer makes even drastic revisions physically easy, but you still need to make the mental effort and decisions that will improve your draft.

You may have received help with this challenge from a classmate or tutor who gave your draft a critical reading. If so, keep this feedback in mind as you decide which parts of your draft need revising and what specific changes you could make. The following suggestions will help you solve problems and strengthen your essay.

To Make the Concept Clearer and More Focused

- If readers are confused or uncertain about the concept's meaning, try defining it more precisely or giving concrete examples.
- If the focus seems too broad, concentrate on one aspect of the concept and explain it in greater depth.
- If the concept seems too narrow, go back to your invention and research notes and look for a larger or more significant aspect of it to focus on.

To Improve the Organization

- If readers have difficulty following the essay, improve the forecasting at the beginning of the essay by listing the topics in the order they will appear.
- If there are places where the topic gets blurred from one sentence or paragraph to the next, make the connections between the sentences or paragraphs clearer.
- If the essay seems to lose steam before it comes to a conclusion, consider again what you want readers to learn from your essay.

To Strengthen the Explanatory Strategies

- If the content seems thin, consider whether you could add any other explanatory strategies or develop more fully the ones you are using already.
- If some of the words you use are new to most readers, take the time to define them now, perhaps explaining how they relate to more familiar terms or adding analogies and examples to make them less abstract.
- If the way you have divided or categorized the information is unusual or unclear, write a sentence or two making explicit what you are doing and why.
- If the concept seems vague to readers, try comparing it to something familiar or applying it to a real-world experience.

To Integrate Quotations Smoothly and Acknowledge Sources Properly

- Revise any sentences where quotations are not smoothly integrated by adding appropriate signal phrases or rewriting the sentences.
- If your critical reader has identified a quotation that could just as effectively be described in your own words, try paraphrasing or summarizing the quote.
- If your sources are not acknowledged properly, check Appendix 2 for the correct citation form.

EDITING AND PROOFREADING

After you have revised your essay, be sure to spend some time checking for errors in usage, punctuation, and mechanics and considering matters of style. If you keep a list of errors you typically make, begin by checking your draft against this list. Ask someone else to proofread your essay before you print out a copy for your instructor or send it electronically.

From our research on student writing, we know that essays explaining concepts tend to have errors in essential or nonessential clauses beginning with *who, which,* or *that,* as well as errors in the use of commas to set off phrases that interrupt the flow of the sentence. Check a writer's handbook for help with these potential problems.

REFLECTING ON WHAT YOU HAVE LEARNED

Explaining Concepts

In this chapter, you have read critically several essays explaining concepts and have written one of your own. To better remember what you have learned, pause now to reflect on the reading and writing activities you completed in this chapter.

1. *Write* a page or so reflecting on what you have learned. *Begin* by describing what you are most pleased with in your essay. Then *explain* what you think contributed to your achievement. *Be specific* about this contribution.
   - If it was something you learned from the readings, *indicate* which readings and specifically what you learned from them.

- If it came from your invention writing, *point out* the section or sections that helped you most.
- If you got good advice from a critical reader, *explain* exactly how the person helped you — perhaps by helping you understand a particular problem in your draft or by adding a new dimension to your writing.

2. Now *reflect* more generally on explaining concepts, a genre of writing that plays an important role in education and in our society. *Consider* that concept explanations attempt to present their information as uncontested truths. *Reflect* on your own essay, and *write* answers to the following questions: When you were doing research on the concept, did you discover that some of the information was being challenged by experts? If so, what were the grounds for this challenge? Did you at any point think that your readers might question any of the information you were presenting? How did you decide what information might seem new or surprising to readers? Did you feel comfortable in your roles as the selector and giver of knowledge? *Describe* how you felt in this role.

CHAPTER 

Evaluation

We make evaluations every day, stating judgments about such things as food, clothes, books, classes, teachers, political candidates, television programs, performers, and films. Most of our everyday judgments simply express our personal preference—"I liked it" or "I didn't like it." But as soon as someone asks "Why?" we realize that evaluation goes beyond individual taste.

If you want others to take your judgment seriously, you have to give reasons for it. Instead of merely asserting that "*Traffic* was fantastic," you might say that the acting in the film was extraordinarily powerful and that its documentary style was appropriate for its subject—drug trafficking, or the smuggling of drugs from Mexico and their distribution and use in the United States.

For readers to find your judgment and reasons convincing, they must recognize that your reasons are appropriate standards for evaluating a movie. An inappropriate reason for the judgment "*Traffic* is a great thriller" would be that the seats in the theater were comfortable. The comfort of the seats may contribute on one occasion to your enjoyment of the theater experience (and, indeed, would be an appropriate reason for judging the quality of a movie theater), but such a reason has nothing to do with the quality of a particular film.

For reasons to be considered appropriate, they must reflect the values or standards typically used in evaluating the kind of thing under consideration, such as a film or a car. The standards you would use for evaluating a film obviously differ from those you would use for evaluating a car. Acting, musical score, and story are common standards for judging films. Handling, safety, and styling are some of the standards used for judging cars.

Readers expect writers of evaluations both to offer appropriate reasons and to support their reasons. If one of your reasons for liking the BMW 330i sports sedan is its quick acceleration, you could cite the *Consumer Reports* road-test results (0 to 60 mph in 6.6 seconds) as evidence. (Statistical support like this, of course, makes sense only when the rate is compared with the acceleration rates of other comparable cars.) Similarly, if one of your reasons for liking *Traffic* is the series of short dramatic scenes featuring soap-opera style close-ups of the actors, you could give examples of several of these short scenes. You might describe the scene where a key witness is poisoned by his room-delivery breakfast on the day he is to testify against a drug lord or the scene where the wealthy father finds his drug-addicted daughter in a hotel room with a man who has paid her for sex. Support is important because it deals in specifics, showing exactly what value terms like *dramatic* and *close-up* mean to you.

As you can see, evaluation of the kind you will read and write in this chapter is intellectually rigorous. In college, you will have many opportunities to write evaluations. You may be asked to critique a book or a journal article, judge a scientific hypothesis against the results of an experiment, assess the value of conflicting interpretations of a historical event or a short story, or evaluate a class you have taken. You will also undoubtedly read evaluative writing in your courses and be tested on what you have read.

Written evaluations will almost certainly play an important part in your work life as well. On the job, you will probably be evaluated periodically and may have to evaluate people whom you supervise. It is also likely that you will be asked your opinion of various plans or proposals under consideration, and your ability to make reasonable, well-supported evaluations will affect your chances for promotion.

As the word *evaluation* suggests, evaluative arguments are basically about values, about what each of us thinks is important. Reading and writing evaluations will help you understand your own values as well as those of others. You will learn that when your basic values conflict with your readers' values, you may not be able to convince readers to accept a judgment different from their own. In such cases, you will usually want to try to bridge the difference by showing respect for their concerns despite your disagreement with them or to clarify the areas of agreement and disagreement.

The readings in this chapter will help you learn a good deal about evaluative writing. From the readings and from the ideas for writing that follow each reading, you will get ideas for your own evaluative essay. As you read and write about the selections, keep in mind the following assignment, which sets out the goals for writing an evaluative essay. To support your writing of this assignment, the chapter concludes with a Guide to Writing Evaluations.

THE WRITING ASSIGNMENT

Evaluation

Choose a subject that you can both evaluate and make a confident judgment about. Write an essay evaluating this subject. State your judgment clearly and back it up with reasons and support. Describe the subject for readers unfamiliar with it, and give them a context for understanding it. Your purpose is to convince readers that your judgment is informed and based on generally accepted standards for this kind of subject.

WRITING SITUATIONS FOR EVALUATION

Following are a few examples to suggest the range of situations that may call for evaluative writing, including academic and work-related situations:

- For a conference on innovation in education, an elementary schoolteacher evaluates *Schoolhouse Rock,* an animated television series developed in the 1970s and reinvented in several new formats: books, CD-ROM learning games, and CDs. She praises the original series as an entertaining way of presenting information, giving two reasons the series remains an effective teaching tool: Witty lyrics and catchy tunes make the information memorable, and cartoonlike visuals make the lessons pleasurable. She supports each reason by showing and discussing videotaped examples of popular *Schoolhouse Rock* segments, such as "Conjunction Junction," "We the People," and "Three Is a Magic Number." She ends by expressing her hope that teachers and developers of educational multimedia will learn from the example of *Schoolhouse Rock.*
- A supervisor reviews the work of a probationary employee. She judges the employee's performance as being adequate overall but still needing improvement in several key areas, particularly completing projects on time and communicating clearly with others. To support her judgment, she describes several problems that the employee has had over the six-month probationary period.
- An older brother, a college junior, sends an email message to his younger brother, a high-school senior who is trying to decide which college to attend. Because the older brother attends one of the colleges being considered and has friends at another, he feels competent to offer advice. He centers his message on the question of what standards to use in evaluating colleges. He argues that if playing football is the primary goal, then college number one is the clear choice. But if having the opportunity to work in an award-winning scientist's genetics lab is more important, then the second college is the better choice.

A Guide to Reading Evaluations

This guide introduces you to evaluative writing. By completing all the activities in it, you will prepare yourself to learn a great deal from the other readings in this chapter about how to read and write an evaluative essay. The guide makes use of "Working at McDonald's," a well-known essay by sociologist Amitai Etzioni one of the founders of the communitarian movement, which advocates that people value group traditions no more than they value national unity. You will read Etzioni's evaluative essay twice. First, you will read it for meaning, looking closely at its content and ideas. Then, you will reread the essay like a writer, analyzing the parts to see how Etzioni crafts his essay and to learn the strategies he uses to make the evaluation informative and convincing. These two activities—reading for meaning and reading like a writer—follow every reading in this chapter.

AMITAI ETZIONI

Working at McDonald's

Amitai Etzioni (b. 1929), who teaches sociology at The George Washington University, has written numerous articles and books reflecting his commitment to a communitarian agenda, including Spirit of Community: Rights, Responsibilities, and the Communitarian Agenda *(1993),* The New Golden Rule: Morality and Community in a Democratic Society *(1998),* Civic Repentance *(1999), and* The Limits of Privacy *(1999). He is also the founder of the* Responsive Community, *a journal.*

The following essay was originally published in 1986 in the Miami Herald, *a major newspaper that circulates in South Florida. The original headnote identifies Etzioni as the father of five sons, including three teenagers, and points out that his son Dari helped Etzioni write this essay—although it does not say what Dari contributed.*

Before you read, think about the part-time jobs you held during high school—not just summer jobs but those you worked during the months when school was in session. Recall the pleasures and disappointments of these jobs. In particular, think about what you learned that might have made you a better student and prepared you for college. Perhaps you worked at a fast-food restaurant. If not, you have probably been in many such places and have observed students working there.

Annotate the essay as you read and as you complete the activities following the selection. For an illustration of the strategies and benefits of annotating, see Appendix 1, pages 518–24.

McDonald's is bad for your kids. I do not mean the flat patties and the white-flour buns; I refer to the jobs teen-agers undertake, mass-producing these choice items. 1

As many as two-thirds of America's high school juniors and seniors now hold down part-time paying jobs, according to studies. 2

Many of these are in fast-food chains, of which McDonald's is the pioneer, trend-setter, and symbol.

3 At first, such jobs may seem right out of the Founding Fathers' educational manual for how to bring up self-reliant, work-ethic-driven, productive youngsters. But in fact, these jobs undermine school attendance and involvement, impart few skills that will be useful in later life, and simultaneously skew the values of teen-agers—especially their ideas about the worth of a dollar.

4 It has been a longstanding American tradition that youngsters ought to get paying jobs. In folklore, few pursuits are more deeply revered than the newspaper route and the sidewalk lemonade stand. Here the youngsters are to learn how sweet are the fruits of labor and self-discipline (papers are delivered early in the morning, rain or shine), and the ways of trade (if you price your lemonade too high or too low . . .).

5 Roy Rogers, Baskin Robbins, Kentucky Fried Chicken, *et al.*, may at first seem nothing but a vast extension of the lemonade stand. They provide very large numbers of teen jobs, provide regular employment, pay quite well compared to many other teen jobs, and, in the modern equivalent of toiling over a hot stove, test one's stamina.

6 Closer examination, however, finds the McDonald's kind of job highly uneducational in several ways. Far from providing opportunities for entrepreneurship (the lemonade stand) or self-discipline, self-supervision, and self-scheduling (the paper route), most teen jobs these days are highly structured—what social scientists call "highly routinized."

7 True, you still have to have the gumption to get yourself over to the hamburger stand, but once you don the prescribed uniform, your task is spelled out in minute detail. The franchise prescribes the shape of the coffee cups; the weight, size, shape, and color of the patties; and the texture of the napkins (if any). Fresh coffee is to be made every eight minutes. And so on. There is no room for initiative, creativity, or even elementary rearrangements. These are breeding grounds for robots working for yesterday's assembly lines, not tomorrow's high-tech posts.

8 There are very few studies of the matter. One of the few is a 1984 study by Ivan Charper and Bryan Shore Fraser. The study relies mainly on what teen-agers write in response to questionnaires rather than actual observations of fast-food jobs. The authors argue that the employees develop many skills such as how to operate a food-preparation machine and a cash register. However, little attention is paid to how long it takes to acquire such a skill, or what its significance is.

What does it matter if you spend 20 minutes to learn to use a cash register, and then—"operate" it? What skill have you acquired? It is a long way from learning to work with a lathe or carpenter tools in the olden days or to program computers in the modern age. 9

A 1980 study by A. V. Harrell and P. W. Wirtz found that, among those students who worked at least 25 hours per week while in school, their unemployment rate four years later was half of that of seniors who did not work. This is an impressive statistic. It must be seen, though, together with the finding that many who begin as part-time employees in fast-food chains drop out of high school and are gobbled up in the world of low-skill jobs. 10

Some say that while these jobs are rather unsuited for college-bound, white, middle-class youngsters, they are "ideal" for lower-class, "non-academic," minority youngsters. Indeed, minorities are "over-represented" in these jobs (21 percent of fast-food employees). While it is true that these places provide income, work, and even some training to such youngsters, they also tend to perpetuate their disadvantaged status. They provide no career ladders, few marketable skills, and undermine school attendance and involvement. 11

The hours are often long. Among those 14 to 17, a third of fast-food employees (including some school dropouts) labor more than 30 hours per week, according to the Charper-Fraser study. Only 20 percent work 15 hours or less. The rest: between 15 to 30 hours. 12

Often the stores close late, and after closing one must clean up and tally up. In affluent Montgomery County, Md., where child labor would not seem to be a widespread economic necessity, 24 percent of the seniors at one high school in 1985 worked as much as five to seven days a week; 27 percent, three to five. There is just no way such amounts of work will not interfere with school work, especially homework. In an informal survey published in the most recent yearbook of the high school, 58 percent of the seniors acknowledged that their jobs interfere with their school work. 13

The Charper-Fraser study sees merit in learning teamwork and working under supervision. The authors have a point here. However, it must be noted that such learning is not automatically educational or wholesome. For example, much of the supervision in fast-food places leans toward teaching one the wrong kinds of compliance: blind obedience, or shared alienation with the "boss." 14

Supervision is often both tight and woefully inappropriate. Today, fast-food chains and other such places of work (record 15 shops, bowling alleys) keep costs down by having teens supervise teens with often no adult on the premises.

16 There is no father or mother figure with which to identify, to emulate, to provide a role model and guidance. The work-culture varies from one place to another: Sometimes it is a tightly run shop (must keep the cash registers ringing); sometimes a rather loose pot party interrupted by customers. However, only rarely is there a master to learn from, or much worth learning. Indeed, far from being places where solid adult work values are being transmitted, these are places where all too often delinquent teen values dominate. Typically, when my son Oren was dishing out ice cream for Baskin Robbins in upper Manhattan, his fellow teen-workers considered him a sucker for not helping himself to the till. Most youngsters felt they were entitled to $50 severance "pay" on their last day on the job.

17 The pay, oddly, is the part of the teen work-world that is most difficult to evaluate. The lemonade stand or paper route money was for your allowance. In the old days, apprentices learning a trade from a master contributed most, if not all of their income to their parents' household. Today, the teen pay may be low by adult standards, but it is often, especially in the middle class, spent largely or wholly by the teens. That is, the youngsters live free at home ("after all, they are high school kids") and are left with very substantial sums of money.

18 Where this money goes is not quite clear. Some use it to support themselves, especially among the poor. More middle-class kids set some money aside to help pay for college, or save it for a major purchase—often a car. But large amounts seem to flow to pay for an early introduction into the most trite aspects of American consumerism: Flimsy punk clothes, trinkets, and whatever else is the last fast-moving teen craze.

19 One may say that this is only fair and square; they are being good American consumers and spend their money on what turns them on. At least, a cynic might add, these funds do not go into illicit drugs and booze. On the other hand, an educator might bemoan that these young, yet unformed individuals, so early in life are driven to buy objects of no intrinsic educational, cultural, or social merit, learn so quickly the dubious merit of keeping up with the Joneses in ever-changing fads, promoted by mass merchandising.

20 Many teens find the instant reward of money, and the youth status symbols it buys, much more alluring than credits in calculus courses, European history, or foreign languages. No wonder quite a few would rather skip school—and certainly homework—

and instead work longer at a Burger King. Thus, most teen work these days is not providing early lessons in work ethic; it fosters escape from school and responsibilities, quick gratification, and a short cut to the consumeristic aspects of adult life.

21 Thus, parents should look at teen employment not as automatically educational. It is an activity—like sports—that can be turned into an educational opportunity. But it can also easily be abused. Youngsters must learn to balance the quest for income with the needs to keep growing and pursue other endeavors that do not pay off instantly—above all education.

22 Go back to school.

READING FOR MEANING

Write to create meanings for Etzioni's evaluation of fast-food jobs as "bad for . . . kids."

Start Making Meaning

Begin by listing two or three of the main reasons Etzioni gives for his judgment that McDonald's-type jobs are problematic for high-school students to work. Continue by writing about anything else in the selection or in your experience that contributes to your understanding of Etzioni's evaluation. As you write, you will need to reread parts of the essay, adding to your annotations as you do so.

If You Are Stuck

If you cannot write at least a page, consider writing about

- the values Etzioni admires (self-reliance, the work ethic, and self-discipline, in paragraphs 3 and 4), considering how your work (in or outside of school) supports or undermines these values.
- Etzioni's judgment that "these jobs . . . skew the values of teen-agers—especially their ideas about the worth of a dollar" (paragraph 3) and his support of this judgment (paragraphs 17–20).
- your experience of working while in high school or college, reflecting on it in light of Etzioni's views about working while going to school.
- Etzioni's contrast between working at McDonald's and selling lemonade or delivering newspapers (paragraphs 4–7 and 17), commenting on the conclusions he draws from the contrast.

READING LIKE A WRITER

This section leads you through an analysis of Etzioni's evaluative writing strategies: *presenting the subject, asserting an overall judgment, giving reasons and support, counterarguing,* and *establishing credibility.* For each strategy, you will be asked to reread and annotate part of Etzioni's essay to see how he uses the strategy in "Working at McDonald's."

When you study the selections later in this chapter, you will see how different writers use these same strategies. The Guide to Writing Evaluations near the end of the chapter suggests ways you can use these strategies in your own writing.

Presenting the Subject

Writers must present the subject so readers know what is being judged. Writers can simply name the subject, but usually they describe it in some detail. A film reviewer, for example, might identify the actors, describe the characters they play, and tell some of the plot. As a critical reader, you may notice that the language used to present the subject also may serve to evaluate it. Therefore, you should look closely at how the subject is presented. Note where the writer's information about the subject comes from, whether the information is reliable, and whether anything important seems to have been left out.

Analyze

1. *Reread* paragraphs 5–7, 9, 12, 15, and 16, and *underline* the factual details that describe who works at fast-food restaurants and what they do. *Ask* yourself the following question as you analyze how Etzioni presents the subject: Where does the writer seem to get his information—from firsthand observation, from conversation with others, or by reading published research?

2. Based on your own knowledge of fast-food jobs, *point to* the details in these paragraphs that you accept as valid as well as to details you think are inaccurate or only partially true. Finally, *consider* whether any information you know about fast-food jobs is missing from Etzioni's presentation of work at fast-food places.

Write

Write several sentences discussing how Etzioni presents the subject to his intended audience—education-minded adults, particularly parents of high-school students—and *give examples* from the reading. Then *write a few more sentences* evaluating Etzioni's presentation of the subject in terms of accuracy and completeness.

Asserting an Overall Judgment

A writer's overall judgment of the subject is the main point of an evaluative essay, asserting that the subject is good or bad, or better or worse, than something comparable. Although readers expect a definitive judgment, they also appreciate a balanced one that acknowledges, for example, some good qualities of a subject judged overall to be bad. Evaluations usually explicitly state the judgment up front in the form of a thesis and may restate it in different ways throughout the essay.

Analyze

1. *Reread* paragraphs 3 and 20–21, where Etzioni states his overall judgment, and *consider* whether you find his statements clear.
2. *Decide* whether Etzioni changes his initial judgment in any way when he restates it in somewhat different language at the end of the essay. *Consider* why he restates his judgment.

Write

Write a few sentences describing and evaluating Etzioni's assertion of his overall judgment.

Giving Reasons and Support

Any evaluative argument must explain and justify the writer's judgment. To be convincing, the reasons given must be recognized by readers as appropriate for evaluating the type of subject under consideration. That is, the reasons must reflect the values or standards of judgment that people typically use in similar situations. The reasons also must be supported by relevant examples, quotations, facts, statistics, or personal anecdotes. This support may come from the writer's own knowledge or experience, from that of other people, and from published materials.

Analyze

1. Etzioni names three principal reasons for his judgment in the final sentence of paragraph 3. *Underline* these reasons, and then *consider* the appropriateness of each one given Etzioni's intended readers—the largely middle-class adult subscribers to the *Miami Herald.* Why do you think they would or

would not likely accept each reason as appropriate for evaluating part-time jobs for teenagers? What objections, if any, might a critical reader have to Etzioni's reasoning?

2. One reason Etzioni gives to clarify his view that working at McDonald's is "bad" for students is that the jobs "impart few skills that will be useful in later life" (paragraph 3). Etzioni then attempts to support (to argue for) this reason in paragraphs 4–9. *Reread* these paragraphs noticing the kinds of support Etzioni relies on.

3. *Evaluate* how well Etzioni supports his argument in paragraphs 4–9. Why do you think his readers will or will not find the argument convincing? Which supporting details might they find most convincing? Least convincing?

Write

Write several sentences reporting what you have learned about how Etzioni uses reasons and support as an evaluative writing strategy in his essay. *Give examples* (from paragraph 3) of the type of support he provides for the "imparting few skills" reason. *Write a few more sentences* explaining how convincing you think his readers will find this support.

Counterarguing

To gain credibility with their readers, writers often anticipate that some readers may resist their judgments, reasons, or support. This strategy, called *counterarguing,* involves responding to or countering readers' likely questions or objections. For example, some parents with children in high school may question Etzioni's reasons for damning an easily available source of income. A relatively poor family, for instance, might firmly oppose his judgment, seeing part-time work at McDonald's as good for high-school students who must buy their own clothes and pay for their entertainment. Other parents may object to Etzioni's comparing a fast-food job unfavorably to a job selling lemonade or delivering newspapers. Still other readers without any personal views on whether high-school students should or should not work part-time may wonder why Etzioni seems unaware that a substantial number of U.S. children live in poverty and must work to help buy food and pay the rent, even if they would rather be doing homework.

Etzioni certainly is aware that some readers have questions and objections in mind. These objections do not cause him to waver in his own judgment, as you have seen, but they do persuade him to anticipate readers' likely questions and objections and to respond to them by counterarguing. There are two basic ways to counterargue: A writer can *refute* readers' objections, arguing that they are simply wrong, or *accommodate* objections, acknowledging that they are justified but do not irreparably damage the writer's reasoning. Etzioni uses both refutation and accommodation in his counterarguments.

Analyze

1. *Reread* paragraphs 8–11, 14, and 19, where Etzioni brings up either a reader's likely objection or an alternative judgment about the worth of part-time work. (Some alternative judgments are attributed to researchers, rather than readers, though it is likely some readers would have similar ideas.) *Underline* the alternative judgment or objection in each of these paragraphs.
2. *Choose* any two of these counterarguments, and then *look closely* at Etzioni's strategy. *Decide* first whether he refutes or accommodates the objection or alternative judgment. Then *note* how he goes about doing so.
3. *Evaluate* whether Etzioni's counterarguments are likely to convince skeptical readers to accept his views.

Write

Write several sentences identifying the objections and alternative judgments against which Etzioni counterargues. *Describe* his counterarguments, and *evaluate* how persuasive they are likely to be with his intended audience.

Establishing Credibility

The success of an evaluation depends to a large extent on readers' confidence in the writer's judgment as well as their willingness to recognize and acknowledge the writer's credibility or authority. Evaluative writers usually try to establish their credibility by showing (1) they know a lot about the subject and (2) their judgment is based on valid values and standards. Biographical information can play a role in establishing a writer's authority by providing facts about his or her educational and professional accomplishments. It is the essay itself, however, that usually tells readers what the writer knows about the subject and from where that knowledge comes.

Analyze

1. Quickly *reread* the biographical headnote and the entire essay. As you do so, *put a checkmark* next to any passages where you believe readers would find Etzioni especially credible or trustworthy, and *place a question mark* next to any passages where you think they might question his credibility.

2. *Look over* the passages you marked, then *underline* the words and bits of information that contribute to your evaluation of Etzioni's credibility with his readers.

Write

Write several sentences summarizing your analysis of Etzioni's credibility with his intended audience—parents with children in high school. *Give examples* from both the headnote and the essay to support your analysis.

Readings

MICHAEL KINSLEY

Email Culture

Michael Kinsley (b. 1951) is the founding editor-in-chief of Slate *(<www.slate.com>), an online general-interest magazine published by Microsoft Corporation. Before joining* Slate, *where he writes a column called "readme," Kinsley served two stints as editor of the* New Republic, *a weekly magazine of politics and the arts. He has also been an editor of three other magazines—*Harper's, *the* Washington Monthly, *and the* Economist*—and a columnist for the* New Republic, *the* Wall Street Journal, *the* Washington Post, *and other newspapers. He has written two books and numerous articles for the* New Yorker, Conde Nast Traveler, Vanity Fair, *and other publications. In addition, he has presided over two political debate shows on television, as moderator of* Firing Line *on PBS and cohost of* Crossfire *on CNN.*

The following essay was originally published in 1996, in Forbes, *a magazine for working professionals. Kinsley gives corporate email culture an enthusiastic endorsement, and he offers several reasons for his positive evaluation. Although Kinsley focuses on email culture in the workplace, email is now widely used in many other settings. For some friends and families, email has almost replaced letters and phone calls. In many colleges, networks enable students to use email to exchange their writing with other students or send it to an instructor. Whether or not you use email, you will want to know why Kinsley believes it to be "a marvelous medium of communication" for people in business.*

The way the new technology has affected my working life most directly has nothing in particular to do with what I am producing. My product happens to be an Internet-based magazine, but this particular innovation would be just as transforming if my business were manufacturing paper clips. The innovation is email. 1

Until I came to Microsoft in January, I had never worked for a big corporation. So I was having a hard time sorting out all my new impressions. What was Microsoft (which prides itself, of course, on being a different kind of corporation) and what was (despite Microsoft's pretensions) corporate America in general? Shortly after I arrived, I met someone who'd just joined Microsoft from Nintendo North America—a similar high tech, postindustrial, 2 shorts-and-sandals sort of company, one would suppose. So I asked him, How is Microsoft different? He said, "At Microsoft, the phone never rings." And it's almost true. The ringing telephones that TV producers use as an all-purpose background noise to signify a business setting are virtually silent at Microsoft. At least in terms of intracompany communications, probably 99 percent take place through email. If you should happen to get an old-fashioned phone call, you may well be informed of that fact by email, even if the person who took the message is within eye-contact range.

3 Microsoft may still be a bit ahead of most of the rest of the country in developing an email culture, but I suspect it's only a tiny bit. Email is inevitable. Nineteen eighty-nine was the year you stopped asking people, "Do you have a fax machine?" and started asking, "What is your fax number?" Nineteen ninety was the year you started being annoyed (and, by around Christmastime), incredulous that anyone in the business or professional world would not have a fax number. Similarly, 1996 is the year you stopped asking people, "Do you have email?" and started asking, "What is your email address?" By the end of 1997 you will be indignant if anyone you're doing business with expects you to go to the trouble of communicating by less convenient methods.

4 This is an almost entirely positive development. Convenience aside, email is a marvelous medium of communication. It combines the immediacy of telephone or face-to-face talk with the thoughtfulness (or at least the opportunity for thoughtfulness) of the written word. At *Slate* we find it a wonderfully productive way to bounce around editorial ideas. And we use it in the online magazine as a medium of policy debate that we find intellectually superior to television chat.

5 Email has eased the burden of putting out a national magazine of politics and culture from Redmond, Washington (which is not the center of the universe, whatever some of its denizens may think). With a small budget and staff, we could not ordinarily afford to have a headquarters in Redmond plus bureaus in Washington and New York. But email enables us to spread the "headquarters" staff over all three places. Our East Coast representatives can pick up the local vibes in the traditional metropolitan manner (i.e., lunch) then plug back into Redmond in the modern manner (i.e., email). If you use email dozens of times a day—and save it—you end up with a pretty complete record of your activities and thoughts. As someone who (like many others) aspires to keep a diary but lacks the self-discipline, I find this

comforting. Lawyers, of course, find it alarming, but you can't please everybody.

6 A social advantage of email is its egalitarianism. It's another blow to the old corporate culture in which Mr. Bigshot dictates letters and memos and the secretary types them, folds them, mails them, opens them at the receiving end, files them, and so on. Is there anyone in the business world who still thinks that he or she is too important to type? If so, that person had better wake up. Refusing to use a keyboard will soon be anachronistic as, say, refusing to speak on the telephone.

7 To be sure, egalitarianism has its limits. The ease and economy of sending email, especially to multiple recipients, makes us all vulnerable to any bore, loony, or commercial or political salesman who can get our email address. It's still a lot less intrusive than the telephone, since you can read and answer or ignore email at your own convenience. But as normal people's email starts mounting into the hundreds daily, which is bound to happen, filtering mechanisms and conventions of etiquette that are still in their primitive stage will be desperately needed.

8 Another supposed disadvantage of email is that it discourages face-to-face communication. At Microsoft, where people routinely send email back and forth all day to the person in the next office, this is certainly true. Some people believe this tendency has more to do with the underdeveloped social skills of computer geeks than with Microsoft's role in developing the technology email relies on. I wouldn't presume to comment on that. Whether you think email replacing live conversation is a good or bad thing depends, I guess, on how much of a misanthrope you are. I like it.

9 Historians looking back on our time, I suspect, will have no doubt that the arrival of email was a good thing. For decades now historians have been complaining about the invention of the telephone. By destroying the art of letter writing, telephones virtually wiped out the historians' principal raw material. Email, however, has reversed that development. Historians of the twenty-first century will be able to mine rich veins of written—and stored—material. People's daily lives will be documented better than ever before. Scholars specializing in the twentieth century will be at a unique disadvantage compared both with their colleagues writing about the nineteenth or earlier centuries and with those writing about the twenty-first or later.

10 So 1996 is not just the year business embraced email. In a way, it is the year history started again.

READING FOR MEANING

Write to create meanings for Kinsley's evaluation of email.

Start Making Meaning

Begin by listing the main reasons Kinsley values email (reasons appear in paragraphs 4–6 and 9). Continue by writing about anything else in the selection or in your experience that contributes to your understanding of Kinsley's evaluation.

If You Are Stuck

If you cannot write at least a page, consider writing about

- Kinsley's acknowledgment of two disadvantages of email (paragraphs 7 and 8), describing the disadvantages briefly and perhaps adding one or more from your own experience.
- Kinsley's comparisons of email with faxes (paragraph 3) and telephones (7).
- your willingness or unwillingness to use email.
- a particular experience you have had with email that illustrates why you do or do not value it as Kinsley does.

READING LIKE A WRITER

GIVING REASONS AND SUPPORT

At the center of every evaluation are the writer's reasons for making a judgment and the support for those reasons. The reasons should be appropriate for evaluating the subject, and they should be convincing to readers. Furthermore, the reasons should be visible: You do not want readers to miss them. As a writer, you make reasons visible by cuing them strongly—for example, by putting them at the beginnings of paragraphs. Kinsley offers several reasons to support the high value he places on email, and he attempts to support each reason.

Analyze

1. *Underline* the reasons Kinsley gives for valuing email in paragraphs 4–6 and 9. *Look for* the one sentence in each paragraph that most concisely states the reason.
2. *Notice* how Kinsley tries to support (to argue for) each of the reasons you have identified.

3. *Consider* whether Kinsley's reasons are likely to seem appropriate and believable to his readers. Then *decide* whether you think the support he offers is convincing. What do you find most and least convincing about the reasons and support he offers?

Write

Write several sentences explaining what you have learned about how Kinsley uses reasons and support to justify his evaluation of email. *Give examples* from the reading. Then *write a few more sentences* evaluating how successfully Kinsley supports his judgment.

CONSIDERING IDEAS FOR YOUR OWN WRITING

Kinsley's evaluation of email culture opens up the possibility of evaluating any device or technology you rely on for communication. Certainly, the telephone is important to you, but you may also have experience with a pager, car phone, cellular phone, or fax machine. You may have used a scanner or digital camera to share photographs via the Internet. Or you may have used a video, audio, or CD recorder to make tapes or CDs for yourself or someone else. Maybe you still handwrite letters or notes regularly. Choose one communication technology to evaluate—to praise or criticize.

How would you interest your readers in this technology and present it to them? For what reasons would you praise or criticize it? You could support these reasons convincingly only if you have considerable experience with the communication technology you are evaluating. What other technologies could you compare or contrast it with?

CHARLES HEROLD

Thief II Stresses Stealth over Strength

Charles Herold (b. 1959) writes reviews of computer game software for the New York Times *and reviews hardware, software, and Web sites for* Time Digital. *He has worked for Time Warner, where he designed Web pages for the company's Internet presence, created Pathfinder, and wrote Perl and Java code. He reports that he has not entirely given up hope of becoming a rock star.*

The following review was published in the New York Times' *weekly electronic section, "Circuits," in 2000. Herold evaluates Thief II: The Metal Age, a computer action game whose hero, Garrett, tries to save the world while stealing from the rich and powerful. Throughout the review, Herold contrasts the permitted actions of Garrett with the violent and destructive actions required in most other action games. He begins the review as a player of the game, taking on the role of Garrett.*

Before you read, think about the computer action games you have played or seen others play. Consider what you found most appealing about the games you played or watched and what you found repelling about them. As you read, notice the reasons Herold gives for liking Thief II. Notice, too, how he acknowledges its weaknesses.

I've just entered the study when I hear a guard moving in the hall outside, whistling tunelessly. Quickly I douse the torch on the wall with one of my water arrows and wait in the dark. The guard passes by, oblivious; I see that he's carrying a key. Planning to pick his pocket, I quickly exit the study, but I've forgotten that between the room and hall carpets there is a brief stretch of wooden floor, and the sound of my boots startles the guard. 1

"Who goes there?" he shouts as I quickly duck back into the study. He enters the room. I press up against the wall and hold my breath. He looks around carefully, but my black cloak blends into the deep shadows. He comes closer and closer, seeming to stare right at me. 2

In any other game, I would pull out my broadsword or laser gun, and the guard would be history. But in Thief II: The Metal Age, a self-described "first-person sneaker" from Looking Glass Studio, brute strength takes a back seat to cunning stealth. So I just keep quiet and hope that he doesn't realize I'm here. 3

"Must have been rats," the guard mutters and turns away. I run up and knock him out with my blackjack, and I drag his body deeper into the study to hide him from the other guards. After I grab the key, I slip out into the hall. 4

If that sounds less exciting than all-out carnage, it isn't. A refreshing alternative to games that glorify violence, Thief II instead glorifies thievery. You play Garrett, a master thief who steals from the wealthy and powerful for a living and saves the world as a hobby. 5

Garrett lives in a world that is part Ivanhoe, part 19th-century mechanics and part information age robotics. An ancient stone castle can be guarded by clanking mechanical beasts that are powered by an internal furnace. 6

In the typical 3-D action game, which Thief II resembles at first glance, a favored technique is to run into a room with supercharged weapons and rain down destruction on your enemies. But in Thief II your weapons are primitive and awkward and if three guards gang up on you, you are dead, pure and simple. 7

Fighting is the surest way to lose the game. Not that Garrett is a pacifist (he can fire off arrows from a safe distance), but it is a lot safer to hide in the shadows or run away. At a higher level of difficulty, you are often required to show even more restraint, completing your mission without leaving any trace of your presence. That means leaving everyone else alive and conscious. 8

The story is slight. Garrett is recruited to help destroy the Mechanists, a cult that worships machines and is turning the poor and disenfranchised into living robots. The overthrow of this cult entails traveling over rooftops and through people's apartments, following Mechanists messengers and reading their communiques. In one of my favorite missions, you follow a dying man by the bloodstains he leaves behind. 9

Whatever else you have to do—frame a corrupt official, find secret documents, kidnap an important Mechanist—you must never forget to steal things. Snatch those golden candlesticks, slip the purse off that woman's belt, pick up a stack of coins from a gambling table. This is your job, and you are very good at it. And after all, saving the world doesn't put food on the table. 10

While most game engines supply rather dimwitted antagonists, the denizens of Thief II give a remarkable impersonation of real intelligence. Guards don't just try to kill you—they get other guards to help. "Come quickly, an intruder," one will shout, and any guard in earshot will come running, sword drawn. A noncombatant will whimper, "Please don't hurt me," then start screaming, "Come quickly—a thief is here." 11

Guards will search for you if they hear your step on a marble floor or find an unconscious body. They peer into every shadow and shout, "Only a coward hides." If they find you, you must 12 escape or fight. If you give a guard a couple of good thrusts with your sword, he will run away and call for assistance.

13 In other ways, Thief II shows its game engine's limitations. Except for highly scripted conversations, the people in the game never acknowledge one another. When a guard passes another guard he never says, "How are the kids?" And while these guards are far smarter than typical game enemies, they still cannot form a posse and methodically hunt you down. They all try to kill you, but they do not really cooperate with one another. (If the guards were that smart, you would never make it out alive.)

14 Much of the fun of Thief II comes from playing fly on the wall. Poking around an office, you might find an exchange of mail from two clerks plotting against their boss, or you might overhear guards debating religion.

15 The world in Thief II is amazingly alive, almost making you feel that the people you are robbing are real characters with lives of their own. They seem so real that leaving them alive may feel like not only the best strategy but also the best moral choice. As that guard crumples to the ground and whimpers, "Help me," you might just feel a little guilty. Poor guy, he was only doing his job.

READING FOR MEANING

Write to create meanings for Herold's evaluation of Thief II.

Start Making Meaning

Begin by listing two or three reasons Herold likes Thief II. Continue by writing about anything else in the selection or in your experience that contributes to your understanding of Herold's evaluation.

If You Are Stuck

If you cannot write at least a page, consider writing about

- the characters and settings of the game.
- the various activities Garrett engages in as he goes about stealing from the rich and saving the world.
- the appeal to you personally of an action game like Thief II that emphasizes stealth and thievery over aggression and murder.

- the role of Garrett as compared to a role you have played in some other computer game.

READING LIKE A WRITER

PRESENTING THE SUBJECT

The subject must be clearly identified if readers are to know what is being evaluated. Therefore, writers of evaluative essays usually begin by naming and describing their subject. As they go on to argue for and support their judgment of the subject, they may give further information about it. Evaluators need provide only enough information to give readers a context for the judgment. However, certain kinds of evaluations—such as book, television, and movie reviews—usually require more information than other kinds of evaluations because reviewers have to assume that readers will be unfamiliar with the subject and will be reading, in part, to learn more about it. Reviewing a just-released computer game, Herold must present it to readers in some detail without giving away all of the protagonist Garrett's key actions or interactions with other characters. Without being able to imagine what Thief II looks like in relation to other similar games, readers have no basis for deciding whether Herold's judgment of it should be taken seriously.

Analyze

1. *Reread* paragraphs 1–4, and *underline* the different elements of the game (scenes, characters, actions, objects) presented in Herold's narrative. (The "I" of the narrative is Herold taking on the player's role of Garrett.)

2. Now *reread* paragraphs 6 and 9, where additional information about the subject is presented. *Contrast* the way information is presented in these two paragraphs with the way it is presented in paragraphs 1–4.

Write

Write several sentences explaining how Herold presents his subject to readers who are unfamiliar with it. *Give examples* from the reading to illustrate your explanation. Then *write one or two more sentences* evaluating how successful you think Herold's presentation of the subject is for his readers, especially his strategy of taking on the role of a player of the game.

A SPECIAL READING STRATEGY

Evaluating the Logic of an Argument

You can learn still more about Herold's evaluation by analyzing and evaluating its logic for appropriateness, believability, and consistency. For detailed guidelines on evaluating the logic of an argument, see Appendix 1 (pp. 545–48).

CONSIDERING IDEAS FOR YOUR OWN WRITING

Consider evaluating a game you own or one you remember from childhood. Examples include computer games (such as Mortal Kombat, Quake, or Myst), board games (Monopoly or Trivial Pursuit), card games (poker), or athletic games (handball or volleyball). The key is to choose a game that you have extensive experience playing and that you are willing to look at critically. Even if the game is easy to play, and even if your first thought about it is simply that it is fun, you still must follow the basic principles for evaluative writing and give substantial reasons explaining why the game works (or does not work) for you. You must judge the game according to such recognized standards, as the visual appeal and skill level, the simplicity or complexity of the rules, the degree of competitiveness or teamwork required, and the pace of the game. You also need to consider the game's strengths and limitations.

RICHARD CORLISS

Run, Chicken Run!

Richard Corliss (b. 1944) is a senior writer at Time *magazine, where he writes about movies, music, sports, theme parks, and other aspects of popular culture. For twenty years he was editor of* Film Comment *magazine, and he has published three books on the movies:* Talking Pictures: Screenwriters in the American Cinema *(1974),* Greta Garbo *(1974), and* Lolita *(1994).*

In this essay from a 2000 issue of Time, *Corliss evaluates a hit movie of that year—*Chicken Run*—in which the main roles are played by plasticine puppet chickens. As Corliss explains, this kind of movie is part of a long tradition of animated films, which include cartoons, Disney-style, hand-drawn animations like* Lady and the Tramp, *and, more recently, computer animations like* Toy Story.

Before you read, think about the animated films you have seen. Consider what you especially liked about the most memorable one. As you read, notice how Corliss informs readers about the movie and its production while evaluating it as a weak or strong movie of its type.

The inmates have tried a dozen ways of escaping from the prison camp. They've tried bouncing over the barbed-wire fence using a hot-water bottle as a trampoline; not enough thrust. They've huddled under the clothes of a giant scarecrow, but the garment ripped, leaving them exposed. After so many failures, the prisoners are distressed and balky. "We haven't tried *not* trying to escape," says Bunty. Babs, her dim friend, nods brightly. "That might work." 1

Ginger, their leader, is not one to chicken out. Told the chances of escaping are a million to one, she replies, "Then there's still a chance." But she knows she faces longer odds than the POWs of *Stalag 17* or *The Great Escape*. Those lads might have been killed. Ginger and her brood—the chickens of Tweedy's Farm—may get cooked. 2

Chicken Run, a comedy-adventure, with feathers, is exactly the picker-upper this macho-movie summer needs. It's a parable of plucky sisterhood: hens who endure life's drab defeats while hoping for a break. The film is funny and touching and beautifully understated; its characters earn big laughs with the subtlest wrinkle of a brow, sobs with a stifled sigh. In a season of nine-figure budgets, the movie was made for chicken feed ($42 million). It also boasts an accent that is defiantly English—Yorkshire, 3 even—with a dash of yank bravado from visiting star Mel Gibson.

4 And while Hollywood goes mad for techno tricks, directors Nick Park and Peter Lord and their team at Aardman Studios of Bristol, England, are still crafting films by hand. *Chicken Run* is one of the few features made in the sublimely masochistic form of animation known as stop motion, in which plasticine puppets on miniature film sets must be adjusted 24 times for every second of film. A live-action feature has perhaps 500 shots; this 82-min. movie has 118,080. "The detail is astonishing," says Lord, still in awe of his colleagues' industry 28 years after co-founding the studio. "There must be more man-hours per film frame here than in anything else known to man." The art of the Aardmen and -women is to make the years of hard work look easy. Viewers don't see the pain; they feel the joy.

5 *Chicken Run* is part of a new vitality and variety in what was once called cartooning. "For decades," says film historian John Canemaker, director of the animation program at New York University, "feature animation was dominated by one style: Disney's. Now a diversity of techniques and styles are gaining acceptance. There are computer-animated features, such as Pixar's *Toy Story* and *A Bug's Life.* There is clay and/or puppet animation—and because of the artistry of Nick Park and Peter Lord, it is going to grab audiences. We are expanding the definition of the form. It's a brave new world in animation."

6 The mood is less brave than bleak on the moor of Tweedy's farm, in the mid-'50s. Mrs. Tweedy, the vicious camp commandant (voiced by Miranda Richardson), and her slow-witted, henpecked husband (Tony Haygarth) have shown her prisoners what happens to a hen who hasn't laid eggs: it becomes a chicken with its head cut off. This fowl existence is driving even Ginger (Julia Sawalha, known to U.S. viewers as young Saffy on the Brit-import sitcom *Absolutely Fabulous*) close to desperation. Then, out of the sky, a savior drops with a thud. He is Rocky Roads (Gibson), the "flying rooster" from a traveling circus, and he vainly promises to teach the hens—this coop of flighty, flightless birds—how to soar to freedom. But while Rocky the flying churl plays up to "all the beautiful English chicks," Mrs. Tweedy has bigger, nastier plans. She has bought a machine that will turn her chicken stalag into a factory for chicken pies. The prison camp is to be a death camp.

7 *Chicken Run*'s style and tone will be endearingly familiar to those who have seen Park's Oscar-winning short work. *Creature Comforts* (1989) attached the comments of zoo visitors to claymated lions, bears and baby hippos, with sad and hilarious re-

sults. The trio *A Grand Day Out* (1989), *The Wrong Trousers* (1993) and *A Close Shave* (1995) were mini-epics starring Wallace, a staid, daft suburban bachelor inventor, and his brilliant, long-suffering dog Gromit. Park has now adapted to feature length his obsession with the forlorn wit of caged animals, with the quiet exasperation of rural English life, with complex machinery destined to go wrong—and with bead-eyed, lipless creatures who have more lower teeth (six or eight) than upper (four). These features give his characters a perpetually dazed expression, as if they've been beaten goofy by life's inequities and iniquities. Simply to keep going is an act of heroism.

Park, Lord and screenwriter Karey Kirkpatrick stocked *Chicken Run* with a cross section of brit types: Bunty (Imelda Staunton) is bossy; silly Babs (Jane Horrocks, who played Bubble on *Ab Fab*) is forever knitting—when she gets morose, she knits a noose. Mac (Lynn Ferguson) is the nearsighted soul of Scottish ingenuity. Fowler (Benjamin Whitrow), a crusty veteran of the RAF,[1] says Yanks can't be trusted: "always late for every war." The hens' lines to the outside world are Nick (Timothy Spall) and Fetcher (Phil Daniels), two music-hall Cockney rats—larcenists with a soft streak. 8

It all might seem fanciful, but for Park, who was raised in rural Lancashire, *Chicken Run* comes close to a childhood memoir. "My family had chickens," he says, "just as pets. They used to come into the porch and eat the food, like a dog really. Or they'd come in the house and steal things. We couldn't bear to eat them; they were characters. Then when I was 16 or 17, I had a summer job at a chicken-packing factory; we had to fold up plucked chickens and pack them in cellophane trays. I also did a day working in a slaughterhouse—it was horrible. Some of what I saw there did get through to the pie machine in the film." 9

A team of 25 animators toiled to achieve two or three seconds of footage a day, as Lord and Park patrolled the tiny sets like the barons of Brobdingnag. The Aardman shop buzzed with the work of painters, press molders and a gent known as the mouth-and-beak-replacement coordinator. 10

And every few weeks, Jeffrey Katzenberg, whose DreamWorks paid for the film, flew in for moral support—"Support," he notes, "means underneath, lifting up, as opposed to on top, holding down"—and to debate the fine points. "Nick and I are English," Lord says. "We don't shout and scream. Whereas Jeffrey says what he thinks immediately and loudly. He wants everything 11

[1]RAF: Royal Air Force. (*Ed.*)

to be argued." Lord finally figured out how to react to the American rooster: "We listen and nod and then go and do our own thing." One thing they did for Katzenberg: a TV spot for the fast-food tie-in with Burger King (you were expecting Kentucky Fried Chicken?). All the hens chorus, "Save the chickens! Eat more beef!"

12 In any format, live action or animation, good films are as scarce as—well, you know. *Chicken Run* is that rare film that advances the art while bathing the audience in smiles. All it took was three years of mind-bending labor to pullet together.

READING FOR MEANING

Write to create meanings for Corliss's evaluation of *Chicken Run.*

Start Making Meaning

Begin by listing the main reasons Corliss likes *Chicken Run.* You will find them in paragraphs 3, 4, and 7. Continue by writing about anything else in the selection or in your experience that contributes to your understanding of why Corliss values the movie.

If You Are Stuck

If you cannot write at least a page, consider writing about

- the animation techniques that make such films possible (see paragraphs 4 and 10).
- the characters in the film, perhaps listing all of those mentioned and adding a phrase after each one that identifies his or her special quality.
- your favorite animation film (Disney, computer, or clay or plasticine puppet), comparing or contrasting it with what you have learned about *Chicken Run* from Corliss's evaluation.

READING LIKE A WRITER

ASSERTING AN OVERALL JUDGMENT

The purpose of an evaluative essay is to assert an overall judgment. To that end, writers can neither hide this judgment nor merely imply it. Instead, they must assert it prominently, usually at or near the beginning of the essay. They also reassert the judgment in various ways later on. Since everything in the essay works toward supporting the overall judgment, writers do not want readers to lose sight of the judgment itself.

Corliss asserts his overall judgment in paragraph 3 and reasserts it in paragraph 12. In between, he presents the reasons for his judgment and the argument and support for each reason, while also continually reminding readers of how much he values *Chicken Run.*

Analyze

1. *Underline* the overall judgment asserted in paragraphs 3 and 12.
2. *Skim the essay,* looking for any other statements that express a positive evaluation of *Chicken Run. Put a checkmark* by these statements.
3. *Consider* how successfully Corliss asserts and reasserts his overall judgment. How does he assert this judgment clearly and unequivocally? How frequently does he remind readers of this positive judgment as his argument moves along? What, if any, weaknesses does he acknowledge about *Chicken Run?*

Write

Write a few sentences explaining how Corliss asserts his overall judgment of the film and reminds readers of this judgment. *Add a sentence or two* evaluating how successful you find Corliss's assertion of his overall judgment.

CONSIDERING IDEAS FOR YOUR OWN WRITING

Consider evaluating a recent or current animated film. In paragraph 7, Corliss mentions four other films by the director of *Chicken Run.* You could find out whether one of these is available in video rental stores, at your college library, or through interlibrary loan. Since *Chicken Run* was a popular film when it was released in 2000, you could also rent it and use it as a basis for comparison with another film by the same director. Alternatively, you could evaluate a full-length animated film (rather than a short cartoon) that was important to you in your childhood, such as *Lady and the Tramp.*

CHRISTINE ROMANO

"Children Need to Play, Not Compete," by Jessica Statsky: An Evaluation

Christine Romano wrote the following essay when she was a first-year college student. In it she evaluates a position paper written by another student, Jessica Statsky's "Children Need to Play, Not Compete," which appears in Chapter 9 of this book (pp. 500–504). Romano focuses not on the writing strategies or basic features of this position paper but rather on its logic—on whether the argument is likely to convince the intended readers. She evaluates the logic of the argument according to the standards presented in Appendix 1 (pp. 545–48). You might want to review these standards before you read Romano's evaluation. Also, if you have not read Statsky's essay, you might want to do so now, thinking about what seems most and least convincing to you about her argument that competitive sports can be harmful to young children .

Parents of young children have a lot to worry about and to hope for. In "Children Need to Play, Not Compete," Jessica Statsky appeals to their worries and hopes in order to convince them that organized competitive sports may harm their children physically and psychologically. Statsky states her thesis clearly and fully forecasts the reasons she will offer to justify her position: Besides causing physical and psychological harm, competitive sports discourage young people from becoming players and fans when they are older and inevitably put parents' needs and fantasies ahead of children's welfare. Statsky also carefully defines her key terms. By *sports,* for example, she means to include both contact and noncontact sports that emphasize competition. The sports may be organized locally at schools or summer sports camps or nationally, as in the examples of Peewee Football and Little League Baseball. She is concerned only with children six to twelve years of age. 1

In this essay, I will evaluate the logic of Statsky's argument, considering whether the support for her thesis is appropriate, believable, consistent, and complete. While her logic *is* appropriate, believable, and consistent, her argument also has weaknesses: it seems incomplete because it neglects to anticipate parents' predictable questions and objections, and because it fails to support certain parts fully. 2

Statsky provides appropriate support for her thesis. Throughout her essay, she relies for support on different kinds of informa- 3 tion (she cites eleven separate sources, including books, newspapers, and Web sites). Her quotations, examples, and statistics all support the reasons she believes competitive sports are bad for children. For example, in paragraph 3, Statsky offers the reason that "overly competitive sports" may damage children's growing bodies and that contact sports, in particular, may be especially hazardous. She supports this reason by paraphrasing Koppett that muscle strain or even lifelong injury may result when a twelve-year-old throws curve balls. She then quotes Tutko on the dangers of tackle football. The opinions of both experts are obviously appropriate. They are relevant to her reason, and we can easily imagine that they would worry many parents.

Not only is Statsky's support appropriate but it is also believable. Statsky quotes or summarizes authorities to support her argument in paragraphs 3–6, 8, 9, and 11. The question is whether readers would find these authorities believable or credible. Since Statsky relies almost entirely on authorities to support her argument, readers must believe these authorities for her argument to succeed. I have not read Statsky's sources, but I think there are good reasons to consider them authoritative. First of all, the newspaper authors she quotes write for two of America's most respected newspapers, the *New York Times* and the *Los Angeles Times.* These newspapers are read across the country by political leaders and financial experts and by people interested in the arts and popular culture. Both have sports reporters who not only report on sports events but also take a critical look at sports issues. In addition, both newspapers have reporters who specialize in children's health and education. Second, Statsky gives background information about the authorities she quotes, information intended to increase the person's believability in the eyes of parents of young children. In paragraph 3, she tells readers that Thomas Tutko is "a psychology professor at San Jose State University and coauthor of the book *"Winning Is Everything and Other American Myths."*" In paragraph 5, she announces that Martin Rablovsky is "a former sports editor for the *New York Times,*" and she notes that he has watched children play organized sports for many years. Third, she quotes from two Web sites—the official Little League site and an AOL message board. Parents are likely to accept the authority of the Little League site and be interested in what other parents and coaches (most of whom are also parents) have to say. 4

In addition to quoting authorities, Statsky relies on examples and anecdotes to support the reasons for her position. If examples and anecdotes are to be believable, they must seem representative 5 to readers, not bizarre or highly unusual or completely unpredictable. Readers can imagine a similar event happening elsewhere. For anecdotes to be believable, they should, in addition, be specific and true to life. All of Statsky's examples and anecdotes fulfill these requirements, and her readers would find them believable. For example, early in her argument, in paragraph 4, Statsky reasons that fear of being hurt greatly reduces children's enjoyment of contact sports. The anecdote comes from Tosches's investigative report on Peewee Football as does the quotation by the mother of an eight-year-old player who says that the children become frightened and pretend to be injured in order to stay out of the game. In the anecdote, a seven-year-old makes himself vomit to avoid playing. Because these echo the familiar "I feel bad" or "I'm sick" excuse children give when they do not want to go somewhere (especially school) or do something, most parents would find them believable. They could easily imagine their own children pretending to be hurt or ill if they were fearful or depressed. The anecdote is also specific. Tosches reports what the boy said and did and what the coach said and did.

6 Other examples provide support for all the major reasons Statsky gives for her position:

- That competitive sports pose psychological dangers—children becoming serious and unplayful when the game starts (paragraph 5)
- That adults' desire to win puts children at risk—parents fighting each other at a Peewee Football game and a coach setting fire to an opposing team's jersey (paragraph 8)
- That organized sports should emphasize cooperation and individual performance instead of winning—a coach banning scoring but finding that parents would not support him and a New York City basketball league in which all children play an equal amount of time and scoring is easier (paragraph 11)

All of these examples are appropriate to the reasons they support. They are also believable. Together, they help Statsky achieve her purpose of convincing parents that organized, competitive sports may be bad for their children and that there are alternatives.

7 If readers are to find an argument logical and convincing, it must be consistent and complete. While there are no inconsistencies or contradictions in Statsky's argument, it is seriously incomplete because it neglects to support fully one of its reasons, it fails to anticipate many predictable questions parents would have, and

it pays too little attention to noncontact competitive team sports. The most obvious example of thin support comes in paragraph 11, where Statsky asserts that many parents are ready for children's team sports that emphasize cooperation and individual performance. Yet the example of a Little League official who failed to win parents' approval to ban scores raises serious questions about just how many parents are ready to embrace noncompetitive sports teams. The other support, a brief description of City Sports for Kids in New York City, is very convincing but will only be logically compelling to those parents who are already inclined to agree with Statsky's position. Parents inclined to disagree with Statsky would need additional evidence. Most parents know that big cities receive special federal funding for evening, weekend, and summer recreation. Brief descriptions of six or eight noncompetitive teams in a variety of sports in cities, rural areas, suburban neighborhoods—some funded publicly, some funded privately—would be more likely to convince skeptics. Statsky is guilty here of failing to accept the burden of proof, a logical fallacy.

8 Statsky's argument is also incomplete in that it fails to anticipate certain objections and questions that some parents, especially those she most wants to convince, are almost sure to raise. In the first sentences of paragraphs 6, 9, and 10, Statsky does show that she is thinking about her readers' questions. She does not go nearly far enough, however, to have a chance of influencing two types of readers: those who themselves are or were fans of and participants in competitive sports and those who want their six- to twelve-year-old children involved in mainstream sports programs despite the risks, especially the national programs that have a certain prestige. Such parents might feel that competitive team sports for young children create a sense of community with a shared purpose, build character through self-sacrifice and commitment to the group, teach children to face their fears early and learn how to deal with them through the support of coaches and team members, and introduce children to the principles of social cooperation and collaboration. Some parents are likely to believe and to know from personal experience that coaches who burn opposing teams' jerseys on the pitching mound before the game starts are the exception, not the rule. Some young children idolize teachers and coaches, and team practice and games are the brightest moments in their lives. Statsky seems not to have considered these reasonable possibilities, and as a result her argument lacks a compelling logic it might have had. By acknowledging that she was aware of many of these objections—and perhaps even

accommodating more of them in her own argument, as she does in paragraph 10, while refuting other objections—she would have strengthened her argument.

9 Finally, Statsky's argument is incomplete because she overlooks examples of noncontact team sports. Track, swimming, and tennis are good examples that some readers would certainly think of. Some elementary schools compete in track meets. Public and private clubs and recreational programs organize competitive swimming and tennis competitions. In these sports, individual performance is the focus. No one gets trampled. Children exert themselves only as much as they are able to. Yet individual performances are scored, and a team score is derived. Because Statsky fails to mention any of these obvious possibilities, her argument is weakened.

10 The logic of Statsky's argument, then, has both strengths and weaknesses. The support she offers is appropriate, believable, and consistent. The major weakness is incompleteness—she fails to anticipate more fully the likely objections of a wide range of readers. Her logic would prevent parents who enjoy and advocate competitive sports from taking her argument seriously. Such parents and their children have probably had positive experiences with team sports, and these experiences would lead them to believe that the gains are worth whatever risks may be involved. Many probably think that the risks Statsky points out can be avoided by careful monitoring. For those parents inclined to agree with her, Statsky's logic is likely to seem sound and complete. An argument that successfully confirms readers' beliefs is certainly valid, and Statsky succeeds admirably at this kind of argument. Because she does not offer compelling counterarguments to the legitimate objections of those inclined not to agree with her, however, her success is limited.

READING FOR MEANING

Write to create meanings for Romano's evaluation of Statsky's position paper.

Start Making Meaning

Begin by describing the major strengths and weaknesses Romano sees in Statsky's argument. Continue by writing about anything else in the selection or in your experience that contributes to your understanding of Romano's evaluation.

If You Are Stuck

If you cannot write at least a page, consider writing about

- why Romano finds Statsky's argument believable (paragraphs 4–6).
- some of the reasons Romano finds Statsky's argument to be incomplete (paragraphs 7–9).
- further reasons why, in your experience, parents of six- to twelve-year-old children might find Statsky's argument incomplete.
- your own experience as a member of an organized sports team for children of the same age group, comparing or contrasting it with what Romano finds believable or incomplete in Statsky's argument.

READING LIKE A WRITER

COUNTERARGUING

Romano clearly admires Statsky's argument, yet she also sees that it is not perfect. Both Michael Kinsley and Charles Herold take a similar approach to evaluating their subjects. All three writers go beyond their first reactions to their subjects in order to consider them critically; that is, with some distance and skepticism. This stance enables each writer to counterargue—to offer a balanced evaluation by expressing reservations about a subject the writer admires. While Romano must have admired Statsky's argument when she first read it—and she does express that admiration at length—she is not blind to its gaps or weaknesses. Consequently, she is able to offer a balanced evaluation of it by both arguing for its apparent strengths and counterarguing weaknesses that some readers would probably see. In counterarguing, Romano tries to convince readers that the weaknesses are real and that they compromise Statsky's evaluation. Romano may have discovered these weaknesses on her own, without thinking about her readers—other students in her writing class and her instructor, all of whom would have read Statsky's essay—but upon reflection she likely realized that some of her readers would share her reservations about the essay and might have considered her naive if she had not brought them up.

Analyze

1. *Reread* paragraphs 7–9, and then *underline* the one sentence in each paragraph that most concisely states a weakness Romano finds in Statsky's evaluation.
2. *Consider* how Romano goes about supporting her counterargument in these paragraphs. *Make notes* in the margin about how many and what kinds of examples she offers.

3. *Evaluate* how successful Romano is in convincing readers that Statsky's argument has major weaknesses. What seems most and least convincing in her counterargument?

Write

Write several sentences reporting on what you have learned about how Romano counterargues weaknesses in Statsky's position paper on children's competitive sports teams. How does Romano bring up the weaknesses, and how does she counterargue? *Add a few more sentences* evaluating how convincing her counterargument is likely to be for her intended readers.

CONSIDERING IDEAS FOR YOUR OWN WRITING

List several texts you would consider evaluating. For example, you might include in your list an essay from one of the chapters in this book. If you choose an argument from Chapters 6 through 9, you could evaluate its logic (as Romano does), emotional appeals, or credibility, relying on the guidelines in Appendix 1 (pp. 545–48). You might prefer to evaluate a children's book you read when you were younger or one you now read to your own children, a magazine for people interested in computers or cars (or another topic), or a scholarly article you read for a research paper. You need not limit yourself to texts written on paper; also consider Internet texts such as the online magazine *Slate* or *Salon.* Choose one possibility from your list, and see whether you can come up with three or four reasons for why you find it a strong or weak text.

SCOTT HYDER

Poltergeist: *It Knows What Scares You*

Scott Hyder wrote this movie review for his first-year writing class. Like all reviewers, he cannot assume readers have seen the subject of his review: Poltergeist, *a movie released in 1982. But he probably assumes that they have seen other horror movies like it.*

As you read the review, think about how Hyder attempts to hold your interest in a movie you might not have seen in a theater or on video.

1 You are an eight-year-old boy all tucked in for the night. Your little sister is sleeping in the bed next to you. Suddenly, you hear a crash of thunder, and through the window, you can see the big, old, growling tree in the lightning. It seems to be, well, to be making faces at you! But, you are a big boy. Nothing scares *you*. Nothing at—BANG! WHOOSH! The tree comes to life as it tumbles through the window, grabbing you with its pulsating, hairy roots from your bed. As you scream for Mommy, the closet door slowly opens and an invisible, windlike presence kidnaps your sister. Your nice, cozy dreamhouse turns into a living hell. Watch out! "They're hee-re!"

2 In June 1982, producer-director-writer Steven Spielberg defined "horror" with a new word: *Poltergeist.* At first and final glance, *Poltergeist* is simply a riveting demonstration of a movie's power to terrify. It creates honest thrills within the confines of a PG rating, reaching for shock effects and the forced suspension of disbelief throughout the movie. Spielberg wrote the story, coproduced it, and supervised the final editing. The directing credit goes to Tobe Hooper, best known for his cult shocker *The Texas Chainsaw Massacre,* which probably explains *Poltergeist's* violence and slight crudeness.

3 Nevertheless, *Poltergeist* cannot be classified in the same horror category with such movies as *A Nightmare on Elm Street,* where a deformed psychotic slashes his victims with razor-edged fingernails. Unlike most horror flicks, *Poltergeist* works! Its success is due to excellent characters, music, and special effects—and to the fact that the story stays within the bounds of believability.

4 The movie takes place in a suburban housing tract. Steve (Craig T. Nelson) and Diane (JoBeth Williams) Freeling have just

purchased a new home when their adorable five-year-old daughter, Carole Anne (Heather O'Rourke), awakes to odd voices coming from the snowy TV screen that Steve falls asleep in front of during the late movie. She calls them the "TV people," and with the help of special-effects producer George Lucas and his Industrial Light and Magic, these people abduct little Carol Anne, provoking turbulence and misery for this once-happy family.

A mere synopsis simply cannot give a real feeling for the story. As Steve Freeling says to the parapsychologists who have come to see the house, "You have to see it to believe it." Each character possesses a unique personality, which contributes to the overall feeling the audience has for the story. The characters are represented to be as normal and American as bologna sandwiches—Dad sells houses, Mom sings along to TV jingles. Spielberg likes these characters, illustrating their go-with-the-flow resilience. When things get suddenly hectic toward the climax, these people can display their fear and anger as well as summon their inner strengths. This is particularly evident when Tangina, the parapsychologist the Freelings hire, instructs Diane to lie to her daughter in order to lure Carol Anne into the light and save her. 5

"Tell her to go into the light," Tangina instructs. "Tell her that *you* are in the light!" 6

"No," Diane replies with betrayed emotions. 7

Tangina immediately puts everything into the proper perspective. "You can't choose between life and death when we're dealing with what's in between! Now tell her before it's too late!" 8

Such scenes clearly illustrate that Spielberg's characters are, in a sense, the ordinary heroes of the movies. 9

A horror movie, however, cannot rely on terror, anger, and disbelief to hold its audience for two hours. Something needs to accompany these emotions, equally expressing the full extent of the characters' fear and anger. Music composer Jerry Goldsmith contributes his share of eeriness with his Academy Award-winning soundtrack. The basic theme is a lullaby (entitled "Carol Anne's Theme") that soothes the watcher, providing a cheerful, childlike innocence to the picture. The inverse is the ghost music that accompanies the abduction of Carol Anne and forces our stomachs to writhe. The music brings a straining, vibrating tone that is responsible for 60 percent of the audience's terror. When the clown doll's hand wraps around Robbie's (Oliver Robbins) neck, the sudden blaring of Goldsmith's orchestra is what makes viewers swallow their stomachs. Without it, the scene would never slap our face or give our necks a backward whiplash. Goldsmith matches the actions and emotions of the characters with 10 the corresponding instrumental music, enabling the audience to parallel its feelings with those delivered on the screen.

11 If a horror movie has a well-developed plot with superior actors and an excellent score to accompany their emotions, then it should be a sure winner at the box office, right? Looking back at such movies as *Rosemary's Baby, The Exorcist,* and the original *Psycho* one would obviously agree. *Poltergeist,* however, doesn't stop here. It goes even further by providing its audience with a special treat. With the help of *Star Wars* creator George Lucas, Spielberg and Hooper whip up a dazzling show of light and magic. There's an eerie parade of poltergeists in chiffons of light marching down the Freelings' staircase to the climactic scene as a huge, bright, nuclear-colored mouth strives to suck the Freeling children into their closet. Hooper's familiarity with film violence surfaces in a grotesque scene in which one of the parapsychologists hallucinates that he is tearing his face. Such shocking, hair-raising scenes as this make a huge contribution to horrifying the audience. Many horror films never achieve such reactions. *Poltergeist*'s precise timing with such effects makes it completely unpredictable as far as what is to come. From the first sign of a ghostlike hand jumping out of the TV to the staggering scene of dead bodies popping out of the half-dug swimming pool, the special-effects team draws every bit of energy out of the audience members, dazzling them and forcing them to believe in the horror on the screen.

12 There have been many movies that possess superior ratings in all of the above. Such movies as John Carpenter's *The Thing* and David Cronenberg's *Scanners* won raves for superior acting, background music, and special effects. Why was *Poltergeist* accepted at the box office more than other such movies? Every movie is forced to set up boundaries of believability through certain actions and concepts, and at one point these boundaries will be accepted by the viewer. In *Indiana Jones and the Temple of Doom,* Spielberg distinguished boundaries within which Indiana Jones defined his heroic stunts. Spielberg, however, unfortunately crossed his boundaries during a scene in which Indiana Jones jumps from one track to another with a moving train cart. From previous observations of Indiana Jones's capabilities, viewers are unable to accept this, nodding their heads with a "give me a break" expression.

13 In *Poltergeist,* Spielberg and Hooper remain within their established boundaries. Unlike most horror movies that have unfeasible killers who are incapable of dying or monsters that pop out of people's stomachs, *Poltergeist* focuses on the supernatural—a

subject with *very wide* boundaries. Because of our lack of knowledge in the area, we are "at the mercy of the writers and directors," as Alfred Hitchcock phrased it. The boundaries can be greater than most horror movies because of *Poltergeist*'s subject matter. The characters' disbelief of their surroundings encourages the audience to accept what is in front of them. Hence, *Poltergeist* successfully stays within its limits, taking them to their maximum, but luring the audience to believe the characters' situation.

14 *Poltergeist* reflects a lot of the fears that most of us grow up with: seeing scary shadows from the light in your closet, making sure your feet are not dangling over the bed, forming scary images of the objects in your room. As Spielberg's *E.T.* reminisces about our childhood dreams, *Poltergeist* surfaces our childhood nightmares. With its characters, music, and special effects, and its clearly distinguished boundaries of belief, *Poltergeist* is able to capture its audience with its unique thrills, allowing viewers to link their most inner-locked fears to those on the screen. *Poltergeist:* It knows what scares you!

READING FOR MEANING

Write to create meanings for Hyder's evaluation of *Poltergeist.*

Start Making Meaning

Begin by describing briefly what you think Hyder hopes to accomplish with his readers in writing this movie review. Continue by writing about anything else in the selection or in your experience that contributes to your understanding of Hyder's evaluation.

If You Are Stuck

If you cannot write at least a page, consider writing about

- Hyder's claim that horror movies must "stay within the bounds of believability" to be considered excellent (paragraph 3).
- Hyder's view that the characters are the heroes of *Poltergeist,* recalling whether this is the case in most horror movies you have seen.
- why you think the director chose an American suburb as the setting for *Poltergeist.*

- a horror movie you have seen recently, comparing it with what you have learned of *Poltergeist* from Hyder's review.

READING LIKE A WRITER

SUPPORTING REASONS WITH EXAMPLES

For a review to be believable and convincing, it must offer readers many examples from the subject. These examples help readers imagine the subject. Perhaps better than anything in the review, examples help readers decide whether they find the reviewer's judgment plausible or worth taking seriously. Beginning writers of evaluations of all kinds usually err on the side of providing too few examples. Think of this fundamental requirement as one of piling up examples, of including a great many, perhaps more than you think readers can stand. If you discover that you have gone an inch or two too far, you can easily drop a few examples when you revise your draft. Hyder provides a good model, offering many examples to support his argument that *Poltergeist* is a fine horror movie.

Analyze

1. Hyder provides many examples to support the reasons for his judgment. In paragraph 5, 10, 11, *or* 12, *underline* each separate example you find in that paragraph. (Some examples are references to other movies, which Hyder seems to assume readers will have seen.) Skipping over the general statements and assertions, *look for* the specific or concrete examples.
2. *Put a checkmark* in the margin by the example that best helps you imagine the movie, and *mark an X* in the margin by the example that you find least helpful.

Write

Write several sentences explaining how Hyder makes use of examples to substantiate his reasoning. *Include* some typical examples. Then *write a few more sentences* evaluating how plausible and convincing the examples are, in your view.

CONSIDERING IDEAS FOR YOUR OWN WRITING

Consider reviewing a current movie. Arrange to see it at least twice before you complete the first draft of your essay and a third time as you are revising. Only in this way can you collect relevant, concrete examples to support your evaluation.

Or you might consider an earlier movie now available at video stores. That way you can view it in segments at home and scan forward or backward to review key scenes. Consider choosing a film in a genre—horror, noir, romance, Western, or another—that you are familiar with. By choosing a film in a recognized genre, your evaluation will be more astute and informed and you will be able to compare your movie with others in its genre, as does Hyder. In the same vein, consider evaluating a movie by a director whose other films you have seen, even one or two of them. These comparisons can strengthen your evaluation.

Which movie might you choose? What arrangements will you need to make in order to see it several times as you are working on your evaluation?

KRISTINE POTTER

Asthma on the Web

Kristine Potter was a college student when she wrote this essay evaluating a Web site related to her son's medical condition.

As you read, notice what Potter looks for in evaluating medical information on the Web. Then consider whether the standards she applies to online research differ from those you would apply to research conducted in the library or through interviews and observations.

The other readings in this chapter are followed by reading and writing activities. Following this reading, however, you are on your own to decide how to read for meaning and read like a writer.

1 The World Wide Web (or WWW) has served as a convenient starting point for much of my college research, but I was still not sure whether it would also be useful for researching questions concerning my personal life. Since my nine-year-old son, Jeremy, suffers from asthma, I am particularly interested in using the Web to learn about the most current treatments for the disease. The Web's up-to-date information and easy accessibility from my home make it an especially attractive research tool. However, I am also aware that Web-based material must be evaluated carefully because anyone with technological know-how can publish on the Web. I have found that when I research medical information on the Web, I need to consider the same basic questions I use when researching for my college courses: (1) Is the information easily accessible? (2) Is it helpful? and (3) Is it reliable? My evaluation of the Canadian Lung Association's *Asthma* Web site, located at < http://www.lung.ca/asthma >, led me to the conclusion that this site successfully meets my criteria for accessible, helpful, and reliable information.

2 I accessed the *Asthma* home page from a list of search results produced by Yahoo!, < http://www.yahoo.com >, a popular Internet search engine, and was happy to learn that one important criterion for Web site usefulness—speedy access to information—was immediately satisfied. Unlike my earlier visit to another asthma-related Web site where I spent an average of thirty seconds waiting for each new page to load, the Canadian Lung Association's *Asthma* home page loaded instantaneously and I could see at a glance that it might be useful for my needs. The page downloaded quickly because it does not use a lot of graphics to attract visitors. Although the information at the other site may

have been useful in my research, graphic downloads took so long that I left in search of other sites that might more efficiently satisfy my research purposes. While the speed at which a Web page loads will vary from one computer to the next, according to Yale's *Web Style Guide,* "research has shown that for most computing tasks the threshold of frustration is around 10 seconds" (Lynch and Horton). Researchers, like myself, who access the Internet from home at less-than-ethernet speeds appreciate quick downloading of information more than fancy graphics. Therefore, the speed at which the Canadian Lung Association's home page appeared in my browser contributed largely to my decision to explore the Web site further.

3 The Canadian Lung Association's *Asthma* Web site seems well designed, incorporating a variety of links and other features that make it easy to navigate the site and find information quickly. As shown in Figure 1, for example, the *Asthma* home page includes several different links to additional pages of information at the site. At the top of the home page are three clickable buttons: "Home," for accessing the Canadian Lung Association home page; "Index," for accessing a list of the site's contents; and "Français," for giving users a choice between the French and English language versions of the Web site. On the left side of the screen are a "Quick Search" option and a lengthy menu of topics. The "Quick Search" option gives users an opportunity to search for information by keywords, while the menu organizes information under various topic headings with hyperlinks to available information at the site. In the center of the *Asthma* home page are two additional sets of hyperlinks for accessing specific information about asthma: first, keywords, underlined and printed in red, within the easy-to-read bulleted text (such as "Asthma Guide") and, second, underlined double arrows in a "Features" box (for example, "Pregnancy & Asthma >>").

4 Other pages at the *Asthma* site also feature useful ways of accessing information. The most important of these is a site map, which displays large buttons as hyperlinks to important topics on asthma. As shown in Figure 2, the *Asthma Resource Guide* page maps out the site's contents. It can be accessed by clicking on the underlined keywords "Asthma Guide" on the *Asthma* home page (Figure 1). The site map reappears at the bottom of every page within the Canadian Lung Association's *Asthma* Web site. Look, for example, at Figure 3, the *Asthma Management* page accessed by clicking on the "Management" button in Figure 2. As you can see, the *Asthma Management* page includes the site map at the bottom of the screen as well as the search and menu options at the

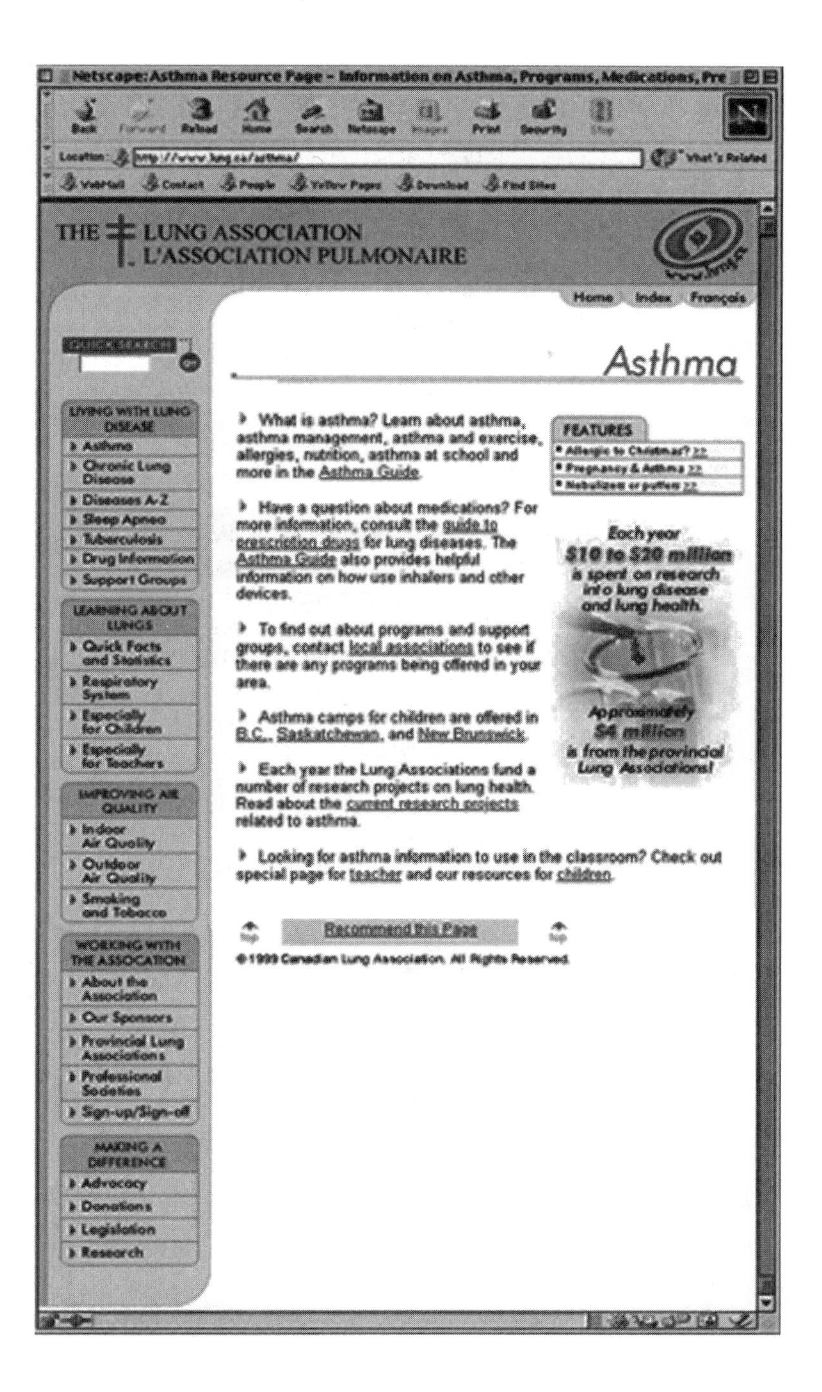

Fig. 1. The Canadian Lung Association's *Asthma* home page.

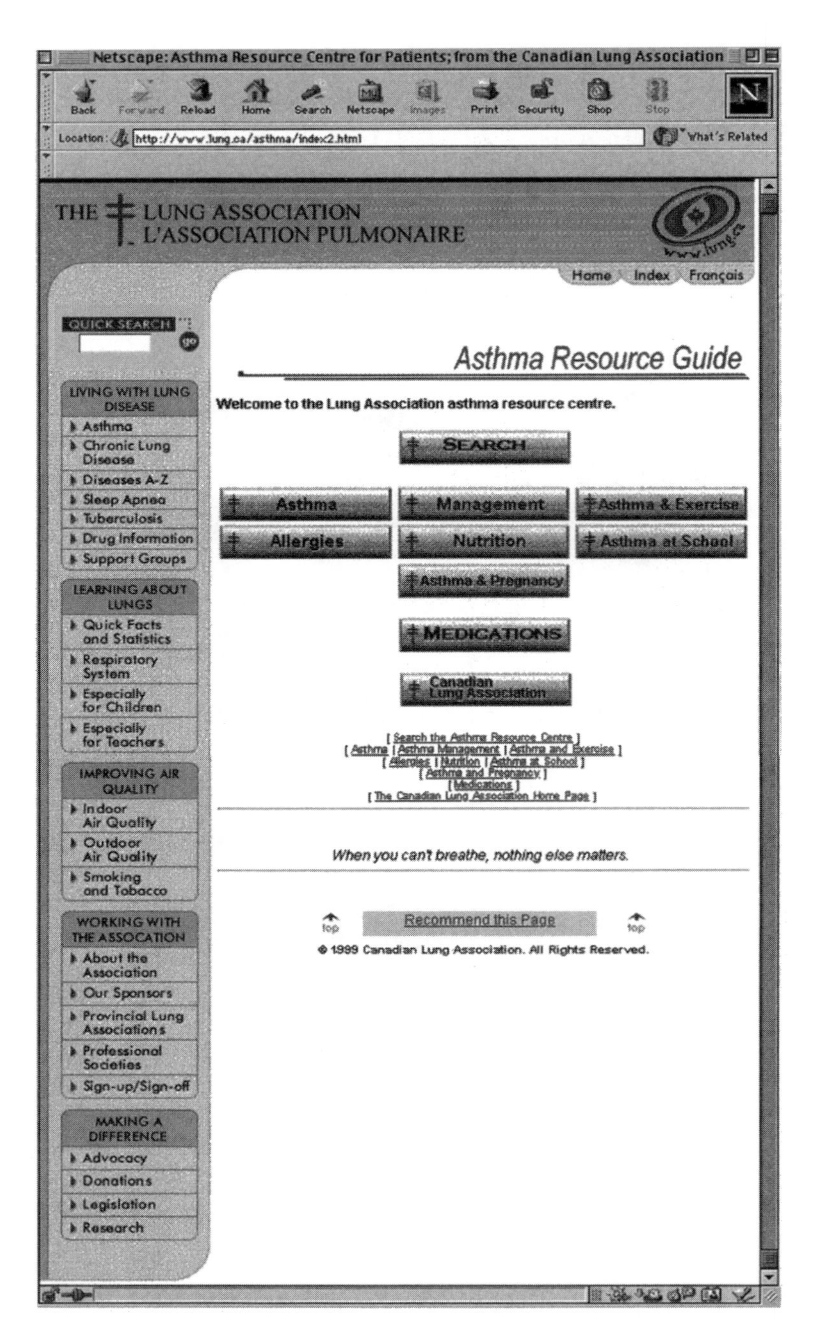

Fig. 2. The Canadian Lung Association's *Asthma Resource Guide* page.

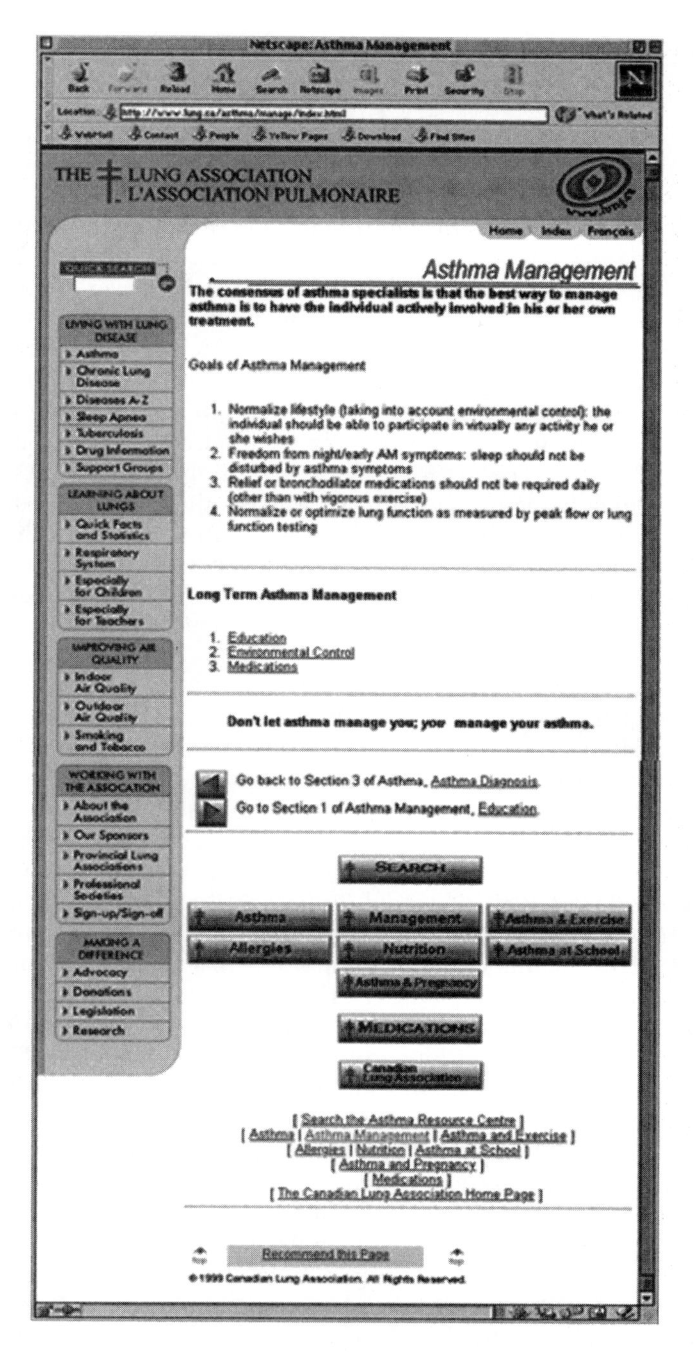

Fig. 3. The Canadian Lung Association's *Asthma Management* page, accessed via the "Management" button shown in Fig. 2.

top and left side of the screen. It also introduces yet another way of maneuvering within the Web site: "Go back" and "Go to" clickable arrows.

5 By giving users a variety of options, the designers of this Web site have made it very easy for users to access information. The site map, in particular, enables users to return to pages they visited earlier by clicking on the corresponding links, rather than having to retype the URL or rely on the "Back" button in their browsers to retrace their steps. I found only one problem in the site's system of hyperlinks. Two buttons, both labeled "Asthma," one in the site map and the other in the left-frame menu, lead to different pages. The site map "Asthma" button correctly links to the *Asthma* home page (Figure 1), whereas the menu "Asthma" button incorrectly links to a general information page on asthma adapted from a 1997 article by a Canadian doctor (see Figure 4). Apart from this one hyperlink problem, the Web site provides easy access to information about the Canadian Lung Association in general and asthma in particular.

6 Furthermore, the hyperlinks at the *Asthma* Web site offer quality information that helped in my research. For example, the "Medications" link on the site map leads to information on various drug treatments and their possible side effects. I was grateful to learn that Jeremy's doctor is not treating him with drugs that produce serious side effects. I also learned about the different causes of asthma and clarified a confusion I had gotten from visiting a different Web site, *Adult/Pediatric Allergy Asthma Center,* < http://www.allergies-asthma.com >, which had led me to misunderstand the importance of symptoms that asthma and allergies have in common (Dantzler). However, according to Jeremy's doctor, my son's asthmatic attacks are responses to viral infections, not allergic reactions to things like dust and pollen. The Canadian Lung Association's site confirmed what the doctor had told me. Now I know which symptoms indicate that Jeremy is having an asthmatic attack and which indicate he is having a harmless allergic reaction to high pollen counts.

7 In addition to confirming information that Jeremy's doctor had already given me, the Canadian *Asthma* site offers useful new information, including the suggestion that I collaborate with the doctor on a "Written 'Rescue' Action Plan." The plan gives instructions on what to do at each stage of an asthmatic attack so as to avoid a "full-blown episode" (Canadian Lung Association). I also learned about the Peak Flow Meter, a device that can detect each stage in an asthmatic attack and that can help implement the action plan appropriately. Because I felt this new information

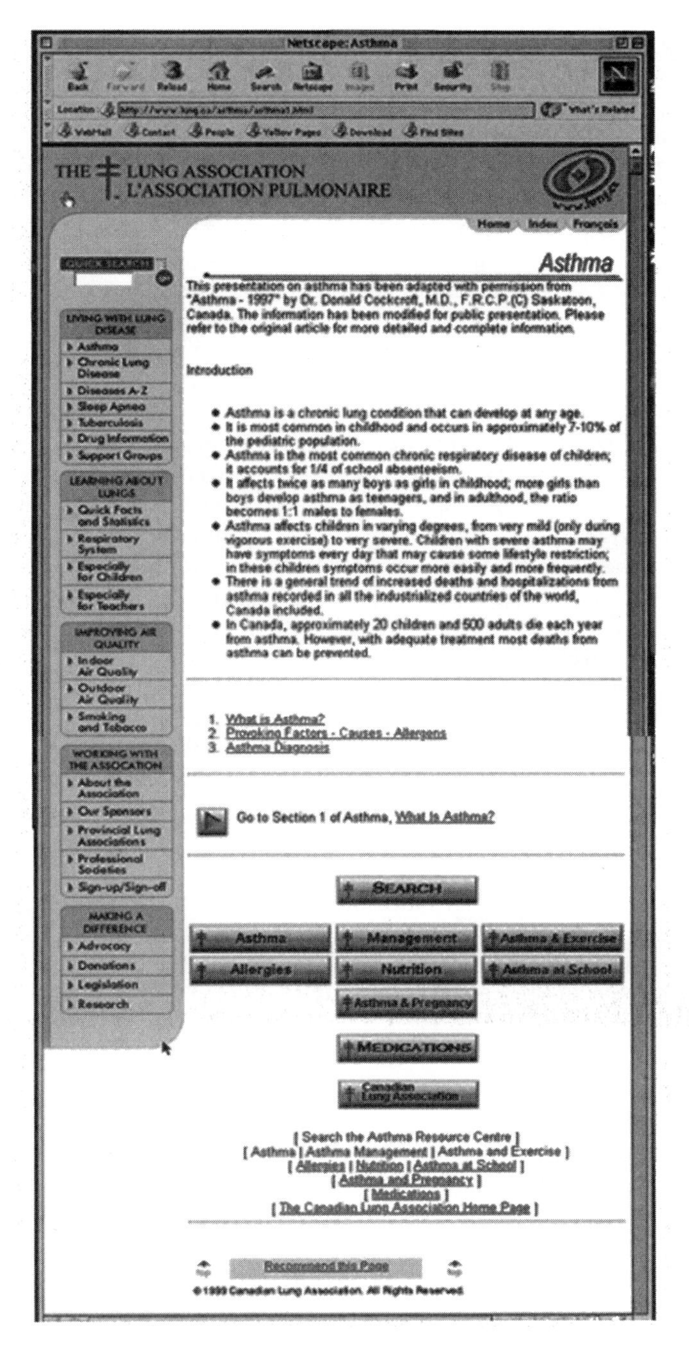

Fig. 4. This Canadian Lung Association general information page was accessed via the left-frame menu "Asthma" button shown in Fig. 1, indicating a hyperlink problem.

might benefit Jeremy, I downloaded the pages to my hard drive and printed them out to bring to Jeremy's next doctor's appointment.

8 Not only is the Canadian Lung Association's *Asthma* Web site easy to access and full of helpful information, but it is also reliable. For a Web site to be reliable, it must have authoritative, up-to-date information and not profit from distributing that information. Although it can be difficult for a layperson to judge the quality and currency of information, most Web sites indicate who has sponsored and authored the site, as well as when it was last revised. The *Asthma* home page, for example, identifies itself as an official site of the Canadian Lung Association, < http://www.lung.ca >, which links to the American Lung Association, < http://www.lungusa.org > (and vice versa), completing a circle that shows that each organization considers the other to be a trustworthy source of information. Although both the Canadian and American Lung Association Web sites solicit donations to help fund research, the information on the *Asthma* site is free and meant to promote healthy lungs, not empty pocketbooks.

9 Because new research in medicine and health care constantly changes, it is important to seek out information that is up-to-date. Of course, currency is supposed to be one of the advantages of researching on the Web. Many Web designers indicate on a general information page when the information at a Web site was created or last updated. A copyright notice at the bottom of the pages at the *Asthma* site indicates it was created in 1999 by the Canadian Lung Association. The general information page shown in Figure 4 has the 1999 copyright but includes a headnote indicating that it is adapted from a 1997 article. The headnote also identifies the author's name, academic credentials, and professional affiliations.

10 The time I have spent at the Canadian Lung Association's *Asthma* Web site has been worthwhile. I consider the information there useful to my research because it provides answers to my questions concerning accessibility, helpfulness, and reliability. Despite the problem with the "Asthma" hyperlink, I find the site to be well organized and efficient (I can move quickly among pages). I also find the material helpful because it substantiates information I already knew about asthma and gives me new and practical ways to monitor Jeremy's health. Finally, the fact that the *Asthma* site is sponsored by the Canadian Lung Association convinces me that it is a reliable source of up-to-date information on successful treatments for asthma.

Works Cited

American Lung Association. 1998. 8 Nov. 1999 < http://www.lungusa.org >.

Canadian Lung Association. *Asthma.* 1999. 18 Nov. 1999 < http://www.lung.ca/asthma >.

Dantzler, Brian S. *Adult/Pediatric Allergy Asthma Center.* 5 July 1999 < http://www.allergies-asthma.com >.

Lynch, Patrick J., and Sarah Horton. *Web Style Guide.* 1997. Yale University. 5 July 1999 < http://info.med.yale.edu/caim/manual/interface/basic_interface2.htm >.

READING FOR MEANING

Write to create meanings for Potter's evaluation of the Canadian Lung Association's *Asthma* Web site.

READING LIKE A WRITER

Writers of evaluative essays

- present the subject.
- assert an overall judgment.
- give reasons and support.
- counterargue.
- establish credibility.

You have seen how important these evaluative writing strategies are in the readings you have read, written about, and discussed in this chapter. Focus on one of these strategies in Potter's essay and analyze it carefully through close rereading and annotating. Then write several sentences explaining what you have learned, giving specific examples from the reading to support your explanation. Add a few sentences evaluating how successfully Potter uses the strategy to evaluate the Canadian Lung Association's *Asthma* Web site.

REVIEWING WHAT MAKES EVALUATIONS EFFECTIVE

In this chapter, you have been learning how to read evaluative essays for meaning and how to read them like a writer. Before going on to write an evaluation of your own, pause here to review and contemplate what you have learned about the elements of effective evaluations.

Analyze

Choose one reading from this chapter that seems to you especially effective. Before rereading the selection, *jot down* one or two reasons you remember it as an example of good evaluative writing.

Reread your chosen selection, adding further annotations about what makes it a particularly successful example of evaluation. *Consider* the selection's purpose and how well it achieves that purpose for its intended readers. (You can make an informed guess about the intended readers and their expectations by noting the publication source of the essay.) Then *focus* on how well the essay

- presents the subject.
- asserts an overall judgment.
- gives reasons and support.
- counterargues.
- establishes credibility.

You can review all of these basic features in the Guide to Reading Evaluations (p. 252).

Your instructor may ask you to complete this activity on your own or to work with a small group of other students who have chosen the same reading. If you work with others, allow enough time initially for all group members to reread the selection thoughtfully and to add their annotations. Then *discuss* as a group what makes the essay effective. *Take notes* on your discussion. One student in your group should then report to the class what the group has learned about the effectiveness of evaluative writing. If you are working individually, write up what you have learned from your analysis.

Write

Write at least a page, supporting your choice of this reading as an example of effective evaluative writing. *Assume* that your readers—your instructor and classmates—have read the selection but will not remember many details about it. They also might not remember it as especially successful. Therefore, you will need to *refer* to details and specific parts of the reading as you explain how it works and as you justify your evaluation of its effectiveness. You need not argue that it is the best essay in the chapter or that it is flawless, only that it is, in your view, a strong example of the genre.

A Guide to Writing Evaluations

The readings in this chapter have helped you learn a great deal about evaluative writing. Now that you have seen how writers of evaluations argue to support their assertions, you are in a good position to approach this type of writing confidently. As you develop your essay, you can review the readings to see how other writers use various strategies to solve the problems you face in your own writing.

This Guide to Writing is designed to assist you in writing an evaluation. Here you will find activities to help you choose a subject and discover what to say about it, organize your ideas and draft the essay, read the draft critically, revise the draft to strengthen your argument, and edit and proofread the essay to improve its readability.

INVENTION

Invention is a process of discovery and planning by which you generate something to say. The following invention activities will help you choose a subject and develop your evaluation of it. A few minutes spent developing each writing activity will improve your chances of producing a detailed and convincing first draft.

Choosing a Subject

Begin by looking over the subjects suggested in the Considering Ideas for Your Own Writing activities in this chapter. The selections suggest several different subjects you could write about. As you have seen, arts and entertainment products are popular subjects for review: fashion, sports, television programs, films, magazines, books, restaurants, and video games included. Technology, since it changes so quickly, is also a source of many possible subjects: new hardware and software, new procedures, and laws. There are countless other possibilities, such as public figures, businesses, educational programs, and types of equipment (cars, sporting gear).

To find a subject, list specific examples in several of the following categories. Although you may be inclined to pick the first idea that comes to mind, try to make your list of possible subjects as long as you can. This will ensure that you have a variety of subjects from which to choose and will encourage you to think of unique subjects.

- A film or group of films by a single director or actor
- A hit song or music CD

- A live or videotaped concert or theatrical performance
- A magazine or newspaper
- A book (perhaps one—either fiction or nonfiction—that you have recently read for one of your classes)
- A club or organized activity—dance instruction, camping or hiking trip, college sports programs, debate group—or a subject (like Etzioni's) that is generally viewed positively but that your experience leads you to evaluate more negatively (or, alternatively, a subject generally viewed negatively that your experience leads you to evaluate more positively)
- A contemporary political movement (perhaps evaluating the movement's methods as well as its goals and achievements)
- A proposed or existing law
- A noteworthy person—someone in the news or a local professional, such as a teacher, doctor, social worker, auto mechanic, or minister (perhaps using your personal experience with the local figure to strengthen your evaluation)
- An artist, a writer, or his or her works
- A local business or businessperson
- Particular brands of machines or equipment with which you are familiar (perhaps comparing a "superior" to an "inferior" brand to make your evaluation more authoritative)
- One of the essays in this book (evaluating it as a strong or weak example of its type) or two essays (arguing that one is better than the other)

After you have a list of possible subjects, consider the following questions as you make your final selection:

- *Do I already know enough about this subject, or can I get the information I need in time?* If, for instance, you decide to review a film, you should be able to see it soon. If you choose to evaluate a brand of machine or equipment, you should already be somewhat familiar with it or have time to learn enough about it to be able to write with some authority.
- *Do I already have a settled judgment about this subject?* It is always easier to write about a subject that you think you can judge confidently, although it is conceivable that you could change your mind as you write. If you choose a subject about which you feel indifferent, you may experience difficulty devising an argument to support your judgment. The more sure you are of your judgment, the more persuasive your evaluation is likely to be.

Developing Your Argument

The writing and research activities that follow will enable you to explore your subject, analyze your readers, and begin developing your evaluation.

Exploring Your Subject. *To find out what you already know about the subject, list the main things you now know about it and then make notes about how you will go about becoming familiar enough with your subject to write about it like an expert or insider.* You may know little or much about your subject, and you may feel uncertain how to learn more about it. For now, discover what you do know.

Analyzing Your Readers. *Make notes about your readers.* Who exactly are your readers? They may be your classmates, or you may want—or be asked by your instructor—to write for another audience. You could write for the general public, as all but one of the writers in this chapter (Romano) seem to be doing. Or you could write for a more narrow audience: parents ready to purchase a new child's learning game, advanced users of email or some other technology, or viewers who have seen (or who have never seen) several other films by the director of the film you are reviewing. How much will your readers know about your subject and others of its type? How can you describe your readers' attitudes and opinions about the subject? What standards might they use to judge a subject like yours?

Considering Your Judgment. *Make a list of the good and bad qualities of your subject.* Then decide whether your judgment will be positive or negative. You can certainly acknowledge both the good and bad qualities in your essay, but your judgment should not be ambivalent throughout. In a movie review, for example, you must ultimately decide whether you do or do not recommend that your readers try to see the film. If your list leaves you feeling genuinely ambivalent, you might want to trust the processes of learning and writing about your subject to help you decide whether you want to praise or criticize it. Another option, of course, is to choose a different subject to evaluate.

If you can judge your subject now, *write a sentence or two asserting your judgment.* At the end of these activities, you will have an opportunity to revise this assertion.

Testing Your Choice. *Pause now to decide whether you have chosen a subject about which you may be able to make a convincing evaluative argument.* At this point, you should be very familiar with your subject—you have viewed the movie again, reread the essay, listened to the music CD, attended another concert, reexamined a machine or piece of equipment, or consumed another meal at the restaurant. It is important that you be able to continue studying your subject as you complete these invention activities and, later, as you draft and revise your essay: The more intimate your knowledge of the subject, the more details you can bring to bear to support your evaluation. If your interest in the subject is growing and you feel increasingly confident about your judgment of it, you have probably made a good choice. If you have not made progress in experiencing and understanding your subject and do not see how you can do so right away, it is probably wise for you to choose another subject.

Listing Reasons. *List all the reasons you might give to persuade your readers of your judgment of the subject.* Reasons answer the question, "Everything considered, why do you evaluate this subject positively [or negatively]?" Write down all the reasons you can think of.

Then look over your list to *consider* which reasons you feel are the most important and which would be most convincing to your readers, given the generally accepted standards for evaluating this type of subject. *Put an asterisk by these convincing reasons.*

Consider this list only a starting point. Continue to revise it as you learn more about your subject. A preliminary list of reasons gives you a head start on planning your essay.

Finding Support for Your Reasons. *Make notes about how to support your most promising reasons.* For support, most evaluations rely largely on details and examples from the subject itself. For that reason, you will have to reexamine the subject closely even if you know it quite well. Depending on the subject, evaluations may also make use of facts, quotations from experts, statistics, or the writer's personal experience.

Work back and forth between your list of reasons and notes for support. The reasons list will remind you of the support you need and help you discover which reasons have substance. The credibility of your argument will depend to a large extent on the amount of specific, relevant support you can bring to your argument.

Considering Visuals. *Consider whether visuals—screen shots, photographs, or drawings—would help you present your subject more effectively to readers or strengthen your evaluation of it.* If you submit your essay electronically to other students and your instructor, or if you post it on a Web site, consider including photographs as well as snippets of film or sound or other memorabilia that might give readers a more vivid sense of your subject. Visual and auditory materials are not at all a requirement of an effective evaluative argument, as you can tell from the readings in this chapter, but they could add a new dimension to your writing. If you want to use photographs or recordings of people, be sure to get permission.

Considering Your Purpose. *Write for a few minutes exploring your purpose for writing an evaluative essay.* The following questions may help you think about your purpose:

- What do I want my readers to believe or do after they read my essay?
- How can I connect to their experience with my subject (or subjects like it)? How can I interest them in a subject that is outside their experience?
- Can I assume that readers will share my standards for judging the subject, or must I explain and justify the standards?
- How can I offer a balanced evaluation that will enhance my credibility with readers?

Formulating a Working Thesis. *Draft a thesis statement.* A working thesis—as opposed to a final, revised thesis—will help you begin drafting your essay purposefully. The thesis statement in an evaluative essay is simply a concise assertion of your overall judgment. Here are two examples from the readings:

- "This is an almost entirely positive development. Convenience aside, email is a marvelous medium of communication" (Kinsley, paragraph 4).
- "Unlike most horror flicks, *Poltergeist* works! Its success is due to excellent characters, music, and special effects—and to the fact that the story stays within the bounds of believability" (Hyder, paragraph 3).

Notice that there is no ambivalence in these statements. They are clear, assertive, and unmistakably positive in their judgments. (An assertive judgment does not preclude a writer's later acknowledging problems or weaknesses in a subject judged positively or anticipating readers' likely reservations about the evaluation.) Hyder's thesis statement illustrates another interesting feature: It forecasts the major reasons for the judgment, the reasons that are at the heart of the evaluation. Forecasts are not required, but readers often find them helpful.

DRAFTING

The following guidelines will help you set goals for your draft and plan its organization.

Setting Goals

Establishing goals for your draft before you begin writing will enable you to make decisions and work more confidently. Consider the following questions now, and keep them in mind as you draft. They will help you set goals for drafting as well as recall how the writers you have read in this chapter tried to achieve similar goals.

- *What is my primary purpose in writing this evaluation?* What do I want to accomplish with my evaluation? Is my primary purpose to make a recommendation, as Herold, Corliss, and Hyder do? Do I want to celebrate my subject, as Kinsley, Hyder, and Potter do, or expose its flaws, as Etzioni? Do I want to strive for a carefully balanced evaluation, as Romano does?

- *How can I present the subject so that I can inform and interest my readers in it?* How much experience evaluating a subject of this kind can I expect my readers to have? Must I provide a full context for my subject, as Potter does, or describe it in a general way, as Hyder does? Can I assume familiarity with it, as does Etzioni? Will readers share my standards, as Hyder seems to assume his readers do, or will I need to explain or define some of my standards, as Potter does? Can I present my subject by showing myself as an engaged user of it, as Kinsley, Herold, and Potter all do?
- *How can I assert my judgment effectively?* How can I construct a clear, unambiguous thesis statement like those in all of the readings in this chapter? Should I assert my judgment in the first sentence and reassert it at the end of my evaluation, as Etzioni does? Or should I first describe my subject or provide a context for evaluating it, as Kinsley, Hyder, Herold, Corliss, and Potter do?
- *How can I give convincing reasons and adequate support for my reasons?* How can I ensure that the reasons I offer to justify my judgment will seem appropriate and convincing to my readers? Should I forecast my reasons, as Etzioni, Romano, Hyder, and Potter do? For my subject, will I offer a wide range of types of support, as Etzioni does? How can I gather an adequate amount of support for my reasons, as do all of the writers in this chapter? Should I rely on comparisons to support my reasoning, as Kinsley, Hyder, and Potter do?
- *How can I anticipate readers' reservations?* Should I pointedly anticipate my readers' likely reservations, objections, and questions, as Etzioni, Kinsley, Herold, and Romano do?
- *How can I establish credibility with my readers?* Should I feature my personal experience with the subject, as Kinsley, Herold, and Potter do? Or should I demonstrate my expertise with the subject by making comparisons with similar subjects, as Kinsley, Corliss, and Hyder do?

Organizing Your Draft

With goals in mind and invention notes at hand, you are ready to make a first outline of your draft. Review the list of reasons you have developed. Tentatively select from that list the reasons you think will most effectively convince your readers of the plausibility of your judgment. Then decide how you will sequence these reasons. Some writers prefer to save their most telling reason or reasons for the end, whereas others try to group the reasons logically (for example, the technical reasons in a movie review). Still other writers like to begin with reasons based on standards of judgment familiar to their readers. Whatever sequence you decide on for your reasons, make sure it will strike your readers as a logical or step-by-step sequence.

READING A DRAFT CRITICALLY

Getting a critical reading of your draft will help you see how to improve it. Your instructor may schedule class time for reading drafts, or you may want to ask a classmate or a tutor in the writing center to read your draft. Ask your reader to use the following guidelines and to write out a response for you to consult during your revision.

Read for a First Impression

1. Read the draft without stopping to annotate or comment, and then write two or three sentences giving your general impression.
2. Identify one aspect of the draft that seems especially effective.

Read Again to Suggest Improvements

1. Recommend ways to strengthen the presentation of the subject.
   - Locate the places in the draft where the subject is described. The description might be spread out over several paragraphs, serving both to identify the subject and to provide support for the argument. Point to any areas where you do not understand what is being said or where you need more detail or explanation.
   - If you are surprised by the way the writer has presented the subject, briefly explain your expectations for reading about this particular subject or subjects of this kind.
   - Indicate whether any of the information given about the subject seems unnecessary.
   - Finally and most important, raise questions wherever information about the subject seems unconvincing, inaccurate, or only partially true.
2. Suggest ways to strengthen the thesis statement.
   - Find and underline the statement of the writer's overall judgment in the draft. If you cannot find a clear thesis, let the writer know.

- If you find several restatements of the thesis, examine them closely for consistency. Look specifically at the value terms the writer uses to see whether they are unclear or waffling.

3. Recommend ways to strengthen the supporting reasons.

   - Highlight the reasons you find in the essay. The reasons in an evaluation may take the form of judgments of the subject's qualities, judgments that in turn need to be explained and supported. Look closely at any reasons that seem problematic and briefly explain what bothers you. Be as specific and constructive as you can, suggesting what the writer might do to solve the problem. For example, if a reason seems inappropriate, indicate what other kind of reason you would expect a writer to use when evaluating this subject.

   - Look for instances of faulty logic. Note whether the writer's argument is based on personal tastes rather than on generally accepted standards of judgment. Point out any areas where you detect *either/or* reasoning (that is, seeing only the good or only the bad qualities) and weak or misleading comparisons.

4. Suggest ways to extend and improve the counterargument.

   - Locate places where the writer anticipates readers' questions, objections, and reservations about the reasons and support. Consider whether these anticipations seem cursory or adequate, logical or questionable, considerate or dismissive. Point to specific problems you see and suggest possible revisions.

   - Look for areas where the writer anticipates readers' alternative judgments of the subject (that is, where readers may value the subject for different reasons or judge the subject in a different way). Note whether the writer addresses readers' alternative judgments responsibly and accurately and responds to them fairly.

   - If the writer does not counterargue, consider where doing so might be appropriate. Help the writer anticipate any reservations and alternative judgments that have been overlooked, providing advice on how to respond to them. Keep in mind that the writer may choose to accommodate *or* refute readers' reservations or alternative judgments.

5. Suggest ways to strengthen the credibility of the writer and the writer's judgment.

   - Ignoring whether you agree or disagree with the writer's judgment on the subject, point to any places in the essay where you do not trust the writer's credibility. For instance, look for areas where the writer seems insufficiently knowledgeable, where the examples seem unconvincing or distorted, or where the writer is being unfair, perhaps criticizing a minor point unnecessarily or emphasizing something beyond the control of the subject's producers.

- Let the writer know whether you think the judgment is sound or based on some idiosyncratic, trivial, or other inappropriate standards of judgment.

6. Suggest how the organizational plan might be improved.

- Consider the overall plan of the draft, perhaps by making a scratch outline. (Scratch outlining is illustrated in Appendix 1, p. 529.) Decide whether the sequence of reasons and counterarguments is logical or whether you can suggest rearrangements to improve it.
- Indicate where new or better transitions might help identify different steps in the argument and keep readers on track.

7. Evaluate the effectiveness of visuals.

- Look at any visuals in the essay, and tell the writer what they contribute to your understanding of the evaluation.
- If any visuals do not seem relevant, or if there seem to be too many visuals, identify the ones that the writer could consider dropping, explaining your thinking.
- If a visual does not seem to be appropriately placed, suggest a better place for it.

REVISING

This section offers suggestions for revising your draft, suggestions that will remind you of the possibilities for developing a well-argued evaluation. Revising means reenvisioning your draft, trying to see it in a new way, given your purpose and readers, in order to develop your evaluation.

The biggest mistake you can make while revising is to focus initially on words or sentences. Instead, first try to see your draft as a whole in order to assess its likely impact on your readers. To improve readability and strengthen your argument, think imaginatively and boldly about cutting unconvincing material, adding new material, and moving material around. Your computer makes even drastic revisions physically easy, but you still need to make the mental effort and decisions that will improve your draft.

You may have received help with this challenge from a classmate or tutor who gave your draft a critical reading. If so, keep this feedback in mind as you decide which parts of your draft need revising and what specific changes you could make. The following suggestions will help you solve problems and strengthen your essay.

To Present the Subject More Effectively

- If more specific information about the subject is needed, review your invention writing to see whether you have forgotten details you could now add to the draft. Or do some further invention work to generate and add new information.
- If critical readers have asked specific questions, consider whether you need to answer those questions in your revision.
- If you have included information that readers regard as unnecessary or redundant, consider cutting it.
- If any of the information strikes readers as inaccurate or only partially true, reconsider its accuracy and completeness and then make any necessary changes to reassure readers.

To Clarify the Overall Judgment

- If your overall judgment is not stated explicitly or clearly, state it more obviously.
- If readers think your restatements of the judgment are contradictory, reread them with a critical eye and, if you agree, make them more consistent.
- If readers think your judgment is unemphatic or waffling, reconsider the value terms you use.
- If your essay discusses both the good and the bad qualities of the subject, be sure that your thesis statement is compatible with what you say about the subject in the essay.

To Strengthen the Reasons and Support

- If a reason seems inappropriate to readers, consider how you might better convince them that the reason is appropriate (for example, that it is used often by others or that it is based on widely shared and valid standards of judgment).
- If readers do not fully understand how a particular reason applies to the subject, make your thinking more explicit.
- If the connection between a reason and its support seems vague or weak, explain why you think the support is relevant.
- Most important, if you have not fully supported your reasons with many examples from your subject, collect further examples by revisiting your sub-

ject (revisit the Web site, see the movie again, reread the text, play the computer game again, and so forth).

To Strengthen the Counterargument

- If you have not anticipated readers' likely questions, objections, or reservations, revise to accommodate or refute them.
- If you have not anticipated alternative judgments that are likely for your particular audience, revise to respond to them.
- If any counterargument seems to attack your readers rather than their ideas, revise it to focus on the ideas.

To Make the Organizational Plan More Effective

- If readers express confusion over your plan, consider a different sequence for your reasons, or forecast your plan more explicitly by giving clear signals like transitions and topic sentences to distinguish the stages of your argument.
- If readers point to gaps in your argument, close the gaps by making connections explicit.
- If readers find your conclusion abrupt or less than helpful, try restating your judgment or summarizing your argument.

To Enhance Credibility

- If readers question your knowledge of the subject or your authority to evaluate it, reassure them by discussing the subject in greater depth and detail and comparing it to other subjects of the same kind.
- If the standards you choose to emphasize seem minor to readers, explain why you think they are important.
- If readers think your essay is too one-sided, consider whether there is any quality of the subject you could either praise or criticize.

EDITING AND PROOFREADING

After you have revised your essay, be sure to spend some time checking for errors in usage, punctuation, and mechanics and considering matters of style. If you keep a list of errors you typically make, begin by checking your draft against this list. Ask someone else to proofread your essay before you print out a copy for your instructor or send it electronically.

From our research on student writing, we know that evaluation essays have frequent problems in sentences that set up comparisons. The comparisons can be incomplete, illogical, or unclear. Edit carefully any sentences that set up comparisons between your subject and others. Check a writer's handbook for help with making all comparisons complete, logical, and clear.

REFLECTING ON WHAT YOU HAVE LEARNED

Evaluation

In this chapter, you have read critically several evaluative essays and have written one of your own. To better remember what you have learned, pause now to reflect on the reading and writing activities you completed in this chapter.

1. *Write* a page or so reflecting on what you have learned. *Begin* by describing what you are most pleased with in your essay. Then *explain* what you think contributed to your achievement. *Be specific* about this contribution.

   - If it was something you learned from the readings, *indicate* which readings and specifically what you learned from them.
   - If it came from your invention writing, *point out* the section or sections that helped you most.
   - If you got good advice from a critical reader, *explain* exactly how the person helped you — perhaps by helping you understand a particular problem in your draft or by adding a new dimension to your writing.

2. Now *reflect* more generally on evaluative essays, a genre of writing that plays an important role in education and in many other areas of life and work in the United States. *Consider* some of the following questions: How confident do you feel about asserting a judgment and supporting it? How comfortable are you playing the role of judge and jury on the subject? How do your personal preferences and values influence your judgment? How might your gender, ethnicity, religious beliefs, age, or social class influence your ideas about the subject? What contribution might evaluative essays make to our society that other genres cannot make?

CHAPTER

Speculating about Causes or Effects

When something surprising occurs, we automatically look to the past and ask, "Why did that happen?" Whether we want to understand it, to make it happen again, or to find a way to prevent its recurrence, we need to speculate about what *caused* it.

Or our focus may shift from cause to *effect,* from "Why did that happen?" to "What is going to happen?" Anticipating possible effects can be useful in planning and decision making.

In many cases, questions about causes and effects are relatively easy to answer. Through personal experience or scientific experimentation, we know what causes some things to happen and what effects they will have. For example, scientists have discovered that the HIV virus causes AIDS, and we all know its potential deadly effects. We cannot be completely certain, however, what causes the virus to develop into AIDS in particular individuals or of the long-term effects of AIDS on society. In these situations, the best we can do is make educated guesses. In this chapter, you will read and write speculative essays about causes and effects that cannot be known for certain.

This kind of speculative cause or effect writing is published every day. A political analyst conjectures about the cause of Vice President Al Gore's defeat in the 2000 presidential election. An economist suggests some likely effects of the 2001 terrorist attacks on the U.S. economy. A sportswriter speculates about why the Pacific Ten nearly always defeats the Big Ten in the Rose Bowl.

Speculation about causes or effects also plays an important role in government, business, and education. To give credit where it is due, a mayor asks the police commission to report on why complaints by African Americans and Latinos against the police have decreased recently. A salesperson writes a memo to the district sales manager explaining why a local advertising campaign may have failed to increase sales of Chevrolet Corvettes. Before proposing changes in the math curriculum, a school principal appoints a committee to investigate the causes of falling math test scores at the school.

Cause or effect speculation is equally important in college study. For example, you might read a history essay in which a noted scholar evaluates other scholars' proposed causes of the Civil War in order to argue for a never-before-considered cause. (If the essay merely summarizes other scholars' proposed causes, the historian would be reporting established information, not speculating about new possibilities.) Or you might encounter a sociological report conjecturing about a recent increase in marriages among the elderly. The writer may not know for certain why this trend exists but could conjecture about its possible causes—and then argue with relevant facts, statistics, or anecdotes to support the conjectures.

Writing an essay in which you speculate about causes or effects involves some of the most challenging problem-solving and decision-making situations a writer can experience. You will test your powers of reasoning and creativity as you search out hidden, underlying causes or speculate about effects that are surprising yet plausible. You will continue to develop a sensitivity to your readers' knowledge and attitudes, anticipating their objections and discovering ways to convince them to take your speculations seriously.

The readings in this chapter will help you see what makes arguments about causes or effects convincing. From the readings and from the ideas for writing that follow each reading, you will get ideas for your own essay speculating about causes or effects. As you read and write about the selections, keep in mind the following assignment, which sets out the goals for writing an essay speculating about causes or effects. To support your writing of this assignment, the chapter concludes with a Guide to Writing Essays Speculating about Causes or Effects.

THE WRITING ASSIGNMENT

Speculating about Causes or Effects

Choose a subject—an event, a phenomenon, or a trend—that invites you to speculate about its causes or effects—why it may have happened or what its effects may be. Write an essay arguing for your proposed causes or effects. Essays about causes look to the past to ponder why something happened, whereas essays about effects guess what is likely to happen in the future. Whether you choose to write about causes or effects, you need to do two things: (1) Establish the existence and significance of the subject, and (2) convince readers that the causes or effects you propose are plausible.

WRITING SITUATIONS FOR ESSAYS SPECULATING ABOUT CAUSES OR EFFECTS

The following examples suggest further the kinds of causal arguments writers typically make:

- A science writer notes that relatively few women get advanced degrees in science and speculates that social conditioning may be the major cause. To support her causal argument, she cites research on the way boys and girls are treated differently in early childhood. She also gives examples to attempt to show that the social pressure to conform to female role expectations may discourage junior-high-school girls from doing well in math and science. She acknowledges that other as-yet-unrecognized causes may contribute as well.
- A student writes in the school newspaper about the rising number of pregnancies among high-school students. Interviews with pregnant students lead her to speculate that the chief cause of the trend is a new requirement that parents must give written consent for minors to get birth-control devices at the local clinic. She explains that many students fail to get birth-control information, let alone devices, because of this regulation. She reports that her interviews do not support alternative explanations that young women have babies to give meaning to their lives, gain status among their peers, or live on their own supported by welfare.
- A psychology student writes about the effects—positive and negative—of extensive video-game playing among preteens. Based on his own experience and observation, he suggests that video games may improve children's hand-eye coordination, as well as their ability to concentrate on a single task. He speculates that, on the negative side, some children's grades may suffer as a result of spending too much time playing video games.

A Guide to Reading Essays Speculating about Causes or Effects

This guide introduces you to written texts that speculate about causes or effects. By completing all of the activities in it, you will prepare yourself to learn a great deal from the other readings in this chapter about how to read and write a speculative essay. The guide makes use of "Why We Crave Horror Movies," a well-known essay by the novelist and screenwriter Stephen King. You will read

King's essay twice. First, you will read it for meaning, looking closely at the content and ideas. Then, you will read the essay like a writer, analyzing the parts to see how King crafts his essay and to learn the strategies he uses to make his speculative writing convincing. These two activities—reading for meaning and reading like a writer—follow every reading in this chapter.

STEPHEN KING

Why We Crave Horror Movies

A preeminent writer of horror novels and films, Stephen King (b. 1947) may be best known for Misery *(1987),* Four Past Midnight *(1990),* Needful Things *(1991), and* Nightmares and Dreamscapes *(1993). More recent books include* Bag of Bones *(1998),* Dreamcatcher *(2001), and* On Writing *(2001). The following essay originally appeared in* Playboy *magazine in 1981.* Playboy *has been the most popular men's magazine in the United States for the last fifty years, and the nature of its format, content, and readers has changed little since 1981. In addition to featuring scantily clad or unclad women, it offers its readers information about health and fitness, social issues, and popular culture. Over the years, it has showcased many well-known writers in addition to Stephen King. Most readers of* Playboy *are men in their twenties to forties.*

As King's title indicates, "Why We Crave Horror Movies" attempts to explain the causes for a common phenomenon: most people's liking—even craving—for horror movies.

Before you read, think about the horror movie that you remember best and consider why it appeals to you. How old were you when you first saw it? What was most terrifying about it? How did you talk about it at the time, and how do you remember it now?

As you read, test King's argument about the appeal of horror movies against your own experience. On first reading, how convincing do you find his causal speculations?

I think that we're all mentally ill; those of us outside the asylums only hide it a little better—and maybe not all that much better, after all. We've all known people who talk to themselves, people who sometimes squinch their faces into horrible grimaces when they believe no one is watching, people who have some hysterical fear—of snakes, the dark, the tight place, the long drop . . . and, of course, those final worms and grubs that are waiting so patiently underground. 1

When we pay our four or five bucks and seat ourselves at tenth-row center in a theater showing a horror movie, we are daring the nightmare. 2

Why? Some of the reasons are simple and obvious. To show that we can, that we are not afraid, that we can ride this roller coaster. Which is not to say that a really good horror movie may not surprise a scream out of us at some point, the way we may scream when the roller coaster twists through a complete 360 or plows through a lake at the bottom of the drop. And horror movies, like roller coasters, have always been the special province of the young; by the time one turns 40 or 50, one's appetite for double twists or 360-degree loops may be considerably depleted. 3

We also go to re-establish our feelings of essential normality; the horror movie is innately conservative, even reactionary. Freda Jackson as the horrible melting woman in *Die, Monster, Die!* confirms for us that no matter how far we may be removed from the beauty of a Robert Redford or a Diana Ross, we are still light-years from true ugliness. 4

And we go to have fun. 5

Ah, but this is where the ground starts to slope away, isn't it? Because this is a very peculiar sort of fun, indeed. The fun comes from seeing others menaced—sometimes killed. One critic has suggested that if pro football has become the voyeur's version of combat, then the horror film has become the modern version of the public lynching. 6

It is true that the mythic, "fairy-tale" horror film intends to take away the shades of gray. . . . It urges us to put away our more civilized and adult penchant for analysis and to become children again, seeing things in pure blacks and whites. It may be that horror movies provide psychic relief on this level because this invitation to lapse into simplicity, irrationality, and even outright madness is extended so rarely. We are told we may allow our emotions a free rein . . . or no rein at all. 7

If we are all insane, then sanity becomes a matter of degree. If your insanity leads you to carve up women like Jack the Ripper or the Cleveland Torso Murderer, we clap you away in the funny farm (but neither of those two amateur-night surgeons was ever caught, heh-heh-heh); if, on the other hand, your insanity leads you only to talk to yourself when you're under stress or to pick your nose on your morning bus, then you are left alone to go about your business . . . though it is doubtful that you will ever be invited to the best parties. 8

The potential lyncher is in almost all of us (excluding saints, past and present; but then, most saints have been crazy in their own ways), and every now and then, he has to be let loose to scream and roll around in the grass. Our emotions and our fears form their own body, and we recognize that it demands its own 9 exercise to maintain proper muscle tone. Certain of these emotional muscles are accepted—even exalted—in civilized society; they are, of course, the emotions that tend to maintain the status quo of civilization itself. Love, friendship, loyalty, kindness—these are all the emotions that we applaud, emotions that have been immortalized in the couplets of Hallmark cards and in the verses (I don't dare call it poetry) of Leonard Nimoy.

When we exhibit these emotions, society showers us with positive reinforcement; we learn this even before we get out of diapers. When, as children, we hug our rotten little puke of a sister and give her a kiss, all the aunts and uncles smile and twit and cry, "Isn't he the sweetest little thing?" Such coveted treats as chocolate-covered graham crackers often follow. But if we deliberately slam the rotten little puke of a sister's fingers in the door, sanctions follow—angry remonstrance from parents, aunts, and uncles; instead of a chocolate-covered graham cracker, a spanking. 10

But anticivilization emotions don't go away, and they demand periodic exercise. We have such "sick" jokes as, "What's the difference between a truckload of bowling balls and a truckload of dead babies?" (You can't unload a truckload of bowling balls with a pitchfork . . . a joke, by the way, that I heard originally from a ten-year-old.) Such a joke may surprise a laugh or a grin out of us even as we recoil, a possibility that confirms the thesis: If we share a brotherhood of man, then we also share an insanity of man. None of which is intended as a defense of either the sick joke or insanity but merely as an explanation of why the best horror films, like the best fairy tales, manage to be reactionary, anarchistic, and revolutionary all at the same time. 11

The mythic horror movie, like the sick joke, has a dirty job to do. It deliberately appeals to all that is worst in us. It is morbidity unchained, our most base instincts let free, our nastiest fantasies realized . . . and it all happens, fittingly enough, in the dark. For those reasons, good liberals often shy away from horror films. For myself, I like to see the most aggressive of them—*Dawn of the Dead,* for instance—as lifting a trap door in the civilized forebrain and throwing a basket of raw meat to the hungry alligators swimming around in that subterranean river beneath. 12

Why bother? Because it keeps them from getting out, man. It keeps them down there and me up here. It was Lennon and McCartney who said that all you need is love, and I would agree with that. 13

As long as you keep the gators fed. 14

READING FOR MEANING

Write to create meanings for King's speculations about why some moviegoers crave horror films.

Start Making Meaning

Begin by restating two or three of the main causes King proposes to explain why some moviegoers crave horror films. Also, given his audience—*Playboy* readers—and his reputation as a writer of horror novels and films, write a sentence or two about what you think King's purpose might be in this essay. Continue by writing about anything else in the selection or in your experience that contributes to your understanding of King's speculations.

If You Are Stuck

If you cannot write at least a page, consider writing about

- the difference between pro- and anti-civilization emotions as King presents them in paragraphs 10–13, indicating what you think about his distinction between these two kinds of emotions.
- King's claim that "all you need is love" so "long as you keep the gators fed" (paragraphs 13 and 14).
- reasons, other than the ones King offers, some moviegoers crave horror films.
- your experience with horror novels or films, making connections to King's argument.

READING LIKE A WRITER

This section guides you through an analysis of King's argument strategies: *presenting the subject, making a cause or effect argument, counterarguing,* and *establishing credibility.* For each strategy you will be asked to reread and annotate part of King's essay to see how King uses the strategy in "Why We Crave Horror Movies."

When you study the selections later in this chapter, you will see how different writers use the same strategies to make causal arguments or speculate about effects. The Guide to Writing Essays Speculating about Causes or Effects near the end of the chapter suggests ways you can use these strategies in your own writing.

Presenting the Subject

In presenting the subject of an essay speculating about causes or effects, the writer must be sure that readers will recognize and understand the subject. In some writing situations, the writer can safely assume that readers will already know a great deal about a familiar subject; in this case, the writer can simply identify the subject and immediately begin the speculations about its causes or effects. In many other cases, however, writers must present an unfamiliar subject in enough detail for readers to understand it fully. On occasion, writers may even need to convince readers that their subject is important and worth speculating about.

When writers decide they need to prove that the trend or phenomenon they are writing about exists, they may describe it in great detail, give examples, offer factual evidence, cite statistics, or quote statements by authorities. To establish the importance of the trend or phenomenon, writers may show that it involves a large number of people or has great importance to certain people.

Analyze

1. How does King present horror movies as a particular movie genre? *Skim* the essay to see which horror movies he mentions by title. Are the few examples he cites sufficient? Do you think readers need to have seen the movies he mentions to get the point? What does King seem to assume about his readers' experiences with horror films?
2. *Consider* how King establishes the importance of his subject. *Underline* one or two comments King makes about the subject that are likely to increase his readers' curiosity about why people crave horror movies.

Write

Write several sentences explaining how King presents his subject.

Making a Cause or Effect Argument

At the heart of an essay speculating about causes or effects is an argument. The argument is made up of at least two parts: the proposed causes or effects, and the reasoning and support for each cause or effect. In addition, the writer may anticipate readers' objections or questions, a strategy we take up in the next section on counterargument. In analyzing King's argument, we will look at some of the causes he proposes and how he supports them.

Writers speculating about causes or effects rarely consider only one possibility. They know that most puzzling phenomena (like people's attraction to horror movies) have multiple possible causes. However, they also know that it would be foolish to try to identify every possible cause. Writers must therefore be selective if they hope to make a convincing argument. The best arguments avoid the obvious. They offer new and imaginative ways of thinking—either proposing causes or effects that will surprise readers or arguing for familiar causes or effects in new ways.

Writers support their arguments with various kinds of evidence: facts, statistical correlations, personal anecdotes, testimony of authorities, examples, and analogies. In this activity, we focus on King's use of analogies.

Analyze

1. *Reread* paragraphs 3 and 12, and *identify* the analogy in each paragraph. An analogy is a special form of comparison in which one part of the comparison is used to explain the other. In arguing by analogy, the writer reasons that if two situations are alike, their causes will also be similar.
2. *Think about* how well the comparisons in paragraphs 3 and 12 hold up. For example, you may be able to use your personal experience to test whether watching a horror movie is much like riding a roller coaster. *Ask yourself* in what ways the two are alike—and different. Are they more alike than different? Also *consider* how you are or are not like a hungry alligator when you watch a horror movie.

Write

Describe and *evaluate* King's support-by-analogy in paragraphs 3 and 12. *Explain* the parts of each analogy—the two separate things being compared. *Evaluate* how well each analogy works logically. In what ways are the two things being compared actually alike? Also *evaluate* what the two analogies contribute to King's causal argument. How is the essay strengthened by them?

Counterarguing

When causes or effects cannot be known for certain, there is bound to be disagreement. Consequently, writers try to anticipate possible objections and alternative causes or effects readers might put forward. Writers bring these objections and alternatives directly into their essays and then either refute (argue against) them or find a way to accommodate them in the argument.

Analyze

1. King anticipates a possible objection from readers when he poses the question "Why bother?" in paragraph 13. *Reread* paragraphs 11 and 12 to

understand the context in which King anticipates the need to pose that question. *Notice* his direct answer to the question in paragraph 13.

2. *Think about* the effectiveness of King's counterargument. *Consider* whether it satisfactorily answers the objection.

Write

Write a few sentences explaining why you think King asks the question at this point in his argument. *Consider* whether some of King's readers would ask themselves this question. *Evaluate* how satisfied they would be with King's response.

Establishing Credibility

Because cause or effect writing is highly speculative, its effectiveness depends in large part on whether readers trust the writer. Readers sometimes use information about the writer's professional and personal accomplishments in forming their judgments about the writer's credibility. The most important information, however, comes from the writing itself, specifically how writers argue for their own proposed causes or effects, as well as how they handle readers' objections.

Writers seek to establish their credibility with readers by making their reasoning clear and logical, their evidence relevant and trustworthy, and their handling of objections fair and balanced. They try to be authoritative (knowledgeable) without appearing authoritarian (opinionated and dogmatic).

Analyze

1. *Reread* the headnote that precedes King's essay, and *reflect on* what his *Playboy* readers might have already known about him. King is more widely known now than he was when "Why We Crave Horror Movies" was published in 1981, but his readers at that time would likely have heard of him.

2. With King's readers in mind, *skim* the essay in order to decide whether the reasoning is clear and logical and the examples and analogies relevant and trustworthy. *Notice* that King's reasoning is psychological: He argues that mental and emotional needs explain why some people crave horror films. Therefore, you, along with King's intended readers, can evaluate King's credibility in light of your own personal experience—your understanding of the role horror novels and films play in your own life. On the basis of your own experience and your evaluation of the logic and consistency of

King's argument, *decide* whether you think most readers would consider him a credible writer on the subject of horror films.

Write

Write several sentences describing the impression readers might get of King from reading both the headnote and his essay on horror films. What might make them trust or distrust what he says about his subject?

Readings

NATALIE ANGIER

Intolerance of Boyish Behavior

One of America's preeminent science writers, Natalie Angier (b. 1958) won a Pulitzer Prize in 1991 for her reports on various scientific topics published in the New York Times, *where she has worked as a reporter since 1990. Her specialties are biology and medicine. Angier began her journalism career in 1980, after graduating* magna cum laude *from Barnard College with a degree in English and physics. As both a staff writer and freelancer she has published articles in several magazines, including* Discovery, Time, *and the* Atlantic. *She has taught in New York University's Graduate Program in Science and Environmental Reporting. Her 1988 book,* Natural Obsessions: The Search for the Oncogene, *won the Lewis Thomas Award for excellence in writing about the life sciences. She is also a 1990 recipient of the International Biomedical Journalism Prize for outstanding media coverage of cancer. Her most recent books are* Natural Obsessions: Striving to Unlock the Deepest Secrets of the Cancer Cell *(1999) and* Woman, an Intimate Geography *(2000).*

The following selection appeared in the New York Times *in 1994. The* Times *is a major newspaper in the New York City region; but because people living in dozens of mid- to large-sized American cities can have it delivered to their homes daily, the* Times *has wide national influence. Politicians, academics, and other journalists give it special attention. Journalists such as Angier who write about scientific topics for newspapers and magazines do not assume that readers have a high level of scientific training; they write for a broad audience, including college students interested in ideas and issues.*

In this reading Angier seeks to explain the increasing intolerance by teachers, parents, counselors, and therapists of certain kinds of behavior that have been labeled "boyish." Angier speculates about the causes of a trend—an increase or decrease in something over time. Unexpected or alarming social trends—such as the increasing use of medication with boys for behavior that was previously tolerated or overlooked—especially invite causal speculation. You will notice that Angier is careful to demonstrate that there is in fact an increasing intolerance of boyish behavior.

As you read, think about your own experience as a sibling, as a friend of other young children, as a student in elementary school, or perhaps even as a parent of a boy with "boyish" behavior. Does Angier convince you that most boys are more rambunctious than most girls? Do you believe that many teachers and parents now see this as a big problem? Consider also how plausible you find

Angier's proposed causes for the growing intolerance of boyish behavior.

Until quite recently, the plain-spun tautology "boys will be boys" summed up everything parents needed to know about their Y-chromosome bundles. Boys will be very noisy and obnoxious. Boys will tear around the house and break heirlooms. They will transform any object longer than it is wide into a laser weapon with eight settings from stun to vaporize. They will swagger and brag and fib and not do their homework and leave their dirty underwear on the bathroom floor. 1

But they will also be . . . boys. They will be adventurous and brave. When they fall down, they'll get up, give a cavalier spit to the side, and try again. Tom Sawyer may have been a slob, a truant and a hedonist; he may have picked fights with strangers for no apparent reason; but he was also resourceful, spirited and deliciously clever. Huckleberry Finn was an illiterate outcast, but as a long-term rafting companion he had no peer. 2

Today, the world is no longer safe for boys. A boy being a shade too boyish risks finding himself under the scrutiny of parents, teachers, guidance counselors, child therapists—all of them on watch for the early glimmerings of a medical syndrome, a bona fide behavioral disorder. Does the boy disregard authority, make snide comments in class, push other kids around and play hooky? Maybe he has a conduct disorder. Is he fidgety, impulsive, disruptive, easily bored? Perhaps he is suffering from attention-deficit hyperactivity disorder, or ADHD, the disease of the hour and the most frequently diagnosed behavioral disorder of childhood. Does he prefer computer games and goofing off to homework? He might have dyslexia or another learning disorder. 3

"There is now an attempt to pathologize what was once considered the normal range of behavior of boys," said Melvin Konner of the departments of anthropology and psychiatry at Emory University in Atlanta. "Today, Tom Sawyer and Huckleberry Finn surely would have been diagnosed with both conduct disorder and ADHD." And both, perhaps, would have been put on Ritalin, the drug of choice for treating attention-deficit disorder. 4

To be fair, many children do have genuine medical problems like ADHD, and they benefit enormously from the proper treatment. Psychiatrists insist that they work very carefully to distinguish between the merely rambunctious child, and the kid who has a serious, organic disorder that is disrupting his life and 5 putting him at risk for all the demons of adulthood: drug addiction, shiftlessness, underemployment, criminality and the like.

6 At the same time, some doctors and social critics cannot help but notice that so many of the childhood syndromes now being diagnosed in record numbers affect far more boys than girls. Attention-deficit disorder, said to afflict 5 percent of all children, is thought to be about three to four times more common in boys than girls. Dyslexia is thought to be about four times more prevalent in boys than girls; and boys practically have the patent on conduct disorders. What is more, most of the traits that brand a child as a potential syndromeur just happen to be traits associated with young males: aggression, rowdiness, restlessness, loud-mouthedness, rebelliousness. None of these characteristics is exclusive to the male sex, of course—for the ultimate display of aggressive intensity, try watching a group of city girls engaged in a serious game of jump-rope—but boys more often will make a spectacle of themselves. And these days, the audience isn't smiling at the show.

7 "People are more sensitized to certain extremes of boyishness," said Dr. John Ratey, a psychiatrist at Harvard Medical School. "It's not as acceptable to be the class clown. You can't cut up. You won't be given slack anymore." Woe to the boy who combines misconduct with rotten grades; he is the likeliest of all to fall under professional observation. "If rowdiness and lack of performance go together, you see the button being pushed much quicker than ever before," he said, particularly in schools where high academic performance is demanded.

8 Lest males of all ages feel unfairly picked upon, researchers point out that boys may be diagnosed with behavioral syndromes and disorders more often than girls for a very good reason: their brains may be more vulnerable. As a boy is developing in the womb, the male hormones released by his tiny testes accelerate the maturation of his brain, locking a lot of the wiring in place early on; a girl's hormonal bath keeps her brain supple far longer. The result is that the infant male brain is a bit less flexible, less able to repair itself after slight injury that might come, for example, during the arduous trek down the birth canal. Hence, boys may well suffer disproportionately from behavioral disorders for reasons unrelated to cultural expectations.

9 However, biological insights can only go so far in explaining why American boyhood is coming to be seen as a state of protodisease. After all, the brains of boys in other countries also were exposed to testosterone in utero, yet non-American doctors are highly unlikely to diagnose a wild boy as having a conduct disorder or ADHD.

"British psychiatrists require a very severe form of hyperactivity before they'll see it as a problem," said Dr. Paul R. McHugh, chairman and director of psychiatry at the Johns Hopkins School of Medicine in Baltimore. "Unless a child is so clearly disturbed that he goes at it until he falls asleep in an inappropriate place like a wastebasket or a drawer, and then wakes up and starts it all over again, he won't be put on medication." Partly as a result of this sharp difference in attitudes, the use of Ritalin-like medications has remained fairly stable in Britain, while pharmaceutical companies here have bumped up production by 250 percent since 1991. 10

Perhaps part of the reason why boyish behavior is suspect these days is Americans' obsessive fear of crime. "We're all really terrified of violence," said Dr. Edward Hallowell, a child psychiatrist at Harvard. "Groups of people who have trouble containing aggression come under suspicion." And what group has more trouble containing aggression than males under the age of 21? Such suspiciousness is not helped by the fact that the rate of violent crime has climbed most steeply among the young, and that everybody seems to own a gun or know where to steal one. Sure, it's perfectly natural for boys to roll around in the dirt fighting and punching and kicking; but toss a firearm into the equation, and suddenly no level of aggression looks healthy. 11

Another cause for the intolerance of boyish behavior is the current school system. It is more group-oriented than ever before, leaving little room for the jokester, the tough, the tortured individualist. American children are said to be excessively coddled and undisciplined, yet in fact they spend less time than their European or Japanese counterparts at recess, where kids can burn off the manic energy they've stored up while trapped in the classroom. Because boys have a somewhat higher average metabolism than do girls, they are likely to become more fidgety when forced to sit still and study. 12

The climate is not likely to improve for the world's Sawyers or Finns or James Deans or any other excessively colorful and unruly specimens of boyhood. Charlotte Tomaino, a clinical neuropsychologist in White Plains, notes that the road to success in this life has gotten increasingly narrow in recent years. "The person who used to have greater latitude in doing one thing and moving onto another suddenly is the person who can't hold a job," she said. "We define success as what you produce, how well you compete, how well you keep up with the tremendous cognitive and technical demands put upon you." The person who will thrive is not the restless version of a human tectonic plate, but the one who can sit 13 still, concentrate and do his job for the 10, 12, 14 hours a day required.

14 A generation or two ago, a guy with a learning disability—or an ornery temperament—could drop out of school, pick up a trade and become, say, the best bridge builder in town. Now, if a guy cannot at the very least manage to finish college, the surging, roaring, indifferent Mississippi of the world's economy is likely to take his little raft, and break it into bits.

READING FOR MEANING

Write to create meanings for Angier's speculations about why adult Americans are increasingly intolerant of boyish behavior.

Start Making Meaning

Begin by listing a few of the basic facts about the trend Angier discusses in her essay. (She presents the trend mainly in paragraphs 1–6.) Then write a sentence or two explaining what you believe to be her purpose in this essay. Continue by writing about anything else in the selection or in your experience that contributes to your understanding of Angier's speculations.

If You Are Stuck

If you cannot write at least a page, consider writing about

- the causes Angier proposes in paragraphs 7, 8, 11, 12, and 13 to explain intolerance of boyish behavior, restating each cause briefly and writing about the one you find most plausible as well as the one you find least plausible.
- how Angier incorporates examples from Mark Twain's novels *Tom Sawyer* and *Huckleberry Finn* and how her use of them contributes to your understanding of the essay.
- Angier's assertion that it is "perfectly natural" (paragraph 11) for boys to fight, punch, and kick.
- a time when you experienced intolerance of boyish behavior, connecting your experience to ideas or examples in Angier's essay.

READING LIKE A WRITER

COUNTERARGUING

Writers speculating about causes must work imaginatively and persistently to support their proposed causes, using all the relevant resources available to them—quoting authorities, citing statistics and research findings, comparing and contrasting, posing rhetorical questions, offering literary allusions, and crafting metaphors, among others. (Angier uses all of the resources in this list.) In addition to supporting their proposed causes, writers usually do more. Because they aim to convince particular readers of the plausibility of their causal argument, writers try to be keenly aware that at every point in the argument their readers will have questions, objections, and other causes in mind. Anticipating and responding to these questions, objections, and alternative causes is known as *counterarguing.*

As readers work their way through a causal argument, nearly all of them will think of questions they would like to ask the writer; or they will resist or object to certain aspects of the support, such as the way the writer uses facts or statistics, relies on an authority, sets up an analogy, or presents an example or personal experience. Readers may doubt whether the support is appropriate, believable, or consistent with the other support provided by the writer. They may come to believe that the writer relies too much on emotional appeals and too little on reason. Readers may also resist or reject the writer's proposed causes, or they may believe that other causes better explain the trend. Experienced writers anticipate all of these predictable concerns. Just as imaginatively as they argue for their proposed causes, writers attempt to answer readers' questions, react to their objections, and evaluate their preferred causes. When you write your essay about causes or effects, anticipating and responding to your readers' concerns will be one of the most challenging and interesting parts of constructing your argument.

Analyze

1. Angier counterargues in at least three places in her causal argument: paragraphs 5, 6, and 8. *Reread* these paragraphs, and *identify* and *underline* the three main objections that Angier anticipates her readers will have to her argument. For example, in the first sentence of paragraph 5, she anticipates readers' likely objection that some boys do have medical problems requiring treatment.

2. *Examine closely* how Angier counterargues readers' objections and questions. For the three objections or questions you identified in paragraphs 5, 6, and 8, *notice* the kinds of support she relies on to argue against each objection. *Decide* whether the support is similar or different among the three cases.

Write

Write several sentences reporting what you have learned about how Angier anticipates her readers' objections. Specifically, in each case, how does she support her counterargument? How appropriate do you, as one of her intended readers, find her support? How believable do you find it?

A SPECIAL READING STRATEGY

Evaluating the Logic of an Argument

To evaluate the logic of an argument speculating about causes, ask yourself three basic questions:

- How appropriate is the support for each cause being speculated about?
- How believable is the support?
- How consistent and complete is the overall argument?

Such an evaluation requires a comprehensive and thoughtful critical reading, but your efforts will help you understand more fully what makes a causal argument successful. To evaluate the logic of Angier's argument, follow the guidelines in Appendix 1 (p. 548). There you will find definitions and explanations as well as an illustration based on an excerpt from a famous essay by Martin Luther King Jr. (the excerpt appears on pp. 519–24).

CONSIDERING IDEAS FOR YOUR OWN WRITING

Think about other groups or categories of people you have the opportunity to observe, and try to identify trends or changes in aspects of their behavior. For example, does it seem to you that girls or women are increasingly interested in math and science or in participating in team sports? If you have been working for a few years, have you noticed that employees have become more docile and more eager to please management? If you have young children, does it seem to you that day-care people have become increasingly professional?

Select one group whose behavior is changing and consider how you would convince readers that the behavior is in fact changing—increasing or decreasing over time. What kind of evidence would you need to gather in the library or on the Internet to corroborate your personal impressions? As a writer speculating about a behavioral change, consider how you would come up with some possible causes for the trend.

ANDREW M. GREELEY

Why Do Catholics Stay in the Church? Because of the Stories

An ordained Roman Catholic priest and a parish priest for over a decade, Andrew M. Greeley (b. 1928) is also a leading American authority on the sociology of religion, with academic appointments at both the University of Arizona and the University of Chicago. He has published hundreds of articles and dozens of books. American universities have awarded him five honorary degrees in recognition of the importance of his scholarly work. As critical of the Catholic church as he is devoted to it, he has been a controversial figure within the church. Greeley's writings include the novels Fall from Grace *(1993) and* Irish Eyes *(2000), religious books such as* The Book of Irish American Prayers and Blessings *(1991) and* Love Affair: A Prayer Journal *(1992), and the highly regarded sociological studies* The Making of the Popes, 1978: The Politics of Intrigue in the Vatican *(1979) and* The Irish Americans: The Rise to Money and Power *(1980), among many others. Greeley has also written an autobiography,* Furthermore! Memories of a Parish Priest *(1999).*

The following essay was published in 1994, in the New York Times Magazine, *a supplement to the Sunday edition of the newspaper. Though most of the paper's readers live in and around New York City, the* Times *is also circulated nationwide and is an important national newspaper. These facts are essential to your understanding of Greeley's argumentative strategies. He assumes that many of his readers are fellow Roman Catholics interested in knowing why people remain Catholic, and that most of his other readers either belong to a different faith or have no religious affiliation. He also expects that a high percentage of Americans may be interested in an argument about the appeal of religious faith, even one different from their own faith. In short, Greeley is writing for a diverse, national audience.*

In this selection, Greeley speculates about the causes of a phenomenon. He wants to try out some ideas about why Catholics remain Catholic. If you are not Catholic or not affiliated with any religious group, think about how Greeley attempts to engage and hold your interest in his argument. Whatever your religious beliefs, as you read notice how carefully and fully Greeley supports the one cause he announces in his title for why Catholics remain faithful.

You can make a persuasive case against Catholicism if you want. The Church is resolutely authoritarian and often seems to be proud of the fact that it "is not a democracy." It discriminates against women and homosexuals. It tries to regulate the bedroom behavior of married men and women. It tries to impose the Catholic position regarding abortion on everyone. It represses dissent and even disagreement. The Vatican seems obsessed with sex. The Pope preaches against birth control in countries with rapidly expanding populations. Catholics often cringe when the local bishop or cardinal pontificates on social policy issues. Bishops and priests are authoritarian and insensitive. Lay people have no control of how their contributions are spent. Priests are unhappy, and many of them leave the priesthood as soon as they can to marry. The Church has covered up sexual abuse by priests for decades. Now it is paying millions of dollars to do penance for the sexual amusements of supposedly celibate priests while it seeks to minimize, if not eliminate altogether, the sexual pleasures of married lay people.

2 One might contend with such arguments. Research indicates that priests are among the happiest men in America. The Church was organized in a democratic structure for the first thousand years and could be so organized again. But let the charges stand for the sake of the argument. They represent the way many of those who are not Catholic see the Catholic Church, and with some nuances and qualifications the way many of those inside the Church see the Catholic institution. Nonetheless this case against Catholicism simply does not compute for most Catholics when they decide whether to leave or stay.

3 Do they in fact remain? Are not Catholics leaving the Church in droves? Prof. Michael Hout of the Survey Research Center at the University of California at Berkeley has demonstrated that the Catholic defection rate has remained constant over 30 years. It was 15 percent in 1960 and it is 15 percent today. Half of those who leave the Church do so when they marry a non-Catholic with stronger religious commitment. The other half leave for reasons of anger, authority and sex—the reasons cited above.

4 How can this be, the outsider wonders. For one thing, as the general population has increased, the number of Catholics has increased proportionately. Still, how can 85 percent of those who are born Catholic remain, one way or another, in the Church? Has Catholicism so brainwashed them that they are unable to leave?

5 The answer is that Catholics like being Catholic. For the last 30 years the hierarchy and the clergy have done just about everything they could to drive the laity out of the Church and have not succeeded. It seems unlikely that they will ever drive the stubborn lay folk out of the Church because the lay folk like being Catholic.

But why do they like being Catholic? 6

First, it must be noted that Americans show remarkable loyalty to their religious heritages. As difficult as it is for members of the academic and media elites to comprehend the fact, religion is important to most Americans. There is no sign that this importance has declined in the last half century (as measured by survey data from the 1940's). Skepticism, agnosticism, atheism are not increasing in America, as disturbing as this truth might be to the denizens of midtown Manhattan. 7

Moreover, while institutional authority, doctrinal propositions and ethical norms[1] are components of a religious heritage—and important components—they do not exhaust the heritage. Religion is experience, image and story before it is anything else and after it is everything else. Catholics like their heritage because it has great stories. 8

If one considers that for much of Christian history the population was illiterate and the clergy semiliterate and that authority was far away, one begins to understand that the heritage for most people most of the time was almost entirely story, ritual, ceremony and eventually art. So it has been for most of human history. So it is, I suggest (and my data back me up), even today. 9

Roger C. Schank, a professor of psychology at Northwestern University who specializes in the study of artificial intelligence, argues in his book *Tell Me a Story* that stories are the way humans explain reality to themselves. The more and better our stories, Schank says, the better our intelligence. 10

Catholicism has great stories because at the center of its heritage is "sacramentalism," the conviction that God discloses Himself in the objects and events and persons of ordinary life. Hence Catholicism is willing to risk stories about angels and saints and souls in purgatory and Mary the Mother of Jesus and stained-glass windows and statues and stations of the cross and rosaries and medals and the whole panoply of images and devotions that were so offensive to the austere leaders of the Reformation.[2] Moreover, the Catholic heritage also has the elaborate ceremonial rituals that mark the passing of the year—Midnight Mass, the 11

[1]*doctrinal propositions:* statements about the basic beliefs of a religion; *ethical norms:* widely shared beliefs about good and bad behavior. (*Ed.*)

[2]*Reformation:* a religious movement that swept Western Europe during the sixteenth century, beginning as a reform movement within the Roman Catholic church and eventuating in the establishment of Protestant churches dissenting from papal authority. (*Ed.*)

Easter Vigil, First Communion, May Crowning, Lent, Advent, grammar-school graduation and the festivals of the saints.

12 Catholicism has also embraced the whole of the human life cycle in Sacraments (with a capital S), which provide rich ceremonial settings, even when indifferently administered for the critical landmarks of life. The Sacrament of Reconciliation (confession that was) and the Sacrament of the Anointing of the Sick (extreme unction that was) embed in ritual and mystery the deeply held Catholic story of second chances.

13 The "sacramentalism" of the Catholic heritage has also led it to absorb as much as it thinks it can from what it finds to be good, true and beautiful in pagan religions: Brigid is converted from the pagan goddess to the Christian patron of spring, poetry and new life in Ireland; Guadalupe is first a pagan and then a Christian shrine in Spain and then our Lady of Guadalupe becomes the patron of poor Mexicans. This "baptism" of pagan metaphors (sometimes done more wisely than at other times) adds yet another overlay of stories to the Catholic heritage.

14 The sometimes inaccurate dictum "once a Catholic, always a Catholic," is based on the fact that the religious images of Catholicism are acquired early in life and are tenacious. You may break with the institution, you may reject the propositions, but you cannot escape the images.

15 The Eucharist (as purists insist we must now call the Mass) is a particularly powerful and appealing Catholic ritual, even when it is done badly (as it often is) and especially when it is done well (which it sometimes is). In the Mass we join a community meal of celebration with our neighbors, our family, our friends, those we love. Such an awareness may not be explicitly on the minds of Catholics when they go to Church on Saturday afternoon or Sunday morning, but it is the nature of metaphor that those who are influenced by it need not be consciously aware of the influence. In a *New York Times*–CBS News Poll last April, 69 percent of Catholics responding said they attend Mass for reasons of meaning rather than obligation.

16 Another important Catholic story is that of the neighborhood parish. Because of the tradition of village parishes with which Catholics came to America, the dense concentration of Catholics in many cities and the small geographical size of the parish, parishes can and often do become intense communities for many Catholics. They actuate what a University of Chicago sociologist, James S. Coleman, calls "social capital," the extra resources of energy, commitment and intelligence that overlapping structures

produce. This social capital, this story of a sacred place in the heart of urban America, becomes even stronger when the parish contains that brilliant American Catholic innovation—the parochial school.

17 Perhaps the Catholic religious sensibility all begins with the Christmas crib. A mother shows her child (perhaps age 3) the crib scene. The child loves it (of course) because it has everything she likes—a mommy, a daddy, a baby, animals, shepherds, shepherd children, angels and men in funny clothes—and with token integration! Who is the baby? the little girl asks. That's Jesus. Who's Jesus? The mother hesitates, not sure of exactly how you explain the communication of idioms to a 3-year-old. Jesus is God. That doesn't bother the little girl at all. Everyone was a baby once. Why not God? Who's the lady holding Jesus? That's Mary. Oh! Who's Mary? The mother throws theological caution to the winds. She's God's mommy. Again the kid has no problem. Everyone has a mommy, why not God?

18 It's a hard story to beat. Later in life the little girl may come to understand that God loves us so much that He takes on human form to be able to walk with us even into the valley of death and that God also loves us the way a mother loves a newborn babe—which is the function of the Mary metaphor in the Catholic tradition.

19 It may seem that I am reducing religion to childishness—to stories and images and rituals and communities. In fact, it is in the poetic, the metaphorical, the experiential dimension of personality that religion finds both its origins and raw power. Because we are reflective creatures we must also reflect on our religious experiences and stories; it is in the (lifelong) interlude of reflection that propositional religion and religious authority become important, indeed indispensable. But then the religiously mature person returns to the imagery, having criticized it, analyzed it, questioned it, to commit the self once more in sophisticated and reflective maturity to the story. . . .

20 When I was in grammar school in the mid-1930's, the nuns told a story that sums up why people stay Catholic. One day Jesus went on a tour of the heavenly city and noted that there were certain new residents who ought not to be there, not until they had put in a long time in purgatory and some of them only on a last-minute appeal. He stormed out to the gate where Peter was checking the day's intake on his Compaq 486DX Deskpro computer (I have edited the nuns' story)—next to which, on his work station, was a fishing pole and a papal crown.

"You've failed again, Simon Peter," said the Lord. 21

"What have I done now?" 22

"You let a lot of people in that don't belong." 23

"I didn't do it." 24

"Well, who did?" 25

"You won't like it." 26

"Tell me anyway." 27

"I turn them away from the front gate and then they go around to the back door and your mother lets them in!" 28

It is the religious sensibility behind that fanciful story that explains why Catholics remain Catholic. It might not be your religious sensibility. But if you want to understand Catholics—and if Catholics want to understand themselves—the starting point is to comprehend the enormous appeal of that sensibility. It's the stories. 29

READING FOR MEANING

Write to create meanings for Greeley's speculations about why so many Catholics stay Catholic.

Start Making Meaning

Begin by explaining what you think Greeley's purpose is in this essay, given his diverse national audience, including yourself as one of his intended readers. Support your explanation with a few details from the essay. Continue by writing about anything else in the selection or in your experience that contributes to your understanding of Greeley's speculations.

If You Are Stuck

If you cannot write at least a page, consider writing about

- Greeley's criticism of the Catholic church (paragraphs 1–5), keeping in mind that the writer is a Catholic priest and that he is addressing an audience made up of non-Catholics as well as Catholics.
- your reaction to the religious story that Greeley claims (in paragraphs 17 and 18) is the most important one for Catholics.
- why you do or do not practice your own religion, comparing or contrasting your choice with why many Catholics stay in the church, according to Greeley.
- criticisms you have of your faith, comparing or contrasting them with Greeley's criticism of Catholicism.

READING LIKE A WRITER

MAKING A CAUSAL ARGUMENT THROUGH EXAMPLES

When writers argue for or support their causes, as Greeley does for his claim that stories keep Catholics faithful to the church, they have many resources available to them. For example, they may use statistics, quote authorities, evoke history, create dialogue, or tell a story. Greeley deploys all of these resources in paragraphs 8–29, where he attempts to convince readers that there is indeed one principal cause for Catholics' loyalty to their faith. However, he relies primarily on examples to support his argument. Because Greeley knows that many of his readers are unfamiliar with the Catholic stories he claims have such power, he names, describes, or tells many of these stories. These are his examples, and they give his argument whatever plausibility it may have with his readers.

Analyze

1. Greeley offers four religious stories from Catholicism as examples to support his speculations: the sacramentalism story (paragraphs 11–14), the Eucharist story (15), the neighborhood parish story (16), and the Christmas crib story (17 and 18). (*Notice* that Greeley uses the story concept broadly, to include narratives with a beginning and an end as well as institutions, events, and rituals.) *Choose one* of these stories to examine closely.
2. *Analyze* how Greeley presents the one story you have chosen. Where does he give examples, quote authorities, present statistics, or tell the story? *Consider* whether you find the story clear and convincing. Does it provide adequate detail? Are all of the details relevant? Do you already have to know something of the story to understand what Greeley writes about it?

Write

Write several sentences reporting what you have learned about Greeley's use of the story to support his argument. Then *add a few more sentences* evaluating how successful this example is in convincing readers that Catholics remain Catholic "because of the stories."

CONSIDERING IDEAS FOR YOUR OWN WRITING

Greeley's essay may suggest to you several ideas for your own essay speculating about causes. For example, consider what might cause other groups of people to do something or to behave in some way: What causes some people to stay in or drop out of college, devote themselves to strenuous exercise programs, abuse their spouses, join cults or gangs, become vegetarians, or listen to talk radio? You should be able to think of other examples.

Like Greeley, you might choose to speculate about why people stay in your religious faith or at your particular church. Or you might speculate about why people leave your faith or church. Because you would be writing for readers of other faiths and those who are nonbelievers, you would need to assume that they might initially consider your faith unusual, if not strange. For your speculations to be convincing, then, you would need to convey a certain detachment or distance from your own beliefs so readers could trust your judgment. You would also need to avoid seeming to recruit others to your faith or attacking other faiths. Your purpose would be to speculate plausibly about why people stay in or leave your faith. Your readers, like Greeley's, would include members of your faith, members of other faiths, and nonbelievers.

EDWARD COHN

Are Men's Fingers Faster?

Edward Cohn (b. 1976) is a graduate student at the University of Chicago, studying the social history of the former Soviet Union. Before entering graduate school, he was a staff writer at the American Prospect, *where he wrote mainly about American politics and culture. He has also written for the* Boston Book Review.

In this essay published in 2000 in the American Prospect, *a magazine with a liberal-progressive slant, Cohn speculates about why most television quiz-show contestants and winners are men. The question he explores asks whether men know more than women or merely push the button for a right answer quicker than women. To support his wide-ranging speculations, Cohn brings in ideas from psychology, test-taking, research, gender differences, and education.*

Before you read, think about your experiences with competitions in school, at work, or at other times when boys and girls, or men and women, competed with each other on the basis of how much information they commanded. How were the competitions organized? (They could have been organized formally or informally.) Were they fair? What were the rewards? (They need not have been monetary.) Did men or women usually win? How did you sometimes explain the outcomes to yourself?

As you read, notice the different causes Cohn offers as possible explanations for why men are more likely than women to become television quiz-show contestants and more likely to succeed when they do so. Think about what you find most convincing—and least convincing—in Cohn's argument.

1 "Can anyone explain this to me?" Regis Philbin asked his *Who Wants to Be a Millionaire* audience of 30 million one evening in February. "Why is it that nearly all of our contestants are white men? I'm a white man, so you know I have nothing against them, but come on. . . . We would really like a little more diversity!" He ended his monologue with an appeal to women and minorities. "So here's the challenge," he said. "Everyone out there who has thought about being on the show—who isn't a white male—dial that 800 number, and let's get into the game."

2 *Who Wants to Be a Millionaire,* of course, has been a runaway hit since ABC imported it from Britain last August. . . . The show begins with a lineup of 10 contestants, who race to answer a "fastest finger" question in the speediest time; the winner then heads to the "hot seat," where he—or, occasionally, she—is asked a series of multiple-choice questions worth from $100 to

$1 million apiece. *Millionaire*'s producers pride themselves on the program's open contestant selection process, in which callers to an 800 number try out by answering timed multiple-choice questions. Much of the show's success derives from its democratic appeal (and its easy, field-leveling questions): Anyone can come home a winner.

3 Anyone, that is, who's white and male. As of this writing, 147 men have sat in the "hot seat," compared to only 21 women; two men, and no women, have won a million dollars; 38 men have won at least $125,000, compared to only three women. "The program looks like a '50s game show in more ways than one," says Robert Thompson, the director of Syracuse University's Center for the study of Popular Television. And Michael Davies, the show's executive producer, admits that the gender gap bothers him, and has considered changes in the show to make the contestants more demographically representative of the country.

4 That may be harder than it sounds because the quiz show gender gap isn't unique to *Millionaire. Jeopardy!*, for example, the grande dame of TV quiz shows, is dominated by men: 80 of the show's top 100 contestants have been male, and only one woman has won *Jeopardy!*'s year-end "tournament of champions" in the 16-year history of the show. And NBC's *Twenty One* and FOX's *Greed*, which aim to copy *Millionaire*'s success, have succeeded in featuring more diverse contestants only by selecting competitors through casting them, not via a blind test.

5 Theories abound for why men dominate these shows. Men, some say, are more competitive and aggressive; women, more nurturing. Men, say others, pursue trivia as a form of adolescent one-upmanship; women have the sense to concentrate on more productive things. A *Washington Post* article even suggested that men's love of trivia was "fueled by the same sublimated aggression and status competition born on the playground."

6 Another possible explanation is that the questions are somehow biased toward men. Critics point to the high number of sports questions, which may favor males; the show's producers reply that *Millionaire* has a diverse team of question writers and that an equal number of questions could be said to favor women.

7 Could the gap derive from the multiple-choice telephone quiz used to decide who goes on the show and the "fastest finger" question that decides who competes for the money? Possibly. In one sense, after all, TV quiz shows are more a test of finger reflexes than a real test of knowledge, and many people suspect that men are better than women at delivering rapid-fire responses to trivia questions. Robert Schaeffer, the director of public educa-

tion at the National Center for Fair and Open Testing (FairTest), uses the literature on standardized tests to support his argument that this type of questioning puts women at a distinct disadvantage. "Fast-paced multiple-choice games with an emphasis on strategic guessing favor a style that is associated with whites and males in our society," he says. The College Board's Advanced Placement exams, for instance, typically include two types of questions: multiple choice and constructed response (involving essays, diagrams, and other more detailed answers). Boys tend to outscore girls on the multiple-choice questions, but "the gender gap narrows, disappears, or reverses," Schaeffer says, when it comes to constructive-response exercises. The reasons for this aren't entirely clear, but, Schaeffer argues, the same dynamic helps men outperform women on *Millionaire*'s qualifying questions.

8 The show's producers dispute this explanation. "There is no evidence that women are any slower than men at the 'fastest finger,'" Davies said at a January press conference. One woman, Shannon McGehee, has logged the best time ever on a "fastest finger" question; another holds the record for the fastest time during a pregame rehearsal. But these women were atypical—they had already made it through two rounds of similar questions. *On average,* men tend to outperform women on speed-based questions—and that may explain the quiz show gender gap.

9 But why should men have "faster fingers"? One theory holds that the men who make it to the show are simply more determined. Anecdotal evidence suggests that there is a class of hypercompetitive men determined to appear on the show—and willing to call back repeatedly in order to do so. Several men have beaten the odds and appeared on the show twice, and one contestant told Rosie O'Donnell that he had called the toll-free number 40 or 50 times before getting on. Another theory postulates that *Millionaire* (and game shows in general) appeal to a distinctive subspecies of the American male, the sci-fi geek, for whom the show's space-age special effects and video-game-like "fast finger" are comfortably familiar.

10 But *Millionaire*'s gender gap may not just be a quirk of game show culture. Here's a discomfiting fact: Males dominate nearly every competition based on the recall of knowledge, at whatever age level, whether or not speed is a factor. Consider the National Geographic Bee, an annual geography competition for children in grades four through eight. The competition begins at over 15,000 elementary and middle schools, each of which crowns a school

champion; each school champion then takes a written exam; the high scorers on the exam head to the state finals; finally, 55 state and territorial winners travel to Washington, D.C., to compete for the grand prize, a $25,000 scholarship. But to the chagrin of the event's sponsor, the National Geographic Society, boys outnumber girls at every level of the competition, with the gender gap increasing at each step along the ladder. Over the bee's 11-year history, in fact, only one girl has won, and every year, at least 50 of the 55 national finalists have been boys.

11 Puzzled by this, the National Geographic Society commissioned a study by two Penn State researchers, geography professor Roger Downs and psychologist Lynn Liben. Their report found that boys and girls entered the bee in roughly equal numbers; that the competitors most likely to succeed were those who loved geography—not those who wanted to win for winning's sake; that the fear of competing in public did not harm the performance of girls; and that boys tended to have slightly better spatial skills and a greater interest in maps. In short, Downs and Liben found that the gender gap in bee winners is probably based on "small, but real" differences in how much boys and girls know about geography.

12 Look at similar competitions, and the pattern repeats itself. Every spring the nation's capital plays host to a series of national academic competitions for elementary- and middle-school students, on topics ranging from spelling and geography to math and civics, but only the National Spelling Bee—the contest with the least emphasis on the recall of knowledge—fields roughly equal numbers of boys and girls. The same is true of the high school and college quiz bowl circuits, where a similarly commanding majority of the competitors are men.

13 Part of the explanation for the gender gap at competitions for younger children presumably lies in the realm of education policy. Many critics argue, for instance, that schools shortchange girls, subtly encouraging boys to act assertively and to dominate classroom discussions. This in turn establishes a series of self-reinforcing assumptions: When girls see boys winning geography bees or trivia contests, they're less likely to join the high school quiz team or try out for *Who Wants to Be a Millionaire* later on.

14 Nevertheless, women have recently begun to appear on *Millionaire* in greater numbers, perhaps because of the show's appeal for diversity. In the month following Regis's plea, in fact, roughly 40 percent of the contestants in the "hot seat" were women. This may just be a temporary blip—and only three of these contestants earned as much as $125,000—but it may be a sign that a little recruitment has helped *Millionaire* buck the trend.

Whatever its origins, the most interesting thing about the quiz show gender gap could be that it had been so widely noticed and discussed. Maybe this isn't surprising. When your co-workers keep asking you, "Is that your final answer?" and your grandmother is offering you lifelines, you know America is in the throes of a pop culture phenomenon that will, for a while, be Topic A of conversation. But given the persistence of more significant gender gaps—in wages, in executive positions, and in a number of other areas—that go generally undiscussed in the popular culture, it's striking how much attention is being lavished on a differential that is, ultimately, trivial. 15

READING FOR MEANING

Write to create meanings for Cohn's speculations about why men have more success than women on television quiz shows.

Start Making Meaning

Cohn speculates about several different causes in paragraphs 5–13. Skim these paragraphs in order to list the causes. Then write two or three sentences about Cohn's purpose. Why do you think he wanted to speculate about this particular phenomenon? What do you think he hopes to achieve with his readers? Continue by writing about anything else in the selection or in your experience that contributes to your understanding of Cohn's speculations.

If You Are Stuck

If you cannot write at least a page, consider writing about

- the statistical evidence given in paragraphs 10–12 supporting the "fact" that "males dominate nearly every competition based on the recall of knowledge, at whatever age level, whether or not speed is a factor."
- the contrasts drawn between men and women in paragraph 5, connecting one or more of the contrasts to your own experience.
- Cohn's conclusion that the gap between men's and women's performances on television quiz shows is "trivial"—that is, less revealing or significant than the gaps in "wages, in executive positions, and in a number of other areas" (paragraph 15), perhaps identifying some of the "other areas" from your own experience or observations.
- other plausible causes Cohn does not mention for men's predominance on television quiz shows.

READING LIKE A WRITER

PRESENTING THE SUBJECT

When writers speculate about the causes of a phenomenon, they must define or describe the phenomenon for readers. Readers must be assured that the phenomenon actually exists. Furthermore, readers are more likely to be engaged by the speculations if they can recognize or be convinced that the phenomenon is important to them personally or that it has some larger significance. In some writing situations, writers may safely assume readers are thoroughly familiar with the phenomenon and therefore need little more than a mention of it. In most other writing situations, however, writers know that readers will require a relatively full presentation of the subject. Because he does not describe a television quiz show in detail, Cohn seems to assume that all, or nearly all, of his readers have seen one. Furthermore, his phrase "of course" in the opening sentence of paragraph 2 suggests he assumes most readers have seen the quiz show *Who Wants to Be a Millionaire.* Perhaps most important is Cohn's assumption that most readers will have neither noticed nor questioned the predominance of men as contestants on the quiz show, and he therefore devotes three of the first four paragraphs to presenting this phenomenon.

Analyze

1. *Reread* paragraphs 1–4, where Cohn presents his subject. *Identify* the different sources of information Cohn relies on in each paragraph. In the margin beside each paragraph, *make notes* about the sources.

2. *Mark* the places where Cohn appears to be trying to establish the importance or significance of his subject. Keep in mind that he may hope to convince readers of its importance to them personally but also of its larger social significance. *Consider* in what ways these paragraphs make you want to read further in order to understand why relatively few women appear on television quiz shows.

Write

Write several sentences explaining how Cohn presents his subject. Then *add a few more sentences* evaluating how successfully he does so. What sources and details in paragraphs 1–4 seem most helpful to readers? What, if anything, seems to be missing from Cohn's presentation? Where is he most successful in declaring or suggesting the importance of his subject?

Compare

Compare the ways Cohn and Natalie Angier present their subjects. *Look back* at Angier's essay (pp. 324–28), and *reread* paragraphs 1–6 about intolerance of boyish behavior. *Notice* the kinds of details and sources Angier uses to present her subject as well as how she attempts to demonstrate its importance or significance. *Write* several sentences comparing the two writers' presentations of their subjects.

CONSIDERING IDEAS FOR YOUR OWN WRITING

Cohn speculates about a persistent difference between women's and men's performance. You too might speculate about a difference in women's and men's performances, achievements, interests, expectations, interactions, or attitudes. For example, you might speculate about why there are so few women trumpet players or drummers in popular-music groups or so few women majors in math or science in college, why men continue to do less housework and provide less child care in marriages where husband and wife hold comparable jobs, or why women want to talk about a problem and men want to solve it. Or, as Cohn suggests, you might speculate about why men earn higher salaries than women for comparable work, or why relatively few women hold corporate executive positions. You would not want to speculate about biological differences that have scientific explanations, differences like why girls mature physically ahead of boys or why women must continue to be the ones to gestate and birth children. Instead, you want to speculate about puzzling social differences that require the special kind of argument known as speculation about causes or effects.

JONATHAN KOZOL

The Human Cost of an Illiterate Society

A well-known critic of American schools, Jonathan Kozol (b. 1936) was in the forefront of educational reformers during the 1970s and 1980s. He has taught in the Boston and Newton, Massachusetts, public schools, as well as at Yale University and the University of Massachusetts at Amherst. In support of his writing and research, he has been awarded numerous prestigious fellowships from the Guggenheim, Ford, and Rockefeller Foundations. Kozol's books include Death at an Early Age *(1967), for which he won the National Book Award,* On Being a Teacher *(1981),* Illiterate America *(1985),* Savage Inequalities: Children in America's Schools *(1991),* Blueprint for a Democratic Education *(1992), and* Ordinary Resurrections: Children in the Years of Hope *(2000).*

The following selection is from Illiterate America, *a comprehensive study of the nature, causes, and effects of illiteracy. The book is intended for a broad readership. Certainly, you are among Kozol's intended readers. In this chapter from the book, Kozol speculates about the human consequences of illiteracy, outlining the limitations and dangers in the lives of adults who cannot read or write. Elsewhere in the book, Kozol conjectures about the causes of illiteracy, but here he concentrates on the effects of the phenomenon, speculating about what life is like for illiterates. He adopts this strategy to argue that the human costs of the problem pose a moral dilemma for our country.*

As you read, decide whether Kozol convinces you that illiteracy is not just a social problem but a special danger to democracy.

PRECAUTIONS. READ BEFORE USING.
Poison: Contains sodium hydroxide (caustic soda-lye).
Corrosive: Causes severe eye and skin damage, may cause blindness.
Harmful or fatal if swallowed.
If swallowed, give large quantities of milk or water.
Do not induce vomiting.
Important: Keep water out of can at all times to prevent contents from violently erupting. . . .

WARNING ON A CAN OF DRANO

Questions of literacy, in Socrates' belief, must at length be judged as matters of morality. Socrates could not have had in mind the moral compromise peculiar to a nation like our own. Some of our Founding Fathers did, however, have this question in their minds. One of the wisest of those Founding Fathers [James Madison] recognized the special dangers that illiteracy would 1 pose to basic equity in the political construction that he helped to shape:

> 2 A people who mean to be their own governors must arm themselves with the power knowledge gives. A popular government without popular information or the means of acquiring it, is but a prologue to a farce or a tragedy, or perhaps both.

3 Tragedy looms larger than farce in the United States today. Illiterate citizens seldom vote. Those who do are forced to cast a vote of questionable worth. They cannot make informed decisions based on serious print information. Sometimes they can be alerted to their interests by aggressive voter education. More frequently, they vote for a face, a smile, or a style, not for a mind or character or body of beliefs.

4 The number of illiterate adults exceeds by 16 million the entire vote cast for the winner in the 1980 presidential contest. If even one third of all illiterates could vote, and read enough and do sufficient math to vote in their self-interest, Ronald Reagan would not likely have been chosen president. There is, of course, no way to know for sure. We do know this: Democracy is a mendacious term when used by those who are prepared to countenance the forced exclusion of one third of our electorate. So long as 60 million people are denied significant participation, the government is neither of, nor for, nor by, the people. It is a government, at best, of those two thirds whose wealth, skin color, or parental privilege allows them opportunity to profit from the provocation and instruction of the written word.

5 The undermining of democracy in the United States is one "expense" that sensitive Americans can easily deplore because it represents a contradiction that endangers citizens of all political positions. The human price is not so obvious at first.

6 Illiterates cannot read the menu in a restaurant.

7 They cannot read the cost of items on the menu in the *window* of the restaurant before they enter.

8 Illiterates cannot read the letters that their children bring home from their teachers. They cannot study school department circulars that tell them of the courses that their children must be taking if they hope to pass the SAT exams. They cannot help with homework. They cannot write a letter to the teacher. They are afraid to visit in the classroom. They do not want to humiliate their child or themselves.

9 Illiterates cannot read instructions on a bottle of prescription medicine. They cannot find out when a medicine is past the year

of safe consumption; nor can they read of allergenic risks, warnings to diabetics, or the potential sedative effect of certain kinds of nonprescription pills. They cannot observe preventive health care admonitions. They cannot read about "the seven warning signs of cancer" or the indications of blood-sugar fluctuations or the risks of eating certain foods that aggravate the likelihood of cardiac arrest.

10 Illiterates live, in more than literal ways, an uninsured existence. They cannot understand the written details on a health insurance form. They cannot read the waivers that they sign preceding surgical procedures. Several women I have known in Boston have entered a slum hospital with the intention of obtaining a tubal ligation and have emerged a few days later after having been subjected to a hysterectomy. Unaware of their rights, incognizant of jargon, intimidated by the unfamiliar air of fear and atmosphere of ether that so many of us find oppressive in the confines even of the most attractive and expensive medical facilities, they have signed their names to documents they could not read and which nobody, in the hectic situation that prevails so often in those overcrowded hospitals that serve the urban poor, had even bothered to explain.

11 Even the roof above one's head, the gas or other fuel for heating that protects the residents of northern city slums against the threat of illness in the winter months become uncertain guarantees. Illiterates cannot read the lease that they must sign to live in an apartment which, too often, they cannot afford. They cannot manage check accounts and therefore seldom pay for anything by mail. Hours and entire days of difficult travel (and the cost of bus or other public transit) must be added to the real cost of whatever they consume. Loss of interest on the check accounts they do not have, and could not manage if they did, must be regarded as another of the excess costs paid by the citizen who is excluded from the common instruments of commerce in a numerate society.

12 "I couldn't understand the bills," a woman in Washington, D.C., reports, "and then I couldn't write the checks to pay them. We signed things we didn't know what they were."

13 Illiterates cannot read the notices that they receive from welfare offices or from the IRS. They must depend on word-of-mouth instruction from the welfare worker—or from other persons whom they have good reason to mistrust. They do not know what rights they have, what deadlines and requirements they face, what options they might choose to exercise. They are half-citizens. Their rights exist in print but not in fact.

14 Illiterates cannot look up numbers in a telephone directory. Even if they can find the names of friends, few possess the sorting

skills to make use of the yellow pages; categories are bewildering and trade names are beyond decoding capabilities for millions of nonreaders. Even the emergency numbers listed on the first page of the phone book—"Ambulance," "Police," and "Fire"—are too frequently beyond the recognition of nonreaders.

15 Many illiterates cannot read the admonition on a pack of cigarettes. Neither the Surgeon General's warning nor its reproduction on the package can alert them to the risks. Although most people learn by word of mouth that smoking is related to a number of grave physical disorders, they do not get the chance to read the detailed stories which can document this danger with the vividness that turns concern into determination to resist. They can see the handsome cowboy or the slim Virginia lady lighting up a filter cigarette; they cannot heed the words that tell them that this product is (not "may be") dangerous to their health. Sixty million men and women are condemned to be the unalerted, high-risk candidates for cancer.

16 Illiterates do not buy "no-name" products in the supermarkets. They must depend on photographs or the familiar logos that are printed on the packages of brand-name groceries. The poorest people, therefore, are denied the benefits of the least costly products.

17 Illiterates depend almost entirely upon label recognition. Many labels, however, are not easy to distinguish. Dozens of different kinds of Campbell's soup appear identical to the nonreader. The purchaser who cannot read and does not dare to ask for help, out of the fear of being stigmatized (a fear which is unfortunately realistic), frequently comes home with something which she never wanted and her family never tasted.

18 Illiterates cannot read instructions on a pack of frozen food. Packages sometimes provide an illustration to explain the cooking preparations; but illustrations are of little help to someone who must "boil water, drop the food—*within* its plastic wrapper—in the boiling water, wait for it to simmer, instantly remove."

19 Even when labels are seemingly clear, they may be easily mistaken. A woman in Detroit brought home a gallon of Crisco for her children's dinner. She thought that she had bought the chicken that was pictured on the label. She had enough Crisco now to last a year—but no more money to go back and buy the food for dinner.

20 Illiterates cannot travel freely. When they attempt to do so, they encounter risks that few of us can dream of. They cannot read traffic signs and, while they often learn to recognize and to decipher symbols, they cannot manage street names which they

haven't seen before. The same is true for bus and subway stops. While ingenuity can sometimes help a man or woman to discern directions from familiar landmarks, buildings, cemeteries, churches, and the like, most illiterates are virtually immobilized. They seldom wander past the streets and neighborhoods they know. Geographical paralysis becomes a bitter metaphor for their entire existence. They are immobilized in almost every sense we can imagine. They can't move up. They can't move out. They cannot see beyond. Illiterates may take an oral test for drivers' permits in most sections of America. It is a questionable concession. Where will they go? How will they get there? How will they get home? Could it be that some of us might like it better if they stayed where they belong?

21 Travel is only one of many instances of circumscribed existence. Choice, in almost all its facets, is diminished in the life of an illiterate adult. Even the printed TV schedule, which provides most people with the luxury of preselection, does not belong within the arsenal of options in illiterate existence. One consequence is that the viewer watches only what appears at moments when he happens to have time to turn the switch. Another consequence, a lot more common, is that the TV set remains in operation night and day. Whatever the program offered at the hour when he walks into the room will be the nutriment that he accepts and swallows. Thus, to passivity, is added frequency—indeed, almost uninterrupted continuity. Freedom to select is no more possible here than in the choice of home or surgery or food.

22 "You don't choose," said one illiterate woman. "You take your wishes from somebody else." Whether in perusal of a menu, selection of highways, purchase of groceries, or determination of affordable enjoyment, illiterate Americans must trust somebody else: a friend, a relative, a stranger on the street, a grocery clerk, a TV copywriter.

23 Billing agencies harass poor people for the payment of the bills for purchases that might have taken place six months before. Utility companies offer an agreement for a staggered payment schedule on a bill past due. "You have to trust them," one man said. Precisely for this reason, you end up by trusting no one and suspecting everyone of possible deceit. A submerged sense of distrust becomes the corollary to a constant need to trust. "They are cheating me . . . I have been tricked . . . I do not know. . . ."

24 *Not knowing:* This is a familiar theme. Not knowing the right word for the right thing at the right time is one form of subjugation. Not knowing the world that lies concealed behind those words is a more terrifying feeling. The longitude and latitude of

one's existence are beyond all easy apprehension. Even the hard, cold stars within the firmament above one's head begin to mock the possibilities for self-location. Where am I? Where did I come from? Where will I go?

25 "I've lost a lot of jobs," one man explains. "Today, even if you're a janitor, there's still reading and writing. . . . They leave a note saying, 'Go to room so-and-so. . . ,' You can't do it. You can't read it. You don't know."

26 "Reading directions, I suffer with. I work with chemicals. . . . That's scary to begin with. . . ."

27 "You sit down. They throw the menu in front of you. Where do you go from there? Nine times out of ten you say, 'Go ahead. Pick out something for the both of us.' I've eaten some weird things, let me tell you!"

28 A landlord tells a woman that her lease allows him to evict her if her baby cries and causes inconvenience to her neighbors. The consequence of challenging his words conveys a danger which appears, unlikely as it seems, even more alarming than the danger of eviction. Once she admits that she can't read, in the desire to maneuver for the time in which to call a friend, she will have defined herself in terms of an explicit importance that she cannot endure. Capitulation in this case is preferable to self-humiliation. Resisting the definition of oneself in terms of what one cannot do, what others take for granted, represents a need so great that other imperatives (even one so urgent as the need to keep one's home in winter's cold) evaporate and fall away in face of fear. Even the loss of home and shelter, in this case, is not so terrifying as the loss of self.

29 Another illiterate, looking back, believes she was not worthy of her teacher's time. She believes that it was wrong of her to take up space within her school. She believes that it was right to leave in order that somebody more deserving could receive her place.

30 People eat what others order, know what others tell them, struggle not to see themselves as they believe the world perceives them. A man in California spoke about his own loss of identity, self-location, definition:

31 "I stood at the bottom of the ramp. My car had broke down on the freeway. There was a phone. I asked for the police. They was nice. They said to tell them where I was. I looked up at the signs. There was one that I had seen before. I read it to them: ONE WAY STREET. They thought it was a joke. I told them I couldn't read. There was other signs above the ramp. They told me to try. I looked around for somebody to help. All the cars was going by real fast. I couldn't make them understand that I was lost. The cop was nice.

He told me: 'Try once more.' I did my best. I couldn't read. I only knew the sign above my head. The cop was trying to be nice. He knew that I was trapped. 'I can't send out a car to you if you can't tell me where you are.' I felt afraid. I nearly cried. I'm forty-eight years old. I only said: 'I'm on a one-way street. . . .'"

Perhaps we might slow down a moment here and look at the realities described above. This is the nation that we live in. This is a society that most of us did not create but which our President and other leaders have been willing to sustain by virtue of malign neglect. Do we possess the character and courage to address a problem which so many nations, poorer than our own, have found it natural to correct? 32

The answers to these questions represent a reasonable test of our belief in the democracy to which we have been asked in public school to swear allegiance. 33

READING FOR MEANING

Write to create meanings for Kozol's speculations about the effects of illiteracy.

Start Making Meaning

Begin by listing the four or five effects of illiteracy Kozol proposes that seem to you most damaging. Then write a few sentences about Kozol's purpose. What seems to be his motivation for writing? Does he seem to be accepting a hopeless situation or hoping for reform? What response do you think he wants from readers? What in the text leads you to your answers? Continue by writing about anything else in the selection or in your experience that contributes to your understanding of Kozol's speculations.

If You Are Stuck

If you cannot write at least a page, consider writing about

- how illiteracy may undermine democracy, summarizing Kozol's main ideas about this danger (from paragraphs 2–4) and, if possible, adding an idea or two of your own.
- Kozol's connection between morality and literacy (paragraph 1), explaining possible connections you see and speculating about whom Kozol seems to be accusing of immoral actions.
- other effects of illiteracy Kozol does not mention.

- "the power that knowledge gives," using examples from your own experience of the ways knowledge gained from reading has contributed to your achievements, sense of identity, or privileges.

READING LIKE A WRITER

SUPPORTING PROPOSED EFFECTS

Kozol proposes many effects of illiteracy. A mere list of possible effects would be interesting, but to convince readers to take all of these effects seriously, Kozol must argue for—or support—them in ways that enhance their plausibility. To do so, all writers speculating about effects have many resources available to them to support their proposed effects: examples, statistics, quotations from authorities, personal anecdotes, analogies, scenarios, quotes from interviews, and more. As a writer speculating about causes or effects, you will need to support your speculations in these ways in order to make them plausible. You can learn more about supporting speculations by analyzing how Kozol does it.

Analyze

1. *Choose* one of Kozol's proposed effects of illiteracy: helplessness in financial affairs (paragraphs 11 and 12), confusion about supermarket purchases (16–19), limited travel (20), or loss of self (28–31).
2. *Examine* the support carefully. What kind of support do you find? More than one kind? Does the support seem to come from many or few sources?
3. *Evaluate* the support. Does it seem appropriate for the proposed effect? Does it seem believable and trustworthy? Does it seem consistent with the other support for the effect? If so, how does it complement the other support?

Write

Write several sentences explaining how Kozol supports the effect you have chosen. Also *evaluate* the plausibility of the support he offers. *Give details* from the paragraphs you have analyzed. As one of Kozol's intended readers, *explain* how convincing you find the support.

CONSIDERING IDEAS FOR YOUR OWN WRITING

Consider speculating, like Kozol does, about the effects of a significant social problem. List several major social problems (local or national) that concern you. Your list might include, for example, the high pregnancy rate among unmarried teenagers, high-school dropout rates, high costs of a college education, unsafe working conditions or high employee turnover at your job, poor academic advising or too many required courses at your college, traffic congestion or uncontrolled development in your community, lack of good bookstores in your area, or limited access to local news because your town has only one daily newspaper. Choose one problem, and consider how you can speculate about its effects. What effects can you argue for? As a writer, how could you convince readers that your proposed effects are plausible? Will you need to research the problem to write about it authoritatively? Remember, your purpose is not to propose a solution to the problem but to speculate about its possible effects.

Alternatively, you could recall a recent controversial decision by college or community leaders that concerns you, such as a decision about campus life (safety, recreation, tutoring, or other special services) or about the future of your community (growth, transportation, safety). List several such decisions, and then choose one you would like to write about. Consider how you would write a letter to your college or community newspaper speculating about the effects or consequences of the decision. What short-term and long-term consequences would you propose? How would you convince readers to take your ideas seriously?

SARAH WEST

The Rise of Reported Incidents of Workplace Sexual Harassment

Sarah West wrote this essay for an assignment in her first-year college writing course.

Like Natalie Angier, West speculates about a trend: a gradual increase in reported incidents of workplace sexual harassment over a thirty-year period. She begins by establishing that the trend exists. Notice that her concern is not whether workplace sexual harassment is increasing but whether reported incidents of it are increasing. She no doubt recognizes that it would be difficult to demonstrate that actual acts of harassment are increasing or decreasing; she may also recognize that such acts are very likely decreasing as reported incidents increase and receive wide publicity. West then launches her speculations about the causes for the increasing number of reports.

As you read, keep in mind that the U.S. Supreme Court has defined illegal sexual harassment as "sufficiently severe or pervasive to alter the conditions of the victim's employment." In other words, it is not a casual or unthreatening one-time incident, but several incidents that create a hostile work environment and undermine victims' trust and ability to do their jobs.

To those students who recently graduated from high school, it may sound like the Dark Ages, but it wasn't: Until 1964, an employee who refused to give in to his or her employer's sexual advances could be fired—legally. An employee being constantly humiliated by a coworker could be forced either to deal with the lewd comments, the stares, and the touching or to just quit his or her job. It is truly strange to think that sexual harassment was perfectly legal in the United States until Congress passed the Civil Rights Act of 1964. 1

But even after 1964, sexual harassment still persisted. It was not widely known exactly what sexual harassment was or that federal laws against it existed. Often when an employee was sexually harassed on the job, he or she felt too alienated and humiliated to speak out against it (Martell and Sullivan 6). During the 1970s and 1980s, however, sexual-harassment victims began coming forward to challenge their harassers. Then suddenly in the 1990s, the number of sexual-harassment complaints and lawsuits sharply rose. According to a 1994 survey conducted by the Society for Human Resource Management, the percentage of 2 human-resource professionals who have reported that their departments handled at least one sexual-harassment complaint rose from 35 percent in 1991 to 65 percent in 1994. Why did this large increase occur in such a short amount of time? Possible answers to this question surely would include growing awareness of the nature of workplace sexual harassment, government action, efforts of companies to establish anti-harassment policies and encourage harassed employees to come forward, and prominence given by the media to many cases of workplace harassment.

3 One significant cause of the rise in reported incidents of sexual harassment was most likely the increased awareness of what constitutes sexual harassment. There are two distinct types of sexual harassment, and although their formal names may be unfamiliar, the situations they describe will most certainly ring a bell. *Hostile environment* sexual harassment occurs when a supervisor or coworker gives the victim "unwelcome sexual attention" that "interferes with (his or her) ability to work or creates an intimidating or offensive atmosphere" (Stanko and Werner 15). *Quid pro quo* sexual harassment occurs when "a workplace superior demands some degree of sexual favor" and either threatens to or does retaliate in a way that "has a tangible effect on the working conditions of the harassment victim" if he or she refuses to comply (Stanko and Werner 15).

4 A fundamental cause of the rise in reports of workplace harassment was government action in 1964 and again in 1991. After the passage of the Civil Rights Act of 1991, which allowed, among other things, larger damage awards for sexually harassed employees, many more employees began coming forward with complaints. They realized that sexual harassment was not legal and they could do something about it. Suddenly, it became possible for a company to lose millions in a single sexual-harassment case. For example, Rena Weeks, a legal secretary in San Francisco, sued the law firm of Baker & McKenzie for $3.5 million after an employee, Martin Greenstein, "dumped candy down the breast pocket of her blouse, groped her, pressed her from behind and pulled her arms back to 'see which one (breast) is bigger'" ("Workplace"). The jury awarded Weeks $7.1 million in punitive damages, twice what she sought in her lawsuit ("Workplace"). In addition, research revealed that the mere existence of sexual harassment in a company could lead to "hidden costs" such as absenteeism, lower productivity, and loss of valuable employees (Stanko and Werner 16). These "hidden costs" could add up to $6 or $7 million a year for a typical large company, according to one survey of Fortune 500 companies (Stanko and Werner 16).

Concerned about these costs, most companies decided to develop and publicize sexual-harassment policies, making every employee aware of the problem and more likely to come forward as early as possible so that employers have a chance to remedy the situation before it gets out of hand (Martell and Sullivan 8). Prior to 1991, sexual-harassment victims were often asked by their employers simply to remain silent (Martell and Sullivan 8). These new policies and procedures, along with training sessions, made it much more likely that employees would report incidents of sexual harassment. And we should not be surprised that the Internet has provided independent information to employees about dealing with workplace sexual harassment ("Handling"; "Sexual"). 5

The media have also contributed to the rise of reports of workplace sexual harassment by giving great attention to a few prominent cases. In 1991, Supreme Court Justice Clarence Thomas in Senate hearings on his nomination had to defend himself from sexual-harassment charges by his former colleague Anita Hill. Later that same year, U.S. male navy officers were accused of sexually harassing female navy officers at the infamous Tailhook Convention, a yearly gathering of navy aviators (Nelton 24). During 1997 and 1998—and probably for many years beyond—Paula Jones's sexual-harassment charges against President Clinton dominated the national news on many days. Jones was an Arkansas state employee at the time she said Clinton, who was then governor, harassed her. These three highly publicized cases made sexual harassment a much-discussed public issue that sparked debate and encouraged victims to come forward. 6

Not everyone believes that there has been an increase in reports of workplace sexual harassment. One journalist has argued that the rise in reported sexual-harassment complaints is actually a sort of illusion caused by insufficient research, since "research on this topic has only been undertaken since the 1970s" (Burke 23). Although this statement is largely true, it is only true because the Civil Rights Act did not exist until 1964. How could sexual harassment be measured and researched if it was not even acknowledged yet by society? 7

It has also been suggested that the trend is the result of a greater percentage of women in the workplace (Martell and Sullivan 5). This may be a sufficient argument since women report sexual harassment in a significantly greater number of cases than men do (men report roughly one-tenth of what women report). It has been noted, however, that there has been a rise in sexual-harassment complaints reported by male victims as well recently. According to the Equal Employment Opportunity Commission, 8 the number of sexual-harassment complaints filed annually by men has more than doubled from 1989 to 1993 (Corey). Sexual harassment is by no means a new occurrence. It has most likely existed since workplace environments have existed. Yet, that there are more women in the workplace today has likely increased the percentage of women workers being sexually harassed, but it is also very plausible that the rise in reported incidents of sexual harassment is because of increased awareness of sexual harassment and the steps that one can legally take to stop it.

9 It has taken thirty years, but American society seems to be making significant progress in bringing a halt to a serious problem. *Sexual harassment,* a phrase that was unfamiliar to most of us only a few years ago, is now mentioned almost daily on television and in newspapers. We can only hope that the problem will end if we continue to hear about, to read about, and, most importantly, to talk about sexual harassment and its negative consequences as we educate each other about sexual harassment. Then, perhaps someday, sexual harassment can be stopped altogether.

Works Cited

Burke, Ronald J. "Incidence and Consequences of Sexual Harassment in a Professional Services Firm." *Employee Counselling Today* Feb. 1995: 23–29.

Corey, Mary. "On-the-Job Sexism Isn't Just a Man's Sin Anymore." *Houston Chronicle* 30 Aug. 1993: D1.

"Handling Sexual Harassment Complaints." *Employer and Employee.* 8 Jan. 1998 < http://www.employer-employee.com/sexhar1.html >.

Martell, Kathryn, and George Sullivan. "Strategies for Managers to Recognize and Remedy Sexual Harassment." *Industrial Management* May/June 1994: 5–8.

Nelton, Sharon. "Sexual Harassment: Reducing the Risks." *Nation's Business* Mar. 1995: 24–26.

"Sexual Harassment: FAQ." *Employment: Workplace Rights and Responsibilities.* 8 Jan. 1998 < http://www.nolo.com/ChunkEMP/emp7.html >.

Stanko, Brian B., and Charles A. Werner. "Sexual Harassment: What Is It? How to Prevent It." *National Public Accountant* June 1995: 14–16.

"Workplace Bias Lawsuits." *USA Today* 30 Nov. 1994: B2.

READING FOR MEANING

Write to create meanings for West's speculations about the rise in reported incidents of sexual harassment in the workplace.

Start Making Meaning

Begin by restating briefly the causes West proposes to explain the increase in reports of sexual harassment at work. She identifies four causes, each in its own paragraph (paragraphs 3–6). Continue by writing about anything else in the selection or in your experience that contributes to your understanding of West's speculations.

If You Are Stuck

If you cannot write at least a page, consider writing about

- your understanding of the two types of workplace sexual harassment described by West (paragraph 3).
- a time when you or someone you know was sexually harassed at work, what happened, and what—if anything—was done about it.
- whether you think the federal government should have a role in protecting people at work.
- the possible implication of workplace sexual-harassment laws for students' interactions on college campuses.

READING LIKE A WRITER

ESTABLISHING CREDIBILITY

To be credible is to be believable. When you write an essay speculating about the causes or effects of something, readers will find your argument believable when they sense that you are able to see the various complexities of your subject. Therefore, if you do not oversimplify, trivialize, or stereotype your subject, if you do not overlook possible alternative causes or effects that will occur to readers, and if you convey more than casual knowledge of your subject and show that you have thought about it deeply and seriously, you will establish your credibility with readers.

Before you attempt your own essay speculating about causes or effects, it will be helpful for you to consider carefully how West establishes her credibility to speculate about the rise in reported incidents of workplace sexual harassment.

Analyze

1. *Reread* this brief essay, and *annotate* it for evidence of credibility or lack of it. (Because you cannot know West personally, you must look closely at the

words, evidence, and arguments of her essay to decide whether she constructs a credible argument.) *Examine closely* how knowledgeable she seems about the subject. Where does her knowledge assure or even impress you as one of her intended readers? Where does her knowledge seem thin? *Consider* especially how she presents the subject and trend (paragraphs 1–3). *Assess* also the sources she relies on and how effectively she uses them.

2. *Look* for evidence that West has not trivialized a complex subject. Keeping in mind that she appropriately limits herself to speculating about possible causes, *note* how her argument reflects the complexity of her subject or fails to do so.
3. *Consider* how West's counterarguments (paragraphs 7 and 8) influence your judgment of her credibility.
4. *Examine* her approach to readers. What assumptions does she make about their knowledge and beliefs? What attitude does she have toward her readers? *Note* evidence of the writer's assumptions and attitude toward readers.

Write

Write several sentences presenting evidence of West's attempts to establish her credibility. Then *write a few more sentences evaluating* how credible her essay is to you as one of her intended readers. To explain your judgment, *point to* parts of the essay and *comment on* the influence of your own attitudes about and knowledge of workplace sexual harassment.

CONSIDERING IDEAS FOR YOUR OWN WRITING

West speculates about a subject of great social significance—sexual harassment. She speculates about the causes of the rise in reported incidents, but she could have speculated about the phenomenon of sexual harassment itself, asking why it happens at all or why there seems to be so much of it in the workplace. Following her lead, you could speculate about the causes of other important social phenomena or trends that influence how people live and work and what their opportunities in life may be. Here are some examples: the increase in the number of students working part-time or full-time to get a college degree; the increase in hateful speech on some campuses; the increase in specific standards to be met before admission to college; the increase in the costs of a college education; the decline of neighborhood or community cohesion; the rise of the political influence of the religious right; the growing gap in wealth between the rich and the rest; the increasing reliance by technology companies on workers trained in other countries; and the stagnant wages over two decades for most workers.

LA DONNA BEATY

What Makes a Serial Killer?

La Donna Beaty was a college student when she wrote this essay speculating about what produces serial killers. Like Natalie Angier and Sarah West, Beaty relies in large part on speculations from a wide range of published research to put together her argument. She is in control of the argument because she selects certain speculations (and not others) and weaves them into her own design.

As you read, notice the wide range of speculations she brings into her argument.

The other readings in this chapter are followed by reading and writing activities. Following this reading, however, you are on your own to decide how to read for meaning and read like a writer.

1 Jeffrey Dahmer, John Wayne Gacy, Mark Allen Smith, Richard Chase, Ted Bundy—the list goes on and on. These five men alone have been responsible for at least ninety deaths, and many suspect that their victims may total twice that number. They are serial killers, the most feared and hated of criminals. What deep, hidden secret makes them lust for blood? What can possibly motivate a person to kill over and over again with no guilt, no remorse, no hint of human compassion? What makes a serial killer?

2 Serial killings are not a new phenomenon. In 1798, for example, Micajah and Wiley Harpe traveled the backwoods of Kentucky and Tennessee in a violent, year-long killing spree that left at least twenty—and possibly as many as thirty-eight—men, women, and children dead. Their crimes were especially chilling as they seemed particularly to enjoy grabbing small children by the ankles and smashing their heads against trees (Holmes and DeBurger 28). In modern society, however, serial killings have grown to near epidemic proportions. Ann Rule, a respected author and expert on serial murders, stated in a seminar at the University of Louisville on serial murder that between 3,500 and 5,000 people become victims of serial murder each year in the United States alone (qtd. in Holmes and DeBurger 21). Many others estimate that there are close to 350 serial killers currently at large in our society (Holmes and DeBurger 22).

3 Fascination with murder and murderers is not new, but researchers in recent years have made great strides in determining the characteristics of criminals. Looking back, we can see how naive early experts were in their evaluations: in 1911, for example, Italian criminologist Cesare Lombrosco concluded that

"murderers as a group [are] biologically degenerate [with] bloodshot eyes, aquiline noses, curly black hair, strong jaws, big ears, thin lips, and menacing grins" (qtd. in Lunde 84). Today, however, we don't expect killers to have fangs that drip human blood, and many realize that the boy-next-door may be doing more than woodworking in his basement. While there are no specific physical characteristics shared by all serial killers, they are almost always male and 92 percent are white. Most are between the ages of twenty-five and thirty-five and often physically attractive. While they may hold a job, many switch employment frequently as they become easily frustrated when advancement does not come as quickly as expected. They tend to believe that they are entitled to whatever they desire but feel that they should have to exert no effort to attain their goals (Samenow 88, 96). What could possibly turn attractive, ambitious human beings into cold-blooded monsters?

4 One popular theory suggests that many murderers are the product of our violent society. Our culture tends to approve of violence and find it acceptable, even preferable, in many circumstances (Holmes and DeBurger 27). According to research done in 1970, one out of every four men and one out of every six women believed that it was appropriate for a husband to hit his wife under certain conditions (Holmes and DeBurger 33). This emphasis on violence is especially prevalent in television programs. Violence occurs in 80 percent of all prime-time shows, while cartoons, presumably made for children, average eighteen violent acts per hour. It is estimated that by the age of eighteen, the average child will have viewed more than 16,000 television murders (Holmes and DeBurger 34). Some experts feel that children demonstrate increasingly aggressive behavior with each violent act they view (Lunde 15) and become so accustomed to violence that these acts seem normal (Lunde 35). In fact, most serial killers do begin to show patterns of aggressive behavior at a young age. It is, therefore, possible that after viewing increasing amounts of violence, such children determine that this is acceptable behavior; when they are then punished for similar actions, they may become confused and angry and eventually lash out by committing horrible, violent acts.

5 Another theory concentrates on the family atmosphere into which the serial killer is born. Most killers state that they experienced psychological abuse as children and never established good relationships with the male figures in their lives (Ressler, Burgess, and Douglas 19). As children, they were often rejected by their parents and received little nurturing (Lunde 94; Holmes and De-

Burger 64–70). It has also been established that the families of serial killers often move repeatedly, never allowing the child to feel a sense of stability; in many cases, they are also forced to live outside the family home before reaching the age of eighteen (Ressler, Burgess, and Douglas 19–20). Our culture's tolerance for violence may overlap with such family dynamics: with 79 percent of the population believing that slapping a twelve-year-old is either necessary, normal, or good, it is no wonder that serial killers relate tales of physical abuse (Holmes and DeBurger 30; Ressler, Burgess, and Douglas 19–20) and view themselves as the "black sheep" of the family. They may even, perhaps unconsciously, assume this same role in society.

6 While the foregoing analysis portrays the serial killer as a lost, lonely, abused little child, another theory, based on the same information, gives an entirely different view. In this analysis, the killer is indeed rejected by his family but only after being repeatedly defiant, sneaky, and threatening. As verbal lies and destructiveness increase, the parents give the child the distance he seems to want in order to maintain a small amount of domestic peace (Samenow 13). This interpretation suggests that the killer shapes his parents much more than his parents shape him. It also denies that the media can influence a child's mind and turn him into something that he doesn't already long to be. Since most children view similar amounts of violence, the argument goes, a responsible child filters what he sees and will not resort to criminal activity no matter how acceptable it seems to be (Samenow 15–18). In 1930, the noted psychologist Alfred Adler seemed to find this true of any criminal. As he put it, "With criminals it is different: they have a private logic, a private intelligence. They are suffering from a wrong outlook upon the world, a wrong estimate of their own importance and the importance of other people" (qtd. in Samenow 20).

7 Most people agree that Jeffrey Dahmer or Ted Bundy had to be "crazy" to commit horrendous multiple murders, and scientists have long maintained that serial killers are indeed mentally disturbed (Lunde 48). While the percentage of murders committed by mental hospital patients is much lower than that among the general population (Lunde 35), it cannot be ignored that the rise in serial killings happened at almost the same time as the deinstitutionalization movement in the mental health care system during the 1960s (Markman and Bosco 266). While reform was greatly needed in the mental health care system, it has now become nearly impossible to hospitalize those with severe problems. In the United States, people have a constitutional right to remain

mentally ill. Involuntary commitment can only be accomplished if the person is deemed dangerous to self, dangerous to others, or gravely disabled. However, in the words of Ronald Markman, "According to the way that the law is interpreted, if you can go to the mailbox to pick up your social security check, you're not gravely disabled even if you think you're living on Mars"; even if a patient is thought to be dangerous, he or she cannot be held longer than ninety days unless it can be proved that the patient actually committed dangerous acts while in the hospital (Markman and Bosco 267). Many of the most heinous criminals have had long histories of mental illness but could not be hospitalized due to these stringent requirements. Richard Chase, the notorious Vampire of Sacramento, believed that he needed blood in order to survive, and while in the care of a psychiatric hospital, he often killed birds and other small animals in order to quench this desire. When he was released, he went on to kill eight people, one of them an eighteen-month-old baby (Biondi and Hecox 206). Edmund Kemper was equally insane. At the age of fifteen, he killed both of his grandparents and spent five years in a psychiatric facility. Doctors determined that he was "cured" and released him into an unsuspecting society. He killed eight women, including his own mother (Lunde 53–56). The world was soon to be disturbed by a cataclysmic earthquake, and Herbert Mullin knew that he had been appointed by God to prevent the catastrophe. The fervor of his religious delusion resulted in a death toll of thirteen (Lunde 63–81). All of these men had been treated for their mental disorders, and all were released by doctors who did not have enough proof to hold them against their will.

8 Recently, studies have given increasing consideration to the genetic makeup of serial killers. The connection between biology and behavior is strengthened by research in which scientists have been able to develop a violently aggressive strain of mice simply through selective inbreeding (Taylor 23). These studies have caused scientists to become increasingly interested in the limbic system of the brain, which houses the amygdala, an almond-shaped structure located in the front of the temporal lobe. It has long been known that surgically altering that portion of the brain, in an operation known as a lobotomy, is one way of controlling behavior. This surgery was used frequently in the 1960s but has since been discontinued as it also erases most of a person's personality. More recent developments, however, have shown that temporal lobe epilepsy causes electrical impulses to be discharged directly into the amygdala. When this electronic stimulation is re-created in the laboratory, it causes violent behavior in lab ani-

mals. Additionally, other forms of epilepsy do not cause abnormalities in behavor, except during seizure activity. Temporal lobe epilepsy is linked with a wide range of antisocial behavior, including anger, paranoia, and aggression. It is also interesting to note that this form of epilepsy produces extremely unusual brain waves. These waves have been found in only 10 to 15 percent of the general population, but over 79 percent of known serial killers test positive for these waves (Taylor 28–33).

9 The look at biological factors that control human behavior is by no means limited to brain waves or other brain abnormalities. Much work is also being done with neurotransmitters, levels of testosterone, and patterns of trace minerals. While none of these studies is conclusive, they all show a high correlation between antisocial behavior and chemical interactions within the body (Taylor 63–69).

10 One of the most common traits that all researchers have noted among serial killers is heavy use of alcohol. Whether this correlation is brought about by external factors or whether alcohol is an actual stimulus that causes certain behavior is still unclear, but the idea deserves consideration. Lunde found that the majority of those who commit murder had been drinking beforehand and commonly had a urine alcohol level of between .20 and .29, nearly twice the legal level of intoxication (31–32). Additionally, 70 percent of the families that reared serial killers had verifiable records of alcohol abuse (Ressler, Burgess, and Douglas 17). Jeffrey Dahmer had been arrested in 1981 on charges of drunkenness, and before his release from prison on sexual assault charges, his father had written a heart-breaking letter pleading that Jeffrey be forced to undergo treatment for alcoholism—a plea that, if heeded, might have changed the course of future events (Davis 70, 103). Whether alcoholism is a learned behavior or an inherited predisposition is still hotly debated, but a 1979 report issued by Harvard Medical School stated that "[a]lcoholism in the biological parent appears to be a more reliable predictor of alcoholism in the children than any other environmental factor examined" (qtd. in Taylor 117). While alcohol was once thought to alleviate anxiety and depression, we now know that it can aggravate and intensify such moods (Taylor 110); for the serial killers this may lead to irrational feelings of powerlessness that are brought under control only when the killer proves he has the ultimate power to control life and death.

11 "Man's inhumanity to man" began when Cain killed Abel, but this legacy has grown to frightening proportions, as evidenced by the vast number of books that line the shelves of modern

bookstores—row after row of titles dealing with death, anger, and blood. We may never know what causes a serial killer to exact his revenge on an unsuspecting society, but we need to continue to probe the interior of the human brain to discover the delicate balance of chemicals that controls behavior; we need to be able to fix what goes wrong. We must also work harder to protect our children. Their cries must not go unheard; their pain must not become so intense that it demands bloody revenge. As today becomes tomorrow, we must remember the words of Ted Bundy, one of the most ruthless serial killers of our time: "Most serial killers are people who kill for the pure pleasure of killing and cannot be rehabilitated. Some of the killers themselves would even say so" (qtd. in Holmes and DeBurger 150).

Works Cited

Biondi, Ray, and Walt Hecox. *The Dracula Killer.* New York: Simon, 1992.

Davis, Ron. *The Milwaukee Murders.* New York: St. Martin's, 1991.

Holmes, Ronald M., and James DeBurger. *Serial Murder.* Newbury Park: Sage, 1988.

Lunde, Donald T. *Murder and Madness.* San Francisco: San Francisco Book, 1976.

Markman, Ronald, and Dominick Bosco. *Alone with the Devil.* New York: Doubleday, 1989.

Ressler, Robert K., Ann W. Burgess, and John E. Douglas. *Sexual Homicide—Patterns and Motives.* Lexington: Heath, 1988.

Samenow, Stanton E. *Inside the Criminal Mind.* New York: Times, 1984.

Taylor, Lawrence. *Born to Crime.* Westport: Greenwood, 1984.

READING FOR MEANING

Write to create meanings for Beaty's speculations about what makes a serial killer.

READING LIKE A WRITER

Writers of essays speculating about causes or effects

- present the subject.
- make a logical, step-by-step cause or effect argument.
- support—or argue for—each cause or effect.
- handle readers' likely objections to the proposed causes or effects.
- evaluate readers' alternative or preferred causes or effects.

You have seen how important these strategies are in the readings you have read, written about, and discussed in this chapter. Focus on one of these strategies in Beaty's essay and analyze it carefully through close rereading and annotating. Then write several sentences explaining what you have learned, giving specific examples from the reading to support your explanation. Add a few sentences evaluating how successfully Beaty uses the strategy to argue convincingly for what makes a serial killer.

REVIEWING WHAT MAKES ESSAYS SPECULATING ABOUT CAUSES OR EFFECTS EFFECTIVE

In this chapter, you have been learning how to read cause or effect arguments for meaning and how to read them like a writer. Before going on to write an essay speculating about causes or effects, pause here to review and contemplate what you have learned about the elements of effective cause or effect essays.

Analyze

Choose one reading from this chapter that seems to you especially effective. Before rereading the selection, *jot down* one or two reasons you remember it as an example of effective cause or effect writing.

Reread your chosen selection, adding further annotations about what makes it particularly effective. *Consider* the selection's purpose and how well it achieves that purpose for its readers. (You can make an informed guess about the intended readers and their expectations by noting the publication source of the essay.) Then *focus* on how well the essay

- presents the subject.
- makes a logical, step-by-step cause or effect argument.
- supports—or argues for—each cause or effect.
- handles readers' likely objections to the proposed causes or effects.
- evaluates readers' alternative or preferred causes or effects.

You can review all of these basic features in the Guide to Reading Essays Speculating about Causes or Effects (p. 315).

Your instructor may ask you to complete this activity on your own or to work with a small group of other students who have chosen the same reading. If you work with others, allow enough time initially for all group members to reread the selection thoughtfully and to add their annotations. Then *discuss* as a group what makes the essay effective. *Take notes* on your discussion. One student in your group should then report to the class what the group has learned about the effectiveness of cause or effect argument. If you are working individually, write up what you have learned from your analysis.

Write

Write at least a page, justifying your choice of this essay as an example of effective cause or effect argument. *Assume* that your readers—your instructor and classmates—have read the selection but will not remember many details about it. They also might not remember it as especially successful. Therefore, you will need to *refer* to details and specific parts of the essay as you explain how it works and as you justify your evaluation of its effectiveness. You need not argue that it is the best essay in the chapter or that it is flawless, only that it is, in your view, a strong example of the genre.

A Guide to Writing Essays Speculating about Causes or Effects

The readings in this chapter have helped you learn a great deal about writing that speculates about causes or effects. Now that you have seen how writers present their subjects to particular readers, propose causes or effects readers may not think of, support those causes or effects so as to make them plausible to readers, and anticipate readers' questions and objections, you can approach this type of writing confidently. The readings remain an important resource for you as you develop your own essay. Use them to review how other writers have solved the problems you face and to rethink the strategies that help writers achieve their purposes.

This Guide to Writing is designed to assist you in writing your essay. Here you will find activities to help you identify a subject and discover what to say about it, organize your ideas and draft the essay, read the draft critically, revise the draft to strengthen your argument, and edit and proofread the essay to improve its readability.

INVENTION

The following invention activities will help you find a subject and begin developing your argument. A few minutes spent completing each writing activity will improve your chances of producing a detailed and convincing first draft. You can decide on a subject for your essay, explore what you presently know about it and gather additional information, think about possible causes or effects, and develop a plausible argument.

Choosing a Subject

The subject of an essay speculating about causes or effects may be a trend, an event, or a phenomenon, as the readings in this chapter illustrate. List the most promising subjects you can think of, beginning with any you listed for the Considering Ideas for Your Own Writing activities following the readings in this chapter. These varied possibilities for analyzing causes or effects may suggest a subject you would like to explore, or you may still need to find an appropriate subject for your essay. Continue listing possible topics. Making such a list often generates ideas: As you list subjects, you will think of new ideas you cannot imagine now.

Even if you feel confident about a subject you have selected, continue listing other possibilities to test your choice. Try to list specific subjects, and make separate lists for trends, events, and phenomena. Here are some other ideas to consider:

Trends

- Changes in men's or women's roles and opportunities in marriage, education, or work
- Changing patterns in leisure, entertainment, life-style, religious life, health, or technology
- Completed artistic or historical trends (various art movements or historical changes)
- Long-term changes in economic conditions or political behavior or attitudes
- Increasing reliance on the Internet for research, entertainment, shopping, and conversation

Events

- A recent college, community, national, or international event that is surrounded by confusion or controversy
- A recent surprising event at your college, such as the closing of a tutorial or health service, the cancellation of popular classes, a change in library hours or dormitory regulations, the loss of a game by a favored team, or some hateful or violent act by one student against another
- A recent puzzling or controversial event in your community, such as the abrupt resignation of a public official, a public protest by an activist group, a change in traffic laws, a zoning decision, or the banning of a book from school libraries
- A historical event about which there is still some dispute as to its causes or effects

Phenomena

- A social problem, such as discrimination, homelessness, child abuse, illiteracy, high-school dropout rates, youth suicides, or teenage pregnancy
- One or more aspects of college life, such as libraries too noisy to study in, large classes, lack of financial aid, difficulties in scheduling classes, shortcomings in student health services, or insufficient availability of housing (in this essay you would not need to solve the problems, only to speculate about their causes or effects)
- A human trait, such as anxiety, selfishness, fear of success or failure, leadership, jealousy, insecurity, envy, opportunism, curiosity, or restlessness

After you have completed your lists, reflect on the possible topics you have compiled. Because an authoritative essay analyzing causes or effects requires sustained thinking, drafting, revising, and possibly even research, you will want to choose a subject to which you can commit yourself enthusiastically for a week or two. Above all, choose a topic that interests you, even if you feel uncertain about how to approach it. Then consider carefully whether you are more interested in the causes or the effects of the event, trend, or phenomenon. Consider, as well, whether the subject in which you are interested invites speculation about its causes or effects or perhaps even precludes speculation about one or the other. For example, you could speculate about the causes for increasing membership in your church, whereas the effects (the results or consequences) of the increase might for now be so uncertain as to discourage plausible speculation. Some subjects invite speculation about both their causes and effects. For this assignment, however, you need not do both.

Developing Your Subject

The writing and research activities that follow will enable you to test your subject choice and to discover what you have to say about it. Each activity takes only a few minutes but will help you produce a fuller, more focused draft.

Exploring Your Subject. *You may discover that you know more about your subject than you suspect if you write about it for a few minutes without stopping.* This brief sustained writing will stimulate your memory, help you probe your interest in the subject, and enable you to test your subject choice. As you write, consider the following questions:

- What interests me in this subject? What about it will interest my readers?
- What do I already know about the subject?
- Why does the trend, event, or phenomenon not already have an accepted explanation for its causes or effects? What causes or effects have others already suggested for this subject?
- How can I learn more about the subject?

Considering Causes or Effects. *Before you research your subject (should you need to), you want to discover which causes or effects you can already imagine. Make a list of possible causes or effects.* For *causes* consider underlying or background causes, immediate or instigating causes, and ongoing causes. For example, if you lost your job delivering pizzas, an underlying cause could be that years ago a plant-closing in your town devastated the local economy, which has never recovered; an immediate cause could be that the pizza-chain outlet you worked for has been hit hard by the recent arrival of a new pizza-chain outlet; an ongoing cause could be that for several years some health-conscious residents regularly eat salad, rather than pizza, for dinner. For *effects,* consider both short-term and long-term consequences, as well as how one effect may lead to another in a kind of chain reaction. Try to think not only of obvious causes or effects but also of ones that are likely to be overlooked in a superficial analysis of your subject.

Identify the most convincing causes or effects in your list. Do you have enough to make a strong argument? Imagine how you might convince readers of the plausibility of some of these causes or effects.

Researching Your Subject. *When developing an essay analyzing causes or effects, you can often gain great advantage by researching your subject.* (See Appendix 2, Strategies for Research and Documentation.) You can gain a greater understanding of the event, trend, or phenomenon; and you can review and evaluate others' proposed causes or effects in case you want to present any of these alternatives in your own essay. Reviewing others' causes or effects may suggest to you plausible causes or effects you have overlooked. You may also find support for your own counterarguments to readers' objections.

Analyzing Your Readers. *Write for a few minutes, identifying who your readers are, what they know about your subject, and how they can be convinced by your proposed causes or effects.* Describe your readers briefly. Mention anything you know about them as a group that might influence the way they would read your essay. Estimate how much they know about your subject, how extensively you will have to present it to them, and what is required to demonstrate to them the importance of the subject. Speculate about how they will respond to your argument.

Rehearsing Part of Your Argument. *Select one of your causes or effects and write several sentences about it, trying out an argument for your readers.* The heart of your essay will be the argument you make for the plausibility of your proposed causes or effects. Like a ballet dancer or baseball pitcher warming up for a performance, you can prepare for your first draft by rehearsing part of the argument you will make. How will you convince readers to take this cause or effect seriously? This writing activity will focus your thinking and encourage you to keep discovering new arguments until you start drafting. It may also lead you to search for additional support for your speculations.

Testing Your Choice. *Pause now to decide whether you have chosen a subject about which you will be able to make a convincing argument.* At this point you have probed your subject in several ways and have some insights into how you would attempt to present and argue for it with particular readers. If your interest in the subject is growing and you are gaining confidence in the argument you want to make, you have probably made a good choice. However, if your interest in the subject is waning or you have been unable to come up with several plausible causes or effects beyond the simply obvious ones, you may want to consider choosing another subject. If your subject does not seem promising, return to your list of possible subjects to select another.

Considering Visuals. *Consider whether visuals—drawings, photographs, tables, or graphs—would strengthen your argument.* You could construct your own visuals, scan materials from books and magazines, or download them from the Internet. If you submit your essay electronically to other students and your instructor, or if you post it on a Web site, consider including photographs as well as snippets of film or sound. Visual and audio materials are not at all a requirement of an effective speculative essay, as you can tell from the readings in this chapter, but they could add a new dimension to your writing. If you want to use photographs or recordings of people, be sure to obtain their permission.

Considering Your Purpose. *Write for several minutes about your purpose for writing this essay.* The following questions will help you think about your purpose:

- What do I hope to accomplish with my readers? What one big idea do I want them to grasp and remember?
- How can I interest them in my subject? How can I help them see its importance or significance? How can I convince them to take my speculations seriously?
- How much resistance should I expect from readers to each of the causes or effects I propose? Will my readers be largely receptive? Skeptical but convinceable? Resistant and perhaps even antagonistic?

Formulating a Working Thesis. *Draft a thesis statement.* A *working*—as opposed to final—*thesis* enables you to bring your invention work into focus and begin your draft with a clearer purpose. At some point during the drafting of your essay, however, you will likely decide to revise your working thesis or even try out a new one. A thesis for an essay speculating about causes or effects nearly always announces the subject; it may also mention the proposed causes or effects and suggest the direction the argument will take. Here are two sample thesis statements from the readings in this chapter.

- "If one considers that for much of Christian history the population was illiterate and the clergy semiliterate and that authority was far away, one begins to understand that the heritage for most people most of the time was almost entirely story, ritual, ceremony and eventually art. So it has been for most of human history. So it is, I suggest (and my data back me up), even today" (Greeley, paragraph 9).

- "According to a 1994 survey conducted by the Society for Human Resource Management, the percentage of human-resource professionals who have reported that their departments handled at least one sexual-harassment complaint rose from 35 percent in 1991 to 65 percent in 1994. Why did this large increase occur in such a short amount of time? Possible answers to this question surely would include growing awareness of the nature of workplace sexual harassment, government action, efforts of companies to establish anti-harassment policies and encourage harassed employees to come forward, and prominence given by the media to many cases of workplace harassment" (West, paragraph 2).

Notice, for instance, that West's thesis clearly announces her subject—workplace sexual harassment—as well as how she will approach the subject: by focusing on the increase in reported incidents and speculating about the causes of the increase. Her thesis also forecasts her speculations, identifying the causes and the order in which she will argue for them in the essay.

DRAFTING

The following guidelines will help you set goals for your draft and plan its organization.

Setting Goals

Establishing goals for your draft before you begin writing will enable you to make decisions and work more confidently. Consider the following questions now, and keep them in mind as you draft. They will help you set goals for drafting as well as recall how the writers you have read in this chapter tried to achieve similar goals.

- *How can I convince my readers that my proposed causes or effects are plausible?* Should I give many examples, like Greeley does, or quote authorities and published research, as Angier, Cohn, West, and Beaty all do? Can I, like Kozol, include personal anecdotes and cases or, like King and Angier, introduce analogies?
- *How should I anticipate readers' objections to my argument?* What should I do about alternative causes or effects? Should I anticipate readers' objections and questions, like Angier does, or answer readers' likely questions, like Greeley? Can I refute alternative causes, as West does? How can I find common ground—shared attitudes, values, and beliefs—with my readers, even with those whose objections or alternative causes I must refute?

- *How much do my readers need to know about my subject?* Do I need to describe my subject in some detail, in the way that Greeley describes Catholicism for non-Catholics or that West describes the legal context for the rise in reported incidents of workplace sexual harassment? Or can I assume that my readers have personal experience with my subject, as King seems to assume? If my subject is a trend, how can I demonstrate that the trend exists?
- *How can I begin engagingly and end conclusively?* Should I begin, as Angier and Beaty do, by emphasizing the importance or timeliness of my subject? Might I begin with an event like Cohn's, or with an unusual statement like King's? How can I conclude by returning to an idea in the opening paragraph (as Kozol does), restating the urgency of the problem (West and Beaty), or repeating the main cause (Greeley)?
- *How can I establish my authority and credibility to argue the causes or effects of my subject?* Can I do this by showing a comprehensive understanding of the likely effects of the phenomenon, as Kozol does, or by showing a willingness to consider a wide range of causes, like Cohn? Or can I do this by displaying my research (Beaty), by counterarguing responsibly (West), or by relying on what I have learned through research and interviews (Angier)?

Organizing Your Draft

With goals in mind and invention notes at hand, you are ready to make a tentative outline of your draft. The sequence of proposed causes or effects will be at the center of your outline, but you may also want to plan where you will consider alternatives or counterargue objections. Notice that some writers who conjecture about causes consider alternative causes—evaluating, refuting, or accepting them—before they present their own. Much of an essay analyzing causes may be devoted to considering alternatives. Both writers who conjecture about causes and writers who speculate about effects usually consider readers' possible objections to their causes or effects along with the argument for each cause or effect. If you must provide readers with a great deal of information about your subject as context for your argument, you may want to outline this information carefully. For your essay, this part of the outline may be a major consideration. Your plan should make the information readily accessible to your readers. This outline is tentative; you may decide to change it after you start drafting.

READING A DRAFT CRITICALLY

Getting a critical reading of your draft will help you see how to improve it. Your instructor may schedule class time for reading drafts, or you may want to ask a classmate or a tutor in the writing center to read your draft. Ask your reader to use the following guidelines and to write out a response for you to consult during your revision.

Read for a First Impression

1. Read the draft without stopping to annotate or comment, and then write two or three sentences giving your general impression.
2. Identify one aspect of the draft that seems particularly effective.

Read Again to Suggest Improvements

1. Recommend ways to make the presentation of the subject more effective.
   - Read the opening paragraphs that present the subject to be speculated about, and then tell the writer what you find most interesting and useful.
   - Point out one or two places where a reader unfamiliar with the subject might need more information.
   - Suggest ways the writer could make the subject seem more interesting or significant.
   - If the subject is a trend, explain what you understand to be the increase or decrease and let the writer know whether you think further evidence is required to demonstrate conclusively that the subject is indeed a trend.
   - If the beginning seems unlikely to engage readers, suggest at least one other way of beginning.
2. Suggest ways to strengthen the cause or effect argument.
   - List the causes or effects. Tell the writer whether there seem to be too many, too few, or just about the right number. Point to one cause or effect that seems especially imaginative or surprising and to one that seems too obvious. Make suggestions for dropping or adding causes or effects.
   - Evaluate the support for each cause or effect separately. To help the writer make every cause or effect plausible to the intended readers, point out where the support seems thin or inadequate. Point to any support that seems less than appropriate or believable or inconsistent with other support. Consider whether the writer has overlooked important resources of support: anecdotes, examples, statistics, analogies, or quotations from publications or interviews.
3. Suggest ways to strengthen the counterargument.
   - Locate every instance of counterargument—places where the writer anticipates readers' objections or questions or evaluates readers' preferred alternative causes. Mark these in the margin of the draft. Review these as a set, and then suggest objections, questions, and alternative causes or effects the writer seems to have overlooked.

- Identify counterarguments that seem weakly supported and suggest ways the writer might strengthen the support.
- Determine whether any of the refutations attack or ridicule readers and suggest ways the writer could refute without insulting or unduly irritating readers.

4. Suggest how credibility can be enhanced.
   - Tell the writer whether the intended readers are likely to find the essay knowledgeable and authoritative. Point to places where it seems most and least authoritative.
   - Identify places where the writer seeks common ground—shared values, beliefs, and attitudes—with readers. Try to identify places where the writer might attempt to do so.
5. Suggest how the organizational plan could be improved.
   - Consider the overall plan, perhaps by making a scratch outline (see Appendix 1). Analyze closely the progression of the causes or effects. Decide whether the causes or effects follow a logical step-by-step sequence.
   - Suggest ways the causes or effects might be more logically sequenced.
   - Review the places where counterarguments appear and consider whether they are smoothly woven into the argument. Give advice on the best places for the counterarguments.
   - Indicate where new or better transitions might cue the steps in the argument and keep readers on track.
6. Evaluate the effectiveness of visuals.
   - Look at any visuals in the essay, and tell the writer what they contribute to your understanding of the writer's speculations.
   - If any visuals do not seem relevant, or if there seem to be too many visuals, identify the ones that the writer could consider dropping, explaining your thinking.
   - If a visual does not seem to be appropriately placed, suggest a better place for it.

REVISING

This section offers suggestions for revising your draft, suggestions that will remind you of the possibilities for developing a plausible cause or effect argument. Revising means reenvisioning your draft, trying to see it in a new way, given your purpose and readers, in order to strengthen your cause or effect argument.

The biggest mistake you can make while revising is to focus initially on words or sentences. Instead, first try to see your draft as a whole in order to assess its likely impact on your readers. Think imaginatively and boldly about cutting unconvincing material, adding new material, and moving material around. Your computer makes even drastic revisions physically easy, but you still need to make the mental effort and decisions that will improve your draft.

You may have received help with this challenge from a classmate or tutor who gave your draft a critical reading. If so, keep this valuable feedback in mind as you decide which parts of your draft need revising and what specific changes you could make. The following suggestions will help you solve problems and strengthen your essay.

To Present the Subject More Effectively

- If readers unfamiliar with the subject may not understand it readily, provide more information.
- If the importance or significance of the subject is not clear, dramatize it with an anecdote or highlight its social or cultural implications.
- If the subject is a trend, show evidence of a significant increase or decrease over an extended period of time.

To Strengthen the Cause or Effect Argument

- If you propose what seem like too many causes or effects, clarify the role of each one or drop one or more that seem too obvious, obscure, or relatively minor.
- If a cause or effect lacks adequate support, come up with further examples, anecdotes, statistics, or quotes from authorities.

To Strengthen the Counterargument

- If you do not anticipate readers' likely questions about your argument and objections to it, do so now. Remember that you can either accommodate these objections and questions in your argument, conceding their insightfulness by making them part of your own argument, or refute them, arguing that they need not be taken seriously.
- If you do not anticipate readers' likely alternative causes or effects, do so now, conceding or refuting each one.
- If you attack or ridicule readers in your refutations, seek ways to refute their ideas decisively while showing respect for them as people.

- If you neglect to establish common ground with your readers, especially those who may think about your subject quite differently from the way you think about it, attempt to show them that you share some common values, attitudes, and beliefs.

To Enhance Credibility

- If readers of your draft question your credibility as a writer of cause or effect argument, learn more about your subject, support your argument more fully, anticipate a wider range of readers' likely objections, or talk with others who can help you think more imaginatively about your speculations.
- If your choice of words or your approach to readers weakens your credibility, consider your word choices throughout the essay and look for ways to show readers respect and to establish common ground with them.

To Organize More Logically and Coherently

- If readers question the logical sequence of your causes or effects, consider strengthening your plan by adding or dropping causes or effects or resequencing them. Ensure that one cause or effect leads to the next in a logically linked chain of reasoning.
- If your logic seems sound but the links are not clear to your readers, provide meaningful transitions from one step in the argument to the next.
- If your various counterarguments are not smoothly integrated into your argument, move them around to make the connections clearer.

EDITING AND PROOFREADING

After you have revised your essay, be sure to spend some time checking for errors in usage, punctuation, and mechanics and considering matters of style. If you keep a list of errors you typically make, begin by checking your draft against this list. Ask someone else to proofread your essay before you print out a copy for your instructor or send it electronically.

From our research on student writing, we know that essays speculating about causes or effects have a high percentage of errors in the use of numbers and "reason is because" sentences. Because you must usually rely on numbers to present statistics when you support your argument or demonstrate the existence of a trend, you may yourself be unsure about the conventions for presenting different kinds of numbers. Because you are usually drawn into "reason is because" sentences when you make a causal argument, you will need to know options for revising such sentences. Refer to a writer's handbook for help with these two potential problems.

REFLECTING ON WHAT YOU HAVE LEARNED

Speculating about Causes or Effects

In this chapter, you have read critically several essays that speculate about causes or effects and have written one of your own. To better remember what you have learned, pause now to reflect on the reading and writing activities you completed in this chapter.

1. *Write* a page or so reflecting on what you have learned. *Begin* by describing what you are most pleased with in your essay. Then *explain* what you think contributed to your achievement. *Be specific* about this contribution.

   - If it was something you learned from the readings, *indicate* which readings and specifically what you learned from them.
   - If it came from your invention writing, *point out* the section or sections that helped you most.
   - If you got good advice from a critical reader, *explain* exactly how the person helped you—perhaps by helping you understand a particular problem in your draft or by adding a new dimension to your writing.

2. Now *reflect* more generally on speculation about causes or effects, a genre of writing that plays an important role in social life and public policy in the United States. *Consider* some of the following questions: Do you tend to adopt a tentative or an assertive stance when making speculations? Why do you think you generally adopt this stance over the other? How might your personal preferences and values influence your speculations? How might your gender, ethnicity, religious beliefs, age, or social class influence your ideas about a subject? What contribution might essays speculating about causes or effects make to our society that other genres cannot make?

CHAPTER 

Proposal to Solve a Problem

Proposals are vital to democratic institutions. By reading and writing proposals, citizens and colleagues learn about problems affecting their well-being and explore possible actions that could be taken to remedy these problems. People read and write proposals every day in government, business, education, and the professions.

Many proposals address social problems and attempt to influence the direction of public policy. For example, a student activist group writes a proposal advocating that all campus food services be restricted from using genetically manufactured foods until the potential health hazards of such foods have been fully researched. A special United Nations task force recommends ways to eliminate acid rain worldwide. The College Entrance Examination Board commissions a report proposing strategies for reversing the decline in Scholastic Assessment Test (SAT) scores. A specialist in children's television writes a book suggesting that the federal government fund the development of new educational programming for preschool and elementary school students.

Proposals are also a basic ingredient of the world's work. A team of engineers and technical writers in a transportation firm, for example, might write a proposal to compete for a contract to build a new subway system. The manager of a fashion outlet might write a memo to a company executive proposing an upgrading of the computer system to include networking within the chain of stores. Seeking funding to support her research on a new cancer treatment, a university professor might write a proposal to the National Institute of Health.

Still other proposals are written by individuals who want to solve problems involving groups or communities to which they belong. A college student irritated by long waits to see a nurse at the campus health clinic writes the clinic director, proposing a more efficient way to schedule and accommodate students. After funding for dance classes has been cut by their school board, students and parents interested in dance write a proposal to the school principal, asking her help in arranging after-school classes taught by a popular high-school teacher who would be paid with community funds. The board of directors of a historical society in a small ranching community proposes to the county board of supervisors that it donate an unused county building to the society so it can display historical records, photographs, and artifacts.

Proposal writing requires a critical questioning attitude—wondering about alternative approaches to bringing about change, puzzling over how a goal might be achieved, questioning why a process unfolds in a particular way, posing challenges to the status quo. In addition, it demands imagination and creativity. To solve a problem, you need to see it anew, to look at it from new perspectives and in new contexts.

Because a proposal tries to convince readers that its way of analyzing and creatively solving the problem makes sense, proposal writers must be sensitive to readers' needs and different perspectives. Readers need to know details of the solution and to be convinced that it will solve the problem and can be implemented. If readers initially favor a different solution, knowing why the writer rejects it will help them decide whether to support or reject the writer's proposed solution. Readers may be wary of costs, demands on their time, superficial changes, and grand schemes.

As you plan and draft a proposal, you will want to determine whether your readers know about the problem and whether they recognize its seriousness. In addition, you will want to consider how your readers might rate other possible solutions. Knowing what your readers know, what their assumptions and biases are, and what kinds of arguments will be appealing to them is crucial to proposal writing, as it is to all good argumentative writing.

Reading the proposal essays in this chapter will help you discover why the genre is so important and how it works. From the readings and from the suggestions for writing that follow each reading, you will get ideas for your own proposal essay. As you read and write about the selections, keep in mind the following assignment, which sets out the goals for writing a proposal. To support your writing of this assignment, the chapter concludes with a Guide to Writing Proposals.

THE WRITING ASSIGNMENT

Proposal

Write an essay proposing a solution to a problem affecting a community or group to which you belong. Your tasks are to analyze the problem and establish that it is serious enough to need solving, to offer a solution that will remedy the problem or at least help solve it, and to lay out the particulars by which your proposed solution would be put into effect. Address your proposal to one or more members of the group or to outsiders who could help solve the problem, being sure to take into account readers' likely objections to your proposed solution as well as their alternative solutions.

WRITING SITUATIONS FOR PROPOSALS

Writing that proposes solutions to problems plays a significant role in college and professional life, as the following examples indicate.

- Frustrated by what they see as the failure of high schools to prepare students for the workplace, managers of a pharmaceuticals company decide to develop a proposal to move vocational and technical training out of an ill-equipped high-school system and onto the plant's floor. Seven divisional managers plus the firm's technical writers meet weekly to plan the proposal. They read about other on-the-job training programs and interview selected high-school teachers and current employees who attended the high-school program they want to replace. After several months' research, they present to the company CEO and to the school board a proposal that includes a timetable for implementing their solution and a detailed budget.
- For a political science class, a college student analyzes the question of presidential term limits. Citing examples from recent history, she argues that U.S. presidents spend the first year of each term getting organized and the fourth year either running for reelection or weakened by their status as a lame duck. Consequently, they are fully productive for only half of their four-year terms. She proposes limiting presidents to one six-year term, claiming that this change would remedy the problem by giving presidents four or five years to put their programs into effect. She acknowledges that it could make presidents less responsive to the public will, but insists that the system of legislative checks and balances would make that problem unlikely.
- For an economics class, a student looks into the many problems arising from *maquiladoras,* new industries in Mexico near the border with the United States that provide foreign exchange for the Mexican government, low-paying jobs for Mexican workers, and profits for American manufacturers. He discovers that in Mexico there are problems of inadequate housing, health care, injuries on the job, and environmental damage. His instructor encourages him to select one of the problems, research it more thoroughly, and propose a solution. Taking injuries on the job as the problem most immediately within the control of American manufacturers, he proposes that they observe standards established by the U.S. Occupational Safety and Health Administration.

A Guide to Reading Proposals

This guide introduces you to proposal writing. By completing all the activities in it, you will prepare yourself to learn a great deal from the other readings in this chapter about how to read and write a proposal. The guide focuses on a proposal by Robert J. Samuelson, a well-known writer on social and economic issues. You will read Samuelson's essay twice. First, you will read it for meaning, seeking to understand Samuelson's argument and the meaning it holds for you. Then, you will reread the essay like a writer, analyzing the parts to see how Samuelson constructs his argument and to learn the strategies he uses to make his proposal effective. These two activities—reading for meaning and reading like a writer—follow every reading in this chapter.

ROBERT J. SAMUELSON

Reforming Schools through a Federal Test for College Aid

Robert J. Samuelson (b. 1945) began his journalism career at the Washington Post *in 1969, after earning a B.A. in government from Harvard, and became a contributing editor for* Newsweek *in 1984. For his syndicated column on economic and social issues, Samuelson has won numerous journalism awards, including four National Headliner Awards, three Gerald Loeb Awards, and a Clarion Award from The Association of Women in Communications. In addition, Samuelson has published two books,* The Good Life and Its Discontents: The American Dream and the Age of Entitlement 1945–1995 *(1996) and* Untruth: Why the Conventional Wisdom Is (Almost Always) Wrong *(2001).*

The following proposal, "Reforming Schools through a Federal Test for College Aid," was first published in Newsweek *in 1991, but the problem it addresses continues today. When Samuelson refers to "the Bush plan," know that he means President George H. W. Bush (1989–1993), not his son, George W. Bush (2001–). Seeking to encourage individual states to voluntarily participate in the National Assessment of Educational Progress (NAEP), the elder Bush proposed a federally funded system of testing students in relation to national standards established for such disciplines as mathematics, reading, science, writing, U.S. history, and geography. This voluntary school testing program was implemented during the Clinton administration, and in 2001 the younger Bush recommended that the testing be made mandatory. You may remember taking these exams periodically when you were in high school. The NAEP tests do not grade students individually; they report grades for the entire school so that school boards, parents, and legislators can assess which schools excel or need improvement. Samuelson argues that such tests do little to improve schools because they fail to motivate students. Instead, he proposes a federal test for college financial aid, which he argues would both motivate students and put pressure on high schools to better prepare students for college.*

Like most of Samuelson's original Newsweek *readers, you have experience with high-school testing that puts you in an excellent position to judge his proposal. As you read it, write your reactions to and questions about his argument in the margins of the text.*

We are not yet serious about school reform. The latest plan from the Bush administration mixes lofty rhetoric (a pledge to "invent new schools") with vague proposals to rate our schools with national tests. It doesn't address the most dreary—and important—fact about American education: our students don't work very hard. The typical high-school senior does less than an hour of homework an evening. No school reform can succeed unless this changes. What's depressing is that we could change it, but probably won't. 1

We could require students receiving federal college aid to pass a qualifying test. This is a huge potential lever. Nearly two-thirds of high-school graduates go to college (including community colleges and vocational schools), and roughly two-fifths—6 million students—get federal aid. In fiscal 1991, government grants and guaranteed loans totaled $18.1 billion. As a practical matter any federal test would also affect many unaided students; most colleges couldn't easily maintain a lower entrance requirement for the rich. The message would be: anyone wanting to go to college can't glide through high school. 2

Just how well our schools perform depends heavily on student attitudes. This is one reason why the Bush plan, which proposes tests to evaluate schools, is so empty. The tests hold no practical consequences for students and, therefore, lack the power to motivate them. When students aren't motivated, they don't treat school seriously. Without serious students, it's hard to attract good people into teaching no matter how much we pay them. And bad teachers ensure educational failure. This is the vicious circle we must break. 3

Unfortunately, we don't now expect much of our students. For most high-school students, it doesn't pay to work hard. Their goal is college, and almost anyone can go to some college. There are perhaps 50 truly selective colleges and universities in the country, Chester Finn Jr., professor of education at Vanderbilt University, writes in his new book, *We Must Take Charge: Our Schools and Our Future*. To survive, the other 3,400 institutions of "higher learning" eagerly recruit students. Entrance requirements are meager and financial assistance from states and the federal government is abundant. 4

"Coast and get into college and have the same opportunities as someone who worked hard," says one senior quoted by Finn. "That is the system." It's this sort of silly rationalization that hurts American students, precisely because they can't always make up what they've missed in the past. Opportunities go only to those who have real skills—not paper credentials or many years spent on campus. The college dropout rate is staggering. After six years, less than half of students at four-year colleges have earned a degree. The graduation rate is even lower for community colleges. 5

Every other advanced society does it differently. "The United States is the only industrial country that doesn't have some (testing) system external to the schools to assess educational achievement," says Max Eckstein, an expert on international education. Their tests, unlike ours, typically determine whether students can continue in school. As the lone holdout, we can compare our system with everyone else's. Well, we rank near the bottom on most international comparisons. 6

In the media, the school "crisis" is often pictured as mainly a problem of providing a better education for the poor and minorities. Stories focus on immigrants and inner-city schools. Almost everyone else is (by omission) presumed to be getting an adequate education. Forget it. In fact, the test scores of our poorest students, though still abysmally low, have improved. Likewise, high-school dropout rates have declined. What we minimize is the slippage of our average schools. 7

COMMON SENSE

When mediocrity is the norm, even good students suffer. In international comparisons, our top students often fare poorly against other countries' top students, notes economist John Bishop of Cornell University. Grade inflation is widespread. In 1990 1.1 million high-school students took the college board exams. These are the best students: 28 percent had A averages, 53 percent B's and the rest C's. Yet, two-fifths of these students scored less than 390 on the verbal SAT. 8

The idea that college-bound students should be required (by test) to demonstrate the ability to do college-level work is common sense. It's hard to see how anyone could object, especially with so much public money at stake. But almost no educators or political leaders advocate it. The American belief in "equality" and "fairness" makes it hard for us to create barriers that block some students. Our approach is more indirect and dishonest: first, we give them meaningless high-school degrees; then we let them drop out of college. 9

The same spirit of self-deception pervades much of the school debate. We skirt the obvious—students will work if there's a good reason—and pursue painless and largely fictitious cures. There's a constant search for new teaching methods and technologies that will, somehow, miraculously mesmerize students and automatically educate them. Computers are a continuing fad. Liberals blame educational failure on inadequate spending; conservatives lambaste public schools as rigid bureaucracies. These familiar critiques are largely irrelevant. 10

Low spending isn't the main problem. Between 1970 and 1990, "real" (inflation adjusted) spending per student in public schools rose 63 percent. In 1989, U.S. educational spending totaled 6.9 percent of gross national product, which equals or exceeds most nations'. As for "vouchers" and "choice"—conservatives' current cure—the experiment has already been tried in higher education. It failed. Government loans and grants are vouchers that allow students choice. The perverse result is that colleges compete by reducing entrance requirements in order to increase enrollments and maximize revenues. 11

A test for college aid would stem this corrosive process. The number of college freshmen would decline, but not—given the high dropout rates—the number of college graduates. Because high-school standards are so lax, the passing grade of any meaningful test would flunk many of today's seniors. Tests are available, because a few state college systems, such as New Jersey's and Tennessee's, give them to freshmen. Failing students must take remedial courses. In 1990, 37 percent of New Jersey freshmen flunked a verbal-skills test and 58 percent an algebra test. 12

AN UPROAR

Who would be hurt? Not students who can pass the test today: that's perhaps 40 to 60 percent of college freshmen. Not students who might pass the test with more study: that's another big fraction. (In New Jersey and Tennessee, most students pass remedial courses. If they can do it at 18 or 19, they can do it at 17.) Some students who now go to college wouldn't. Often, these students drop out after saddling themselves with a hefty student loan. Would they be worse off? On college loans, default rates range as high as 25 percent. 13

But let's be candid. None of this is about to happen soon. Requiring tests for college aid would cause an uproar. There would be charges of elitism, maybe racism. Colleges and universities would resist. They depend on the current open-ended flow of students and, without it, some would have to shut down. This wouldn't be bad for the country, because we now overinvest in 14 higher education. With one-fifth the students, colleges and universities account for two-fifths of all educational spending. But today's waste has spawned a huge constituency.

15 Little wonder that President Bush—and all politicians—steer clear of this sort of reform. It's too direct. It wouldn't cure all our educational problems, but it would make a start. It would jolt students, parents and teachers. It would foster a climate that rewards effort. It would create pressures for real achievement, not just inflated grades. It would force schools to pay more attention to non-college-bound students, rather than assuming everyone can go somewhere. It would strip away our illusions, which, sadly, are precisely what we cherish most.

READING FOR MEANING

Write to create meanings for Samuelson's proposal that students take a test administered by the federal government in order to receive federal aid for college.

Start Making Meaning

Begin by writing about Samuelson's definition of the problem as one of student motivation (paragraphs 3–6), restating briefly what he has to say and describing your reaction to it. Continue by writing about anything else in the essay or in your experience that contributes to your understanding of and response to Samuelson's proposal.

If You Are Stuck

If you cannot write at least a page, consider writing about

- the "vicious circle" (paragraph 3), explaining what Samuelson means to convey with that phrase and evaluating it from your perspective as a former high-school student.
- Samuelson's statement, "When mediocrity is the norm, even good students suffer" (paragraph 8).
- the alternative solutions Samuelson refutes in paragraphs 10 and 11, describing one or two of them and giving your opinion about their potential value in improving high-school students' preparation for college.
- the "uproar" Samuelson expects would greet his proposal, commenting on his prediction that "there would be charges of elitism, maybe racism" (paragraph 14).

READING LIKE A WRITER

This section guides you through an analysis of Samuelson's argumentative strategies: *introducing the problem; presenting the solution; arguing directly for the proposed solution; counterarguing readers' objections, questions, and preferred solutions;* and *establishing credibility.* For each strategy you will be asked to reread and annotate part of Samuelson's essay to see how he uses the strategy in "Reforming Schools through a Federal Test for College Aid."

When you study the selections later in this chapter, you will see how different writers use these same strategies. The Guide to Writing Proposals near the end of the chapter suggests ways you can use these strategies in writing your own proposal.

Introducing the Problem

Every proposal begins with a problem. Depending on what their readers know about the problem, writers may explain how it came to be or what attempts have been made to solve it. Sometimes, readers are already aware of a problem, especially if it affects them directly. In such cases, the writer can merely identify the problem and move directly to presenting a solution. At other times, readers may be unaware that the problem exists or may have difficulty imagining the problem. In these situations, the writer may have to describe the problem in detail, helping readers recognize its importance and the consequences of failing to solve it.

Writers may also believe that readers misunderstand the problem, failing to recognize it for what it really is. They may then decide that their first task is to redefine the problem in a way that helps readers see it in a different way. Samuelson does precisely that. Because he believes that efforts to reform American schools are doomed because they fail to recognize the real problem, his opening strategy must be to redefine the problem.

Analyze

1. *Reread* paragraphs 3–6, noting in the margin which kinds of support Samuelson uses to convince readers that the problem should be redefined as one of student motivation. Where does he point to causes of the problem and to its consequences, rely on comparisons, quote authorities, give examples, make use of statistics, or make judgments?

2. *Consider* how effectively Samuelson redefines the problem. As one of his intended readers, *explain* why you are or are not convinced of his redefinition. In what ways might he have made his argument more convincing?

Write

Write several sentences explaining Samuelson's strategy for introducing the problem and evaluating how convincing you find his argument. *Give details* from the reading.

Presenting the Solution

The proposal writer's primary purposes are to convince readers of the wisdom of the proposal solution and to take action on its implementation. In order to achieve these purposes, the writer must ensure that readers can imagine the solution being implemented.

Some proposals have little chance of success unless every small step for implementing them is detailed for readers. For this reason, a proposed solution to a highly technical engineering problem might run many pages in length. In contrast, a more general proposal, such as Samuelson's idea for encouraging greater student preparedness for college through federal testing and incentives, could be brief. This type of proposal seeks to gain readers' adherence to the principle of testing and defers the implementation—the types of tests, when they would be offered, how they would be evaluated, and so forth—to specialists who would work out the details later. Although the writer may think that detailing the implementation is premature, some critical readers might be skeptical that the tests Samuelson proposes would escape the problems that already exist for similar national tests such as the SAT. As you look closely at the way Samuelson presents his solution, you will want to consider how well he handles the question of implementation given his purpose, his space limitations, and his *Newsweek* readers' expectations.

Analyze

1. *Reread* paragraph 12, and *underline* the few details Samuelson gives about his proposed solution.
2. Keeping in mind his space constraints, *list* two or three additional key details Samuelson might have included to help readers more easily imagine how his proposed solution would be implemented.

Write

List the details Samuelson gives about his proposed federal test for financial aid. Then *add a few sentences* evaluating whether Samuelson gives enough details for you to imagine how the solution might be implemented, even though it is not spelled out.

Arguing Directly for the Proposed Solution

In arguing for solutions, writers rely on two interrelated strategies: arguing directly for the proposed solution and counterarguing readers' likely objections, questions, and preferred solutions. (We take up the second strategy, counterargument, in the next section.)

A proposal is not a proposal without some argument supporting the solution. It may describe a situation well or complain with great feeling about a problem; if it goes no further, however, it cannot be a proposal. Writers must try to convince readers that the solution presented will actually alleviate the problem. The solution should appear feasible, cost-effective, and more promising than alternative solutions.

Proposal writers should ask themselves why the solution would work and support their argument. Such support may include personal experience, hypothetical cases and scenarios, statistics, facts, assertions, examples, speculations about causes or consequences, and quotations from authorities. The most convincing support surprises readers: They see it and think, "I never thought of it that way."

Whatever else proposal writers do, they must argue energetically, imaginatively, and sensitively for their proposed solutions. Although Samuelson describes his solution only briefly and says almost nothing about how it might be implemented, he does argue energetically for it, relying on a variety of strategies.

Analyze

1. *Reread* paragraphs 8, 12, 13, and 15, where Samuelson argues directly for his solution. In each of these paragraphs, *underline* the one main reason Samuelson gives for advocating his solution.

2. *Review* these paragraphs, this time noting in the margin the kinds of support Samuelson offers.

3. *Consider* the strengths of Samuelson's direct argument for his solution. What do you find most and least convincing in his reasons and support?

Write

Write several sentences describing and evaluating Samuelson's argument in the paragraphs you analyzed. What kinds of reasons and support does he use? *Give examples* from the reading. *Conclude with a few more sentences* that evaluate the effectiveness of Samuelson's argument.

Counterarguing Readers' Objections, Questions, and Preferred Solutions

As they argue for their solutions, experienced writers are continually aware of readers' objections to the argument or questions about it. Writers may *accommodate* readers' likely objections and questions by modifying their own arguments. What better way to disarm a skeptical or antagonistic reader! Or writers may *refute* readers' objections and questions; that is, try to show them to be wrong. Experienced arguers bring their readers' questions and objections right into their arguments. They do not ignore their reader's concerns or conveniently assume that readers are on their side.

Experienced proposal writers may also acknowledge other solutions. When a writer knows or suspects readers may have alternative solutions in mind, it is best to discuss them directly in the argument. If Samuelson had failed to acknowledge obvious alternative solutions, readers would have regarded him as ill-informed about the problem. A writer can integrate all or part of an alternative solution into his or her own solution, or refute or dismiss the alternative as unworkable.

Analyze

1. *Reread* paragraphs 7 and 13, where Samuelson anticipates readers' likely objections and questions. *Underline* the specific objections or questions against which Samuelson seems to be counterarguing. Then *note in the margin* whether he accommodates or refutes the objections and the strategies he uses to do so.
2. *Reread* paragraphs 10 and 11, where Samuelson opposes some popular alternative solutions. *Identify* the alternative solutions. Then *consider* whether Samuelson accommodates or refutes the alternatives and how he goes about doing so.

Write

Write a few sentences explaining how Samuelson counterargues. *Give examples* of both objections or questions and alternative solutions. Then *write a few more sentences* evaluating Samuelson's counterarguments. How successfully do you think he handles readers' likely objections or questions? How do you think advocates of the alternative solutions Samuelson evaluates would respond to his counterargument?

Establishing Credibility

For an argument to be considered credible by readers, they must find it authoritative, believable, or trustworthy. Readers have many ways of deciding whether an argument is credible. They may already know the writer by reputation. They may have confidence in the magazine or book where the argument is published. They may learn current information about the writer—jobs held, degrees earned, books published, awards won, and so on—from a biographical note published with the reading. The most important basis for readers' judgments about credibility, however, is the argument itself—the attitudes toward readers revealed in the writer's choice of wording and use of sources, the ring of truth in interview quotes and personal experience stories, the step-by-step logic of the argument, the plausibility of reasons, the adequacy of support, and the sensitivity in handling readers' likely questions, objections, and preferred solutions.

Analyze

1. *Reread* the biographical note introducing Samuelson's essay. How do the facts given there contribute to the credibility of his argument? What do you know about the publications he has worked for and published in? What more might you want to know?

2. Keeping in mind that you are among the intended readers of Samuelson's argument, *skim the essay* with a focus on assessing the credibility of the writer and his argument. *Note in the margin* your impressions and judgments.

Write

Write several sentences describing the impression you have of Samuelson from both the biographical headnote and his essay. What makes you trust or distrust his argument? *Give examples* from his argument to support your answer.

Readings

ROB RYDER

10 Is a Crowd, So Change the Game

Rob Ryder writes screenplays and directs movies. Because of his experience playing and coaching basketball, he has served as an adviser on several hoop-related movies.

Ryder's proposal to turn basketball into an eight-player game was originally published in 1998, in the New York Times *sports section. His style is informal, like that of a sports announcer at work. The sentences and paragraphs tend to be short, and the words are familiar ones, except for a few technical terms from basketball. Ryder mentions several professional basketball players and coaches, but you need not recognize them or know much about the game to follow his proposal. Your experience with any sport will help you understand Ryder's attempt to make basketball a more challenging and entertaining game.*

As you read, think about how Ryder attempts to convince readers that there is a problem with basketball as it is currently played and that his proposed solution would improve the game.

Along with about a billion other people on this planet, I've had a lifelong love affair with basketball. I've known the game as a player (Princeton), as a coach (Hollywood Y.M.C.A. 5- to 8-year-olds), and as a basketball supervisor for the movies (*White Men Can't Jump*, *Blue Chips*, and *Eddie* among others). 1

So, it is with deep regret that I must finally go public with the truth: Basketball is a mess. A muddled, boring, chaotic, overcrowded, utterly predictable game of slapping, clawing, double and triple-teaming, endless stoppages, timeouts, whistles, whining, and countless trips to the free-throw line where players continue to stupefy us with their ineptitude. 2

Yet the game is still punctuated by enough moments of pure poetry, grace, power and creativity to keep us coming back for more. 3

So, now that we can admit the game is flawed, let's fix it. 4

I'm not tinkering here—this is no "raise the rim," "widen the lane" Band-Aid I'm proposing. Rather, I'm going straight to the heart of the problem. It's just too crowded out there. Basketball is meant to be played four on four. 5

Too radical? You're forgetting your American heritage. It's our game. We invented it; we can change it if we want to. (I'm sure 6 there was a lot of groaning when the forward pass was introduced to football.)

When I ran the concept of four-on-four basketball, or 8-Ball, by Doc Rivers during the filming of *Eddie,* his eyes lighted up. 7

"Guards would rule," he said. Not necessarily, but we'll get to that later. Working on another movie, *The Sixth Man,* I proposed the change to Jerry Tarkanian, who replied: "I've been saying that for years. I've been saying that for years." When I asked Marty Blake, the crusty old N.B.A. war horse, he responded, "What, are you nuts?" 8

Yeah. And so was James Naismith. The man almost got it right. But how many realize that in the old days, there was a jump ball after every basket scored? Or that teams were allowed to hold the ball indefinitely? Or that there wasn't always a 3-point shot? 9

The new game will be a lean, sleek, fluid game—dominated by high-flying superbly coordinated athletes, with no room for defensive ends. Charles Oakley, I love your work ethic, but you're going to have trouble keeping up. 10

Kobe Bryant, Tim Duncan, Keith Van Horn, Ray Allen, the future is yours. 11

Lisa Leslie, Teresa Edwards, Venus Lacey, you too will love 8-Ball. As will all the little kids out there whose Saturday morning games often resemble two swarms of bees fighting over a Rollo. 12

Remember the pick-and-roll?—now it's more commonly known as the pick-and-collide-into-two-defenders-coming-from-the-weak-side. In 8-Ball, the pick-and-roll will rule. Help from the weak side leaves the defense much more vulnerable without the fifth defender there to rotate over the passing lane. 13

The old back-door play (which only Princeton seems to pull off regularly these days) will be back. Only now, there will be a cleaner path to the basket. Defenders, deny your man the ball at your own peril. 14

But what about Doc Rivers's comment that guards would rule playing four on four? Tell that to Hakeem Olajuwon, who cannot only run the floor but will now also have enough room for his dazzling array of post-up moves. 15

You see, everybody wins: The big men will finally have some space, the shooters will get plenty of open looks from the 3-point line, and the slashers, like Eddie Jones, should have a field day with one fewer defender out there to clog the lane. 16

So just what are we sacrificing by going to four on four? 17

Well, the lumbering big man will go the way of the dinosaur. Sorry, George Mhuresan, but no one's going to cover for you 18 when your man releases and beats you downcourt. A four on three is infinitely tougher to defend than a five on four.

19 And for you little guys, if you can't shoot, you're a liability.

20 There'll be a lot less room for the role player out there because 8-Ball will demand that every player on the floor polish his or her overall skills.

21 So where's the downside? Nolan Richardson knows—as Arkansas' 94-feet-of-hell amoeba defense will be reduced to a quick detour through purgatory. It'll be a lot tougher to press full court with only four defenders. Any good ballhandler will be able to break the press, and this will definitely hurt the college and high school game.

22 For the pros, it's a moot point—full-court pressure disappeared years ago. Even Rick Pitino's on his way to discovering how tough it is to ask pro athletes to press full court over an 82-game season.

23 But will this mean a reduction of the 12-man roster, reduced playing time and howls from the N.B.A. Players' Association?

24 Not at all, for two reasons. One, 8-Ball will be a running game, and in some ways may adopt the more exciting characteristics of hockey (yes, hockey). Coaches may actually find themselves injecting four new players into a game simultaneously (a line change)—a nifty way to ratchet up the action while giving your starters a rest.

25 And secondly, in the world of 8-Ball, the time of game will expand; in the pros, from 48 to 60 minutes. But how do you keep these games from running over three hours?

26 In 8-Ball, the time wasted on stupor-inducing foul shooting will be reduced by two-thirds, allowing for extra minutes of real action. Whenever a player is fouled but not in the act of shooting, his team automatically gets the ball out of bounds. When fouled in the act of shooting, a player gets one free throw worth 2 points or 3 points, depending on the shot he was taking. But in both cases, the offensive team gets the option of skipping the foul line and taking the ball out of bounds.

27 This will eliminate the ugly strategy of intentional fouling, choke-induced shooting and subhuman fan behavior all in one easy stroke.

28 A good basketball game is about rhythm, and 8-Ball will flow.

29 The substitutions will make for marvelous matchups. We'll see more fast breaks, cleaner inside moves, purer shooting, more offensive rebounding, fewer turnovers, a lot less standing around, more minutes of actual action, and more scoring.

30 Plus, 8-Ball would bring forth the elimination of what must be the stupidest addition to N.B.A. rules: the illegal defense viola-

tion. Just try playing a four-man zone in 8-Ball. It'll turn to a man-to-man real fast.

There it is, 8-Ball. Is there any realistic chance that the N.C.A.A. or the N.B.A. will change over to four on four? "Never happen," Dick Vitale answered. 31

That's why a group of former Princeton players is launching a professional basketball league—the "8BL." Look for it in '99 following a televised exhibition this fall. In the meantime, all you rec league and intramural players out there—with your smaller courts and running clocks and purists' love for the game—8-Ball's for you, too. Show us the way. 32

READING FOR MEANING

Write to create meanings for Ryder's proposal to make basketball a game with eight players.

Start Making Meaning

Begin by explaining the problem Ryder has with current-day basketball, listing a few of the changes he envisions (paragraphs 10–16, 21, 24, 25, and 29). Continue by writing about anything else in the essay or in your experience that contributes to your understanding of Ryder's proposal.

If You Are Stuck

If you cannot write at least a page, consider writing about

- why Ryder refers to the introduction of the forward pass in football (paragraph 6) when his focus is basketball.
- the changes you imagine in eight-player basketball beyond those mentioned by Ryder or a specific change you would like to see in some other established sport, relating the change to the one Ryder proposes.
- why you think Ryder mentions people like Doc Rivers and James Naismith and brings up his own experience as a "basketball supervisor for the movies" (paragraph 1).
- how your personal experience of playing or watching basketball contributes to your understanding of and response to Ryder's proposal.

READING LIKE A WRITER

COUNTERARGUING READERS' OBJECTIONS, QUESTIONS, AND PREFERRED SOLUTIONS

Because proposal writers want their readers to accept their proposed solutions and sometimes even take action to help implement them, they must make an extraordinary effort to anticipate their readers' objections and questions. This task is a major part of what is known as *counterarguing.* From trying out his proposal on several basketball experts (see paragraphs 7, 8, and 31), Ryder knows that some readers will resist it. In recognizing that he is "not tinkering" but proposing a substantial change, he assumes that most readers will at least be startled by his proposal, raising many questions if not also objections. In fact, the first question he anticipates—"Too radical?" (paragraph 6)—confirms that he knows his proposal will be a hard sell. Consequently, Ryder devotes a large part of his essay to counterargument. The following activity will guide you in analyzing his approach. It will also prepare you for counterarguing convincingly in your own proposal.

Analyze

1. *Reread* paragraphs 17, 21, 23, and 25, and *underline* the four readers' questions Ryder mentions in order to counterargue. *Choose two* of these questions and counterarguments to analyze closely.
2. *Notice* that Ryder answers the questions by countering them with the advantages of his proposal. For the two questions you have chosen, *underline* the specific advantages to the game he mentions in his attempt to allay readers' concerns.
3. *Evaluate* how successfully Ryder answers the two questions you have chosen. Does he offer enough advantages to the game to make his answer convincing? Which answer seems more convincing and why? What other questions do you have that Ryder overlooks?

Write

Write several sentences explaining how Ryder anticipates and responds to readers' questions. *Cite examples* from the reading. Then *add a few sentences* describing how successful you find Ryder's answers to the two questions you focused on in your analysis.

CONSIDERING IDEAS FOR YOUR OWN WRITING

Following Ryder's lead, consider proposing a way to improve a popular sport. Your idea need not revolutionize the sport, though it might. Or it could offer only a small refinement such as changing a rule or adding a feature to the game. (Relatively recent developments such as the designated hitter in baseball and instant replays to resolve disputed official calls in football were originally subjects of proposals.) Your proposal could seek to improve the safety of the game for participants, the way records are kept, the way athletes are recruited into the sport, the way athletes are treated, or the entertainment value of the game to spectators. You could focus on either a professional or amateur sport, a team sport or individual competition, high-school or college teams, or the National Hockey League. You could address your proposal to players, officials, fans, or the general public.

Another idea for writing is to identify a problem that needs to be solved in some activity or enterprise that everyone seems to think is working nearly perfectly, that no one seems to be questioning, or that people would initially strongly resist changing in any way. Capture readers' interest, as Ryder does, by announcing to readers that an activity as widely—and wildly—popular as playing basketball could be improved. Such a proposal would be in the respected American tradition of debunking authorities. Possible topics include the convention of taking a honeymoon after a wedding, commuting to work or school by car, the institution of small-claims court, food or service at the most popular place to eat on or near campus, or the youth program at a local church.

EDWARD J. LOUGHRAN

Prevention of Delinquency

Edward J. Loughran (b. 1939) served as commissioner of the Massachusetts Department of Youth Services from 1985 to 1993. From 1993 to 1996, for the Robert F. Kennedy Memorial Foundation he administered the National Juvenile Justice Project to assist corrections agencies throughout the country. He is presently executive director of the Council of Juvenile Correctional Administrators and president of Loughran and Associates, a consulting firm. In addition to consulting, teaching, and lecturing, Loughran writes on the subject of juvenile justice. Balancing Juvenile Justice, *written with Professor Susan Gorino-Ghezzi, was published in 1995.*

The following proposal first appeared in Education Week *in 1990, a newspaper read by public and private school administrators, school board members, and state and federal education policymakers. For Loughran, a specialist in youth services, the problem is the increasing number of young people who are jailed (or, as he says, "incarcerated" or "institutionalized") each year. He has in mind a solution that requires early attention to troubled eight- to twelve-year-olds in their homes, schools, and neighborhoods. You will be interested to see the range of specific programs he recommends, one of them involving college students as paid tutors and mentors.*

Loughran begins by contrasting two responses to the problem of teenage delinquency: putting offenders in jail versus assigning them to community-based programs. As you read, pay close attention to how the writer presents the problem and argues for its seriousness.

1 The National Council on Crime and Delinquency recently reported that the number of young people incarcerated in the United States reached 53,000 last year—the highest number in the nation's history, despite a decline over the last decade in the juvenile population.

2 Many of these youths are placed in large, overcrowded facilities, where physical and sexual abuse and substandard correctional practices are on the rise. Educational and clinical programs in these settings are often ineffective.

3 The study found that young people treated in such institutions had a significantly higher rate of recidivism[1] than those in community-based, rehabilitative programs. In a comparison between California's institutional system and Massachusetts' community-based program, the council determined that 62

[1]*recidivism:* a return to delinquent behavior. *(Ed.)*

percent of the former state's sample, as opposed to only 23 percent in Massachusetts, were re-incarcerated after leaving a facility.

4 Most states continue to operate large institutions as their primary response to juvenile crime. But many are now examining the community-based approach as an alternative, for reasons of cost as well as rehabilitation. The shift in focus from correction to prevention that underlies such changes is essential if we are to help those children most likely to become delinquents.

5 Today's juvenile offenders, reflecting a growing underclass, have a complex profile. They typically are poor and virtually illiterate. Chronic truants or dropouts, they possess no marketable job skills. Many are children of teenage parents, and nearly 50 percent of them have already repeated that cycle. Though years below the legal drinking age, most have serious drug and alcohol problems.

6 Like most states, Massachusetts has seen a dramatic increase in the number of young people coming into its youth-services system. Since 1982, the number of juveniles detained with the youth-services department while awaiting trial has doubled, from 1,500 to 3,044 in 1989. In addition, there were 835 new commitments to the department in 1989—121 more than in the preceding year. Yet these increases come at a time when the juvenile population in the state and in the nation is shrinking. In 1990, there are fewer than 500,000 juveniles in Massachusetts; in 1970, there were 750,000. Even more perplexing, juvenile arraignments on delinquency charges have also dropped significantly in the state, from 25,943 in 1980 to 18,902 in 1989.

7 These numbers show that something is wrong with the way that juvenile-justice systems, courts, schools, and social-service agencies are addressing the problem of delinquency.

8 Two primary factors explain the growing numbers of juvenile offenders. First, there is indeed a rise in serious crime among young people, fueled by the steady stream of drugs and weapons into their hands. These dangerous offenders are committed—legitimately—to juvenile-correction agencies for long-term custody or treatment.

9 But a second, larger group is also contributing to the increase. It consists of 11-, 12-, and 13-year-old first-time offenders who have failed at home, failed in school, and fallen through the cracks of state and community social-service agencies. These are not serious offenders, or even typical delinquents. But they are coming into the correctional system because we have ignored the warning signs among them.

10 Each year in Massachusetts, roughly 20,000 youths become involved with the justice system. Although many of them will not

receive probation or commitment to the department, each is signaling a need for help. Studies indicate that youths at risk to offend will begin to show signs as early as 2nd or 3rd grade. School failure, child abuse and neglect, drug abuse, and teenage pregnancy may all be indicators of a future involving crime.

11 Waiting for "problem children" to outgrow negative behavior is a mistake—in most cases, they don't. Unless intensive community supports are developed to improve their school experiences and the quality of life in their families and neighborhoods, as many as one in four American young people—some 7 million youths—are in danger of destroying their opportunities in life.

12 If we want to interrupt criminal paths and reduce the number of juveniles launching criminal careers, a shift in our priorities is necessary. States must invest their money in delinquency-prevention programs—at the front end rather than the back end of problems. These efforts should be targeted at elementary-school students from poor, high-crime neighborhoods, where traditional avenues to success are blocked.

13 For youths appearing in court on petty larceny or trespassing charges, we should develop restitution programs or innovative alternatives to costly lockups. Young people will learn something positive from a work assignment in the community, but not from 15 days' incarceration spent rubbing shoulders with more sophisticated offenders. And—at a time when correction resources are scarce—states will spend less money, gaining a greater return on investment.

14 Our department spends an average of $60,000 a year on each of its most serious offenders; much needs to be done in a short period of time to change behavior reinforced over many years. Less serious offenders are placed in group homes, at half the cost of secure facilities. For the least serious offenders, we operate day-treatment and outreach and tracking programs, which annually cost between $9,000 and $15,000 per youth. All of these programs include intensive educational and clinical components tailored to the individual.

15 The cost of constructing a 30-bed secure facility for juvenile offenders in Massachusetts is approximately $6 million; annual operating expenses are $1.8 million. A delinquency-prevention program costs about $10,000 per year.

16 The efforts of youth-services departments must necessarily remain accountable for public safety. But the juvenile-justice system should join together with local schools and social-service and religious organizations to implement prevention and intervention strategies such as the following:

17
- *Home-builders:* Dispatch workers to the homes of children who have been abused, neglected, or recently released from a

juvenile-detention program. Keep workers in homes at times of high stress: early in the morning, when the children might resist leaving for school, and after school, to supervise homework and nightly curfews. The annual cost for 1 worker to supervise 1 family is $4,000, with each worker responsible for 4 to 5 families.

- *Mentors:* Assign a teaching assistant or college student to work with youths who are beginning to fail in school. Mentors would serve as adult companions, helping children with homework and supervising them during after-school hours. The annual cost of 1 mentor working with 4 youngsters is $8,500. Public schools should employ students from local colleges or citizens in the community as part-time mentors. 18

- *Restitution:* Establish a plan whereby youths are assigned a community service or job to reimburse their victims, as well as serve justice and instill a sense of accountability in the offenders. A restitution program would also introduce a young offender to the world of work. 19

- *Streetworkers:* More and more 8- to 12-year-olds are being swept up in the excitement and status that accompany gang membership and urban violence. To counter the influence of gang leaders and reduce incidents of violence among these youngsters, hire full-time "streetworkers"—residents of the target areas who are street savvy and who want change in their neighborhood. Estimated cost is $8,000 per youth. 20

- *After-school employment:* Arrange for local businesses to hire high-school students as paid interns to work with a designated professional and learn a particular aspect of business. This would not only expose youths to professional opportunities but also provide positive role models. These private-public ventures could be overseen by community and state agencies, and by the larger businesses. 21

There are many other possibilities. The important thing is to begin reaching kids sooner. We must refocus our efforts from correcting the problem after the crime to creating alternatives that prevent the crime—not only in the interest of dollars but also for the sake of lives. 22

READING FOR MEANING

Write to create meanings for Loughran's proposal for a community-based approach to reducing juvenile crime.

Start Making Meaning

Begin by listing the advantages that Loughran attributes to his solution (paragraphs 12–15). Continue by writing about anything else in the essay or in your experience that contributes to your understanding of Loughran's proposal.

If You Are Stuck

If you cannot write at least a page, consider writing about

- Loughran's argument that young "problem children" need special help (paragraphs 9–11).
- the one activity among those outlined in paragraphs 17–21 that you would most like to participate in, describing its possibilities and explaining why it appeals to you.
- the unstated assumptions in Loughran's argument, one example being that the state should be responsible for preventing delinquency.
- a personal experience (or that of a friend or family member) with the juvenile justice system, describing what happened and evaluating it in light of Loughran's recommendations.

READING LIKE A WRITER

INTRODUCING THE PROBLEM

In introducing the problem, writers may define or describe it as well as argue for its seriousness. Depending on their purpose and readers, writers must decide whether they need to identify the problem briefly (as Samuelson does) or introduce it at some length (as Loughran does). In the latter case, writers may present its history and speculate about its causes. Loughran devotes a relatively large portion of his proposal to introducing the problem.

Analyze

1. *Reread* paragraphs 8–11, a key part of Loughran's introduction of the problem. *Annotate* each paragraph by writing in the margin a phrase or two identifying its topic or purpose. *Notice* the contrast Loughran sets up in paragraphs 8 and 9.
2. *Analyze* how, in paragraphs 8–11, Loughran establishes the importance of helping especially young offenders. *Note* the statements and evidence he gives to convince readers that helping young offenders is in their best interests.

Write

Write several sentences describing how Loughran introduces the problem and emphasizes its importance in paragraphs 8–11. What strategies and kinds of evidence does he use? *Give details* from the reading to support your answer. *Conclude with a few sentences* evaluating Loughran's presentation of the problem. Given his purpose and readers, how successful do you find his argument? Which parts do you find most convincing? Least convincing?

Compare

Read Mark Hertsgaard's proposal, "A Global Green Deal" (pp. 406–9). Then compare how Loughran introduces the problem with the way Hertsgaard introduces the problem in his proposal (paragraphs 1–2 and 5–7). *Notice* that unlike Loughran, Hertsgaard assumes that his readers are familiar with environmental problems and that they are likely to feel defeated by them, or "resigned to passivity" as he puts it in paragraph 2. *Annotate* the three "facts" Hertsgaard tries to focus readers' attention on in paragraphs 5–7, and *consider* how he uses these facts to argue for his proposed solution. Then *write* several sentences explaining how the two writers use their introductions to the problem as the foundation for their argument to convince readers to support their proposed solutions. *Cite a few examples* from each reading.

CONSIDERING IDEAS FOR YOUR OWN WRITING

Consider writing about the local implications of a large social problem such as juvenile crime, homelessness, or the lack of affordable child care for children of college students or working parents. Although problems like these often are national in scope, you may be able to propose a practical solution for your campus community or neighborhood. You would want to start by talking with people who experience the problem in order to enlarge your understanding of it. For example, you might interview a homeless person as well as someone who works for an agency or shelter for the homeless. Through interviews and observations, you can learn about the practical difficulties that homeless people encounter, discover alternative solutions and assess their strengths and weaknesses, and identify the individuals or groups to whom you might address your proposal.

MARK HERTSGAARD

A Global Green Deal

A freelance journalist and political commentator for National Public Radio, Mark Hertsgaard (b. 1956) contributes articles to numerous newspapers and magazines such as the New York Times, New Yorker, Atlantic Monthly, Outside, Rolling Stone, *and* Nation. *He also teaches nonfiction writing at Johns Hopkins University and has written four books, including* Nuclear, Inc.: The Men and Money behind Nuclear Energy *(1983),* On Bended Knee: The Press and the Reagan Presidency *(1988), and* A Day in the Life: The Music and Artistry of the Beatles *(1995).*

His most recent book, Earth Odyssey: Around the World in Search of Our Environmental Future *(1999), is based on his extensive research on environmental problems faced by people in nineteen countries around the world and how the problems are solved or addressed by local communities and businesses. "A Global Green Deal," which was published in* Time *magazine's Special Earth Day edition in April–May 2000, also reflects extensive research. Hertsgaard's title indicates that he wants readers to see his proposal as similar to President Franklin Roosevelt's "New Deal," which aimed to help the United States recover from the depression of the 1930s. Hertsgaard proposes that governments of wealthy countries like the United States should encourage businesses to develop and use new technologies that are both economically profitable and environmentally safe.*

As you read the essay, notice that Hertsgaard addresses his argument to the business community as well as to voters generally. He tries to convince businesspeople that solving environmental problems is in their best interests and can be done with existing technologies. At the same time, he tries to convince the voting public that government can and should play a role.

The bad news is that we have to change our ways—and fast. Here's the good news: it could be a hugely profitable enterprise. 1

So what do we do? Everyone knows the planet is in bad shape, but most people are resigned to passivity. Changing course, they reason, would require economic sacrifice and provoke stiff resistance from corporations and consumers alike, so why bother? It's easier to ignore the gathering storm clouds and hope the problem magically takes care of itself. 2

Such fatalism is not only dangerous but mistaken. For much of the 1990s I traveled the world to write a book about our environmental predicament. I returned home sobered by the extent of the damage we are causing and by the speed at which it is occurring. But there is nothing inevitable about our self-destructive 3 behavior. Not only could we dramatically reduce our burden on the air, water and other natural systems, we could make money doing so. If we're smart, we could make restoring the environment the biggest economic enterprise of our time, a huge source of jobs, profits and poverty alleviation.

4 What we need is a Global Green Deal: a program to renovate our civilization environmentally from top to bottom in rich and poor countries alike. Making use of both market incentives and government leadership, a 21st century Global Green Deal would do for environmental technologies what government and industry have recently done so well for computer and Internet technologies: launch their commercial takeoff.

5 Getting it done will take work, and before we begin we need to understand three facts about the reality facing us. First, we have no time to lose. While we've made progress in certain areas, air pollution is down in the U.S. —big environmental problems like climate change, water scarcity and species extinction are getting worse, and faster than ever. Thus we have to change our ways profoundly—and very soon.

6 Second, poverty is central to the problem. Four billion of the planet's 6 billion people face deprivation inconceivable to the wealthiest 1 billion. To paraphrase Thomas Jefferson, nothing is more certainly written in the book of fate than that the bottom two-thirds of humanity will strive to improve their lot. As they demand adequate heat and food, not to mention cars and CD players, humanity's environmental footprint will grow. Our challenge is to accommodate this mass ascent from poverty without wrecking the natural systems that make life possible.

7 Third, some good news: we have in hand most of the technologies needed to chart a new course. We know how to use oil, wood, water and other resources much more efficiently than we do now. Increased efficiency—doing more with less—will enable us to use fewer resources and produce less pollution per capita, buying us the time to bring solar power, hydrogen fuel cells and other futuristic technologies on line.

8 Efficiency may not sound like a rallying cry for environmental revolution, but it packs a financial punch. As Joseph J. Romm reports in his book *Cool Companies*, Xerox, Compaq and 3M are among many firms that have recognized they can cut their greenhouse-gas emissions in half—and enjoy 50% and higher returns on investment through improved efficiency, better lighting and insulation and smarter motors and building design. The rest of us (small businesses, homeowners, city governments, schools) can reap the same benefits.

9 Super-refrigerators use 87% less electricity than older, standard models while costing the same (assuming mass production) and performing better, as Paul Hawken, L. Hunter Lovins, and Amory Lovins explain in their book *Natural Capitalism*. In Amsterdam the headquarters of ING Bank, one of Holland's largest banks, uses one-fifth as much energy per square meter as a nearby bank, even though the buildings cost the same to construct. The ING center boasts efficient windows and insulation and a design that enables solar energy to provide much of the building's needs, even in cloudy Northern Europe.

10 Examples like these lead even such mainstream voices as AT&T and Japan's energy planning agency, NEDO, to predict that environmental restoration could be a source of virtually limitless profit. The idea is to retrofit our farms, factories, shops, houses, offices and everything inside them. The economic activity generated would be enormous. Better yet, it would be labor intensive; investments in energy efficiency yield two to 10 times more jobs than investments in fossil fuel and nuclear power. In a world where 1 billion people lack gainful employment, creating jobs is essential to fighting the poverty that retards environmental progress.

11 But this transition will not happen by itself—too many entrenched interests stand in the way. Automakers often talk green but make only token efforts to develop green cars because gas-guzzling sport-utility vehicles are hugely profitable. But every year the U.S. government buys 56,000 new vehicles for official use from Detroit. Under the Global Green Deal, Washington would tell Detroit that from now on the cars have to be hybrid-electric or hydrogen-fuel-cell cars. Detroit might scream and holler, but if Washington stood firm, carmakers soon would be climbing the learning curve and offering the competitively priced green cars that consumers say they want.

12 We know such government pump-priming works; it's why so many of us have computers today. America's computer companies began learning to produce today's affordable systems during the 1960s while benefiting from subsidies and guaranteed markets under contracts with the Pentagon and the space program. And the cyberboom has fueled the biggest economic expansion in history.

13 The Global Green Deal must not be solely an American project, however. China and India, with their gigantic populations and ambitious development plans, could by themselves doom everyone else to severe global warming. Already, China is the world's second

largest producer of greenhouse gases (after the U.S.). But China would use 50% less coal if it simply installed today's energy-efficient technologies. Under the Global Green Deal, Europe, America and Japan would help China buy these technologies, not only because that would reduce global warming but also because it would create jobs and profits for workers and companies back home.

14 Governments would not have to spend more money, only shift existing subsidies away from environmentally dead-end technologies like coal and nuclear power. If even half the $500 billion to $900 billion in environmentally destructive subsidies now offered by the world's governments were redirected, the Global Green Deal would be off to a roaring start. Governments need to establish "rules of the road" so that market prices reflect the real social costs of clear-cut forests and other environmental abominations. Again, such a shift could be revenue neutral. Higher taxes on, say, coal burning would be offset by cuts in payroll and profits taxes, thus encouraging jobs and investment while discouraging pollution. A portion of the revenues should be set aside to assure a just transition for workers and companies now engaged in inherently anti-environmental activities like coal mining.

15 All this sounds easy enough on paper, but in the real world it is not so simple. Beneficiaries of the current system—be they U.S. corporate-welfare recipients, redundant German coal miners, or cut-throat Asian logging interests—will resist. Which is why progress is unlikely absent a broader agenda of change, including real democracy: assuring the human rights of environmental activists and neutralizing the power of Big Money through campaign-finance reform.

16 The Global Green Deal is no silver bullet. It can, however, buy us time to make the more deep-seated changes—in our often excessive appetites, in our curious belief that humans are the center of the universe, in our sheer numbers—that will be necessary to repair our relationship with our environment.

17 None of this will happen without an aroused citizenry. But a Global Green Deal is in the common interest, and it is a slogan easily grasped by the media and the public. Moreover, it should appeal across political, class and national boundaries, for it would stimulate both jobs and business throughout the world in the name of a universal value: leaving our children a livable planet. The history of environmentalism is largely the story of ordinary people pushing for change while governments, corporations and other established interests reluctantly follow behind. It's time to repeat that history on behalf of a Global Green Deal.

READING FOR MEANING

Write to create meanings for Hertsgaard's proposal for what he calls "a Global Green Deal."

Start Making Meaning

Begin by briefly listing the elements of Hertsgaard's Global Green Deal. Continue by writing about anything else in the selection or in your experience that contributes to your understanding of Hertsgaard's proposal.

If You Are Stuck

If you cannot write at least a page, consider writing about

- what you know about environmental problems in this country and around the world, and how your knowledge influences your response to Hertsgaard's proposal.
- the idea that as people around the world raise themselves out of poverty, environmental problems grow because more people demand necessities like "adequate heat and food," and want luxuries like "cars and CD players" (paragraph 6).
- the claim that energy efficiency can be an effective "rallying cry" for business because efficiency not only conserves resources but also "packs a financial punch" (paragraph 8).
- your own willingness as a consumer to make "buying green" a priority, perhaps recalling relevant purchases you, your friends, or family have made and how these experiences affect your reading of Hertsgaard's proposal.

READING LIKE A WRITER

ESTABLISHING CREDIBILITY

To be taken seriously, a proposal must demonstrate to readers that the writer fully understands the problem and has seriously considered possible objections and alternative solutions. One way Hertsgaard tries to establish credibility is by telling readers that his proposal is based on his extensive research. He announces in paragraph 3 that he has spent "much of the 1990s" studying environmental problems throughout the world. In addition to this firsthand observation, Hertsgaard shows that he is well read on the subject; for example, in paragraphs 8 and 9, he refers to two related books by other authors. Readers' trust is likely to be enhanced by the fact that Hertsgaard's research has been published in a book as well as in this article in *Time*, a respected newsmagazine.

Finally, knowing that Hertsgaard has written other books and other articles for prestigious journals further bolsters his credibility. The following activity invites you to analyze still other ways that Hertsgaard tries to establish credibility: by challenging readers to see the seriousness of the problem, and by attempting to convince them that something can be done about the problem.

Analyze

1. *Reread* paragraphs 1–3, and *underline* words like *passivity* (paragraph 2) and *fatalism* (3) that Hertsgaard uses to characterize the attitude he assumes his readers have about "our environmental predicament" (3).
2. *Look for* and *mark* places elsewhere in the essay where Hertsgaard shifts into more positive language (for example, in paragraphs 5 and 6, he talks about the problem as a "challenge" requiring effort and hard work).
3. *Examine* the concluding paragraphs (16 and 17) to see how Hertsgaard represents his own proposal as "no silver bullet."

Write

Write several sentences describing what you have learned about Hertsgaard's representation of readers' negative attitude as well as his own more positive attitude. *Explain* the effect you think this shift in tone might have on his credibility with readers. *Conclude with a few sentences* describing the writer's tone at the end of the essay and speculating about its possible effects on readers.

CONSIDERING IDEAS FOR YOUR OWN WRITING

Hertsgaard's admittedly limited proposal might suggest to you other ideas that might help in even a small way to solve environmental problems. For example, you might consider writing a proposal for increasing the use of carpools on campus, reducing energy consumption in dormitories, or instituting a campus recycling program. You might interview people in your community about the feasibility of subsidizing alternative energy sources, such as solar-heating panels that could be installed in public buildings and parks. You might also research new technologies for a proposal addressed to your college administration encouraging use of promising technologies.

KATHERINE S. NEWMAN

Dead-End Jobs: A Way Out

Katherine S. Newman (b. 1953) is the Ford Professor of Urban Studies in the John F. Kennedy School of Government at Harvard University. She is also the director of Harvard's joint doctoral program in sociology, government, and social policy. Chair of the National Science Foundation training program on inequality and social policy, Newman has written several books on middle-class economic insecurity, including Falling from Grace *(1988) and* Declining Fortunes: The Withering of the American Dream *(1993). Her 1999 book,* No Shame in My Game: The Working Poor in the Inner City, *which focuses on the job-search strategies, work experiences, and family lives of African American and Latino youths and adults in Harlem, was awarded the Sidney Hillman Book Prize and the Robert F. Kennedy Book Award.*

The following proposal comes out of Newman's study of inner-city fast-food workers, in which she learned that many such workers experience great difficulty finding better, higher-paying jobs because the "social networks"—the connections they depend on for job information and referrals—help them make only lateral moves or lead them into industries that were economically vital a generation ago but are now shrinking. In this proposal, originally published in 1995 in the Brookings Review, *a journal concerned with public policy, Newman proposes that managers of inner-city fast-food businesses form an "employer consortium" to give their most successful employees "upward mobility."*

As you read the proposal, think about your own experience job hunting and whether you have been helped by knowing someone who could serve as a reference or give you useful inside information about a job. Do you think a system that depends so much on who you know is beneficial and fair? What would you suggest to replace it?

Millions of Americans work full-time, year-round in jobs that still leave them stranded in poverty. Though they pound the pavement looking for better jobs, they consistently come up empty-handed. Many of these workers are in our nation's inner cities. 1

I know, because I have spent two years finding out what working life is like for 200 employees—about half African-American, half Latino—at fast food restaurants in Harlem. Many work only part-time, though they would happily take longer hours if they could get them. Those who do work full-time earn about $8,840 (before taxes)—well below the poverty threshold for a family of four. 2

These fast food workers make persistent efforts to get better jobs, particularly in retail and higher-paid service-sector occupations. They take civil service examinations and apply for jobs with the electric company or the phone company. Sometimes their efforts bear fruit. More often they don't. 3

A few workers make their way into the lower managerial ranks of the fast food industry, where wages are marginally better. An even smaller number graduate into higher management, a path made possible by the internal promotion patterns long practiced by these firms. As in any industry, however, senior management opportunities are limited. Hence most workers, even those with track records as reliable employees, are locked inside a low-wage environment. Contrary to those who preach the benefits of work and persistence, the human capital these workers build up—experience in food production, inventory management, cash register operation, customer relations, minor machinery repair, and cleaning—does not pay off. These workers are often unable to move upward out of poverty. And their experience is not unusual. Hundreds of thousands of low-wage workers in American cities run into the same brick wall. Why? And what can we do about it? 4

STAGNATION IN THE INNER CITY

Harlem, like many inner-city communities, has lost the manufacturing job base that once sustained its neighborhoods. Service industries that cater to neighborhood consumers, coupled with now dwindling government jobs, largely make up the local economy. With official jobless rates hovering around 18 percent (114 people apply for every minimum wage fast food job in Harlem), employers can select from the very top of the preference "queue." Once hired, even experienced workers have virtually nowhere to go. 5

One reason for their lack of mobility is that many employers in the primary labor market outside Harlem consider "hamburger flipper" jobs worthless. At most, employers credit the fast food industry with training people to turn up for work on time and to fill out job applications. The real skills these workers have developed go unrecognized. However inaccurate the unflattering stereotypes, they help keep experienced workers from "graduating" out of low-wage work to more remunerative employment. . . . 6

As Harry Holzer, an economist at Michigan State University, has shown, "central city" employers insist on specific work experience, references, and particular kinds of formal training in addition to literacy and numeracy skills, even for jobs that do not require a college degree. Demands of this kind, more stringent in 7 the big-city labor markets than in the surrounding suburbs, clearly limit the upward mobility of the working poor in urban areas. If the only kind of job available does not provide the "right" work experience or formal training, many better jobs will be foreclosed.

8 Racial stereotypes also weaken mobility prospects. Employers view ghetto blacks, especially men, as a bad risk or a troublesome element in the workplace. They prefer immigrants or nonblack minorities, of which there are many in the Harlem labor force, who appear to them more deferential and willing to work harder for low wages. As Joleen Kirshenman and Kathryn Neckerman found in their study of Chicago workplaces, stereotypes abound among employers who have become wary of the "underclass." Primary employers exercise these preferences by discriminating against black applicants, particularly those who live in housing projects, on the grounds of perceived group characteristics. The "losers" are not given an opportunity to prove themselves. . . .

SOCIAL NETWORKS

9 Social networks are crucial in finding work. Friends and acquaintances are far more useful sources of information than are want ads. The literature on the urban underclass suggests that inner-city neighborhoods are bereft of these critical links to the work world. My work, however, suggests a different picture: the working poor in Harlem have access to two types of occupational social networks, but neither provides upward mobility. The first is a homogeneous *lateral* network of age mates and acquaintances, employed and unemployed. It provides contacts that allow workers to move sideways in the labor market—from Kentucky Fried Chicken to Burger King or McDonald's—but not to move to jobs of higher quality. Lateral networks are useful, particularly for poor people who have to move frequently, for they help ensure a certain amount of portability in the low-wage labor market. But they do not lift workers out of poverty; they merely facilitate "churning" laterally in the low-wage world.

10 Young workers in Harlem also participate in more heterogeneous *vertical* networks with their older family members who long ago moved to suburban communities or better urban neighborhoods to become homeowners on the strength of jobs that were more widely available 20 and 30 years ago. Successful grandparents, great-aunts and uncles, and distant cousins, relatives now in their 50s and 60s, often have (or have retired from) jobs in the post office, the public sector, the transportation system, public

utilities, the military, hospitals, and factories that pay union wages. But these industries are now shedding workers, not hiring them. As a result, older generations are typically unable to help job-hunting young relatives.

11 Although little is known about the social and business networks of minority business owners and managers in the inner city, it seems that Harlem's business community, particularly its small business sector, is also walled off from the wider economy of midtown. Fast food owners know the other people in their franchise system. They do business with banks and security firms inside the inner city. But they appear less likely to interact with firms outside the ghetto.

12 For that reason, a good recommendation from a McDonald's owner may represent a calling card that extends no farther than the general reputation of the firm and a prospective employer's perception—poor, as I have noted—of the skills that such work represents. It can move someone from an entry-level job in one restaurant to the same kind of job in another, but not into a good job elsewhere in the city.

13 Lacking personal or business-based ties that facilitate upward mobility, workers in Harlem's fast food market find themselves on the outside looking in when it comes to the world of "good jobs." They search diligently for them, they complete many job applications, but it is the rare individual who finds a job that pays a family wage. Those who do are either workers who have been selected for internal promotion or men and women who have had the luxury of devoting their earnings solely to improving their own educational or craft credentials. Since most low-wage service workers are under pressure to support their families or contribute to the support of their parents' households, this kind of human capital investment is often difficult. As a result, the best most can do is to churn from one low-wage job to another.

THE EMPLOYER CONSORTIUM

14 Some of the social ills that keep Harlem's fast food workers at the bottom of a short job ladder—a poor urban job base, increasing downward mobility, discrimination, structural problems in the inner-city business sector—are too complex to solve quickly enough to help most of the workers I've followed. But the problem of poor social networks may be amenable to solution if formal organizations linking primary and secondary labor market employers can be developed. An "employer consortium" could help to move hardworking inner-city employees into richer job

markets by providing the job information and precious referrals that "come naturally" to middle-class Americans.

15 How would an employer consortium function? It would include both inner-city employers of the working poor and downtown businesses or nonprofit institutions with higher-paid employees. Employers in the inner city would periodically select employees they consider reliable, punctual, hard-working, and motivated. Workers who have successfully completed at least one year of work would be placed in a pool of workers eligible for hiring by a set of linked employers who have better jobs to offer. Entry-level employers would, in essence, put their own good name behind successful workers as they pass them on to their consortium partners in the primary sector.

16 Primary-sector employers, for their part, would agree to hire from the pool and meet periodically with their partners in the low-wage industries to review applications and follow up on the performance of those hired through the consortium. Employers "up the line" would provide training or educational opportunities to enhance the employee's skills. These training investments would make it more likely that hirees would continue to move up the new job ladders.

17 As they move up, the new hirees would clear the way for others to follow. First, their performance would reinforce the reputation of the employers who recommended them. Second, their achievements on the job might begin to lessen the stigma or fear their new employers may feel toward the inner-city workforce. On both counts, other consortium-based workers from the inner city would be more likely to get the same opportunities, following in a form of managed chain migration out of the inner-city labor market. Meanwhile, the attractiveness of fast food jobs, now no better reputed among inner-city residents than among the rest of society, would grow as they became, at least potentially, a gateway to something better.

ADVANTAGES FOR EMPLOYERS

18 Fast food employers in Harlem run businesses in highly competitive markets. Constant pressure on prices and profit discourage them from paying wages high enough to keep a steady workforce. In fact, most such employers regard the jobs they fill as temporary placements: they *expect* successful employees to leave. And despite the simple production processes used within the fast food industry to minimize the damage of turnover, sudden departures of knowledgeable workers still disrupt business and cause considerable frustration and exhaustion.

An employer consortium gives these employers—who *can't* raise wages if they hope to stay in business—a way to compete for workers who will stay with them longer than usual. In lieu of higher pay, employers can offer access to the consortium hiring pool and the prospect of a more skilled and ultimately better-paying job upon graduation from this real world "boot camp." . . . 19

Consortiums would also appeal to the civic spirit of minority business owners, who often choose to locate in places like Harlem rather than in less risky neighborhoods because they want to provide job opportunities for their own community. The big franchise operations mandate some attention to civic responsibility as well. Some fast food firms have licensing requirements for franchisees that require demonstrated community involvement. 20

At a time when much of the public is voicing opposition to heavy-handed government efforts to prevent employment discrimination, employer consortiums have the advantage of encouraging minority hiring based on private-sector relationships. Institutional employers in particular—for example, universities and hospitals, often among the larger employers in East Coast cities—should find the consortiums especially valuable. These employers typically retain a strong commitment to workforce diversity but are often put off by the reputation of secondary-sector workers as unskilled, unmotivated, and less worthy of consideration. 21

The practical advantages for primary-sector managers are clear. Hirees have been vetted and tested. Skills have been assessed and certified in the most real world of settings. A valuable base of experience and skills stands ready for further training and advancement. The consortium assures that the employers making and receiving recommendations would come to know one another, thus reinforcing the value of recommendations—a cost-effective strategy for primary-sector managers who must make significant training investments in their workers. 22

MINIMAL GOVERNMENT INVOLVEMENT

Despite the evident advantages for both primary and secondary labor market employers, it may be necessary for governments to provide modest incentives to encourage wide participation. Secondary-sector business owners in the inner city, for example, might be deterred from participating by the prospect of losing some of their best employees at the end of a year. Guaranteeing these employers a lump sum or a tax break for every worker they promote into management internally or successfully place with a consortium participant could help break down such reluctance. 23

Primary-sector employers, who would have to provide support for training and possibly for schooling of their consortium employees, may also require some kind of tax break to subsidize their efforts at skill enhancement. Demonstration projects could experiment with various sorts of financial incentives for both sets of employers by providing grants to underwrite the costs of training new workers. 24

Local governments could also help publicize the efforts of participating employers. Most big-city mayors, for example, would be happy to shower credit on business people looking to boost the prospects of the deserving (read working) poor. 25

Government involvement, however, would be minimal. Employer consortiums could probably be assembled out of the existing economic development offices of U.S. cities, or with the help of the Chamber of Commerce and other local institutions that encourage private-sector activity. Industry- or sector-specific consortiums could probably be put together with the aid of local industry councils. 26

Moreover, some of the negative effects of prior experiments with wage subsidies for the "hard to employ"—efforts that foundered on the stigma assigned to these workers and the paperwork irritants to employers—would be reversed here. Consortium employees would be singled out for doing well, for being the cream of the crop. And the private sector domination of employer consortiums would augur against extensive paperwork burdens. 27

BUILDING BRIDGES

The inner-city fast food workers that I have been following in Harlem have proven themselves in difficult jobs. They have shown that they are reliable, they clearly relish their economic independence, and they are willing to work hard. Still, work offers them no escape from poverty. Trapped in a minimum-wage job market, they lack bridges to the kind of work that can enable them to support their families and begin to move out of poverty. For reasons I have discussed, those bridges have not evolved naturally in our inner cities. But where they are lacking, they must be created and fostered. And we can begin with employer consortiums, to the benefit of everyone, workers and employers alike. 28

READING FOR MEANING

Write to create meanings for Newman's proposal for creating inner-city "employer consortiums."

Start Making Meaning

Begin by explaining in your own words how, according to Newman, an employer consortium would help solve the problem of "dead-end jobs" for inner-city fast-food workers. Continue by writing about anything else in the essay or in your experience that contributes to your understanding of Newman's proposal.

If You Are Stuck

If you cannot write at least a page, consider writing about

- the "unflattering stereotypes" of "'hamburger flipper' jobs" (paragraph 6) and whether you think fast-food workers learn useful and marketable skills, as Newman suggests in paragraph 4.
- the idea that people in "dead-end" fast-food jobs would be willing to forgo the immediate gratification of "higher pay" for the future "prospect of a more skilled and ultimately better-paying job" (paragraph 19).
- Newman's argument, in paragraphs 23–27, that her proposal is preferable to the old welfare system that gave "wage subsidies" to unemployed and underemployed people, but that giving tax-break subsidies to businesses that participate in the employee consortium would be justifiable.
- Newman's assertion about the importance of "social networks" in job hunting and the distinction she makes between "lateral" and "vertical" networks (paragraphs 9 and 10), perhaps in relation to your own experience and observation of family and friends.

READING LIKE A WRITER

PRESENTING THE SOLUTION

Proposal writers often go into detail explaining how the proposed solution would work and arguing that the changes would be beneficial. Presenting the solution in an attractive way becomes especially difficult when the chief beneficiary is a third party and not the readers who are being addressed in the proposal. This is the case in Newman's proposal to form an employer consortium. She is writing to employers about her proposal to help employees move into better jobs. Convincing managers of any organization—including fast-food businesses—to make fundamental changes in their policies or practices is a daunting task for any proposal writer. It is especially challenging to convince managers that making changes designed primarily to help their employees get other jobs will benefit and not harm their businesses. The following activity will help you see how Newman tries to present her proposed solution in a way that reduces the concerns of her intended readers—inner-city employers.

Analyze

1. *Reread* paragraphs 14–22, where Newman provides many details about how an employer consortium would function. *Annotate* the information she presents on how the solution would be implemented—the different roles that would be played by "entry-level employers" who would recommend their best employees for advancement and by "primary-sector employers" who would hire successful employees. Also *annotate* the "advantages" Newman argues her proposal would have for both sets of employers, particularly for "entry-level employers" who are being asked to give up their best workers.
2. *Evaluate* Newman's success, in paragraphs 14–22, in presenting the solution to inner-city employers at entry and advanced levels. Where does Newman's argument seem most successful? Least successful?

Write

Write several sentences explaining how Newman presents the solution in paragraphs 14–22. *Include specific examples* from these paragraphs. Also briefly *evaluate* the success of Newman's presentation.

CONSIDERING IDEAS FOR YOUR OWN WRITING

Newman's topic suggests a type of proposal you might want to consider for your essay—a proposal to improve the living or working conditions of a group of people. You could focus on a particular category of people and a problem that they face. For example, you might think of ways to help elderly and infirm people in your community who need transportation, or you might want to help elementary school kids who have no after-school programs to organize their time. Newman's proposal might also suggest the possibility of other kinds of job-training and referral programs to help college students find work to support their education. You could find out what resources are available on your campus and check the Internet to discover if there are any services other campuses provide that might be useful on your campus. You might also interview students as well as employers in the community to see whether a new campus job-referral service could be developed or an existing one could be improved.

You might also consider writing a proposal to improve the functioning of a goal-directed organization such as a sports team, business, or public institution (small-claims court, traffic offenders' school, welfare office, recreation center, or school). You could propose a solution to a problem in an institution in which you participated regularly or one in which you had a single disappointing experience. Your goal is not to ridicule or complain, but to attempt to bring about change that would make the organization more humane, efficient, productive, or successful in fulfilling its goals. Do not limit yourself to your own experience. Seek out former and current members who experienced the problem; they can help you understand the problem in a deeper way, refine your presentation of a solution, and strengthen your argument for the solution.

PATRICK O'MALLEY

More Testing, More Learning

Patrick O'Malley wrote the following proposal while he was a first-year college student. He proposes that college professors give students frequent brief examinations in addition to the usual midterm and final exams. After discussing his unusual rhetorical situation—a student advising teachers on how to plan their courses—with his instructor, O'Malley decided to revise the essay into the form of an open letter to professors on his campus, a letter that might appear in the campus newspaper.

O'Malley's essay may strike you as unusually authoritative. This air of authority is due in large part to what O'Malley learned from interviewing two professors (his writing instructor and the writing program director) and several students in his classes. As you read, notice particularly how O'Malley responds to the objections to his proposal he expects many professors to raise as well as their preferred solutions to the problem he identifies.

It's late at night. The final's tomorrow. You got a *C* on the midterm, so this one will make or break you. Will it be like the midterm? Did you study enough? Did you study the right things? It's too late to drop the course. So what happens if you fail? No time to worry about that now—you've got a ton of notes to go over. 1

Although this last-minute anxiety about midterm and final exams is only too familiar to most college students, many professors may not realize how such major, infrequent, high-stakes exams work against the best interests of students both psychologically and intellectually. They cause unnecessary amounts of stress, placing too much importance on one or two days in the students' entire term, judging ability on a single or dual performance. They don't encourage frequent study and they fail to inspire students' best performance. If professors gave additional brief exams at frequent intervals, students would learn more, study more regularly, worry less, and perform better on midterms, finals, and other papers and projects. 2

Ideally, a professor would give an in-class test or quiz after each unit, chapter, or focus of study, depending on the type of class and course material. A physics class might require a test on concepts after every chapter covered, while a history class could necessitate quizzes covering certain time periods or major events. These exams should be given weekly, or at least twice monthly. Whenever possible, they should consist of two or three essay 3 questions rather than many multiple-choice or short-answer questions. To preserve class time for lecture and discussion, exams should take no more than 15 or 20 minutes.

4 The main reason professors should give frequent exams is that when they do, and when they provide feedback to students on how well they are doing, students learn more in the course and perform better on major exams, projects, and papers. It makes sense that in a challenging course containing a great deal of material, students will learn more of it and put it to better use if they have to apply or "practice" it frequently on exams, which also helps them find out how much they are learning and what they need to go over again. A recent Harvard study notes students' "strong preference for frequent evaluation in a course." Harvard students feel they learn least in courses that have "only a midterm and a final exam, with no other personal evaluation." They believe they learn most in courses with "many opportunities to see how they are doing" (Light, 1990, p. 32). In a review of a number of studies of student learning, Frederiksen (1984) reports that students who take weekly quizzes achieve higher scores on final exams than students who take only a midterm exam and that testing increases retention of material tested.

5 Another, closely related argument in favor of multiple exams is that they encourage students to improve their study habits. Greater frequency in test taking means greater frequency in studying for tests. Students prone to cramming will be required—or at least strongly motivated—to open their textbooks and notebooks more often, making them less likely to resort to long, kamikaze nights of studying for major exams. Since there is so much to be learned in the typical course, it makes sense that frequent, careful study and review are highly beneficial. But students need motivation to study regularly, and nothing works like an exam. If students had frequent exams in all their courses, they would have to schedule study time each week and gradually would develop a habit of frequent study. It might be argued that students are adults who have to learn how to manage their own lives, but learning history or physics is more complicated than learning to drive a car or balance a checkbook. Students need coaching and practice in learning. The right way to learn new material needs to become a habit, and I believe that frequent exams are key to developing good habits of study and learning. The Harvard study concludes that "tying regular evaluations to good course organization enables students to plan their work more than a few days in advance. If quizzes and homework are scheduled on specific days, students plan their work to capitalize on them" (Light, 1990, p. 33).

6 By encouraging regular study habits, frequent exams would also decrease anxiety by reducing the procrastination that produces anxiety. Students would benefit psychologically if they were not subjected to the emotional ups and downs caused by major exams, when after being virtually worry-free for weeks they are suddenly ready to check into the psychiatric ward. Researchers at the University of Vermont found a strong relationship among procrastination, anxiety, and achievement. Students who regularly put off studying for exams had continuing high anxiety and lower grades than students who procrastinated less. The researchers found that even "low" procrastinators did not study regularly and recommended that professors give frequent assignments and exams to reduce procrastination and increase achievement (Rothblum, Solomon, & Murakami, 1986, pp. 393, 394).

7 Research supports my proposed solution to the problems I have described. Common sense as well as my experience and that of many of my friends support it. Why, then, do so few professors give frequent brief exams? Some believe that such exams take up too much of the limited class time available to cover the material in the course. Most courses meet 150 minutes a week—three times a week for 50 minutes each time. A 20-minute weekly exam might take 30 minutes to administer, and that is one-fifth of each week's class time. From the student's perspective, however, this time is well spent. Better learning and greater confidence about the course seem a good trade-off for another 30 minutes of lecture. Moreover, time lost to lecturing or discussion could easily be made up in students' learning on their own through careful regular study for the weekly exams. If weekly exams still seem too time-consuming to some professors, their frequency could be reduced to every other week or their length to 5 or 10 minutes. In courses where multiple-choice exams are appropriate, several questions could be designed to take only a few minutes to answer.

8 Another objection professors have to frequent exams is that they take too much time to read and grade. In a 20-minute essay exam, a well-prepared student can easily write two pages. A relatively small class of 30 students might then produce 60 pages, no small amount of material to read each week. A large class of 100 or more students would produce an insurmountable pile of material. There are a number of responses to this objection. Again, professors could give exams every other week or make them very short. Instead of reading them closely they could skim them quickly to see whether students understand an idea or can apply it to an unfamiliar problem; and instead of numerical or letter grades they could give a plus, check, or minus. Exams could be

collected and responded to only every third or fourth week. Professors who have readers or teaching assistants could rely on them to grade or check exams. And the Scranton machine is always available for instant grading of multiple-choice exams. Finally, frequent exams could be given *in place of* a midterm exam or out-of-class essay assignment.

9 Since frequent exams seem to some professors to create many problems, however, it is reasonable to consider alternative ways to achieve the same goals. One alternative solution is to implement a program that would improve study skills. While such a program might teach students to study for exams, it cannot prevent procrastination or reduce "large test anxiety" by a substantial amount. One research team studying anxiety and test performance found that study skills training was "not effective in reducing anxiety or improving performance" (Dendato & Diener, 1986, p. 134). This team, which also reviewed other research that reached the same conclusion, did find that a combination of "cognitive/relaxation therapy" and study skills training was effective. This possible solution seems complicated, however, not to mention time-consuming and expensive. It seems much easier and more effective to change the cause of the bad habit than treat the habit itself. That is, it would make more sense to solve the problem at its root: the method of learning and evaluation.

10 Still another solution might be to provide frequent study questions for students to answer. These would no doubt be helpful in focusing students' time studying, but students would probably not actually write out the answers unless they were required to. To get students to complete the questions in a timely way, professors would have to collect and check the answers. In that case, however, they might as well devote the time to grading an exam. Even if it asks the same questions, a scheduled exam is preferable to a set of study questions because it takes far less time to write in class, compared to the time students would devote to responding to questions at home. In-class exams also ensure that each student produces his or her own work.

11 Another possible solution would be to help students prepare for midterm and final exams by providing sets of questions from which the exam questions will be selected or announcing possible exam topics at the beginning of the course. This solution would have the advantage of reducing students' anxiety about learning every fact in the textbook, and it would clarify the course goals, but it would not motivate students to study carefully each new unit, concept, or text chapter in the course. I see this as a way of complementing frequent exams, not as substituting for them.

12 From the evidence and from my talks with professors and students, I see frequent, brief in-class exams as the only way to improve students' study habits and learning, reduce their anxiety and procrastination, and increase their satisfaction with college. These exams are not a panacea, but only more parking spaces and a winning football team would do as much to improve college life. Professors can't do much about parking or football, but they can give more frequent exams. Campus administrators should get behind this effort, and professors should get together to consider giving exams more frequently. It would make a difference.

References

Dendato, K. M., & Diener, D. (1986). Effectiveness of cognitive/relaxation therapy and study-skills training in reducing self-reported anxiety and improving the academic performance of test-anxious students. *Journal of Counseling Psychology, 33,* 131–135.

Frederiksen, N. (1984). The real test bias: Influences of testing on teaching and learning. *American Psychologist, 39,* 193–202.

Light, R. J. (1990). *Explorations with students and faculty about teaching, learning, and student life.* Cambridge, MA: Harvard University Graduate School of Education and Kennedy School of Government.

Rothblum, E. D., Solomon, L., & Murakami, J. (1986). Affective, cognitive, and behavioral differences between high and low procrastinators. *Journal of Counseling Psychology, 33,* 387–394.

READING FOR MEANING

Write to create meanings for O'Malley's proposal for improving students' learning and study habits.

Start Making Meaning

Begin by describing briefly the problem O'Malley sees and the solution he proposes (paragraphs 1–3). Then list the alternative solutions that O'Malley counterargues (paragraphs 9–11). Continue by writing about anything else in the essay or in your experience that contributes to your understanding of O'Malley's proposal.

If You Are Stuck

If you cannot write at least a page, consider writing about

- the reasons so few professors give frequent exams, listing the main reasons O'Malley offers (paragraphs 7 and 8) and commenting on one or two of his responses (paragraphs 9–11).

- the relation O'Malley attempts to establish between high-pressure exams and poor performance (paragraph 2), testing it against your own experience.
- which classes, in your experience, are and are not suited to frequent brief exams.
- your own experience preparing for major exams such as midterms and finals, comparing it with the scenario O'Malley describes in paragraph 1.

READING LIKE A WRITER

ARGUING DIRECTLY FOR THE PROPOSED SOLUTION

Arguing directly for the proposed solution, like counterarguing readers' likely questions and preferred solutions, is especially important in proposals. Writers argue directly for a proposed solution by explaining the reasons it should be implemented and then supporting those reasons with evidence or examples. Many types of support are available: personal experience, assertions, research, reviews of research, quotes from authorities, effects or consequences, benefits, contrasts, analogies, and causes. O'Malley makes use of all of these types of support.

Analyze

1. *Skim* paragraphs 4–6. In each paragraph, *underline* the sentence that announces the reason for the solution.
2. *Note in the margin* the kinds of support O'Malley relies on. *Categorize* all of his support.
3. *Evaluate* how effectively O'Malley argues to support his solution. Do the reasons seem plausible? Is one reason more convincing to you than the others? How believable do you find the support?

Write

Write several sentences explaining what you have learned about O'Malley's attempt to convince readers to take his proposed solution seriously. *Give examples* from the reading. Then *add a few more sentences* evaluating how convincing you find his argument. Which parts do you find most convincing? Least convincing? *Explain* your choices.

CONSIDERING IDEAS FOR YOUR OWN WRITING

Much of what happens in high school and college is predictable and conventional. Examples of conventional practices that have changed very little over the years are exams, classroom lectures, graduation ceremonies, required courses, and lower admission requirements for athletes. Think of additional examples of established practices in high school or college; then select one that you believe needs to be improved or refined in some way. What changes would you propose? What individual or group might be convinced to take action on your proposal for improvement? What questions or objections should you anticipate? How could you discover whether others have previously proposed improvements in the practice you are concerned with? Whom might you interview to learn more about the practice and the likelihood of changing it?

SHANNON LONG

Wheelchair Hell: A Look at Campus Accessibility

Shannon Long wrote this essay for a first-year composition course at the University of Kentucky and later sent her proposal to campus administrators. In it, she tries to convince readers that there is a serious accessibility problem for wheelchair-bound students on campus. She painstakingly documents the problem and offers a simple but practical solution. As you read Long's essay, think about how accessible your own campus is for students in wheelchairs.

The other readings in this chapter are followed by reading and writing activities. Following this reading, however, you are on your own to decide how to read for meaning and read like a writer.

It was my first week of college, and I was on my way to the third floor of the library to meet up with someone to study. After entering the library, I went to the elevator and hit the button calling it. A few seconds later, the elevator door opened, and I rolled inside. The doors closed behind me. Expecting the buttons to be down in front of me, I suddenly noticed that they were behind me—and too high to reach. There I was stuck in the elevator with no way to call for help. Finally, someone got on at the fourth floor. I'd been waiting fifteen minutes. 1

I'm not the only one who has been a victim of inaccessibility on campus. The University of Kentucky (UK) currently has twelve buildings that are inaccessible to students in wheelchairs (Karnes). Many other UK buildings, like the library, are accessible, but have elevators that are inoperable by handicapped students. Yet, Section 504 of the Rehabilitation Act of 1973 states that 2

> No qualified handicapped person shall, because a recipient's facilities are inaccessible to or unusable by handicapped persons, be denied the benefits of, be excluded from participation in, or otherwise be subjected to discrimination under any program or activity receiving Federal financial assistance. (qtd. in *Federal Register* 22681)

When this law went into effect in 1977, the University of Kentucky started a renovation process in which close to $1 million was spent on handicap modifications (Karnes). Even though that much money has been spent, there are still many 3 more modifications needed. Many buildings remain inaccessible to wheelchair-bound students: the Administration building, Alumni House, Barker Hall, Bowman Hall, Bradley Hall, Engineering Quadrangle, Gillis building, Kinkead Hall, Miller Hall, Safety and Security building, Scovell Hall, and several residence halls.

4 The inaccessibility of so many buildings on campus creates many unnecessary problems for UK students in wheelchairs. For example, handicapped students who want to meet with an administrator must make an appointment for somewhere else on campus because the Administration building is not accessible. Making appointments is usually not a problem, but there is still the fact that able-bodied students have no problem entering the Administration building while handicapped students cannot. Although handicapped students can enter the Gillis building, they cannot go beyond the ground floor and even have to push a button to get someone to come downstairs to help them. Finally, for handicapped students to get counseling from the Career Planning Center, they must set up an appointment to meet with someone at another place. Some of these students might not use the center's counseling services because of the extra effort and inconvenience involved (Croucher).

5 Even many of the buildings that are accessible have elevators, water fountains, and door handles that are inoperable by handicapped students, forcing them to ask somebody for assistance. If there is nobody around to ask, the handicapped student simply has to wait. In the Chemistry and Physics building, for example, a key is needed to operate the elevator, forcing wheelchair-bound students to ride up and down the hall to find somebody to help them. Many water fountains are inaccessible to people in wheelchairs, and some buildings have only one accessible water fountain. Finally, hardly any buildings have doorknobs that students with hand and arm impairments can operate independently.

6 In addition, many residence halls, such as Boyd, Donovan, Patterson, and Keenland, are completely inaccessible. When handicapped students want to drop by and see friends or attend a party in one of these dorms, they have to be carried up the steps. Kirivan Tower and Blanding Tower have no accessible bathrooms. Also, in Kirivan Tower the elevators are so small that someone has to lift the back of the wheelchair into the elevator. The complex low-rises—Shawneetown, Commonwealth Village, and Cooperstown Apartments—are also inaccessible. Cooperstown has some accessible first-floor apartments, but a handicapped student couldn't very well live there because the

bathrooms are inaccessible. All eleven sorority houses are inaccessible, and only five of the sixteen fraternity houses are accessible. Since the land that these sorority and fraternity houses are on is owned by the university, Section 504 of the Rehabilitation Act requires that the houses be accessible to handicapped students (University 14, 15).

7 With so many places on campus still inaccessible to wheelchair-bound UK students, it is obvious that hundreds of modifications need to be done. According to Jake Karnes, assistant dean of students and director of Handicap Student Services, "it will probably take close to $1 million to make UK totally accessible." UK's current budget allows for just $10,000 per year to go toward handicap modifications (Karnes). If no other source of funds is sought, the renovation process could be strung out for many years.

8 A possible solution could be the use of tuition. If only $2 were collected from each UK student's tuition, there would be almost $50,000 extra per semester for handicap modifications. Tuition is already used to pay for things ranging from teacher salaries to the funding of the campus radio station. This plan could be started with the upcoming fall semester. The money could be taken from each of the existing programs the tuition now pays for, so there would be no need for an increase in tuition. Also, this would not be a permanent expense because with an extra $50,000 a semester, all of the needed modifications could be completed within ten years. After that, the amount taken from the tuition could be lowered to fifty cents to help cover the upkeep costs of the campus improvements. This plan is practical—and more importantly, it is ethical. Surely if part of our tuition already goes to fund a radio station, some of it can be used to make UK a more accessible place. Which is more important, having a radio station to play alternative music or having a campus that is accessible to all students?

9 June 1980 was the deadline for meeting the requirements of Section 504 (Robinson 28). In compliance with the law, the University of Kentucky has spent almost $1 million making its campus more accessible. But there are still many more changes needed. These changes will take a lot of money, but if $2 could be used out of each student's tuition, the money would be there. Handicapped students often work to overachieve to prove their abilities. All they ask for is a chance, and that chance should not be blocked by high buttons, heavy doors, or steps.

Works Cited

Croucher, Lisa. "Accountability at UK for Handicapped Still Can Be Better." *Kentucky Kernal* n.d.: n. pag.

Karnes, Jake. Personal interview. 17 Oct. 1989.
Rehabilitation Act of 1973. Title 5 of Pub. L. 93–112. 26 Sept. 1973. 87 stat. 355; 24 USC 794 as amended. *Federal Register* 24 (4 May 1977): 22681.
Robinson, Rita. "For the Handicapped: Renovation Report Card." *American School and University* Apr. 1980: 28.
University of Kentucky. Transition Plan. Report. N.d.

READING FOR MEANING

Write to create meanings for Long's proposal for improving wheelchair-bound students' life on campus.

READING LIKE A WRITER

Writers of proposals

- introduce the problem.
- present the solution.
- argue directly for the proposed solution.
- counterargue readers' objections, questions, and preferred solutions.
- establish credibility.

You have seen how important these writing strategies are in the proposal essays you have read, written about, and discussed in this chapter. Focus on one of these strategies in Long's essay, and analyze it carefully through close rereading and annotating. Then write several sentences explaining what you have learned about the strategy, giving specific examples from the reading to support your explanation. Add a few sentences evaluating how successfully Long uses the strategy to construct a persuasive argument.

REVIEWING WHAT MAKES PROPOSALS EFFECTIVE

In this chapter, you have been learning how to read proposals for meaning and how to read them like a writer. Before going on to write a proposal of your own, pause here to review and contemplate what you have learned about the elements of effective proposal writing.

Analyze

Choose one reading from this chapter that seems to you especially effective. Before rereading the selection, *jot down* one or two reasons you remember it as an example of good proposal writing.

Reread your chosen selection, adding further annotations about what makes it a particularly successful example of proposal writing. *Consider* the selection's purpose and how well it achieves that purpose for its intended readers. (You can make an informed guess about the intended readers and their expectations by noting the publication source of the essay.) Then *focus* on how well the essay

- introduces the problem.
- presents the solution.
- argues directly for the proposed solution.
- counterargues readers' objections, questions, and preferred solutions.
- establishes credibility.

You can review all of these basic features in the Guide to Reading Proposals (p. 383).

Your instructor may ask you to complete this activity on your own or to work with a small group of other students who have chosen the same reading. If you work with others, allow enough time initially for all group members to reread the selection thoughtfully and to add their annotations. Then *discuss* as a group what makes the essay effective. *Take notes* on your discussion. One student in your group should then report to the class what the group has learned about the effectiveness of proposal writing. If you are working individually, write up what you have learned from your analysis.

Write

Write at least a page explaining your choice of this reading as an example of effective proposal writing. *Assume* that your readers—your instructor and classmates—have read the selection but will not remember many details about it. They also may not remember it as especially successful. Therefore, you will need to *refer* to details and specific parts of the reading as you explain how it works and as you justify your evaluation of its effectiveness. You need not argue that it is the best essay in the chapter or that it is flawless, only that it is, in your view, a strong example of the genre.

A Guide to Writing Proposals

The readings in this chapter have helped you learn a great deal about proposal writing. A proposal has two basic features: the problem and the solution. Now that you have seen how writers establish that the problem exists and is serious, offer a detailed analysis of the problem, attempt to convince readers to accept the solution offered, and demonstrate how the proposed solution can be implemented, you can approach this type of writing confidently. Using these strategies will help you develop a convincing proposal of your own.

This Guide to Writing is designed to assist you in writing your essay. Here you will find activities to help you identify a subject and discover what to say about it, organize your ideas and draft the essay, read the draft critically, revise the draft to strengthen your argument, and edit and proofread the essay to improve readability.

INVENTION

Invention is a process of discovery and planning by which you generate something to say. The following invention activities will help you choose a problem for study, analyze the problem and identify a solution, consider your readers, develop an argument for your proposed solution, and research your proposal. A few minutes spent completing each writing activity will improve your chances of producing a detailed and convincing first draft.

Choosing a Problem

Begin the selection process by reviewing what you wrote under "Considering Ideas for Your Own Writing." Then, try listing several groups or organizations to which you presently belong—for instance, a neighborhood or town, film society, dormitory, sports team, biology class. For each group, list as many problems facing it as you can. If you cannot think of any problems for a particular organization, consult with other members. Then reflect on your list of problems, and choose the one for which you would most like to find a solution. It can be a problem that everyone already knows about or one about which only you are aware.

Proposing to solve a problem in a group or community to which you belong gives you an important advantage: You can write as an expert, an insider. You know about the history of the problem, have felt the urgency to solve it, and perhaps have already thought of possible solutions. Equally important, you know precisely where to send the proposal and who would most benefit from it. You have the access needed to interview others in the group, people who can contribute different, even dissenting viewpoints about your problem and solution. You are in a position of knowledge and authority—from which comes confident, convincing writing. If you choose a problem that affects a wider group, concentrate on one with which you have direct experience and for which you can suggest a detailed plan of action.

Developing Your Proposal

The writing and research activities that follow will enable you to test your problem and proposal and develop an argument that your readers will take seriously.

Analyzing the Problem. Write a few sentences in response to each of these questions:

- Does the problem really exist? How can you tell?
- What caused this problem? Consider immediate and deeper causes.
- What is the history of the problem?
- What are the negative consequences of the problem?
- Who in the community or group is affected by the problem?
- Does anyone benefit from the existence of the problem?

Considering Your Readers. *With your understanding of the problem in mind, write for a few minutes about your intended readers.* Will you be writing to all members of your group or to only some of them? To an outside committee that might supervise or evaluate the group, or to an individual in a position of authority inside or outside the group? Briefly justify your choice of readers. Then gauge how much they already know about the problem and what solutions they might prefer. Consider the problem's direct or indirect impact on them. Comment on what values and attitudes you share with your readers and how they have responded to similar problems in the past.

Finding a Tentative Solution. *List at least three possible solutions to the problem.* Think about solutions that have already been tried as well as solutions that have been proposed for related problems. Find, if you can, solutions that eliminate causes of the problem. Also consider solutions that reduce the symptoms of the problem. If the problem seems too complex to be solved all at once, list solutions for one or more parts of the problem. Maybe a series of solutions is required and a key solution should be proposed first. From your list, choose the solution that seems to you most timely and practicable and write two or three sentences describing it.

Anticipating Readers' Objections. *Write a few sentences defending your solution against each of the following predictable objections.* For your proposal to succeed, readers must be convinced to take the solution seriously. Try to imagine how your prospective readers will respond.

- It won't really solve the problem.
- I'm comfortable with things as they are.
- We can't afford it.
- It will take too long.
- People won't do it.
- Too few people will benefit.
- I don't see how to get started on your solution.
- It's already been tried, with unsatisfactory results.
- You're making this proposal because it will benefit you personally.

Counterarguing Alternative Solutions. *Identify two or three likely solutions to the problem that your readers may prefer, solutions different from your own.* Choose the one that poses the most serious challenge to your solution. Then write a few sentences comparing your solution with the alternative solution, weighing the strengths and weaknesses of each. Explain how you might demonstrate to readers that your solution has more advantages and fewer disadvantages than the alternative solution.

Supporting Your Solution. *Write down every plausible reason your solution should be heard or tried.* Then review your list and highlight the strongest reasons, the ones most likely to persuade your readers. Write for a few minutes about the single most convincing reason for your solution. Support this reason in any way you can. You want to build an argument that readers will take seriously.

Researching Your Proposal. *Try out your proposal on members of the group, or go to the library to research a larger social or political problem.* If you are writing about a problem affecting a group to which you belong, talk with other members of the group to learn more about their understanding of the problem. Try out your solution on one or two people; their objections and questions will help you counterargue and support your argument more successfully.

If you are writing about a larger social or political problem, you should do research to confirm what you remember and to learn more about the problem. You can probably locate all the information you need in a good research library or on the Internet; you could also interview an expert on the problem. Readers will not take you seriously unless you are well informed.

Formulating a Working Thesis. *Draft a thesis statement.* A working thesis helps you begin drafting your essay purposefully. The thesis statement in a proposal is simply a statement of the solution you propose. Keep in mind that you may need to revise your thesis as you develop a first draft and learn more about your proposal. Here are three examples from the readings:

- "I'm not tinkering here—this is no 'raise the rim,' 'widen the lane' Band-Aid I'm proposing. Rather, I'm going straight to the heart of the problem. It's just too crowded out there. Basketball is meant to be played four on four" (Ryder, paragraph 5).
- "If we want to interrupt criminal paths and reduce the number of juveniles launching criminal careers, a shift in our priorities is necessary. States must invest their money in delinquency-prevention programs—at the front end rather than the back end of problems. These efforts should be targeted at elementary-school students from poor, high-crime neighborhoods, where traditional avenues to success are blocked" (Loughran, paragraph 12).
- "If professors gave additional brief exams at frequent intervals, students would learn more, study more regularly, worry less, and perform better on midterms, finals, and other papers and projects" (O'Malley, paragraph 2).

Notice that each of these thesis statements makes clear what the writer is proposing. Each thesis also mentions or implies the problem to be solved, even though it has already been described in the essay. Note that O'Malley's thesis statement forecasts the benefits of solving the problem, a strategy that helps readers anticipate how the argument is sequenced.

Considering Visuals. *Consider whether visuals—drawings, photographs, tables, or graphs—would strengthen your proposal.* You could construct your own visuals, scan materials from books and magazines, or download them from the Internet. If you submit your essay electronically to other students and your instructor, or if you post it on a Web site, consider including photographs as well as snippets of film or sound. Visual and auditory materials are not at all a requirement of a successful proposal, as you can tell from the readings in this chapter, but they could add a new dimension to your writing. If you want to use photographs or recordings of people, though, be sure to obtain their permission.

DRAFTING

The following guidelines will help you set goals for your draft and plan its organization.

Setting Goals

Establishing goals for your draft before you begin writing will enable you to make decisions and work more confidently. Consider the following questions now, and keep them in mind as you draft. They will help you set goals for drafting as well as recall how the writers you have read in this chapter tried to achieve similar goals.

- *How can I introduce the problem in a way that interests my readers and convinces them that it needs to be solved?* Like Ryder, do I have to convince my readers that there really is a problem? Like Newman, should I draw on my authority from having observed the group carefully for some time? Must I describe the problem at length, as Loughran does, or merely identify it, as O'Malley does?
- *How should I present the solution?* Should I describe in detail how the solution might be implemented, as do Loughran and Newman? Or need I describe the solution only briefly, like Samuelson, Ryder, and O'Malley do, letting other interested parties work out the details and take action?
- *How can I argue convincingly for my proposed solution?* Should I give examples of similar solutions that have proven successful, as Hertsgaard does? Describe the benefits of my solution, as Newman and O'Malley do? Offer statistics, like Loughran and Long? Provide scenarios for what the solution could look like, as Ryder does? Or, like O'Malley, refer to research?
- *How should I anticipate readers' objections and their preferred alternative solutions?* Should I refute readers' likely objections to the argument for my solution, as O'Malley and Samuelson do? Should I attempt to answer readers' questions, as Ryder does? Should I accommodate objections from my readers, as Hertsgaard does when he acknowledges that his proposal is not a "silver bullet"? Should I consider and refute alternative solutions, as O'Malley and Samuelson do?
- *How can I establish my credibility so that my readers will want to join me in taking action to solve the problem?* Should I feature my firsthand experience with the problem, as Loughran, O'Malley, and Long do? Should I set up a logical step-by-step argument, as all the writers in this chapter do? Should I show my respect for and knowledge of my readers by counterarguing at length, as Ryder and O'Malley do? Can I reveal my efforts to learn about the problem by quoting some of the people I interviewed (as Ryder and Long do) or by showing what I learned from published sources (as O'Malley and Hertsgaard do)?

Organizing Your Draft

With goals in mind and invention notes at hand, you are ready to make a first outline of your draft. The basic parts are quite simple: the problem, the solution, and the reasons in support of the solution. This simple plan is nearly always complicated by other factors, however. In outlining your material, you must take into consideration many other details, such as whether readers already recognize the problem, how much agreement exists on the need to solve the problem, how much attention should be given to alternative solutions, and how many objections and questions by readers should be expected.

Your outline should reflect your own writing situation. You should not hesitate to change this outline after you start drafting. For example, you might discover a more convincing way to order the reasons for adopting your proposal, or you might realize that counterargument must play a larger role than you first imagined. The purpose of an outline is to identify the basic features of your proposal, not to lock you in to a particular structure.

READING A DRAFT CRITICALLY

Getting a critical reading of your draft will help you see how to improve it. Your instructor may schedule class time for reading drafts, or you may want to ask a classmate or a tutor in the writing center to read your draft. Ask your reader to use the following guidelines and to write out a response for you to consult during your revision.

Read for a First Impression

1. Read the draft without stopping to annotate or comment, and then write two or three sentences giving your general impression.
2. Identify one aspect of the draft that seems to you particularly effective.

Read Again to Suggest Improvements

1. Recommend ways to present the problem more effectively.
   - Locate places in the draft where the problem is defined and described. Point to places where you believe the intended readers will need more explanation or where the presentation seems unclear or confusing.
   - Consider whether readers might want to know more about the causes or effects of the problem. Suggest ways the writer might do more to establish the seriousness of the problem, creating a sense of urgency to gain readers' support and to excite their curiosity about solutions.
2. Suggest ways to present the solution more effectively.
   - Find the solution, and notice whether it is immediately clear and readable. Point to places where it could be made clearer and more readable.

- Advise the writer whether it would help to lay out steps for implementation.
- Tell the writer how to make the solution seem more practical, workable, and cost-effective.

3. Recommend ways to strengthen the argument for the solution.
   - List the reasons the writer gives for adopting the solution or considering it seriously. Point out the reasons most and least likely to be convincing. Let the writer know whether there are too many or too few reasons. If the reasons are not sequenced in a logical, step-by-step sequence, suggest a new order.
   - Evaluate the support for each reason. Point out any passages where the support seems insufficient, and recommend further kinds of support.
4. Suggest ways to extend and improve the counterargument.
   - Locate places where the writer anticipates readers' objections to and questions about the proposal. Keeping in mind that the writer can accommodate or refute each objection or question, evaluate how successfully the writer does so. Recommend ways to make the response to each question or objection more convincing.
   - Suggest any likely objections and questions the writer has overlooked.
   - Identify any alternative solutions the writer mentions. Give advice on how the writer can present these alternative solutions more clearly and responsibly, and suggest ways to accommodate or refute them more convincingly.
5. Suggest ways to make the argument more credible.
   - Tell the writer whether the intended readers are likely to find the proposal knowledgeable and authoritative. Point to places where it seems most and least authoritative.
   - Identify places where the writer seems most insightful in anticipating what readers need to know, what questions and objections they may have, and what alternative solutions they may prefer. Note whether the writer responds to readers' concerns responsibly and respectfully.
6. Suggest how the organization might be improved.
   - Consider the overall plan, perhaps by making a scratch outline (see Appendix 1, p. 527, for advice on scratch outlining). Decide whether the reasons and counterarguments follow a logical, step-by-step sequence. Suggest a more logical sequence, if necessary.
   - Indicate where new or better transitions might help identify steps in the argument and keep readers on track.

7. Evaluate the effectiveness of visuals.
   - Look at any visuals in the essay, and tell the writer what they contribute to your understanding of the writer's argument.
   - If any visuals do not seem relevant, or if there seem to be too many visuals, identify the ones that the writer could consider dropping, explaining your thinking.
   - If a visual does not seem to be appropriately placed, suggest a better place for it.

REVISING

This section offers suggestions for revising your draft, suggestions that will remind you of the possibilities for developing a convincing proposal. Revising means reenvisioning your draft, trying to see it in a new way, given your purpose and readers, in order to develop your argument.

The biggest mistake you can make while revising is to focus initially on words or sentences. Instead, first try to see your draft as a whole in order to assess its likely impact on readers. Think imaginatively and boldly about cutting unconvincing material, adding new material, and moving material around to improve readability and strengthen your argument. Your computer makes even drastic revisions physically easy, but you still need to make the mental effort and decisions that will improve your draft.

You may have received help with this challenge from a classmate or tutor who gave your draft a critical reading. If so, keep this valuable feedback in mind as you decide which parts of your draft need revising and what specific changes you could make. The following suggestions will help you solve problems and strengthen your essay.

To Introduce the Problem More Effectively

- If readers are unfamiliar with the problem or doubt that it exists, briefly address its history or describe it in some detail to make its impact seem real.
- If readers know about the problem but believe it is insignificant, argue for its seriousness, perhaps by dramatizing its current and long-term effects. Or speculate about the complications that might arise in the future if the problem is not solved.

To Present the Solution More Effectively

- If readers cannot see how to implement your proposed solution, outline the steps of its implementation. Lead them through it chronologically.

Demonstrate that the first step is easy to take; or, if it is unavoidably challenging, propose ways to ease the difficulty.

- If a solution is beyond your expertise, explain where the experts can be found and how they can be put to use.
- If all readers can readily imagine how the solution would be implemented and how it would look once in place, reduce the amount of space you give to presenting the solution.

To Strengthen the Argument for the Proposed Solution

- If you have not given adequate reasons for proposing the solution, give more reasons.
- If your reasons are hidden among other material, move them to the foreground. Consider announcing them explicitly at the beginnings of paragraphs (the first reason why, the second, the third; the main reason why; the chief reason for; and so on).
- If your argument seems unconvincing, support your reasoning and argument with examples, anecdotes, statistics, quotes from authorities or members of the group, or any other appropriate support.

To Strengthen the Counterarguments

- If you have not anticipated all of your readers' weighty objections and questions, do so now. Consider carefully whether you can accommodate some objections by either granting their wisdom or adapting your solution in response to them. If you refute objections or dismiss questions, do so in a spirit of continuing collaboration with members of your group; there is no need to be adversarial. You want readers to support your solution and perhaps even to join with you in implementing it.
- If you have neglected to mention alternative solutions that are popular with readers, do so now. You may accommodate or reject these alternatives, or—a compromise—incorporate some of their better points. If you must reject all aspects of an alternative, do so through reasoned argument, without questioning the character or intelligence of those who prefer the alternative. You may be able to convince some of them that your solution is the better one.

To Enhance Credibility

- If critical readers of your draft questioned your credibility, learn more about the problem, seek advice on presenting the solution in a more compelling way, make the feasibility of the solution clearer, and talk with more members of the group so that you can incorporate or address more viewpoints.

- If your attitude toward your readers weakens your credibility, look for ways to show readers more respect and to establish a common ground with them.

To Organize More Logically and Coherently

- If your argument lacks logical progression, reorganize the reasons supporting your proposed solution.
- If your various counterarguments are not smoothly integrated into your argument, try another sequence or add better transitions.

EDITING AND PROOFREADING

After you have revised your essay, be sure to spend some time checking for errors in usage, punctuation, and mechanics and considering matters of style. If you keep a list of errors you typically make, begin by checking your draft against this list. Ask someone else to proofread your essay before you print out a copy for your instructor or send it electronically.

From our research on student writing, we know that proposal writers tend to refer to the problem or solution by using the pronoun *this* or *that* ambiguously. Edit carefully any sentences with *this* or *that* to ensure that a noun immediately follows the pronoun to make the reference clear. Check a writer's handbook for help with avoiding ambiguous pronoun reference.

REFLECTING ON WHAT YOU HAVE LEARNED

Proposal to Solve a Problem

In this chapter, you have read critically several proposals and have written one of your own. To better remember what you have learned, pause now to reflect on the reading and writing activities you completed in this chapter.

1. *Write* a page or so reflecting on what you have learned. *Begin* by describing what you are most pleased with in your essay. Then *explain* what you think contributed to your achievement. *Be specific* about this contribution.
    - If it was something you learned from the readings, *indicate* which readings and specifically what you learned from them.

- If it came from your invention writing, *point out* the section or sections that helped you most.
- If you got good advice from a critical reader, *explain* exactly how the person helped you—perhaps by helping you understand a particular problem in your draft or by adding a new dimension to your writing.

Try to write about your achievement in terms of what you have learned about the genre.

2. Now *reflect* more generally on proposals, a genre of writing that plays an important role in our society. *Consider* some of the following questions: How confident do you feel about making a proposal that might lead to improvements in the functioning of an entire group or community? Does your proposal attempt fundamental or minor change in the group? How necessary is your proposed change in the scheme of things? Whose interest would be served by the solution you propose? Who else might be affected? In what ways does your proposal challenge the status quo in the group? What contribution might essays proposing solutions to problems make to our society that other genres of writing cannot make?

CHAPTER 

Position Paper

You may associate arguing with quarreling or with the in-your-face debating we hear so often on radio and television talk shows. These ways of arguing may let us vent strong feelings, but they seldom lead us to consider seriously other points of view, let alone to look critically at our own thinking or learn anything new.

This chapter presents a more deliberative way of arguing that we call *reasoned argument* because it depends on giving reasons rather than raising voices. It demands that positions be supported rather than merely asserted. It also commands respect for the right of others to disagree with you as you may disagree with them. Reasoned argument requires more thought than quarreling, but no less passion or commitment, as you will see when you read the position papers in this chapter.

Controversial issues are, by definition, issues about which people have strong feelings and sometimes disagree vehemently. The issue may involve a practice that has been accepted for some time, like naming sports teams for Native American tribes, or it may concern a newly proposed or recently instituted policy, like federal limits on embryonic stem cell research. People may agree about goals but disagree about the best way to achieve them, as in the perennial debate over how to guarantee adequate health care for all citizens. Or they may disagree about fundamental values and beliefs, as in the debate over affirmative action in college admissions.

As these examples suggest, position papers take on controversial issues that have no obvious "right" answer, no truth everyone accepts, no single authority everyone trusts. Consequently, simply gathering information—finding the facts or learning from experts—will not settle these disputes because ultimately they are matters of opinion and judgment.

Although it is not possible to prove that a position on a controversial issue is right or wrong, it is possible through argument to convince others to consider a particular position seriously or to accept or reject a position. To be convincing, a position paper must argue for its position by giving readers strong reasons and solid support. It also must anticipate opposing arguments.

As you read and discuss the selections in this chapter, you will discover why position papers play such an important role in college, the workplace, and civic life. You will also learn how position papers work. From the essays and from the ideas for writing that follow each selection, you will get many ideas for taking a position on an issue that you care about. As you read and write about the selections, keep in mind the following assignment, which sets out the goals for writing a position paper. The Guide to Writing Position Papers, which follows the readings, supports your writing of this assignment.

THE WRITING ASSIGNMENT

Arguing a Position on an Issue

Choose an issue about which you have strong feelings. Write an essay arguing your position on this issue. Your purpose is to try to convince your readers to take your argument seriously. Therefore, you will want to acknowledge readers' opposing views as well as any objections or questions they might have.

WRITING SITUATIONS FOR POSITION PAPERS

Writing that takes a position on a controversial issue plays a significant role in college work and professional life, as the following examples indicate:

- A committee made up of business and community leaders investigates the issue of regulating urban growth. After reviewing the arguments for and against government regulation, committee members argue against it on the grounds that supply and demand alone will regulate development, that landowners should be permitted to sell their property to the highest bidder, and that developers are guided by the needs of the market and thus serve the people.

- For a sociology class, a student writes a term paper on surrogate mothering. She first learns about the subject from television news, but she knows that she needs more information to write a paper on the topic. In the library, she finds several newspaper and magazine articles that help her understand better the debate over the issue. In her paper, she presents the strongest arguments on each side but concludes that, from a sociological perspective, surrogate mothering should not be allowed because it exploits poor women by creating a class of professional breeders.

- For a political science class, a student is assigned to write an essay on public employees' right to strike. Having no well-defined position herself, she discusses the issue with her mother, a nurse in a county hospital, and her uncle, a firefighter. Her mother believes that public employees like hospital workers and teachers should have the right to strike, but that police officers and firefighters should not because public safety would be endangered. The uncle disagrees, arguing that allowing hospital workers to strike would jeopardize public safety as much as allowing firefighters to strike. He insists that the central issue is not public safety, but individual rights. In her essay, the student supports the right of public employees to strike, but she argues that the timing of a strike should be arbitrated whenever a strike might jeopardize public safety.

A Guide to Reading Position Papers

This guide introduces you to essays that take a position on controversial issues. By completing all of the activities, you will prepare yourself to learn a great deal from the other readings in this chapter about how to read and write a position paper. The guide focuses on a brief but forceful argument by Richard Estrada against the practice of naming sports teams and mascots after Native Americans.

You will read Estrada's essay twice. First, you will read it for meaning, seeking to understand and respond to Estrada's argument. Then, you will read the essay like a writer, analyzing the parts to see how Estrada crafts his essay and to learn the strategies he uses to make his argument convincing. These two activities—reading for meaning and reading like a writer—follow every reading in this chapter.

RICHARD ESTRADA

Sticks and Stones and Sports Team Names

Richard Estrada (1951–1999) wrote a nationally syndicated newspaper column. This essay was first published in the Dallas Morning News *on October 29, 1995, during the baseball World Series in which the Atlanta Braves played the Cleveland Indians. The series between these teams drew attention to a long-standing debate in the United States over sports teams using names associated with Native Americans, as well as dressing team mascots like Native Americans on the warpath and encouraging fans to rally their teams with gestures like the "tomahawk chop" and pep yells like the "Indian chant." Various high schools and at least one university, Stanford, have changed the names of their sports teams in recent years because of this ongoing controversy.*

The title of the essay, as you may know, refers to a children's chant: "Sticks and stones will break my bones, but words will never hurt me." As you read, consider why Estrada thought this title was appropriate.

When I was a kid living in Baltimore in the late 1950s, there was only one professional sports team worth following. Anyone who ever saw the movie *Diner* knows which one it was. Back when we liked Ike, the Colts were the gods of the grid-iron and Memorial Stadium was their Mount Olympus. 1

Ah, yes: The Colts. The Lions. Da Bears. Back when defensive tackle Big Daddy Lipscomb was letting running backs know exactly what time it was, a young fan could easily forget that in a game where men were men, the teams they played on were not invariably named after animals. Among others, the Packers, the Steelers and the distant 49ers were cases in point. But in the roll call of pro teams, one name in particular always discomfited me: the Washington Redskins. Still, however willing I may have been to go along with the name as a kid, as an adult I have concluded that using an ethnic group essentially as a sports mascot is wrong. 2

The Redskins, along with baseball teams like the Atlanta Braves, the Cleveland Indians and the Kansas City Chiefs, should find other names that avoid highlighting ethnicity. 3

By no means were such names originally meant to disparage Native Americans. The noble symbols of the Redskins or college football's Florida Seminoles or the Illinois Illini are meant to be strong and proud. Yet, ultimately, the practice of using a people as mascots is dehumanizing. It sets them apart from the rest of society. It promotes the politics of racial aggrievement at a moment when our storehouse is running over with it. 4

The World Series between the Cleveland Indians and the Atlanta Braves reignited the debate. In the chill night air of October, tomahawk chops and war chants suddenly became far more familiar to millions of fans, along with the ridiculous and offensive cartoon logo of Cleveland's "Chief Wahoo." 5

The defenders of team names that use variations on the Indian theme argue that tradition should not be sacrificed at the altar of political correctness. In truth, the nation's No. 1 P.C. [politically correct] school, Stanford University, helped matters some when it changed its team nickname from "the Indians" to "the Cardinals." To be sure, Stanford did the right thing, but the school's status as P.C. without peer tainted the decision for those who still need to do the right thing. 6

Another argument is that ethnic group leaders are too inclined to cry wolf in alleging racial insensitivity. Often, this is the case. But no one should overlook genuine cases of political insensitivity in an attempt to avoid accusations of hypersensitivity and political correctness. 7

The real world is different from the world of sports entertainment. I recently heard a father who happened to be a Native American complain on the radio that his child was being pressured into participating in celebrations of Braves baseball. At his kid's school, certain days are set aside on which all children are told to dress in Indian garb and celebrate with tomahawk chops and the like. 8

That father should be forgiven for not wanting his family to serve as somebody's mascot. The desire to avoid ridicule is legitimate and understandable. Nobody likes to be trivialized or deprived of their dignity. This has nothing to do with political correctness and the provocations of militant leaders. 9

Against this backdrop, the decision by newspapers in Minneapolis, Seattle and Portland to ban references to Native American nicknames is more reasonable than some might think. 10

What makes naming teams after ethnic groups, particularly minorities, reprehensible is that politically impotent groups continue to be targeted, while politically powerful ones who bite back are left alone. How long does anyone think the name "Washington Blackskins" would last? Or how about "the New York Jews"? 11

With no fewer than 10 Latino ballplayers on the Cleveland Indians' roster, the team could change its name to "the Banditos." The trouble is, they would be missing the point: Latinos would correctly object to that stereotype, just as they rightly protested against Frito-Lay's use of the "Frito Bandito" character years ago. 12

It seems to me that what Native Americans are saying is that what would be intolerable for Jews, blacks, Latinos and others is no less offensive to them. Theirs is a request not only for dignified treatment, but for fair treatment as well. For America to ignore the complaints of a numerically small segment of the population because it is small is neither dignified nor fair. 13

READING FOR MEANING

Write to create meanings for Estrada's argument against using Native American names for sports teams.

Start Making Meaning

Begin by explaining briefly what you believe to be Estrada's purpose in writing this essay. What does he seem to want to accomplish with his particular readers? How does he hope to influence them? Give a few details from the reading to support your explanation. Then list the main reasons Estrada takes the position that he does (look for these reasons in paragraphs 4 and 11). Continue by writing about anything else in the essay or in your experience that contributes to your understanding of Estrada's argument. As you write, you may want to reread parts of the essay and add further annotations.

If You Are Stuck

If you cannot write at least a page, consider writing about

- the apparent contradiction between Estrada's assumption (in paragraph 4) that naming a sports team "the Redskins" was originally intended to be admiring and not disparaging, and his assertion in the next sentence that "ultimately, the practice of using a people as mascots is dehumanizing."
- the term "political correctness" (paragraph 6)—what you think it means and how Estrada's argument relates to it.
- the power of words to hurt, especially words that make people feel different or inferior, perhaps relating to your own experience of being called demeaning names.
- a question you would like to ask Estrada, an addition you would make to his argument, or an alternative position you would argue for.

READING LIKE A WRITER

This section guides you through an analysis of Estrada's argumentative writing strategies: *presenting the issue; asserting a clear, unequivocal position; arguing directly for the position; counterarguing objections and opposing positions;* and *establishing credibility.* For each strategy you will be asked to reread and annotate part of Estrada's essay to see how he uses the strategy in "Sticks and Stones and Sports Team Names."

When you study the selections later in this chapter, you will see how different writers use the same strategies to develop a position paper. The Guide to Writing Position Papers near the end of this chapter suggests ways you can use these strategies in your own writing.

Presenting the Issue

For position papers published in the midst of an ongoing public debate, writers may need only to mention the issue. In most cases, however, writers need to identify the issue as well as explain it to readers. To present the issue, writers may provide several kinds of information. They may, for example, place the issue in its historical or cultural context, cite specific instances to make the issue seem less abstract, show their personal interest in the debate, or establish or redefine the terms of the debate.

Analyze

1. *Reread* paragraphs 1 and 2, where Estrada introduces the issue, and *make notes* about the approach he takes.
2. Then, *reread* paragraph 5, where Estrada describes the events at the World Series that "reignited the debate." *Look closely* at his description of the television images, and *underline* any words that might lead readers to take his argument seriously.

Write

Write several sentences describing how Estrada presents the issue. Specifically, how does he introduce the issue and connect it to his readers' experiences and interests? Then *add a few sentences* evaluating how successfully Estrada presents the issue and prepares readers for his argument.

Asserting a Clear, Unequivocal Position

Writers of position papers always take sides. Their primary purpose is to assert a position of their own and to influence readers' thinking. This assertion is the main point of the essay, its thesis. Writers try to state the thesis simply and directly, although they may qualify the thesis by limiting its applicability. For example, a thesis in favor of the death penalty might limit capital punishment to certain kinds of crimes. The thesis statement often forecasts the stages of the argument as well, identifying the main reason or reasons that will be developed and supported in the essay.

Where the thesis is placed depends on various factors. Most likely, you will want to place the thesis early in the essay to let readers know right away where you stand. But when you need to spend more time presenting the issue or defining the terms of the debate, you might postpone introducing your own position. Restating the thesis at various points and at the end can also help keep readers oriented.

Analyze

1. *Find* the first place where Estrada explicitly asserts his position (at the end of paragraph 2), and *underline* the sentence that states the thesis.
2. *Skim* paragraphs 3, 4, 9, and 13, and *put brackets around* the sentences in these paragraphs that restate the thesis.
3. *Examine* the context for each of these restatements. *Look closely* at the language he uses to see whether he repeats key words, uses synonyms, or adds new words.

Write

Write a few sentences explaining what you have learned about how Estrada states and restates his position. *Describe* the different contexts in which he restates the thesis and how the wording changes. *Cite examples* from the reading. Then *write a few more sentences* speculating about the possible reasons for reasserting a thesis so often in a brief essay like this one.

Arguing Directly for the Position

Not only do writers of position papers explicitly assert their positions, but they also give reasons for them. Moreover, they usually support their reasons with facts, statistics, examples, anecdotes, quotes from authorities, and analogies.

Facts are statements that can be proven objectively to be true; but readers may need to be reassured that the facts indeed come from trustworthy sources. Although *statistics* may be mistaken for facts, they often are only interpretations or correlations of numerical data. Their reliability depends on how and by whom the information was collected and interpreted. *Examples* and *anecdotes,* in contrast, tend *not* to make truth claims or pretend to apply to everyone. Instead, they present particular stories and vivid images that work by appealing to readers' emotions. Somewhere in between these two extremes are expert opinions and analogies. Readers must decide whether to regard *quotes from experts* as credible and authoritative. They must also decide how much weight to give *analogies,* comparisons that encourage readers to assume that what is true about one thing is also true about something to which it is compared. As a critical reader, you should look skeptically at analogies to determine whether they are logical as well as persuasive.

Analyze

1. *Reread* paragraphs 11–13, where Estrada develops his final reason for opposing the use of Native American names for sports teams. *Find* the first place where Estrada explicitly asserts his reason, and *put brackets around* the

sentence or sentences that state the topic sentence of this part of his argument.

2. *Look at* how Estrada supports this reason with analogy. *Underline* the three sports team names that he facetiously proposes in paragraphs 11 and 12, and then *compare* them to the actual teams named after Native Americans that he mentions in paragraphs 2–4.

3. *Consider* how persuasive his analogies are in paragraphs 11 and 12.

Write

Write several sentences briefly describing Estrada's strategy of argument by analogy. *Cite examples* of his analogies. Then *add a few sentences* speculating about the persuasiveness of his strategy of arguing by analogy. Why do you think some readers would find the argument in this part of the essay compelling and other readers would not?

Counterarguing Objections and Opposing Positions

Writers of position papers often try to anticipate likely objections and questions readers might raise as well as opposing positions. Writers may concede points with which they agree and may even modify a thesis to accommodate valid objections. But when they think the criticism is groundless or opposing arguments are flawed, writers counterargue aggressively. They refute the challenges to their argument by poking holes in their opponents' reasoning and support.

Analyze

1. *Reread* paragraphs 6 and 7, where Estrada introduces two opposing arguments to his position. *Underline* the sentence in each paragraph that best states the opposing positions.

2. *Examine* paragraphs 6–9 to see how Estrada counterargues these two predictable opposing arguments. For example, *notice* that he both concedes and refutes, and *consider* why he would attempt to do both. What seems to be his attitude toward those who disagree with him or, at least, object to parts of his argument?

3. *Consider* how well the anecdote about a Native American father (paragraphs 8 and 9) supports Estrada's counterargument, particularly why the anecdote might appeal to his *Dallas Morning News* readers.

Write

Write several sentences briefly explaining Estrada's counterargument. Then *add a few sentences* evaluating the probable success of this strategy with his newspaper readers.

Establishing Credibility

Readers judge the credibility of a position paper about a controversial issue by the way it presents the issue, argues for the position, and counterargues objections and opposing positions. Critical readers expect writers to advocate forcefully for their position, but at the same time they expect writers to avoid misrepresenting other points of view, attacking opponents personally, or manipulating readers' emotions. To establish credibility, writers thus aim instead to support their argument responsibly with the help of authoritative sources and a well-reasoned, well-supported argument.

Another factor that can influence readers' judgment of an argument's credibility is whether the writer seems to share at least some of their values, beliefs, attitudes, and ideals. Readers often are more willing to trust a writer who expresses concerns they also have about an issue. Many readers respect arguments based on strong values even if they do not share those particular values or hold to them as strictly. Yet readers also tend to dislike moralizing and resent a condescending or belittling tone as much as a shrill or hectoring one. Instead, readers usually appreciate a tone that acknowledges legitimate differences of opinion, while seeking to establish common ground where possible.

Analyze

1. Quickly *reread* Estrada's entire essay. As you read, *put a question mark* in the margin next to any passages where you doubt Estrada's credibility, and *put a checkmark* next to any passages where he seems especially trustworthy.
2. *Review* the passages you marked. Where possible, *note in the margin* a word or phrase that describes the dominant tone of each marked passage.
3. Then *consider* what language, information, or other element in the marked passages contributes to your judgment of Estrada's credibility.

Write

Write several sentences describing your impression of Estrada's credibility. *Cite examples* from the reading to support your view.

Readings

MICHAEL SANDEL

Bad Bet

Michael Sandel (b. 1953) is a professor of government at Harvard University. A Rhodes Scholar, he earned a doctorate from Oxford University. He writes frequently for general publications such as the Atlantic Monthly, New York Times, *and* New Republic. *His books include* Democracy's Discontent: America in Search of a Public Philosophy *(1996),* Liberalism and Its Critics *(1984), and* Liberalism and the Limits of Justice *(1999).*

In this essay published in the New Republic *in 1997, Sandel takes a position on state-sponsored lotteries: He opposes such lotteries, defining them as a form of civic corruption that undermines democracy. By "civic" he means those activities available to all citizens of a democracy regardless of their religious or political affiliations—activities like voting, going to school, joining various organizations, seeking information about local or national problems and issues, exercising rights of speech or assembly, and supporting an admired public official or working to defeat a disliked one.*

Before you read, think about your own experiences with gambling—perhaps with friends, on the Internet, or in clubs and casinos—or with state lotteries. Have you or members of your family purchased lottery tickets? With what result? What do you know about how your state's lottery operates? What programs does it offer, and how does it advertise them? What are your personal views about gambling and lotteries?

As you read, notice how Sandel presents the views of lottery proponents or defenders, while arguing energetically for his own views.

1 Political corruption comes in two forms. Most familiar is the hand-in-the-till variety: bribes, payoffs, influence-peddling, lobbyists lining the pockets of public officials in exchange for access and favors. This corruption thrives in secrecy, and is usually condemned when exposed.

2 But another kind of corruption arises, by degree, in full public view. It involves no theft or fraud, but rather a change in the habits of citizens, a turning away from public responsibilities. This second, civic corruption, is more insidious than the first. It violates no law, but enervates the spirit on which good laws depend. And by the time it becomes apparent, the new habits may be too pervasive to reverse.

3 Consider the most fateful change in public finance since the income tax: the rampant proliferation of state lotteries. Illegal in every state for most of the century, lotteries have suddenly become the fastest-growing source of state revenue. In 1970, two states ran lotteries; today, thirty-seven states and the District of Columbia run them. Nationwide, lottery sales exceed $34 billion a year, up from $9 billion in 1985.

4 The traditional objection to lotteries is that gambling is a vice. This objection has lost force in recent decades, partly because notions of sin have changed but also because Americans are more reluctant than they once were to legislate morality. Even people who find gambling morally objectionable shy away from banning it on that ground alone, absent some harmful effect on society as a whole.

5 Freed from the traditional, paternalistic objections to gambling, proponents of state lotteries advance three seemingly attractive arguments: first, lotteries are a painless way of raising revenue for important public services without raising taxes; unlike taxes, lotteries are a matter of choice, not coercion. Second, they are a popular form of entertainment. Third, they generate business for the retail outlets that sell lottery tickets (such as convenience stores, gas stations and supermarkets) and for the advertising firms and media outlets that promote them.

6 What, then, is wrong with state-run lotteries? For one thing, they rely, hypocritically, on a residual moral disapproval of gambling that their defenders officially reject. State lotteries generate enormous profits because they are monopolies, and they are monopolies because privately operated numbers games are prohibited, on traditional moral grounds. (In Las Vegas, where casinos compete with one another, the slot machines and blackjack tables pay out around 90 percent of their take in winnings. State lotteries, being monopolies, only pay out about 50 percent.) Libertarian defenders of state lotteries can't have it both ways. If a lottery is, like dry cleaning, a morally legitimate business, then why should it not be open to private enterprise? If a lottery is, like prostitution, a morally objectionable business, then why should the state be engaged in it?

7 Lottery defenders usually reply that people should be free to decide the moral status of gambling for themselves. No one is forced to play, they point out, and those who object can simply abstain. To those troubled by the thought that the state derives revenue from sin, advocates reply that government often imposes "sin taxes" on products (like liquor and tobacco) that many regard as undesirable. Lotteries are better than taxes, the argument goes, because they are wholly voluntary, a matter of choice.

8 But the actual conduct of lotteries departs sharply from this laissez-faire ideal. States do not simply provide their citizens the opportunity to gamble; they actively promote and encourage them to do so. The nearly $400 million spent on lottery advertising each year puts lotteries among the largest advertisers in the country. If lotteries are a form of "sin tax," they are the only kind in which the state spends huge sums to encourage its citizens to commit the sin.

9 Not surprisingly, lotteries direct their most aggressive advertising at their best customers—the working class, minorities and the poor. A billboard touting the Illinois lottery in a Chicago ghetto declared, "This could be your ticket out." Ads often evoke the fantasy of winning the big jackpot and never having to work again. Lottery advertising floods the airwaves around the first of each month, when Social Security and welfare payments swell the checking accounts of recipients. In sharp contrast to most other government amenities (say, police protection), lottery ticket outlets saturate poor and blue-collar neighborhoods and offer less service to affluent ones.

10 Massachusetts, with the highest grossing per capita lottery sales in the country, offers stark evidence of the blue-collar bias. A recent series in *The Boston Globe* found that Chelsea, one of the poorest towns in the state, has one lottery agent for every 363 residents; upscale Wellesley, by contrast, has one agent for every 3,063 residents. In Massachusetts, as elsewhere, this "painless" alternative to taxation is a sharply regressive way of raising revenue. Residents of Chelsea spent a staggering $915 per capita on lottery tickets last year, almost 8 percent of their income. Residents of Lincoln, an affluent suburb, spent only $30 per person, one-tenth of 1 percent of their income.

11 For growing numbers of people, playing the lottery is not the free, voluntary choice its promoters claim. Instant games such as scratch tickets and Keno (a video numbers game with drawings every five minutes), now the biggest money-makers for the lottery, are a leading cause of compulsive gambling, rivaling casinos and racetracks. Swelling the ranks of Gamblers Anonymous are lottery addicts, like the man who scratched $1,500 worth of tickets per day, exhausted his retirement savings and ran up debt on eleven credit cards.

12 Meanwhile, the state has grown as addicted to the lottery as its problem gamblers. Lottery proceeds now account for 13 percent of state revenues in Massachusetts, making radical change all but unthinkable. No politician, however troubled by the lottery's harmful effects, would dare raise taxes or cut spending sufficiently to offset the revenue the lottery brings in.

13 With states hooked on the money, they have no choice but to continue to bombard their citizens, especially the most vulnerable ones, with a message at odds with the ethic of work, sacrifice and moral responsibility that sustains democratic life. This civic corruption is the gravest harm that lotteries bring. It degrades the public realm by casting the government as the purveyor of a perverse civic education. To keep the money flowing, state governments across America must now use their authority and influence not to cultivate civic virtue but to peddle false hope. They must persuade their citizens that with a little luck they can escape the world of work to which only misfortune consigns them.

READING FOR MEANING

Write to create meanings for Sandel's position paper on the issue of state-sponsored lotteries.

Start Making Meaning

Begin by explaining briefly what you think Sandel's purpose is for writing this essay. What does he seem to want to accomplish with his readers? Then list the main reasons he advances to support his position (you will find the main reasons in paragraphs 6, 8, 9, and 11–13). Continue by writing about anything else in the selection or in your experience that contributes to your understanding of Sandel's argument.

If You Are Stuck

If you cannot write at least a page, consider writing about

- Sandel's charge of hypocrisy in paragraphs 6–8, defining *hypocrisy* and explaining who is being hypocritical and in what ways.
- whether state governments should attempt to define civic virtue and sustain democratic life by encouraging an "ethic of work, sacrifice and moral responsibility" (paragraph 13)—and if so how, in your opinion, they might do so.
- Sandel's claim that states' lottery ticket outlets far outnumber other state government "amenities"—benefits or services—in poor neighborhoods (paragraph 9), perhaps testing his claim against your own experience.
- Your own or your friends' or family's participation in a state lottery, reflecting on your experience in light of Sandel's argument.

READING LIKE A WRITER

COUNTERARGUING OBJECTIONS AND OPPOSING POSITIONS

Although counterarguing occasionally involves modifying your position to accommodate objections you consider valid, most often it simply means refuting opposing arguments. Refutation can be a small part of an argument or it can dominate the argument. Experienced writers know that a refutation's effectiveness depends largely on how staunch readers are in defending their opinions. If a reader's position is based on fundamental values and beliefs, then even the most compelling reasons and support are unlikely to shake his or her ideological foundations. But if a reader is at all uncertain, then supplying good counterarguments could influence his or her thinking on the issue.

Because refutation risks antagonizing readers, the tone of the argument is especially important. A tone perceived as hostile or sarcastic could be alienating, whereas a witty or easygoing tone could have the opposite effect of disarming readers, making them less defensive and more open to considering new ideas. Sandel organizes his argument around refutation. He outlines three opposing positions favored by proponents of state lotteries, and then he devotes nearly every sentence in the argument for his position to refuting these positions favored by his opponents.

Analyze

1. *Reread* paragraph 5, where Sandel lists the three positions favored by his opponents. *Underline* the first position, the one beginning with "lotteries are a painless way. . . ."

2. *Reread* from the last sentence in paragraph 7 to the end of paragraph 11, where Sandel attempts to refute the position that playing the lottery is a matter of choice and a painless way for citizens to pay part of their taxes. As you read, *notice* whether Sandel consistently refutes this opposing position or whether he even once concedes that there may be something useful in it. *Notice* also the tone he adopts: What seems to be his attitude toward his opponents?

3. Sandel relies on examples, statistics, and one research study to support his counterargument. *Reread* paragraphs 8–11, and *identify* these strategies. For instance, four examples are offered in paragraphs 8 and 9, the research study is cited in paragraph 10, and statistics are featured in nearly all four of these paragraphs.

4. *Evaluate* Sandel's success in this part of his counterargument, keeping in mind his readers and purpose.

Write

Write several sentences describing what you have learned about how Sandel counterargues. *Cite examples* from the reading. Then *write a few more sentences* telling whether you think his strategy is effective and why.

CONSIDERING IDEAS FOR YOUR OWN WRITING

Sandel is concerned about "a turning away from public responsibilities." Consider writing about a local civic issue related to this concern. Here are some possibilities: Should communities provide homeless people with free food and shelter? Should community growth be limited? Should height and design restrictions be placed on new commercial buildings? Should there be a police review board to handle complaints against the police? Should skateboarding be banned from all sidewalks? Should parents be held responsible legally and financially for crimes committed by their children under age eighteen? One major advantage of writing a position paper on a local civic issue is that you can gather information by researching the issue in local newspapers and talking with community leaders and residents.

MARI J. MATSUDA

Assaultive Speech and Academic Freedom

Well known for writing and speaking about constitutional law, hate speech, affirmative action, and feminist theory, Mari J. Matsuda is a law professor at Georgetown University Law Center. Before coming to Georgetown, she taught law at the University of California, Los Angeles. Her books include We Won't Go Back: Making the Case for Affirmative Action *(1997, edited with Charles R. Lawrence III and Kimberle Williams Crenshaw) and* Where Is Your Body?: And Other Essays on Race, Gender, and Law *(1997). She is currently working on a book about her father and his family, who were sent to Japanese American concentration camps in the United States during World War II.*

The following selection, first published in Where Is Your Body?, *is the text of a speech that Matsuda delivered at several universities in the late 1980s and early 1990s. Engaging an issue that was much debated during these years and one that is still of concern today, Matsuda takes the position that colleges should attempt to regulate students' speech in order to prevent assaultive or hateful speech on campus. As soon as you start reading, you will discover that Matsuda explores the issue primarily in terms of the effects of hateful speech on students at whom it is directed. As a constitutional lawyer, she is careful to make clear that she understands the speech guarantees in the First Amendment to the Constitution, but she insists on giving equal weight to the ideals of equality of access and equality of participation enshrined in the Constitution, ideals corrupted, in her view, by colleges that allow students to be harassed and intimidated by hateful speech. Toward the end of her essay, Matsuda gives reasons why she thinks colleges should take responsibility for protecting students by legislating speech codes or restrictions. So far, the courts have insisted that such restrictions violate the speech protections in the Constitution.*

Before you read, reflect on times in high school, in college, or at a workplace when another student or co-worker said (or wrote) something to you for the apparent purpose of insulting, hurting, frightening, silencing, or banning you. If you have not personally experienced this kind of hateful speech, perhaps you have heard it directed at others. Think particularly of any hateful speech that was aimed at you because you are a man or woman; a member of some religious, ethnic, or racial group; gay or lesbian; or somehow outside the norms for dress, interests, body type, or language use.

As you read, notice how Matsuda presents the issue in constitutional or legal terms, focusing on a major Supreme Court decision of the 1950s that ended racially segregated public schools and on the First Amendment protections for free speech. Because early attempts by colleges to write and enforce speech regulations were overturned by the courts, Matsuda makes a special effort to convince her listeners that, properly interpreted, as she sees it, the First Amendment supports speech regulation on college campuses.

What is a university, what is academic freedom, and how do people with different worldviews come together in the pursuit of knowledge? These are the questions I hope to address today as I consider the problem of campus regulation of racist, sexist, and homophobic speech. 1

First, I believe we should read the Constitution and the Bill of Rights as a whole. The values of equality and personhood run throughout our founding document. Equality of access and equality of participation are ideals that are central to and definitive of American democracy, particularly in the twentieth century. Hate speech on campus cuts deeply into equality of access for minority group members. To understand this, it is necessary to look at both the quantity and the quality of hate activity on campus. The quantity has increased to the point where few students of color can expect to go through four years of undergraduate education without encountering hate speech. By hate speech I refer to speech the only function of which is to wound and degrade by asserting the inherent inferiority of a group. Similarly, few women will leave our universities without encountering sexual harassment in the form of unwanted advances or a hostile environment created by sexist comments, pornography, or misogynist speech. 2

Exposure to these kinds of hate leaves lasting impressions on university students who come to the academy at a formative time in their lives. Students are a population particularly at risk for psychological harm. Younger students are forming their identities, abandoning old peer ties, and seeking out new ones. They are in a transitional stage vis-à-vis families, coming to a new understanding about what is good and bad in relationships with parents and siblings; playing out old dramas of interpersonal relationships with new characters; seeking self-knowledge; and considering what they want to do with their adult lives. Older students face the financial uncertainty and self-doubt that comes from returning to school. Many students—younger and older—are economically at risk, holding down part-time jobs, taking out loans, and hoping for financial aid. Some have partners or children or parents whom they are supporting. Some are academically at risk, unsure about how to make it in the maze of large classes, inacces- 3 sible professors, fancy-talking classmates, and cultural or class differences that make up the academic world. Even those excelling academically face self-doubt generated by examinations, grades, and job interviewing. Many emotional disorders manifest for the first time in college. Coming to the university is a major life stress event.

This is not the time to subject someone to psychological assault. It is not the time for a student to come back to her dorm room and find an anonymous note calling her ancestors filth, not a time for a student to come to class and find posters advocating the genocide of everyone of his religion, not a time to walk down the street and face shouts and threats and demeaning and hateful things said about one's body. The administrators and counselors on the front lines of dealing with students, those who know about the students who have changed majors, moved out of the dorm, dropped classes, gone into therapy, and left the university because of harassment know that the problem is a serious one. 4

A student in Texas told me of studying in her carrel at the library, getting up for a break, and coming back to find someone had drawn swastikas in the margin of her textbook and on her notes. 5

Another women, a white woman, told me of walking to school with her moot court partner, an African-American woman, when a passing motorist called out, "Get that n—— bitch off this campus." 6

A student writer at UCLA spoke of sitting in class listening to a lecture and discovering that someone had written on the wall next to her desk, "Kill all the jews." 7

On their way to a reception in my honor when I received tenure at UCLA, students who rode the elevator were confronted with graffiti that said, "I want Asian c——nt." 8

In each of these cases, students were participating in essential activities and daily life at the university—studying, walking to class, listening to the lecture, or attending a social event—when they were attacked out of the blue with a hateful and degrading message. They were ambushed, making the space that once seemed familiar and safe seem threatening and not one's own. 9

These students are supposed to keep functioning, and most of them do. Look away from the death threat, refocus on the lecture, and keep on taking notes. Turn the page, keep studying, ignore the swastikas. Continue down the street with your moot court partner, do not be late for class, and forget that someone felt compelled to threaten you and hate you in a public and aggressive way. Feel your knees go weak when the stranger yells from the car and keep walking, head erect, like you have a right to be there. 10

People manage, but they manage under a burden. Maybe they do not hear all the lecture. Maybe they do not get a full night's sleep, and maybe they do not do as well on the calculus exam. There is a cost, a burden, a price paid for the epidemic of assaultive speech on our campuses, and the cost is paid disproportionately by historically subordinated groups. 11

The principles of equality and liberty recognize the worth of every human being and the right of each to participate in the institutions of our nation. As Professor Charles Lawrence has pointed out, the case of *Brown v. Board of Education* was, at its core, a case about the way in which racist messages violate the rights of equality and liberty. In *Brown,* the court recognized that no matter how equal the schools, separating children on the basis of race was never constitutionally permissible. Why was this? We separate children all the time, by district, by birth date, and by ability. The reason it was not permissible to separate children by race was that segregation represented a racist ideology. Jim Crow embodied white supremacy: white is pure and must remain untainted by the dirt, by the filth, of the Other. The Supreme Court knew this when it decided *Brown,* and it considered substantial testimony about the psychological harm caused by segregation. Separate is never equal, the court found, because of the damage caused by *the message* of racial inferiority. *Brown* thus sets up a set of competing values at odds with the protection of racist speech. 12

In addition to the liberty and equality interests implicated by hate-speech regulations, there are also First Amendment reasons to ban hate speech. The goal of the First Amendment is to protect dissent, to maximize public discourse, and to achieve the great flowering of debate and of ideas that we need for democracy to work. Hate speech impedes these goals because hate speech is intended to and has the effect of cutting off debate. When someone calls you a hate name, they are not trying to get into a debate or even a rancorous argument with you. They are telling you that you are less than human, that you have no right to be here, and that your speech is worthless. The typical responses to racist hate speech include fear, flight, or fistfights. People use these words precisely because of the wounding, silencing effect. I suggest that there are some forms of speech we need to limit precisely because we value speech. 13

Let me give you some examples of hate speech limiting free speech. One of my students was discussing gay-rights issues with friends in a restaurant. A stranger came up to him and said aggressively, "Are you a f——gg——t?" My student said, yes, he is gay and proud of it. Then the assailant escalated his verbal abuse, 14 finally assaulting my student physically. Since the incident, the student tells me, his friends look over their shoulders and size up the room before they discuss gay issues. They speak in hushed tones; sometimes they do not speak. In this case, responding to hate speech with counterspeech resulted in physical assault.

15 Because physical abuse so often follows verbal abuse in our violent and patriarchal culture, it does not require actual physical assault for assaultive speech to silence. In San Francisco's Chinatown, community members who testified at a public hearing, many of them participating in the political process for the first time, found that their names and a racist, anti-Asian message were broadcast on the White Aryan Resistance hotline. Many of the speakers feared for their lives. They will think twice before testifying again.

16 Any university professor who has tried to promote classroom discussion about race, gender, and homosexuality knows how hard it is to get students to express their ideas, feelings, and disagreements about these topics. Our ability to speak across cultural divides is impeded by the feelings of animosity growing on our campuses. Hate speech shuts down conversations and keeps us from the important work of learning to talk across difference.

17 Let me emphasize that I believe in the First Amendment. It is absolutely critical, particularly in these days of economic collapse, that citizens retain the right of dissent, the right to criticize the government. In suggesting that the ugliest forms of hate speech should fall outside First Amendment protection, I make a distinction between dissent, or criticism directed against the powerful institutions that affect our lives, and hate speech, or speech directed against the least powerful segment of our communities.

18 It is the lawyer's job to make distinctions in principled ways, and the principle I suggest is that of antisubordination. Our minority students are already at risk for a variety of historical reasons. Many of them come from economically disadvantaged backgrounds. Many are of the first generation in their families to go to college. The antisubordination principle recognizes the historical reality that some members of our community are less powerful and have less access to education. The universities have come a long way in recognizing this, making commitments to affirmative action and to outreach programs to help less advantaged students. Protecting these students from psychological attack is part of that same ethical goal of equal opportunity and inclusion.

19 Universities bear special obligations for several reasons. First, universities are part of the public trust. They receive government

support in the form of subsidies and tax advantages. State universities are supported by taxpayers—by all taxpayers, including the working poor and immigrants who are less often the beneficiaries of a university education. Second, university students are a captive audience. Students cannot choose not to come to class, not to go to their mailboxes, and not to study in the library. When hate speech invades the campus, students have no choice, no place to go to escape the speech. Students are encouraged to think of the university as their home. The university encourages activities in and out of class and promotes a host of extracurricular clubs and events that are critical to the educational experience. The physical confines of the campus are not the anonymous places that city streets are. They are home. And to have ugly messages of hate posted on the walls of a home is much more of an intrusion than, say, a racist march downtown. "Invasion" is a word often used by people who have received hate messages in their dorms, in their churches or synagogues, and in their homes. The right to a sense of personal security in the geographic confines of a home place is something we owe our students.

20 Finally, universities are not neutral, relativistic, amoral institutions. They stand for something. They stand for the pursuit of knowledge. They stand for ethical striving. They stand for equal opportunity. We wave these values in letterheads, mottos, and catalogs used to recruit students. . . . We are about the pursuit of knowledge and ethics. We do teach values. . . .

21 A belief in human dignity is at the heart of what we do. Why else try to study and to know all the phenomena of the universe if we do not believe, ultimately, in the glory of life on this planet and the grace of knowing all we can about how to live decent lives while we are here? There is no value-free reason for our existence. We do stand for human dignity, and we must protect the dignity of each of our students. . . .

22 The unfortunate pattern of response to hate speech has been to do nothing until a serious incident creates a crisis. The crisis is then followed by hastily enacted rules or, worse yet, ex post facto discipline. These hate incidents are not going to go away. . . . We need to start by gathering information. Every campus should have a system for collecting data about hate incidents. We should provide fora for students to speak out about the discrimination they feel. We need to share this information among campuses, to get a clear picture of the extent of the problem and to develop proactive strategies for dealing with hate. I believe we should draft narrow regulations that will penalize the worst forms of assaultive speech, and I would challenge those who disagree with me to

come up with concrete alternative responses to hate speech, including strong nondisciplinary condemnation of bigotry, affirmative action programs, curriculum reform, and other means to improve the campus climate for underrepresented groups. There is a range of alternatives open to us, and I hope we continue to debate and consider them all.

23 The theme of this lecture is academic freedom. . . . Academic freedom must include freedom from racist and sexist oppression unless we mean that academic freedom is the sole property of the powerful. I think that the origin of the concept is exactly the opposite. It was the freedom to say that the planets revolve around the sun, even when the church insisted it was the other way around. It was the freedom to expose government corruption, even when the government is paying your salary. This courageous tradition is one we must preserve. It is not the same as the freedom to hurt and degrade the powerless.

24 Many will disagree with what I have said. I hope we can continue to argue with and learn from one another, letting our speech fill the space made by academic freedom.

READING FOR MEANING

Write to create meanings for Matsuda's position paper on the issue of whether colleges should restrict hateful, assaultive speech on campus to protect the students at whom it is directed.

Start Making Meaning

Begin by speculating about Matsuda's purpose. What do you think she wants her readers—all of the members of a campus community including students, professors, and administrators—to understand or do? If she wants them to take action, why do you suppose she gives so little attention to her listeners' points of view on the issue, to their likely objections to or questions about her position, and to their opposing arguments? Then list the main reasons Matsuda gives in support of her position (you will find these reasons in paragraphs 19 and 20). Continue by writing about anything else in the selection or in your experience that contributes to your understanding of Matsuda's argument.

If You Are Stuck

If you cannot write at least a page, consider writing about

- why Matsuda believes college students are especially vulnerable to hate speech (paragraphs 3–13), testing her conclusions against your own experience.

- a question you would like to ask Matsuda or an objection you have to some part of her argument, explaining why the question or objection is important to you.
- Matsuda's confidence that hate speech can and should be regulated on college campuses through rules that make clear what kinds of speech are unacceptable and how students who break the rules would be punished (paragraph 22), saying whether you agree or disagree with her and explaining why.
- your own experience with assaultive or hateful speech directed at you in high school, in college, or at a workplace, narrating what happened (where you were, who was there, what was said, what you said and did) and connecting your experience to Matsuda's argument.

READING LIKE A WRITER

PRESENTING THE ISSUE

Every position paper begins with an issue. Consequently, in planning and drafting a position paper, one of the first questions a writer must answer is how much readers know about the issue. If they are very familiar with the issue, the writer may need to tell them very little about it. If they are unfamiliar with the issue, however, the writer may need to present it in great detail. Whether they are familiar or unfamiliar with the issue, readers may benefit from knowing about its history. They may also appreciate the writer's speculations about the larger social significance of the issue and even the likely immediate personal importance of it to readers. Writers need not—and probably should not—assume that readers will find an issue immediately engaging and worth their time to learn more about. Writers may therefore open a position paper not with a straightforward description of the issue, but with an interesting anecdote, arresting quotation, troubling fact, doomsday scenario, rhetorical question, or something else that is likely to engage readers.

Besides meeting all of these readerly demands, writers must answer for themselves another important question: how to define the issue. Often, writers seek to redefine a familiar issue, in order to convince readers to look at it in a new way. If they succeed, then they can argue to support the issue in their own terms, as they have redefined it. Matsuda's position paper offers a very good example of this strategy. In fact, her lengthy presentation of the issue is an extended attempt to redefine the issue in a way that makes it seem more dangerous than her listeners may have thought and at the same more solvable than they had imagined, given the courts' refusal to support campus hate speech regulations. Matsuda begins by carefully defining hate speech and explaining what it means to become a college student. Then, more ambitiously, she attempts to define the issue not as one solely of speech restrictions but at least equally one of constraints on liberty and equality. Then, introducing the principle of "antisubordination," she argues that because hate speech impedes the goals of the First Amendment, it can be banned, not protected, by the First Amendment. It is easy to imagine that many of her listeners would be skeptical of these redefinitions of the issue because they are so unexpected. For you as a writer of a position paper, it will be instructive to analyze the strategies Matsuda adopts to achieve one of these redefinitions.

Analyze

1. *Underline* the sentence in paragraph 2 that defines "hate speech."
2. In paragraphs 13 and 17, Matsuda makes a distinction between "dissent" and "hate speech." *Underline* the words and phrases that help you understand this distinction.
3. Beginning in paragraph 13, Matsuda attempts to redefine the First Amendment as an amendment that both protects certain kinds of speech and bans other kinds of speech, particularly hate speech, because it limits free speech. *Reread* paragraphs 13–17, and *look closely* at how she supports this redefinition of free speech.

Write

Write several sentences explaining how Matsuda attempts to define hate speech in a way that would make it seem reasonable and constitutional to exclude it from the speech protections in the First Amendment. *Give details* from her argument to support your explanation. Then *add a few sentences* evaluating how successful this redefinition of free speech is likely to be with Matsuda's listeners.

CONSIDERING IDEAS FOR YOUR OWN WRITING

Consider answering Matsuda. For example, you could offer a different definition of a university from the one she proposes or a different view of what it is like to be a college student. The issue between the two of you would be how to define a university or what it is like to be a college student. On one of these issues, you would take a position opposing her position. Or you could take the position that it is unwise for colleges to attempt to regulate students' speech, arguing that hate speech is not really a problem, at least in your experience on your college campus, that her view of college life and the purpose of a college education is too limited, and that it is neither practical nor constitutional to regulate speech on college campuses.

Or you could consider taking a position on other school or college issues. Here are some possibilities: Should handicapped students receive special assignments to accommodate their abilities? Should pregnant students receive prenatal care and students with newborns receive day-care services at school? Should students who lack fluency in English receive education in bilingual classrooms? Should school districts offer Afrocentric courses or curricula? Should some students be able to avoid certain science subjects and activities, like evolution or dissecting a cat? Should teenagers be required to get their parents' permission to obtain birth-control information and contraceptives? Should training in music, drama, or art (drawing, painting, sculpting) be required of all high-school students? Should college admission be based solely on academic achievement in high school? Should students attending public colleges be required to pay higher tuition fees if they do not graduate within four years? Should colleges require students to perform community service as a condition of graduation? Should students choose a college or courses that would confirm or challenge their beliefs and values?

RANDALL KENNEDY

You Can't Judge a Crook by His Color

Randall Kennedy (b. 1954) is a law professor at Harvard University Law School. In 1983 and 1984, he was a law clerk for Supreme Court Justice Thurgood Marshall. Kennedy writes occasionally for general publications such as the New Republic, Time, *the* Boston Globe, *and the* Wall Street Journal. *He has also written* Race, Crime, and the Law *(1997), which won the 1998 Robert F. Kennedy Book Award, and* Interracial Intimacies *(2001). His honors include election to the American Academy of Arts and Sciences and an honorary degree from Haverford College.*

Kennedy wrote the following position paper for the New Republic *in 1999. In it he addresses the controversial issue of racial profiling, a law-enforcement strategy that relies on a suspect's race as a reason to question, search, or arrest that person. A lawyer, like Mari J. Matsuda, Kennedy is interested in the legal, social, and moral implications of racial profiling. Unlike Matsuda, however, he fully reviews the opposing position on this important current issue. In fact, readers must wait for several paragraphs to discover Kennedy's position, which may come as something of a surprise following his respectful presentation of the opposing position.*

Before you read, reflect on a time when you were stopped by the police but were not doing anything illegal. Why do you think you were stopped? What happened? What was your reaction at the time? How did it influence your attitude toward police officers and toward law enforcement in general?

As you read, be patient with Kennedy's careful, unhurried consideration of many aspects of this explosive issue. Because he has thought and written about racial profiling for several years, you are in the hands of a respected expert who is not going to oversimplify a complex issue. Be assured that he is writing not for fellow legal scholars but for readers like you.

1 In Kansas City, a Drug Enforcement Administration officer stops and questions a young man who has just stepped off a flight from Los Angeles. The officer has focused on this man because intelligence reports indicate that black gangs in L.A. are flooding the Kansas City area with illegal drugs. Young, toughly dressed, and appearing nervous, he paid for his ticket in cash, checked no luggage, brought two carry-on bags, and made a beeline for a taxi when he arrived. Oh, and one other thing: The young man is black. When asked why he decided to question this man, the officer declares that he considered race, along with other factors,

because doing so helps him allocate limited time and resources efficiently.

2 Should we applaud the officer's conduct? Permit it? Prohibit it? This is not a hypothetical example. Encounters like this take place every day, all over the country, as police battle street crime, drug trafficking, and illegal immigration. And this particular case study happens to be the real-life scenario presented in a federal lawsuit of the early '90s, *United States v. Weaver,* in which the 8th U.S. Circuit Court of Appeals upheld the constitutionality of the officer's action.

3 "Large groups of our citizens," the court declared, "should not be regarded by law enforcement officers as presumptively criminal based upon their race." The court went on to say, however, that "facts are not to be ignored simply because they may be unpleasant." According to the court, the circumstances were such that the young man's race, considered in conjunction with other signals, was a legitimate factor in the decision to approach and ultimately detain him. "We wish it were otherwise," the court maintained, "but we take the facts as they are presented to us, not as we would like them to be." Other courts have agreed that the Constitution does not prohibit police from considering race, as long as they do so for bona fide purposes of law enforcement (not racial harassment) and as long as it is only one of several factors.

4 These decisions have been welcome news to the many law enforcement officials who consider what has come to be known as racial profiling an essential weapon in the war on crime. They maintain that, in areas where young African American males commit a disproportionate number of the street crimes, the cops are justified in scrutinizing that sector of the population more closely than others—just as they are generally justified in scrutinizing men more closely than they do women.

5 As Bernard Parks, chief of the Los Angeles Police Department, explained to Jeffrey Goldberg of *The New York Times Magazine:* "We have an issue of violent crime against jewelry salespeople. . . . The predominant suspects are Colombians. We don't find Mexican Americans, or blacks, or other immigrants. It's a collection of several hundred Colombians who commit this crime. If you see six in a car in front of the Jewelry Mart, and they're waiting and watching people with briefcases, should we play the percentages and follow them? It's common sense."

6 Cops like Parks say that racial profiling is a sensible, statistically based tool. Profiling lowers the cost of obtaining and processing crime information, which in turn lowers the overall cost of doing the business of policing. And the fact that a number of

WANTED
SUSPECT
POLICE

cops who support racial profiling are black, including Parks, buttresses claims that the practice isn't motivated by bigotry. Indeed, these police officers note that racial profiling is race-*neutral* in that it can be applied to persons of all races, depending on the circumstances. In predominantly black neighborhoods in which white people stick out (as potential drug customers or racist hooligans, for example), whiteness can become part of a profile. In the southwestern United States, where Latinos often traffic in illegal immigrants, apparent Latin American ancestry can become part of a profile.

7 But the defenders of racial profiling are wrong. Ever since the Black and Latino Caucus of the New Jersey Legislature held a series of hearings, complete with testimony from victims of what they claimed was the New Jersey state police force's overly aggressive racial profiling, the air has been thick with public denunciations of the practice. In June 1999, at a forum organized by the Justice Department on racial problems in law enforcement, President Clinton condemned racial profiling as a "morally indefensible, deeply corrosive practice." Vice President Al Gore has promised that, if he is elected president, he will see to it that the first civil rights act of the new century would end racial profiling. His rival for the Democratic nomination, Bill Bradley, has countered that Gore should prepare an executive order and ask the president to sign it *now*.

8 Unfortunately, though, many who condemn racial profiling do so without really thinking the issue through. One common complaint is that using race (say, blackness) as one factor in selecting surveillance targets is fundamentally racist. But selectivity of this sort can be defended on nonracist grounds. "There is nothing more painful to me at this stage in my life," Jesse Jackson said in 1993, "than to walk down the street and hear footsteps and start to think about robbery and then look around and see somebody white and feel relieved." Jackson was relieved not because he dislikes black people, but because he estimated that he stood a somewhat greater risk of being robbed by a black person than by a white person. Statistics confirm that African Americans—particularly young black men—commit a dramatically disproportionate share of street crime in the United States. This is a sociological fact, not a figment of a racist media (or police) imagination. In recent years, victims report blacks as perpetrators of around 25 percent of violent crimes, although blacks constitute only about 12 percent of the nation's population.

9 So, if racial profiling isn't bigoted, and if the empirical claim upon which the practice rests is sound, why is it wrong?

10 Racial distinctions are and should be different from other lines of social stratification. That is why, since the civil rights revolu-

tion of the 1960s, courts have typically ruled—based on the 14th Amendment's equal protection clause—that mere reasonableness is an insufficient justification for officials to discriminate on racial grounds. In such cases, courts have generally insisted on applying "strict scrutiny"—the most intense level of judicial review—to government actions. Under this tough standard, the use of race in governmental decision making may be upheld only if it serves a compelling government objective and only if it is "narrowly tailored" to advance that objective.

11 A disturbing feature of this debate is that many people, including judges, are suggesting that decisions based on racial distinctions do not constitute unlawful racial discrimination—as long as race is not the only reason a person was treated objectionably. The court that upheld the DEA agent's action at the Kansas City airport, for instance, declined to describe it as racially discriminatory and thus evaded strict scrutiny.

12 But racially discriminatory decisions typically stem from mixed motives. For example, an employer who prefers white candidates to black candidates—except for those black candidates with superior experience and test scores—is engaging in racial discrimination, even though race is not the only factor he considers (since he selects black superstars). In some cases, race is a marginal factor; in others it is the only factor. The distinction may have a bearing on the moral or logical justification, but taking race into account at all means engaging in discrimination.

13 Because both law and morality discourage racial discrimination, proponents should persuade the public that racial profiling is justifiable. Instead, they frequently neglect its costs and minimize the extent to which it adds to the resentment blacks feel toward the law enforcement establishment. When O. J. Simpson was acquitted, many recognized the danger of a large sector of Americans feeling cynical and angry toward the system. Such alienation creates witnesses who fail to cooperate with police, citizens who view prosecutors as the enemy, lawyers who disdain the rules they have sworn to uphold, and jurors who yearn to get even with a system that has, in their eyes, consistently mistreated them. Racial profiling helps keep this pool of accumulated rage filled to the brim.

14 The courts have not been sufficiently mindful of this risk. In rejecting a 1976 constitutional challenge that accused U.S. Border Patrol officers in California of selecting cars for inspection partly on the basis of drivers' apparent Mexican ancestry, the Supreme Court noted in part that, of the motorists passing the checkpoint, fewer than 1 percent were stopped. It also noted that, of the 820 vehicles inspected during the period in question, roughly 20 percent contained illegal aliens.

15 Justice William J. Brennan dissented, however, saying the Court did not indicate the ancestral makeup of *all* the persons the Border Patrol stopped. It is likely that many of the innocent people who were questioned were of apparent Mexican ancestry who then had to prove their obedience to the law just because others of the same ethnic background have broken laws in the past.

16 The practice of racial profiling undercuts a good idea that needs more support from both society and the law: Individuals should be judged by public authorities on the basis of their own conduct and not on the basis of racial generalization. Race-dependent policing retards the development of bias-free thinking; indeed, it encourages the opposite.

17 What about the fact that in some communities people associated with a given racial group commit a disproportionately large number of crimes? Our commitment to a just social order should prompt us to end racial profiling even if the generalizations on which the technique is based are supported by empirical evidence. This is not as risky as it may sound. There are actually many contexts in which the law properly enjoins us to forswear playing racial odds even when doing so would advance legitimate goals.

18 For example, public opinion surveys have established that blacks distrust law enforcement more than whites. Thus, it would be rational—and not necessarily racist—for a prosecutor to use ethnic origin as a factor in excluding black potential jurors. Fortunately, the Supreme Court has outlawed racial discrimination of this sort. And because demographics show that in the United States, whites tend to live longer than blacks, it would be perfectly rational for insurers to charge blacks higher life-insurance premiums. Fortunately, the law forbids that, too.

19 The point here is that racial equality, like all good things in life, costs something. Politicians suggest that all Americans need to do in order to attain racial justice is forswear bigotry. But they must also demand equal treatment before the law even when unequal treatment is defensible in the name of nonracist goals—and even when their effort will be costly.

20 Since abandoning racial profiling would make policing more expensive and perhaps less effective, those of us who oppose it must advocate a responsible alternative. Mine is simply to spend more money on other means of enforcement—and then spread the cost on some nonracial basis. One way to do that would be to hire more police officers. Another way would be to subject everyone to closer surveillance. A benefit of the second option would be to acquaint more whites with the burden of police intrusion, which might prompt more of them to insist on limiting police power. As it stands now, the burden is unfairly placed on minori-

ties—imposing on Mexican Americans, blacks, and others a special kind of tax for the war against illegal immigration, drugs, and other crimes. The racial element of that tax should be repealed.

21 I'm not saying that police should never be able to use race as a guideline. If a young white man with blue hair robs me, the police should certainly be able to use a description of the perpetrator's race. In this situation, though, whiteness is a trait linked to a particular person with respect to a particular incident. It is not a free-floating accusation that hovers over young white men practically all the time—which is the predicament young black men currently face. Nor am I saying that race could never be legitimately relied upon as a signal of increased danger. In an extraordinary circumstance in which plausible alternatives appear to be absent, officials might need to resort to racial profiling. This is a far cry from routine profiling that is subjected to little scrutiny.

22 Now that racial profiling is a hot issue, the prospects for policy change have improved. President Clinton directed federal law enforcement agencies to determine the extent to which their officers focus on individuals on the basis of race. The Customs Service is rethinking its practice of using ethnicity or nationality as a basis for selecting subjects for investigation. The Federal Aviation Administration has been re-evaluating its recommended security procedures; it wants the airlines to combat terrorism with computer profiling, which is purportedly less race-based than random checks by airport personnel. Unfortunately, though, a minefield of complexity lies beneath these options. Unless we understand the complexities, this opportunity will be wasted.

23 To protect ourselves against race-based policing requires no real confrontation with the status quo, because hardly anyone defends police surveillance triggered *solely* by race. Much of the talk about police "targeting" suspects on the basis of race is, in this sense, misguided and harmful. It diverts attention to a side issue. Another danger is the threat of demagoguery through oversimplification. When politicians talk about "racial profiling," we must insist that they define precisely what they mean. Evasion—putting off hard decisions under the guise of needing more information—is also a danger.

24 Even if routine racial profiling is prohibited, the practice will not cease quickly. An officer who makes a given decision partly on a racial basis is unlikely to acknowledge having done so, and supervisors and judges are loath to reject officers' statements. Nevertheless, it would be helpful for President Clinton to initiate a strict anti-discrimination directive to send a signal to conscientious, law-abiding officers that there are certain criteria they ought not use.

To be sure, creating a norm that can't be fully enforced isn't ideal, but it might encourage us all to work toward closing the gap between our laws and the conduct of public authorities. A new rule prohibiting racial profiling might be made to be broken, but it could set a new standard for legitimate government. 25

READING FOR MEANING

Write to create meanings for Kennedy's position paper on the issue of racial profiling.

Start Making Meaning

Begin by explaining what you think Kennedy hopes to accomplish with his readers, well-informed citizens and policymakers. How does he want to influence their thinking about this difficult policy issue of racial profiling? Then list the main reasons he opposes racial profiling (you will find these reasons in paragraphs 10, 12, 13, and 16). Continue by writing about anything else in the selection or in your experience that contributes to your understanding of Kennedy's argument.

If You Are Stuck

If you cannot write at least a page, consider writing about

- your reaction to Kennedy's argument in paragraph 16 that "race-dependent policing" encourages racial bias.
- the presentation of the issue in paragraphs 1–8, where Kennedy presents a position he cannot support, listing the important features of this position and telling how these paragraphs influenced your reading of Kennedy's argument in support of his own position.
- your personal experience of being questioned by the police or denied a job, narrating what happened and speculating about why it happened.
- what the drawing adds to your understanding of Kennedy's argument.

READING LIKE A WRITER

ASSERTING A CLEAR, UNEQUIVOCAL POSITION

The writer's statement of position is the one sentence (or two or three) that lights up a position paper. Like moons and planets, the other sentences reflect the light of this position statement. Without it, the essay would be only a faint explanation of the debate on an issue, not a luminous argument for a position on it. Writers usually (but not always) assert their positions early in the argument. To keep readers in focus, they may reassert the position later in the essay and nearly always in the conclusion. Because readers must be able to understand readily and unambiguously just what the writer's position is, it must be stated clearly and without equivocation or waffling. That is not to say, however, that the position cannot be carefully qualified. Key terms must be precisely defined unless there is little likelihood that readers will differ over what the key terms mean. (As noted earlier in this chapter, the position statement is also the thesis statement in a position paper.)

Analyze

1. *Underline* Kennedy's statement, restatements, and qualifications of his position (you will find these sentences at the beginnings of paragraphs 7, 9, and 21 and in the third-from-last sentence of paragraph 21).
2. *Consider* whether the writer's position statements are clear and unequivocal. *Think about* where they are located in relation to the other parts of his argument.

Write

Write several sentences reporting what you have learned about how Kennedy asserts his position on the issue of racial profiling. What sentence forms do his statements take? What does each statement add to the others? Then *add a few sentences* evaluating how effectively Kennedy asserts his position for his particular readers. *Make judgments* about the clarity of the statements. What does Kennedy gain or lose by waiting so long to assert and reassert his position and to qualify it?

CONSIDERING IDEAS FOR YOUR OWN WRITING

Consider writing a position paper on a current law that you consider unfair or unjust. Here are some examples: Should the "three strikes" law that sends a criminal to jail for life on his or her third felony conviction remain in force or be modified? Should cancer patients be able to purchase marijuana legally for use in reducing their nausea and pain? Should term limits for elected officials be maintained or eliminated? Should state laws recognizing gay and lesbian marriages be supported or opposed? Should motor vehicle laws be changed to make it more difficult for older drivers to renew their licenses?

DENNIS PRAGER

The Soul-Corrupting Anti-Tobacco Crusade

Focusing on moral and ethical issues, Dennis Prager hosts a nationally syndicated talk show on radio station KABL in Los Angeles. From 1995 to 2000, he wrote "The Prager Perspective," a newsletter. He appears frequently on television and writes for general publications such as Commentary, *the* Weekly Standard, *the* Wall Street Journal, *and the* Los Angeles Times. *Prager's books include* Think a Second Time *(1996),* Happiness Is a Serious Problem *(1998), and* Why the Jews? The Reason for Antisemitism *(1983).*

The following selection appeared in 1998 in the Weekly Standard, *a politically conservative magazine published in Washington, D.C. In the essay, Prager argues, surprisingly, that the widespread campaign against tobacco smoking is wrong and should be stopped. For most readers, especially the nonsmokers, this argument may be difficult to read calmly. Yet nearly all readers will agree that Prager makes a skillful argument: He gives several reasons for his position and employs wide knowledge and diverse argumentative strategies in supporting his reasons. Nevertheless, his position does not bring an end to the debate, and he does not seem to assume that it will. Therefore, even if you are a smoker, you will want to read his argument critically, asking questions, noting unstated assumptions (for example, cigars are not as dangerous as cigarettes), and raising objections. Annotate these responses as you read.*

Before you read, consider what you know about the dangers of smoking tobacco and of breathing secondhand smoke. What have been your main sources of information over the years? Reflect on the advertising you have seen designed to discourage smoking. If you are a tobacco smoker, when did you begin and what attempts, if any, have you made to quit? If you have never smoked tobacco, what is the principal reason?

I have never been a cigarette smoker. I have never doubted that cigarette smoking is dangerous. I believe that American tobacco companies have systematically lied about the dangers of cigarettes. I accept the public-health statistic that one out of three cigarette smokers will die prematurely. 1

I have smoked a pipe and cigars since I was a teenager. The joy and relaxation that cigars and pipes have brought me are very great. I do not regret having begun smoking. Life does not afford us an unlimited number of daily pleasures that are as largely innocuous as cigar and pipe smoking. As for my three children, I would not be particularly concerned if they decided to smoke cigars or pipes, and while I would be unhappy if they took up 2 cigarette smoking and became addicted to nicotine, I would not be unduly so. I would be considerably more unhappy if they became addicted to television. In fact, if smoking cigarettes is the most dangerous activity or worst vice my children ever engage in, I will rejoice.

3 I therefore do not consider cigarette smoking, let alone cigar or pipe smoking, to be worthy of the crusade society is waging against it. A simple commonsense health problem has been transformed into America's great moral cause. In the process, the war against smoking is playing havoc with moral values—with the truth, with science and scientists, with children's moral education, with the war on real drugs, with the principle of personal freedom and much more that we hold dear. The war against tobacco, in short, has come to be far more dangerous than tobacco itself.

4 One particularly irresponsible aspect of the war against tobacco is the now commonplace equating of tobacco use with drug use. In California, which leads the country in sums spent on anti-smoking ads, billboards throughout the state proclaim that cigarettes and tobacco are drugs—implicitly no different from marijuana or even heroin and cocaine. In fact, it has become a staple of anti-smoking rhetoric that it is harder to end nicotine addiction than heroin addiction. Now the anti-smoking forces want the Food and Drug Administration to regulate nicotine as a drug.

5 The only conceivable consequence of equating hard drugs, which can destroy the mind and soul, with tobacco, which can actually have positive effects on the mind and has no deleterious effect on the soul, is to lessen the fear of real drugs among young people. How could it not? If taking heroin, cocaine, and marijuana is the moral, personal, and social equivalent of smoking cigarettes, then how bad can heroin, cocaine, and marijuana be? After all, young people see adults smoking cigarettes all the time without destroying their lives.

6 The truth is that tobacco doesn't interfere with the soul, mind, conscience, or emotional growth of a smoker. As for the one trait cigarettes and drugs share—addictiveness—this tells us little. Human beings are addicted to a plethora of substances and activities. These include coffee, sugar, alcohol, gambling, sex, food, spending, and virtually every other human endeavor that brings immediate gratification and that people cannot, or choose not to, control.

7 In the past, when the moral compass of our society functioned more accurately, we fought the addictions that lead to social

breakdown far more vigorously than those that can lead to ill health. Today American society and government do the opposite: They fight health dangers—and actually encourage social dangers. For example, government now encourages gambling (by instituting lotteries and legalizing casinos, which advertise more freely than tobacco); government largely ignores alcohol, the addiction most associated with child abuse, spousal abuse, and violent crime; and it fails in its efforts to curb real drug addiction. All the while, it wages its most ubiquitous war against cigarette smokers, who pose no danger to society or family life.

8 Another irresponsible aspect of the war against tobacco is the demonization of smokers. In the span of a few years, smokers have been transformed from people engaged in a somewhat dangerous but morally innocuous habit into drug addicts, child abusers, and killers. Smoking has become, incredibly, an issue of moral character, not merely of health.

9 Here is one result:

> Judges in divorce cases are increasingly considering smoking as a factor in deciding where to put the kids and retaining custody. . . . If a judge is so inclined, he can depict smoking as negative in two ways: dirtying the child's air and *showing poor character.*
>
> In Knox County, Tenn., the Circuit Court has adopted a rule for all custody cases, and *not just those in which the child has a health problem:* "If children are exposed to smoke, it will be strong evidence that the exposing parent does not take good care of them."
>
> That rule led last year to a criminal contempt conviction—and a loss of all visitation rights—for a father who smoked during his time with his daughter. [Associated Press, April 18, 1997, italics added.]

10 Think of it: A thoroughly decent person and loving parent can now lose custody of his or her child solely because of smoking. This is moral idiocy, and it hinges on the fraudulent theory of secondhand smoke.

11 Since the Environmental Protection Agency listed secondhand smoke as a first-class human carcinogen in 1993, numerous eminent scientists have expressed skepticism. They include epidemiologists Dimitrios Trichopoulos of the Harvard School of Public Health and Alvan Feinstein of Yale Medical School. Dr. Philippe Shubik, editor in chief of *Teratogenesis, Carcinogenesis and Mutagenesis,* published at Oxford University, contrasts cigarette smoking—"an unequivocal human cancer hazard"—with envi-

ronmental smoke. Officially designating the latter a human carcinogen, he writes, "is not only unjustified but establishes a scientifically unsound principle."

12 In other words, anti-tobacco activities who ascribe murderous carcinogenic qualities to secondhand smoke are engaging in junk science and propaganda, just as were the pro-tobacco spokesmen who denied the carcinogenic properties of smoking.

13 Instilling fear in children has been one of the few successful educational techniques in America over the past generation. Educators frightened young children first about dying in a nuclear war; then about dying from heterosexually transmitted AIDS; then about being sexually harassed; then about being abused (hence teachers and day-care providers are told not to hug children); then about "stranger danger"; and now schools tell our children that their parent who smokes will die and may even kill them.

14 After frightening young children, the anti-smoking crusaders attempt to use them: Children's grasp of the issue is not terribly sophisticated, which makes them all the more easily brainwashed and all the more useful as foot soldiers in the war against smoking.

15 Massachusetts—a state that prides itself on its commitment to "question authority"—puts its students to work unquestioningly on behalf of anti-smoking authority. Thus, second-graders in Mattapan are told to express their support for a smoking ban in restaurants. Fifth-graders in Chelsea are instructed to use an approach reminiscent of the Chinese Cultural Revolution, namely, "to knock on the doors of friends and parents who smoke to educate them about the dangers of smoking."

16 But frightening children is hardly the only abuse of which the anti-smoking zealots are guilty. Lies, half-truths, exaggerations, and distortions characterize the anti-smoking campaign—as much as they ever characterized the tobacco companies.

17 The first manipulation of truth concerns the number of Americans said to die from smoking. We are told repeatedly that 500,000 Americans die each year from "tobacco-related illnesses." Even if the figure is accurate, citing it as if it were the only relevant statistic is dishonest.

18 What if anti-smoking billboards and ads told the truth about the two statistics that truly matter to anyone contemplating smoking: What are the chances that any individual smoker will die prematurely? And how many years does the average pack-a-day cigarette smoker lose? If anti-smoking announcements dealt with these questions, they would have to declare something like this: "One out of every three cigarette smokers will die

prematurely," and, "While the average American male who never smoked a cigarette will live until age 78, males who smoke a pack a day will, on average, live only until age 71."

19 That's it. The justification for all this hysteria—all the laws restricting speech in advertisements, all the bans on smoking sections in private businesses, all the regressive taxes, all this frightening of children about their lives and those of their parents—is that one-third of cigarette smokers die prematurely, at an average loss of seven years. And that may overstate the case. According to *The Costs of Poor Health Habits,* a RAND study published in 1991 by Harvard University Press, smoking cigarettes "reduces the life expectancy of a 20-year-old by about 4.3 years."

20 Another claim, repeated by President Clinton in a radio broadcast in June [1998], is that we must fight tobacco in order to "save the lives of one million young people." I will leave it to others to determine whether this qualifies as a lie or sophistry. Whichever, it is untrue. Unlike drugs, drunk driving, and murder, which annually kill many thousands of young people, cigarettes do not kill a single young person. Those young people who die from cigarettes will do so at an average age of over 70. Tell that to the young.

21 One of the greatest distortions of truth by the anti-smoking crusade—one that can only be characterized as a Big Lie, since it is repeated so often, by so many, and has led to a money grab of unprecedented proportions—is how much it costs the public to cover the medical care of smokers.

22 We are told that treatment of sick smokers costs government billions of dollars a year. Unlike the claim of 500,000 a year dead from "tobacco-related diseases," which is only misleading and can be neither proved nor disproved, this claim is easily exposed as a lie. Smokers actually save the public money. On purely financial grounds, the public is a net gainer from cigarette smokers. To put it differently: If everyone stopped smoking, the public would lose substantial sums.

23 This is because government makes a great deal of money from cigarette taxes, and it saves enormous sums upon the death of cigarette smokers, most of whom die at an age when they would otherwise collect Social Security and other public benefits. Moreover, as hard as it is for the anti-smoking movement to acknowledge, non-smokers impose great costs on society in their last months of life, just as smokers do.

24 Society has always had two means of discouraging behavior: punishment and stigma. What a society punishes and stigmatizes reveals what it values.

25 Consider a recent cover story in *People* magazine. The cover featured a photograph of actress Jody Foster, who is pregnant. The magazine overflowed with enthusiasm about her pregnancy and quoted one source after another welcoming the future Foster child.

26 This article would have been inconceivable a generation ago. For not only is Jody Foster unmarried, there is not even an identifiable father (presumably some anonymous sperm donor) for the child she is bringing into the world.

27 Yet this means nothing to elite America. Hooray for the deliberately fatherless child! Hooray for unwed motherhood! Those are the messages sent to America's young women and girls and to its young men and boys.

28 *People* magazine, a pretty accurate reflection of America's social attitudes, knew it ran no risk by celebrating a fatherless pregnancy. But there is one photo it would probably never dare show on its cover: Jody Foster smoking a cigarette.

29 America has made its choice: It reserves its stigma for cigarette smokers and is entirely nonjudgmental about bringing children into the world without a father. When I see smokers shivering outside buildings and regarded by many as pathetic or even dangerous people while unwed mothers are celebrated, I worry about America's future.

America reserves its stigma for cigarette smoking and is entirely nonjudgmental about deliberate single motherhood.

30 Here's another example of the misplaced priorities that the hysteria over cigarette smoking has wrought. The president of the United States and the country's surgeon general summoned the national media to the White House for what they deemed a highly significant announcement: Smoking among black and other minority youths has increased. President Clinton and Surgeon General David Satcher appeared with a group of non-white children and spoke in the gravest tones about this threat to them.

31 But in six years in office, the president has never convened a White House conference to lament the plague of unwed

motherhood. The majority of black children grow up without their father in their home. This is easily the greatest obstacle to black progress. Yet the president and the media focus on the increase in cigarette smoking among young blacks—and black smoking rates are *lower* than those of whites.

A question: Which would improve black life more—for every single black youth to stop smoking while the illegitimacy rate remained the same, or for every black youth to smoke cigarettes while growing up from birth to adulthood with both of his parents? With the nation morally at sea, many Americans may find this question difficult to answer. 32

At the heart of the anti-smoking lawsuits against the tobacco industry is the denial that smokers are personally responsible for smoking. They allegedly had no knowledge of the dangers of cigarette smoking and began smoking because venal tobacco companies used mind-numbing ads to convince them cigarettes were healthy. 33

The last thing America needs is a massive campaign further eroding personal responsibility. We already live in a country that regularly teaches its citizens to blame others—government, ads, parents, schools, movies, genes, sugar, tobacco, alcohol, sexism, racism—for their poor decisions and problems. Now we have the largest public-relations campaign in American history teaching Americans this: If you smoke, you are in no way responsible for what happens to you. You are entirely a victim. 34

The war against tobacco is telling teenagers in particular to look for others to blame. The latest ad campaign, in Florida—funded by tens of millions of public dollars—is directed to teens. It tells them that if they smoke, they do so solely because they have been manipulated by tobacco-company ads. This is the theme of all the approaches to young people by the anti-smoking forces: You kids have been manipulated by a cartoon camel. 35

This approach not only sends the destructive message to young people that they are not responsible for their behavior, that they are helpless when confronted with a billboard for Marlboro cigarettes, it also is intellectually dishonest. If young people are powerless in the face of tobacco billboards—tobacco ads are already banned from television, radio, and youth-oriented magazines—they are presumably powerless in the face of all advertisements. Why then allow advertisements for liquor, wine, beer, or R-rated movies? Aren't young people equally powerless in the face of these ads? Why allow ads showing sexually suggestive gestures or behavior? Won't those ads make young people engage in sex? Or 36 is teen sex less worrisome than teen smoking? Isn't the message that young people are not responsible for behaving as billboards urge them to behave a *disempowering* message?

37 The ultimate question is this: Why, given the far greater ills of American society and the minimal harm caused by tobacco, is America obsessed with smoking? The reason is that our moral compass is broken. Two generations ago, when our value system was comparatively sound, the vice America fought was alcohol, not tobacco. America understood that the effects of alcohol are incomparably worse than the effects of tobacco.

38 Cigarettes can lead to premature death. Alcohol can lead to murder, rape, child abuse, spousal beatings, family rupture, and permanent pathologies in the children of alcoholics. If all alcoholic beverages were miraculously removed from the earth, the amount of rape, murder, child abuse, and spousal beating would plummet, and no child would ever again suffer the permanently debilitating effects of having been raised by an alcoholic. If all tobacco products miraculously disappeared from the earth, the amount of rape, murder, child abuse, and spousal beating would remain identical, and millions of children would continue to suffer the horrors of growing up in alcoholic homes. In other words, morally speaking, little would change if tobacco miraculously disappeared.

39 In a more religious age, social activists fought alcohol; in our secular age, social activists fight tobacco—and a few other select ills, such as restrictions on abortion. Indeed, America's elites now consider it immoral to let a bar owner choose whether to allow smoking in his bar. But the same elites are pro-choice when it comes to letting the alcohol flow in those bars and allowing mothers to extinguish nascent human life for any reason they please.

40 The same president who vetoed a bill outlawing "partial-birth" abortions, which are usually performed in mid- or late pregnancy, vigorously opposes choice about smoking in nearly all privately owned businesses. In California at the end of the twentieth century, third-trimester abortions are legal, but smoking in bars and outdoor stadiums is not. I happen to favor keeping first-trimester abortions legal, but even I can see that it is quite a statement about a society's sense of right and wrong when it deems secondhand smoke more worthy of legal restriction than the killing of human fetuses.

41 As early as 1994, *New York Times* columnist Russell Baker foresaw the dangers of the anti-smoking crusade. He wrote:

> Crusades typically start by being admirable, proceed to being foolish and end by being dangerous. The crusade against smoking is now clearly well into the second stage where foolishness abounds.
>
> Now something very sinister is developing. Some businesses are refusing to hire workers who smoke outside the workplace, on the ground that smokers' health problems are bad for their employers.
>
> This is an illustration of a crusade entering its dangerous stage. Give employers the right to control the habits of their workers outside the workplace, and you set the stage for a tyranny even worse than the evils of too much government which keep conservatives so alarmed.

Put this crusade in perspective. In the 1920s, America waged a war against alcohol. In the 1930s, it battled economic depression. In the 1940s, it fought fascism. In the 1950s and 1960s, it led the struggle against communism. In the 1970s, America grappled with its own racism and bigotry. In the 1980s, it ensured the defeat of the Soviet empire. 42

The next generation will ask: What preoccupied America in the final decade of the twentieth century—while unprecedented numbers of its children were being raised without fathers, while the country was living with rates of murder far higher than in any other advanced democracy, while its public schools were graduating semi-literates, while its ability to fight two wars was being eviscerated even as rogue nations built stocks of chemical and biological weapons and new countries were acquiring nuclear weapons? The editors of America's leading editorial pages and the majority of its national politicians, state attorneys general, and educators will be able to answer together, "We fought tobacco." Shame on them all. 43

READING FOR MEANING

Write to create meanings for Prager's position paper on government intervention in citizens' personal habits, particulary their smoking of cigarettes.

Start Making Meaning

Begin by explaining what you think Prager's purpose is for writing this essay. You can reasonably assume that most of his readers do not smoke cigarettes because it is terribly dangerous to do so. With that in mind, list the reasons Prager selects to make his position seem at least plausible to readers (you will find his reasons within paragraphs 4, 8, 13, 16, 24, 33–34, and 37). Continue by writing about anything else in the selection or in your experience that contributes to your understanding of Prager's argument.

If You Are Stuck

If you cannot write at least a page, consider writing about

- Prager's argument (in paragraphs 3 and 5–7) that the campaign against tobacco products plays havoc "with the war on real drugs."
- Prager's claims that opponents of smoking behave irresponsibly (paragraphs 7–15) and manipulate the truth (paragraphs 16–23), explaining what you find convincing or unconvincing in this part of his argument and why.
- what the photographs add to your understanding of Prager's argument.
- an addiction of your own, explaining how you acquired it, what kind of pleasure you get from it, and what, if anything, you have done to control or shake it, relating your insights to some of the ideas in Prager's position paper.

READING LIKE A WRITER

ARGUING DIRECTLY FOR THE POSITION

As suggested throughout this chapter, a writer has much to do to create a successful position paper. Central to this effort, however, must be developing a strong argument in support of the writer's position on the issue. A writer may counterargue readers' questions, objections, and opposing positions, but that does not complete the argument. Readers also want to know in positive terms why the writer holds his or her particular position and what sort of reasoned argument the writer can devise—in brief, readers expect reasons and support.

Prager's essay shows how writers of position papers usually make use of several strategies to support their reasons. Prager makes good use of many supporting strategies; reporting on or speculating about results or effects, citing statistics, quoting authorities, giving examples, setting up comparisons or contrasts, and creating analogies.

Analyze

1. *Reread* the following groups of paragraphs, looking for examples of the strategies Prager uses to support his reasons: reporting on or speculating about results (in paragraphs 5, 9, and 10), citing statistics (17–20 and 22), quoting authorities (11, 19, 41), giving examples (15, 25, 26, 30, 35), setting

up comparisons or contrasts (2, 4, 7, 31, 32, 38), and creating analogies (36, 38).

2. *Select two* of these strategies to analyze and evaluate. *Look closely* at the relevant paragraphs to see how Prager uses each strategy. *Make notes* in the margin about how he develops the strategy. What kinds of details does he include, and what sorts of sentences does he rely on?

3. *Evaluate* how effectively Prager uses each strategy to support his reasons. What is most and least convincing about the support? What does it contribute to the overall argument? How essential is it?

Write

Write several sentences explaining Prager's use of the two strategies you analyzed. *Support* your explanation with details from the paragraphs. Then *add a few sentences* evaluating how successfully Prager uses the strategies.

Compare

Compare Prager's use of statistics, examples, and analogies to support his reasons with Sandel's use of the same strategies in "Bad Bet." In Sandel's position paper, you will find statistics used in paragraphs 3, 6, 8, 10, and 12; examples in paragraphs 9 and 11; and analogies in paragraphs 1, 2, and 6. (For the locations of the same strategies in Prager's essay, look in Analyze, step 1, in the preceding section.) *Reread* the relevant paragraphs in both essays, and *make notes* in the margin about how the writers develop each strategy. What kinds of details does each writer include, and what sorts of sentences does each one rely on? Then *write a few sentences* about what the strategies contribute to the overall argument in both position papers. Finally, *write several sentences* comparing and contrasting how the two writers employ these three writing strategies. *Give examples* from each reading.

CONSIDERING IDEAS FOR YOUR OWN WRITING

Consider answering Prager in a position paper defending the current antitobacco campaigns by state and federal governments. Give reasons why you think the campaigns are necessary and counterargue Prager's reasons for thinking otherwise. Or consider taking a position on other issues involving curbs on personal freedoms or changes in people's behavior. Here are some examples: Should the religious beliefs of a few students define the kind of science all students study? Should parent groups or school boards ban certain books from high-school reading lists? Should condoms be distributed free in high schools? Should access to sexually explicit material on the Internet be limited? Should health officials mount a campaign to discourage people from drinking alcohol? Should school officials try to convince more parents of young children to read aloud to them? Should motorized scooters be banned, or should helmets be required when riding them?

BRENT KNUTSON

Auto Liberation

Brent Knutson wrote this position paper for his first-year college composition course. In it he addresses the issue of whether national speed limits are necessary on U.S. interstate highways and argues that, on the basis of his experience driving German autobahns, the speed limits are unnecessary. You will discover that Knutson asserts his position boldly and seems confident that he has a convincing argument to support it. Yet he applies much of his argument to counterarguing two particular objections he expects his readers will raise.

Because Knutson's instructor asked him to cite sources formally, Knutson does so within the text of his position paper. These in-text citations refer to the published sources in the works-cited list at the end of his essay. Previous position papers in this chapter refer to sources informally within the text of the argument. They need not adopt a formal citation style like the one Knutson relies on because the conventions of newspaper and magazine publishing usually do not require it.

Before you read, consider whether interstate highways in your part of the country could accommodate cars traveling at unlimited speeds. What problems do you see? What advantages might there be?

The driver of a late-model Japanese sports car grins as he downshifts into third gear, blips the throttle with his heel, and releases the clutch. The car's rear end abruptly steps out in the wide, sweeping corner. He cranks the wheel, gathering the tail while eagerly stabbing the accelerator. The engine emits a metallic wail and barks angrily as the driver pulls the gearshift into fourth. Controlled pandemonium ensues as the secondary turbocharger engages and slams the driver's cranium against the headrest. With adrenaline thumping in his temples, he watches the needle on the speedometer sweep urgently toward the end of the scale. The driver then flicks the turn signal and blasts onto the interstate like a guided missile launching from a fighter jet. Today, he will not be late for work. 1

This scenario may seem a bit far-fetched, enough so that one might conclude that the driver is unnecessarily risking his life and the lives of other people on the road. But, on Germany's autobahns, people normally drive in excess of 80 miles per hour. Yet, these German superhighways are the safest in the world, filled with German drivers who are skilled, competent, and courteous. Using the autobahn system as a model, it is possible to examine whether national speed limits in the United States are necessary. 2

3 In fact, there is solid reasoning to support the claim that the speed limits on U.S. interstate highways should be repealed. Not only are American speed limits unnecessarily restrictive, but also they infringe on the personal freedoms of American citizens. Although there are locations where speed limits are appropriate, in most cases these limits are arbitrarily imposed and sporadically enforced. Modern automobiles are capable of traveling safely at high speeds, and despite what the auto-insurance companies would have us believe, speed does not kill. With proper training, American drivers could be capable of driving "at speed" responsibly. Perhaps the most compelling reason to lift the national speed limit is the simplest: driving fast is enjoyable.

4 Those opposed to lifting the national speed limit argue that removing such restrictions would result in mayhem on the freeways; they're convinced that the countryside would be littered with the carcasses of people who achieved terminal velocity only to careen off the road and explode into flames. Speed limit advocates also argue that American drivers do not possess the skill or capacity to drive at autobahn speeds. They contend that our driver-education programs do not sufficiently prepare drivers to operate vehicles and that obtaining a driver's license in most states is comically easy; therefore, lifting the speed limit would be irresponsible.

5 The belief that a "no speed limit" highway system would result in widespread carnage appears to be based more on fear than fact. In 1987, Idaho Senator Steve Symms introduced legislation allowing states to raise speed limits on rural interstates to 65 miles per hour (Csere, "Free"). Auto-insurance industry advocates responded that the accident rates would skyrocket and the number of fatalities caused by auto accidents would increase accordingly. Ironically, the Insurance Institute for Highway Safety (IIHS) reported in July 1994 that "[o]nly 39,235 deaths resulting from auto-related accidents were reported during 1992, the lowest number since 1961. The institute found that 1992 was the fourth year in which automotive deaths consistently declined" (qtd. in "Highways" 51). Coincidentally, that decline in fatalities began two years after many states raised interstate speed limits. Unfortunately, the insurance industry has made it a habit to manipulate statistics to suit its purposes. Later in the essay, I'll discuss evidence of this propensity to deceive.

6 The contention that American drivers are not capable of driving safely at higher speeds has some merit. During a drive around any city in this country, one is bound to witness numerous displays of behind-the-wheel carelessness. Because of poor

driver-education programs, as well as general apathy, Americans have earned their high standing among the worst drivers in the world. Regarding our poor driving habits, automotive journalist Csaba Csere wrote in the April 1994 issue of *Car and Driver* that "American drivers choose their lanes randomly, much in the way cows inexplicably pick a patch of grass on which to graze" ("Drivers"). Fortunately, Americans' poor driving habits can be remedied. Through intensive driver-education programs, stringent licensing criteria, and public-service announcement campaigns, we can learn to drive more proficiently.

7 I recently returned from a four-year stay in Kaiserslautern, Germany. While there, I learned the pleasure of high-speed motoring. I was particularly impressed by the skill and discipline demonstrated by virtually all drivers traveling on the network of superhighways that make up the autobahn system. Germany's automobile regulatory laws are efficient, practical, and serve as an example for all countries to follow. It is striking that automobiles and driving fast are such integral components of German culture. Germans possess a passion for cars that is so contagious I didn't want to leave the country. German Chancellor Helmut Kohl summed up the German attitude regarding speed limits quite concisely: "For millions of people, a car is part of their personal freedom" (qtd. in Cote 12).

8 It is apparent in the United States that there are not many old, junky cars left on the road. The majority of vehicles operating in the United States are newer cars that have benefited from automotive engineering technology designed to increase the performance of the average vehicle. With the advent of independent suspension, electronic engine-management systems, passive restraints, and other technological improvements, modern automobiles are more capable than ever of traveling at high speeds safely. Indeed, the stringent safety requirements imposed by the Department of Transportation for vehicles sold in the United States ensure that our cars and trucks are the safest in the world.

9 One of the biggest fallacies perpetrated by the auto-insurance industry and car-fearing legislators is that "speed kills." Driving fast in itself, however, is not a hazard; speed combined with incompetence, alcohol, or hazardous conditions is dangerous. A skilled motor-vehicle operator traveling at 90 miles per hour, in light traffic, on a divided highway does not present a significant risk. Psychologist and compensation theorist G. J. Wilde "developed the RHT (Risk Homeostasis Theory) to account for the apparent propensity of drivers to maintain a constant level of experienced accident risk" (qtd. in Jackson and Blackman 950).

During a driving-simulation experiment in which he changed "non-motivational factors," Wilde determined that "[n]either speed limit nor speeding fine had a significant impact on accident loss" (qtd. in Jackson and Blackman 956). Wilde's theory is convincing because he emphasizes the human tendency toward self-preservation. The impact of RHT could be far-reaching. As Wilde says, "The notion that drivers compensate fully for non-motivational safety countermeasures is significant because it is tantamount to the claim that most legislated safety measures will not permanently reduce the total population traffic accident loss" (qtd. in Jackson and Blackman 951). What this means is that drivers would not increase their personal risk by driving faster than their capabilities dictate, regardless of the speed limit.

10 Unfortunately, the IIHS doesn't see things this way. It has been busy manipulating statistics in an attempt to convince people that raising the interstate speed limits to 65 miles per hour has resulted in a veritable bloodbath. A headline in a recent edition of the IIHS status report states, "For Sixth Year in a row, Deaths on U.S. Rural Interstates Are Much Higher Than Before Speed Limits Were Raised to 65 mph" (qtd. in Bedard 20). That claim is more than a little misleading because it does not compensate for the increased number of drivers on the road. Patrick Bedard explains: "What's the real conclusion? Rural interstate fatalities over the whole United States increased 19 percent between 1982 and 1992. But driving increased 44 percent. So the fatality rate is on a definite downward trend from 1.5 to 1.2 [percent]" (21).

11 One might ask what the insurance industry stands to gain by misrepresenting auto-fatality statistics. The real issue is what it stands to lose if speed limits are deregulated. The lifting of speed limits translates into fewer traffic citations issued by police. Fewer tickets means fewer points assessed on Americans' driving records, which would remove the insurance industry's primary tool for raising premiums. Needless to say, auto-insurance companies aren't thrilled about the prospect of less money in their coffers.

12 There is one lucid and persuasive argument for abolishing interstate speed limits: Driving fast is pure, unadulterated, rip-snortin' fun. I experienced the thrill of a lifetime behind the wheel of a 1992 Ford Mustang while chasing a BMW 525i on the Frankfurt–Mainz Autobahn. I remember my heart racing as I glanced at my speedometer, which read 120 mph. When I looked up, I saw the high-beam flash of headlights in my rearview mirror. Moments after I pulled into the right lane, a bloodred Ferrari F-40 passed in a surreal symphony of sound, color, and power,

marked by the enraged howl of a finely tuned Italian motor running fullout. At that moment, I was acutely aware of every nerve ending in my body, as I experienced the automotive equivalent of Zen consciousness. It was a sort of convergence of psyche and body that left me light-headed and giddy for ten minutes afterward. I was glad to discover that my reaction to driving fast was not unique:

> Few people can describe in words the mixture of sensations they experience, but for some the effect is so psychologically intense that no other experience can match it. . . . For some people the psychological effects are experienced as pure fear. For others, however, this basic emotional state is modified to give a sharply tingling experience which is perceived as intensely pleasurable. The fear, and the state of alertness are still there—but they have been mastered. (Marsh and Collett 179)

Repealing interstate speed limits is an objective that every driver should carefully consider. At a time when our elected officials are striving to control virtually every aspect of our lives, it is imperative that we fight to regain our freedom behind the wheel. Like Germans, Americans have a rich automotive culture and heritage. The automobile represents our ingenuity, determination, and independence. It is time to return control of the automobile to the driver, and "free us from our speed slavery once and for all" (Csere, "Free"). 13

Works Cited

Bedard, Patrick. "Auto Insurance Figures Don't Lie, but Liars Figure." Editorial. *Car and Driver* Mar. 1994: 20–21.

Cote, Kevin. "Heartbrake on Autobahn." *Advertising Age* 26 Sept. 1994: 1+.

Csere, Csaba. "Drivers We Love to Hate." Editorial. *Car and Driver* Apr. 1994: 9.

———. "Free the Speed Slaves." Editorial. *Car and Driver* Nov. 1993: 9.

"Highways Become Safer." *Futurist* Jan.–Feb. 1994: 51–52.

Jackson, Jeremy S. H., and Roger Blackman. "A Driving Simulator Test of Wilde's Risk Homeostasis Theory." *Journal of Applied Psychology* 79.6 (1994): 950–58.

Marsh, Peter, and Peter Collett. *Driving Passion.* Winchester: Faber, 1987.

READING FOR MEANING

Write to create meanings for Knutson's position paper on the issue of whether speed limits are necessary on U.S. interstate highways.

Start Making Meaning

Begin by speculating about Knutson's purpose for writing this position paper. What does he seem to assume about his readers? How does he hope to influence them? Then list the main reasons for Knutson's position (you will find well-supported reasons in paragraphs 8, 9, and 12). Continue by writing about anything else in the selection or in your experience that contributes to your understanding of Knutson's argument.

If You Are Stuck

If you cannot write at least a page, consider writing about

- what you find most or least convincing about Knutson's comparisons between drivers of German autobahns (freeways) and drivers of U.S. interstate highways.
- a question you would like to ask Knutson or an objection you have to his argument, explaining your thinking and connecting it to some aspect of his argument.
- the driving conditions on highways in your part of the country, considering whether highways could accommodate unlimited speeds and whether drivers could adjust to them.
- a particular driving experience of your own that supports or challenges Knutson's advocacy of unlimited speed limits on U.S. highways.

READING LIKE A WRITER

COUNTERARGUING OBJECTIONS AND OPPOSING POSITIONS

One of the challenges—and pleasures—of writing position papers is that in nearly every writing situation writers recognize that some or many or even all of their readers will hold opposing positions or, if they have no position, will question or object to some part of the argument. Therefore, one of the special challenges of the position paper is to counterargue readers' positions, objections, or questions. To do so convincingly, writers must succeed with two basic moves: (1) demonstrate that they understand their readers' opposing positions and recognize their readers' objections or questions and (2) either concede or refute those positions, objections, or questions without exasperating, insulting, or harassing readers. To *concede* is to admit the usefulness or wisdom of readers' views. To *refute* is to attempt to argue that readers' views are limited or flawed. (For more on counterarguing, turn to the Reading Like a Writer sections following the Estrada and Sandel selections in this chapter.)

Knutson counterargues extensively. In fact, he organizes his entire argument around two particular objections he anticipates his readers to raise.

Analyze

1. In paragraph 4, *underline* the first sentence (up to the semicolon) and the second sentence. These sentences introduce the two (interrelated) reader objections that Knutson counterargues throughout his essay. In thinking about his readers, he seems to assume that his argument cannot succeed unless he convincingly refutes these two objections.
2. *Reread* paragraphs 5, 8, 10, and 11, where Knutson attempts to counterargue the mayhem objection (*mayhem* can mean both "permanent crippling or disfigurement" and "disorder or violence"). *Make notes* in the margins about what strategies Knutson deploys, whether he only refutes and never concedes, and what his attitude seems to be toward the Insurance Institute for Highway Safety.
3. *Reread* paragraphs 6, 7, and 9, where Knutson attempts to counterargue the lack of skill objection. *Make notes* in the margins about what strategies Knutson deploys, noticing where he refutes and where he concedes.

Write

Write several sentences explaining what you have learned about how Knutson counterargues. *Give examples* from the reading. Then *add a few sentences* evaluating how convincingly Knutson counterargues. What do you find most or least convincing in his counterargument—and why?

A SPECIAL READING STRATEGY

Evaluating the Logic of an Argument

To evaluate the logic of an argument, apply the ABC test by asking yourself three basic questions:

A. How *appropriate* is the support for each reason offered?
B. How *believable* is the support?
C. How *consistent and complete* is the overall argument?

Such an evaluation requires a comprehensive, thoughtful critical reading, but your efforts will help you understand more fully what makes a position paper successful. Follow the detailed guidelines for evaluating the logic of an argument in Appendix 1. There you will find definitions and explanations (pp. 545–48) as well as an illustration based on an excerpt from a famous essay by Martin Luther King Jr. (p. 548).

CONSIDERING IDEAS FOR YOUR OWN WRITING

Consider other rights or cultural and economic practices from other countries that we might adopt in the United States. Here are some examples: Should we legislate national health care, as in Germany, Canada, and England? Should we have a national curriculum in all schools, as in France? Should we follow Sweden's lead and give new parents a paid year off from work immediately following the birth of a child? Should we have a nationwide system of preschool education based on the one in France? Should required secondary education end at our current grade 10, as in Germany? Should competitive sports programs be transferred from public schools to voluntary programs sponsored by town or city sports organizations, as in Italy? Should the price of gasoline more closely reflect the costs of maintaining and policing roads and highways and cleaning the air from smog created by cars and trucks, as in England and Japan? Should our tax system be more progressive, as in Germany? Should all public school students study one other language for at least ten years, as in Norway and Sweden?

JESSICA STATSKY

Children Need to Play, Not Compete

Jessica Statsky was a college student when she wrote this position paper in which she takes the position that organized sports are not good for children between the ages of six and twelve. Before you read, recall your own experiences as an elementary school student playing competitive sports, either in or out of school. If you were not actively involved yourself, did you know anyone who was? Looking back, do you recall whether winning was unduly emphasized? What value was placed on having a good time? On learning to get along with others? On developing athletic skills and confidence?

As you read, notice how Statsky supports the reasons for her position and how she handles readers' likely objections to her argument. Also pay attention to the visible cues Statsky provides to guide you through her argument step by step.

The other readings in this chapter are followed by reading and writing activities. Following this reading, however, you are on your own to decide how to read for meaning and read like a writer.

Over the past three decades, organized sports for children have increased dramatically in the United States. And though many adults regard Little League Baseball and Peewee Football as a basic part of childhood, the games are not always joyous ones. When overzealous parents and coaches impose adult standards on children's sports, the result can be activities that are neither satisfying nor beneficial to children. 1

I am concerned about all organized sports activities for children between the ages of six and twelve. The damage I see results from noncontact as well as contact sports, from sports organized locally to those organized nationally. Highly organized competitive sports such as Peewee Football and Little League Baseball are too often played to adult standards, which are developmentally inappropriate for children and can be both physically and psychologically harmful. Furthermore, because they eliminate many children from organized sports before they are ready to compete, they are actually counterproductive for developing either future players or fans. Finally, because they emphasize competition and winning, they unfortunately provide occasions for some parents and coaches to place their own fantasies and needs ahead of children's welfare. 2

One readily understandable danger of overly competitive sports is that they entice children into physical actions that are bad for growing bodies. Although the official *Little League Online* 3

Web site acknowledges that children do risk injury playing baseball, they insist that severe injuries are infrequent, "far less than the risk of riding a skateboard, a bicycle, or even the school bus" ("What about My Child"). Nevertheless, Leonard Koppett in *Sports Illusion, Sports Reality* claims that a twelve-year-old trying to throw a curve ball, for example, may put abnormal strain on developing arm and shoulder muscles, sometimes resulting in lifelong injuries (294). Contact sports like football can be even more hazardous. Thomas Tutko, a psychology professor at San Jose State University and coauthor of the book *Winning Is Everything and Other American Myths,* writes:

> I am strongly opposed to young kids playing tackle football. It is not the right stage of development for them to be taught to crash into other kids. Kids under the age of fourteen are not by nature physical. Their main concern is self-preservation. They don't want to meet head on and slam into each other. But tackle football absolutely requires that they try to hit each other as hard as they can. And it is too traumatic for young kids. (qtd. in Tosches A1)

4 As Tutko indicates, even when children are not injured, fear of being hurt detracts from their enjoyment of the sport. *Little League Online* ranks fear of injury as the seventh of seven reasons children quit ("What about My Child"). One mother of an eight-year-old Peewee Football player explained, "The kids get so scared. They get hit once and they don't want anything to do with football anymore. They'll sit on the bench and pretend their leg hurts . . ." (qtd. in Tosches A1). Some children are driven to even more desperate measures. For example, in one Peewee Football game, a reporter watched the following scene as a player took himself out of the game:

> "Coach, my tummy hurts. I can't play," he said. The coach told the player to get back onto the field. "There's nothing wrong with your stomach," he said. When the coach turned his head the seven-year-old stuck a finger down his throat and made himself vomit. When the coach turned back, the boy pointed to the ground and told him, "Yes there is, coach. See?" (Tosches A33)

5 Besides physical hazards and anxieties, competitive sports pose psychological dangers for children. Martin Rablovsky, a former sports editor for the *New York Times,* says that in all his years of watching young children play organized sports, he has noticed very few of them smiling. "I've seen children enjoying a

spontaneous pre-practice scrimmage become somber and serious when the coach's whistle blows," Rablovsky says. "The spirit of play suddenly disappears, and sport becomes joblike" (qtd. in Coakley 94). The primary goal of a professional athlete—winning—is not appropriate for children. Their goals should be having fun, learning, and being with friends. Although winning does add to the fun, too many adults lose sight of what matters and make winning the most important goal. Several studies have shown that when children are asked whether they would rather be warming the bench on a winning team or playing regularly on a losing team, about 90 percent choose the latter (Smith, Smith, and Smoll 11).

Winning and losing may be an inevitable part of adult life, but they should not be part of childhood. Too much competition too early in life can affect a child's development. Children are easily influenced, and when they sense that their competence and worth are based on their ability to live up to their parents' and coaches' high expectations—and on their ability to win—they can become discouraged and depressed. Little League advises parents to "keep winning in perspective" (*Little League Online,* "Your Role"), noting that the most common reasons children give for quitting, aside from change in interest, are lack of playing time, failure and fear of failure, disapproval by significant others, and psychological stress (*Little League Online,* "What about My Child"). According to Dr. Glyn C. Roberts, a professor of kinesiology at the Institute of Child Behavior and Development at the University of Illinois, 80 to 90 percent of children who play competitive sports at a young age drop out by sixteen (Kutner C8). 6

This statistic illustrates another reason I oppose competitive sports for children: because they are so highly selective, very few children get to participate. Far too soon, a few children are singled out for their athletic promise, while many others, who may be on the verge of developing the necessary strength and ability, are screened out and discouraged from trying out again. Like adults, children fear failure, and so even those with good physical skills may stay away because they lack self-confidence. Consequently, teams lose many promising players who with some encouragement and experience might have become stars. The problem is that many parent-sponsored, out-of-school programs give more importance to having a winning team than to developing children's physical skills and self-esteem. 7

Indeed, it is no secret that too often scorekeeping, league standings, and the drive to win bring out the worst in adults who are more absorbed in living out their own fantasies than in enhancing 8 the quality of the experience for children (Smith, Smith, and Smoll 9). Recent newspaper articles on children's sports contain plenty of horror stories. *Los Angeles Times* reporter Rich Tosches, for example, tells the story of a brawl among seventy-five parents following a Peewee Football game (A33). As a result of the brawl, which began when a parent from one team confronted a player from the other team, the teams are now thinking of hiring security guards for future games. Another example is provided by an *L.A. Times* editorial about a Little League manager who intimidated the opposing team by setting fire to one of their team's jerseys on the pitching mound before the game began. As the editorial writer commented, the manager showed his young team that "intimidation could substitute for playing well" ("The Bad News" B6).

9 Although not all parents or coaches behave so inappropriately, the seriousness of the problem is illustrated by the fact that Adelphi University in Garden City, New York, offers a sports psychology workshop for Little League coaches, designed to balance their "animal instincts" with "educational theory" in hopes of reducing the "screaming and hollering," in the words of Harold Weisman, manager of sixteen Little Leagues in New York City (Schmitt B2). In a three-and-one-half-hour Sunday morning workshop, coaches learn how to make practices more fun, treat injuries, deal with irate parents, and be "more sensitive to their young players' fears, emotional frailties, and need for recognition." Little League is to be credited with recognizing the need for such workshops.

10 Some parents would no doubt argue that children cannot start too soon preparing to live in a competitive free-market economy. After all, secondary schools and colleges require students to compete for grades, and college admission is extremely competitive. And it is perfectly obvious how important competitive skills are in finding a job. Yet the ability to cooperate is also important for success in life. Before children are psychologically ready for competition, maybe we should emphasize cooperation and individual performance in team sports rather than winning.

11 Many people are ready for such an emphasis. In 1988, one New York Little League official who had attended the Adelphi workshop tried to ban scoring from six- to eight-year-olds' games—but parents wouldn't support him (Schmitt B2). An innovative children's sports program in New York City, City Sports for Kids, emphasizes fitness, self-esteem, and sportsmanship. In this program's basketball games, every member on a team plays at least two of six eight-minute periods. The basket is seven feet from the floor, rather than ten feet, and a player can score a point just by hitting the rim (Bloch C12). I believe this kind of local program

should replace overly competitive programs like Peewee Football and Little League Baseball. As one coach explains, significant improvements can result from a few simple rule changes, such as including every player in the batting order and giving every player, regardless of age or ability, the opportunity to play at least four innings a game (Frank).

12 Authorities have clearly documented the excesses and dangers of many competitive sports programs for children. It would seem that few children benefit from these programs and that those who do would benefit even more from programs emphasizing fitness, cooperation, sportsmanship, and individual performance. Thirteen- and fourteen-year-olds may be eager for competition, but few younger children are. These younger children deserve sports programs designed specifically for their needs and abilities.

Works Cited

"The Bad News Pyromaniacs?" Editorial. *Los Angeles Times* 16 June 1990: B6.

Bloch, Gordon B. "Thrill of Victory Is Secondary to Fun." *New York Times* 2 Apr. 1990, late ed.: C12.

Coakley, Jay J. *Sport in Society: Issues and Controversies.* St. Louis: Mosby, 1982.

Frank, L. "Contributions from Parents and Coaches." CYB Message Board 8 July 1997, 14 May 1999 <http://members.aol.com/JohnHoelter/b-parent.html>.

Koppett, Leonard. *Sports Illusion, Sports Reality.* Boston: Houghton, 1981.

Kutner, Lawrence. "Athletics, through a Child's Eyes." *New York Times* 23 Mar. 1989, late ed.: C8.

Little League Online. "Your Role as a Little League Parent." Little League Baseball, Incorporated 1999, 30 June 1999 <http://www.littleleague.org/about/parents/yourrole.htm>.

———. "What about My Child." Little League Baseball, Incorporated 1999. 30 June 1999 <http://www.littleleague.org/about/parents/yourchild.htm>.

Schmitt, Eric. "Psychologists Take Seat on Little League Bench." *New York Times* 14 Mar. 1988, late ed.: B2.

Smith, Nathan, Ronald Smith, and Frank Smoll. *Kidsports: A Survival Guide for Parents.* Reading: Addison, 1983.

Tosches, Rich. "Peewee Football: Is It Time to Blow the Whistle?" *Los Angeles Times* 3 Dec. 1988: A1+.

READING FOR MEANING

Write to create meanings for Statsky's position paper on the physical and psychological dangers of competitive sports for young children.

READING LIKE A WRITER

Writers of position papers

- present the issue.
- assert a clear, unequivocal position.
- argue directly for the position.
- counterargue objections and opposing positions.
- establish credibility.

You have seen how important these argumentative strategies are in the readings you have read, written about, and discussed in this chapter. Focus on one of these strategies in Statsky's essay, and analyze it carefully through close rereading and annotating. Then write several sentences explaining what you have learned, giving specific examples from the reading to support your explanation. Add a few sentences evaluating how successfully Statsky uses the strategy to argue convincingly for her position.

REVIEWING WHAT MAKES POSITION PAPERS EFFECTIVE

In this chapter, you have been learning how to read position papers for meaning and how to read them like a writer. Before going on to write a position paper, pause here to review and contemplate what you have learned about the elements of effective position papers.

Analyze

Choose one reading from this chapter that seems to you especially effective. Before rereading the selection, *jot down* one or two reasons you remember it as an example of an effective position paper.

Reread your chosen selection, adding further annotations about what makes it a particularly effective example of the genre. *Consider* the selection's purpose and how well it achieves that purpose for its intended readers. (You can make an informed guess about the intended readers and their expectations by noting the publication source of the essay.) Then *focus* on how well the essay

- presents the issue.
- asserts a clear, unequivocal position.
- argues directly for the position.
- counterargues objections and opposing positions.
- establishes credibility.

You can review all of these basic features in the Guide to Reading Position Papers (p. 447).

Your instructor may ask you to complete this activity on your own or to work with a small group of other students who have chosen the same reading. If you work with others, allow enough time initially for all group members to reread the selection thoughtfully and to add their annotations. Then *discuss* as a group what makes the essay effective. *Take notes* on your discussion. One student in your group should then report to the class what the group has learned about the effectiveness of position papers. If you are working individually, write up what you have learned from your analysis.

Write

Write at least a page supporting your choice of this reading as an example of an effective position paper. *Assume* that your readers—your instructor and classmates—have read the selection but will not remember many details about it. They also might not remember it as especially successful. Therefore, you will need to *refer* to details and specific parts of the essay as you explain how it works and as you justify your evaluation of its effectiveness. You need not argue that it is the best essay in the chapter or that it is flawless, only that it is, in your view, a strong example of the genre.

A Guide to Writing Position Papers

The readings in this chapter have helped you learn a great deal about position papers. Now that you have seen how writers construct arguments supporting their position on issues for their particular readers, you can approach this type of writing confidently. The readings will remain an important resource for you as you develop your own position paper. Use them to review how other writers solved the types of problems you will encounter in your writing.

This Guide to Writing is designed to assist you in writing your position paper. Here you will find activities to help you choose an issue and discover what to say about it, organize your ideas and draft the essay, read the draft critically, revise the draft to strengthen your argument, and edit and proofread the essay to improve readability.

INVENTION

The following invention activities will help you choose an issue to write about and develop an argument to support your position on the issue. You will also explore what you already know about the issue and determine whether you need to learn more about it through extended research. A few minutes spent completing each writing activity will improve your chances of producing a detailed and convincing first draft.

Choosing an Issue

Rather than limiting yourself to the first issue that comes to mind, widen your options by making a list of the issues that interest you. List the most promising issues you can think of, beginning with any you listed for the Considering Ideas for Your Own Writing activities following the readings in this chapter. Continue listing other possible issues. Making such a list often generates still other ideas: As you list ideas, you will think of new issues you cannot imagine now.

List the issues in the form of questions, like these:

- Should local school boards have the power to ban such books as *The Adventures of Huckleberry Finn* and *Of Mice and Men* from school libraries?
- Should teenagers be required to get their parents' permission to obtain birth-control information and contraceptives?
- Should businesses remain loyal to their communities or should they move to wherever labor costs, taxes, and other conditions are more favorable?

After you have completed your list, reflect on the possible issues you have compiled. Choose an arguable issue, one about which people disagree but that cannot be resolved simply with facts or by authorities. Your choice also may be influenced by whether you have time for research and whether your instructor requires it. Issues that have been written about extensively—such as whether weapon searches should be conducted on high-school campuses or whether affirmative action should be continued in college admissions—make excellent topics for extended research. Other issues—such as whether students should be required to perform community service or discouraged from taking part-time jobs that interfere with their studies—may be confidently based on personal experience.

Developing Your Argument

The writing and research activities that follow will enable you to test your choice of an issue and discover good ways to argue for your position on the issue.

Defining the Issue. *To see how you can define the issue, write nonstop for a few minutes.* This brief but intensive writing will help stimulate your memory, letting you see what you already know about the issue and whether you will need to do research to discover more about it.

Considering Your Own Position and Reasons for It. *Briefly state your current position on the issue and give a few reasons you take this position.* You may change your position as you develop your ideas and learn more about the issue, but for now say as directly as you can where you stand and why.

Researching the Issue. *If your instructor requires you to research the issue, or if you decide your essay would benefit from research, consult Appendix 2, Strategies for Research and Documentation, for guidelines on finding library and Internet sources.* Research can help you look critically at your own thinking and help you anticipate your readers' arguments and their possible objections to your argument.

Analyzing Your Readers. *Write for a few minutes identifying who your readers are, what they know about the issue, and how they can be convinced that your position may be plausible.* Describe your readers briefly. Mention anything you know about them as a group that might influence the way they would read your position paper. Speculate about how they will respond to your argument.

Rehearsing the Argument for Your Position. *Consider the reasons you could give for your position, and then write for a few minutes about the one reason you think would be most convincing to your readers.* Which reason do you think is the strongest? Which is most likely to appeal to your readers? As you write, try to show your readers why they should take this reason seriously.

Rehearsing Your Counterargument. *List what will likely be the one or two strongest opposing arguments or objections to your argument, and then write for a few minutes either conceding or refuting each one.* Try to think of arguments or objections your readers will expect you to know about and respond to, especially any criticism that could seriously undermine your argument.

Testing Your Choice. *Pause now to decide whether you have chosen an issue about which you will be able to make a convincing argument.* At this point you have some insights into how you will attempt to present the issue and argue to support your position on it for your particular readers. If your interest in the issue is growing and you are gaining confidence in the argument you want to make, you have probably made a good choice. However, if your interest in the issue is waning and you have been unable to come up with at least two or three plausible reasons why you take the position you do, you may want to consider choosing another issue. If your issue does not seem promising, return to your list of possible subjects to select another.

Considering Visuals. *Consider whether visuals—drawings, photographs, tables, or graphs—would strengthen your argument.* You could construct your own visuals, scan materials from books and magazines, or download them from the Internet. If you submit your essay electronically to other students and your instructor, or if you post it on a Web site, consider including photographs as well as snippets of film or sound. Visual and auditory materials are not at all a requirement of a successful position paper, as you can tell from the readings in this chapter, but they could add a new dimension to your writing. If you want to use photographs or recordings of people, though, be sure to obtain their permission.

Considering Your Purpose. *Write for several minutes about your purpose for writing this position paper.* The following questions will help you think about your purpose:

- What do I hope to accomplish with my readers? How do I want to influence their thinking? What one big idea do I want them to grasp and remember?
- How much resistance to my argument should I expect from my readers? Will they be largely receptive? Skeptical but convincible? Resistant and perhaps even antagonistic?
- How can I interest my readers in the issue? How can I help my readers see its significance—both to society at large and to them personally?

Formulating a Working Thesis. *Draft a thesis, or position, statement.* A working thesis—as opposed to a final or revised thesis—will help you bring your invention writing into focus and begin your draft with a clear purpose. As you draft and revise your essay, you may decide to modify your position and reformulate your thesis. Remember that the thesis for a position paper should assert your position on the issue and may define or qualify that position. In addition, the thesis usually forecasts your argument; it might also forecast your counterargument. The thesis and forecasting statements, therefore, may occupy several sentences. Here are three examples from the readings:

- "Still, however willing I may have been to go along with the name [Washington Redskins] as a kid, as an adult I have concluded that using an ethnic group essentially as a sports mascot is wrong" (Estrada, paragraph 2).
- "I therefore do not consider cigarette smoking, let alone cigar or pipe smoking, to be worthy of the crusade society is waging against it" (Prager, paragraph 3).
- "When overzealous parents and coaches impose adult standards on children's sports, the result can be activities that are neither satisfying nor beneficial to children. I am concerned about all organized sports activities for children between the ages of six and twelve. The damage I see results from noncontact as well as contact sports, from sports organized locally to those organized nationally. Highly organized competitive sports such as Peewee Football and Little League Baseball are too often played to adult standards, which are developmentally inappropriate for children and can be both physically and psychologically harmful. Furthermore, because they eliminate many children from organized sports before they are ready to compete, they are actually counterproductive for developing either future players or fans. Finally, because they emphasize competition and winning, they unfortunately provide occasions for some parents and coaches to place their own fantasies and needs ahead of children's welfare" (Statsky, paragraphs 1 and 2).

DRAFTING

The following guidelines will help you set goals for your draft and plan its organization.

Setting Goals

Establishing goals for your draft before you begin writing will enable you to make decisions and work more confidently. Consider the following questions now, and keep them in mind as you draft. They will help you set goals for drafting as well as recall how the writers you have read in this chapter tried to achieve similar goals.

- *How can I present the issue in a way that will interest my readers?* Should I open with an anecdote (as Kennedy does), a scenario (as Knutson does), or a connection to my personal experience (as both Estrada and Prager do)? Do I need to define the issue explicitly, perhaps by distinguishing between terms (like Sandel) or redefining familiar activities or institutions (like Matsuda)? Should I present the issue in a historical context, as Kennedy and Statsky do? Or should I start with alarming statistics, as Sandel does?
- *How can I support my argument in a way that will win the respect of my readers?* Should I quote authorities or offer statistics from research studies, as Sandel, Matsuda, Prager, Knutson, and Statsky do? Should I argue that my position is based on shared values, as all the writers in this chapter do? Should I create analogies, as Sandel, Matsuda, Kennedy, and Prager do? Should I provide examples, like all the writers? Should I speculate about consequences, like all the writers? Should I support my argument with personal experience, as Matsuda, Prager, and Knutson do?
- *How can I counterargue effectively?* Should I introduce my argument by reviewing readers' opposing positions and likely objections, as Sandel, Kennedy, and Knutson do? Should I concede the wisdom of readers' views, as Sandel and Knutson do? Or should I attempt to refute readers' views, as Sandel, Kennedy, Knutson, and Statsky do?
- *How can I establish my authority and credibility on the issue?* Should I support my argument through research, as all the writers in this chapter do? Should I risk bringing in my personal experience, as Estrada, Prager, and Knutson do? How can I refute readers' views without attacking them, as Sandel and Kennedy manage to do? Should I make an appeal to possible shared moral values with readers, as Estrada, Sandel, and Matsuda do?

Organizing Your Draft

With goals in mind and invention notes in hand, you are ready to make a tentative outline of your draft. First list the reasons you plan to use as support for your argument. Decide how you will sequence these reasons. Writers of position papers often end with the strongest reasons because this organization gives the best reasons the greatest emphasis. Then add to your outline the opposing positions or objections that you plan to counterargue.

READING A DRAFT CRITICALLY

Getting a critical reading of your draft will help you see how to improve it. Your instructor may schedule class time for reading drafts, or you may want to ask a classmate or a tutor in the writing center to read your draft. Ask your reader to use the following guidelines and to write out a response for you to consult during revision.

Read for a First Impression

1. Read the draft without stopping to annotate or comment, and then write two or three sentences giving your general impression.
2. Identify one aspect of the draft that seems particularly effective.

Read Again to Suggest Improvements

1. Suggest ways of presenting the issue more effectively.
   - Read the paragraphs that present the issue, and tell the writer how they help you understand the issue or fail to help you.
   - Point to any key terms used to present the issue that seem surprising, confusing, antagonizing, or unnecessarily loaded.
2. Recommend ways of asserting the position more clearly and unequivocally.
   - Find the writer's thesis, or position statement, and underline it. If you cannot find a clear thesis, let the writer know.
   - If you find several restatements of the thesis, examine them closely for consistency.
   - If the position seems extreme or overstated, suggest how it might be qualified and made more reasonable.
3. Help the writer argue more directly for the position and strengthen the argument.
   - Indicate any reasons that seem unconvincing, and explain briefly why you think so.
   - Look at the support the writer provides for each reason. If you find any of it ineffective, briefly explain why you think so and how it could be strengthened.
   - If you find places in the draft where support is lacking, suggest what kinds of support (facts, statistics, quotations, anecdotes, examples, or analogies) the writer might consider adding—and why.
4. Suggest ways of improving the counterargument.
   - If any part of the refutation could be strengthened, suggest what the writer could add or change.

- If only the weakest objections or opposing positions have been acknowledged, remind the writer of the stronger ones that should be taken into account.

5. Suggest how credibility can be enhanced.

- Tell the writer whether the intended readers are likely to find the essay authoritative and trustworthy. Point to places where the argument seems most and least trustworthy.
- Identify places where the writer seeks to establish a common ground of shared values, beliefs, and attitudes with readers. Point to other places where the writer might attempt to do so without undermining the position being argued.

6. Suggest ways of improving readability.

- Consider whether the beginning adequately sets the stage for the argument, perhaps by establishing the tone or forecasting the argument.
- If the organization does not seem to follow a logical plan, suggest how it might be rearranged or where transitions could be inserted to clarify logical connections.
- Note whether the ending gives the argument a satisfactory sense of closure.

7. Evaluate the effectiveness of visuals.

- Look at any visuals in the essay, and tell the writer what they contribute to your understanding of the argument.
- If any visuals do not seem relevant, or if there seem to be too many visuals, identify the ones that the writer could consider dropping, explaining your thinking.
- If a visual does not seem to be appropriately placed, suggest a better place for it.

REVISING

This section offers suggestions for revising your draft, suggestions that will remind you of the possibilities for developing a well-argued position paper. Revising means reenvisioning your draft, trying to see it in a new way, given your purpose and readers, in order to develop your argument.

The biggest mistake you can make while revising is to focus initially on words or sentences. Instead, first try to see your draft as a whole in order to assess its likely impact on your readers. Think imaginatively and boldly about cutting unconvincing material, adding new material, and moving material around to enhance clarity and strengthen your argument. Your computer makes even drastic revisions physically easy, but you still need to make the mental effort and decisions that will improve your draft.

You may have received help with this challenge from a classmate or tutor who gave your draft a critical reading. If so, keep this valuable feedback in mind as you decide which parts of your draft need revising and what specific changes you could make. The following suggestions will help you solve problems and strengthen your essay.

To Present the Issue More Effectively

- If readers do not fully understand what is at stake in the issue, consider adding anecdotes, examples, or facts to make the issue more specific and vivid, or try explaining more systematically why you see the issue as you do.
- If the terms you use to present the issue are surprising, antagonizing, or unnecessarily loaded, consider revising your presentation of the issue in more familiar or neutral terms.

To Assert the Position More Clearly and Unequivocally

- If your position on the issue seems unclear to readers, try reformulating it or spelling it out in more detail.
- If your thesis statement is not easy for readers to find, try stating it more directly to avoid misunderstanding.
- If your thesis is not appropriately qualified to account for valid opposing arguments or objections, modify it by limiting its scope.

To Argue More Directly for the Position and Strengthen the Argument

- If a reason seems unconvincing, try clarifying its relevance to the argument.
- If you need better support, review your invention notes or do more research to find facts, statistics, quotations, examples, or other types of support that will help bolster your argument.

To Improve the Counterargument

- If your refutation seems unconvincing, provide more or better support (such as facts and statistics from reputable sources) to convince readers that your counterargument is not idiosyncratic or personal. Avoid attacking your opponents on a personal level; refute only their ideas.

- If your counterargument ignores any strong, opposing positions or reasonable objections, revise your essay to address them directly. If you cannot refute them, acknowledge their validity—and, if necessary, modify your position to accommodate them.
- If you can make any concessions without doing injustice to your own views, consider doing so now.

To Enhance Credibility

- If readers find any of your sources questionable, either establish these sources' credibility or choose more reliable sources to back up your argument.
- If readers think you ignore any opposing arguments, demonstrate to readers that you know and understand, even if you do not accept, these different points of view on the issue.
- If readers find your tone harsh or off-putting, consider the implications and potential offensiveness of your word choices; then look for ways to show respect for and establish common ground with readers, revising your essay to achieve a more accommodating tone.

To Improve Readability

- If the beginning seems dull or unfocused, rewrite it, perhaps by adding a surprising or vivid anecdote.
- If readers have trouble following your argument, consider adding a brief forecast of your main points at the beginning of your essay.
- If the reasons and counterarguments are not logically arranged, reorder them. Consider announcing each reason more explicitly or adding transitions to make the connections clearer.
- If the ending seems weak, search your invention and research notes for a memorable quotation or a vivid example that will strengthen your ending.

EDITING AND PROOFREADING

After you have revised your essay, be sure to spend some time checking for errors in usage, punctuation, and mechanics and considering matters of style. If you keep a list of errors you typically make, begin by checking your draft against this list. Ask someone else to proofread your essay before you print out a copy for your instructor or send it electronically.

From our research on student writing, we know that essays arguing positions have a high percentage of sentence fragment errors involving subordinating conjunctions as well as punctuation errors involving conjunctive adverbs. Because arguing a position often requires you to use subordinating conjunctions (such as *because, although,* and *since*) and conjunctive adverbs (such as *therefore, however,* and *thus*), you want to be sure you know the conventions for punctuating sentences that include these types of words. Check a writer's handbook for help with avoiding sentence fragments and using punctuation correctly in sentences with subordinating conjunctions and conjunctive adverbs.

REFLECTING ON WHAT YOU HAVE LEARNED

Position Paper

In this chapter, you have read critically several position papers and have written one of your own. To better remember what you have learned, pause now to reflect on the reading and writing activities you completed in this chapter.

1. *Write* a page or so reflecting on what you have learned. *Begin* by describing what you are most pleased with in your essay. Then *explain* what you think contributed to your achievement. *Be specific* about this contribution.
   - If it was something you learned from the readings, *indicate* which readings and specifically what you learned from them.
   - If it came from your invention writing, *point out* the section or sections that helped you most.
   - If you got good advice from a critical reader, *explain* exactly how the person helped you—perhaps by helping you understand a particular problem in your draft or by adding a new dimension to your writing.
   - *Try to write* about your achievement in terms of what you have learned about the genre.
2. Now *reflect* more generally on position papers, a genre of writing that plays an important role in our society. *Consider* some of the following questions: As a reader and writer of position papers, how important are reasons and supporting evidence? When people on television and radio talk shows argue their positions, do they tend to emphasize reasons and support? If not, what do they emphasize? How do you think their purpose differs from the purpose of the writers you read in this chapter and from your own purpose in writing a position paper? What contribution might position papers make to our society that other genres of writing cannot make?

APPENDIX 1

A Catalog of Critical Reading Strategies

Serious study of a text requires a pencil in hand—
how much pride that pencil carries.

IRVING HOWE

Here we present fifteen specific strategies for reading critically, strategies that you can learn readily and then apply not only to the selections in this book but also to your other college reading. Mastering these strategies may not make the critical reading process any easier, but it can make reading much more satisfying and productive and thus help you handle difficult material with confidence. These strategies are:

- *Annotating:* recording your reactions to and questions about a text directly on the page
- *Previewing:* learning about a text before reading it closely
- *Outlining:* listing the main idea of each paragraph to see the organization of a text
- *Summarizing:* briefly presenting the main ideas of a text
- *Paraphrasing:* restating and clarifying the meaning of a few sentences from a text
- *Synthesizing:* combining ideas and information selected from different texts
- *Questioning to understand and remember:* inquiring about the content
- *Contextualizing:* placing a text within an appropriate historical and cultural framework
- *Reflecting on challenges to your beliefs and values:* examining your responses to reveal your own unexamined assumptions and attitudes
- *Exploring the significance of figurative language:* seeing how metaphors, similes, and symbols enhance meaning

- *Looking for patterns of opposition:* discovering what a text values by analyzing its system of binaries/contrasts
- *Evaluating the logic of an argument:* testing the argument of a text to see whether it makes sense
- *Recognizing emotional manipulation:* looking for false or exaggerated appeals
- *Judging the writer's credibility:* determining whether a text can be trusted
- *Comparing and contrasting related readings:* exploring likenesses and differences between texts to understand them better

ANNOTATING

For each of these strategies, annotating directly on the page is fundamental. *Annotating* means underlining key words, phrases, or sentences; writing comments or questions in the margins; bracketing important sections of the text; connecting ideas with lines or arrows; numbering related points in sequence; and making note of anything that strikes you as interesting, important, or questionable. (If writing on the text itself is impossible or undesirable, you can annotate a photocopy.)

Most readers annotate in layers, adding further annotations on second and third readings. Annotations can be light or heavy, depending on a reader's purpose and the difficulty of the material.

For several of the strategies in this appendix, you will need to build on and extend annotating by *taking inventory:* analyzing and classifying your annotations, searching systematically for patterns in the text, and interpreting their significance. An inventory is basically a list. When you take inventory, you make various kinds of lists in order to find meaning in a text. As you inventory your annotations on a particular reading, you may discover that the language and ideas cluster in various ways.

Inventorying annotations is a three-step process:

1. Examine your annotations for patterns or repetitions of any kind, such as recurring images or stylistic features, related words and phrases, similar examples, or reliance on authorities.
2. Try out different ways of grouping the items.
3. Consider what the patterns you have found suggest about the writer's meaning or rhetorical choices.

The patterns you discover will depend on the kind of reading you are analyzing and on the purpose of your analysis. (See Exploring the Significance of Figurative Language, p. 539, and Looking for Patterns of Opposition, p. 542, for examples of inventorying annotations.) These patterns can help you reach a deeper understanding of the text.

The following selection has been annotated to demonstrate the processes required by the critical reading strategies we describe in the remainder of Appendix 1. As you read about each strategy, you will refer back to this annotated example.

MARTIN LUTHER KING JR.

An Annotated Sample from "Letter from Birmingham Jail"

Martin Luther King Jr. (1929–1968) first came to national notice in 1955, when he led a successful boycott against back-of-the-bus seating of African Americans in Montgomery, Alabama, where he was minister of a Baptist church. He subsequently formed a national organization, the Southern Christian Leadership Conference, that brought people of all races from across the country to the South to fight nonviolently for racial integration. In 1963, King led demonstrations in Birmingham that were met with violence: A black church was bombed, killing four little girls. King was arrested and, while in prison, he wrote the famous "Letter from Birmingham Jail" to answer local clergy's criticism. King begins by discussing his disappointment with the lack of support he received from white moderates, such as the group of clergymen who published their criticism in the local newspaper (the complete text of the clergymen's published criticism appears at the end of this appendix).

The following brief excerpt from King's "Letter" is annotated to illustrate some of the ways you can annotate as you read. Since annotating is the first step for all critical reading strategies in this catalog, these annotations are referred to throughout this appendix. As you read, add your own annotations in the right-hand margin.

¶1 White moderates block progress

Order vs. justice

Negative vs. positive

1 . . . I must confess that over the past few years I have been gravely disappointed with the white moderate. I have almost reached the regrettable conclusion that the Negro's [great stumbling block in his stride toward freedom] is not the White Citizen's Counciler or the Ku Klux Klanner, but the white moderate, who is more devoted to "order" than to justice; who prefers a negative peace which is the absence of tension to a positive peace which is the presence of justice; who constantly says: "I agree with you in the goal you seek,

Ends vs. means
Treating others like children

but I cannot agree with your methods of direct action"; who paternalistically believes he can set the timetable for another man's freedom; who lives by a mythical concept of time and who constantly advises the Negro to wait for a "more convenient season." Shallow understanding from people of good will is more frustrating than absolute misunderstanding from people of ill will. [Lukewarm acceptance is much more bewildering than outright rejection.]

¶12 Tension necessary for progress

Tension already exists

Simile: hidden tension is "like a boil"

True?

2 I had hoped that the white moderate would understand that law and order exist for the purpose of establishing justice and that when they fail in this purpose they become the [dangerously structured dams that block the flow of social progress.] I had hoped that the white moderate would understand that the present tension in the South is a necessary phase of the transition from an [obnoxious negative peace,] in which the Negro passively accepted his unjust plight, to a [substantive and positive peace,] in which all men will respect the dignity and worth of human personality. Actually, we who engage in nonviolent direct action are not the creators of tension. We merely bring to the surface the hidden tension that is already alive. We bring it out in the open, where it can be seen and dealt with. [Like a boil that can never be cured so long as it is covered up but must be opened with all its ugliness to the natural medicines of air and light, injustice must be exposed, with all the tension its exposure creates, to the light of human conscience and the air of national opinion before it can be cured.]

¶13 King questions clergymen's logic of blaming the victim

Yes!

3 In your statement you assert that our actions, even though peaceful, must be condemned because they precipitate violence. But is this a logical assertion? Isn't this like condemning [a robbed man] because his possession of money precipitated the evil act of robbery? Isn't this like condemning [Socrates] because his unswerving commitment to truth and his philosophical inquiries precipitated the act by the misguided populace in which they made him drink hemlock? Isn't this like condemning [Jesus] because his unique God-consciousness and never-ceasing devotion to God's will precipitated the evil act of crucifixion? We must come to see that, as the federal courts have consistently affirmed, it is wrong to urge an individual to cease his efforts to gain his basic constitutional rights because the question may precipitate violence. [Society must protect the robbed and punish the robber.]

¶14 Justifies urgency

Quotes white moderate as example

Critiques assumptions

Silence is as bad as hateful words and actions

Not moving

Elegy = death; psalm = celebration

Metaphors: quicksand, rock

4

I had also hoped that the white moderate would reject the myth concerning time in relation to the struggle for freedom. I have just received a letter from a white brother in Texas. He writes: "All Christians know that the colored people will receive equal rights eventually, but it is possible that you are in too great a religious hurry. It has taken Christianity almost two thousand years to accomplish what it has. The teachings of Christ take time to come to earth." Such an attitude stems from a tragic misconception of time, from the strangely irrational notion that there is something in the very flow of time that will inevitably cure all ills. [Actually, time itself is neutral; it can be used either destructively or constructively.] More and more I feel that the people of ill will have used time much more effectively than have the people of good will. We will have to repent in this generation not merely for the [hateful words and actions of the bad people] but for the [appalling silence of the good people.] Human progress never rolls in on [wheels of inevitability;] it comes through the tireless efforts of men willing to be co-workers with God, and without this hard work, time itself becomes an ally of the forces of social stagnation. [We must use time creatively, in the knowledge that the time is always ripe to do right.] Now is the time to make real the promise of democracy and transform our pending [national elegy] into a creative [psalm of brotherhood.] Now is the time to lift our national policy from the [quicksand of racial injustice] to the [solid rock of human dignity.]

¶15 Refutes criticism, King not an extremist

Complacency vs. hatred

5

You speak of our activity in Birmingham as extreme. At first I was rather disappointed that fellow clergymen would see my nonviolent efforts as those of an extremist. I began thinking about the fact that I stand in the middle of two opposing forces in the Negro community. One is a [force of complacency,] made up in part of Negroes who, as a result of long years of oppression, are so drained of self-respect and a sense of "somebodiness" that they have adjusted to segregation; and in part of a few middle-class Negroes, who because of a degree of academic and economic security and because in some ways they profit by segregation, have become insensitive to the problems of the masses. The other [force is one of bitterness and hatred,] and it comes perilously close to advocating violence. It is expressed in the various black nationalist [groups that are springing up]

Malcolm X?

across the nation, the largest and best-known being Elijah Muhammad's Muslim movement. Nourished by the Negro's frustration over the continued existence of racial discrimination, this movement is made up of people who have lost faith in America, who have absolutely repudiated Christianity, and who have concluded that the white man is an incorrigible "devil."

¶6 Claims to offer better choice

6 I have tried to stand between these two forces, saying that we need emulate neither the "do-nothingism" of the complacent nor the hatred and despair of the black nationalist. For there is the more excellent way of love and nonviolent protest. I am grateful to God that, through the influence of the Negro church, the way of nonviolence became an integral part of our struggle.

¶7 Claims his movement prevents racial violence

If . . . then . . . Veiled threat?

7 If this philosophy had not emerged, by now many streets of the South would, I am convinced, be flowing with blood. And I am further convinced that if our white brothers dismiss as "rabble-rousers" and "outside agitators" those of us who employ nonviolent direct action, and if they refuse to support our nonviolent efforts, millions of Negroes will, out of frustration and despair, seek solace and security in black-nationalist ideologies—a development that would inevitably lead to a frightening racial nightmare.

¶8 Change inevitable: evolution or revolution?

Spirit of the times Worldwide uprising against injustice

Why "he," not "I"?

Repeats "let him"

Not a threat?

"I" channel discontent

8 [Oppressed people cannot remain oppressed forever.] The yearning for freedom eventually manifests itself, and that is what has happened to the American Negro. Something within has reminded him of his birthright of freedom, and something without has reminded him that it can be gained. Consciously or unconsciously, he has been caught up by the *Zeitgeist*, and with his black brothers of Africa and his brown and yellow brothers of Asia, South America and the Caribbean, the United States Negro is moving with a sense of great urgency toward the [promised land of racial justice.] If one recognizes this [vital urge that has engulfed the Negro community,] one should readily understand why public demonstrations are taking place. The Negro has many [pent-up resentments] and latent frustrations, and he must release them. So let him march; let him make prayer pilgrimages to the city hall; let him go on freedom rides—and try to understand why he must do so. If his repressed emotions are not released in nonviolent ways, they will seek expression through violence; this is not a threat but a fact of history. So I have not said to my people: "Get rid of your discontent." Rather, I have tried to say that this normal and

healthy discontent can be [channeled into the creative outlet of nonviolent direct action.] And now this approach is being termed extremist.

¶9 Justifies extremism for righteous ends

9 But though I was initially disappointed at being categorized as an extremist, as I continued to think about the matter I gradually gained a measure of satisfaction from the label. Was not Jesus an extremist for love: "Love your enemies, bless them that curse you, do good to them that hate you, and pray for them which despitefully use you, and persecute you." Was not Amos an extremist for justice: "Let justice roll down like waters and righteousness like an ever-flowing stream." Was not Paul an extremist for the Christian gospel: "I bear in my body the marks of the Lord Jesus." Was not Martin Luther an extremist: "Here I stand; I cannot do otherwise, so help me God." And John Bunyan: "I will stay in jail to the end of my days before I make a butchery of my conscience." And Abraham Lincoln: "This nation cannot survive half slave and half free." And Thomas Jefferson: "We hold these truths to be self-evident, that all men are created equal. . . ." [So the question is not whether we will be extremists, but what kind of extremists we will be.] Will we be extremists for hate or for love? Will we be extremists for the preservation of injustice or for the extension of justice? In that dramatic scene on Calvary's hill three men were crucified. We must never forget that all three were crucified for the same crime—the crime of extremism. Two were extremists for immorality, and thus fell below their environment. The other, Jesus Christ, was an extremist for love, truth and goodness, and thereby rose above his environment. Perhaps the South, [the nation and the world are in dire need of creative extremists.]

Hebrew prophet

Christ's disciple

Founded Protestantism

English preacher

Freed slaves

Wrote Declaration of Independence

Redeemer — all extremists for good

¶10 Disappointed in white moderate critics; thanks supporters

10 I had hoped that the white moderate would see this need. Perhaps I was too optimistic; perhaps I expected too much. I suppose I should have realized that few members of the oppressor race can understand the deep groans and passionate yearnings of the oppressed race, and still fewer have the vision to see that [injustice must be rooted out] by strong, persistent and determined action. I am thankful, however, that some of our white brothers in the South have grasped the meaning of this social revolution and committed themselves to it. They are still all too few in quantity, but they are big in quality. Some — such as Ralph McGill, Lillian Smith, Harry Golden, James McBride Dabbs, Ann Braden and Sarah Patton Boyle — have written about our struggle in

Who are they?

Left unaided

Framing—recalls boil simile

eloquent and prophetic terms. Others have marched with us down nameless streets of the South. They have (languished) in filthy, roach-infested jails, suffering the abuse and brutality of policemen who view them as "dirty nigger-lovers." Unlike so many of their moderate brothers and sisters, they have recognized the urgency of the movement and sensed the need for powerful ["action" antidotes] to combat the [disease of segregation.]

CHECKLIST

Annotating

To annotate a reading:

1. Mark the text using notations.
   - Circle words to be defined in the margin.
   - Underline key words and phrases.
   - Bracket important sentences and passages.
   - Use lines or arrows to connect ideas or words.
   - Use question marks to note any confusion or disagreement.
2. Write marginal comments.
   - Number each paragraph for future reference.
   - State the main idea of each paragraph.
   - Define unfamiliar words.
   - Note responses and questions.
   - Identify interesting writing strategies.
   - Point out patterns.
3. Layer additional markings on the text and comments in the margins as you reread for different purposes.

PREVIEWING

Previewing enables you to get a sense of what the text is about and how it is organized before reading it closely. This simple critical reading strategy includes seeing what you can learn from headnotes, biographical notes about the author, or other introductory material; skimming to get an overview of the content and organization; and identifying the genre and rhetorical situation.

Learning from Headnotes

Many texts provide some introductory material to orient readers. Books often have brief blurbs on the cover describing the content and author, as well as a preface, an introduction, and a table of contents. Articles in professional and academic journals usually provide some background information. Scientific articles, for example, typically begin with an abstract summarizing the main points. In this book, as in many textbooks, headnotes introducing the author and identifying the circumstances under which the selection was originally published precede the reading selections.

Because Martin Luther King Jr. is a well-known figure, the headnote might not tell you anything you do not already know. If you know something else about the author that could help you better understand the selection, you might want to make a note of it. As a critical reader, you should think about whether the writer has authority and credibility on the subject. Information about the writer's education, professional experience, and other publications can help. If you need to know more about a particular author, you could consult a biographical dictionary or encyclopedia in the library, such as *Who's Who, Biographical Index, Current Biography, Dictionary of American Biography,* or *Contemporary Authors.*

Skimming for an Overview

When you *skim* a text, you give it a quick, selective, superficial reading. For most explanations and arguments, a good strategy is to read the opening and closing paragraphs; the first usually introduces the subject and may forecast the main points, while the last typically summarizes what is most important in the essay. You should also glance at the first sentence of every internal paragraph because it may serve as a topic sentence, introducing the point discussed in the paragraph. Because narrative writing is usually organized chronologically rather than logically, often you can get a sense of the progression by skimming for time markers such as *then, after,* and *later.* Heads and subheads, figures, charts, and the like also provide clues for skimming.

To illustrate, turn back to the King excerpt and skim it. Notice that the opening paragraph establishes the subject: the white moderate's criticism of Dr. King's efforts. It also forecasts many of the main points that are taken up in subsequent paragraphs; for example, the moderate's greater devotion to order than to justice (paragraph 2), the moderate's criticism that King's methods, though nonviolent, precipitate violence (paragraph 3), and the moderate's "paternalistic" timetable (paragraph 4).

Identifying the Genre and Rhetorical Situation

Reading an unfamiliar text is like traveling in unknown territory: You can use a map to check what you see against what you expect to find. In much the same way, previewing for genre equips you with a set of expectations to guide your reading. *Genre* means "kind" or "type," and is generally used to classify pieces of writing according to their particular social function. Nonfiction prose genres include autobiography, observation, reflection, explanations of concepts, and various forms of argument, such as evaluation, analysis of causes or effects, proposals to solve a problem, and position papers on controversial issues. These genres are illustrated in Chapters 2 through 9 with guidelines to help you analyze and evaluate their effectiveness. After working through these chapters, you will be able to identify the genre of most unfamiliar pieces of writing you encounter.

You can make a tentative decision about the genre of a text by first looking at why the piece was written and to whom it was addressed. These two elements—purpose and audience—constitute the rhetorical or writing situation. Consider the writing of "Letter from Birmingham Jail." The title explicitly identifies this particular selection as a letter. We know that letters are usually written with a particular reader in mind, but can also be written for the reading public (as in a letter to the editor of a magazine); that they may be part of an ongoing correspondence; and that they may be informal or formal.

Read the clergymen's statement at the end of this appendix (pp. 555–57) to gain some insight into the situation in which King wrote his letter and some understanding of his specific purpose for writing. As a public letter written in response to a public statement, "Letter from Birmingham Jail" may be classified as a position paper, one that argues for a particular point of view on a controversial issue.

Even without reading the clergymen's statement, you can get a sense of the rhetorical situation from the opening paragraph of the King excerpt. You would not be able to identify the "white moderate" with the clergymen who criticized King, but you would see clearly that he is referring to people he had hoped would support his cause but who, instead, have become an obstacle. King's feelings about the white moderate's lack of support are evident in the first paragraph, where he uses such words as *gravely disappointed, regrettable conclusion, frustrating,* and *bewildering.* The opening paragraph, as noted earlier, also identifies the white moderate's specific objections to King's methods. Therefore, you not only learn very quickly that this is a position paper, but you also learn the points of disagreement between the two sides and the writer's attitude toward those with whom he disagrees.

Knowing that this is an excerpt from a position paper allows you to appreciate the controversiality of the subject King is writing about and the sensitivity of the rhetorical situation. You can see how he asserts his own position at the same time that he tries to bridge the gap separating him from his critics. You can then evaluate the kinds of points King makes and the persuasiveness of his argument.

CHECKLIST

Previewing

To orient yourself before reading closely:

1. See what you can learn from headnotes or other introductory material.
2. Skim the text to get an overview of the content and organization.
3. Identify the genre and rhetorical situation.

OUTLINING

Outlining is an especially helpful critical reading strategy for understanding the content and structure of a reading. Outlining, which identifies and organizes the text's main ideas, may be done as part of the annotating process, or it may be done separately. Writing an outline in the margins of the text as you read and annotate makes it easier to find information later. Writing an outline on a separate piece of paper gives you more space to work with and thus usually includes more detail.

The key to effective outlining is distinguishing between the main ideas and the supporting material, such as examples, factual evidence, and explanations. The main ideas form the backbone that holds the various parts and pieces of the text together. Outlining the main ideas helps you uncover this structure.

Making an outline, however, is not simple. The reader must exercise judgment in deciding which are the most important ideas. Reading is never a passive or neutral act; the process of outlining shows how active reading can be.

You may make either a *formal, multileveled outline* with roman (I, II) and arabic (1, 2) numerals together with capital and lowercase letters, or you can make an *informal, scratch outline* that lists the main idea of each paragraph. A formal outline is harder to make and much more time-consuming than a scratch outline. You might choose to make a formal outline of a reading about which you are writing an in-depth analysis or evaluation. For example, here is a formal outline a student wrote for a paper evaluating the logic of the King excerpt. Notice that the student uses roman numerals for the main ideas or claims, capital letters for the reasons, and arabic numerals for supporting evidence and explanation.

Formal Outline

I. The Negro's great stumbling block in his stride toward freedom is . . . the white moderate

- A. *Because* the white moderate is more devoted to "order" than to justice (paragraph 2)
    1. Law and order should exist to establish justice
    2. Law and order compare to dangerously structured dams that block the flow of social progress
- B. *Because* the white moderate prefers a negative peace (absence of tension) to a positive peace (justice) (paragraph 2)
    1. The tension already exists
    2. It is not created by nonviolent direct action
    3. Society that does not eliminate injustice compares to a boil that hides its infections. Both can be cured only by exposure (boil simile)
- C. *Because* even though the white moderates agree with the goals, they do not support the means to achieve them (paragraph 3)
    1. The argument that the means—nonviolent direct action—are wrong because they precipitate violence is flawed
    2. Analogy of the robbed man condemned because he had money
    3. Comparison with Socrates and Jesus
- D. *Because* the white moderates paternalistically believe they can set a timetable for another man's freedom (paragraph 4)
    1. Rebuts the white moderate's argument that Christianity will cure man's ills and man must wait patiently for that to happen
    2. Argues that time is neutral and that man must use time creatively for constructive rather than destructive ends

II. Creative extremism is preferable to moderation

- A. Classifies himself as a moderate (paragraphs 5–8)
    1. I stand between two forces: the white moderate's complacency and the black Muslim's rage
    2. If nonviolent direct action were stopped, more violence, not less, would result
    3. "Millions of Negroes will, out of frustration and despair, seek solace and security in black-nationalist ideologies" (paragraph 7)
    4. Repressed emotions will be expressed—if not in nonviolent ways, then through violence (paragraph 8)
- B. Redefines himself as a "creative extremist" (paragraph 9)
    1. Extremism for love, truth, and goodness is creative extremism
    2. Identifies himself with the creative extremists Jesus, Amos, Paul, Martin Luther, John Bunyan, Abraham Lincoln, and Thomas Jefferson
- C. Not all whites are moderates; many are creative extremists (paragraph 10)
    1. Lists names of white writers
    2. Refers to white activists

Making a scratch outline, in contrast to a formal outline, takes less time but still requires careful reading. A scratch outline will not record as much information as a formal outline, but it is sufficient for most critical reading purposes. To make a scratch outline, you need to locate the topic of each paragraph. The topic is usually stated in a word or phrase, and it may be repeated or referred to throughout the paragraph. For example, the opening paragraph of the King excerpt (pp. 519–20) makes clear that its topic is the white moderate.

After you have found the topic of the paragraph, figure out what is being said about it. To return to our example: If the white moderate is the topic of the opening paragraph, then what King says about the topic can be found in the second sentence, where he announces the conclusion he has come to—namely, that the white moderate is "the Negro's great stumbling block in his stride toward freedom." The rest of the paragraph specifies the ways the white moderate blocks progress.

When you make an outline, you can use the writer's words, your own words, or a combination of the two. A paragraph-by-paragraph outline appears in the margins of the selection, with numbers for each paragraph (see pp. 519–24). Here is the same outline as it might appear on a separate piece of paper, slightly expanded and reworded:

Paragraph Scratch Outline

¶1 White moderates block progress in the struggle for racial justice
¶2 Tension is necessary for progress
¶3 The clergymen's criticism is not logical
¶4 King justifies urgent use of time
¶5 Clergymen accuse King of being extreme, but he claims to stand between two extreme forces in the black community
¶6 King offers a better choice
¶7 King's movement has prevented racial violence by blacks
¶8 Discontent is normal and healthy but must be channeled creatively rather than destructively
¶9 Creative extremists are needed
¶10 Some whites have supported King

CHECKLIST

Outlining

To make a scratch outline of a text:

1. Reread each paragraph systematically, identifying the topic and what is being said about it. Do not include examples, specific details, quotations, or other explanatory and supporting material.

2. List the main ideas in the margin of the text or on a separate piece of paper.

SUMMARIZING

Summarizing is one of the most widely used strategies for critical reading because it helps you understand and remember what is most important in a text. Another advantage of summarizing is that it creates a condensed version of the reading's ideas and information, which you can refer to later or insert into your own written text. Along with quoting and paraphrasing, summarizing enables you to refer to and integrate other writers' ideas into your own writing.

Relatively brief restatements of the reading's main ideas, summaries have many functions, depending on context. When you search for sources through your college library's online catalog, summaries help you decide whether you want to read the complete source. You may also notice summaries at key points in your textbooks, points where the author wants you to review information covered in previous pages. When you begin using journal articles in your field of study, brief summaries called abstracts can help you tell right away whether the report is relevant to your research.

Summaries also vary in length. Some summaries are very brief—a sentence or even a subordinate clause. For example, if you were referring to the excerpt from "Letter from Birmingham Jail" and simply needed to indicate how it relates to your other sources, your summary might focus on only one aspect of the reading. It might look something like this:

> There have always been advocates of extremism in politics. Martin Luther King Jr., in "Letter from Birmingham Jail," for instance, defends nonviolent civil disobedience as an extreme but necessary means of bringing about racial justice.

If, however, you were surveying the important texts of the civil rights movement, you might write a longer, more detailed summary, one that not only identifies the reading's main ideas but also shows how the ideas relate to one another.

Many writers find it useful to outline the reading as a preliminary to writing a summary. A paragraph-by-paragraph scratch outline (like the one illustrated on the preceding page) lists the reading's main ideas following the sequence in which they appear in the original. But writing a summary requires more than merely stringing together the entries in an outline. A summary has to make explicit the logical connections between the ideas. Writing a summary shows how reading critically is a truly constructive process of interpretation involving both close analysis and creative synthesis.

To summarize, you need to segregate the main ideas from the supporting material, usually by making an outline of the reading. You want to use your own words for the most part because doing so confirms that you understand the material you have read, but you may also use key words and phrases from the reading. You may also want to cite the title and refer to the author by name, using verbs like *expresses, acknowledges,* and *explains* to indicate the writer's purpose and strategy at each point in the argument.

Following is a sample summary of the King excerpt. It is based on the outline on pages 527–28, but is much more detailed. Most important, it fills in connections between the ideas that King left for readers to make.

> King expresses his disappointment with white moderates who, by opposing his program of nonviolent direct action, have blocked progress toward racial justice. He acknowledges that his program has raised tension in the South, but he explains that tension is necessary to bring about change. Furthermore, he argues that tension already exists. But because it has been unexpressed, it is unhealthy and potentially dangerous.
>
> He defends his actions against the clergymen's criticisms, particularly their argument that he is in too much of a hurry. Responding to charges of extremism, King claims that he has actually prevented racial violence by channeling the natural frustrations of oppressed blacks into nonviolent protest. He asserts that extremism is precisely what is needed now—but it must be creative, rather than destructive, extremism. He concludes by again expressing disappointment with white moderates for not joining his effort as many other whites have.

CHECKLIST

Summarizing

To restate briefly the main ideas in a text:

1. Make an outline.
2. Write a paragraph or more that presents the main ideas largely in your own words. Use the outline as a guide, but reread parts of the original text as necessary.
3. To make the summary coherent, fill in connections between ideas.

PARAPHRASING

Unlike a summary, which is much briefer than the original text, a *paraphrase* is generally as long as the original and often longer. Whereas summarizing seeks to present the gist or essence of the reading and leave out everything else, paraphrasing tries to be comprehensive and leave out nothing that contributes to the meaning. (For more on summarizing, see pp. 530–31).

Paraphrasing works as a critical reading strategy for especially complex and obscure passages. Because it requires a word-for-word or phrase-by-phrase rewording of the original text, paraphrasing is too time consuming and labor intensive to use with long texts. But it is perfect for making sure you understand the important passages of a difficult reading. To paraphrase, you need to work systematically through the text, looking up in a good college dictionary many of the key words, even those you are somewhat familiar with. You can quote the author's words, but if you do, put quotation marks around them and be sure to define them.

Following are two passages. The first is excerpted from paragraph 2 of "Letter from Birmingham Jail." The second passage paraphrases the first.

Original

> I had hoped that the white moderate would understand that law and order exist for the purpose of establishing justice and that when they fail in this purpose they become the dangerously structured dams that block the flow of social progress. I had hoped that the white moderate would understand that the present tension in the South is a necessary phase of the transition from an obnoxious negative peace, in which the Negro passively accepted his unjust plight, to a substantive and positive peace, in which all men will respect the dignity and worth of human personality.

Paraphrase

> King writes that he had hoped for more understanding from the white moderate—specifically that they would recognize that law and order are not ends in themselves but means to the greater end of establishing justice. When law and order do not serve this greater end, they stand in the way of progress. King expected the white moderate to recognize that the current tense situation in the South is part of a transition that is necessary for progress. The current situation is bad because although there is peace, it is an "obnoxious" and "negative" kind of peace based on blacks passively accepting the injustice of the status quo. A better kind of peace, one that is "substantive," real and not imaginary, as well as "positive," requires that all people, regardless of race, be valued.

When you compare the paraphrase to the original, you can see that the paraphrase tries to remain true to the original by including *all* the important information and ideas. It also tries to be neutral, to avoid inserting the reader's opinions or distorting the original writer's ideas. But because paraphrasing requires the use of different words and putting those words together into different sentences, the resulting paraphrase will be different from the original. The paraphrase always, intentionally or not, expresses the reader's interpretation of the original text's meaning.

CHECKLIST

Paraphrasing

To paraphrase information in a text:

1. Reread the passage to be paraphrased, looking up unknown words in a college dictionary.
2. Relying on key words in the passage, translate the information into your own sentences.
3. Revise to ensure coherence.

SYNTHESIZING

Synthesizing involves combining ideas and information gleaned from different sources. As a critical reading strategy, synthesizing can help you see how different sources relate to one another—for example, by offering supporting details or opposing arguments.

When you synthesize material from different sources, you construct a conversation among your sources, a conversation in which you also participate. Synthesizing contributes most to critical thinking when writers use sources not only to support their ideas but to challenge and extend them as well.

In the following example, the reader uses a variety of sources related to the King passage (pp. 519–24). The synthesis brings the sources together around a central idea. Notice how quotation, paraphrase, and summary are all used to present King's and the other sources' ideas.

> When King defends his campaign of nonviolent direct action against the clergymen's criticism that "our actions, even though peaceful, must be condemned because they precipitate violence" (King excerpt, paragraph 3), he is using what Vinit Haksar calls Mohandas Gandhi's "safety-valve argument" ("Civil Disobedience and Non-Cooperation" 117). According to Haksar, Gandhi gave a "non-threatening warning of worse things to come" if his demands were not met. King similarly makes clear that advocates of actions more extreme than those he advocates are waiting in the wings: "The other force is one of bitterness and hatred, and it comes perilously close to advocating violence" (King excerpt, paragraph 5). King identifies this force with Elijah Muhammad, and although he does not name him, King's contemporary readers would have known that he was referring also to Malcolm X who, according to Herbert J. Storing, "urged that Negroes

take seriously the idea of revolution" ("The Case against Civil Disobedience" 90). In fact, Malcolm X accused King of being a modern-day Uncle Tom, trying "to keep us under control, to keep us passive and peaceful and nonviolent" (*Malcolm X Speaks* 12).

CHECKLIST

Synthesizing

To synthesize ideas and information:

1. Find and read a variety of sources on your topic, annotating the passages that give you ideas about the topic.
2. Look for patterns among your sources, possibly supporting or refuting your ideas or those of other sources.
3. Write a paragraph or more synthesizing your sources, using quotation, paraphrase, and summary to present what they say on the topic.

QUESTIONING TO UNDERSTAND AND REMEMBER

As a student, you are accustomed to teachers asking you questions about your reading. These questions are designed to help you understand a reading and respond to it more fully, and often they work. When you need to understand and use new information, however, it may be more beneficial for *you* to write the questions. Using this strategy, you can write questions while you read a text the first time. In difficult academic reading, you will understand the material better and remember it longer if you write a question for every paragraph or brief section.

We can demonstrate how this strategy works by returning to the excerpt from "Letter from Birmingham Jail" and examining, paragraph by paragraph, some questions that might be written about it. Reread the King selection (pp. 519–24). When you finish each paragraph, look at the question numbered to match that paragraph in the following list. Assume for this rereading that your goal is to comprehend the information and ideas. Notice that each question in the list asks about the content of a paragraph and that you can answer the question with information from that paragraph.

Paragraph	*Question*
1	How can white moderates be more of a barrier to racial equality than the Ku Klux Klan?
2	How can community tension resulting from nonviolent direct action benefit the civil rights movement?
3	How can peaceful actions be justified even if they cause violence?
4	Why should civil rights activists take action now instead of waiting for white moderates to support them?
5	How are complacent members of the community different from black nationalist groups?
6	What is King's position in relation to these two forces of complacency and anger?
7	What would have happened if King's nonviolent direct action movement had not started?
8	What is the focus of the protest, and what do King and others who are protesting hope to achieve?
9	What other creative extremists does King associate himself with?
10	Who are the whites who have supported King, and what has happened to some of them?

Each question focuses on the main idea in the paragraph, not on illustrations or details. Note, too, that each question is expressed partly in the reader's own words, not just copied from parts of the paragraph.

How can writing questions during reading help you understand and remember the content—the ideas and information—of the reading? Researchers studying the ways people learn from their reading have found that writing questions during reading enables readers to remember more than they would by reading the selection twice. Researchers who have compared the results of readers who write brief summary sentences for a paragraph with readers who write questions have found that readers who write questions learn more and remember the information longer. These researchers conjecture that writing a question involves reviewing or rehearsing information in a way that allows it to enter long-term memory, where it is more easily recalled. The result is that you clarify and "file" the information as you go along. You can then read more confidently because you have more of a base on which to build your understanding, a base that allows meaning to develop and that enables you to predict what is coming next and add it readily to what you have already learned.

This way of reading informational material is very slow, and at first it may seem inefficient. In those reading situations where you must use the information in an exam or a class discussion, it can be very efficient, however. Because this reading strategy is relatively time-consuming, you will, of course, want to use it selectively.

CHECKLIST

Questioning to Understand and Remember

To use questioning to understand and remember a reading, especially one that is unfamiliar or difficult:

1. Pause at the end of each paragraph to review the information.
2. Try to identify the most important information—the main ideas or gist of the discussion.
3. Write a question that can be answered by the main idea or ideas in the paragraph.
4. Move on to the next paragraph, repeating the process.

CONTEXTUALIZING

The texts you read were all written sometime in the past and often embody historical and cultural assumptions, values, and attitudes different from your own. To read critically, you need to become aware of these differences. *Contextualizing* is a critical reading strategy that involves making inferences about a reading's historical and cultural contexts and examining the differences between those contexts and your own.

We can divide the process of contextualizing into two steps:

1. Reread the text to see how it represents the historical and cultural situation. Compare the way the text presents the situation with what you know about the situation from other sources—such as what you have read in other books and articles, seen on television or in the movies, and learned in school or from talking with people who were directly involved.

   Write a few sentences, describing your understanding of what it was like at that particular time and place. Note how the representation of the time and place in the text differs in significant ways from the other representations with which you are familiar.

2. Consider how much and in what ways the situation has changed. Write another sentence or two, exploring the historical and cultural differences.

The excerpt from "Letter from Birmingham Jail" is a good example of a text that benefits from being read contextually. If you knew little about the history of slavery and segregation in the United States, Martin Luther King Jr., or the civil rights movement, it would be very difficult to understand the passion for justice and the impatience with delay expressed in the King selection. Most Americans, however, have read about Martin Luther King Jr. and the civil rights movement, or they have seen television histories such as *Eyes on the Prize* or films such as Spike Lee's *Malcolm X*.

Here is how one reader contextualized the excerpt from "Letter from Birmingham Jail":

> 1. I am not old enough to remember what it was like in the early 1960s when Dr. King was leading marches and sit-ins, but I have seen television documentaries of newsclips showing demonstrators being attacked by dogs, doused by fire hoses, beaten and dragged by helmeted police. Such images give me a sense of the violence, fear, and hatred that King was responding to.
>
> The tension King writes about comes across in his writing. He uses his anger and frustration creatively to inspire his critics. He also threatens them, although he denies it. I saw a film on Malcolm X, so I could see that King was giving white people a choice between his nonviolent way and Malcolm's more confrontational way.
>
> 2. Things have certainly changed since the sixties. Legal segregation has ended. The term *Negro* is no longer used, but there still are racists like the detective in the O. J. Simpson case. African Americans like Secretary of State Colin Powell are highly respected and powerful. The civil rights movement is over. So when I'm reading King, I'm reading history.
>
> But then again, police officers still beat black men like Rodney King, and extremists like Ice T still threaten violence. I don't know who's playing Dr. King's role today (Jesse Jackson?).

CHECKLIST

Contextualizing

To contextualize:

1. Describe the historical and cultural situation as it is represented in the reading and in other sources with which you are familiar.

2. Compare the text's historical and cultural contexts to your own historical and cultural situations.

REFLECTING ON CHALLENGES TO YOUR BELIEFS AND VALUES

Reading often challenges our attitudes, our unconsciously held beliefs, or our positions on current issues. We may feel anxious, irritable, or disturbed; threatened or vulnerable; ashamed or combative. We may feel suddenly wary or alert. When we experience these feelings as we read, we are reacting in terms of our personal or family values, religious beliefs, racial or ethnic group, gender, sexual orientation, social class, or regional experience.

You can grow intellectually, emotionally, and in social understanding if you are willing (at least occasionally) to *reflect on* these challenges instead of simply resisting them. Learning to question your unexamined assumptions and attitudes is an important part of becoming a critical thinker.

This reading strategy involves marking the text where you feel challenged, and then reflecting on why you feel challenged. As you read a text for the first time, simply mark an *X* in the margin at each point where you sense a challenge to your attitudes, beliefs, or values. Make a brief note in the margin about what you feel at that point or about what in the text seems to create the challenge. The challenge you feel may be mild or strong. It may come frequently or only occasionally.

Review the places you have marked in the text where you felt challenged in some way. Consider what connections you can make among these places or among the feelings you experienced at each place. For example, you might notice that you object to only a limited part of a writer's argument, resist nearly all of an authority's quoted statements, or dispute implied judgments about your gender or social class.

Write about what you have learned. Begin by describing briefly the part or parts of the text that make you feel challenged. Then write several sentences, reflecting on your responses. Keep the focus on your feelings. You need not defend or justify your feelings. Instead, try to give them a voice. Where do they come from? Why are they important to you? Although the purpose is to explore why you feel as you do, you may find that thinking about your values, attitudes, and beliefs sends you back to the text for help with defining your own position.

Here, for example, is how one writer responded to the excerpt from "Letter from Birmingham Jail":

> I'm troubled and confused by the way King uses the labels *moderate* and *extremist.* He says he doesn't like being labeled an extremist but he labels the clergymen moderate. How could it be okay for King to be moderate and not okay for the clergymen? What does *moderate* mean anyway? My dictionary defines *moderate* as "keeping within reasonable or proper limits; not extreme, excessive, or intense." Being a moderate sounds a lot better than being an extremist. I was taught not to act rashly or to go off the deep end. I'm also troubled that King makes a threat (although he says he does not).

CHECKLIST

Reflecting on Challenges to Your Beliefs and Values

To reflect on challenges to your beliefs and values:

1. Identify the challenges by marking where in the text you feel your beliefs and values are being opposed, criticized, or unfairly characterized.
2. Select one or two of the most troubling challenges you have identified and write a few sentences describing why you feel as you do. Do not attempt to defend your feelings; instead, analyze them to see where they come from.

EXPLORING THE SIGNIFICANCE OF FIGURATIVE LANGUAGE

Figurative language—metaphors, similes, and symbols—takes words literally associated with one object or idea and applies them to another object or idea. Because it embodies abstract ideas in vivid images, figurative language can often communicate more dramatically than direct statement. Figurative language also enriches meaning by drawing on a complex of feeling and association, indicating relations of resemblance and likeness. Here are definitions and examples of the most common figures of speech.

Metaphor implicitly compares two things by identifying them with each other. For instance, when King calls the white moderate "the Negro's great stumbling block in his stride toward freedom" (paragraph 1), he does not mean that the white moderate literally trips the Negro who is attempting to walk toward freedom. The sentence makes sense only when it is understood figuratively: The white moderate trips up the Negro by frustrating every effort to eliminate injustice. Similarly, King uses the image of a dam to express the abstract idea of the blockage of justice (paragraph 2).

Simile, a more explicit form of comparison, uses *like* or *as* to signal the relation of two seemingly unrelated things. King uses simile when he says that injustice is "like a boil that can never be cured so long as it is covered up" (paragraph 2). This simile makes several points of comparison between injustice and a boil. It suggests that injustice is a disease of society, as a boil is a disease of the body, and that injustice, like a boil, must be exposed or it will fester and worsen. A simile with many points of comparison is called an *extended simile* or *conceit.*

A *symbol* is something that stands for or represents something else. Critics do not agree about the differences between a metaphor and a symbol, but one popular line of thought is that a symbol relates two or more items that already have a strong recognized alliance or affinity; metaphor, more general, would be the association of two related or unrelated items. By this definition, King uses the white moderate as a symbol for supposed liberals and would-be supporters of civil rights who are actually frustrating the cause.

How these figures of speech are used in a text reveals something of the writer's feelings about the subject and attitude toward prospective readers, and may even suggest the writer's feelings about the act of writing. Annotating and taking inventory of patterns of figurative language can thus provide insight into the tone and intended emotional effect of the writing.

Exploring the patterns of figurative language involves (1) annotating and then listing all the metaphors, similes, and symbols you find in the reading; (2) grouping the figures of speech that appear to express similar feelings and attitudes, and labeling each group; and (3) writing to explore the meaning of the patterns you have found.

The following sample inventory and analysis of the King excerpt demonstrate the process of exploring the significance of figurative language.

Listing Figures of Speech

Step 1 produced the following inventory:

order is a dangerously structured dam that blocks the flow

social progress should flow

stumbling block in the stride toward freedom

injustice is like a boil that can never be cured

the light of human conscience and air of national opinion

time is something to be used, neutral, an ally, ripe quicksand of racial injustice

the solid rock of human dignity

human progress never rolls in on wheels of inevitability

men are co-workers with God

groups springing up

promised land of racial justice

vital urge engulfed

pent-up resentments

normal and healthy discontent can be channeled into the creative outlet of nonviolent direct action

root out injustice

powerful action is an antidote

disease of segregation

Grouping Figures of Speech

Step 2 yielded three common themes:

Sickness: segregation is a disease; action is healthy, the only antidote; injustice is like a boil

Underground: tension is hidden; injustice must be rooted out; extremist groups are springing up; discontent can be channeled into a creative outlet

Blockage: forward movement is impeded by obstacles—the dam, stumbling block; human progress never rolls in on wheels of inevitability; social progress should flow

Exploring Patterns

Step 3 entailed about ten minutes of writing to explore the themes listed in step 2:

> The patterns of *blockage* and *underground* suggest a feeling of frustration. Inertia is a problem; movement forward toward progress or upward toward the promised land is stalled. There seems to be a strong need to break through the resistance, the passivity, the discontent, and to be creative, active, vital. These are probably King's feelings both about his attempt to lead purposeful, effective demonstrations and his effort to write a convincing letter.
>
> The simile of injustice being like a boil links the two patterns of *underground* and *sickness,* suggesting something bad, a disease, is inside the people or the society. The cure is to expose, to root out, the blocked hatred and injustice and to release the tension or emotion that has so long been repressed. This implies that repression itself is the evil, not simply what is repressed.

CHECKLIST

Exploring the Significance of Figurative Language

To understand how figurative language—metaphors, similes, and symbols—contributes to a reading's meaning:

1. Annotate and then list all the figures of speech you find.
2. Group them and label each group.
3. Write to explore the meaning of the patterns you have found.

LOOKING FOR PATTERNS OF OPPOSITION

All texts contain *voices* or *patterns of opposition.* These voices may echo the views and values of critical readers the writer anticipates or predecessors to which the writer is responding; they may even reflect the writer's own conflicting values. You may need to look closely for such a dialogue of opposing voices within the text.

When we think of oppositions, we ordinarily think of polarities such as *yes* and *no, up* and *down, black* and *white, new* and *old.* Some oppositions, however, may be more subtle. The excerpt from "Letter from Birmingham Jail" is rich in such oppositions: *moderate* versus *extremist, order* versus *justice, direct action* versus *passive acceptance, expression* versus *repression.* These oppositions are not accidental; they form a significant pattern that gives a critical reader important information about King's letter.

A careful reading shows that one of the two terms in an opposition is nearly always valued over the other. In the King excerpt, for example, *extremist* is valued over *moderate* (paragraph 9). This preference for extremism is surprising. The critical reader should ask why, when white extremists like the Ku Klux Klan have committed so many outrages against black southerners, King would prefer extremism. If King is trying to convince his readers to accept his point of view, why would he represent himself as an extremist? Moreover, why would a clergyman advocate extremism instead of moderation?

By studying the patterns of opposition, you can answer these questions more fully. You can see that King sets up this opposition to force his readers to examine their own values and realize that they are in fact misplaced. Instead of working toward justice, he says, those who support law and order maintain the unjust status quo. Getting his readers to think of the white moderate as blocking rather than facilitating peaceful change brings them to align themselves with King and perhaps even embrace his strategy of nonviolent resistance.

Looking for patterns of opposition is a four-step method of analysis:

1. Divide a piece of paper in half lengthwise by drawing a line down the middle. In the left-hand column, list those words and phrases from the text that you have annotated as indicating oppositions. Enter in the right-hand column the word or phrase that seems, according to this writer, the opposite of each word or phrase in the left-hand column. You may have to paraphrase or even supply this opposite word or phrase if it is not stated directly in the text.

2. For each pair of words or phrases, put an asterisk next to the one that seems to be preferred by the writer.

3. Study the list of preferred words or phrases, and identify what you think is the predominant system of values put forth by the text. Do the same for the other list, identifying the alternative system or systems of values implied in the text. Take about ten minutes to describe the oppositions in writing.

4. To explore these conflicting points of view, write a few sentences presenting one side, and then write a few more sentences presenting the other side. Use as many of the words or phrases from the list as you can—explaining, extending, and justifying the values they imply. You may also, if you wish, quarrel with the choice of words or phrases on the grounds that they are loaded or oversimplify the issue.

The following sample inventory and analysis of the King excerpt demonstrate the method for exploring patterns of opposition in a text.

Listing Oppositions

Steps 1 and 2: This list of oppositions uses asterisks to identify King's preferred word or phrase in each pair:

white moderate	*extremist
order	*justice
negative peace	*positive peace
absence of justice	*presence of justice
goals	*methods
*direct action	passive acceptance
*exposed tension	hidden tension
*robbed	robber
*individual	society
*words	silence
*expression	repression
*extension of justice	preservation of injustice
*extremist for love, truth, and justice	extremist for immorality

Analyzing Oppositions

Step 3 produced the following description of the conflicting points of view:

In this reading, King addresses as "white moderates" the clergymen who criticized him. He sees the moderate position in essentially negative terms, whereas extremism can be either negative or positive. Moderation is equated with passivity, acceptance of the status quo, fear of disorder, perhaps even fear of any change. The moderates believe justice can wait, whereas law and order cannot. Yet, as King points out, there is no law and order for blacks who are victimized and denied their constitutional rights.

The argument King has with the white moderates is basically over means and ends. Both agree on the ends but disagree on the means that should be taken to secure those ends. What means are justified to achieve one's goals? How does one decide? King is willing to risk a certain amount of tension and disorder to bring about justice; he suggests that if progress is not made, more disorder, not less, is bound to result. In a sense, King represents himself as a moderate caught between the two extremes—the white moderates' "do-nothingism" and the black extremists' radicalism.

At the same time, King substitutes the opposition between moderation and extremism with an opposition between two kinds of extremism, one for love and the other for hate. In fact, he represents himself as an extremist willing to make whatever sacrifices—and perhaps even to take whatever means—are necessary to reach his goal of justice.

Considering Alternative Points of View

Step 4 entailed a few minutes of exploratory writing about the opposing point of view, and then several more minutes of writing about King's possible response to the opposition's argument:

The moderates' side: I can sympathize with the moderates' fear of further disorder and violence. Even though King advocates nonviolence, violence does result. He may not cause it, but it does occur because of him. Moderates do not really advocate passive acceptance of injustice, but want to pursue justice through legal means. These methods may be slow, but since ours is a system of law, the only way to make change is through that system. King wants to shake up the system, to force it to move quickly for fear of violence. That strikes me as blackmail, as bad as if he were committing violence himself. Couldn't public opinion be brought to bear on the legal system to move more quickly? Can't we elect officials who will change unjust laws and see that the just ones are obeyed? The *vote* should be the weapon in a democracy, shouldn't it?

King's possible response: He would probably have argued that the opposing viewpoint was naive. One of the major injustices at that time was that blacks were prevented from voting, and no elected official would risk going against those who voted for him or her. King would probably have agreed that public opinion needed to be changed, that people needed to be educated, but he would also have argued that education was not enough when people were being systematically deprived of their legal rights. The very system of law that should have protected people was being used as a weapon against blacks in the South. The only way to get something done was to shake people up, make them aware of the injustice they were allowing to continue. Seeing their own police officers committing violence should have made people question their own values and begin to take action to right the wrongs.

CHECKLIST

Looking for Patterns of Opposition

To explore and analyze the patterns of opposition in a reading:

1. Annotate the selection to identify the oppositions, and list the pairs on a separate page.
2. Put an asterisk next to the writer's preferred word or phrase in each pair of opposing terms.
3. Examine the pattern of preferred terms to discover the system of values the pattern implies; then do the same for the unpreferred terms.
4. Write to analyze and evaluate these opposing points of view or, in the case of reading that does not take a position, alternative systems of value.

EVALUATING THE LOGIC OF AN ARGUMENT

An *argument* has two essential parts: the claim and support. The *claim* asserts a conclusion—an idea, an opinion, a judgment, or a point of view—that the writer wants readers to accept. The *support* includes *reasons* (shared beliefs, assumptions, and values) and *evidence* (facts, examples, statistics, and authorities) that give readers the basis for accepting the writer's conclusion.

When you assess the logic of an argument, you are concerned about the process of reasoning as well as the argument's truthfulness. Three conditions must be met for an argument to be considered logically acceptable—what we call the ABC test:

A. The support must be *appropriate* to the claim.
B. All of the statements must be *believable.*
C. The argument must be *consistent* and *complete.*

A. Testing for Appropriateness

To assess whether a writer's reasoning is appropriate, you look to see if all of the evidence is relevant to the claim it supports. For example, if a writer claims that children must be allowed certain legal rights, readers could readily accept as appropriate support quotations from Supreme Court justices' decisions but might question quotations from a writer of popular children's books. Readers could probably accept the reasoning that if women have certain legal rights then so should children, but few readers would agree that all human rights under the law should be extended to animals.

As these examples illustrate, appropriateness of support comes most often into question when the writer is invoking authority or arguing by analogy. For example, in the excerpt from "Letter from Birmingham Jail," King argues by analogy and, at the same time, invokes authority: "Isn't this like condemning Socrates because his unswerving commitment to truth and his philosophical inquiries precipitated the act by the misguided populace in which they made him drink hemlock?" (paragraph 3). Readers not only must judge the appropriateness of comparing the Greek populace's condemnation of Socrates to the white moderates' condemnation of King's action, but also must judge whether it is appropriate to accept Socrates as an authority on this subject. Because Socrates is generally respected for his teaching on justice, his words and actions are likely to be considered appropriate to King's situation in Birmingham.

In paragraph 2, King argues that if law and order fail to establish justice, "they become the dangerously structured dams that block the flow of social progress." The analogy asserts a logical relationship: that law and order are to social justice what a dam is to water. If readers do not accept this analogy, then the argument fails the test of appropriateness. Arguing by analogy is usually considered a weak kind of argument because most analogies are parallel only up to a point, beyond which they may fail.

B. Testing for Believability

Believability is a measure of the degree to which readers are willing to accept the assertions supporting the claim. Whereas some assertions are obviously true, most depend on the readers' sharing certain values, beliefs, and assumptions with the writer. Readers who agree with the white moderate that maintaining law and order is more important than establishing justice are not going to accept King's claim that the white moderate is blocking progress.

Other statements, such as those asserting facts, statistics, examples, and authorities, present evidence to support a claim. Readers must put all of these kinds of evidence to the test of believability.

Facts are statements that can be proven objectively to be true. The believability of facts depends on their *accuracy* (they should not distort or misrepresent reality), their *completeness* (they should not omit important details), and the *trustworthiness* of their sources (sources should be qualified and unbiased). In the excerpt from "Letter from Birmingham Jail," for instance, King asserts as fact that the African American will not wait much longer for racial justice (paragraph 8). His critics might question the factuality of this assertion by asking: Is it true of all African Americans? How much longer will they wait? How does King know what the African American will and will not do?

Statistics are often assumed to be factual, but they are really only interpretations of numerical data. The believability of statistics depends on the *accuracy* of the methods of gathering and analyzing data (representative samples should be used and variables accounted for), the *trustworthiness* of the sources (sources should be qualified and unbiased), and often on the *comparability* of the data (are apples being compared to oranges?).

Examples and *anecdotes* are particular instances that if accepted as believable lead readers to accept the general claim. The power of examples depends on their *representativeness* (whether they are truly typical and thus generalizable) and their *specificity* (whether particular details make them seem true to life). Even if a vivid example or gripping anecdote does not convince readers, it strengthens argumentative writing by bringing home the point dramatically. In paragraph 5, for example, King supports his generalization that there are black nationalist extremists motivated by bitterness and hatred by citing the specific example of Elijah Muhammad's Muslim movement. Conversely, in paragraph 9, he refers to Jesus, Paul, Luther, and others as examples of extremists motivated by love. These examples support his assertion that extremism is not in itself wrong, that any judgment must depend on the cause for which one is an extremist.

Authorities are people whom the writer consults for expertise on a given subject. Such authorities not only must be appropriate, as mentioned earlier, but must be believable as well. The believability of authorities, their *credibility,* depends on whether the reader accepts them as experts on the topic. King cites authorities repeatedly throughout the essay, referring not only to religious leaders such as Jesus and Luther but also to American political leaders such as Lincoln and Jefferson. These figures are certain to have a high degree of credibility among King's readers.

C. Testing for Consistency and Completeness

Be sure that all the support works together, that no supporting statement contradicts any of the others, and that no important objection or opposing argument is unacknowledged. To test for consistency and completeness, ask yourself: Are any of the supporting statements contradictory? Are there any objections or opposing arguments that are not refuted?

In his essay, a potential contradiction is King's characterizing himself first as a moderate between the forces of complacency and violence, and later as an extremist opposed to the forces of violence. King attempts to reconcile this apparent contradiction by explicitly redefining extremism in paragraph 9. Similarly, the fact that King fails to examine and refute every legal recourse available to his cause might allow a critical reader to question the sufficiency of his supporting arguments.

Following is one student's written evaluation of the logic of King's argument. The student wrote these paragraphs after applying the ABC test, evaluating the appropriateness, believability, consistency, and completeness of King's supporting reasons and evidence.

King writes both to the ministers who published the letter in the Birmingham newspaper and to the people of Birmingham. He seems to want to justify his group's actions. He challenges white moderates, but he also tries to avoid antagonizing them. Given this purpose and his readers, his supporting statements are generally appropriate. He relies mainly on assertions of shared belief with his readers and on memorable analogies. For example, he knows his readers will accept assertions like "law and order exist for the purpose of establishing justice"; it is good to be an extremist for "love, truth, and goodness"; and progress is not inevitable, but results from tireless work and creativity. His analogies also seem acceptable and are based on appropriate comparisons. For example, he compares injustice to a boil that nonviolent action must expose to the air if it is to be healed. Throughout his argument, King avoids fallacies of inappropriateness.

Likewise, his support is believable in terms of the well-known authorities he cites (Socrates, Jesus, Amos, Paul, Luther, Bunyan, Lincoln, Jefferson); the facts he asserts (for example, that racial tension results from injustice, not from nonviolent action); and the examples he offers (such as his assertion that extremism is not in itself wrong—as exemplified by Jesus, Paul, and Luther). If there is an inconsistency in the argument, it is the contradiction between King's portraits of himself both as a moderating force and as an "extremist for love"; but his redefinition of extremism as a positive value for any social change is central to the overall persuasiveness of his logical appeal to white moderates.

CHECKLIST

Evaluating the Logic of an Argument

To determine whether an argument makes sense, apply the ABC test:

1. *Test for appropriateness* by checking to be sure that each piece of evidence is clearly and directly related to the claim it is supposed to support.

2. *Test for believability* by deciding whether you can accept as true facts, statistics, and expert testimony, and whether you can accept generalizations based on the examples given.

3. *Test for consistency and completeness* by ascertaining whether there are any contradictions in the argument and whether any important objections or opposing arguments have been ignored.

Then write a few sentences exploring the appropriateness, believability, consistency, and completeness of the argument.

RECOGNIZING EMOTIONAL MANIPULATION

Writers often try to arouse emotions in readers—to excite their interest, make them care, move them to action. Although nothing is wrong with appealing to readers' emotions, it is wrong to manipulate readers with false or exaggerated emotional appeals.

Many words have connotations, associations that enrich their meaning and give words much of their emotional power. For example, we use the word *manipulation* in naming this particular critical reading strategy to arouse an emotional response in readers like you. No one wants to be manipulated. Everyone wants to feel in control of his or her attitudes and opinions. This is especially true in reading arguments: We want to be convinced, not tricked.

Emotional manipulation often works by distracting readers from relevant reasons and evidence. To keep from being distracted, you want to pay close attention as you read and try to distinguish between emotional appeals that are acceptable and those that you consider manipulative or excessive.

Here is an example of one student's reaction to the emotional appeal of the excerpt from "Letter from Birmingham Jail":

> As someone King would probably identify as a white moderate, I can't help reacting negatively to some of the language he uses in this reading. For example, in the first paragraph, he equates white moderates with members of the Ku Klux Klan even though he admits that white moderates were in favor of racial equality and justice. He also puts down white moderates for being paternalistic. Finally, he uses scare tactics when he threatens "a frightening racial nightmare."

CHECKLIST

Recognizing Emotional Manipulation

To assess whether emotional appeals are unfairly manipulative:

1. Annotate places in the text where you sense emotional appeals are being used.
2. Write a few sentences identifying the kinds of appeals you have found and exploring your responses to them.

JUDGING THE WRITER'S CREDIBILITY

Writers often try to persuade readers to respect and believe them. Because readers may not know them personally or even by reputation, writers must present an image of themselves in their writing that will gain their readers' confidence. This image cannot be made directly but must be made indirectly, through the arguments, language, and the system of values and beliefs implied in the writing. Writers establish *credibility* in several ways:

- By showing their understanding of the subject
- By building common ground with readers
- By responding fairly to objections and opposing arguments

Testing for Knowledge

Writers demonstrate their knowledge through the facts and statistics they marshal, the sources they rely on for information, and the scope and depth of their understanding. As a critical reader, you may not be sufficiently expert on the subject yourself to know whether the facts are accurate, the sources reliable, and the understanding sufficient. You may need to do some research to see what others are saying about the subject. You can also check credentials—the writer's educational and professional qualifications, the respectability of the publication in which the selection first appeared, any reviews of the writer's work—to determine whether the writer is a respected authority in the field. King brings with him the authority that comes from being a member of the clergy and a respected leader of the Southern Christian Leadership Conference.

Testing for Common Ground

One way writers can establish common ground with their readers is by basing their reasoning on shared values, beliefs, and attitudes. They use language that includes their readers (*we*) rather than excludes them (*they*). They qualify their assertions to keep them from being too extreme. Above all, they acknowledge differences of opinion and try to make room in their argument to accommodate reasonable differences. As a reader, you will be affected by such appeals.

King creates common ground with readers by using the inclusive pronoun *we*, suggesting shared concerns between himself and his audience. Notice, however, his use of masculine pronouns and other references ("the Negro . . . he," "our brothers"). Although King intended this letter to be published in the local newspaper, where it would be read by an audience of both men and women, he addressed it to male clergy. By using language that excludes women, King missed the opportunity to build common ground with half his readers.

Testing for Fairness

Writers display their character by how they handle objections to their arguments. As a critical reader, you want to pay particular attention to how writers treat possible differences of opinion. Be suspicious of those who ignore differences and pretend everyone agrees with their viewpoints. When objections or opposing views are represented, you should consider whether they have been distorted in any way; if they are refuted, you want to be sure they are challenged fairly—with sound reasoning and solid evidence.

One way to gauge an author's credibility is to identify the tone of the argument. *Tone,* the writer's attitude toward the subject and toward the reader, is concerned not so much with what is said as with how it is said. By reading sensitively, you should be able to detect the writer's tone. To identify the tone, list whatever descriptive adjectives come to mind in response to either of these questions: How would you characterize the attitude of this selection? What sort of emotion does the writer bring to his or her writing? Judging from this piece of writing, what kind of person does the author seem to be?

Here is one student's answer to the second question, based on the excerpt from "Letter from Birmingham Jail":

> I know something about King from television programs on the civil rights movement. But if I were to talk about my impression of him from this passage, I'd use words like *patient, thoughtful, well educated, moral, confident.* He doesn't lose his temper but tries to convince his readers by making a case that is reasoned carefully and painstakingly. He's trying to change people's attitudes; no matter how annoyed he might be with them, he treats them with respect. It's as if he believes that their hearts are right, but they're just confused. If he can just set them straight, everything will be fine. Of course, he also sounds a little pompous when he compares himself to Jesus and Socrates, and the threat he appears to make in paragraph 8 seems out of character. Maybe he's losing control of his self-image at those moments.

CHECKLIST

Judging the Writer's Credibility

To decide whether you can trust the writer:

1. As you read and annotate, consider the writer's knowledge of the subject, how well the writer establishes common ground with readers, and whether the writer deals fairly with objections and opposing arguments.
2. Write a few sentences exploring what you discover.

COMPARING AND CONTRASTING RELATED READINGS

When you *compare* two reading selections, you look for similarities. When you *contrast* them, you look for differences. As critical reading strategies, comparing and contrasting enable you to see both texts more clearly.

Both strategies depend on how imaginative you are in preparing the grounds or basis for comparison. We often hear that it is fruitless, so to speak, to compare apples and oranges. It is true that you cannot add or multiply them, but you can put one against the other and come up with some interesting similarities and differences. For example, comparing apples and oranges in terms of their roles as symbols in Western culture (say, the apple of Adam and Eve compared to the symbol for Apple computers) could be quite productive. The grounds or basis for comparison, like a camera lens, brings some things into focus while blurring others.

To demonstrate how this strategy works, we compare and contrast the excerpt from "Letter from Birmingham Jail" (pp. 519–24) with the following selection by Lewis H. Van Dusen Jr.

LEWIS H. VAN DUSEN JR.

Legitimate Pressures and Illegitimate Results

A respected attorney and legal scholar, Lewis H. Van Dusen Jr. has served as chair of the American Bar Association Committee on Ethics and Professional Responsibility. This selection comes from the essay "Civil Disobedience: Destroyer of Democracy," which first appeared in the American Bar Association Journal *in 1969. As you read, notice the annotations we made comparing this essay to the one by King.*

There are many civil rights leaders who show impatience with the process of democracy. They rely on the sit-in, boycott, or mass picketing to gain speedier solutions to the problems that face every citizen. But we must realize that the legitimate pressures that [won concessions in the past] can easily escalate into the illegitimate power plays that might [extort demands in the future.] The victories of these civil rights leaders must not shake our confidence in the democratic procedures, as the pressures of demonstration are desirable only if they take place within the limits

1

To get something by force or intimidation

allowed by law. Civil rights gains should continue to be won by the persuasion of Congress and other legislative bodies and by the decision of courts. Any illegal entreaty for the [rights of some] can be an injury to the [rights of others,] for mass demonstrations often trigger violence.

2 Those who advocate [taking the law into their own hands] should reflect that when they are disobeying what they consider to be an immoral law, they are deciding on a possibly immoral course. Their answer is that the process for democratic relief is too slow, that only mass confrontation can bring immediate action, and that any injuries are the inevitable cost of the pursuit of justice. Their answer is, simply put, that the end justifies the means. It is this justification of any form of demonstration as a form of dissent that threatens to destroy a society built on the rule of law.

King's concern with time

Ends vs. means debate Any form?

3 Our Bill of Rights guarantees wide opportunities to use mass meetings, public parades and organized demonstrations to stimulate sentiment, to dramatize issues and to cause change. The Washington freedom march of 1963 was such a call for action. But the rights of free expression cannot be mere force cloaked in the garb of free speech. As the courts have decreed in labor cases, free assembly does not mean mass picketing or sit-down strikes. These rights are subject to limitations of time and place so as to secure the rights of others. When militant students storm a college president's office to achieve demands, when certain groups plan rush-hour car stalling to protest discrimination in employment, these are not dissent, but a denial of rights to others. Neither is it the lawful use of mass protest, but rather the unlawful use of mob power.

These are legal

Right to demonstrate is limited

Can't deny others' rights

4 Justice Black, one of the foremost advocates and defenders of the right of protest and dissent, has said:

> . . . Experience demonstrates that it is not a far step from what to many seems to be the earnest, honest, patriotic, kind-spirited multitude of today, to the fanatical, threatening, lawless mob of tomorrow. And the crowds that press in the streets for noble goals today can be supplanted tomorrow by street mobs pressuring the courts for precisely opposite ends.

5 Society must censure those demonstrators who would trespass on the public peace, as it must condemn those rioters whose pillage would destroy the public peace. But more ambivalent is society's posture toward the civil disobedient.

Unlike the rioter, the true civil disobedient commits no violence. Unlike the mob demonstrator, he commits no trespass on others' rights. The civil disobedient, while deliberately violating a law, shows an oblique respect for the law by voluntarily submitting to its sanctions. He neither resists arrest nor evades punishment. Thus, he breaches the law but not the peace.

Isn't he contradicting himself?

6 But civil disobedience, whatever the ethical rationalization, is still an assault on our democratic society, an affront to our legal order and an attack on our constitutional government. To indulge civil disobedience is to invite anarchy, and the permissive arbitrariness of anarchy is hardly less tolerable than the repressive arbitrariness of tyranny. Too often the license of liberty is followed by the loss of liberty, because into the desert of anarchy comes the man on horseback, a Mussolini or a Hitler.

Threatens repression as retaliation

We had already read and annotated the King excerpt, so we read the Van Dusen selection looking for a basis for comparison. We decided to base our contrast on the writers' different views of nonviolent direct action. We carefully reread the Van Dusen selection, annotating aspects of his argument against the use of nonviolent direct action. These annotations led directly to the first paragraph of our contrast, which summarizes Van Dusen's argument. Then we reread the King excerpt, looking for how he justifies nonviolent direct action. The second paragraph of our contrast presents King's defense, plus some of our own ideas on how he could have responded to Van Dusen.

King and Van Dusen present radically different views of legal, nonviolent direct action, such as parades, demonstrations, boycotts, sit-ins, or pickets. Although Van Dusen acknowledges that direct action is legal, he nevertheless fears it; and he challenges it energetically in these paragraphs. He seems most concerned about the ways direct action disturbs the peace, infringes on others' rights, and threatens violence. He worries that, even though some groups make gains through direct action, the end result is that everyone else begins to doubt the validity of the usual democratic procedures of relying on legislation and the courts. He condemns advocates of direct action like King for believing that the end (in this case, racial justice) justifies the means (direct action). Van Dusen argues that demonstrations often end violently and that an organized movement like King's can in the beginning win concessions through direct action but then end up extorting demands through threats and illegal uses of power.

In contrast, King argues that nonviolent direct action preserves the peace by bringing hidden tensions and prejudices to the surface where they can be acknowledged and addressed. Direct action enhances democracy by changing its unjust laws and thereby strengthening it.

Since direct action is entirely legal, to forgo it as a strategy for change would be to turn one's back on a basic democratic principle. Although it may inconvenience people, its end (a more just social order) is entirely justified by its means (direct action). King would no doubt insist that the occasional violence that follows direct action results always from aggressive, unlawful interference with demonstrations, interference sometimes led by police officers. He might also argue that neither anarchy nor extortion followed from his group's actions.

Notice that these paragraphs address each writer's argument separately. An alternative plan would have been to compare and contrast the two writers' arguments point by point.

CHECKLIST

Comparing and Contrasting Related Readings

To compare and contrast two reading selections:

1. Read them both to decide on a basis or grounds for comparison or contrast.
2. Reread and annotate one selection to identify points of comparison or contrast.
3. Reread the second selection, annotating for the points you have already identified.
4. Write up your analyses of the two selections, revising your analysis of the first selection to correspond to any new insights you have gained. Or write a point-by-point comparison or contrast of the two selections.

Martin Luther King Jr. wrote "Letter from Birmingham Jail" in response to the following public statement by eight Alabama clergymen.

Public Statement by Eight Alabama Clergymen

April 12, 1963

1 We the undersigned clergymen are among those who, in January, issued "An Appeal for Law and Order and Common Sense,"

in dealing with racial problems in Alabama. We expressed understanding that honest convictions in racial matters could properly be pursued in the courts, but urged that decisions of those courts should in the meantime be peacefully obeyed.

2 Since that time there has been some evidence of increased forebearance and a willingness to face facts. Responsible citizens have undertaken to work on various problems which cause racial friction and unrest. In Birmingham, recent public events have given indication that we all have opportunity for a new constructive and realistic approach to racial problems.

3 However, we are now confronted by a series of demonstrations by some of our Negro citizens, directed and led in part by outsiders. We recognize the natural impatience of people who feel that their hopes are slow in being realized. But we are convinced that these demonstrations are unwise and untimely.

4 We agree rather with certain local Negro leadership which has called for honest and open negotiation of racial issues in our area. And we believe this kind of facing of issues can best be accomplished by citizens of our own metropolitan area, white and Negro, meeting with their knowledge and experience of the local situation. All of us need to face that responsibility and find proper channels for its accomplishment.

5 Just as we formerly pointed out that "hatred and violence have no sanction in our religious and political traditions," we also point out that such actions as incite to hatred and violence, however technically peaceful those actions may be, have not contributed to the resolution of our local problems. We do not believe that these days of new hope are days when extreme measures are justified in Birmingham.

6 We commend the community as a whole, and the local news media and law enforcement officials in particular, on the calm manner in which these demonstrations have been handled. We urge the public to continue to show restraint should the demonstrations continue, and the law enforcement officials to remain calm and continue to protect our city from violence.

7 We further strongly urge our own Negro community to withdraw support from these demonstrations, and to unite locally in working peacefully for a better Birmingham. When rights are consistently denied, a cause should be pressed in the courts and in negotiations among local leaders, and not in the streets. We appeal to both our white and Negro citizenry to observe the principles of law and order and common sense.

Signed by:

C. C. J. CARPENTER, D.D., LL.D., *Bishop of Alabama*

JOSEPH A. DURICK, D.D., *Auxiliary Bishop, Diocese of Mobile-Birmingham*

Rabbi MILTON L. GRAFMAN, *Temple Emanu-El, Birmingham, Alabama*

Bishop PAUL HARDIN, *Bishop of the Alabama-West Florida Conference of the Methodist Church*

Bishop NOLAN B. HARMON, *Bishop of the North Alabama Conference of the Methodist Church*

GEORGE M. MURRAY, D.D., LL.D., *Bishop Coadjutor, Episcopal Diocese of Alabama*

EDWARD V. RAMAGE, *Moderator, Synod of the Alabama Presbyterian Church in the United States*

EARL STALLINGS, *Pastor, First Baptist Church, Birmingham, Alabama*

APPENDIX 2

Strategies for Research and Documentation

As many of the essays in *Reading Critically, Writing Well* show, writers often rely on research to expand and test their own ideas about a topic. This appendix offers advice on conducting research, evaluating potential sources, integrating source material you decide to use with your own writing, and documenting this material in an acceptable way.

CONDUCTING RESEARCH

In your college career, you may have opportunities to do many different kinds of research, including laboratory experiments and statistical surveys. Here we introduce the three basic types of research you are most likely to use to satisfy the assignments in *Reading Critically, Writing Well* and to fulfill requirements of other lower-division courses: field research using observation and interview, library research, and Internet research.

Field Research

Observation and *interview* are the two major kinds of *field* or *ethnographic research*. The observational essays in Chapter 3 illustrate some of the ways you might use field research. You might also use these research techniques when proposing a solution to a problem (Chapter 8) or when arguing a position on a controversial issue (Chapter 9). You may be asked to read and write essays based on field research in other courses as well, such as in sociology, political science, anthropology, psychology, communication, or business.

Observation

Following are guidelines for planning an observational visit, taking notes on your observations, and reflecting on what you observed.

PLANNING THE VISIT

To ensure that you use your time productively during observational visits, you must plan them carefully.

Getting Access. If the place you propose to visit is public, you probably will have easy access to it. Ask yourself whether everything you need to see is within casual view. If not, you have encountered a potential problem of access. If you require special access or permission, you will need to call ahead or make a get-acquainted visit to introduce yourself and explain your purpose.

Announcing Your Intentions. Explain politely who you are, where you are from, and why you would like access. You may be surprised at how receptive people can be to a student on assignment from a college course. Not every place you wish to visit will welcome you, however. A variety of constraints on outside visitors exist in private businesses as well as public institutions. But generally, if people know your intentions, they may be able to tell you about aspects of a place or an activity you would not have thought to observe.

Bringing Tools. Take a notebook with a firm back so that you will have a steady writing surface, perhaps a small stenographer's pad with a spiral binding across the top. Take a few pens or pencils. If you prefer to use a tape recorder to note your observations, bring along extra tapes and batteries. Also take a notebook in case something goes wrong with the tape recorder.

OBSERVING AND TAKING NOTES

Here are some practical suggestions for making observations and taking notes.

Observing. Some activities invite multiple vantage points, whereas others seem to limit the observer to a single perspective. Explore the space as much as possible, taking advantage of every vantage point available to you. Consider it from different angles, both literally and figuratively. Since your purposes are to analyze as well as to describe your subject, look for its typical and atypical features, how it is like and unlike similar subjects. Think also about what would make the subject interesting to your readers.

Notetaking. You undoubtedly will find your own style of notetaking, but here are a few pointers:

- Write only on one side of the page. Later, when you organize your notes, you may want to cut up the pages and file notes under different headings.
- Along with writing words, phrases, or sentences, draw diagrams and sketches that will help you see and recall the place later on.
- Use abbreviations as much as you like, but use them consistently and clearly.

- Note any ideas or questions that occur to you.
- Use quotation marks around any overheard conversation you take down.

Because you can later reorganize your observational notes easily, you do not need to record them in any planned or systematic way. Your notes should include information about the place, the people, and your personal reactions to both:

The Place. Begin by listing objects you see. Then add details of some of these objects—color, shape, size, texture, function, relation to similar or dissimilar objects. Although visual details will probably dominate your notes, you might also want to note sounds and smells. Be sure to include some notes about the shape, dimensions, and layout of the place. How big is it? How is it organized?

The People. Note the number of people and their activities, movements, and behavior. Describe their appearance or dress. Record parts of overheard conversations. Note whether you see more men than women, more people of one racial group than of another, more older than younger people. Most important, note anything surprising or unusual about people in the scene and how they interact with one another.

Your Impressions. Include in your notes the feelings, ideas, or insights you have about what you observe.

REFLECTING ON YOUR OBSERVATIONS

Immediately after your visit (within a few minutes, if possible), find a quiet place to reflect on what you saw, review your notes, and add any images, details, insights, or questions you now recall. Give yourself at least a half hour for quiet thought. Finally, review all your notes, and write a few sentences about your main impressions of the place. What did you learn? How did this visit change or confirm your preconceptions? What impression of the place and people would you like to convey to readers?

Interview

Here are guidelines for planning and setting up an interview, conducting an interview, and reflecting on what you learned.

PLANNING THE INTERVIEW

Choosing an Interview Subject. If you will be interviewing a person who is the focus of your research, consider beginning with one or two background interviews with other people. If several people play important roles, be sure to interview as many of them as possible. Try to be flexible, however, because you may be unable to speak with the people you targeted initially and may wind up interviewing someone else—an assistant, perhaps. You might even learn more from an assistant than you would from the person in charge.

Arranging an Interview. You may be nervous about phoning a busy person and asking for some of his or her time. Indeed, you may get turned down. If so, do ask if someone else might talk with you: Many people are genuinely flattered to be asked about themselves and their work. Moreover, because you are a college student on assignment, some people may feel that they are doing a public service by allowing you to interview them. When arranging the interview, introduce yourself with a short, simple, and enthusiastic description of your project.

Keep in mind that the person you want to interview will be donating time to you. When you call ahead to arrange a specific time for the interview, be sure to ask what time is most convenient. Arrive at the appointed time and bring all the materials you will need to conduct the interview. Remember, too, to express your thanks when the interview has ended.

Preparing for the Interview. Make any necessary observational visits and do any essential background reading before the interview. Consider your objectives: For example, do you want the "big picture," answers to specific questions, or clarification of something you observed, read, or heard about in another interview?

The key to good interviewing is flexibility. You may be looking for facts, but your interview subject may not have any to offer. In that case, you should be able to shift gears and go after whatever insight your subject does have to offer.

Composing Interview Questions. You probably will want to mix *specific questions* requesting factual information with *open-ended questions,* which are likely to generate anecdotes and reveal attitudes that could lead to other, more penetrating questions. In interviewing a small-business owner, for example, you might begin with a specific question about when the business was established and then follow up with an open-ended question, such as "Could you take a few minutes to tell me something about your early days in the business? I'd be interested to hear about how you got started, what your hopes were, and what problems you had to face." Also consider asking directly for an anecdote ("What happened when your employees threatened to strike?"), encouraging reflection ("What do you think has helped you most? What has hampered you?"), or soliciting advice ("What advice would you give someone trying to start a new business today?").

The best questions encourage the interview subject to talk freely but to the point. If the answer strays too far from the point, a follow-up question may be necessary to refocus the talk. Another way to direct the conversation is to rephrase the subject's answer, saying something like "Let me see if I have this right . . ." or "Am I correct in saying that you feel. . . ?" Often, the interview subject will take this opportunity to amplify the original response by adding just the anecdote or quotation you have been looking for.

One type of question to avoid during interviewing is the *leading question.* Such questions assume too much. Consider, for example, this question: "Do you think the increase in the occurrence of rape is due to the fact that women are perceived as competitors in a severely depressed economy?" The question makes several assumptions, including that there is an increase in the occurrence of rape, that women are perceived (apparently by rapists) as competitors, and that the economy is severely depressed. A better way of asking the question might be to make the assumptions more explicit by dividing the question into its parts: "Do you think there is an increase in the occurrence of rape? What could have caused it? I've heard some people argue that the economy has something to do with it. Do you think so? Do you think rapists perceive women as competitors? Could the current economic situation have made this competition more severe?" This form of questioning allows you to voice what others have said without bullying your subject into echoing your terms.

Bringing Tools. You will need several pencils or pens and a notebook with a firm back so you can write without a table. We recommend dividing the page into two columns. Use the left-hand column (one-third of the page) to note your impressions and descriptions of the scene, the person, and the mood of the interview. Title this column *Impressions.* Title the wider right-hand column *Information.* Before the interview, write down a few basic questions to jog your memory. During the interview, however, listen and ask questions based on what your interview subject says. Do not mechanically go through your list of questions.

TAKING NOTES DURING THE INTERVIEW

Your interview notes might include a few full quotations, key words, and phrases to jog your memory, as well as descriptive jottings about the scene, the person, and the mood of the interview. Remember that how something is said may be as important as what is said. Do not try to record everything your subject says during the interview. Except for the occasional quotation that you will cite directly, you do not want to make a verbatim transcript of the interview. You may not have much confidence in your memory, but if you pay close attention to your subject you are likely to recall a good deal of the conversation immediately after the interview, when you should take the time to add to your notes.

REFLECTING ON THE INTERVIEW

Soon after the interview has concluded, find a quiet place to review your notes. Spend at least half an hour adding to your notes and thinking about what you learned. At the end of this time, write a few sentences about your main impressions from the interview:

- What were the highlights of the interview for you?
- Which questions did not get as much of a response as you anticipated or seem less important to you now?

- How did the interview change your attitude toward or understanding of the subject?
- How has this experience influenced your plans to interview others or to reinterview this person?

Library Research

Library research involves a variety of activities: checking the card or online catalog, browsing in the stacks, consulting bibliographical indexes, and evaluating sources. Although librarians are there to help, all college students should learn basic library research skills. You should familiarize yourself with your college library's resources and keep careful notes as you research so that you will not have to go back over the same ground later on.

Library research can be useful at various stages of the writing process, depending on the kind of essay you are writing and the special needs of your subject. You may, for example, need to do research immediately to choose a subject. Or you may choose a topic without the benefit of research, and then use the library to find specific information to develop and support your thesis. But no matter when you enter the stacks, you need to follow a systematic strategy: Keep a working bibliography; prepare to search for sources by determining the appropriate subject headings or other criteria; consult standard reference works, such as bibliographical indexes and computer databases; and search for books, articles, and other sources on your topic. Later in Appendix 2, in Evaluating Sources Critically (pp. 575–79), you will find guidelines to help you evaluate the relevancy and credibility of these and other sources.

Keep a Working Bibliography

A *working bibliography* is a preliminary, ongoing record of all the references you consult as you research, even including those that you do not plan to cite in your essay. Encyclopedias, bibliographies, and indexes, for example, should go into the working bibliography, though you will not list these resources in your final bibliography. The working bibliography is a record of the *research process* as a whole; the final bibliography is a record of the *research paper* that you ultimately write.

Since the working bibliography is a first draft of your final list of sources, it is a good idea to use the same documentation style from the start. In Documenting Sources (pp. 589–614), later in this appendix, two styles of documentation are discussed and illustrated: the style adopted by the Modern Language Association (MLA) and widely used in the humanities, and the style advocated by the American Psychological Association (APA) for use in the social sciences. Individual disciplines often have their own preferred styles of documentation, which your instructor may wish you to use.

You can keep your working bibliography on index cards, in a notebook, or in a computer file. Whatever method you choose, make your entries accurate and complete. If the call number for a book is missing a single digit, for example, you might not be able to find the book in the stacks.

Prepare to Search for Sources

To find sources in the library, you first need to determine subject headings and possibly other search criteria.

HOW TO SEARCH BY SUBJECT HEADINGS

Most information in libraries is referenced by *subject headings*. Book catalogs as well as periodical and newspaper indexes are arranged by subject. Therefore, when you begin library research, you need to identify possible subject headings, the specific words and phrases under which information on your topic is categorized. You might start with the *Library of Congress Subject Headings (LCSH),* a reference book that lists the standard subject headings used in catalogs and indexes and in many encyclopedias and bibliographies. Here is what the *LCSH* entry for "Home schooling" looks like:

Home schooling (*May Subd Geog*) Place names may follow heading

Here are entered works on the provision of compulsory education in the home by parents as an alternative to traditional public or private schooling. General works on the provision of education in the home by educational personnel are entered under Domestic Education.

Used for → **UF** Education, Home
Home-based education
Home education **NT** ← Narrower term
Home instruction **SA** ← See also
Home teaching by parents
Homeschooling
Instruction, Home
Schooling, Home

Broader term → **BT** Education

Related term → **RT** Education—United States
Education—Parent participation

To find relevant sources, you also may need to break your topic into subtopics (also known as *subdivisions* or *subheadings*) and browse in related subject areas. For example, you would find the following subdivisions for "Home schooling" in *Academic Index,* an index of magazine and journal articles:

Home schooling

- Athletics
- Demographic aspects
- Equipment and supplies
- Finance
- History
- Laws, regulations, etc.
- Moral and ethical aspects
- Services

Most subject listings in catalogs and indexes include cross-references: related terms or "see also" lines that point you to more information. Note in the preceding example from the *LCSH* that "Education—Parent participation" is listed as a related term for "Home schooling."

SELECTING OTHER SEARCH CRITERIA

In addition to subject searches, you may be able to use other search criteria, such as author's name, title, call number, location, type of media (audiotape, videotape, CD-ROM), and publication date. You could search by author name for a particular author mentioned frequently in your sources, search by library call number to determine what other sources are available in a specific subject area, or search by date in a newspaper index to research a particular event—for example, "May 1980" would yield references to the eruption of Mount Saint Helens.

Consult Standard Reference Works

To get an overview of your topic, look up your subject headings in *standard reference works.* Usually, these resources are found in the reference section of the library and cannot be checked out, so budget your library time for consulting reference works accordingly.

The most useful standard reference works include *specialized encyclopedias, disciplinary guides, government publications,* and *bibliographies.* In addition, a general encyclopedia such as *Encyclopedia Americana* might help provide a very general overview of your topic, while almanacs, atlases, and dictionaries are sometimes useful as well.

SPECIALIZED ENCYCLOPEDIAS

A specialized encyclopedia, such as *Encyclopedia of Crime and Justice,* or a disciplinary guide, such as *Social Sciences: A Cross-Disciplinary Guide to Selected Sources,* can offer background on your subject and starting points for further research. Specialized encyclopedias often include an explanation of issues related to the topic, definitions of specialized terminology, and selective bibliographies naming additional sources. Specialized encyclopedias can be found in the catalog under the subject heading for the discipline, such as "psychology," and the subheading "dictionaries and encyclopedias." Three particular reference sources can help you identify specialized encyclopedias covering your topic:

- *ARBA Guide to Subject Encyclopedias and Dictionaries* (1997). Lists specialized encyclopedias by broad subject category, with descriptions of coverage, focus, and any special features.
- *First Stop: The Master Index to Subject Encyclopedias* (1989). Lists specialized encyclopedias by broad subject category and provides access to individual articles within them. By looking under the key terms that describe a topic, you can find references to specific articles in any of over four hundred specialized encyclopedias.
- *Kister's Best Encyclopedias: A Comparative Guide to General and Specialized Encyclopedias* (1994). Describes over a thousand encyclopedias, both print and electronic. Includes major foreign-language encyclopedias.

DISCIPLINARY GUIDES

Disciplinary guides can help you locate the major handbooks, encyclopedias, bibliographies, journals, periodical indexes, and computer databases in various academic fields. These types of works are published rarely and are not known for their currency. However, they can be valuable references, if you take the time to check dates and supplement your sources as needed. Here is a sample of disciplinary guides:

- *The Humanities: A Selective Guide to Information Sources*, 4th ed. (2000). By Ron Blazek and Elizabeth S. Aversa.
- *Introduction to Library Research in Anthropology*, 2nd ed. (1998). By John M. Weeks.
- *The American Historical Association's Guide to Historical Literature*, 3rd ed. (1995). Edited by Mary Beth Norton and Pamela Gerardi.
- *Political Science: A Guide to Reference and Information Sources* (1990). By Henry E. York.
- *Literary Research Guide: A Guide to Reference Sources for the Study of Literatures in English and Related Topics*, 3rd ed. (1998). By James L. Harner.

GOVERNMENT RESOURCES

Some government publications and statistical reports may be found in the reference section or in a special government documents section of your college library. If you are researching current issues, for example, you might want to consult *Congressional Quarterly Almanac* or *Congressional Quarterly Weekly Report.* On the Internet, try the home page of the U.S. Congress for the *Congressional Record* (<http://thomas.loc.gov/home/thomas2.html>). For compilations of statistics, try *Statistical Abstract of the United States, Statistical Reference Index,* or *The Gallup Poll: Public Opinion.* The Gallup Web site (<http://www.gallup.com>) provides descriptions of some of its most recent polls.

BIBLIOGRAPHIES

A bibliography is simply a list of books on a given topic, which can be more or less exhaustive depending on its purpose. (To discover how selections were made, check the bibliography's preface or introduction.) A good way to locate a comprehensive, up-to-date bibliography on your subject is to look in the *Bibliographic Index.* A master list of bibliographies that contain fifty or more titles, the *Bibliographic Index* draws from articles, books, and government publications. The index, published yearly, is not cumulative, so check the most recent volume for current information.

Search for Books

The primary source of information on books is the library's *online catalog.* Just over a decade ago a library's catalog consisted of small file cards organized alphabetically into rows of drawers, by subject, title, and author's name. Today the same type of information is organized electronically in an online catalog. The online catalog provides more flexibility in searching and often tells you whether the book is available or checked out. Another distinct advantage is that you can print out source information, making it unnecessary for you to copy it by hand. You should, however, check to make sure that the online catalog goes far enough back in time for your purposes. If the computerized records do not date far enough back, see whether your library has maintained its hard-copy card catalog for the period in question.

Each catalog or computer entry gives the same basic information: the name of the author, the title of the book, the subject heading(s) related to the book, and the call number you will need to find the book on the library shelves. Most libraries provide a map showing where the various call numbers are shelved. On the next page is one college library's online catalog display of the author entry for a book on home schooling. Notice the call number in the middle of the bottom line. (On cards, look for the call number in the upper left-hand corner.)

Even if you attend a large research university, your library is unlikely to hold every book or journal article you might need. Remember that your library's online catalog and serial record (a list of the periodicals the library holds) include only records of the books and periodicals it holds. As you will learn in the following section on Internet research, you can access the online

AUTHOR: Guterson, David, 1951-
TITLE: Family matters: Why homeschooling makes sense
EDITION: 1st Harvest ed.
PUBLISHER: San Diego: Harcourt Brace & Co., c1992
PHYSICAL DESC: x, 254 p.; 18 cm.
NOTES: Includes bibliographical references and index.
SUBJECTS: Education—United States
Education—parent participation
Teaching methods
LOCATION/CALL NUMBER STATUS
UCSD Undergrad/649.68 g 1993 Available

catalogs of other libraries to find sources not within your library's holdings. At that point, you can request an interlibrary loan from another college library, a procedure handled by email or in person at the reference desk. Keep in mind, however, that it may take up to a couple of weeks to obtain a source by way of interlibrary loan.

Search for Articles

Articles published in periodicals (magazines or journals that publish periodically) and in newspapers usually are not listed in the library catalog. To find them, you will want to use *periodical indexes*, which originally appeared only in book form but today are likely to take the form of a CD-ROM, an online database, or a hybrid of the two. As computer technology becomes more sophisticated, some database services have begun to offer full-text articles along with the listings of articles. *Indexes* list citations of articles; *abstracts* summarize the articles as well. *Full-text retrieval* means you can view an entire article online and potentially download it (often excluding graphics) for reading offline.

Following is a list of some of the computer database services that your library might subscribe to:

- *Readers' Guide to Periodical Literature* (1900–; CD-ROM, 1983–; online). The classic index for periodicals, updated quarterly, offering about two hundred popular periodicals. (<http://www.silverplatter.com/catalog/wipl.htm>)
- *ERIC (Educational Resources Information Center)* (1969–; online). Houses indexes, abstracts, and the full text of selected articles from 750 education journals. (<http://www.ericir.syr.edu>)
- *Business Periodicals Ondisc* (1988–), and *ABI/INFORM* (1988–). Provides the full text of articles from business periodicals. If your library has a printer attached to a terminal, you can print out articles, including illustrations.

- *Carl/Uncover* (1988–; online). An online document delivery service that lists over three million articles from twelve thousand journals. For a fee, you can receive the full text of the article by fax, usually within a few hours. (<http://www.carl.org>)
- *Lexis-Nexis* (1973–; online and CD-ROM). An information service for journalists, lawyers, and financial analysts. (<http://www.lexis-nexis.com>)
- *InfoTrac* (online and CD-ROM). An information supplier that provides access to the following three indexes: (1) *General Periodicals Index*, which lists information on over twelve hundred general-interest publications; (2) *Academic Index*, which provides the full text of articles from five hundred popular and academic periodicals; and (3) *National Newspaper Index*, which covers the *Christian Science Monitor, Los Angeles Times, New York Times, Wall Street Journal,* and *Washington Post.* (<http://www.infotrac-college.com/wadsworth/access.html>)

Using *Academic Index* to do a search for "home schooling" would yield several listings, including the two examples shown here. Notice that the results specify whether an abstract is available and where the periodical can be found in the library.

```
   Home Schooling
   Mommy, what's a classroom? (the merits of home
schooling are still being debated) Bill Roorback.
The New York Times Magazine, Feb 2, 1997 p30 col1
(112 col in).
   —Abstract Available—
   Holdings: 10/92—present Periodicals—1st Floor
Paper 01/66—present Microfilm (Room #162)

   Microfilm
   The natural curriculum. (educating children at
home) Rosie Benson-Bunch. Times Education Supplement,
Dec 27, 1996 n4200 pA25(1).
   —Abstract Available—
```

While InfoTrac is intended for popular and academic reference purposes, *Business Periodicals Ondisc* and ERIC are designed for use within specific disciplines. Other discipline-specific databases include *Accountant's Index, Art Index, Education Index, Historical Abstracts, MLA International Bibliography* (literature), *Psychological Abstracts,* and *Sociological Abstracts.* For current events and topics in the news, you can use news-specific databases, including *Newsbank, Newspaper Abstracts Ondisc,* and *Alternative Press Index.* Most of these resources use the Library of Congress subject headings, but some have their own systems of classification. *Sociological Abstracts,* for example, has a separate volume for subject headings. Check the opening pages of the index or abstract you are using or, to see how subjects are classified, refer to the system documentation.

When you look for the periodicals in your library, you will typically find them arranged alphabetically by title in a particular section of the building. For previous years' collections of popular magazines and many scholarly journals, look for bound annual volumes rather than individual issues. Some older periodicals and newspapers may be stored on microfilm (reels) or microfiche (cards) that must be read in viewing machines.

Internet Research

The *Internet* is a global computer network that enables users to store and share information and resources from the comfort of their own computers. The World Wide Web is a network of Web sites, each with its own address, or *uniform resource locator (URL)*. You may be able to gain access to the Internet through your library or through a commercial Internet service provider. To search the Web, you also need access to a Web browser such as Netscape Navigator or Internet Explorer.

Research on the Internet is very different from library research. As you use the Internet for conducting research, be sure to keep the following concerns and guidelines in mind:

- *The Internet has no central system of organization.* On the Internet, a vast amount of information is stored on many different networks, on different servers, and in different formats, each with its own system of organization. There is no central catalog, reference librarian, or standard classification system for the vast resources available on the Internet.
- *Internet sources are generally less reliable than print sources.* Because it is relatively easy for anyone with a Web page to "publish" on the Internet, judging the reliability of online information is a special concern. Depending on your topic, purpose, and audience, the sources you find on the Internet may not be as credible or authoritative as library sources, and for some topics most of what you find may be written by amateurs. In most cases, you will probably want to balance or supplement Internet sources with print sources. When in doubt about the reliability of online sources for a particular assignment, check with your instructor. (See Evaluating Sources Critically, p. 575, for more specific suggestions.)
- *Internet sources must be documented.* The requirements for documenting source material found on the Internet are the same as for more traditional sources, though the formats are slightly different. As with print sources you locate in the library, you will need to follow appropriate conventions for quoting, paraphrasing, and documenting the online sources you cite. (See Documenting Sources, p. 589, for guidelines.)

As with library research, you will need to follow a systematic research strategy: Keep a working bibliography; learn how to navigate the Web; prepare to search the Web by determining appropriate keywords and using online search engines; access online library catalogs; and use email to contact other researchers and experts. Later in this appendix, in Evaluating Sources Critically (pp. 575–79), you will find guidelines to help you evaluate the relevancy and credibility of Internet sources.

Keep a Working Bibliography

A working bibliography for Internet research serves the same purpose as one for library research: supplying an ongoing record of all the sources you discover as you research your subject. This working bibliography becomes the draft for the list of works cited at the end of your essay, even though you may not list these resources in your final bibliography. In this case, it also helps you keep track of the URLs for Web sites you visit. You can store URLs as bookmarks or favorites in your Web browser or copy them to a text file.

You will notice that some documents you find on the Web are untitled and that some do not make the name of their author obvious. You may be able to create a title from the first words or heading of the text, or you can give the source a descriptive title. For an unnamed document, look for an email address or open the document's source information window to find the document's "owner." In addition, you should be sure to note each document's publication date (or date of last revision or modification) as well as the date you accessed it.

Learn How to Navigate the Web

For many academic users, an especially useful feature of the World Wide Web is that it allows *hypertext links* to other documents or files, so that with a simple click of the mouse a reader might find more detailed information on a subject or access a related document. Most material on the Web is available twenty-four hours a day, as long as your server is up and running.

A *Web browser* is a software program that allows you to display and navigate Web pages on your computer. Web browsers have evolved from basic text-driven browsers such as Lynx (still used today) into graphical, point-and-click interfaces such as Netscape Navigator and Microsoft Internet Explorer, which support not only text and hypertext links but also images, sound, animation, and even video.

A browser lets you move around a *Web site,* a set of connected pages (programming files) made available to the public. The central or starting point for a Web site is often called its *home page.* Web sites may be sponsored by companies, institutions, government agencies, organizations, clubs, or individuals.

As noted earlier, each Web site has its own address or uniform resource locator (URL). The URL for the Ecology Action Centre is typical:

http://www.cfn.cs.dal.ca/Environment/EAC/EAC-Home.html

The first part of a URL usually consists of the abbreviation *http://* that tells the sending and receiving computers the type of information being sent and how to transfer it. The second part usually includes the standard *www.* to establish that the location being accessed is on the World Wide Web, and the country, if outside of the United States, where the document is located. After a slash, the rest of the URL gives the address of the directory and file where the page is found as well as the name of the page itself, separated by slashes. URLs can be rather long, so you may need to break them between lines when citing them in an essay. *Wired Style* (1999) recommends breaking a URL after the *http://* or before a punctuation mark such as a period or slash. In the MLA style, however (see p. 590), a URL within a list of works cited should be broken only after a slash. Whatever style you follow, do not use a hyphen to indicate the break, and if your word-processing program adds a hyphen, delete it.

Many organizational and resource sites list the URLs of their home pages in print publications so that readers can access the Web sites for further information. Keep an eye out for such resources related to your research projects.

Prepare to Search the Web

To find sources on the Web you need to use search engines, which are typically based on keyword searches.

DETERMINING HOW TO SEARCH THE WEB BY KEYWORD

Search engines on the World Wide Web and other specialized software allow you to enter keywords to retrieve related information. Before you can use a search engine, however, you need to identify possible *keywords*—words you think are likely to appear in a title, summary, full-text document, or Web page related to your subject. In a *keyword search,* you direct the software to search a database and list any resources that match your terms. On the Internet, keyword searches are more useful than focused subject searches of the kind you would do in the library because information on the Web is not organized systematically by subject.

Some keyword-search software programs look for the specified terms in the whole document, whereas others search only headings, summaries, or titles. Read the instructions on the screen or ask your reference librarian or instructor for help. To launch a keyword search, type in the search terms. In most cases, a logical connector such as *and, or,* or *not* can be used to focus the search. For example, the keywords *home schooling and socialization* will retrieve references to documents that contain both of those terms. If you are researching the topic of euthanasia and want to find instances of assisted suicide other than those involving Dr. Jack Kevorkian (a doctor famous for helping terminally ill patients commit suicide), entering the phrase *euthanasia not Kevorkian* will yield references to sources containing the term *euthanasia,* but excluding sources that also contain the term *Kevorkian.* Some search software allows you to search by phrases, asking you to enclose a phrase in quotation marks. For example, if the phrase *"working mothers"* is entered, only references containing that phrase will be returned. Use capital letters for proper nouns and titles, and remember that correct spelling is essential.

USING SEARCH ENGINES TO LOCATE SOURCES

Once you have some keywords about your topic in mind, you can choose any number of search engines to locate sources. In most cases, you will want to use several search engines because the results can vary considerably. You might begin by clicking *Search* on the home page for either Netscape Navigator or Microsoft Internet Explorer, where you can access a list of links to such popular search engines as Infoseek, Lycos, and Yahoo! Or you can access these and other common search engines directly at their URL addresses:

AltaVista	http://www.altavista.com
Excite	http://www.excite.com
Google	http://www.google.com
HotBot	http://www.hotbot.com
Infoseek	http://www.infoseek.com
Lycos	http://www.lycos.com
Magellan	http://www.magellan.excite.com
WebCrawler	http://www.webcrawler.com
Yahoo!	http://www.yahoo.com

The functions of a search engine are to scan its directory of the Web for your keyword and to produce a list of direct links to Web pages containing the keyword. Most programs search both the titles of Web pages and the actual text of those pages for the keyword. Usually, the list of search results includes a brief description of each page. By clicking on the links in the list, you can directly access the Web pages. When you find a page you think might be useful, you should create a bookmark for it in your Web browser. Bookmarks (or favorites) record the locations of Web pages within your browser so that you can return to a page later just by clicking on its bookmark. By bookmarking potentially useful Web pages you can keep track of your Internet research and maintain a working bibliography of your Internet sources.

Keep in mind that each search engine works a bit differently and will yield different results from the same keyword. Therefore, before you enter your keyword, read the on-screen instructions or help information for each search engine to see how it works. Also, try more than one search engine. Several search engines can perform meta-searches, collecting the results from multiple search engines simultaneously. These include the following:

Dogpile	http://www.dogpile.com
Ask Jeeves!	http://www.ask.com
MetaCrawler	http://www.metacrawler.com

The success of a Web search and the number of hits or responses it yields depends on the keywords you choose and the comprehensiveness of the search engine. If a search yields too few sources or too many irrelevant ones, try rephrasing your keywords or choosing more specific ones to locate the most useful information. If your topic is ecology, for example, you might find information by searching with the keywords *ecosystem, environment, pollution,* and *endangered species,* among others. As with library searches, however, you should narrow your topic if the number of sources becomes unmanageable. Most search engines invite you to refine your search and help by offering related keywords. For instance, when an AltaVista search using the keyword *ecology* resulted in 374,576 matches, a series of keyword groups with percentages was provided. If you choose the *ecology, biology, biological research, and genetics* group, you cut down to 88 percent of the matches, but if you choose *habitats, freshwater, extinction* group, you cut down to 15 percent of the original 374,576 possibilities. You could refine your search this way in several stages and wind up with a manageable number of sources.

A useful alternative to searching the Internet with keywords is to browse or search subject directories, which let you choose from broad categories that lead to more focused directories. Subject directories include the following:

Argus Clearinghouse	http://www.clearinghouse.net
Inter-Links	http://alabanza.com/kabacoff/Inter-Links/index.html
Refdesk	http://www.refdesk.com

For current events and other topics in the news, you can narrow your results by starting with a local or national newspaper or one whose coverage you respect. The following newspapers have high-powered search engines on their own sites:

Chicago Tribune	http://www.chicagotribune.com
Los Angeles Times	http://www.latimes.com
New York Times	http://www.nytimes.com
San Francisco Chronicle	http://www.sfgate.com
San Jose Mercury News	http://www.mercurycenter.com
Washington Post	http://www.washingtonpost.com

Be warned, though, that some online news publishers now charge a fee for the full-text retrieval of articles. Finding the article is usually free of charge, but downloading the full text of an article to your computer will cost a small fee. Whichever search engines you choose, allow yourself enough time to sort through the results.

Access Online Library Catalogs

Many library catalogs throughout the world can be accessed online, whether by a Web browser, a telnet connection, or direct modem-to-modem dialing. Contact your college library to see whether it offers Web-based, telnet, or modem access to the online catalogs of other libraries. Searches of the book catalogs of local and remote libraries may yield lists of valuable resources or, in some cases, complete articles. For more information, as well as a comprehensive list of links to searchable library catalogs, visit the Library of Congress site at <http://lcweb.loc.gov>. The Library of Congress Web site, as well as such other sites as the WWW Virtual Library at <http://vlib.org/Overview.html> and the Internet Public Library (IPL) at <http://www.ipl.org/ref/index.text.html>, provide an extensive list of subjects arranged according to the LCSH. An added advantage to the IPL site is that librarians are available to answer your questions by email.

Use Email to Contact Other Researchers and Experts

You can contact others directly through *email* (electronic mail). Some authors include their email addresses along with their articles, so you may be able to write to them for further information. Web pages often include email links to individuals who have further information on specific topics.

Another important email resource for some projects, *newsgroups,* are interest groups in which people post messages in a public forum for discussion. The messages are usually posted on the Internet for anyone to read and respond to, much like a public bulletin board. A *listserv* is like a newsgroup except that listserv messages are not posted in a public forum but are sent automatically to all subscribers of the group by private email. In addition, the discussion that takes place on a listserv tends to be more serious and focused than that of newsgroups. One student researching language acquisition, for instance, subscribed to a listserv made up primarily of teachers of English as a second language. She read the group's email discussions for a while to determine whether her questions would be appropriate to the list, rather than posting her message immediately. She decided to post a message to the listserv with questions related to her research. In return, she received a great deal of useful information from professionals in the field.

Finally, note that most newsgroups and some listservs maintain searchable archives of previous postings. Contact a reference librarian for help in identifying useful email research tools, or start with a search engine that specializes in newsgroups, such as Deja News at <http://www.dejanews.com>. If all else fails, you can try a keyword search online combining the keyword *listserv* or *newsgroup* with your topic to see what you can find.

EVALUATING SOURCES CRITICALLY

From the very beginning of your search for sources, you should evaluate each potential source to determine whether it will be useful and relevant to your essay. Obviously, you must decide which sources provide information relevant to the topic, but you also must read sources with a critical eye to decide how credible or trustworthy they are. Just because a book or essay appears in print or an article is posted on a Web site does not necessarily mean the information or opinions within it are reliable.

Criteria for Evaluating Sources

To help you evaluate the sources you have found, try using the following criteria. Your goal is to determine the relevance, currency, range of viewpoints, and authoritativeness of each potential source. In addition, you want to take special care when evaluating sources gathered from the Internet.

Determine the Relevance of Potential Sources

Begin your evaluation of sources by narrowing your working bibliography to the most relevant works. To decide how relevant a particular source is to your topic, you need to examine the source in depth. Do not depend on title alone, for it may be misleading. If the source is a book, check its table of contents and index to see how many pages are devoted to the precise subject you are exploring. In most cases you will want an in-depth, not a superficial, treatment of the subject. Read the preface or introduction to a book, the abstract or opening paragraphs of an article, and any biographical information given about the author to determine the author's basic or distinctive approach to the subject. As you look at all these elements, consider the following questions:

- Does the source provide a general overview or a specialized point of view? General sources are helpful early in your research, but ultimately you will need the authoritative and up-to-date coverage of specialized sources (excluding those that are overly technical).
- Is the source long enough to provide adequate detail?
- Is the source written for general readers or specialists? Advocates or critics?
- Is the author an expert on the topic? Does the author's way of looking at the topic support or challenge other views?

Determine the Currency of Potential Sources

Currency—or the timeliness of a source—is more important for some topics than for others. In an essay about changes in tax laws, for instance, you would need to use the most current information available to describe changes in the law. Although you should always consult the most up-to-date sources available on your subject, older sources often establish the principles, theories, and data on which later work is based and may provide a useful perspective for evaluating more current sources. For an Internet source, check the publication date and any revision or modification dates. Also make a note of the date you accessed the site.

Determine the Viewpoint of Potential Sources

Your sources should represent a variety of viewpoints on the topic. Just as you would not depend on a single author for all of your information, you would not want to use authors who all belong to the same school of thought. Authors come to their subjects with particular viewpoints derived from their philosophies, experiences, educational backgrounds, and affiliations. In evaluating your sources, then, consider carefully how these viewpoints are reflected in the writing and how they affect the way authors present their arguments.

Although the text of a source gives you the most precise indication of the author's viewpoint, you can often get a good idea by also looking at the preface or introduction or at the sources the author cites. You will want to determine whether the document fairly represents other views on the topic with which you are familiar. When you examine a reference, you can often determine the point of view it represents by considering the following elements:

- *Title:* Look closely at the title and subtitle to see if they use words that indicate a particular viewpoint. Watch for "loaded" words or confrontational phrasing. Keep in mind, however, that titles and subtitles are often determined by editors or publishers rather than authors, especially in the case of newspaper and magazine articles.
- *Author:* Consider how the author's professional affiliation might affect his or her perspective on the topic. Look also at the tone of the writing and any biographical information provided about the author.
- *Editorial slant:* Notice where the selection was published. To determine the editorial slant of a newspaper or periodical, all you have to do is read some of its editorials, opinion columns, or letters to the editor. You can also check such sources as the *Gale Directory of Publications and Broadcast Media* (2001) and *Magazines for Libraries,* 11th ed. (2001). For books, read the preface or introduction as well as the acknowledgments and sources cited to get an idea of how the authors position themselves in relation to other specialists in the field. For Internet sources, notice what organization, if any, stands behind the author's work.

Determine Whether the Sources Are Authoritative

Just because a book or essay appears in print or online does not guarantee that it is a reliable source of information. Check the author's professional credentials, background, and publication history to verify that he or she is an established voice in the field. To help determine which authors are established, note whether they are cited in encyclopedia articles, bibliographies, and recent works on the subject. For books, you can also look up reviews in newspapers or academic journals.

Experts will (and should) disagree on topics, and each author will naturally see the topic in his or her own way. Yet authoritative authors will explain and support, not just assert, their opinions. They will also cite their sources. Because articles published in most academic journals and books published by university presses are judged by other experts in the field, you can assume that these authors' views are respected even if they are controversial. Allowing for differences of viewpoint, information about the topic provided in the source should be consistent with information you have found on the topic in other sources.

Use Special Care in Evaluating Internet Sources

Unlike most published print resources, which have been reviewed and selected by editors in a "filtering" process to ensure their accuracy and credibility, most publications on the Internet have been through no comparable filtering process. Anyone who can upload material to a server can publish on the Internet. Web sites may be sponsored by academic institutions, government agencies, companies, organizations, clubs, or individuals—for recreational or professional use. This variety makes it essential that you take extra care in evaluating the credentials of the author and the credibility of the information before you use an Internet publication as a source.

Often, the information needed to evaluate Internet sources is more difficult to locate than it is for print sources. Books, for example, display the name of their publisher on the spine and the title page, include information about the author in the beginning or at the end of the book, and often make the purpose of the work clear in a preface or introduction. Determining the publisher, the purpose, and sometimes even the author of a Web page, however, can often be more difficult because of the technical differences between print and online media. For example, Web pages that are part of a larger Web site might—when they are accessed by a search engine—give few pointers to the rest of the site. These Web pages may carry little or no indication of who published or sponsored the site or of its overall purpose or author. In this situation, the researcher should not use the source unless more information about the Web site can be tracked down. The following specialized techniques for reading and evaluating Web pages will help:

- *Look for a Web site that provides information on its history.* Look for the following information on any online articles you retrieve: the author's professional title, affiliation, and other credentials; the sponsor of the page and the Web site; a link to the site's home page; and the date the site was created or last revised. Check the title, headers, and footers of the Web page for this information. If it is provided, it may indicate a willingness to publish in a professional manner, and it will help you evaluate the source according to the criteria discussed earlier. Checking the home page of the Web site will help you discover, for example, if its purpose is commercial (a site published to sell radar detectors) or one of public safety (a site established by the Highway Patrol to give information on speed limits).

- *Alter the URL in the browser's "location" box, and try to contact the sponsoring institution.* By deleting all but the initial directory from a lengthy URL, you may be able to determine the sponsoring institution for the Web page. For example, in <http://lcweb.loc.gov/z3950/gateway.html>, taking away the subdirectory (z3950) and filename (gateway.html) will reveal the sponsoring computer's address: <http://lcweb.loc.gov> (which in this case is the Library of Congress home page). Enter the abbreviated URL address in your browser to access the site and to determine where the information comes from.
- *Follow links out from the site to others.* Internet sources sometimes provide direct links to other sources so you can see the context from which a fact, statistic, or quotation has been taken. Many also link to Web site "consumer reports" that have rated the site favorably, but you need to consider whether the site doing the ratings is trustworthy.
- *Use any other evaluation techniques available.* Even if you cannot discover the author's credentials, you can check his or her facts, details, and presentation: Does the information make sense to you? Can you verify the facts? You may find that, even though the author is not a recognized expert in the field, he or she offers information valuable to your project. One advantage of the Web is that anyone, not just recognized experts, can express views and relate firsthand experiences that may be useful in developing your topic.

INTEGRATING SOURCES WITH YOUR OWN WRITING

Writers commonly use sources by quoting directly, by paraphrasing, and by summarizing. This section provides guidelines for deciding when to use each of these three methods and how to do so effectively.

Deciding Whether to Quote, Paraphrase, or Summarize

As a general rule, quote only in these situations: (1) when the wording of the source is particularly memorable or vivid or expresses a point so well that you cannot improve it without destroying the meaning, (2) when the words of reliable and respected authorities would lend support to your position, (3) when you wish to highlight the author's opinions, (4) when you wish to cite an author whose opinions challenge or vary greatly from those of other experts, or (5) when you are going to discuss the source's choice of words. Paraphrase passages whose details you wish to note completely but whose language is not particularly striking. Summarize any long passages whose main points you wish to record selectively as background or general support for a point you are making.

Quoting

Quotations should duplicate the source exactly. If the source has an error, copy it and add the notation *sic* (Latin for "thus") in brackets immediately after the error to indicate that it is not your error but your source's:

```
According to a recent newspaper article, "Plagirism [sic] is a
problem among journalists and scholars as well as students"
(Berensen 62).
```

However, you can change quotations (1) to emphasize particular words by underlining or italicizing them, (2) to omit irrelevant information or to make the quotation conform grammatically to your sentence by using ellipsis marks, and (3) to make the quotation conform grammatically or to insert information by using brackets.

Underlining or Italicizing for Emphasis

You may underline or italicize any words in the quotation that you want to emphasize, and add the words *emphasis added* (in regular type, not italicized or underlined) in brackets immediately after the words you want to emphasize.

```
In his introduction, Studs Terkel (1972) claims that his book
is about a search for "daily meaning as well as daily bread,
for recognition as well as cash, for astonishment rather than
torpor [emphasis added]; in short, for a sort of life rather
than a Monday through Friday sort of dying" (p. xi).
```

Using Ellipsis Marks for Omissions

Ellipsis marks—three spaced periods (. . .)—signal that something has been left out of a quotation. When you omit words from within a quotation, you must use ellipsis marks in place of the missing words. If you are following the MLA style, place brackets around ellipses you have inserted to distinguish them from any ellipsis marks the author may have used. When the omission occurs within the sentence, include a space before the first bracket and after the closing bracket. There should also be spaces between the three ellipsis marks, but not between the opening bracket and the first ellipsis point or between the closing bracket and the last ellipsis point.

```
Ellen Ruppel Shell claims in "Does Civilization Cause Asthma?"
that what asthma "lacks in lethality, it more than makes up
for in morbidity: it wears people down [. . .] and threatens
their livelihood" (90).
```

When the omission falls at the end of a sentence, place a sentence period *directly after* the closing bracket.

```
But Grimaldi's recent commentary on Aristotle contends that
for Aristotle, rhetoric, like dialectic, had "no limited and
unique subject matter upon which it must be exercised [. . .].
Instead, rhetoric as an art transcends all specific disci-
plines and may be brought into play in them" (6).
```

A period plus ellipsis marks can indicate the omission of the rest of the sentence as well as whole sentences, paragraphs, or even pages.

When a parenthetical reference follows the ellipsis marks at the end of a sentence, place the three spaced periods after the quotation, and place the sentence period after the final parenthesis:

```
But Grimaldi's recent commentary on Aristotle contends that for
Aristotle, rhetoric, like dialectic, had "no limited and unique
subject matter upon which it must be exercised [. . .]" (6).
```

Of course, you may decide to leave certain words out of a quotation because they are not relevant to the point being made or because they add information readers will not need in the context in which the quotation is being used. When you quote only single words or phrases, you do not need to use ellipsis marks because it will be obvious that you have left out some of the original.

```
According to Geoffrey Nunberg, many people believe that the
Web is "just one more route along which English will march on
an ineluctable course of world conquest" (40).
```

Using Brackets for Insertions or Changes

Use brackets around an insertion or a change needed to make a quotation conform grammatically to your sentence, such as a change in the tense of a verb, in the capitalization of the first letter of the first word of a quotation, or in a pronoun. In this example from an essay on James Joyce's "Araby," the writer adapts Joyce's phrases "we played till our bodies glowed" and "shook music from the buckled harness" to fit the tense of her sentences:

```
In the dark, cold streets during the "short days of winter,"
the boys must generate their own heat by "[playing] till
```

[their] bodies glowed." Music is "[shaken] from the buckled harness" as if it were unnatural, and the singers in the market chant nasally of "the troubles in our native land" (30).

You may also use brackets to add or substitute explanatory material in a quotation:

Guterson notes that among Native Americans in Florida, "education was in the home; learning by doing was reinforced by the myths and legends which repeated the basic value system of their [the Seminoles] way of life" (159).

Several kinds of changes necessary to make a quotation conform grammatically to another sentence may be made without any signal to readers: (1) A period at the end of a quotation may be changed to a comma if you are using the quotation within your own sentence, and (2) double quotation marks enclosing a quotation may be changed to single quotation marks when the quotation is enclosed within a longer quotation.

Integrating Quotations

Depending on its length, a quotation may be incorporated into your text by enclosing it in quotation marks or setting it off from your text in block format without quotation marks. In either case, be sure to blend the quotation into your essay rather than dropping it in without appropriate integration.

In-Text Quotations

Incorporate brief quotations (no more than four typed lines of prose or three lines of poetry) into your text. You may place the quotation virtually anywhere in your sentence:

At the Beginning

"To live a life is not to cross a field," Sutherland quotes Pasternak at the beginning of her narrative (11).

In the Middle

Anna Quindlen argues that "booze and beer are not the same as illegal drugs. They're worse" (88)--a claim that meets much resistance from students and parents alike.

At the End

In The Second Sex, Simone de Beauvoir describes such an experience as one in which the girl "becomes as object, and she sees herself as object" (378).

Divided by Your Own Words

```
"Science usually prefers the literal to the nonliteral term,"
Kinneavy writes, "--that is, figures of speech are often out
of place in science" (177).
```

When you quote poetry within your text, use a slash (/) with spaces before and after to signal the end of each line of verse:

```
Alluding to St. Augustine's distinction between the City of
God and the Earthly City, Lowell writes that "much against my
will / I left the City of God where it belongs" (4-5).
```

Block Quotations

In the MLA style, put in block form prose quotations of five or more typed lines and poetry quotations of four or more lines. In the APA style, use block form for quotations of forty words or more. If you are using the MLA style, indent the quotation an inch (ten character spaces) from the left margin, as shown in the following example. If you are using the APA style, indent the block quotation five to seven spaces, keeping your indents consistent throughout your paper.

In a block quotation, double-space between lines just as you do in your text. *Do not* enclose the passage within quotation marks. Use a colon to introduce a block quotation, unless the context calls for another punctuation mark or none at all. When quoting a single paragraph or part of one in the MLA style, do not indent the first line of the quotation more than the rest. In quoting two or more paragraphs, indent the first line of each paragraph an extra quarter inch (three spaces). If you are using the APA style, the first line of subsequent paragraphs in the block quotation indents an additional five to seven spaces from the block quotation indent.

```
In "A Literary Legacy from Dunbar to Baraka," Margaret Walker
says of Paul Lawrence Dunbar's dialect poems:
          He realized that the white world in the United
          States tolerated his literary genius only because of
          his "jingles in a broken tongue," and they found the
          old "darky" tales and speech amusing and within the
          vein of folklore into which they wished to classify
          all Negro life. This troubled Dunbar because he re-
          alized that white America was denigrating him as a
          writer and as a man. (70)
```

Punctuating Introductory Statements

Statements that introduce quotations take a range of punctuation marks and lead-in words. Let us look at some examples of ways writers typically introduce quotations.

INTRODUCING A STATEMENT WITH A COLON

A colon usually follows an independent clause placed before the quotation.

```
As George Williams notes, protection of white privilege is
critical to patterns of discrimination: "Whenever a number of
persons within a society have enjoyed for a considerable
period of time certain opportunities for getting wealth, for
exercising power and authority, and for successfully claiming
prestige and social deference, there is a strong tendency for
these people to feel that these benefits are theirs "by
right'" (727).
```

INTRODUCING A STATEMENT WITH A COMMA

A comma usually follows an introduction that incorporates the quotation in its sentence structure.

```
Similarly, Duncan Turner asserts, "As matters now stand, it is
unwise to talk about communication without some understanding
of Burke" (259).
```

INTRODUCING A STATEMENT USING *THAT*

No punctuation is generally needed with *that,* and no capital letter is used to begin the quotation.

```
Noting this failure, Alice Miller asserts that "the reason for
her despair was not her suffering but the impossibility of
communicating her suffering to another person" (255).
```

INTRODUCING A STATEMENT USING *AS . . . SAID*

Using *as* to introduce a quotation places the time of the statement in the past tense, not the present. Without *as,* generally use the present tense to describe authors speaking through their writing. Use the past tense for historical events.

```
We need to continue to fight against racial profiling, for as
Randall Kennedy has said, "The practice of racial profiling
undercuts a good idea that needs more support from both
society and the law: Individuals should be judged by public
authorities on the basis of their own conduct and not on the
basis of racial generalization" (74).
```

Punctuating within Quotations

Although punctuation within a quotation should reproduce the original, some adaptations may be necessary. Use single quotation marks for quotations within the quotation:

Original from Guterson (16–17)

> E. D. Hirsch also recognizes the connection between family and learning, suggesting in his discussion of family background and academic achievement "that the significant part of our children's education has been going on outside rather than inside the schools."

Quoted Version

```
Guterson claims that E. D. Hirsch "also recognizes the connec-
tion between family and learning, suggesting in his discussion
of family background and academic achievement 'that the sig-
nificant part of our children's education has been going on
outside rather than inside the schools'" (16-17).
```

When a quotation ends with a question mark or an exclamation point, retain the original punctuation:

```
"Did you think I loved you?" Edith later asks Dombey (566).
```

When a quotation ending with a question mark or an exclamation point concludes your sentence, retain the question mark or exclamation point, and put the parenthetical reference and sentence period outside the quotation marks:

```
Edith later asks Dombey, "Did you think I loved you?" (566).
```

Avoiding Grammatical Tangles

When you incorporate quotations into your writing, and especially when you omit words from quotations, you run the risk of creating ungrammatical sentences. Three common errors you should try to avoid are *verb incompatibility, ungrammatical omissions,* and *sentence fragments.*

Verb Incompatibility

When this error occurs, the verb form in the introductory statement is grammatically incompatible with the verb form in the quotation. When your quotation has a verb form that does not fit in with your text, it is usually possible to use just part of the quotation, thus avoiding verb incompatibility.

```
The narrator suggests his bitter disappointment when [he describes seeing himself] ~~"I saw myself~~ "as a creature driven and derided by vanity" (35).
```

As this sentence illustrates, use the present tense when you refer to events in a literary work.

Ungrammatical Omission

Sometimes omitting text from a quotation leaves you with an ungrammatical sentence. Two ways of correcting the grammar are (1) adapting the quotation (with brackets) so that its parts fit together grammatically and (2) using only one part of the quotation.

```
From the moment of the boy's arrival in Araby, the bazaar is presented as a commercial enterprise: "I could not find any sixpenny entrance and [. . .] [hand[ed]] ~~handing~~ a shilling to a weary-looking man" (34).
```

```
From the moment of the boy's arrival in Araby, the bazaar is presented as a commercial enterprise: [He "] ~~"I~~ could not find any sixpenny entrance" and [so had to pay a shilling to get in (34).] ~~[. . .] handing a shilling to a weary-looking man" (34).~~
```

Sentence Fragment

Sometimes when a quotation is a complete sentence, writers neglect the sentence that introduces the quote—for example, by forgetting to include a verb. It is important to make sure that the quotation is introduced by a complete sentence.

```
The girl's interest in the bazaar [leads] ~~leading~~ the narrator to make what amounts to a sacred oath: "If I go [. . .] I will bring you something" (32).
```

Paraphrasing and Summarizing

In addition to quoting sources, writers have the option of paraphrasing or summarizing what others have written. In a *paraphrase,* the writer restates primarily in his or her own words all the relevant information from a few sentences of a text, without any additional comments or elaborations. A paraphrase is useful for recording details of the text when the order of the details is important but the source's wording is not. Because all the details of the text are included, a paraphrase is often about the same length as the original text.

In a *summary,* the writer boils down a long text—several pages or even a whole chapter or book—to its main ideas. Unlike a paraphrase, a summary conveys the gist of a source, using just enough information to record the points the summarizer chooses to emphasize. In choosing what to include in a summary, be sure not to distort the author's meaning. Whereas a paraphrase may be as long as or even longer than the original, a summary is generally much shorter than the original text.

To avoid plagiarizing inadvertently, you must rely mainly on *your own words and sentence structures* when paraphrasing or summarizing. If you include an author's original expressions, enclose them in quotation marks. In the following examples, notice that the names for the two groups—"discovery theorists" and "assimilationist theorists"—are in quotation marks. Even when a paraphrase or a summary is restated in your own words, you still need to include a citation in your text that identifies the original source of the ideas. If you are uncertain about a particular paraphrase or summary, ask your instructor for help while you are still drafting your paper.

Here is a passage from a book on home schooling and an example of a paraphrase:

Original Text

> Bruner and the discovery theorists have also illuminated conditions that apparently pave the way for learning. It is significant that these conditions are unique to each learner, so unique, in fact, that in many cases classrooms can't provide them. Bruner also contends that the more one discovers information in a great variety of circumstances, the more likely one is to develop the inner categories required to organize that information. Yet life at school, which is for the most part generic and predictable, daily keeps many children from the great variety of circumstances they need to learn well.
>
> —David Guterson, *Family Matters: Why Homeschooling Makes Sense,* p. 172

Paraphrase

According to Guterson (172), the "discovery theorists," particularly Bruner, have identified the conditions that allow learning to take place. Because these conditions are specific to each individual, many children are not able to learn in the classroom. According to Bruner, when people can explore information in different situations, they learn to classify and order what they discover. The general routine of the school day, however, does not provide children with the diverse activities and situations that would allow them to learn these skills.

Here is an example of a summary of the longer section that contains the original text:

Summary

In looking at different theories of learning that discuss individual-based programs (such as home schooling) versus the public school system, Guterson describes the disagreements among "cognitivist" theorists. One group, the "discovery theorists," believes that individual children learn by creating their own ways of sorting the information they take in from their experiences. Schools should help students develop better ways of organizing new material, not just present them with material that is already categorized, as traditional schools do. "Assimilationist theorists," by contrast, believe that children learn by linking what they don't know to information they already know. These theorists claim that traditional schools help students learn when they present information in ways that allow children to fit the new material into categories they have already developed (171-75).

Introducing Cited Material

Notice in the preceding examples that the source is acknowledged by name. Even when you use your own words to present someone else's information, you must acknowledge that you borrowed the information. The only types of information that do not require acknowledgment are common knowledge (John F. Kennedy was assassinated in Dallas), familiar sayings ("Haste makes waste"), and well-known quotations ("To be or not to be. That is the question").

The documentation guidelines later in this appendix (pp. 589–614) present various ways of citing the sources you quote, paraphrase, and summarize; the important thing is that your readers can tell where words or ideas that are not your own begin and end. You can accomplish this most readily by separating your words from those of the source with *signal phrases* such as "According to

Smith," "Peters claims," and "As Olmos asserts." When you cite a source for the first time, you may use the author's full name; after that, use just the last name.

Avoiding Plagiarism

Writers—students and professionals alike—occasionally fail to acknowledge sources properly. The word *plagiarism,* which derives from the Latin word for "kidnapping," refers to the unacknowledged use of another's words, ideas, or information. Students sometimes get into trouble because they mistakenly assume that plagiarizing occurs only when another writer's exact words are used without acknowledgment. In fact, plagiarism applies to such diverse forms of expression as musical compositions and visual images as well as ideas and statistics. So keep in mind that you must indicate the source of any information or ideas you use in your essay, whether you have paraphrased, summarized, or quoted directly from the source.

Some people plagiarize simply because they do not know the conventions for using and acknowledging sources. The following section, Documenting Sources, makes clear how to incorporate sources into your writing and how to acknowledge your use of those sources. Others plagiarize because they keep sloppy notes and thus fail to distinguish between their own and their sources' ideas. Either they neglect to enclose their sources' words in quotation marks, or they fail to indicate when they are paraphrasing or summarizing a source's ideas and information. If you keep a working bibliography and careful notes, you will not make this serious mistake.

Another reason some people plagiarize is that they doubt their ability to write the essay by themselves. They feel intimidated by the writing task or the deadline or their own and others' expectations. If you experience this same anxiety about your work, speak to your instructor. Do not run the risk of failing a course or being expelled because of plagiarism. If you are confused about what is and what is not plagiarism, be sure to ask your instructor.

DOCUMENTING SOURCES

Although there is no universally accepted system for acknowledging sources, there is agreement on both the need for documentation and the details that should be included. Writers should acknowledge sources for three reasons: to give credit to those sources, to enable readers to consult those sources for further information, and to give credibility and authority to the work they produce.

The following guidelines cover two popular styles of documentation: the *Modern Language Association (MLA)* system, which is used in English and the humanities, and the *American Psychological Association (APA)* system, which is used in the social sciences.

Document Sources Using MLA Style

The following guidelines are sufficient for most college research assignments in English and other humanities courses that call for MLA-style documentation. For additional information, see the *MLA Handbook for Writers of Research Papers,* Fifth Edition (1999), or check the MLA Web site at <http://www.mla.org>.

Use In-Text Citations to Show Where You Have Used Material from Sources

In-text citations mark places in the text of an essay where information, ideas, or quotations from sources are included. Each in-text citation has a corresponding entry in the list of sources at the end of the essay that tells readers how to find the source. In the MLA style this list is titled *Works Cited.*

Place an in-text citation in parentheses as near as possible to the borrowed material without disrupting your sentence. Include a citation each time you refer to a source, except when all of the sentences in a single paragraph refer to the same source—and no reference to another page in the source or to another source intervenes. In this case, you may use a single parenthetical citation, positioned after the last reference in the paragraph. Do not cite common knowledge or personal knowledge.

USE THE FOLLOWING MODELS FOR IN-TEXT CITATIONS

1. When the author is indicated in a signal phrase

"Despite his immense working vocabulary, Shakespeare did not mention chocolate at all," Sokolov points out, even though by 1569 chocolate was available in England (134).

2. When the author and page are indicated in a parenthetical citation

Dr. James is described as a "not-too-skeletal Ichabod Crane" (Simon 68).

While automotive design improvements have made American cars safer than ever at high speeds (Kaye 73), speed limits in many places still remain low.

3. When the source has more than one author

Dyal, Corning, and Willows identify several types of students, including the "Authority-Rebel" (4).

Authority-rebels see themselves as "superior to other students in the class" (Dyal, Corning, and Willows 4).

The drug AZT has been shown to reduce the risk of transmission from HIV-positive mothers to their infants by as much as two-thirds (Van de Perre et al. 4-5).

For three or more authors, you may list everyone or only the first author followed by *et al.*, as in the example above.

4. When the author is not named

In 1992, five years after the Symms legislation, the number of deaths from automobile accidents reached a thirty-year low ("Highways" 51).

5. When the source has a corporate or government author

A tuition increase has been proposed for community and technical colleges to offset budget deficits from Initiative 601 (Washington State Board for Community and Technical Colleges 4).

6. When two or more works by the same author are cited

When old paint becomes transparent, it sometimes shows the artist's original plans: "A tree will show through a woman's dress" (Hellman, Pentimento 1).

Because more than one of Hellman's works is included in the list of works cited, the title follows the author's name in the parentheses.

7. When two or more authors have the same last name

According to Edgar V. Roberts, Chaplin's Modern Times provides a good example of montage used to make an editorial statement (246).

Chaplin's Modern Times provides a good example of montage used to make an editorial statement (E. V. Roberts 246).

Note that Roberts's first and middle initials are included in the parentheses because another author with the same last name is included in the list of works cited.

8. When a work without page numbers is cited

The average speed on Montana's interstate highways, for example, has risen by only 2 miles per hour since the repeal of the federal speed limit, with most drivers topping out at 75 (Schmid).

There is no page number available for this source because it comes from the Internet.

9. When a quotation is taken from a secondary source

Chancellor Helmut Kohl summed up the German attitude: "For millions of people, a car is part of their personal freedom" (qtd. in Cote 12).

Create a works-cited entry for the secondary source in which you found the quote, rather than for the original source (for this example, an entry for Cote, not Kohl, would appear in the list of works cited).

10. When a citation comes from a multivolume work

"Double meaning," according to Freud, "is one of the most fertile sources for [...] jokes" (8: 56).

In the parentheses, the number 8 indicates the volume and *56* indicates the page. (For a works-cited entry for a single volume in a multivolume work, see p. 595, entry 8.)

11. When the source is a literary work

For a novel or other prose work available in various editions, provide the page numbers from the edition used. To help readers locate the quotation in another edition, add the part and/or chapter number.

In Hard Times, Tom reveals his utter narcissism by blaming Louisa for his own failure: "'You have regularly given me up. You never cared for me'" (Dickens 262; bk. 3, ch. 9).

For a play in verse, such as a Shakespearean play, indicate the act, scene, and line numbers instead of the page numbers.

At the beginning, Regan's fawning rhetoric hides her true attitude toward Lear: "I profess / Myself an enemy to all other joys/ [...] / And find I am alone felicitate / In your dear highness' love" (King Lear I.i.74-75, 77-78).

For a poem, indicate the line numbers and stanzas (if they are numbered), instead of the page numbers.

In "Song of Myself," Whitman finds poetic details in busy urban settings, as when he describes "the blab of the pave, tires of carts [...]/[...] the driver with his interrogating thumb" (8.153-54).

If the source gives only line numbers, use the term *lines* in the first citation; in subsequent citations, give only the numbers.

12. When the citation comes from a work in an anthology

```
In "Six Days: Some Rememberings," Grace Paley recalls that
when she was in jail for protesting the Vietnam War, her pen
and paper were taken away and she felt "a terrible pain in the
area of my heart--a nausea" (191).
```

If you are discussing the editor's *preface* or *introduction,* name the editor.

13. When two or more works are cited in the same parentheses

When two or more different sources are used in the same passage, it may be necessary to cite them in the same parentheses. Separate the citations with a semicolon.

```
A few studies have considered differences between oral and
written discourse production (Scardamalia, Bereiter, and Goel-
man; Gould).
```

```
The scene registers conflicts in English law as well, for
while the medieval Westminster statutes also distinguish
between lawful and unlawful exchanges of women, sixteenth-
century statutes begin to redefine rape as a violent crime
against a woman rather than as a property crime against her
guardians (Maitland 2:490-91; Post; Bashar; Gossett).
```

14. When an entire work is cited

```
In The Structure of Scientific Revolutions, Thomas Kuhn dis-
cusses how scientists change their thinking.
```

15. When material from the Internet is cited

```
In handling livestock, "many people attempt to restrain ani-
mals with sheer force instead of using behavioral principles"
(Grandin).
```

If the author is not named, give the document title. Include page or paragraph numbers, if available.

Include All of Your Sources in a Works-Cited List at the End of Your Essay

The works-cited list provides information that enables readers to find the sources cited in the essay. Every source referred to in the text of your essay must have a corresponding entry in the list of works cited at the end of your essay. Conversely, every entry in the works-cited list must correspond to at least one in-text citation in the essay.

Although there are many varieties of works-cited entries, the information generally follows this order:

BASIC ENTRY FOR A BOOK

Author's last name, First name, Middle initial. Book Title. City of publication: Publisher's name, year published.

Copy the author's name and the title from the book's title page or the first page of the article. Do not worry about including information that is unavailable within the source, such as the author's middle initial or the issue number for a periodical. If your instructor permits, you may italicize rather than underline book titles and periodical names. *Note:* The MLA recommends that the list of works cited be placed at the end of the paper, beginning on a new page with pages numbered consecutively; that the first line of each entry begins flush with the left margin; that subsequent lines of the same entry indent five character spaces; and that the entire list be double-spaced, between and within entries.

USE THE FOLLOWING MODELS FOR BOOKS

1. A book by a single author

Arnold, Marion I. Women and Art in South Africa. New York: St. Martin's, 1996.

2. Multiple works by the same author (or same group of authors)

Vidal, Gore. Empire. New York: Random, 1987.

---. Lincoln. New York: Random, 1984.

3. A book by an agency, organization, or corporation

Association for Research in Nervous and Mental Disease. The Circulation of the Brain and Spinal Cord: A Symposium on Blood Supply. New York: Hafner, 1966.

4. A book by two or more authors

For two or three authors:

Gottfredson, Stephen D., and Sean McConville. America's Correctional Crisis. Westport: Greenwood, 1987.

For three or more authors, name all the authors or only the first author plus *et al.* ("and others"):

Belenky, Mary F., Blythe M. Clinchy, Nancy R. Goldberger, and Jill M. Tarule. Women's Ways of Knowing: The Development of Self, Voice, and Mind. New York: Basic Books, 1986.

Belenky, Mary F., et al. Women's Ways of Knowing: The Development of Self, Voice, and Mind. New York: Basic Books, 1986.

5. A book with an unlisted author

Rand McNally Commercial Atlas. Skokie: Rand, 1993.

6. A book with one or more editors

Axelrod, Steven Gould, and Helen Deese, eds. Robert Lowell: Essays on the Poetry. Cambridge: Cambridge UP, 1986.

7. A book with an author and an editor

If you refer to the work itself:

Arnold, Matthew. Culture and Anarchy. Ed. J. Dover Wilson. Cambridge: Cambridge UP, 1966.

If you discuss the editor's work in your essay:

Wilson, J. Dover, ed. Culture and Anarchy. By Matthew Arnold. Cambridge: Cambridge UP, 1966.

8. One volume of a multivolume work

If only one volume from a multivolume set is used, indicate the volume number after the title:

Freud, Sigmund. The Complete Psychological Works of Sigmund Freud. Vol. 8. Trans. James Strachey. London: Hogarth, 1962.

9. Two or more volumes of a multivolume work

Sandburg, Carl. Abraham Lincoln. 6 vols. New York: Scribner's, 1939.

10. A book that is part of a series

Include the series name, without underlining or quotation marks, followed by the series number. If the word *Series* is part of the name, include the abbreviation *Ser.* before the number.

Kirsch, Gesa, and Duane H. Roen. A Sense of Audience in Written Communication. Written Communication Annual: An Intl.

Survey of Research and Theory 5. Newbury Park: Sage, 1990.

11. A republished book

Provide the original publication date after the title of the book, followed by normal publication information for the current edition:

Takaki, Ronald. Strangers from a Different Shore: A History of Asian Americans. 1989. New York: Penguin, 1990.

12. A later edition of a book

Rottenberg, Annette T. The Structure of Argument. 2nd ed. Boston: Bedford, 1997.

13. A book with a title in its title

Do not underline a title normally underlined when it appears within the title of a book or other work that is underlined:

Kinney, Arthur F. Go Down Moses: The Miscegenation of Time. New York: Twayne, 1996.

Brooker, Jewel Spears, and Joseph Bentley. Reading The Waste Land: Modernism and the Limits of Interpretation. Amherst: U of Mass P, 1990.

Use quotation marks around a work normally enclosed in quotation marks when it appears in the title of a book or other work that is underlined:

Miller, Edwin Haviland. Walt Whitman's "Song of Myself": A Mosaic of Interpretations. Iowa City: U of Iowa P, 1989.

14. A work in an anthology or a collection

Fairbairn-Dunlop, Peggy. "Women and Agriculture in Western Samoa." Different Places, Different Voices. Ed. Janet H. Momsen and Vivian Kinnaird. London: Routledge, 1993. 211-26.

15. Two or more works from the same anthology

To avoid repetition, you may create an entry for the collection and cite the collection's editors to cross-reference individual works to the entry:

Atwan, Robert, and Jamaica Kincaid, eds. The Best American Essays, 1995. New York: Houghton, 1995.

Paley, Grace. "Six Days: Some Rememberings." Atwan and Kincaid 187-92.

16. A translation

If you refer to the work itself:

Tolstoy, Leo. War and Peace. Trans. Constance Garnett. London: Pan, 1972.

If you discuss the translation in your essay:

Garnett, Constance, trans. War and Peace. By Leo Tolstoy. London: Pan, 1972.

17. An article in a reference book

Suber, Howard. "Motion Picture." The Encyclopedia Americana. 1991 ed.

18. An introduction, preface, foreword, or afterword

Holt, John. Introduction. Better than School. By Nancy Wallace. Burnett: Larson, 1983. 9-14.

BASIC ENTRY FOR AN ARTICLE

Author's last name, First name, Middle initial. "Title of the Article." Journal Name Volume number.Issue number (year published): page range.

USE THE FOLLOWING MODELS FOR ARTICLES

19. An article from a newspaper

Wilford, John Noble. "Corn in the New World: A Relative Latecomer." New York Times 7 Mar. 1995, late ed.: C1+.

20. An article from a weekly or biweekly magazine

Kaye, Steven D. "Hello 75, So Long 55." U.S. News and World Report 18 Dec. 1995: 71-75.

21. An article from a monthly or bimonthly magazine

Spencer, Paula. "No More Whining." Parenting Apr. 1997: 151-56.

22. An article in a scholarly journal with continuous annual pagination

Jackson, Jeremy S. H., and Roger Blackman. "A Driving Simulator Test of Wilde's Risk Homeostasis Theory." Journal of Applied Psychology 79 (1994): 950-58.

23. An article in a scholarly journal that paginates each issue separately

Epstein, Alexandra. "Teen Parents: What They Need to Know." High/Scope Resource 1.2 (1982): 6.

24. An article by an unidentified author

"Highways Become Safer." Futurist Jan.-Feb. 1994: 51-52.

25. An editorial

"Meth Lab Charades." Editorial. Press-Enterprise [Riverside] 2 Oct. 1997: A8.

26. A letter to the editor

Rissman, Edward M. Letter. Los Angeles Times 29 June 1989: B5.

27. A review

If the review is titled:

Anders, Jaroslaw. "Dogma and Democracy." Rev. of The Church and the Left, by Adam Minchik. New Republic 17 May 1993: 42-48.

If the review is untitled:

Lane, Anthony. Rev. of The English Patient, dir. Anthony Minghella. New Yorker 25 Nov. 1996: 118-21.

If the review has no title and no named author, start with the words *Rev. of* and the title of the work being reviewed.

BASIC ENTRY FOR AN ELECTRONIC SOURCE

Although there are many varieties of Internet works-cited entries, the information generally follows this order:

Author's last name, First name, Middle initial. "Title of Short Work." Title of Book, Periodical, or Web Site. Publication date or date of last revision. Page numbers or number of paragraphs. Name of sponsoring institution or organization. Date of access. <URL>.

USE THE FOLLOWING MODELS FOR ELECTRONIC SOURCES

Most of the following guidelines for citing Internet sources are derived from the *MLA Handbook for Writers of Research Papers,* Fifth Edition (1999), and the MLA Web site at <http://www.mla.org>. Models for citing a few other kinds of

Internet sources not covered by the MLA guidelines are based on Andrew Harnack and Eugene Kleppinger, *Online! A Reference Guide to Using Internet Sources* (New York: Bedford/St. Martin's, 2000).

28. A professional or personal Web site

Professional Web site:

Center for Immigration Studies. 8 Sept. 1998. 12 Dec 1998 <http://www.cis.org>.

Personal Web site:

Johnson, Suzanne H. Home page. 5 Oct. 1997. 23 July 1999 <http://members.aol.com/suzannehi/hello.htm>.

29. A book or poem available online

Book:

Blind, Mathilde. Dramas in Miniature. London: Chatto & Windus, 1891. Victorian Women Writers Project. Ed. Perry Willett. 3 Oct. 1997. Indiana U. 13 Oct. 1997 <http://www.indiana.edu/-letrs/vwwp/blind/dramas.html>.

Poem:

Mosko, Marc. "Muir Woods." Home page. 1996. 13 Oct. 1997 <http://www.tear.com/poems/mosko/muirwoods.html>.

30. An article in a reference database

Linsk. "Thrills Spills." Investigative Reporters and Editors, Inc. IRE Resource Center. 12338. Aug. 1995. Asbury Free P. 15 pages. 8 July 1996 <http://www.ire.org/resources/center/search.html>.

31. An article from an online journal

Killiam, Rosemary. "Cognitive Dissonance: Should Twentieth-Century Women Composers Be Grouped with Foucault's Mad Criminals?" Music Theory Online 3.2 (1997): 30 pars. 10 May 1997 <http://smt.ucsb.edu/mto/mtohome.html>.

32. An article from an online magazine

Keillor, Garrison. "Why Did They Ever Ban a Book This Bad?" Salon 13 Oct. 1997. 14 Oct. 1997 <http://www.salon1999.com/feature/>.

33. A posting to a discussion list

A newsgroup posting:

Conrad, Ed. "Proof of Life after Death." Online posting. 8 July 1996. 9 July 1996 <news:sci.archeology>.

A listserv posting:

Martin, Francesca Alys. "Wait--Did Somebody Say 'Buffy'?" Online posting. 8 Mar. 2000.cultstud-l. 8 Mar. 2000 <http://lists.accomp.usf.edu/cgi-bin/lyris.pl?visit=cultstud-l&id=111011221>.

34. An online scholarly project

The Ovid Project. Ed. Hope Greenberg. 13 Mar. 1996. U of Vermont. 13 Oct. 1997 <http://www.uvm.edu/hag/ovid/index.html>.

35. Material from a CD-ROM database

Braus, Patricia. "Sex and the Single Spender." American Demographics 15.11 (1993): 28-34. ABI/INFORM. CD-ROM. UMI-ProQuest. 1993.

If no print version is available, include the author, title, and date (if provided) along with information about the electronic source.

36. Material published on a CD-ROM, magnetic tape, or diskette

Picasso: The Man, His Works, the Legend. CD-ROM. Danbury: Grolier Interactive, 1996.

37. Material from an online subscription service

Fineman, Howard. "A Brawl on Tobacco Road: How Bill Clinton--and the Democrats' 'Butt Man'--Is Maneuvering to Turn Joe Camel into Bob Dole's Willie Horton." Newsweek 15 July 1996. America Online. 11 July 1996. Keyword: Joe Camel.

If no print version is available, include the author, title, and date (if it is provided), along with information about the electronic source.

USE THE FOLLOWING MODELS FOR OTHER SOURCES

38. An interview

Published interview:

Lowell, Robert. "Robert Lowell." Interview with Frederick Seidel. Paris Review 25 (1975): 56-95.

Personal interview:

Harkness, Edward. Personal interview. 7 May 1996.

Broadcast interview:

Calloway, Cab. Interview with Rich Conaty. The Big Broadcast. WFUV, New York. 10 Dec. 1990.

39. A lecture or public address

Timothy, Kristen. "The Changing Roles of Women's Community Organizations in Sustainable Development and in the United Nations." UN Assn. of the US. Seattle. 7 May 1997.

40. A government document

United States. Dept. of Health and Human Services. Clinical Classifications for Health Policy Research, Version 2: Hospital Inpatient Statistics. Rockville: AHCPR Publications Clearinghouse, 1996.

If the author is known, the author's name may either come first or be placed after the title and introduced with the word *By*.

41. A pamphlet

Harborview Injury Prevention and Research Center. A Decade of Injury Control. Seattle: Harborview Medical Center, 1995.

42. A published doctoral dissertation

Hilfinger, Paul N. Abstraction Mechanisms and Language Design. Diss. Carnegie-Mellon U, 1981. Cambridge: MIT P, 1983.

43. An unpublished doctoral dissertation

Bullock, Barbara. "Basic Needs Fulfillment among Less Developed Countries: Social Progress over Two Decades of Growth." Diss. Vanderbilt U, 1986.

44. A dissertation abstract

Bernstein, Stephen David. "Fugitive Genre: Gothicism, Ideology, and Intertextuality." Diss. Yale U, 1991. DAI 51 (1991): 3078-79A.

45. Published proceedings of a conference

Duffett, John, ed. Against the Crime of Silence. Proc. of the Intl. War Crimes Tribunal, Nov. 1967, Stockholm. New York: Clarion-Simon, 1970.

If the name of the conference is part of the title of the publication, it should not be repeated. Use the format for a work in an anthology (see model entry 14) to cite an individual presentation.

46. A letter

Hamilton, Alexander. "To William Seton." 3 Dec. 1790. The Papers of Alexander Hamilton. Ed. Harold C. Syrett. Vol. 7. New York: Columbia UP, 1969. 190.

Hannah, Barry. Letter to the author. 10 May 1990.

47. A map or chart

Mineral King, California. Map. Berkeley: Wilderness P, 1979.

48. A cartoon

Wilson, Gahan. Cartoon. New Yorker 14 July 1997: 74.

Provide the cartoon's title (if given) in quotes.

49. An advertisement

Reliance National Employment Practices Liability. Advertisement. Wired May 1997: 196.

50. A work of art or a musical composition

De Goya, Francisco. The Sleep of Reason Produces Monsters. Norton Simon Museum, Pasadena.

Beethoven, Ludwig van. Violin Concerto in D Major, op. 61.

Gershwin, George. Porgy and Bess.

51. A performance

Hamlet. By William Shakespeare. Dir. Jonathan Kent. Perf. Ralph Fiennes. Belasco Theatre, New York. 20 June 1995.

Include the names of any performers or other contributors who are relevant to or cited in your essay.

52. A television or radio program

"The Universe Within." Nova. Narr. Stacy Keach. Writ. Beth Hoppe and Bill Lattanzi. Dir. Goro Koide. PBS. WNET, New York. 7 Mar. 1995.

Include the names of any contributors who are relevant to or cited in your essay. If you are discussing the work of a particular person (for example, the director or writer), begin the entry with that person's name.

53. A film or videotape

Othello. Perf. Laurence Fishburne, Irene Jacob, and Kenneth Branagh. Castle Rock Entertainment, 1995.

Casablanca. Dir. Michael Curtiz. Perf. Humphrey Bogart. 1942. Videocassette. MGM-UA Home Video, 1992.

Include the names of any performers or other contributors who are relevant to or cited in your essay. If you are discussing the work of a particular person (for example, an actor), begin the entry with that person's name:

Bogart, Humphrey, perf. Casablanca. Dir. Michael Curtiz. 1942. Videocassette. MGM-UA Home Video, 1992.

54. A sound recording

Bach, Johann Sebastian. Italian Concerto in F, Partita No. 1, and Tocata in D. Dubravka Tomsic, piano. Polyband, 1987.

Jane's Addiction. "Been Caught Stealing." Ritual de lo Habitual. Audiocassette. Warner Brothers, 1990.

If the year of issue is not known, add *n.d.*

Document Sources Using APA Style

The following guidelines are sufficient for most college research reports that call for APA-style documentation. For additional information, see the *Publication Manual of the American Psychological Association,* Fifth Edition (2001), or check the APA Web site at <http://www.apa.org>.

Use In-Text Citations to Show Where You Have Used Material from Sources

In-text citations mark places in the text of an essay where information, ideas, or quotations from sources are included. Each in-text citation has a corresponding entry in the list of sources at the end of the essay that tells readers how to find the source. In the APA style this list is titled *References.*

Place an in-text citation as near as possible to the borrowed material without disrupting your sentence. Include a citation each time you refer to a source, except when all of the sentences in a single paragraph refer to the same source—and no mention of another source intervenes. In this case, you may use a single parenthetical citation for the entire paragraph. Do not cite common knowledge or personal knowledge. Always give page numbers for quotations but not for more general references. For electronic texts or other works without page numbers, paragraph numbers may be used instead, preceded by the ¶ symbol or the abbreviation *para.*

USE THE FOLLOWING MODELS FOR IN-TEXT CITATIONS

1. When the author is indicated in a signal phrase

As Allis (1990) noted about home-schooling environments, "There are no drugs in the bathroom or switchblades in the hallways" (p. 85).

Denes (1980, ¶1) claimed that psychotherapy is an art that is "volatile, unpredictable, standardless in its outcome, subjective in its worth."

2. When the author and year are indicated in a parenthetical citation

"The children in my class made fun of my braids, so Sister Victoire, the principal, sent a note home to my mother asking her to comb my hair in a more 'becoming' fashion" (Lorde, 1982, pp. 59-60).

While home schoolers are a diverse group--libertarians, conservatives, Christian fundamentalists, and a growing number of ethnic minorities (Wahisi, 1995)--most cite one of two reasons as their primary motive for home schooling.

3. When the source has two authors

Gallup and Elam (1988) show that lack of proper financial support ranked third on the list of the problems in public schools, while poor curriculum and poor standards ranked fifth on the list.

In a 1988 Gallup poll, lack of proper financial support ranked third on the list of the problems in public schools; poor curriculum and poor standards ranked fifth on the list (Gallup & Elam).

When a source with two or more authors is cited parenthetically, use an ampersand (&) instead of the word *and* before the last author's name, as shown in the preceding example.

4. When the source has three or more authors

First citation for a source with three to five authors:

```
Dyal, Corning, and Willows (1975) identify several types of
students, including the "Authority-Rebel" (p. 4).
```

```
One type of student that can be identified is the "Authority-
Rebel" (Dyal, Corning, & Willows, 1975, p. 4).
```

Subsequent citations for a source with three to five authors:

```
According to Dyal et al. (1975), Authority-Rebels "see them-
selves as superior to other students in the class" (p. 4).
```

```
Authority-Rebels "see themselves as superior to other students
in the class" (Dyal et al., 1975, p. 4).
```

For a source with six or more authors, use the last name of the first author and *et al.* in all in-text citations. But in the list of references, give all the authors' names, regardless of the number.

5. When the author is not named

```
As reported in the 1994 Economist article "Classless Society,"
estimates as late as 1993 placed the number of home-schooled
children in the 350,000 to 500,000 range.
```

```
An international pollution treaty still to be ratified would
prohibit all plastic garbage from being dumped at sea
("Awash," 1987).
```

6. When the source has a corporate author

First in-text citation, with signal phrase:

```
According to the Washington State Board for Community and
Technical Colleges, a tuition increase has been proposed to
offset budget deficits from Initiative 601 (1995).
```

First parenthetical citation:

```
Tuition increases proposed for Washington community and tech-
nical colleges would help offset budget deficits brought about
by Initiative 601 (Washington State Board of Community and
Technical Colleges [WSBCTC], 1995).
```

Subsequent parenthetical citation:

```
The tuition increases would amount to about 3 percent and
would still not cover the loss of revenue (WSBCTC, 1995).
```

7. When two or more authors have the same last name

```
"Women are more in the public world, the heretofore male
world, than at any previous moment in history," transforming
"the lives of women and men to an extent probably unparalleled
by any other social or political movement" (W. Brown, 1988,
pp. 1, 3).
```

If two or more primary authors with the same last name are listed in the references, include the authors' first initial in all text citations, even if the year of publication of the authors' works differs.

8. When two or more works are cited in the same parentheses

```
Through support organizations and programs offered by public
schools, home-schooled children are also able to take part in
social activities outside the home, such as field trips and
sports (Guterson, 1992; Hahn & Hasson, 1996).
```

When citing two or more works by different authors, arrange them alphabetically by the authors' last names, as in the preceding example. However, when citing multiple works by the same author in the same parentheses, order the citations by date, with the oldest reference first: (*Postman, 1979, 1986*).

9. When two or more works by the same author are cited

```
When old paint becomes transparent, it sometimes shows the
artist's original plans: "A tree will show through a woman's
dress" (Hellman, 1973b, p. 1).
```

When two or more works by the same author or authors are cited, the years of publication are usually enough to distinguish them. An exception occurs when the works share the same publication date. In this case, arrange the works alphabetically by title, and then add *a*, *b*, *c*, and so on after the years to distinguish works published in the same year by the same author(s).

10. When a quotation is taken from a secondary source

```
Forster says "the collapse of all civilization, so realistic
for us, sounded in Matthew Arnold's ears like a distant and
harmonious cataract" (as cited in Trilling, 1955, p. 11).
```

Create an entry in the list of references for the secondary source in which you found the quote, not for the original source.

11. When material from the Internet is cited

```
Each type of welfare recipient "requires specific services or
assistance to make the transition from welfare to work"
(Armato & Halpern, 1996, para. 7).
```

12. When an email or other personal communication is cited

```
According to L. Jones (personal communication, May 2, 1997),
some parents believe they must maximize their day-care value
and leave their children at day-care centers for up to ten
hours a day, even on their days off.
```

In addition to emails, personal communications include letters, memos, personal interviews, telephone conversations, and postings on electronic discussion groups or bulletin boards that are not archived. Give the initial(s) as well as the surname of the communicator, and provide as exact a date as possible. Personal communications are cited only in the text; do not include them in your list of references.

Include All of Your Sources in a References List at the End of Your Essay

This list, inserted on a separate page titled *References,* provides information that enables readers to find the sources cited in the essay. Every source referred to in the text of your essay (except a personal communication) must have a corresponding entry in the list of references at the end of your essay. Likewise, every entry in the references list must correspond to at least one in-text citation in the essay. If you want to show the sources you consulted but did not cite in the essay, list them on a separate page titled *Bibliography.*

Although there are many varieties of references, the information generally follows this order:

BASIC ENTRY FOR A BOOK

```
Author's last name, First initial. Middle initial. (year pub-
     lished). Book title. City of publication: Publisher's
     name.
```

Copy the author's name and the title from the first or title page of the source but do not use first names, only initials. Do not worry about including information that is unavailable, such as the author's middle initial and the issue number for a journal article. *Note:* The APA recommends that all references be double-spaced and that students use a *hanging indent:* The first line of the entry is not indented, but subsequent lines are indented five to seven spaces. The examples in this section demonstrate the hanging-indent style. The APA encourages use of italics, but your instructor may approve of or even prefer underlining. The underlined titles and other elements in the models that follow can be italicized instead of underlined.

USE THE FOLLOWING MODELS FOR BOOKS

1. A book by a single author

Guterson, D. (1992). Family matters: Why homeschooling makes sense. San Diego: Harcourt.

2. A book by more than one author

Gottfredson, S. D., & McConville, S. (1987). America's correctional crisis. Westport, CT: Greenwood.

Dyal, J. A., Corning, W. C., & Willows, D. M. (1975). Readings in psychology: The search for alternatives (3rd ed.). New York: McGraw-Hill.

3. A book by an agency, organization, or corporation

Association for Research in Nervous and Mental Disease. (1966). The circulation of the brain and spinal cord: A symposium on blood supply. New York: Hafner.

4. A book with an unlisted author

Rand McNally commercial atlas. (1993). Skokie, IL: Rand McNally.

When the word *Anonymous* appears on the title page, cite the author as *Anonymous.*

5. A later edition of a book

Lewis, I. M. (1996). Religion in context: Cults and charisma (2nd ed.). New York: Cambridge University Press.

6. Multiple works by the same author (or same group of authors)

Ritzer, G. (1993). The McDonaldization of society. Newbury Park, CA: Pine Forge Press.

Ritzer, G. (1994). Sociological beginnings: On the origins of key ideas in sociology. New York: McGraw-Hill.

Two or more works published by the same author or authors are listed in chronological order, as shown above. However, when the works also have the same publication date, arrange them alphabetically by title and add a lowercase letter after the date: *1996a, 1996b.*

7. A multivolume work

Sandburg, C. (1939). Abraham Lincoln: Vol. 2. The war years. New York: Scribner's.

Sandburg, C. (1939). Abraham Lincoln (Vols. 1-6). New York: Scribner's.

8. A book with an author and an editor

Baum, L. F. (1996). Our landlady (N. T. Koupal, Ed.). Lincoln: University of Nebraska Press.

9. An edited collection

Carter, K., & Spitzack, C. (Eds.). (1989). Doing research on women's communication. Norwood, NJ: Ablex.

10. A work in an anthology or a collection

Fairbairn-Dunlop, P. (1993). Women and agriculture in western Samoa. In J. H. Momsen & V. Kinnaird (Eds.), Different places, different voices (pp. 211-226). London: Routledge.

11. A republished book

Arnold, M. (1966). Culture and anarchy (J. D. Wilson, Ed.). Cambridge: Cambridge University Press. (Original work published 1869)

Note: Both the original and the republished dates are included in the in-text citation, separated by a slash: (*Arnold, 1869/1966*).

12. A translation

Tolstoy, L. (1972). War and peace (C. Garnett, Trans.). London: Pan Books. (Original work published 1869)

Note: Both the original publication date and the publication date for the translation are included in the in-text citation, separated by a slash: *(Tolstoy, 1869/1972).*

13. An article in a reference book

Suber, H. (1991). Motion picture. In Encyclopedia Americana (Vol. 19, pp. 505-539). Danbury, CT: Grolier.

14. An introduction, preface, foreword, or afterword

Holt, J. (1983). Introduction. In N. Wallace, Better than school (pp. 9–14). Burnett, NY: Larson.

BASIC ENTRY FOR AN ARTICLE

Author's last name, First initial. Middle initial. (publication date). Title of the article. Journal Name, volume number(issue number), page range.

USE THE FOLLOWING MODELS FOR ARTICLES

15. An article in a scholarly journal with continuous annual pagination

Natale, J. A. (1993). Understanding home schooling. Education Digest, 9, 58–61.

16. An article in a scholarly journal that paginates each issue separately

Mayberry, M., & Knowles, J. G. (1989). Family unit objectives of parents who teach their children: Ideological and pedagogical orientations to home schooling. Urban Review, 21(4), 209–225.

17. An article from a newspaper

Wilford, J. N. (1995, March 7). Corn in the New World: A relative latecomer. The New York Times, pp. C1, C5.

18. An article from a magazine

Rohn, A. (1988, April). Home schooling. Atlantic Monthly, 261, 20–25.

19. An unsigned article

Awash in garbage. (1987, August 15). The New York Times, p. A26.

20. A review

Anders, J. (1993, May 17). Dogma and democracy [Review of the book The church and the left]. The New Republic, 208, 42–48.

If the review is untitled, use the bracketed information as the title, retaining the brackets.

21. An editorial or a letter to the editor

Meader, R. (1997, May 11). Hard to see how consumers will benefit from deregulation [Letter to the editor]. Seattle Post-Intelligencer, p. E3.

22. Two or more articles by the same author in the same year

Selimuddin, A. K. (1989a, March 25). The selling of America. USA Today, pp. 12-14.

Selimuddin, A. K. (1989b, September). Will America become #2? USA Today Magazine, 14-16.

BASIC ENTRY FOR AN ELECTRONIC SOURCE

Author's last name, First initial. Middle initial. (Publication date). Title of document. Title of complete document. [Retrieved] date of retrieval [from] URL

USE THE FOLLOWING MODELS FOR ELECTRONIC SOURCES

The APA *Publication Manual* notes that it can be difficult to identify appropriate citation information for many electronic sources, but it recommends that for Internet sources you should at least provide a title or description of the electronic document, the date it was published or most recently updated or the date you retrieved it, and an address, or URL. If possible, include the author of the document as well. The APA also recommends that you check the URLs of your Internet sources frequently to make sure that they still provide access to the source, updating them as necessary.

23. An Internet article based on a print source

If you believe the Internet version is the same as the print version:

Banker, B. S., & Gaertner, S. L. (1998). Achieving stepfamily harmony: An intergroup relations approach. [Electronic version]. Journal of Family Psychology, 12, 3, 310-325.

If you have reason to believe the Internet version is not the same as the print version:

Banker, B. S., & Gaertner, S. L. (1998). Achieving stepfamily harmony: An intergroup relations approach. Journal of Family Psychology, 12, 3, 310-325. Retrieved October 4, 2001, from http://www.apa.org/journals/fam/998ab.html

24. An article from a journal that appears only on the Internet

Kamradt, T. (2001, September 28). Lyme disease and current aspects of immunization. Arthritis Research. Retrieved

October 4, 2001, from http://arthritis-research.com/content/AR-4-1-kamradt/abstract

25. A document on the Web site of a university program or department

Voigt, L. (1999, January). Bridging the gap between language and literature. Retrieved October 4, 2001, from Brown University, Harriet W. Sheridan Center for Teaching and Learning Web site: http://sheridan-center.stg.brown.edu/teachingexchange/TE_bridgegap.shtml

26. A Web document with no author or date identified

Begin the entry with the title of the document, and put *n.d.* in parentheses where the date of publication or update normally appears.

NUA Internet Survey: How many online? (n.d.). Retrieved October 4, 2001, from http://www.nua.ie/surveys/how_many_online

27. A U.S. government report available on a government agency Web site, no date

U.S. Department of Labor Bureau of Labor Statistics. (n.d.). Occupational outlook handbook 2000-01. Retrieved October 4, 2001, from http://stats.bls.gov/ocohome.htm

28. A posting to a newsgroup, electronic mailing list, or other online forum or discussion group

Postings to Usenet newsgroups, electronic mailing lists (also called "listservs"), and other online discussion forums should be included in your reference list only if they are archived, so that readers can retrieve them. Otherwise, they should be cited only in the text, as personal communications. Include the author's name (use the screen name if the real name is not available), the date of the posting, its subject line, and any identifying number (in square brackets).

Sand, P. (1996, April 20). Java disabled by default in Linux Netscape. Message posted to news://Keokuk.unh.edu

Crispen, P. (2001, September 2). The Hunger Site/Windows RG/WebElements. Message posted to The Internet Tourbus, archived at http://www.tourbus.com

29. An abstract retrieved from an electronic database

Natchez, G. (1987). Frida Kahlo and Diego Rivera: The transformation of catastrophe to creativity. Psychotherapy-

Patient, 8, 153-174. Abstract retrieved October 4, 2001, from PsychLIT database.

30. A newspaper article retrieved from an electronic database

Chass, M. (1998, September 8). Big bang: McGwire breaks Maris's home run record. New York Times. Retrieved September 9, 1998, from http://www.nytimes.com

31. An email message

The APA's *Publication Manual* discourages including email in a list of references and suggests citing email only in text as personal communication (see entry 12).

32. A software or computer program

McAfee Office 2000. Version 2.0 [Computer software]. (1999). Santa Clara, CA: Network Associates.

USE THE FOLLOWING MODELS FOR OTHER SOURCES

33. An interview

Do not list personal interviews in your references list. Cite the person's name in your text, and give the notation *personal communication.* Cite a published interview like an article from a magazine (see model entry 18).

34. A government document

U.S. Department of Health, Education and Welfare. (1979). Healthy people: The surgeon general's report on health promotion (DHEW Publication No. 79-55071). Washington, DC: U.S. Government Printing Office.

35. A dissertation abstract

Fairhall, J. L. (1989). James Joyce, history, and the political unconscious. (Doctoral dissertation, State University of New York at Stony Brook, 1989). Dissertation Abstracts International, 51, 3582A.

36. An unpublished doctoral dissertation

Bullock, B. (1986). Basic needs fulfillment among less developed countries: Social progress over two decades of growth. Unpublished doctoral dissertation, Vanderbilt University, Nashville.

37. Published proceedings of a conference

Bingman, C. F. (1985). The president as manager of the federal government. In C. L. Harriss (Ed.), Control of federal spending (pp. 146-161). New York: Proceedings of the Academy of Political Science.

38. A technical or research report

Brown, B. B., Kohrs, D., & Lazarro, C. (1991, April). The academic costs and consequences of extracurricular participation in high school. Chicago: American Education Research Association.

39. A television program

Hoppe, B., & Lattanzi, B. (Writers). (1995). The universe within (G. Koide, Director). In P. Apsell (Producer), Nova. Boston: WGBH.

40. A film or videotape

Parker, O. (Director). (1995). Othello [Film]. New York: Castle Rock Entertainment.

Acknowledgments (continued from copyright page)

Beth L. Bailey. "Dating." Taken from *Front Porch to Back Seat: Courtship in 20th Century America* by Beth L. Bailey. Copyright ©1983 by Beth L. Bailey. Used by permission of Johns Hopkins University Press.

Rick Bragg. "100 Miles per Hour, Upside Down and Sideways." From *All Over But the Shoutin'* by Rick Bragg. Copyright © 1997 by Rick Bragg. Used by permission of Pantheon Books, a division of Random House, Inc.

Edward Cohn. "Are Men's Fingers Faster?" From *The American Prospect,* Volume II, Number 11, April 24, 2000. The American Prospect, 5 Broad Street, Boston, MA 02109. All rights reserved. Reprinted by permission of The American Prospect and the author.

Richard Corliss. "Run, *Chicken Run*!" From *Time,* June 19, 2000, pp. 124–126. Copyright © 2000 Time, Inc. Reprinted by permission.

Amanda Coyne. "The Long Good-Bye: Mother's Day in Federal Prison." Copyright © 1997 by *Harper's Magazine.* All rights reserved. Reproduced from the May issue by special permission.

Annie Dillard. "A Chase." Taken from *An American Childhood* by Annie Dillard. Copyright © 1987 by Annie Dillard. Reprinted by permission of HarperCollins Publishers, Inc.

John T. Edge. "I'm Not Leaving Until I Eat This Thing." From *The Oxford American* (September/October 1999). Copyright © 1999 by John T. Edge. Reprinted by permission of the author.

Barbara Ehrenreich. "Are Families Dangerous?" From *Time,* July 18, 1994. Originally titled "Oh, Those Family Values." "Copyright © 1994 Time, Inc. Reprinted by permission.

Richard Estrada. "Sticks and Stones and Sports Team Names." From *The Los Angeles Times,* October 29, 1995. Copyright © 2000 Washington Post Writers Group. Reprinted with permission.

Amitai Etzioni. "Working at McDonald's." From *The Miami Herald,* August 24, 1986. Reprinted by permission of the author.

Christopher John Farley. "Rave New World." From *Time,* June 5, 2000, pp. 69–72. Copyright © 2000 Time, Inc. Reprinted by permission.

Ian Frazier. "Dearly Disconnected." From *Mother Jones,* January/February 2000. Copyright © 2000 Foundation for National Progress. Reprinted by permission of Foundation for National Progress.

Andrew M. Greeley. "Why Do Catholics Stay in the Church? Because of the Stories." From *The New York Times Magazine,* July 10, 1994. Copyright © 1994 by The New York Times Company. Reprinted by permission.

Charles Herold. "Thief II Stresses Stealth over Strength." From *The New York Times,* July 6, 2000. Copyright © 2000 by The New York Times Company. Reprinted by permission.

Mark Hertsgaard. "A Global Green Deal." From *Time,* April/May 2000. Copyright © 2000 Time, Inc. Reprinted by permission.

Randall Kennedy. "You Can't Judge a Crook by His Color." From *The New Republic,* September 13, 1999. © 1999 The New Republic, Inc. Reprinted by permission of The New Republic.

Stephen King. "Why We Crave Horror Movies." Originally appeared in *Playboy* (1982). © Stephen King. Reprinted with permission. All rights reserved.

Michael Kinsley. "Email Culture." From *Forbes ASAP,* December 2, 1996. Reprinted by permission of the author.

Jonathan Kozol. "The Human Cost of an Illiterate Society." From *Illiterate America* by Jonathan Kozol. Copyright © 1985 by Jonathan Kozol. Used by permission of Doubleday, a division of Bantam Doubleday Dell Publishing Group, Inc.

John Leland. "Monster Factory." From *Newsweek,* February 7, 2000, pp. 54–55. © 2000 Newsweek, Inc. All rights reserved. Reprinted by permission.

Michael D. Lemonick. "Will Tiny Robots Build Diamonds One Atom at a Time?" From *Time,* June 19, 2000. © 2000 Time, Inc. Reprinted by permission.

Audre Lorde. "That Summer I Left Childhood Was White." From *Zami: A New Spelling of My Name* by Audre Lorde. Copyright © 1982 by Audre Lorde. Published by The Crossing Press.

Edward J. Loughran. "Prevention of Delinquency." Reprinted by permission of the author.

Mari J. Matsuda. "Assaultive Speech and Academic Freedom." From *Where Is Your Body?: And Other Essays on Race, Gender, and the Law.* Copyright © 1996 by Mari J. Matsuda. Reprinted with the permission of Beacon Press, Boston.

John McPhee. "The New York Pickpocket Academy" (our title). Excerpt from *Giving Good Weight* by John McPhee. Copyright © 1979 by John McPhee. Reprinted by permission of Farrar, Straus & Giroux, L.L.C. Published in Canada by Macfarlane Walter & Ross, Toronto.

Katherine S. Newman. "Dead-End Jobs: A Way Out." From *The Brookings Review,* Fall 1995. Copyright © 1995 by The Brookings Institution. Reprinted with the permission of the publisher.

The New Yorker. "Soup." Originally titled "Slave" from *The Talk of the Town* in *The New Yorker,* January 23, 1989. Copyright © 1989 The New Yorker Magazine, Inc. All rights reserved. Reprinted by permission.

Dennis Prager. "The Soul-Corrupting Anti-Tobacco Crusade." From *The Weekly Standard,* July 20, 1998, pp. 17–23. Reprinted by permission.

David Quammen. "Is Sex Necessary? Virgin Birth and Opportunism in the Garden." This article originally appeared in *Outside* magazine. Copyright © 1982 by David Quammen. All rights reserved. Reprinted by permission of David Quammen.

Rob Ryder. "10 Is a Crowd, So Change the Game." From *The New York Times,* March 8, 1998. Copyright © 1998 by The New York Times Company. Reprinted by permission.

Robert J. Samuelson. "Reforming Schools through a Federal Test for College Aid." From *Newsweek,* May 27, 1991. © 1991 Newsweek, Inc. All rights reserved. Reprinted with permission.

Brent Staples. "Black Men and Public Space." Copyright © 1987 by Brent Staples. Reprinted by permission of the author, Brent Staples, who holds a Ph.D. in psychology from the University of Chicago, is a member of the Editorial Board of *The New York Times,* and is the author of the memoir *Parallel Time: Growing Up in Black and White.*

Deborah Tannen. "Marked Women." Originally "Marked Women, Unmarked Men" from *The New York Times Magazine,* June 20, 1993. Copyright © 1993 by Deborah Tannen. Reprinted by permission of the author.

Lewis H. Van Dusen Jr. "Legitimate Pressures and Illegitimate Results." From *ABA Journal,* February 1969. Reprinted by permission.

Suzanne Winckler. "A Savage Life." From *The New York Times Magazine,* February 7, 1999. Copyright © 1999 by Suzanne Winckler. Reprinted by permission.

Amy Wu. "A Different Kind of Mother." From *Chinese American Forum* 9:26. Reprinted by permission of the author.

Index to Methods of Development

This index lists the readings in the text according to the methods of writing the authors used to develop their ideas. For readings relying predominately on one method or strategy, we indicate the first page of the reading. If a method plays a minor role in a reading, we provide both the first page of the reading as well as the paragraph number(s) where the method is put to use.

Argument

Cause or Effect

Comparison and Contrast

Definition

Description

Division and Classification

Example

Narration

Index of Authors, Titles, and Terms

Research and Writing Online

Whether you want to investigate the ideas behind a thought-provoking essay or conduct in-depth research for a paper, the Web resources for *Reading Critically, Writing Well* can help you find what you need—and then use it once you find it.

The English Research Room for Navigating the Web

www.bedfordstmartins.com/english_research

The Web brings a flood of information to your screen, but it takes skill to track down the best sources. Not only does *The English Research Room* point you to some reliable starting places for Web investigations, but it also lets you tune up your skills with interactive tutorials.

- Want to improve your skill at searching electronic databases, online catalogs, and the Web? Try the *Interactive Tutorials* for some hands-on practice.
- Need quick access to online search engines, reference sources, and research sites? Explore *Research Links* for some good starting places.
- Have questions on evaluating the sources you find, navigating the Web, or conducting research in general? Consult one of our *Reference Units* for authoritative advice.

Research and Documentation Online for Incorporating Sources

www.bedfordstmartins.com/resdoc

Incorporating sources correctly in a paper is often a challenge, and the Web has made it even more complex. This online version of the popular booklet *Research and Documentation in the Electronic Age,* by Diana Hacker, provides clear advice for the humanities, social sciences, history, and the sciences on

- which Web and library sources are relevant to your topic (with links to Web sources)
- how to integrate outside material into your paper
- how to cite sources correctly, using the appropriate documentation style
- what the format for the final paper should be